Succeeding in Business™ with Microsoft® Access® 2013:
A Problem-Solving Approach

"With knowledge comes opportunity, with opportunity comes success."
– Anonymous

Sandra Cable
Texas A&M University – Commerce

CENGAGE
Learning®

Australia • Brazil • Japan • Korea • Mexico • Singapore • Spain • United Kingdom • United States

**Succeeding in Business™ with Microsoft®
Access® 2013: A Problem-Solving Approach**
Sandra Cable

Senior Product Team Manager: Donna Gridley

Content Developer: Jon Farnham

Associate Content Developer: Angela Lang

Product Assistant: Melissa Stehler

Development Editor: Ann Fisher

Director of Production: Patty Stephan

Senior Content Project Manager: Matthew
  Hutchinson

Manufacturing Planner: Fola Orekoya

Market Development Manager: Kristie Clark

Market Development Manager: Gretchen
  Swann

Composition: GEX Publishing Services

Art Director: GEX Publishing Services

Text Designer: Tim Blackburn

Cover Designer: GEX Publishing Services

Cover Illustration: GEX Publishing Services

Copy Editor: GEX Publishing Services

Proofreader: Kathy Orrino

Indexer: Sharon Hilgenberg

For product information and technology assistance, contact us at
Cengage Learning Customer & Sales Support, 1-800-354-9706

For permission to use material from this text or product,
submit all requests online at **cengage.com/permissions**
Further permissions questions can be emailed to
permissionrequest@cengage.com

Library of Congress Control Number: 2013953094
ISBN-13: 978-1-285-07758-1
ISBN-10: 1-285-07758-X

Cengage Learning
200 First Stamford Place, 4th Floor
Stamford, CT 06902
USA

Cengage Learning is a leading provider of customized learning solutions
with office locations around the globe, including Singapore, the United
Kingdom, Australia, Mexico, Brazil, and Japan. Locate your local office at:
www.cengage.com/global

Cengage Learning products are represented in Canada by Nelson
Education, Ltd.

For your course and learning solutions, visit **www.cengage.com**

Purchase any of our products at your local college store or at our
preferred online store **www.cengagebrain.com**

Printed in the United States of America
1 2 3 4 5 6 7 17 16 15 14

Brief
Contents

Table of **Contents**

Preface

THE SUCCEEDING IN BUSINESS™ SERIES

Because you're ready for more.

Increasingly students are coming into the classroom with stronger computer skills. As a result, they are ready to move beyond "point and click" skills and learn to use these tools in a way that will assist them in the business world.

You've told us you and your students want more: more of a business focus, more realistic case problems, more emphasis on application of software skills, and more problem-solving. For this reason, we created the **Succeeding in Business Series.**

The **Succeeding in Business Series** is the first of its kind designed to prepare the technology-savvy student for life after college. In the business world, your students' ability to use available tools to analyze data and solve problems is one of the most important factors in determining their success. The books in this series engage students who have mastered basic computer and applications skills by challenging them to think critically and find effective solutions to realistic business problems.

We're excited about the new classroom opportunities this new approach affords, and we hope you are too. We look forward to hearing about your successes!

The Succeeding in Business Team

The Succeeding in Business Series Instructor Resources

A unique approach requires unique instructor support; and we have you covered. We take the next step in providing you with outstanding Instructor Resources—developed by educators and experts and tested through our rigorous Quality Assurance process. Whether you use one resource or all the resources provided, our goal is to make the teaching and learning experience in your classroom the best it can be. With Cengage Learning's resources, you'll spend less time preparing, and more time teaching.

To access any of the items mentioned below, go to www.cengage.com/login.

Instructor's Manual

The instructor's manual offers guidance through each level of each chapter. You will find lecture notes that provide an overview of the chapter content along with background information and teaching tips. Also included are classroom activities and discussion questions that will get your students thinking about the business scenarios and decisions presented in the book.

Test Bank

ExamView features a user-friendly testing environment that allows you to not only publish traditional paper and LAN-based tests, but also Web-deliverable exams. In addition to the traditional multiple-choice, true/false, completion, short answer, and essay questions, the **Succeeding in Business** series emphasizes new critical thinking questions. Like the textbook, these questions challenge your students by going beyond defining key terms and focusing more on the real-world decision-making process they will face in business, while keeping the convenience of automatic grading for you.

Student Data Files and Solution Files

All student data files necessary to complete the hands-on portion of each level and the end-of chapter material are provided along with the solutions files.

Annotated Solution Files and Rubrics

Challenging your students shouldn't make it more difficult to set grading criteria. Each student assignment in your textbook will have a correlating Annotated Solution File that highlights what to look for in your students' submissions. Grading Rubrics list these criteria in an auto-calculating table that can be customized to fit the needs of your class. The electronic file format of both of these tools offers the flexibility of online or paper-based grading. This complete grading solution will save you time and effort on grading.

PowerPoint Presentations

The PowerPoint presentations deliver visually impressive lectures filled with the business and application concepts and skills introduced in the text. Use these to engage your students in discussion regarding the content covered in each chapter. You can also distribute or post these files for your students to use as an additional study aid.

Figure Files

Every figure in the text is provided in an easy to use file format. Use these to customize your PowerPoint Presentations, create overheads, and to enhance your course.

Sample Syllabus

A sample syllabus is provided to help you get your course started. Provided in a Word document, you can use the syllabus as is or modify it for your own course.

Succeeding in Business Series Walk-Through

The Succeeding in Business approach is unique. It moves beyond point-and-click exercises to give your students more real-world problem-solving skills that they can apply in business. In the following pages, step through *Succeeding in Business with Microsoft Access 2013* to learn more about the series pedagogy, features, design, and reinforcement exercises.

Thought-provoking quotes at the beginning of each chapter set the stage for the concepts to be presented.

The Learning Objectives provide a quick reference for topics covered in the chapter.

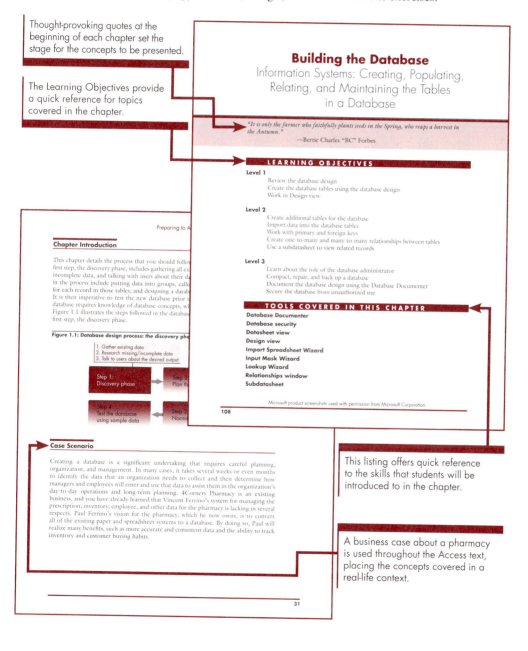

Building the Database
Information Systems: Creating, Populating, Relating, and Maintaining the Tables in a Database

"It is only the farmer who faithfully plants seeds in the Spring, who reaps a harvest in the Autumn."
—Bertie Charles "BC" Forbes

LEARNING OBJECTIVES

Level 1
Review the database design
Create the database tables using the database design
Work in Design view

Level 2
Create additional tables for the database
Import data into the database tables
Work with primary and foreign keys
Create one-to-many and many-to-many relationships between tables
Use a subdatasheet to view related records

Level 3
Learn about the role of the database administrator
Compact, repair, and back up a database
Document the database design using the Database Documenter
Secure the database from unauthorized use

TOOLS COVERED IN THIS CHAPTER
Database Documenter
Database security
Datasheet view
Design view
Import Spreadsheet Wizard
Input Mask Wizard
Lookup Wizard
Relationships window
Subdatasheet

Microsoft product screenshots used with permission from Microsoft Corporation.

108

Chapter Introduction

This chapter details the process that you should follow
first step, the discovery phase, includes gathering all ex
incomplete data, and talking with users about their da
in the process include putting data into groups, calle
for each record in those tables; and designing a datab
It is then imperative to test the new database prior t
database requires knowledge of database concepts, wi
Figure 1.1 illustrates the steps followed in the databas
first step, the discovery phase.

Figure 1.1: Database design process: the discovery pha

1. Gather existing data
2. Research missing/incomplete data
3. Talk to users about the desired output

Step 1:
Discovery phase

Step 2
Plan th

Step 4:
Test the database
using sample data

Step 3
Norma

This listing offers quick reference to the skills that students will be introduced to in the chapter.

Case Scenario

Creating a database is a significant undertaking that requires careful planning, organization, and management. In many cases, it takes several weeks or even months to identify the data that an organization needs to collect and then determine how managers and employees will enter and use that data to assist them in the organization's day-to-day operations and long-term planning. 4Corners Pharmacy is an existing business, and you have already learned that Vincent Ferrino's system for managing the prescription, inventory, employee, and other data for the pharmacy is lacking in several respects. Paul Ferrino's vision for the pharmacy, which he now owns, is to convert all of the existing paper and spreadsheet systems to a database. By doing so, Paul will realize many benefits, such as more accurate and consistent data and the ability to track inventory and customer buying habits.

A business case about a pharmacy is used throughout the Access text, placing the concepts covered in a real-life context.

31

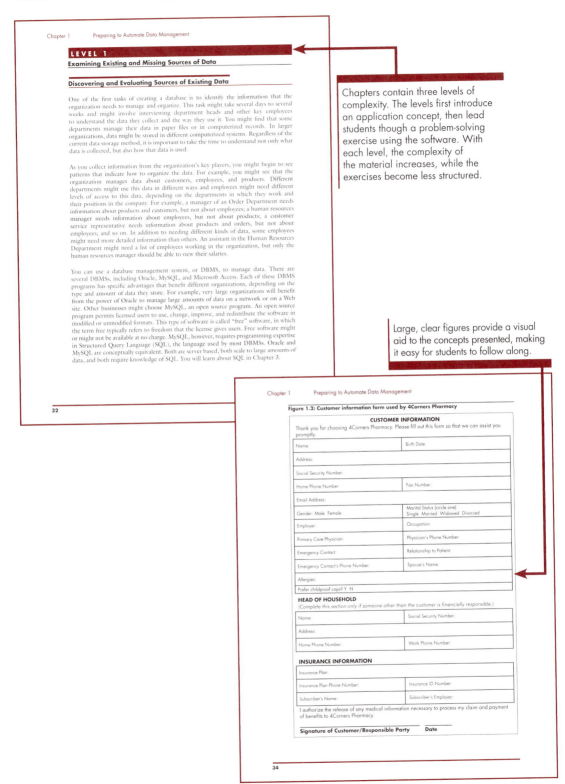

Chapter 1   Preparing to Automate Data Management

LEVEL 1

Examining Existing and Missing Sources of Data

Discovering and Evaluating Sources of Existing Data

One of the first tasks of creating a database is to identify the information that the organization needs to manage and organize. This task might take several days to several weeks and might involve interviewing department heads and other key employees to understand the data they collect and the way they use it. You might find that some departments manage their data in paper files or in computerized records. In larger organizations, data might be stored in different computerized systems. Regardless of the current data storage method, it is important to take the time to understand not only what data is collected, but also how that data is used.

As you collect information from the organization's key players, you might begin to see patterns that indicate how to organize the data. For example, you might see that the organization manages data about customers, employees, and products. Different departments might use this data in different ways and employees might need different levels of access to this data, depending on the departments in which they work and their positions in the company. For example, a manager of an Order Department needs information about products and customers, but not about employees; a human resources manager needs information about employees, but not about products; a customer service representative needs information about products and orders, but not about employees; and so on. In addition to needing different kinds of data, some employees might need more detailed information than others. An assistant in the Human Resources Department might need a list of employees working in the organization, but only the human resources manager should be able to view their salaries.

You can use a database management system, or DBMS, to manage data. There are several DBMSs, including Oracle, MySQL, and Microsoft Access. Each of these DBMS programs has specific advantages that benefit different organizations, depending on the type and amount of data they store. For example, very large organizations will benefit from the power of Oracle to manage large amounts of data on a network or on a Web site. Other businesses might choose MySQL, an open source program. An open source program permits licensed users to use, change, improve, and redistribute the software in modified or unmodified formats. This type of software is called "free" software, in which the term free typically refers to freedom that the license gives users. Free software might or might not be available at no charge. MySQL, however, requires programming expertise in Structured Query Language (SQL), the language used by most DBMSs. Oracle and MySQL are conceptually equivalent. Both are server based; both scale to large amounts of data, and both require knowledge of SQL. You will learn about SQL in Chapter 3.

32

Chapters contain three levels of complexity. The levels first introduce an application concept, then lead students though a problem-solving exercise using the software. With each level, the complexity of the material increases, while the exercises become less structured.

Large, clear figures provide a visual aid to the concepts presented, making it easy for students to follow along.

Chapter 1   Preparing to Automate Data Management

Figure 1.2: Customer information form used by 4Corners Pharmacy

CUSTOMER INFORMATION

Thank you for choosing 4Corners Pharmacy. Please fill out this form so that we can assist you promptly.

Name:	Birth Date:
Address:	
Social Security Number:	
Home Phone Number:	Fax Number:
Email Address:	
Gender: Male Female	Marital Status (circle one): Single Married Widowed Divorced
Employer:	Occupation:
Primary Care Physician:	Physician's Phone Number:
Emergency Contact:	Relationship to Patient:
Emergency Contact's Phone Number:	Spouse's Name:
Allergies:	
Prefer childproof caps? Y N	

HEAD OF HOUSEHOLD

(Complete this section only if someone other than the customer is financially responsible.)

Name:	Social Security Number:
Address:	
Home Phone Number:	Work Phone Number:

INSURANCE INFORMATION

Insurance Plan:	
Insurance Plan Phone Number:	Insurance ID Number:
Subscriber's Name:	Subscriber's Employer:

I authorize the release of any medical information necessary to process my claim and payment of benefits to 4Corners Pharmacy.

_____   _____

Signature of Customer/Responsible Party   Date

34

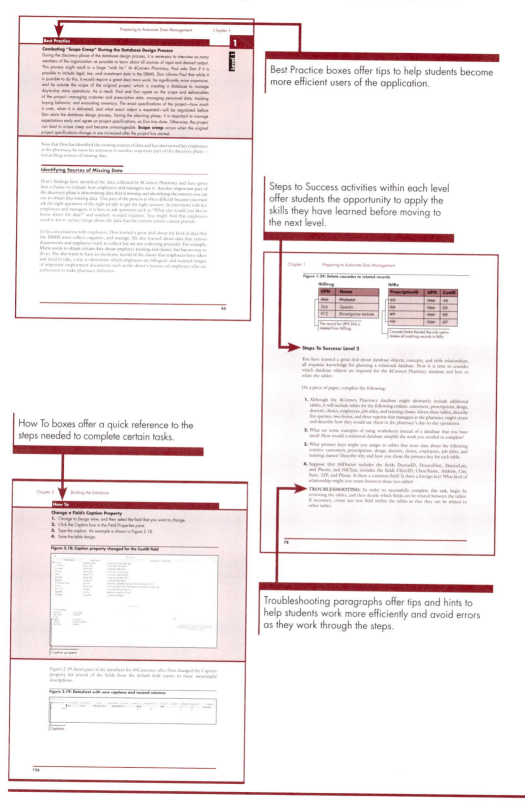

Best Practice boxes offer tips to help students become more efficient users of the application.

Steps to Success activities within each level offer students the opportunity to apply the skills they have learned before moving to the next level.

How To boxes offer a quick reference to the steps needed to complete certain tasks.

Troubleshooting paragraphs offer tips and hints to help students work more efficiently and avoid errors as they work through the steps.

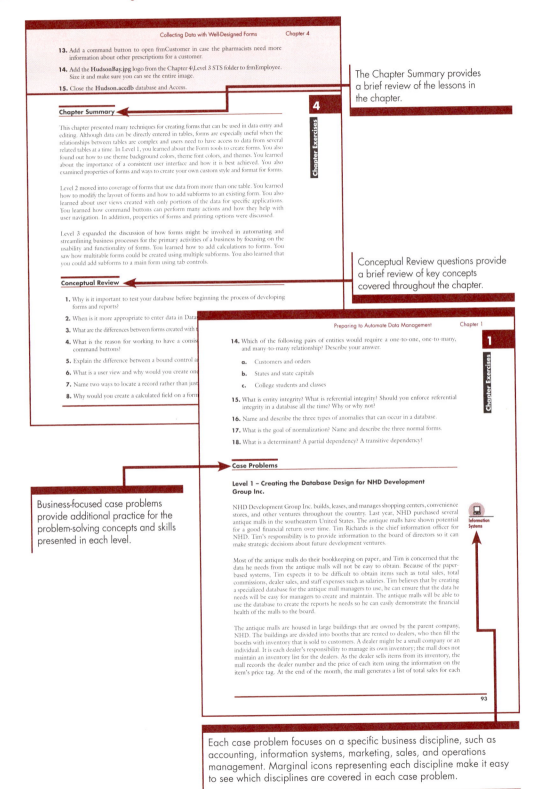

Collecting Data with Well-Designed Forms   Chapter 4

13. Add a command button to open frmCustomer in case the pharmacists need more information about other prescriptions for a customer.

14. Add the **HudsonBay.jpg** logo from the Chapter 4\Level 3 STS folder to frmEmployee. Size it and make sure you can see the entire image.

15. Close the **Hudson.accdb** database and Access.

4

Chapter Exercises

The Chapter Summary provides a brief review of the lessons in the chapter.

Chapter Summary

This chapter presented many techniques for creating forms that can be used in data entry and editing. Although data can be directly entered in tables, forms are especially useful when the relationships between tables are complex and users need to have access to data from several related tables at a time. In Level 1, you learned about the Form tools to create forms. You also found out how to use theme background colors, theme font colors, and themes. You learned about the importance of a consistent user interface and how it is best achieved. You also examined properties of forms and ways to create your own custom style and format for forms.

Level 2 moved into coverage of forms that use data from more than one table. You learned how to modify the layout of forms and how to add subforms to an existing form. You also learned about user views created with only portions of the data for specific applications. You learned how command buttons can perform many actions and how they help with user navigation. In addition, properties of forms and printing options were discussed.

Level 3 expanded the discussion of how forms might be involved in automating and streamlining business processes for the primary activities of a business by focusing on the usability and functionality of forms. You learned how to add calculations to forms. You saw how multitable forms could be created using multiple subforms. You also learned that you could add subforms to a main form using tab controls.

Conceptual Review questions provide a brief review of key concepts covered throughout the chapter.

Conceptual Review

1. Why is it important to test your database before beginning the process of developing forms and reports?

2. When is it more appropriate to enter data in Data

3. What are the differences between forms created with

4. What is the reason for working to have a consist command buttons?

5. Explain the difference between a bound control a

6. What is a user view and why would you create one

7. Name two ways to locate a record rather than just

8. Why would you create a calculated field on a form

Preparing to Automate Data Management   Chapter 1

1

Chapter Exercises

14. Which of the following pairs of entities would require a one-to-one, one-to-many, and many-to-many relationship? Describe your answer.

   a. Customers and orders

   b. States and state capitals

   c. College students and classes

15. What is entity integrity? What is referential integrity? Should you enforce referential integrity in a database all the time? Why or why not?

16. Name and describe the three types of anomalies that can occur in a database.

17. What is the goal of normalization? Name and describe the three normal forms.

18. What is a determinant? A partial dependency? A transitive dependency?

Case Problems

Level 1 – Creating the Database Design for NHD Development Group Inc.

NHD Development Group Inc. builds, leases, and manages shopping centers, convenience stores, and other ventures throughout the country. Last year, NHD purchased several antique malls in the southeastern United States. The antique malls have shown potential for a good financial return over time. Tim Richards is the chief information officer for NHD. Tim's responsibility is to provide information to the board of directors so it can make strategic decisions about future development ventures.

Most of the antique malls do their bookkeeping on paper, and Tim is concerned that the data he needs from the antique malls will not be easy to obtain. Because of the paper-based systems, Tim expects it to be difficult to obtain items such as total sales, total commissions, dealer sales, and staff expenses such as salaries. Tim believes that by creating a specialized database for the antique mall managers to use, he can ensure that the data he needs will be easy for managers to create and maintain. The antique malls will be able to use the database to create the reports he needs so he can easily demonstrate the financial health of the malls to the board.

The antique malls are housed in large buildings that are owned by the parent company, NHD. The buildings are divided into booths that are rented to dealers, who then fill the booths with inventory that is sold to customers. A dealer might be a small company or an individual. It is each dealer's responsibility to manage its own inventory; the mall does not maintain an inventory list for the dealers. As the dealer sells items from its inventory, the mall records the dealer number and the price of each item using the information on the item's price tag. At the end of the month, the mall generates a list of total sales for each

Information Systems

93

Business-focused case problems provide additional practice for the problem-solving concepts and skills presented in each level.

Each case problem focuses on a specific business discipline, such as accounting, information systems, marketing, sales, and operations management. Marginal icons representing each discipline make it easy to see which disciplines are covered in each case problem.

About the Author

Sandra Cable Texas A&M University – Commerce

Sandra Cable received her doctorate in Education from Texas A&M University – Commerce in 2003. She currently teaches computer classes to businesses, colleges, and career colleges promoting simple approaches to using computer applications. In addition, she volunteers teaching computer seminars to non-profit organizations.

Author Acknowledgements

This book is the result of many people's efforts. To the thousands of students and clients that I have taught over the years, many thanks for your encouragement and for all you have taught me. I am also very grateful to my family for their support, Keith and Meridith Albright, and Miller Keplinger. Thank you for your love and support throughout the years.

I would also like to thank the great team at Cengage Learning, including: Donna Gridley, Senior Product Team Manager; Jon Farnham, Content Developer; Angela Lang, Associate Content Developer; Melissa Stehler, Product Assistant; Matthew Hutchinson, Senior Content Project Manager; and Chris Scriver, Manuscript Quality Assurance Project Leader, and his team of MQA testers: John Freitas, Danielle Shaw, Serge Palladino, and Susan Pedicini. This team at Cengage is truly a terrific team!

I would also like to give special thanks to Ann Fisher, my Development Editor. Thank you so much for keeping the project on track and for all of your great comments! It's always terrific working with a great person with wonderful ideas.

Introduction to Data Management with Microsoft Access 2013

"To succeed in life in today's world, you must have the will and tenacity to finish the job."
—Chin-Ning Chu

LEARNING OBJECTIVES

Introduce the features in Access 2013
Introduce the company used in this book
Identify how an organization manages data
Describe how problem solving is presented in this book
Understand the roles of data consumers in an organization
Determine how data is interlinked throughout an organization
Understand the current deficiencies in an organization's data
Introduce the companies used in this book's end-of-chapter case problems

About This Book and Microsoft Office Access 2013

Traditional study of computer applications has mostly involved acquiring skills related to an application's features and functions. Although this approach is important in teaching the mechanics required to perform certain tasks, it does not address *when* a particular tool is most appropriate or *how* it should best be utilized in solving a specific problem.

Although this book focuses on learning how to organize data using Microsoft Office Access 2013, the concepts and tasks presented in this book could apply to other database programs as well. Access is a relational database program in which data is stored in tables that are related to each other using relationships. You will learn about tables and relationships in Chapters 1 and 2. This idea is important, because tables can store a great deal of related information in one location and display the information in many ways. Access stores information in one database and lets the user manipulate that information to see as much or as little of it as desired and in many ways. For example, Access can provide you with a list of employees living in the same city or a report showing sales organized by product category.

What is information and where does it come from? The term "information" can mean different things to different people. For the purpose of this discussion, **information** is defined as data that is organized in a meaningful way. **Data** can be words, images, numbers, or even sounds. Using data to make decisions depends on an organization's ability to collect, organize, and otherwise transform data into information that can be used to support those decisions—a process more commonly referred to as **analysis**. A **data analyst** is a person in an organization who transforms data into information by sorting, filtering, and performing calculations on it to perform this analysis.

The amount of information available in a company can overwhelm many decision makers as they try to determine which sets of data and information are important and which should be ignored. The result is a complex world in which decision makers can no longer rely on intuition and calculations on paper to make effective decisions; they need tools that support decision making and help to solve problems.

Introduction to Access 2013

Access 2013 offers innovative features that assist you in creating professional databases and performing calculations. You may already be familiar with some of the application features such as the Ribbon, the .accdb file type, Intellisense, and the FILE tab. New features include an improved Backstage view, easier navigation between Backstage view, other Ribbon tabs, and Web apps. This introduction presents these and other features you'll encounter when working with Access 2013.

Starting Access 2013 in Windows 8 or Windows 8.1

You start Access 2013 in Windows 8 using the Start button located on the Charms bar. The Charms bar has five buttons on it: Search, Share, Start, Devices, and Settings, as shown in Figure 1.

If you are using Windows 8.1 and the new Start screen appears when you log in, simply start typing the word *Access*. When Access appear in the Search box, press Enter to start Access. See Figures 2 and 3.

Figure 1: Charms bar in Windows 8

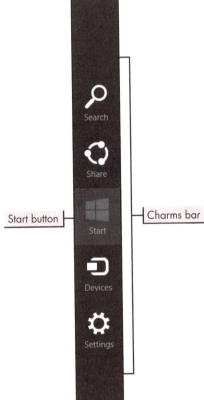

Figure 2: Windows 8.1 Start screen

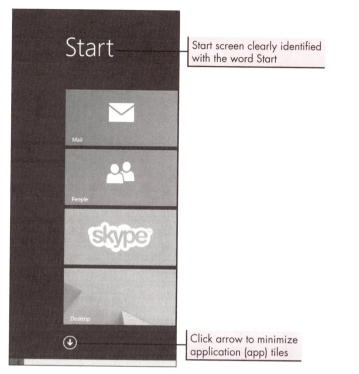

Start screen clearly identified with the word Start

Click arrow to minimize application (app) tiles

Figure 3: Windows 8.1 Search box

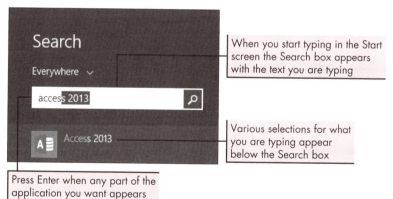

When you start typing in the Start screen the Search box appears with the text you are typing

Various selections for what you are typing appear below the Search box

Press Enter when any part of the application you want appears

If the Desktop window appears when you start Windows 8.1 as shown in Figure 4, click the Start button, start typing the word Access, then press Enter when Access appears in the Search box.

Figure 4: Windows 8.1 default Desktop

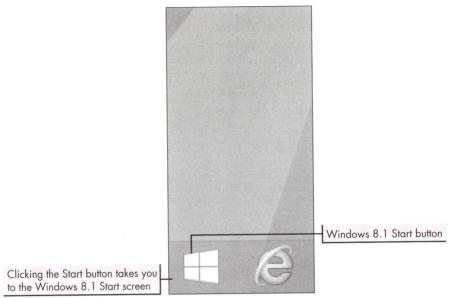

Windows 8.1 Start button

Clicking the Start button takes you to the Windows 8.1 Start screen

Starting Access 2013 in Windows 7 or Vista

This book was written using the Windows 8 operating system with additional text and figures added for Windows 8.1. However, you may follow along using Access 2013 in Windows 7 or earlier versions.

There are four ways to display the Charms bar:

1. Position the mouse in the lower-right corner of the screen. When you see the outline of the Charms bar, click to display the Charms bar.
2. Press the Windows key ⊞ + C
3. On a touchscreen, swipe your finger to the right edge of the screen until the Charms bar appears.
4. In the Start window of Windows 8.1, start typing Access, then press Enter.

How To

Start Access

1. Position the mouse in the lower-right or upper-right corner of the screen. When you see the outline of the Charms bar, click to display the Charms bar.
   TIP: Use any of the three methods to display the Charms bar.
2. Click the **Start** button ⊞ .
3. Drag the light gray scroll bar at the bottom of the screen to the right until the Office 2013 apps appear, as shown in Figure 5, then click the **Access 2013** app button.

Figure 5: Office 2013 apps in the Start screen

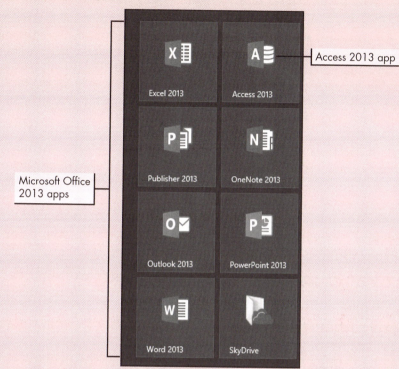

OR

1. Press the Windows key ⊞ +C to display the Charms bar.
2. Press the up or down arrow keys until the Start button in highlighted.
3. Press Enter.
4. Press the right arrow key until the Office 2013 programs appear.
5. Press the up or down arrow keys until the Access 2013 icon is highlighted, and then press Enter.

When you start Access for the first time, you will need to register the program, which you can do automatically, if you are on the Internet. However, if you are not connected to the Internet when starting Access, you may follow the steps in the Activation Wizard to register the program.

If you want the Access program icon to be located on the Taskbar menu, simply right-click the Microsoft Access 2013 icon and then click Pin this program to taskbar.

Using the Backstage View and Quick Access Toolbar

When the FILE tab is selected, the improved Backstage view displays. The Backstage view includes the Navigation bar and the Navigation pane. The contents of the Navigation pane display options for whichever command is selected on the Navigation bar. For example, when the Open command is selected, as shown in Figure 6, the Navigation pane displays all of the options for opening existing Access database files. Selecting Open also shows recent databases that were open. You can also click Computer, then Browse to navigate to the location of an existing database on your computer.

A new feature in Backstage view is the navigation arrow that appears at the top of the Navigation bar. Clicking this arrow quickly takes you back to the database window.

Selecting New in the Navigation bar offers a variety of options to the right of the Navigation pane. You can start a new blank database, a new Web database, or select a database template. Selecting SkyDrive lets you view your personal cloud or SkyDrive location to select a database.

Figure 6: Backstage view with the Open command selected

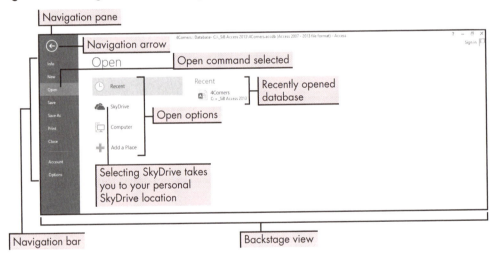

Clicking the Navigation arrow located at the top of the Navigation bar takes you back to the database window, as shown in Figure 7. Notice that the Quick Access toolbar appears above the Ribbon with the Access program button located to the left of the toolbar.

Figure 7: Database window

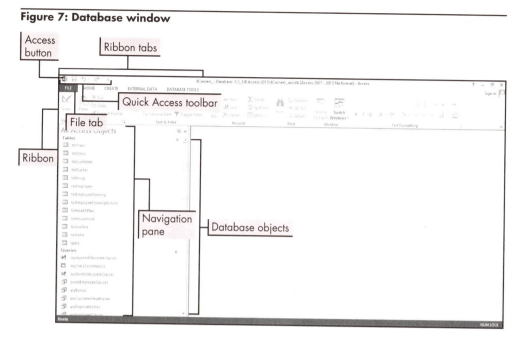

Selecting the Access program button displays options to Restore, Move, Size, Minimize, Maximize, or Close the database window. The Quick Access toolbar provides quick access to frequently used features, such as Save, Undo, and Redo. This toolbar appears at the top-left corner of the screen.

Opening and Closing Files in Access 2013

The default file format for Access 2013 is .accdb. Using Access 2013, you can open files created in previous versions of Access. You can also save files in earlier versions of Access. However, if you save a file as an Access 2002–2003 or Access 2000 format, it will not include all the functionality available in the Access 2013 format.

When you click Open on the Navigation bar in Backstage view, any Access 2013 files that you have saved will appear in the Navigation pane. You can click Computer, then Browse to open the Open dialog box like the one shown in Figure 8. Your Open dialog box may appear slightly different depending on the default database folder. By default, Access displays the most recently used database file at the top of the file list.

Figure 8: Open dialog box

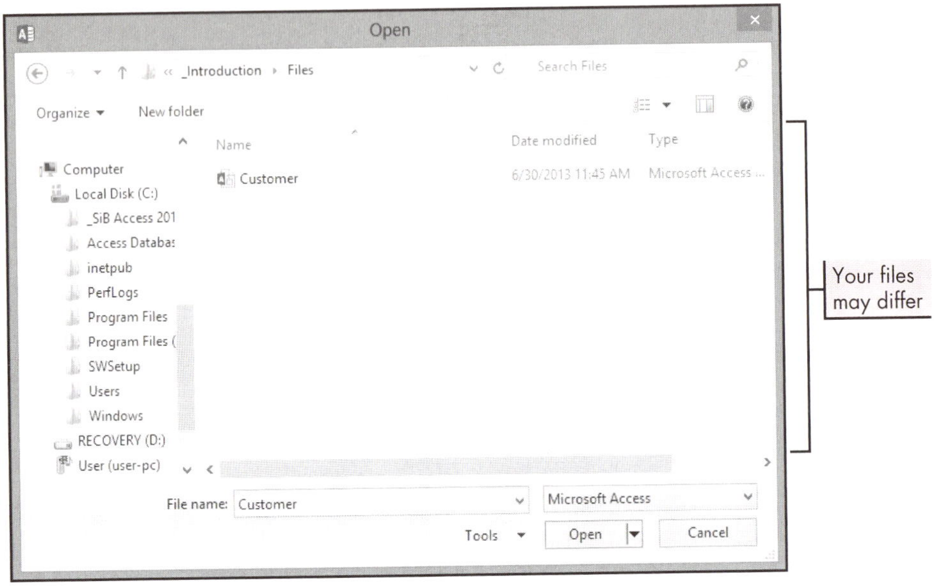

How To

Open a File

1. Click the FILE tab.
2. Click Open.
3. If you see the database you wish to open next to Recent, simply click on the database file to open it. If you want to open another database, click Computer.
4. Click the Browse button, navigate to the drive and folder location for the Customer.accdb file.
5. Click the Customer.accdb file.
6. Click the Open button.

How To

Close a File

1. Click the FILE tab.
2. Click Close.

Saving Files in Access 2013

When you create a new database in Access 2013, it is saved in the .accdb database format by default. However, you can also save it in the .mdb file format—the file format for earlier versions of Access. Saving a file in the .mdb format may limit the options that are available in the database.

How To

Save an Existing File in Access 2013 Format

1. Open the Customer_1 database that was not created in the .accdb format.
2. Click the FILE tab.
3. Click Save As. Make sure Access Database is highlighted to the right of Save Database As.
4. Click the Save As button. The Save As dialog box appears. See Figure 9.

Figure 9: Save As dialog box

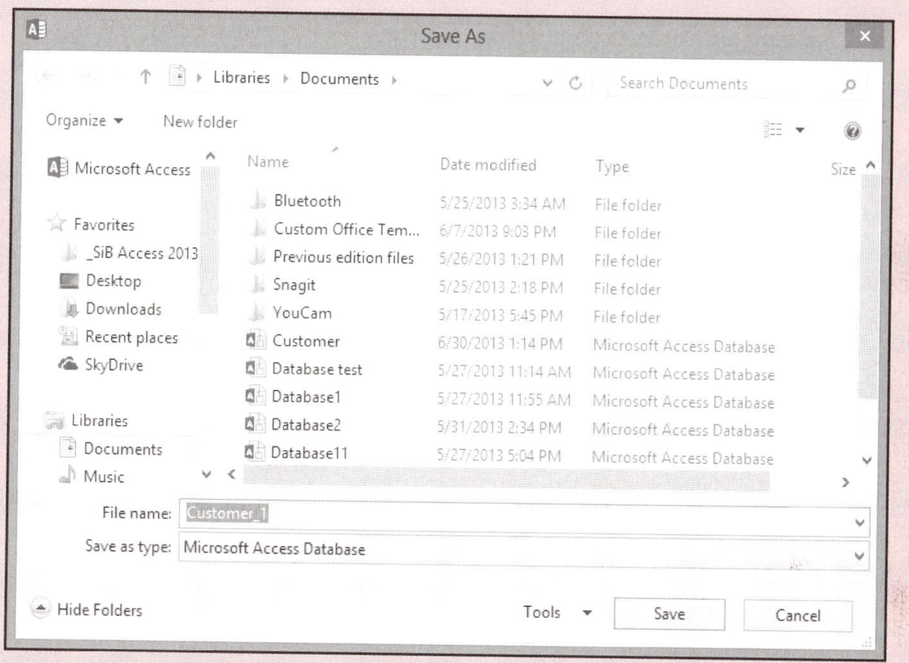

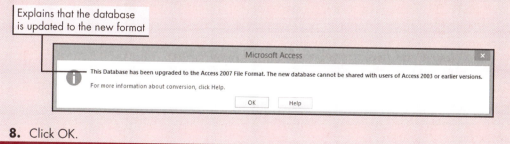

5. If necessary, enter the name for the database in the File name text box.
6. Click the Save button.
7. A Message box appears letting you know that the format upgraded as shown in Figure 10.

Figure 10: Upgrade message box

Explains that the database is updated to the new format

Microsoft Access

This Database has been upgraded to the Access 2007 File Format. The new database cannot be shared with users of Access 2003 or earlier versions.

For more information about conversion, click Help.

OK   Help

8. Click OK.

How To

Create a New Blank Desktop Database

When you create a new blank database, it only has one table object. Once you enter data into this table, you can create other objects based on the table, such as queries, forms, reports, and macros.

1. In Backstage view, click New, then click the Blank desktop database option. The Blank desktop database dialog box opens as shown in Figure 11.

Figure 11: Blank desktop database dialog box

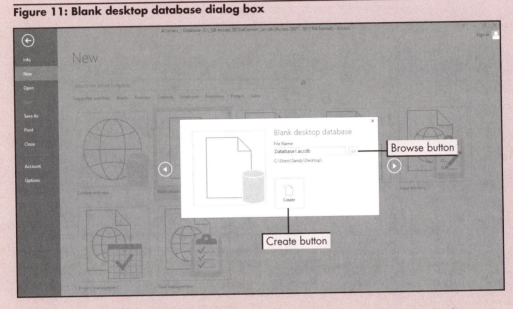

2. Click the Browse button then navigate to location where you want to save the database.
3. Type a filename in the File name box, then click OK.
4. Click the Create button.

Using Templates to Create Databases

Access 2013 provides templates for both local databases and Web databases. When you use a template, a complete ready-to-use database is created. In a template, the tables, relationships, forms, and reports are already built. You simply enter the data and begin analyzing it. These templates provide a starting point for the database and can be customized for optimal use.

The local templates are installed when you install Access. Online templates are available at the Microsoft website.

Creating Databases for the Web

With Access 2013, you can create a database to be used on the Web with relative ease. When you design a database for the Web, the Ribbon and available options change because the database is in a dynamic HTML format. You can then publish the database to Access Services, which places the database on a SharePoint site. You can then set up permissions for the users who are allowed to access the information in the database. SharePoint is a Microsoft technology solution that can be used to host websites and allows the database to be available on the Internet. To use the SharePoint services, you need to load the SharePoint program on your computer or server.

Understanding Intellisense

In Access, you build expressions to perform calculations or tasks with the data. When you create an expression, you use fields from the database. **Intellisense** is an Access feature that appears when you start to create an expression. As you start typing an expression, such as Sum or Avg, a list of expressions appears from which you can make a selection.

As you type the field name into the expression, Access fills in the complete field name, much like autocomplete features in other programs, significantly reducing potential typing errors.

The Ribbon

The Ribbon, which first appeared in Access 2007, replaces menus and toolbars formerly in earlier versions of Access, and makes finding options easier than ever. The Ribbon allows Access users, both experienced and novice, to find features without searching through endless menus. Instead, the Ribbon organizes them into tabs and groups. Each time you launch Access 2013 five tabs initially appear on the Ribbon: FILE, HOME, CREATE, EXTERNAL DATA, and DATABASE TOOLS, as shown in Figure 12.

Figure 12: Access Ribbon with HOME tab displayed

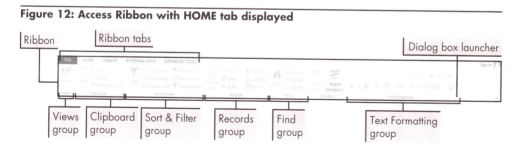

On each Ribbon tab, commands are organized into groups. On the Home tab, for example, you'll find the View button, which enables you to switch between Design, Datasheet, and other views. Depending on the selected table, form, report, or query, the View menu will change. The Clipboard group, also found on the HOME tab, includes commands for moving and copying data and formats, and the Text Formatting group contains commands for enhancing font formats. Groups are identified by labels which indicate the types of commands in the group.

Remember that the Ribbon is not static. As you perform various tasks, additional Ribbon tabs appear. For example, if you import Excel data to create an Access table, two additional contextual tabs that are related to Excel, will appear on the Ribbon. Contextual tabs are displayed when you create or select various features, such as forms, reports, or queries. Table 1 gives an overview of the Ribbon tabs.

Table 1: Tabs on the Ribbon in Access

Ribbon Tab	Description
FILE	Displays Backstage view with the Navigation pane located on the left side with tab options you can select. Depending on the tab selected in the Navigation pane, the right side of the screen displays options from which to select commands and other features.
HOME	Includes the most frequently used editing and data manipulation commands, such as Cut, Copy, Paste, Filter, and Ascending and Descending sort options. It also includes commands for adding, deleting, and finding records, as well as text formatting commands.
CREATE	Includes buttons for creating new objects in the database, such as tables, forms, and reports. It also provides options for selecting different templates.
EXTERNAL DATA	Contains commands for importing data and objects into the current database, exporting data and objects, and collecting data. This tab also lets you import data through e-mail in Microsoft Outlook or a SharePoint list.
DATABASE TOOLS	Includes buttons for creating and managing relationships between tables, documenting and analyzing a database, adding security to a database, and compacting and repairing a database.

© 2014 Cengage Learning

Some group tabs display a small arrow in the lower-right corner, called a Dialog Box Launcher button. Clicking a Dialog Box Launcher opens a dialog box or task pane for the group, with the full set of features and options available for that group. For example, to see additional font options that are available on the HOME tab on the Ribbon, simply click the Dialog Box Launcher in the Text Formatting group, and the Datasheet Formatting dialog box opens, as shown in Figure 13.

Figure 13: Datasheet Formatting dialog box

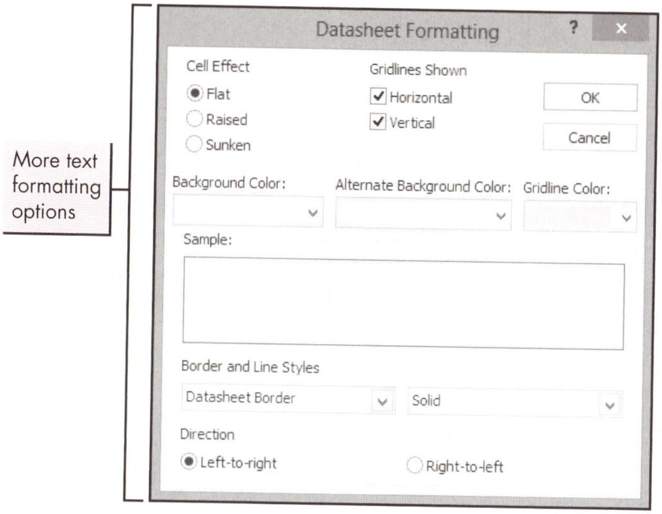

More text formatting options

If you need more room on the screen for your database, you can minimize the Ribbon so that only the tabs are displayed. You can press Ctrl+F1 to collapse the Ribbon and then press Ctrl+F1 to redisplay the Ribbon. You can right-click the Ribbon and then select Collapse the Ribbon.

How To

Collapse or Redisplay the Ribbon
1. Press Ctrl+F1.

OR

1. Right-click the Quick Access toolbar or the Ribbon.
2. Click Collapse the Ribbon.

Using the Keyboard to Initiate Commands

If you like using the keyboard to initiate commands, you can do so using some of the same access keys available in previous versions of Office applications. If you press the Alt key, Access displays KeyTips next to each command on the Quick Access toolbar and next to each tab on the Ribbon. **KeyTips** display the access key for a particular command or tab. Figure 14 shows the KeyTips that appear when you press Alt. Then simply type the desired key to invoke a command on the Quick Access toolbar or to choose a tab. For example, you can press 1 to save the database object or the letter H to display the KeyTips on the HOME tab.

Figure 14: KeyTips on the Ribbon

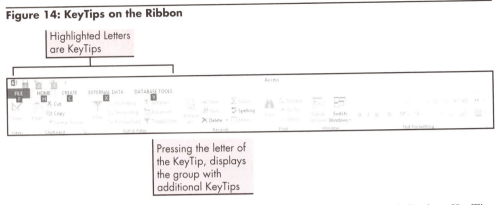

Highlighted Letters are KeyTips

Pressing the letter of the KeyTip, displays the group with additional KeyTips

If you choose to display KeyTips for a particular tab, the tab opens and displays KeyTips for all commands for which an access key is available.

Switching between tabs and commands can also be accomplished using the arrow and Tab keys. After pressing the Alt key, you can then use the right and left arrow keys to move to adjacent tabs. After the desired tab is selected, simply press the down arrow key to move down into the options for that tab. Using the arrow keys, Tab key, or the key combination [Shift]+[Tab] allow you to navigate between the various options. To select a command, simply press the [Enter] key.

Table 2 shows shortcut key combinations for several popular commands in Access 2013.

Table 2: Ctrl key combinations

Key Combination	Action
Ctrl+O	Open
Ctrl+S	Save
Ctrl+C	Copy
Ctrl+X	Cut
Ctrl+V	Paste
Ctrl+B	Bold
Ctrl+I	Italic
Ctrl+U	Underline
Ctrl+Z	Undo

© 2014 Cengage Learning

Additional key combinations can be found on the Microsoft website at *www.microsoft.com/Access.*

Adding Commands to the Quick Access Toolbar

When you first start Access 2013, three tools appear on the Quick Access toolbar by default: Save, Undo, and Redo. You can customize the toolbar by adding or removing commands and moving it below the Ribbon. After adding several commands to the Quick Access toolbar, you may want to move it below the Ribbon. Positioning the Quick Access toolbar below the Ribbon allows you quick access to the commands.

How To

Add Commands to the Quick Access Toolbar

1. Right-click any command on the Ribbon, then click Add to Quick Access Toolbar.

OR

1. Click the Customize Quick Access Toolbar button located on the right side of the Quick Access toolbar.
2. If you see the command on the Customize Quick Access Toolbar button menu, then simply click the command and it will appear on the toolbar. Notice that the Save, Undo, and Redo options have a check mark in front of them indicating that they are already on the Quick Access toolbar.

OR

1. If you do not see the command you want on the Customize Quick Access Toolbar button menu, click More Commands. The Access Options dialog box opens.
2. By default, the Popular Commands list appears in the Choose commands from list box at the top of the dialog box. If you see the command you want, double-click to move it to the list on the right side of the dialog box with the other options that are on the toolbar. If you do not see the desired command in the Popular Commands category, click the Choose commands from down arrow and choose the category for the command.
3. Click the OK button.

OR

1. Right-click any group on the Ribbon, then click Add to Quick Access Toolbar to add the group to the Quick Access toolbar.

How To

Remove Commands from the Quick Access Toolbar

1. Right-click the Quick Access Toolbar command you want to remove.
2. Click Remove from Quick Access Toolbar.

How To

Move the Quick Access Toolbar Below the Ribbon

1. Click the Customize Quick Access Toolbar button ⏷ .
2. Click Show Below the Ribbon.

OR

1. Right-click the Quick Access toolbar or the Ribbon.
2. On the shortcut menu, click Show Quick Access Toolbar Below the Ribbon.

Changing Views

Access provides you with a variety of buttons to change the view of a current object. The View button on the HOME tab lets you switch between the current view and the most recently used view. If you need additional views, simply select the arrow located at the bottom of the View button and a drop-down list of available view options will be displayed.

Getting Help

You have many options for getting help as you work in Access 2013. For most of the buttons and dialog box launchers, Access displays a context-sensitive ScreenTip about the feature when the mouse pointer is over it. To open the Access Help dialog box, you can click the Help button ? located on the right end of the Ribbon. There is a Help button in most dialog boxes. You can also open Help at any time by pressing the F1 key.

When the Help dialog box first opens, Access tries to connect to online help at the Microsoft Office Online website. If you cannot connect to the website, you will still have access to the offline Help system. See Figure 15.

Figure 15: Online Access Help dialog box

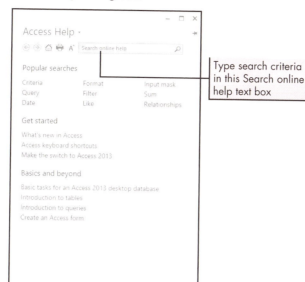

Type search criteria in this Search online help text box

How To

Get Help

1. Click the Help button [?] on the Ribbon or in a dialog box, or press the F1 key.
2. Type the first one or two words of the task you need help with in the Search box, and then click the Search button or press the Enter key.

OR

1. Click a topic in the Search online help list, and then click additional links to navigate to the desired topic.

The Fictional Company Used in this Book

The problems to be solved in this book are presented within the context of the fictional company, 4Corners Pharmacy, which is so named because it is located in southwestern Colorado on the border of the four corners connecting the states of Arizona, Colorado, New Mexico, and Utah. Case scenarios involving 4Corners Pharmacy are used to provide real-world business examples to illustrate the lessons in each chapter. They are not based on real people or real events. You will be guided through the solutions to solve realistic business problems for various people working for this company. These "employees" work in a variety of business departments: accounting, finance, human resources, information systems, marketing, operations management, and sales. Context is an important factor to consider when solving the problems in this book. The following background on 4Corners Pharmacy provides perspective on the situations that you will encounter throughout this book.

Vincent Ferrino opened 4Corners Pharmacy in 1994. Over the years, Vincent's business evolved from a small "mom-and-pop" corner drugstore to the busiest pharmacy in the area. Vincent's son, Paul Ferrino, has worked at the pharmacy in different capacities since 1995. After graduating with a degree in pharmacology and becoming licensed by the state of Colorado, Paul worked as a pharmacist in his father's store, and then took two years off to earn an MBA from Thunderbird University in Arizona. When Vincent retired, he sold the store to Paul, but continues to work as a part-time pharmacist.

Paul envisions expanding his father's business to take advantage of the growing pharmaceutical industry. Paul was encouraged recently by a study indicating that 47% of Americans take prescription drugs on a regular basis. He sees the trend increasing as life expectancy rises and as aging baby boomers need more prescriptions. Although he was a shrewd and successful businessperson, Vincent ran the day-to-day operations of the business with little help from computers, primarily because he was never trained to use them and never realized the benefits they could offer his business. Consequently, the pharmacy's recordkeeping, although meticulous and professional, is inefficient. Maintaining the growing business using mostly manual systems is becoming more costly for two reasons. The pharmacy has had to hire additional employees to meet industry regulations regarding the Health Insurance Portability and Accountability Act (HIPAA) and because of federal and state regulations that affect the sale, storage, and dispensing of prescription drugs. Although Paul succeeded in automating some of the pharmacy's data management in Excel workbooks, he knows that a more substantial change is needed to properly maintain and store the company's data.

Key Players

Paul Ferrino—Pharmacist and Owner

Paul began working as a pharmacist at 4Corners Pharmacy in January 1995, and bought the store from his father in May 2014. Paul is the head pharmacist, and as such, he manages a dedicated and capable group of experienced pharmacists, pharmacy technicians, and sales assistants. Paul's vision for the pharmacy is to continue his father's lifelong pledge of providing excellent customer service and "giving back" to the community. Vincent regularly sponsored and underwrote local events for kids and senior citizens, which resulted in several community service awards for Vincent and multiple wins in the "best pharmacy" category by a reader's poll sponsored by the local newspaper. The pharmacy also earned three awards from the local Chamber of Commerce. Although there are other big chain drugstores in the area, Vincent has managed to hang on to generations of customers because of his community involvement and excellent rapport with his customers. Paul is dedicated to continuing his father's traditions.

Donald Linebarger—Information Systems Director

After purchasing the store, Paul's first order of business was hiring someone who could overhaul the pharmacy's manual recordkeeping systems. Don Linebarger worked for many years as a systems analyst for a large business in the area. He was the perfect choice to work at 4Corners Pharmacy, not only because he is capable and experienced, but also because he has been a satisfied customer of 4Corners Pharmacy for many years. After developing the recordkeeping system for 4Corners Pharmacy, Don will train employees to use it, perform system maintenance, make any necessary changes, and maintain all of the records necessary for the business.

Maria Garcia—Human Resources Manager

Maria Garcia has been the human resources manager at 4Corners Pharmacy since 2013. She is responsible for interviewing and hiring employees; maintaining data about certifications for pharmacists and pharmacy technicians; monitoring attendance and sick days; and maintaining and administering company benefits, including life and health insurance, 401(k) programs, and bonuses.

Elaine Estes—Store/Operations Manager

Elaine Estes has worked at 4Corners Pharmacy since 2004. During this time, she has been the store's general manager and operations manager. Elaine maintains the inventory of prescription and nonprescription items, places orders for additional stock, and disposes of drugs when they are stocked past their expiration dates. Elaine also supervises the 4Corners Pharmacy staff and reports their achievements and any problems to Maria.

Company Goal: Expand Operations into Other Areas

The strength of 4Corners Pharmacy has always been Vincent's dedication to his customers and his community. Paul wants to continue this tradition by sponsoring local events and ensuring that his customers and their families never have a reason to seek another pharmacy. Paul also wants to open a second store in Colorado by the end of the year, possibly by acquiring an existing business. With the addition of another store on the horizon, Don needs to ensure that the database created to run 4Corners Pharmacy is easily expandable and adaptable to run the operations at a second location.

How Will Access Be Used at 4Corners Pharmacy?

Employees at 4Corners Pharmacy will use Access in many ways to assist them with the daily operations of the pharmacy. Specific examples of how a database will improve store operations and customer service are as follows:

- **Accounting**

  As the store manager, Elaine needs reports that detail how much inventory remains for each prescription and nonprescription item in the store. She also needs to know the value of the existing inventory for insurance purposes. She can use Access to compute information about sales and create a report from the information that is current and easy to read.

Accounting

- **Finance**

  Elaine and Paul need to ensure the pharmacy's financial reserve is sufficient. As a result, they will be able to use Access to produce reports that accurately detail the pharmacy's sales figures, salary commitments, and similar financial data to determine the financial health of the pharmacy.

Finance

Human Resources

- **Human Resources**

  As the human resources manager, Maria needs to manage all of the data about employees. Some of this data is descriptive, such as the employee's name and address. Other data is sensitive, such as the employee's Social Security number, salary, and information about job performance, and needs to be protected from unauthorized access. Maria can use Access to manage data about employees and ensure that sensitive data is protected from fraud and abuse.

Information Systems

- **Information Systems**

  Don's goal for the new database at 4Corners Pharmacy is to produce a system that meets user needs, stores and manages the correct information, displays information in the correct format, and is easy for employees to use. He will use the tools available in Access to secure, back up, and maintain the database to ensure that it is properly protected from unauthorized access, loss, and failure. In addition, Don will ensure that the database will be expandable for future increased business.

Marketing

- **Marketing**

  As the store's marketing contact, Elaine works with an outside advertising agency to produce the store's weekly ads that run in the local newspaper and on the company website. Elaine can use Access to determine how store items are selling and determine which products to add to the store's advertising. She can also use Access to produce reports about the buying behavior and demographics of 4Corners Pharmacy customers. Although this data exists within the pharmacy, it is not currently organized in a format that makes it easy to analyze for determining market trends and demographic buying behavior.

Operations Management

- **Operations Management**

  Elaine needs to be able to determine which drugs to order from suppliers and in what quantities. She frequently evaluates the store's inventory for low-drug volumes and expired drugs. Customer health is of great importance to the pharmacy. Although no one has ever been injured as a result of pharmacist negligence at 4Corners Pharmacy, increased federal regulations and legal liability issues mandate that pharmacy employees are properly certified and diligently inform customers of dosage instructions, possible side effects, and adverse interactions for each prescription sold. The pharmacy already keeps meticulous records about pharmacist certifications, and pharmacists and pharmacy technicians diligently inform their customers about the drugs they dispense. But with the increase in hiring and the possible expansion of the company, Don can use Access to put formal processes, to track and implement these requirements, into place.

Sales

- **Sales**

  Customers are also data consumers at the pharmacy. They receive data from the pharmacists detailing drug information and potential interactions. Some customers participate in flexible spending accounts (FSAs) that allow them to pay for prescriptions with pre-tax dollars. Participating customers frequently request a list of the prescriptions ordered by their households on a quarterly or annual basis. Elaine and Paul can use Access to manage these requests by creating reports of all drugs ordered by a single customer or household.

All of these business areas of the pharmacy are related, just as the tables in the database are related. For example, when a customer's prescription is filled, different parts of the database are affected, as shown in Figure 16.

Figure 16: Data to store in the database at 4Corners Pharmacy

1. Doctor writes a prescription for patient. Doctor and clinic data is stored in the database.

2. Patient presents prescription to pharmacist. Data about pharmacists and other employees is stored in the database.

3. Pharmacy staff enters customer, insurance, and prescription data into the database.

4. Pharmacist fills prescription. The database records the prescription and reduces the drug inventory by the correct amount.

5. Customer picks up prescription and makes payment. The database stores the cost and price of the drug, which are used to generate the profit amount.

© 2014 Cengage Learning

The customer requests the prescription, either by presenting a written order from a doctor to a pharmacist or asking for a refill of an existing prescription. The pharmacist adds this request to the system by getting the required information to fill it, including information about the drug, customer, customer's insurance plan, and so on. The prescription also affects the inventory that is tracked by operations and the profile of buying behavior that is tracked for marketing purposes. Eventually, the prescription affects the pharmacy's financial health by contributing revenue and profit to the store. In Chapter 1, you will learn how 4Corners Pharmacy manages its data and create a plan for storing this data in a database.

Managing Data for the Organization

All organizations must deal with how best to collect, store, and manage their data. There are several problems at 4Corners Pharmacy. First, not all data is gathered for managers to make informed business decisions. For example, marketing data is scarce and dispersed throughout the organization. Several departments import and export data to each other and then maintain that data separately, resulting in errors and redundancy of data.

Also, the operations department manages inventory based on data entered by the pharmacists. However, this data is not updated on a regular basis, resulting in orders placed too early, too frequently, or not frequently enough. Moreover, redundancy occurs in the customer list as each customer is listed with his own address, despite the fact that several people might live at the same address. Therefore, if one person submits a change of address or phone number, this data is not updated for people living in the same household. This problem leads to erroneous data that might result in undelivered mail sent to customers from 4Corners Pharmacy or the pharmacist not being able to reach a customer because of an incorrect phone number.

The business motivation for gathering all the data used in 4Corners Pharmacy and storing it in one relational database is to save time and money and to prevent errors and redundancy. But, why is using a database program such as Access a superior method for organizing data? Why not use Excel to manage this data? After all, it is possible to sort, filter, and manipulate a significant amount of data in an Excel worksheet.

There are many benefits to using a relational database to address the data deficiencies at 4Corners Pharmacy. First, the pharmacy produces too much data to store effectively in an Excel workbook. 4Corners Pharmacy gathers data about employees, customers, drugs, health plans, and doctors, each of which is its own unique category and should have its own worksheet. It would be difficult to list all the pharmacy's employees, customers, and prescribing doctors in one Excel worksheet, much less all the drug and health plan data.

Excel is limited in the structure of its data; you cannot easily manage all of this data in one workbook, but you can do so in one database. A database might contain dozens of tables, just as an Excel workbook might contain dozens of worksheets. However, through a process of relating tables to each other, you can join together multiple tables in Access if they share common data, and then query those tables as though they were one big table, presenting a huge advantage over managing data in multiple worksheets in Excel. For example, 4Corners Pharmacy will use three tables to store and manage data about employees, customers, and doctors; a table to store and manage data about prescriptions that pharmacists fill for customers; and a table to store and manage data about the drugs prescribed, such as the drug's name, dosage, expiration date, cost, and so on. All of these tables have a relationship that connects them to the others, as shown in Figure 17.

Figure 17: Interlinked data at 4Corners Pharmacy

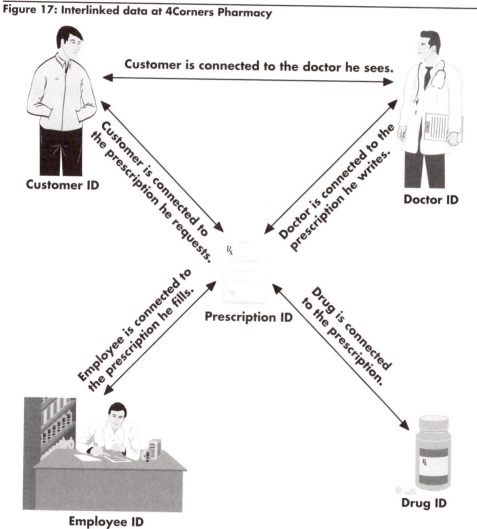

© 2014 Cengage Learning

Figure 17 shows that a customer brings in a prescription, and then a pharmacist fills the prescription. In the database, the customer's data is stored in a table that stores all customer information. The prescription table contains data about prescriptions and a reference to the customer table (such as a customer identification number) to indicate the customer who purchased the prescription. The prescription table contains a reference (such as a prescription identification number) to the table that stores data about pharmacists, a reference to which pharmacist filled the prescription, and a reference (such as a drug identification number) to the table that stores data about drugs. Finally, the doctor table contains a reference to the prescription table, indicating which doctor wrote the prescription.

The benefit of designing tables and then creating relationships between them is that you are able to retrieve the data stored in these tables easily and quickly. For example, you can select any prescription and find out which doctor wrote it, which pharmacist filled it, and which customer purchased it. This type of querying simply isn't possible in Excel.

Problem Solving in This Book

Throughout this book, you will be presented with various problems to solve or analyses to complete using different Access tools. Each chapter in this book presents three levels of problem solving with Access. Level 1 deals with basic problems or analyses that require the application of one or more database tools, focusing on the implementation of those tools. However, problem solving not only requires you to know *how* to use a tool, but, more importantly, *why* or *when* to use *which* tool. So, with Level 2 the problems and analyses presented increase in complexity. By the time you reach Level 3, the complexity increases further, providing you with opportunities for more advanced critical thinking and problem solving.

In the hands-on portions of each chapter—the "Steps To Success" sections at the end of each level and the Case Problems at the end of each chapter—the degree of complexity increases, matching how the material is presented in each level. In addition, while the complexity *increases*, the structure of the problem to be solved *decreases* in the hands-on sections for each level. Figure 18 illustrates this approach to problem solving in this book.

Figure 18: Pedagogical model for problem solving

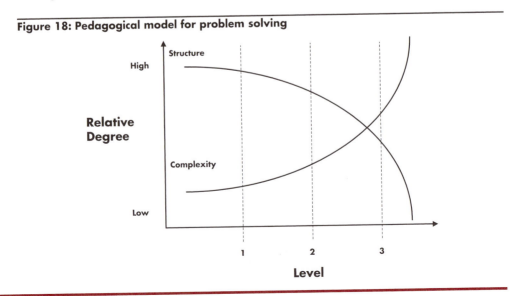

In this model, structure can be thought of as the way that various parts of a problem are held or put together. In a highly structured situation, almost every part of the problem is defined, and it is up to you to put the last few pieces in place to reach a solution. As the amount of structure is reduced, you need to understand more of the pieces and how they fit together to reach a solution. As structure is further reduced (more missing pieces of the puzzle) and complexity is increased (more pieces to understand), the difficulty of solving the problem increases. You can measure this difficulty in the time, number of steps, and decisions required to reach a solution. The goal is to increase your problem-solving skills while moving you toward an environment that is more like the real business world you will encounter during internships and upon graduation from college.

Steps To Success Exercises

As you read each level in a chapter, you will see how business problems are evaluated and solved at 4Corners Pharmacy using a database. At the end of each level, you will complete the exercises in the Steps To Success section to reinforce what you learned in the level. However, to ensure that you have a way to practice everything you learned in each level, the Steps To Success exercises are completed in a separate database for a similar business, Hudson Bay Pharmacy, which has slightly different data needs and requirements. Hudson Bay Pharmacy is located in Edmonton, Alberta (Canada). This pharmacy has similar needs to those of 4Corners Pharmacy, but because Canada has different requirements for the data it collects about employees and drugs, you will need to develop the database with these needs in mind. You will create this database in the Steps To Success exercises in Level 1 of Chapter 2, and then do all subsequent work for the Steps To Success exercises in your copy of the database. This approach makes it possible for you to develop a database from scratch and practice everything you learned in the chapter in your copy of the database. Because the database has slightly different requirements, you will be faced with decisions and problems that are unique to that database but are not specifically taught in the levels.

End-Of-Chapter Continuing Case Problems

At the end of each chapter, there are three Case Problems that let you apply the skills that you learned in the chapter to problems faced by different kinds of businesses. All three Case Problems put you in the position of working for the company and making decisions about how best to store, analyze, and manage the data for the business. Instead of asking you to perform certain skills to arrive at a result, these Case Problems ask you to analyze a situation, evaluate the choices, and determine the correct way to reach a certain goal.

Although all three Case Problems are challenging, they are arranged so that the first Case Problem provides the most structure and requires skills learned in all of Level 1 and some of Level 2 as necessary to complete the tasks. Level 2 Case Problem is less structured and requires skills learned in all of Levels 1 and 2. Level 3 Case Problem is the most challenging, as it requires you to evaluate a problem and make most of the decisions to solve it. This Case Problem requires skills from all three levels in the chapter, and as such, it is the most comprehensive.

As you work through the chapters in this book, you should complete the same Case Problem in each chapter using the database you first create in Chapter 2. For example, when you begin working in Chapter 3, you will open the database you created in Chapter 2 and continue your work.

LEVEL 1 CASE PROBLEM: NHD Development Group Inc.

NHD Development Group Inc. develops commercial properties throughout the United States. Tim Richards, the company's (CEO) Chief Executive Officer, is charged with scouting prospective projects and evaluating current ones. He has identified a current investment, a series of shopping malls that sell antiques, as being deficient in reporting financial returns, making it difficult to determine their profitability. Consequently, he seeks to design a database that manages the malls' data and produces the reports he needs. Tim chose a mall in Tennessee as a pilot project. If successful at this mall, NHD will use the database at other malls in the investment portfolio. Your assistance is required to create objects within the database and to produce the financial reports required by the business.

LEVEL 2 CASE PROBLEM: MovinOn Inc.

MovinOn Inc. is a moving and storage company based in the northwestern United States. Having grown from a start-up venture consisting of one vehicle and one warehouse in Oregon, the company is burgeoning into other states and is outgrowing its paper-based recordkeeping system. David Bowers, the CEO of MovinOn Inc., hired an information systems manager to design a database to manage employee, driver, customer, and order data. Your assistance is required to design the objects in the database so that the present inefficient system is replaced and the new system is reliable upon implementation. You will also assist in securing the database so that the company's data is not accidentally or maliciously deleted.

LEVEL 3 CASE PROBLEM: Hershey College Intramural Department

Hershey College is a four-year liberal arts college in Hershey, Pennsylvania. Having received a grant to promote health and wellness, the college seeks to expand its athletic and fitness offerings by creating an intramural department. The college appointed Marianna Fuentes, an assistant coach for the women's basketball team, as the intramural department's director. She needs to build and maintain a database of teams, coaches, and captains so that she can report information about the department's popularity and usage to grant administrators and the college administration. It is important that her participation reporting is accurate, professional, and timely, as the grant will not be renewed without it. Because the intramural department is new, Marianna's challenge is to develop a system from scratch without the benefit of evaluating an existing system. Your assistance is required to design this database.

Chapter Summary

This Introduction presented how to use Access 2013 and some of the new features. After you get comfortable with the latest aspects, you'll find you're spending less time performing common tasks. You will no longer need to search for commands that are used for the entire database because they are readily available in Backstage view. If you prefer using the keyboard, you are still able to use shortcut key combinations with the KeyTips. The Quick Access toolbar still makes it easy to find your frequently used commands. You'll also discover creating expressions are exceptionally easy with the new enhanced Intellisense tool.

In the chapters ahead, you will practice using these new features as you build databases, make calculations, and present information effectively. The enhanced interface and features will make it easier for you to find the commands and complete tasks in record time.

Conceptual Review

1. What is a data analyst?

2. What kinds of data about yourself do you think the data analysts at your school or work place may use?

3. How might data analysts at your school or work place relate the data they collect about you?

4. What are some examples of data deficiencies that might occur about the data collected at your school or work place?

5. Explain the benefit of designing tables and then creating relationships between them.

6. Explain how tables can be related to each other.

7. When tables are related, they can be queried as one large table. Explain the advantage of managing data in this manner versus trying to manage data in multiple worksheets in Excel.

8. Describe the motivations that a business, such as the 4Corners Pharmacy, might have for gathering all of their data and storing it in one relational database.

9. Give an example of how data redundancy might occur in a table.

10. Give an example of how erroneous data might result using Excel workbooks versus an Access database.

Preparing to Automate Data Management
Information Services: Gathering Data and Planning the Database Design

LEARNING OBJECTIVES

Level 1

Discover and evaluate sources of existing data

Research sources of missing data

Assign data to tables and use field types and sizes to define data

Level 2

Understand relational database objects and concepts

Create table relationships

Understand referential integrity

Level 3

Learn the techniques for normalizing data

Evaluate fields that are used as keys

Test the database design

Chapter Introduction

This chapter details the process that you should follow prior to creating a database. The first step, the discovery phase, includes gathering all existing data, researching missing and incomplete data, and talking with users about their data output needs. Subsequent steps in the process include putting data into groups, called tables; identifying unique values for each record in those tables; and designing a database to produce the desired output. It is then imperative to test the new database prior to its implementation. Designing a database requires knowledge of database concepts, which are introduced in this chapter. Figure 1.1 illustrates the steps followed in the database design process and highlights the first step, the discovery phase.

Figure 1.1: Database design process: the discovery phase

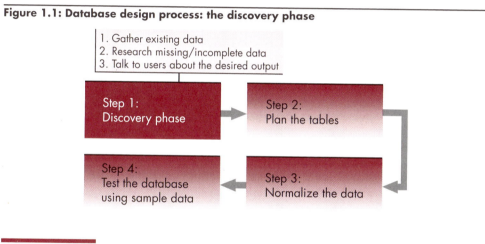

1. Gather existing data
2. Research missing/incomplete data
3. Talk to users about the desired output

Step 1:
Discovery phase

Step 2:
Plan the tables

Step 4:
Test the database
using sample data

Step 3:
Normalize the data

Case Scenario

Creating a database is a significant undertaking that requires careful planning, organization, and management. In many cases, it takes several weeks or even months to identify the data that an organization needs to collect and then determine how managers and employees will enter and use that data to assist them in the organization's day-to-day operations and long-term planning. 4Corners Pharmacy is an existing business, and you have already learned that Vincent Ferrino's system for managing the prescription, inventory, employee, and other data for the pharmacy is lacking in several respects. Paul Ferrino's vision for the pharmacy, which he now owns, is to convert all of the existing paper and spreadsheet systems to a database. By doing so, Paul will realize many benefits, such as more accurate and consistent data and the ability to track inventory and customer buying habits.

LEVEL 1
Examining Existing and Missing Sources of Data

Discovering and Evaluating Sources of Existing Data

One of the first tasks of creating a database is to identify the information that the organization needs to manage and organize. This task might take several days to several weeks and might involve interviewing department heads and other key employees to understand the data they collect and the way they use it. You might find that some departments manage their data in paper files or in computerized records. In larger organizations, data might be stored in different computerized systems. Regardless of the current data storage method, it is important to take the time to understand not only what data is collected, but also how that data is used.

As you collect information from the organization's key players, you might begin to see patterns that indicate how to organize the data. For example, you might see that the organization manages data about customers, employees, and products. Different departments might use this data in different ways and employees might need different levels of access to this data, depending on the departments in which they work and their positions in the company. For example, a manager of an Order Department needs information about products and customers, but not about employees; a human resources manager needs information about employees, but not about products; a customer service representative needs information about products and orders, but not about employees; and so on. In addition to needing different kinds of data, some employees might need more detailed information than others. An assistant in the Human Resources Department might need a list of employees working in the organization, but only the human resources manager should be able to view their salaries.

You can use a database management system, or DBMS, to manage data. There are several DBMSs, including Oracle, MySQL, and Microsoft Access. Each of these DBMS programs has specific advantages that benefit different organizations, depending on the type and amount of data they store. For example, very large organizations will benefit from the power of Oracle to manage large amounts of data on a network or on a Web site. Other businesses might choose MySQL, an open source program. An open source program permits licensed users to use, change, improve, and redistribute the software in modified or unmodified formats. This type of software is called "free" software, in which the term free typically refers to freedom that the license gives users. Free software might or might not be available at no charge. MySQL, however, requires programming expertise in Structured Query Language (SQL), the language used by most DBMSs. Oracle and MySQL are conceptually equivalent. Both are server based, both scale to large amounts of data, and both require knowledge of SQL. You will learn about SQL in Chapter 3.

Some midsized and smaller organizations might choose to use Access because this DBMS, part of the Microsoft Office suite of programs, is fairly easy to use and quite powerful, but does not require extensive programming knowledge. Access can also be differentiated because it is an integrated DBMS, which includes both forms and reports along with storing the data. In addition, Access integrates very well with the other Microsoft Office programs, such as Excel. Access uses the SQL language but makes using it a simpler task compared to other programs that require programming expertise.

Because 4Corners Pharmacy is a small business, the company's information systems director, Don Linebarger, selected Access as the DBMS to manage the pharmacy's database. As the business grows in the future, Don might choose another DBMS, but for now, Access will handle the pharmacy's data management needs.

Before he gets started, Don needs to determine how the pharmacy collects and stores data about prescription transactions, drug inventories, customers, and employees. Don also needs to determine if there are other data needs at the pharmacy that are currently going unfulfilled and determine how the data will be collected. After extensive consulting with Vincent and Paul Ferrino, Don learns that data is managed in many ways and realizes that entering customer data at 4Corners Pharmacy is a manual and time-consuming process. When new customers visit the pharmacy to fill a prescription, they complete a customer information form by hand. A pharmacy technician enters the information into an Excel worksheet. Figure 1.2 shows the pharmacy's customer information form.

Figure 1.2: Customer information form used by 4Corners Pharmacy

CUSTOMER INFORMATION

Thank you for choosing 4Corners Pharmacy. Please fill out this form so that we can assist you promptly.

Name:	Birth Date:
Address:	
Social Security Number:	
Home Phone Number:	Fax Number:
Email Address:	
Gender: Male Female	Marital Status (circle one): Single Married Widowed Divorced
Employer:	Occupation:
Primary Care Physician:	Physician's Phone Number:
Emergency Contact:	Relationship to Patient:
Emergency Contact's Phone Number:	Spouse's Name:
Allergies:	
Prefer childproof caps? Y N	

HEAD OF HOUSEHOLD

(Complete this section only if someone other than the customer is financially responsible.)

Name:	Social Security Number:
Address:	
Home Phone Number:	Work Phone Number:

INSURANCE INFORMATION

Insurance Plan:	
Insurance Plan Phone Number:	Insurance ID Number:
Subscriber's Name:	Subscriber's Employer:

I authorize the release of any medical information necessary to process my claim and payment of benefits to 4Corners Pharmacy.

_____   _____

Signature of Customer/Responsible Party   Date

After entering the data from the customer information form into the worksheet, the technician stores the form in a filing cabinet in one of 26 file folders arranged by the first letter of the customer's last name. This system makes it difficult to find individual customer information later when forms require an update, such as a change of address, a change in insurance information, or a new drug allergy. Vincent's original objective was to have one row in the worksheet for each customer, as shown in Figure 1.3.

Figure 1.3: Customer data maintained in an Excel worksheet

One row per customer

	A	B	C	D	E	F	G	H
1	SSN (Last 4)	First Name	Last Name	Birth Date	Address	City	State	ZIP
2	2243	Anders	Aannestad	9/11/1974	623 South Hampton Way	Farmington	NM	87499
3	6289	Jonathan	Cardenas	8/22/2004	620 East Empire	Kayenta	AZ	86033
4	6234	Dallas	Coats	10/31/1972	912 North Hampton Ave	Yellow Jacket	CO	81335
5	5623	Octavia	Coats	6/30/1976	912 North Hampton Ave	Yellow Jacket	CO	81335
6	0975	Isabel	Lopez	8/30/1949	633 Empire Street	Flora Vista	NM	87415
7	1329	Danny	Cardenas	5/12/2002	620 East Empire	Kayenta	AZ	86033
8	0979	Geoffrey	Baaz	12/31/2001	1233 Myrna Place	Kirtland	NM	87417
9	2943	Rose	Baaz	4/12/1970	1233 Myrna Place	Kirtland	NM	87417
10	1413	Albert	Cardenas	10/14/1965	620 East Empire	Kayenta	AZ	86033
11	1156	Dana	Coats	8/16/2002	912 North Hampton Ave	Yellow Jacket	CO	81335
12	1064	Sonia	Cardenas	4/12/1968	620 East Empire	Kayenta	AZ	86033
13	1329	Daniel	Cardenas	5/12/2002	620 East Empire	Kayenta	AZ	86033

Don knows from experience that the existing recordkeeping system is error-prone, as it is possible to store two records for the same customer without realizing the mistake. For example, if a customer has a formal name and a nickname or goes by a middle name, it might be possible to store two separate records for the same individual without realizing that these records are for the same person. This problem might also occur if the person who entered the record misspelled a customer's name on one or more occasions. This phenomenon is known as **data duplication** and it is undesirable, not only because it takes up additional space in the database, but because it often leads to inconsistent and inaccurate data. For example, a pharmacist might indicate that the customer named John W. Jackson has a drug allergy, but the record for J. William Jackson—the same person but with a different version of his name—might not indicate this important fact. This situation might not seem important for billing or correspondence issues, but a serious error occurs when the pharmacist accesses the duplicate customer record that does not include the important information about the customer's drug allergy and gives the customer a prescription to which he is allergic. Don's first order of business is to work to avoid data duplication in the database.

In addition to deleting duplicate records for customers, Don also notes that he needs to find a way to group and store the address and phone information for people in the same household. This repetition is known as **data redundancy** and is to be avoided. When one member of a household reports a new address or change of insurance that also affects other people in the household, the database must update the records for everyone affected by the change. Figure 1.4 shows the customer data shown in Figure 1.3, but it is sorted alphabetically by last name.

Figure 1.4: Sorted customer data illustrates data duplication and redundancy errors

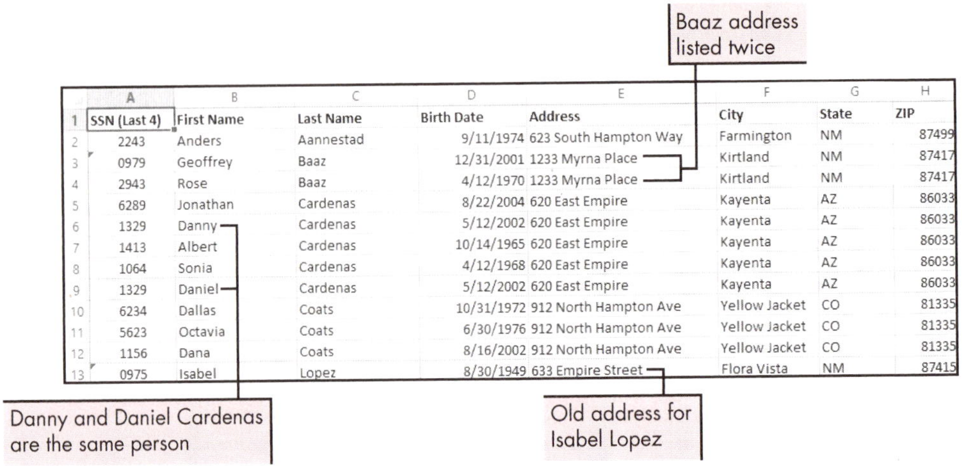

Baaz address listed twice

	A	B	C	D	E	F	G	H
1	SSN (Last 4)	First Name	Last Name	Birth Date	Address	City	State	ZIP
2	2243	Anders	Aannestad	9/11/1974	623 South Hampton Way	Farmington	NM	87499
3	0979	Geoffrey	Baaz	12/31/2001	1233 Myrna Place	Kirtland	NM	87417
4	2943	Rose	Baaz	4/12/1970	1233 Myrna Place	Kirtland	NM	87417
5	6289	Jonathan	Cardenas	8/22/2004	620 East Empire	Kayenta	AZ	86033
6	1329	Danny	Cardenas	5/12/2002	620 East Empire	Kayenta	AZ	86033
7	1413	Albert	Cardenas	10/14/1965	620 East Empire	Kayenta	AZ	86033
8	1064	Sonia	Cardenas	4/12/1968	620 East Empire	Kayenta	AZ	86033
9	1329	Daniel	Cardenas	5/12/2002	620 East Empire	Kayenta	AZ	86033
10	6234	Dallas	Coats	10/31/1972	912 North Hampton Ave	Yellow Jacket	CO	81335
11	5623	Octavia	Coats	6/30/1976	912 North Hampton Ave	Yellow Jacket	CO	81335
12	1156	Dana	Coats	8/16/2002	912 North Hampton Ave	Yellow Jacket	CO	81335
13	0975	Isabel	Lopez	8/30/1949	633 Empire Street	Flora Vista	NM	87415

Danny and Daniel Cardenas are the same person

Old address for Isabel Lopez

Don spots several errors when the data is arranged in this different way. For example, Don suspects that Daniel and Danny Cardenas might be the same person. Although it is possible that two similarly named boys live in Kayenta, Arizona, a closer look reveals that they share the same date of birth and address. Don imagines that the first record is the boy's formal name and the second is his nickname. Further evidence supports Don's belief: Daniel and Danny share the same last four digits of their Social Security numbers. Don must devise a way to eliminate this repetition while at the same time preserving the customer's prescription history.

Don also notices cases of data redundancy. For example, there are two records for people with the last name Baaz, and both people share the same address. As mentioned earlier, this duplication requires that the address be changed for both family members if they move. Don also notices that the address for Isabel Lopez is not showing as her current address based on her most recent prescription. Don found this error when he compared her customer information with her latest customer prescription worksheet.

Concerned that other errors might exist in the 4Corners Pharmacy recordkeeping system, Don asks Paul about the method he uses to manage new prescriptions and prescription refills that are brought to the pharmacy by customers or that are phoned in or faxed from doctors' offices. Paul explains that prescriptions are logged in a separate worksheet for each day the pharmacy is open. For each prescription filled by the pharmacy, the worksheet contains one row that includes the customer's first and last names, address, phone number, and insurance information; the prescription number, drug name, instructions, fill date, expiration date, and number of refills authorized by the physician; and the prescribing physician's name, address, clinic affiliation, and phone number. Figure 1.5 shows the worksheet from January 2, 2016.

Figure 1.5: Prescription data managed in an Excel worksheet

Anders Aannestad
is listed five times

	A	B	C	D	E
	First Name	Last Name	Prescription ID	Name	Instructions
1	First Name	Last Name		Name	Instructions
2	Anders	Aannestad	2	Dyotex	1 pill every 6 hours
3	Ted	Sabus	4	Phalastat	1 teaspoon every 4 hours
4	Steven	Nguyen	5	Clonazepam	2 pills daily
5	Anders	Aannestad	72	Epronix	2 pills every 12 hours
6	Anders	Aannestad	60	Syocil	2 pills every 6 hours with food
7	Rose	Baaz	61	Diazapam	2 pills every 6 hours
8	Geoffrey	Baaz	56	Glimepiride	1 teaspoon every 6 hours
9	Albert	Cardenas	70	Almotriptan	2 teaspoons every 5 hours
10	Paula	Hargus	47	Myobuterol	2 teaspoons every 4 hours
11	Christina	Hargus	55	Oxaprozin	2 teaspoons every 6 hours
12	Malena	D'Ambrosio	10	Didanosine	2 pills every 6 hours with food
13	Anders	Aannestad	52	Tvalaxec	2 pills daily
14	Gina	Mercado	19	Rivastigmine tartrate	2 pills every 4 hours with food
15	William	Gabel	3	Rizatriptan Benzoate	1 pill every 8 hours
16	Maria	Gabel	18	Phalastat	1 teaspoon every 4 hours
17	Anders	Aannestad	24	Clonazepam	2 pills daily
18	Dusty	Alkier	33	Diazapam	2 pills every 6 hours
19	Kevin	Wachter	63	Glimepiride	1 teaspoon every 6 hours
20	Cesar	Lopez	39	Almotriptan	2 teaspoons every 5 hours
21	Josefina	Hernandez	14	Myobuterol	2 teaspoons every 4 hours
22	Jennifer	Ramsey	57	Diazapam	2 teaspoons every 6 hours

Jan 2, 2016 Prescriptions ⊕

Don sorted the worksheet by last name and in doing so notices that Anders Aannestad is listed five times. Don also realizes that the table is unwieldy because it requires hiding columns or scrolling frequently to see the details of a given prescription, such as which doctor prescribed which drug for which customer.

Don reviews the columns of customer address and insurance information so he can see prescription details. An audit of the insurance information reveals additional errors. Figure 1.6 shows another view of the prescription worksheet from January 2, 2016, with the customer health plan identification numbers displayed.

Figure 1.6: Incorrect customer addresses and Plan ID

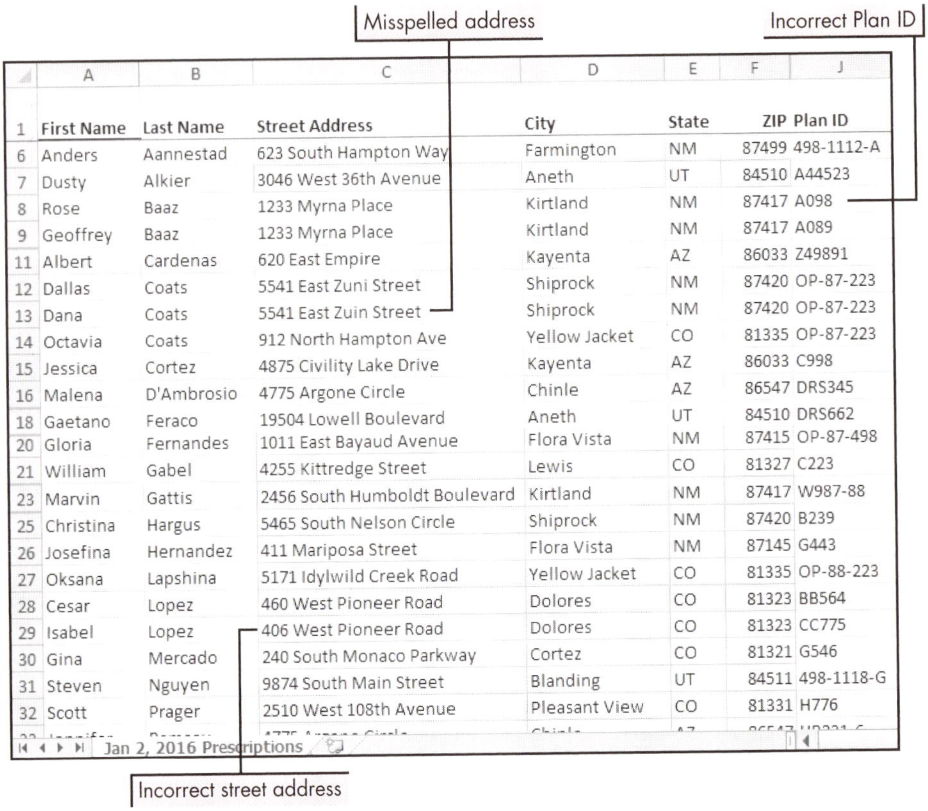

Misspelled address   Incorrect Plan ID

	A	B	C	D	E	F	J
1	First Name	Last Name	Street Address	City	State	ZIP	Plan ID
6	Anders	Aannestad	623 South Hampton Way	Farmington	NM	87499	498-1112-A
7	Dusty	Alkier	3046 West 36th Avenue	Aneth	UT	84510	A44523
8	Rose	Baaz	1233 Myrna Place	Kirtland	NM	87417	A098
9	Geoffrey	Baaz	1233 Myrna Place	Kirtland	NM	87417	A089
11	Albert	Cardenas	620 East Empire	Kayenta	AZ	86033	Z49891
12	Dallas	Coats	5541 East Zuni Street	Shiprock	NM	87420	OP-87-223
13	Dana	Coats	5541 East Zuin Street	Shiprock	NM	87420	OP-87-223
14	Octavia	Coats	912 North Hampton Ave	Yellow Jacket	CO	81335	OP-87-223
15	Jessica	Cortez	4875 Civility Lake Drive	Kayenta	AZ	86033	C998
16	Malena	D'Ambrosio	4775 Argone Circle	Chinle	AZ	86547	DRS345
18	Gaetano	Feraco	19504 Lowell Boulevard	Aneth	UT	84510	DRS662
20	Gloria	Fernandes	1011 East Bayaud Avenue	Flora Vista	NM	87415	OP-87-498
21	William	Gabel	4255 Kittredge Street	Lewis	CO	81327	C223
23	Marvin	Gattis	2456 South Humboldt Boulevard	Kirtland	NM	87417	W987-88
25	Christina	Hargus	5465 South Nelson Circle	Shiprock	NM	87420	B239
26	Josefina	Hernandez	411 Mariposa Street	Flora Vista	NM	87145	G443
27	Oksana	Lapshina	5171 Idylwild Creek Road	Yellow Jacket	CO	81335	OP-88-223
28	Cesar	Lopez	460 West Pioneer Road	Dolores	CO	81323	BB564
29	Isabel	Lopez	406 West Pioneer Road	Dolores	CO	81323	CC775
30	Gina	Mercado	240 South Monaco Parkway	Cortez	CO	81321	G546
31	Steven	Nguyen	9874 South Main Street	Blanding	UT	84511	498-1118-G
32	Scott	Prager	2510 West 108th Avenue	Pleasant View	CO	81331	H776

Jan 2, 2016 Prescriptions

Incorrect street address

Figure 1.6 shows multiple data entry errors and some design problems that create redundant data. The address data for each customer is redundant in the Prescriptions worksheet; these addresses already exist in the Customers worksheet shown in Figure 1.4. This problem is compounded when data entry mistakes are made. In looking at the data shown in Figure 1.6, Don sees that Dana Coats lives on either Zuni or Zuin Street, Isabel Lopez lives in house number 406 or 460, and Geoffrey Baaz's health insurance is a plan with the identification number A089 or A098.

Don continues examining the prescriptions data by scrolling and hiding columns as necessary and notes the many mistakes it contains. Figure 1.7 details more errors Don found in this part of the discovery phase. He suspects that the doctor is named either Chinn or Chin. These problems are probably the result of typographical errors.

Figure 1.7: Prescription data with doctor name errors

Incorrect spelling
of doctor's name

	First Name	Last Name	Street Address	City	State	ZIP	Plan ID	Doctor
1	First Name	Last Name	Street Address	City	State	ZIP	Plan ID	Doctor
2	Anders	Aannestad	623 South Hampton Way	Farmington	NM	87499	498-1112-A	Allen
3	Anders	Aannestad	623 South Hampton Way	Farmington	NM	87499	498-1112-A	Freitag
4	Anders	Aannestad	623 South Hampton Way	Farmington	NM	87499	498-1112-A	Freitag
5	Anders	Aannestad	623 South Hampton Way	Farmington	NM	87499	498-1112-A	Freitag
6	Anders	Aannestad	623 South Hampton Way	Farmington	NM	87499	498-1112-A	Freitag
7	Dusty	Alkier	3046 West 36th Avenue	Aneth	UT	84510	A44523	Pifer
8	Rose	Baaz	1233 Myrna Place	Kirtland	NM	87417	A098	Freitag
9	Geoffrey	Baaz	1233 Myrna Place	Kirtland	NM	87417	A089	Freitag
11	Albert	Cardenas	620 East Empire	Kayenta	AZ	86033	Z49891	Loke
12	Dallas	Coats	5541 East Zuni Street	Shiprock	NM	87420	OP-87-223	Floyd
13	Dana	Coats	5541 East Zuin Street	Shiprock	NM	87420	OP-87-223	Chinn
14	Octavia	Coats	912 North Hampton Ave	Yellow Jacket	CO	81335	OP-87-223	Chin
15	Jessica	Cortez	4875 Civility Lake Drive	Kayenta	AZ	86033	C998	Wilson
16	Malena	D'Ambrosio	4775 Argone Circle	Chinle	AZ	86547	DRS345	Zamarron
18	Gaetano	Feraco	19504 Lowell Boulevard	Aneth	UT	84510	DRS662	Huddleson
20	Gloria	Fernandes	1011 East Bayaud Avenue	Flora Vista	NM	87415	OP-87-498	Banan
21	William	Gabel	4255 Kittredge Street	Lewis	CO	81327	C223	Faust-Perez
23	Marvin	Gattis	2456 South Humboldt Boulevard	Kirtland	NM	87417	W987-88	Jurski
25	Christina	Hargus	5465 South Nelson Circle	Shiprock	NM	87420	B239	Baechle
26	Josefina	Hernandez	411 Mariposa Street	Flora Vista	NM	87145	G443	Gomez
27	Oksana	Lapshina	5171 Idylwild Creek Road	Yellow Jacket	CO	81335	OP-88-223	Banan
28	Cesar	Lopez	460 West Pioneer Road	Dolores	CO	81323	RR564	Gomez

Jan 2, 2016 Prescriptions   (+)

Don sees some serious problems with the current process of logging prescriptions using this system. First, there is no method to control the duplication of data. If a customer fills three prescriptions on the same day, there will be three rows in the worksheet—one row for each prescription filled. The name, address, and phone number can vary in each of these three rows because there is no built-in method in a worksheet to prevent this problem from occurring. It is possible to have similar variances in the doctor's name, address, clinic affiliation, and phone number. Second, data is difficult to track and gather together. For example, because the pharmacy creates new worksheets for each day's prescriptions, pharmacists would need to know the original fill date for a prescription to find out how many refills the doctor authorized. Aggregating, or gathering, data by customer, doctor, or drug would also be difficult.

After finishing his exploration of the current system, Don asks Paul for other changes that he wants to make and types of data that he wants to add to the database that is currently not in the system. Paul tells Don that in the new database system, he would like to be able to do the following:

- Eliminate paper registration forms
- Make it easier to update customer information
- Have quick access to a customer's prescription history (without searching a paper file)

- Print a list of drug names
- Create a way to ensure that the person entering a customer's information inquired about the customer's allergies
- Verify that the pharmacist explained interactions with other drugs to a customer
- Prove that the pharmacist provided counseling about using the drug to the customer
- Print a list of doctors and their contact information

In talking with the pharmacy staff, Don also learns that in the past it has been difficult to generate items for the marketing department. Elaine sends notices to customers about pharmacy events, drug recalls, and local health fairs. She needs to be able to obtain addresses of customers and physicians to create mailing labels. Don also learns from the pharmacy technicians that some customers have requested year-end reports identifying all of the prescriptions and their total cost for each family member. The customers would like to have the total prescription drug costs to use when reconciling with flexible spending accounts (FSAs) provided by their employers. Because the current system has no way to account for this data, this need is going unmet.

After examining the pharmacy's records and discovering all of the problems with data entry errors and data duplication, Don moves on to look at how Paul manages the pharmacy's inventory of prescription drugs. He talks with Paul and Vincent about their method for tracking the value and number of each item in inventory. He also discusses the system they use for reordering out-of-stock items, evaluating items that do not sell well and discontinuing them, and making sure that items on sale are stocked in appropriate quantities before the sale is advertised. Figure 1.8 shows the worksheet that Paul uses to track prescription drug inventory.

Figure 1.8: Prescription drug inventory data

UPN	Name	Generic	Description	Unit	Dosage	DosageForm	Cost	Price	Interactions	PregCategory	Supplier
102	Ampicillin	Yes	Antibiotic	Pill	250	mg	0.75	1.45	Calcium	B	Inundate Pharmaceuticals
121	Tolbutamide	No	Bacterial infections	Pill	2	mcg	0.24	0.90		C	Kwekker Pharmaceuticals
224	Avatocin	No	Allergies	Pill	100	mg	0.65	1.40	Alcohol	A	TJR Labs
247	Acebutolol hydrochloride	No	Arthritis	Pill	400	mg	0.55	1.10		A	Pulman Labs
256	Dseurton	Yes	High blood pressure	Pill	175	mg	0.60	1.20	Sedatives	C	Cranston Pharmaceuticals
289	Levothyroxine	Yes	Thyroid disorders	Pill	25	mg	0.70	1.40		B	Vacer Labs
311	Dyotex	No	Tonsillitis	Bottle	2	tsp	0.25	1.05		D	Frankmeir Pharmaceuticals
366	Phalastat	No	Allergies	Bottle	1	tsp	0.75	1.60		A	Swinton Labs
398	Clonazepam	No	Epilepsy	Pill	4	mcg	0.65	1.20		A	TJR Labs
412	Epronix	No	Pain	Pill	500	mg	0.85	1.50	Grapefruit	C	Vacer Labs
444	Syocil	Yes	Diabetes	Pill	120	mg	0.45	1.10		D	Kwekker Pharmaceuticals
452	Diazapam	Yes	Anxiety	Pill	5	mg	0.45	1.12		D	Esterman Pharmaceuticals
467	Glimepiride	Yes	Diabetes	Pill	2	mg	0.25	0.90		X	Nerman Pharmaceuticals
523	Xeroflarol	Yes	Acid reflux	Bottle	1	tsp	0.50	1.05		X	Wilper Labs
524	Cefixime	Yes	Antihistamine	Pill	400	mg	0.95	1.60	Sedatives	A	Ranston Pharmaceuticals
566	Quentix	Yes	High blood pressure	Pill	50	mg	0.50	1.25	Alcohol	A	Esterman Pharmaceuticals
587	Haloperidol	No	Diuretic	Pill	6	mcg	0.70	1.30		C	Valfer Pharmaceuticals
622	Tiron	No	Beta blocker	Pill	150	mcg	0.75	1.30		A	Opherman Labs
642	Montelukast sodium	Yes	Acne	Pill	10	mcg	0.32	0.90	Alcohol	B	Gilman Labs
644	Hyometadol	No	Asthma	Bottle	2	tsp	0.65	1.35		B	Ranston Pharmaceuticals
654	Warfarin Sodium	Yes	Bronchitis	Pill	4	mg	0.65	1.40		D	Swinton Labs
711	Nvalax	Yes	Depression	Pill	200	mg	0.30	0.90	Grapefruit	C	Pulman Labs

tblDrug

Because the data in this worksheet isn't connected to the systems that the pharmacists and cashiers use to sell prescription drugs and other items, sales volume cannot be calculated electronically. Indeed, Vincent has always performed a bimonthly hand count of inventory and then built temporary columns in Excel to determine costs and profits. Paul has continued to use the same method for tracking inventory. Don suspects that it would be difficult to use this worksheet to determine how much inventory exists for any given item in the store or prescription drug in the pharmacy, and imagines that it is unlikely that Vincent could accurately account for any product in stock. Thus, not only is it difficult to determine the quantity or volume of drugs in stock and the overall value of the inventory, there is no way to determine which items sell well and which sell poorly. Consequently, Don guesses that reordering occurs only when a pharmacist or other employee notices that a product's inventory is low or nonexistent. Don wants the database to address all of these problems by providing timely and accurate information about sales volume, inventory levels, and drug expiration dates. Furthermore, he wants to incorporate a list of interactions, pregnancy risks, and suppliers of each drug in the inventory, as presently these must be cross-referenced with data found online or in proprietary databases.

Vincent explains to Don that his system has worked fine for the nearly two decades in which he has been in business. However, Don knows that Paul wants to automate all of the business processes that must occur to run the pharmacy. Paul knows that Vincent's systems do not work well enough to ensure timely and accurate information. Paul also knows that his father's systems contain many errors and as the owner of the pharmacy, Paul wants to increase the efficiency of these systems.

Don continues his research by talking with Maria Garcia, who manages all of the pharmacy's employment records, including applications, employee reviews, benefits, certifications, training, and salary and tax-related information. Maria tells Don that as the pharmacy grows, it is becoming increasingly difficult to manage employee records. Currently, she maintains employee data in paper forms and in three programs. As shown in Figure 1.9, Maria uses Microsoft Outlook's contacts feature to maintain employee address and telephone information.

Figure 1.9: Employee contact information in Outlook

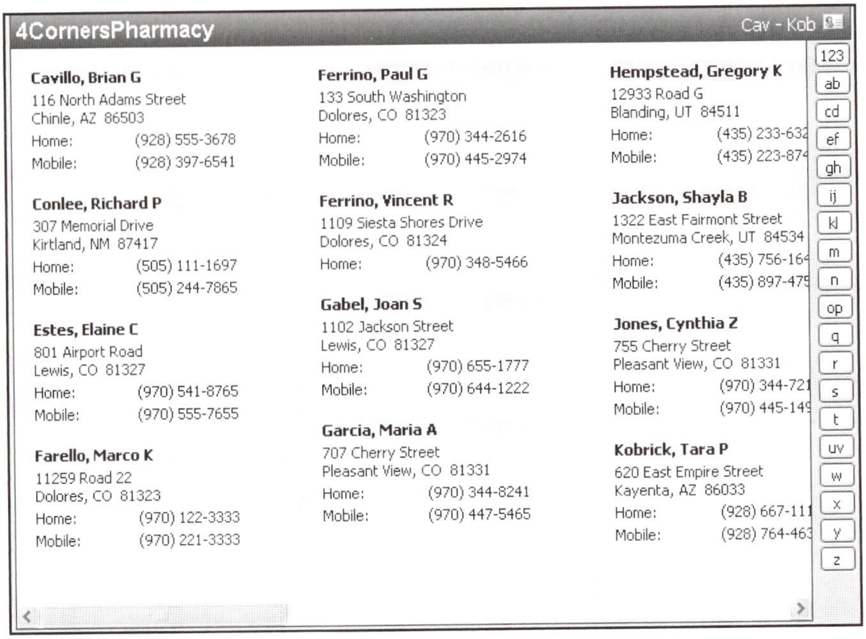

Maria uses Excel for tracking key employee dates, such as date of birth, date of hire, termination date, and date of the employee's last personnel review. Maria also uses Excel for recording salary data. Because this worksheet contains sensitive information—in addition to salaries, the table lists employee Social Security numbers—Maria keeps this file in its own password-protected workbook that only she has access to. Figure 1.10 shows Maria's Excel worksheets.

Figure 1.10: Employee date and salary data in Excel worksheets

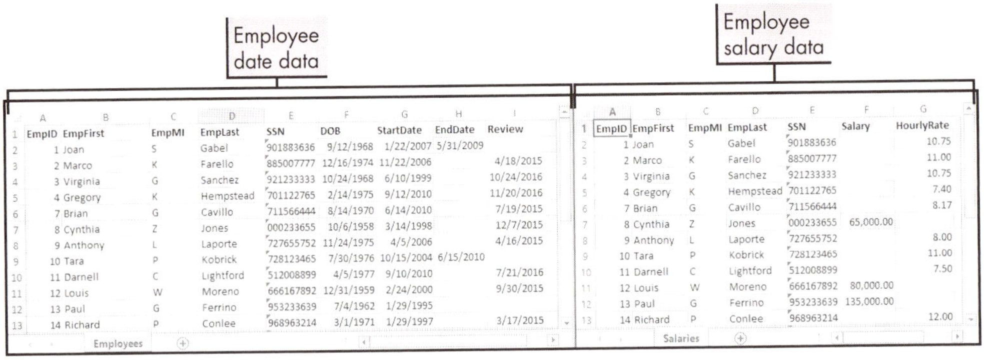

EmpID	EmpFirst	EmpMI	EmpLast	SSN	DOB	StartDate	EndDate	Review
1	Joan	S	Gabel	901883636	9/12/1968	1/22/2007	5/31/2009	
2	Marco	K	Farello	885007777	12/16/1974	11/22/2006		4/18/2015
3	Virginia	G	Sanchez	921233333	10/24/1968	6/10/1999		10/24/2016
4	Gregory	K	Hempstead	701122765	2/14/1975	9/12/2010		11/20/2016
7	Brian	G	Cavillo	711566444	8/14/1970	6/14/2010		7/19/2015
8	Cynthia	Z	Jones	000233655	10/6/1958	3/14/1998		12/7/2015
9	Anthony	L	Laporte	727655752	11/24/1975	4/5/2006		4/16/2015
10	Tara	P	Kobrick	728123465	7/30/1976	10/15/2004	6/15/2010	
11	Darnell	C	Lightford	512008899	4/5/1977	9/10/2010		7/21/2016
12	Louis	W	Moreno	666167892	12/31/1959	2/24/2000		9/30/2015
13	Paul	G	Ferrino	953233639	7/4/1962	1/29/1995		
14	Richard	P	Conlee	968963214	3/1/1971	1/29/1997		3/17/2015

EmpID	EmpFirst	EmpMI	EmpLast	SSN	Salary	HourlyRate
1	Joan	S	Gabel	901883636		10.75
2	Marco	K	Farello	885007777		11.00
3	Virginia	G	Sanchez	921233333		10.75
4	Gregory	K	Hempstead	701122765		7.40
7	Brian	G	Cavillo	711566444		8.17
8	Cynthia	Z	Jones	000233655	65,000.00	
9	Anthony	L	Laporte	727655752		8.00
10	Tara	P	Kobrick	728123465		11.00
11	Darnell	C	Lightford	512008899		7.50
12	Louis	W	Moreno	666167892	80,000.00	
13	Paul	G	Ferrino	953233639	135,000.00	
14	Richard	P	Conlee	968963214		12.00

In addition to using Outlook and Excel, Maria keeps several employee records in Word, including a list of bilingual employees at 4Corners Pharmacy. If a bilingual employee is not on duty, pharmacists can refer to this list and call these employees when Spanish-speaking customers request assistance. She also keeps a Word document to track absenteeism. Although absenteeism is not a large problem at 4Corners Pharmacy, Maria is aware that Paul plans to expand the company and documentation should be in place as the employee base grows. Figure 1.11 shows both of these documents.

Figure 1.11: Bilingual employees and absentee report

Bilingual Employees

Name	Language	Proficiency
Joan Gabel	Spanish	Fluent
Maria Garcia	Spanish	Fluent
Darnell Lightford	Spanish & Chinese	Fluent

Absentee/Tardy

Name	Date	Absent/Tardy
Dominique Latour	3/4/2016	Tardy
Shayla Jackson	10/15/2016	Absent
Gregory Hempstead	11/14/2016	Tardy

Maria is also responsible for monitoring staff development, a time-consuming task. Each pharmacist and pharmacy technician must maintain the proper license and certification as mandated by Colorado state law. Maria is responsible for ensuring that employees take the required classes to maintain their certifications. In addition, she must manage the employee performance reviews, which occur every 90 days, 6 months, or 12 months, depending on their job titles and the number of years they have worked at the pharmacy. She also serves as the pharmacy's benefits coordinator and manages requests for sick days and vacation, extended leaves of absence, pension benefits, and life insurance benefits.

Although Maria's various documents and worksheets seem to manage the information she needs, Don worries that these systems will not work well if the pharmacy grows as expected and adds additional stores and employees. Don sees that Maria could also benefit from storing and managing personnel data in a database.

After talking extensively with Vincent, Paul, and Maria, Don took a few days to talk to other employees in the store to understand and view the data that they use and need to perform their jobs. Upon concluding his discovery phase of the database design process, Don learned many things. First, there are many paper-based and handwritten methods of gathering data at 4Corners Pharmacy that use various forms, faxes, and memos. Second, many employees copy and paste data from one worksheet to another or import and export data from one program to another, thereby creating redundant data. This process occasionally leads to errors. Finally, Don suspects that the pharmacy is not collecting data that it needs to produce reports for outside consultants, such as the value of inventory in the pharmacy for insurance purposes or the value of business capital for local tax authorities. Don also sees that some data collected by the customer information form (Figure 1.2), such as insurance information, is never recorded in detail. As the business grows, it will be important to automate all of the processes at the pharmacy. Don knows that a DBMS will serve this function better than hiring a large staff of people to manage the growing data needs of 4Corners Pharmacy and that using a DBMS will make Paul's business run more smoothly and more efficiently.

Concluding the first part of the discovery phase, Don details his findings to Paul. Table 1.1 lists the expectations of the database as Don understands them.

Table 1.1: Preliminary database expectations for 4Corners Pharmacy

Department	Expectation
Pharmacy	• Eliminate paper forms • Provide quick access to prescription history • Print list of drug names • Ensure pharmacist consulted with customer about dosage instructions, allergies, and drug interactions • Print doctor contact information
Marketing	• Print customer mailing labels • Print physician mailing labels • Use customer data to gather data information about customer buying habits
Operations	• Track inventory • Identify poor-selling items
Human Resources	• Monitor staff development • Confirm certifications • Create employee performance reviews
Customers	• Print a year-end report of all prescriptions purchased by an individual or household
Accounting and Finance	• Determine profit and loss for individual sale items • Value the store's inventory • Track the business profit

© 2014 Cengage Learning

Best Practice

Combating "Scope Creep" During the Database Design Process

During the discovery phase of the database design process, it is necessary to interview as many members of the organization as possible to learn about all sources of input and desired output. This process might result in a large "wish list." At 4Corners Pharmacy, Paul asks Don if it is possible to include legal, tax, and investment data in the DBMS. Don informs Paul that while it is possible to do this, it would require a great deal more work, be significantly more expensive, and lie outside the scope of the original project, which is creating a database to manage day-to-day store operations. As a result, Paul and Don agree on the scope and deliverables of the project—managing customer and prescription data, managing personnel data, tracking buying behavior, and evaluating inventory. The exact specifications of the project—how much it costs, when it is delivered, and what exact output is expected—will be negotiated before Don starts the database design process. During the planning phase, it is important to manage expectations early and agree on project specifications, as Don has done. Otherwise, the project can lead to scope creep and become unmanageable. **Scope creep** occurs when the original project specifications change or are increased after the project has started.

Now that Don has identified the existing sources of data and has interviewed key employees at the pharmacy, he turns his attention to another important part of the discovery phase—researching sources of missing data.

Identifying Sources of Missing Data

Don's findings have identified the data collected by 4Corners Pharmacy and have given him a chance to evaluate how employees and managers use it. Another important part of the discovery phase is determining data that is missing and identifying the sources you can use to obtain that missing data. This part of the process is often difficult because you must ask the right questions of the right people to get the right answers. In interviews with key employees and managers, it is best to ask questions such as "What else would you like to know about the data?" and similarly worded inquiries. You might find that employees need to know certain things about the data that the current system cannot provide.

In his conversations with employees, Don learned a great deal about the kind of data that the DBMS must collect, organize, and manage. He also learned about data that various departments and employees want to collect but are not collecting presently. For example, Maria needs to obtain certain data about employee training and classes, but has no way to do so. She also wants to have an electronic record of the classes that employees have taken and need to take, a way to determine which employees are bilingual, and scanned images of important employment documents such as the driver's licenses of employees who are authorized to make pharmacy deliveries.

Determining Output

When you interview members of an organization during the discovery phase of database design, listen closely to their needs. Few people are familiar with database concepts. Consequently, they will speak of needing lists, reports, files, printouts, records, and other terms. Your job is to translate those needs into database deliverables. You will learn database terms later in this chapter, but it is important to remember that no one you interview will direct you to "employ the 'and' logical operator in a select query to list the customers in Colorado who are allergic to aspirin." People don't talk that way. They will say, "I need a printout of every customer who can't take aspirin and who's either been a customer for a long time or who spends a lot of money at the pharmacy. I want to send these customers a free sample of a new aspirin substitute." It becomes your job to translate this information into database commands.

Databases are not created in a vacuum; it is essential to interview employees, managers, and potential users of the database to learn how data is gathered and stored in an organization and to seek feedback regarding what output and functionality they want to obtain from the database. After gathering this information, you will better understand which users require access to which data, how that data should be stored and formatted, and how to organize the data into logical groups.

Assimilating the Available Information and Planning the Database

Now that Don has completed his interviews with the various managers and key employees at 4Corners Pharmacy, he is ready to start planning the database. His notes include sample documents showing how and which data is currently stored, data that should be collected but currently is not, and information that suggests possible additions and desires from future users of the system. With all of this information, Don has a good understanding of how 4Corners will store, manage, and use the data it collects, so he is ready to move into the next phase of database development—planning the database design.

The first step in database design is to determine the best way to organize the data that you collected in the discovery phase into logical groups of fields. These logical groups of fields are known as entities. An **entity** is a person, place, thing, or idea. In a database, a **field** (or **column**) is a single characteristic of an entity. For example, the fields to describe a customer would be ones such as first name, last name, address, city, state, and so on. When all the fields about an entity are grouped together, they create a **record** (or **row**). A **table** (also called a **relation**) is a collection of records that describe one entity. A **database** is a collection of one or more tables.

When a database contains tables, related through fields that contain identical data, the database is called a **relational database**. For example, a table that stores customer data might be named Customer and contain a field that stores unique identification numbers for each customer; this field might be named Customer ID. To relate customers to the sales representatives who represent them, the database might also contain a table named Rep that includes information about sales representatives. To relate the Customer and Rep tables to each other, so you can determine which representative represents which customers, the Customer table would also contain a field named RepID and this field would contain identical values in both tables. You will learn more about tables and relationships later in this chapter.

Evaluating Field Values and Assigning Appropriate Data Types

After identifying the fields that describe the data that will be stored in the tables in the database, the next step is to determine the data type to assign to each field. A database stores data in different ways; a **data type** determines how to store the data in the field. Some fields store text values, such as a person's name; other fields store numbers, such as quantity sold. A database might also store objects such as pictures or fields that contain hyperlinks to Internet or file locations. In Table 1.2, Access data type names are listed in the first column.

Table 1.2: Access data types and their descriptions

Data Type	Description	Example
Short Text	Text or alphanumeric combinations of data and numbers that are not used in calculations	Names, addresses, phone numbers, Social Security numbers, and ZIP codes
Long Text	Long passages of data containing text and alphanumeric characters	Employee review information and detailed product descriptions
Number	Numbers that are used in calculations	Quantity ordered and number of refills
Date/Time	Dates or date and time combinations	Inventory expiration dates and birth dates
Currency	Monetary amounts (not available in all DBMSs)	Item cost and item price
AutoNumber	An automatically generated number that produces unique values for each record (not available in all DBMSs)	Any number that is necessary to uniquely identify records, such as a product ID number that is not assigned by another method
Yes/No	A field value that is limited to yes or no, on or off, and true or false values (not available in all DBMSs)	Responses to indicate whether childproof caps are whether the employ (both require yes or
OLE Object (Object Linking and Embedding)	Linked or embedded objects that are created in another program (not available in all DBMSs)	Photographs, sounds and video
Hyperlink	Text that contains a hyperlink to an Internet or file location (not available in all DBMSs)	Web pages, e-mail ac on network or worksta

48

Table 1.2: Access data types and their descriptions (cont.)

Data Type	Description	Example
Attachment	Many types of documents and files can be attached to the database	Pictures, documents, spreadsheets, charts, or sounds
Calculated	Computes data from fields in the same table	Order Cost is determined by the Quantity Order field multiplied by the Item Cost field; when an amount in either field is added or changed, the calculated field is updated with the new value
Lookup Wizard	A field that lets you look up data in another table or in a list of values created for the field (not available in all DBMSs)	Predefined list of drug codes, categories of information, and state abbreviations

How do you determine which data type to assign each field? Doing so depends on what function you want to derive from that data because each data type has different properties. For example, 4Corners Pharmacy requires name and address data for employees, customers, and doctors. Don will create separate tables for each of these entities. Within each table, he will create fields for first names, last names, street addresses, cities, states, and ZIP codes. The data stored in each field and its intended use determine what data type to assign to the field, as explained in the following sections.

Short Text and Long Text Data Types

A primary goal in designing a database is to keep it small by assigning the data type to each field that is large enough to hold the data required in that field without wasting additional space. That is why it is important to understand the difference between the Short Text and Long Text data types. Short Text data type stores a maximum of 255 characters. Don will assign the **Short Text** data type to the fields that store a person's name because names are composed of letters. He will also assign the Short Text data type to the street address as it is often an alphanumeric combination. A ZIP code is a number, but this number is not used in calculations—you would never add, subtract, multiply, or divide one customer's ZIP code by another, so the appropriate data type is Short Text.

Maria wants to enter comments about disciplinary actions for employees in the database. Don will need to create a field in the Employee table for this and assign it the **Long Text** data type because this data type can store long passages of text. Long Text data type can effectively store over 65,000 characters. Long Text fields can also contain rich text, which is text that supports formatting, such as bold, italic, colors, and various fonts. Thus, names, addresses, descriptions, and so on generally require the Short Text data type, whereas notes and comments generally require the Long Text data type.

Because it is the most commonly assigned data type, the Short Text data type is the default for all fields created in an Access database.

Number Data Type

Don will also create a table to store the details for every prescription filled at 4Corners Pharmacy, including the number of prescriptions filled for each customer and the number of refills authorized by the doctor. Don will assign the **Number** data type to these fields because Paul will want to use them to calculate how many prescriptions were filled in a given period or perhaps to calculate the average refill allowance per drug type.

The Number data type stores both positive and negative numbers in a field containing up to 15 digits. A simple way to remember the purpose of the Number data type is that it is typically used for numbers that you need to use in calculations. As mentioned earlier, data such as telephone numbers, Social Security numbers, and ZIP codes, despite their appearance and the fact that most people identify these values as numbers, are not used in calculations and are not assigned the Number data type, but rather the Short Text data type. Also, if the ZIP code starts with a leading zero, such as 07705, Access will drop the leading zero if the field is set to a Number data type rather than a Short Text data type.

Currency Data Type

Another important consideration is that monetary values are assigned the Currency data type, not the Number data type. Despite the fact that monetary values are numbers and used in calculations, the Currency data type includes two decimal places and displays values with a dollar sign by default. Thus, Don will assign the Currency data type to fields that store the costs and prices for drugs and the salaries and wages for employees so that these amounts will display as currency values.

Date/Time Data Type

Don will include a field in the Employee and Customer tables to store a person's date of birth. He will assign this field the **Date/Time** data type. By default, fields assigned the Date/Time data type display values in the format mm/dd/yyyy and hh:mm:ss, but they can also include the date or time in different formats. Dates can be used in calculations if necessary to calculate the number of days between a starting date and an ending date, or to determine a person's age. Just as he is able to modify other data types, Don may also change the default formatting of the Date/Time data type to display date and time values in different formats.

AutoNumber Data Type

The **AutoNumber** data type is a number automatically generated by Access that produces unique values for each record. This data type is useful when you need to distinguish two records that share identical information. For example, two prescriptions of the same drug, in the same amount, filled on the same day might be entered into a Prescription table. It might be difficult to tell these prescriptions apart, but if assigned the AutoNumber data type, this unique value created for each record would differentiate them.

Yes/No Data Type

The **Yes/No** data type is assigned to those fields requiring a yes/no, true/false, or on/off answer. This field can also be customized with other values, such as always/never. Don will assign the Yes/No data type to the field in the Customer table that indicates whether the customer prefers childproof caps on prescription bottles. The Yes/No field will make data entry easy; a user only needs to click the check box to place a check mark in it to represent a "yes" value. Using a check box also saves space, as each field takes only one character of space compared with the 15 characters that would be required to type the words "childproof caps."

OLE Object Data Type

The **OLE object** data type is used to identify files that are created in another program and then linked or embedded in the database. Don might use this data type if he needs to link an employee's record to a scanned image of the employee driver's license necessary for delivering prescriptions.

Hyperlink Data Type

The **Hyperlink** data type is assigned to fields that contain hyperlinks to Web pages and email addresses when clicked. Don can use this data type when creating fields that link to websites for health plans or doctors.

Attachment Data Type

This data type lets you attach files such as pictures, documents, charts, and spreadsheets. The **Attachment** data type can store one or more files for each record in the database. Attachments open in the program they were created in. For example, selecting an Excel spreadsheet attachment opens the Excel program so that you can view the attachment. Because attachments open their original programs, they do not require additional database space for anything other than the attachment link. Don can use the Attachment data type to store information about prescription drugs and medical reports about drug interactions.

Calculated Data Type

The **Calculated** data type uses data from fields in the same table to perform calculations, a few of which include addition, subtraction, multiplication, and division. Don will use this field to view the cost of inventory items by multiplying an Item Cost field by the Quantity on Hand field. When Calculated is selected as the data type, the Expression Builder opens so that you can create the calculation or expression. You will learn more about the Expression Builder and the Calculated data type in Chapter 3.

Lookup Data Type

The **Lookup** data type creates fields that let you look up data in another table or in a list of values created for the field. Don might use the Lookup data type in a Customer table to display the two-letter abbreviations for each state so the user could choose the correct state from a drop-down menu. A lookup field accomplishes two things—it makes data entry easy and ensures that valid data is entered into the field. The user cannot misspell the state and cannot enter more or fewer letters than are available in the drop-down menu. For example, if you have a lookup table that stores state values, it is impossible for end-users to make mistakes, such as entering the abbreviation for Mississippi as MI when in fact that abbreviation is for Michigan. In addition, you won't have erroneous entries. For example, a user will not be able to enter CL for California or Colorado. They will only be able to choose from a list of allowable values, such as CA for California and CO for Colorado.

Selecting the Correct Data Type

Choosing the appropriate data type for each field in a table is essential for two reasons. First, it helps store the correct data in the correct format while using the least amount of space. Second, it facilitates data entry and interactivity with data because choosing the appropriate data types results in user-friendly, interactive features, such as drop-down menus, check boxes, and hyperlinks. Choosing the appropriate data type also lets you correctly manipulate the data. For example, say the pharmacy decides to start a customer loyalty program: The pharmacy will reward longtime customers who spend a set amount at the pharmacy by giving them a coupon to save 10% off their next pharmacy purchase. Don will need a way to calculate the sum of all orders placed by each customer. If the database can calculate the total for each pharmacy order, Don can use it to create yearly or monthly totals by customer. If this field uses the Text data type, these calculations would not be possible because a database cannot perform calculations on text values, even if they contain numbers. If this field uses the Currency data type, these calculations are possible.

Data types are important not only for manipulating data, but also for entering data into the database. For example, Maria might want to include a field in a table that identifies available training classes and course descriptions. To accomplish this goal, she might need to use a field with the Long Text data type to have room to include a complete course description that includes the course objectives, prerequisites, and requirements.

The Yes/No and Lookup data types ease data entry by controlling what data a user can enter into a field. The Yes/No data type accepts the values "yes" and "no." This restriction is valuable for answering such questions as "Did the pharmacist ask the customer about her allergies?" In this case, the pharmacist simply clicks the check box to indicate that he asked the question. Either the pharmacist followed or did not follow the procedures— there is no other choice for this field. The Yes/No data type provides a nice audit trail in this case.

What happens when the answer to a question is not always yes or no? What if the answer could be "undetermined," "undecided," or "maybe"? If any of these answers are possible, you should use the Short Text data type.

The Lookup data type also ensures accurate data, but can be more flexible than the Yes/No data type. For example, if the majority of 4Corners Pharmacy customers reside in the four nearby states of Colorado, Utah, New Mexico, and Arizona, it might be convenient to list those four states in a lookup field that provides a drop-down menu allowing the pharmacist to choose among them. The menu saves a great deal of typing for the pharmacist and ensures that the state abbreviations are entered correctly and in the appropriate format into the State field. In Chapter 2, you will learn more about ways to override the lookup field.

Assigning the Correct Field Size for Text Fields

As mentioned earlier, it is important to consider field size when assigning data types and to minimize the space reserved for each record by assigning the smallest data type possible. For example, to store the number of years worked you would need to create a field with the Short Text data type and a field size of two characters. In this case, the Lookup field size not only saves space, but also prohibits someone from entering "100" instead of "10" into the field for number of years worked. It is important to be conservative when assigning field sizes, but not too conservative. For example, how many spaces should be allowed for a person's last name? Upon first consideration, you might choose a field size of 10 or 12 characters and safely store the names "Jefferson" (requiring nine characters) or "O'Callaghan" (requiring 11 characters). But what happens when you try to store the names "Thangsuphanich," "Traiwatanapong," or "Jefferson-O'Callaghan," which require 21 characters? Storing a last name with 21 characters in a field designed to store 12 characters would result in almost half of the name being truncated, or cut off. On the other hand, you would not want to leave the last name field at the maximum of 255 characters as this field size would waste space and violate a cardinal rule of database design. A good compromise is to define fields that store last names with 30 to 40 characters.

Assigning the Correct Field Size for Number Fields

Just as you must be aware of preserving storage space when assigning the Short Text data type, you must also be conservative when assigning the Number data type, as there are seven choices for Number field sizes. Table 1.3 describes the different field sizes for fields with the Number data type.

Table 1.3: Field sizes for the Number data type

Field Size	Values Allowed	Decimal Precision	Storage Size
Byte	Whole numbers between 0 to 255 (excludes fractions)	None	1 byte
Integer	–32,768 to 32,767 (excludes fractions)	None	2 bytes
Long Integer	–2,147,483,648 to 2,147,483,647 (excludes fractions)	None	4 bytes
Single	$–3.4 \times 10^{38}$ for negative values through 3.4×10^{38} for positive values	7	4 bytes
Double	$–1.797 \times 10^{308}$ for negative values through 1.797×10^{308} for positive values	15	8 bytes
Decimal	$–9.999 \times 10^{27}$ for negative values through 9.999×10^{27}	28	12 bytes
Replication ID	Globally unique identifiers (GUID) are used to identify replicas, replica sets, tables, records, and other objects. Replication appears as a Number format option; however, it is not supported in the .accdb file format.	N/A	16 bytes

© 2014 Cengage Learning

To determine the correct field size, you must evaluate the data stored in a Number field just as you would evaluate the data stored in a Text field. For example, Don might assign the Number data type to a Dependents field in the Customer table and then set the field size to Byte. A Byte field stores only positive numbers up to 255. Because a customer cannot have a negative number of dependents, a fractional number of dependents, or more than 255 dependents, this is the correct field size because it stores the correct data using the least amount of space possible.

It is important to choose the correct data type prior to entering data into a table. Although it is possible to change a field's data type after entering data into a table, you might lose some of the data if you decrease a field size after data has been entered. For example, a last name may be truncated if it requires more space than the revised field size allows.

Dividing the Existing and Missing Data into Tables

Now that the discovery phase is over, Don will create the tables to be used in the 4Corners Pharmacy database. Figure 1.12 details the four steps involved in this process.

Figure 1.12: Database design process: planning the tables

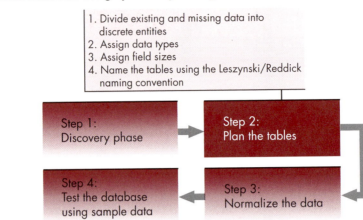

Tables are the single most important component of the database; all objects in a database are based on tables. A database can be as simple as one table containing only one field and only one record in it, such as your first name. Such a database wouldn't be terribly useful, but it would still be a database. Most databases contain multiple tables and hundreds or even thousands of records.

In the discovery phase, Don interviewed 4Corners Pharmacy employees so he could understand the desired database output. Now he needs to divide the existing and missing data into discrete entities, break those entities into smaller fields that describe an attribute, assign data types to the fields, modify the field sizes as necessary, and then name each table according to standard conventions.

Don focuses first on the employee data that Maria collects because it is currently the most fragmented. Recall that Maria keeps personnel records in Outlook, Excel, Word, and on paper, with much of the data, such as the employee's name, appearing in all of these sources. Don lists the type of data that Maria identified about employees in the discovery phase:

- Name
- Age
- Years with company
- Address
- Position
- Job description
- Pay rate
- Annual review
- Training classes attended
- Other information (such as whether the employee is bilingual and attendance information)
- The type of prescription that can be filled by a pharmacist or a pharmacy technician

After listing the items Maria provided, Don analyzes the list provided by Maria and finds five problem areas.

1. Missing Field for Telephone Numbers

Maria needs to print telephone lists of bilingual employees so that they can be called if necessary to assist with translation. This telephone list would be impossible to create as Don did not include a phone number in his initial field list. Thus, it is imperative to review the desired output and then ensure that you have the necessary data to produce it. Don expands the list to include one field for telephone number and another field for cell phone number, as most employees have both. Even if he does not have all employee cell phone numbers, he knows they can be added later.

2. Primary Key Field Needed

Don did not identify a primary key field. A **primary key** is one field (or perhaps a combination of fields) that creates a unique value in each record so you can identify each record in the table. The employees at 4Corners Pharmacy have unique last names, and at first it appears that the last name will uniquely identify each record. However, if two employees have the last name, "Garcia," there would be no way to use the last name field to distinguish between them. In addition, if Paul opens additional stores, the likelihood of having employees with the same last name increases. To create a unique value in each employee's record, Don could expand Maria's list to include an employee ID field, into which he will enter a unique value for each employee, and establish this field as the primary key.

3. Fields Listed Are Too Broad

The fields Don listed are too broad. For example, if an employee's first and last names are in one field called Name, you are limited to what you can do with the data. For example, Maria sends quarterly updates to all employees informing them of how many sick days and holidays they have accrued. Having recently learned how to perform a mail merge in Word, Maria wants to customize the contents of the letter to include each employee's first name only in the greeting. However, in Don's initial list above, Name is only one field. If Maria used the Name field in the mail merge, the salutation would read "Dear Maria Garcia," which would be too formal, the exact opposite of Maria's intention of writing the more customary and personal "Dear Maria." Thus, Don decides that the Name field should be broken down into at least two fields to store the first name and last name. Indeed, he could break down the Name field further, including additional fields to store the employee's title, middle name, suffix, and preferred name. For the Employee table, Don includes fields for first name, middle initial, and last name. Following this principle, Don also divides Address into multiple fields (address, city, state, and ZIP code) and Pay rate into multiple fields (salary and hourly rate).

4. Age and Years with Company Should be Calculated Fields

Don realizes a fourth problem with the proposed fields in the Employee table: employee age is stored as a whole number, which means it will become outdated within a year. Don knows that employees' ages should be stored using their birth dates. By storing a person's birth date, you can calculate the person's age by subtracting the birth date from today's date. Don changes the Age field to Date of Birth and then changes the Years with company field—another value that he can calculate—to Start Date and End Date. He realizes that with the Calculated data type he could use these fields in his calculation for age and years with the company. A Calculated field actually computes the value. In this case it would calculate the difference between the Start Date and the End Date and it would subtract their Date of Birth from the current date to show their age.

5. Data Redundancy

The fifth and final problem with the proposed fields for the Employee table is data redundancy. Don realizes that some of the fields will have data redundancy and should not be part of the Employee Table. For example, in Figure 1.13 it shows that 14 people have taken the same training class.

Figure 1.13: Employee training data

	A	B	C	D
1	EmpFirst	EmpLast	Description	Date
2	Joan	Gabel	Adult CPR	2/6/2012
3	Tara	Kobrick	Adult CPR	4/10/2012
4	Rachel	Thompson	Adult CPR	3/17/2012
5	Amy	Urquiza	Adult CPR	6/20/2012
6	Marco	Farello	Child/Infant CPR	1/30/2012
7	Cynthia	Jones	Child/Infant CPR	11/21/2014
8	Tara	Kobrick	Child/Infant CPR	11/15/2012
9	Dora	Langston	Child/Infant CPR	6/9/2012
10	Marco	Farello	Adult CPR Recertification	2/1/2014
11	Virginia	Sanchez	Adult CPR Recertification	6/1/2015
12	Virginia	Sanchez	Adult CPR Recertification	6/29/2016
13	Tara	Kobrick	Adult CPR Recertification	4/12/2013
14	Louis	Moreno	Adult CPR Recertification	4/1/2014
15	Paul	Ferrino	Adult CPR Recertification	2/5/2015
16	Rachel	Thompson	Adult CPR Recertification	3/16/2013
17	Amy	Urquiza	Adult CPR Recertification	6/21/2013
18	Amy	Urquiza	Adult CPR Recertification	3/10/2014
19	Dora	Langston	Adult CPR Recertification	6/15/2014
20	Dora	Langston	Adult CPR Recertification	3/5/2015
21	Vincent	Ferrino	Adult CPR Recertification	2/2/2013
22	Vincent	Ferrino	Adult CPR Recertification	4/2/2015
23	Vincent	Ferrino	Adult CPR Recertification	4/5/2016

Redundant data: "Adult CPR Recertification" appears 14 times

Typing the same information into each employee's record is a waste of time for Maria and exactly what Don seeks to avoid by designing a relational database. Retyping "Adult CPR Recertification" 14 times is inefficient and could result in inconsistent data. Don is glad that he spotted this redundancy now and knows that this is why the brainstorming component of database design, though often time consuming, is imperative and well worth the effort. By foreseeing this potential redundancy, Don will avoid it by creating a separate table to store data about the class descriptions, cost, provider, and any other pertinent data, which will be linked to the current table.

Don sees a similar issue with the Position field because multiple employees can share the same job title. To fix this, he creates a table to store all of the job descriptions at 4Corners Pharmacy. He also needs a way to identify which employee filled which prescription, so he creates another table to store information about prescriptions.

As you can see, Don's brainstorming about employees resulted in the creation of three additional tables and several more fields. Don will complete this brainstorming process for each table that he creates, making sure to include all necessary fields, identify primary keys, split broad fields into smaller discrete components, and avoid data redundancy. He will create as many tables as necessary to avoid repeating any information in the database. The result of Don's brainstorming is shown in Table 1.4, with the fields for the Employee table and their corresponding data types.

Table 1.4: Field names and data types for the Employee table

Field Name	Data Type
Employee ID	Number
First Name	Short Text
Middle Initial	Short Text
Last Name	Short Text
Social Security Number	Short Text
Date of Birth	Date/Time
Start Date	Date/Time
End Date	Date/Time
Address	Short Text
City	Short Text
State	Short Text
ZIP	Short Text
Comments	Long Text
Phone	Short Text
Cell	Short Text
Salary	Currency
Hourly Rate	Currency
Review Date	Date/Time

© 2014 Cengage Learning

The data about training classes attended, job positions, and prescriptions filled, which originally appeared in the Employee table, will become fields in their own tables.

Naming Conventions

After brainstorming the employee fields and grouping them together, Don must name the table. Database tables must have unique names and follow established naming conventions for the DBMS in which they are stored. Some general rules for naming objects (including tables) are as follows:

- Object names cannot exceed 64 alpha numeric characters and cannot start with a number. Try to keep object names as short as possible.
- Object names must not include a period (.), exclamation point (!), accent grave (`), or brackets ([ ]).
- Object names should preferably not include spaces. Instead, most database developers capitalize the first letter of each word when a table name includes two words, such as EmployeeTraining.

In general, field names follow the same naming rules. For example, in the Employee table, Don will change the field name First Name (which includes a space) to FirstName.

Most developers use the Leszynski/Reddick naming convention in which a prefix or tag precedes the object name to further define it. Instead of naming the table Employee, Don uses the Leszynski/Reddick naming conventions, shown in Table 1.5, and names the table tblEmployee.

Table 1.5: Leszynski/Reddick naming conventions for database objects

Database Object	Prefix	Example
Table	tbl	tblEmployee
Query	qry	qryPharmacists
Form	frm	frmCustomer
Report	rpt	rptBilingualPharmacists
Macro	mcr	mcrUpdateClasses
Module	bas	basInventory

© 2014 Cengage Learning

Some developers also use a prefix to identify the fields in a table, such as changing the field name LastName to txtLastName to identify the field as having the Short Text data type. Don decides not to use this convention because it will increase the time it takes to type the field names.

Changing a Field Name

Don knows that it is possible to change a field name after a database has been created but it will be better to change the name sooner rather than later after numerous queries, reports, and forms are established. However, Don knows that Access offers a protection feature, Name AutoCorrect, to ensure that field names are systematically changed throughout the database. When he creates the database, Don will turn this feature on by checking Perform name AutoCorrect check box in the Access Options/Current Database dialog box.

Although it will take some time to build all the tables, Paul is encouraged by the benefits that a DBMS will offer the pharmacy. Don interviewed as many key players at 4Corners Pharmacy as possible, gathered the existing data, researched sources of missing data, and talked to users about desired output. He and Paul agreed on expectations and then Don began planning the tables by dividing existing and missing data into discrete entities, naming the fields, and assigning data types to these fields.

Steps To Success: Level 1

After concluding the discovery phase of database design, Don began brainstorming about the tables he needs to create and which specific fields within those tables are necessary to capture all data required for the desired output he identified. Don created tblEmployee. He asks you to create the table designs for the remaining tables in the database by grouping the existing and missing data he identified into tables, creating field names and data types, and naming the fields and tables according to the standards he established.

On a piece of paper, complete the following:

1. Plan the Employee and Customer tables needed in the 4Corners Pharmacy database using the information Don garnered during the discovery phase. Planning each table in this database will be a time-consuming process. After you complete these two tables, challenge yourself to plan other tables.

2. Name the Employee and Customer tables according to their contents and the Leszynski/Reddick naming conventions.

3. List the fields in each table.

4. Designate data types for each field in each table.

5. Look at the plan you created for 4Corners Pharmacy and look for any missing or incomplete data. What other changes would you suggest making, and why?

LEVEL 2
Understanding and Creating Table Relationships

Understanding Relational Database Objects

The four main objects in an Access database are tables, queries, forms, and reports. Users can view the data that is stored in tables by opening the table or by creating other objects.

Tables

You learned in Level 1 that the data in a relational database is stored in one or more tables. You can view the data in a table by opening it and scrolling through its records. However, most of the time you will use one of the three other main database objects—queries, forms, and reports—to display the data from one or more tables in a format that matches your needs.

Queries

A **query** is a question that you ask about the data. For example, the question might be "Which customers live in Colorado?" If you use a query to find the answer to this question frequently, you can save the query in the database and use it again to list the customers who live in Colorado: The query searches each record in tblCustomer and lists in the results each one with the value CO in the State field. The query results look similar to a table, with fields displayed in columns and records displayed in rows. (This arrangement of data in Access is called a **datasheet**.) There are four main types of queries: select queries, action queries, crosstab queries, and SQL-specific queries.

The **select query** is the most commonly used query. As the name suggests, data is selected from the table on which the query is based (also called the **base table** or the **underlying table**), and is displayed in a datasheet. A query can select basic information or very specific information. For example, a select query might select all customers who live in Colorado. A more specific select query might select all customers who are older than 55 and live in the 81323 ZIP code in Colorado. When you run a select query, the query results are dynamic; that is, they change each time the query is run. For example, if every customer living in Colorado moves to another state, the datasheet will display no matching records the next time you run a query that selects customers living in Colorado. On the other hand, if 1,000 new Colorado customers were entered into tblCustomer, running a query that selects customers living in Colorado would display 1,000 new records.

A two-way relationship exists between a table and queries that are based on the table. If a record is changed in a query, it will be updated in the table it came from and if a record is deleted from a query, it will also be deleted from the table it came from. For example, if a pharmacist viewing a query that selects customers living in Colorado changes the value in the State field from CO to AZ for a customer, the customer's record is updated in tblCustomer. When he runs the query again, that customer's record will no longer appear in the query results because it no longer satisfies the requirements for being included. If a pharmacist accidentally deletes a record from the query results, that record is also deleted from tblCustomer.

An **action query**, as its name implies, performs an action on the table on which it is based. Some action queries let you select specific records in a table and update them in some way, such as increasing the price of a drug by 10%. Other action queries let you select data from one table and append (add) it to another table; you can use this type of query to create a new table or add records to an existing table. You can also use an action query to delete records from a table, such as deleting all customer records from a table when the customer's account has been inactive for a specific length of time.

A **crosstab query** performs calculations on the values in a field and displays the results in a datasheet. A crosstab query might sum sales of a product and then show the sales totals by month. This type of query adds another level of grouping to allow for additional analysis of the data.

Finally, a **SQL-specific query** is a type of query that must be written in SQL code. Even though queries have underlying SQL statements, most queries can be created in Design view. After creating the query in Design view, you can then switch to SQL view to see the SQL statements. SQL-specific queries, however, need to be written using SQL in the SQL VIEW OBJECT tab. Union queries, pass-through queries, and data-definition queries are all types of SQL-specific queries. You will learn more about queries in Chapter 3.

Forms

A **form** is used to view, add, delete, and update records in a database. A form is based on a table or a query. Often a form displays many or all the fields from the table on which it is based, and you can enter data into the form to add a record to the table. Depending on how a form is created, it might have a two-way relationship with a table, because changing data in a form might update the data in the table on which the form is based. A form based on tblCustomer is shown in Figure 1.14.

Figure 1.14: Form based on a table

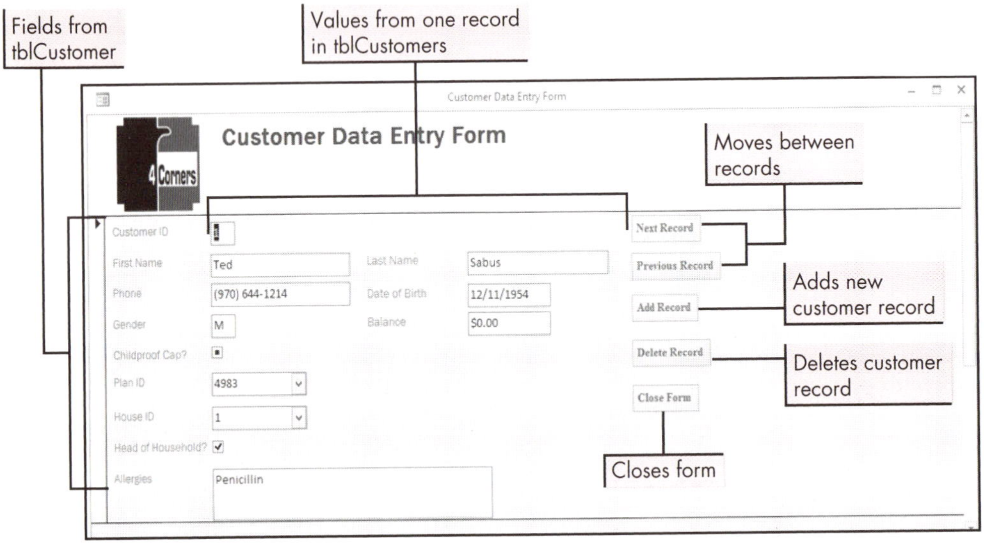

Fields from tblCustomer

Values from one record in tblCustomers

Moves between records

Adds new customer record

Deletes customer record

Closes form

Customer Data Entry Form

Customer ID	
First Name	Ted
Phone	(970) 644-1214
Gender	M
Childproof Cap?	☐
Plan ID	4983
House ID	1
Head of Household?	☑
Allergies	Penicillin

Last Name: Sabus
Date of Birth: 12/11/1954
Balance: $0.00

Next Record
Previous Record
Add Record
Delete Record
Close Form

Don could use the clinic information form he obtained during the discovery phase to create its database counterpart. Using the form object, the pharmacy staff could add a new clinic to the database, update fields as necessary, find and view a clinic's data, and then make any necessary changes. You will learn more about forms in Chapter 4.

Another benefit of using a form to display data is that the interface is more attractive than the table datasheet and you can customize a form's appearance with instructions and command buttons. The command buttons shown in Figure 1.14 offer the ability to add a new clinic, find an existing clinic, and close the form. As a result, even the least-experienced user of a database can feel confident when entering or viewing data.

Forms can also be used as a type of welcome menu to a database; when used in this capacity, it is called a navigation form or switchboard. A **navigation form** is a form that is displayed when you open a database and provides a controlled method for users to open the objects in a database. Users click buttons to open existing objects, which is more user friendly than using the database interface. You will learn how to create and use a navigation form in Chapter 6.

Reports

A **report** is a formatted presentation of data, from a table or query, that can be printed or viewed on-screen. A report might contain an employee telephone directory, inventory summaries, or mailing labels. The data displayed by a report is usually based on a query, although you can also base a report on a table. Reports are dynamic, reflecting the latest data from the object on which they are based. However, unlike forms, you can only view the data in a report; you cannot change the data or use a report to add a new record. The amount of data in a report varies—a report might list the top five best-selling drugs at 4Corners Pharmacy or all customers at the pharmacy who take a certain drug. When a report exceeds more than one page, the user must use the page navigation features to view the pages on-screen. Figure 1.15 shows a report that displays the accounts receivable data for customers with outstanding balances.

Figure 1.15: Accounts Receivable report for customers with outstanding balances

Outstanding Balance

Balance	CustID	First Name	Last Name
$40.00	20	Kevin	Wachter
$35.00	18	Anders	Aannestad
$30.00	33	James	Fernandes
$30.00	4	Steven	Nguyen
$24.00	11	Paula	Hargus
$20.00	41	Marisella	Velasquez
$20.00	40	John	Velasquez
$20.00	31	Dana	Coats
$15.00	29	Marvin	Gattis
$15.00	25	Adriane	Walters
$12.00	15	Gina	Mercado
$10.00	37	Isabel	Lopez

The report shown in Figure 1.15 is based on the query shown in Figure 1.16. As you can see, the data in the report and query are the same, but the report format makes the data easier to read. The report contains a title to identify its contents. You can also add page numbers, headers, and footers to a report. You will learn more about reports in Chapter 5.

Figure 1.16: Query datasheet

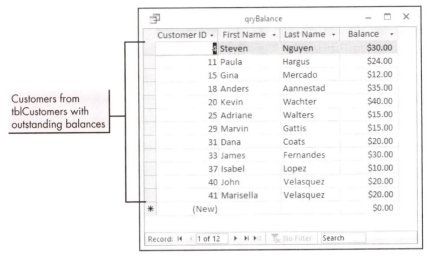

Customers from tblCustomers with outstanding balances

Customer ID ▾	First Name ▾	Last Name ▾	Balance ▾
4	Steven	Nguyen	$30.00
11	Paula	Hargus	$24.00
15	Gina	Mercado	$12.00
18	Anders	Aannestad	$35.00
20	Kevin	Wachter	$40.00
25	Adriane	Walters	$15.00
29	Marvin	Gattis	$15.00
31	Dana	Coats	$20.00
33	James	Fernandes	$30.00
37	Isabel	Lopez	$10.00
40	John	Velasquez	$20.00
41	Marisella	Velasquez	$20.00
*	(New)		$0.00

Record: I◄ ◄ 1 of 12 ► ►I ►▭ No Filter | Search

Some reports are simple to create, such as generating telephone lists. Other types of reports, such as inventory summaries, are more complex. Paul also needs reports showing the pharmacy's daily, monthly, quarterly, and yearly revenues. If Paul opens one or more additional stores, he'll need this same information, but grouped by location.

Other Database Objects

Most users interact regularly with the tables, queries, forms, and reports in a database, but you might also use other objects. Microsoft has moved toward SharePoint Services for sharing data on company intranets and on the Web. Authorized employees in a company can share and access information. For example, you can create a database for use on a SharePoint site to be accessed by authorized individuals. You will see the option to use SharePoint in the Backstage view on the FILE tab. Figure 1.17 shows the SharePoint option located on the FILE tab.

Figure 1.17: SharePoint option in Backstage view

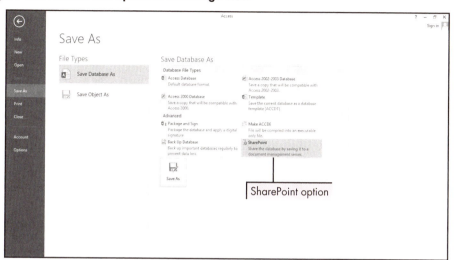

A **macro** is a set of instructions that you specify to automate certain database tasks. A macro might contain instructions to open a specific form or query in the database when you click a command button on a form. A macro can also contain instructions to close an object, find a record, print an object, or close Access. You will learn more about using and creating macros in Chapter 6.

A **module** is another object that contains instructions to automate a database task. Modules are written in **Visual Basic for Applications (VBA)**, the programming language for Microsoft Office programs, including Access. A macro usually automates a simple task, such as opening or closing a form. A module performs more sophisticated actions, such as verifying the data entered into a field before storing it in the database. You will learn more about modules in Chapter 7.

Using a Database Instead of Excel Spreadsheets

The Excel worksheet and other systems used by 4Corners Pharmacy in the past indicate that Paul and Vincent are not familiar with a relational database. A relational database contains multiple tables to store related information. When most people are faced with a task that requires some kind of data management, they often open Excel and start entering data into a worksheet with columns to define the different fields for each row in the worksheet. Figure 1.18 shows a worksheet that Vincent created using Excel.

Figure 1.18: Worksheet with rows containing duplicate information for one household

Redundant data for same customer

	A	B	C	D	E	F	G
6	Anders	Aannestad	623 South Hampton Way	Farmington	NM	87499	498-1112-A
7	Anders	Aannestad	623 South Hampton Way	Farmington	NM	87499	498-1112-A
8	Anders	Aannestad	623 South Hampton Way	Farmington	NM	87499	498-1112-A
9	Byron	Buescher	4165 Umatilla Avenue	Pleasant View	CO	81331	B1621
10	Cesar	Lopez	460 West Pioneer Road	Dolores	CO	81323	BB564
11	Chloe	Feraco	19504 Lowell Boulevard	Aneth	UT	84510	17-22-GH
12	Christina	Hargus	5465 South Nelson Circle	Shiprock	NM	87420	B239
13	Dallas	Coats	5541 East Zuni Street	Shiprock	NM	87420	OP-87-223
14	Dana	Coats	5541 East Zuin Street	Shiprock	NM	87420	OP-87-223
15	Dusty	Alkier	3046 West 36th Avenue	Aneth	UT	84510	A44523
16	Gaetano	Feraco	19504 Lowell Boulevard	Aneth	UT	84510	DRS662
17	Geoffrey	Baaz	123 Myrna Place	Kirtland	NM	87417	A089
18	Gina	Mercado	240 South Monaco Parkway	Cortez	CO	81321	G546
20	Gloria	Fernandes	1011 East Bayaud Avenue	Flora Vista	NM	87415	OP-87-498
21	Isabel	Lopez	406 West Pioneer Road	Dolores	CO	81323	CC775
22	Jennifer	Ramsey	4775 Argone Circle	Chinle	AZ	86547	HR231-6
23	Jessica	Cortez	4875 Civility Lake Drive	Kayenta	AZ	86033	C998
24	John	Velasquez	54213 Oak Drive	Kirtland	NM	87417	2233-pl77y
25	Josefina	Hernandez	411 Mariposa Street	Flora Vista	NM	87145	G443
26	Josiah	Sanchez	4875 Civility Lake Drive	Kayenta	AZ	86033	1922-DX5
27	Kevin	Wachter	2931 East Narcissus Way	Montezuma Creek	UT	84534	1983GH
28	Kimberley	Schultz	411 East Cornish Court	Chinle	AZ	86507	554497G
29	Malena	D'Ambrosio	4775 Argone Circle	Chinle	AZ	86547	DRS345
20	Maria	Gabel	4255 Kittredge Street	Lewis	CO	81327	C223

Jan 2, 2016 Prescriptions   (+)

Redundant and inconsistent data for people living in the same household

Figure 1.18 shows two members of one household entered separately into the worksheet, resulting in the duplication of the family address. This method creates at least three problems. First, the pharmacist wastes time by entering the name, address, phone number, and data for each prescription the customer fills. Notice that Anders Aannestad filled two prescriptions. The pharmacist entered Ander's name, address, and health plan information into both records, even though this data is the same for both records.

Second, and more important, this process is prone to errors. Notice that Cesar and Isabel Lopez who filled prescriptions on the same day, seem to be related but live at different house numbers, suggesting that one or both of these house numbers contain an error. Such errors are common occurrences in worksheets because of the amount of data repetition and data redundancy.

Third, what if Anders or the Lopezes move or change health plans? The pharmacist would need to locate every row in the worksheet containing this data for these customers and change the corresponding data—another waste of time and another opportunity for inconsistent data to occur. You might think that a solution to this problem would be to add columns for additional prescriptions to the worksheet, instead of rows, as shown in Figure 1.19.

Figure 1.19: Worksheet with multiple columns added for new prescriptions

	A	B	C	D	E	F	G	H	I	J
			Prescription			Dosage	Prescription			Dosage
1	First Name	Last Name	ID	Name	Dosage	Form	ID	Name	Dosage	Form
2	Adriane	Walters	104	Ampicillin	250	mg		79 Epronix	500	mg
3	Albert	Cardenas	66	Tolbutamide	2	mcg				
4	Anders	Aannestad	23	Avatocin	100	mg		101 Xeroflarol	1	tsp

If this design were adopted, however, 4Corners Pharmacy could track all prescriptions in one worksheet instead of creating a new worksheet daily to detail each day's prescriptions. Although this method will work for some time, the table will become too large after months and years of adding new columns. Moreover, this system would only work if the customer has the same doctor write all his prescriptions, as each row includes a field for prescribing doctor. If Adriane is prescribed migraine medicine from a general practitioner and eye drops from an ophthalmologist, then the pharmacy could not use this table, or it would need to modify the table to include a prescribing doctor field for each prescription. This field would contain duplicate data for most customers, thereby defeating the purpose of the new design.

If Don were creating these tables in Access, he could create tables to store the data and then relate the tables to find information from several tables. He would not be limited by separate worksheets. What if you attempt to solve these problems by creating two worksheets to store orders? One worksheet would store customer data and the other worksheet would store prescription data, as shown in Figure 1.20.

Figure 1.20: Storing customer and prescription data in separate worksheets

Customers

	A	B	C	D	E	F	G	H
1	SSN (Last 4)	First Name	Last Name	Birth Date	Address	City	State	ZIP
2	2243	Anders	Aannestad	9/11/1974	623 South Hampton Way	Farmington	NM	87499
3	0979	Geoffrey	Baaz	12/31/2001	1233 Myrna Place	Kirtland	NM	87417
4	2943	Rose	Baaz	4/12/1970	1233 Myrna Place	Kirtland	NM	87417
5	6289	Jonathan	Cardenas	8/22/2004	620 East Empire	Kayenta	AZ	86033
6	1329	Danny	Cardenas	5/12/2002	620 East Empire	Kayenta	AZ	86033
7	1413	Albert	Cardenas	10/14/1965	620 East Empire	Kayenta	AZ	86033
8	1064	Sonia	Cardenas	4/12/1968	620 East Empire	Kayenta	AZ	86033
9	1329	Daniel	Cardenas	5/12/2002	620 East Empire	Kayenta	AZ	86033
10	6234	Dallas	Coats	10/31/1972	912 North Hampton Ave	Yellow Jacket	CO	81335
11	5623	Octavia	Coats	6/30/1976	912 North Hampton Ave	Yellow Jacket	CO	81335
12	1156	Dana	Coats	8/16/2002	912 North Hampton Ave	Yellow Jacket	CO	81335
13	0975	Isabel	Lopez	8/30/1949	633 Empire Street	Flora Vista	NM	87415

Prescriptions

	A	B	C	D	E	F	G	H	I
1	PrescriptionID	UPN	Quantity	Unit	Date	ExpireDate	Refills	AutoRefill	RefillsUsed
2	1	224	1	mg	9/10/2012	6/10/2013	2	Yes	1
3	2	828	1	ml	12/15/2012	12/11/2013	3	No	1
4	3	711	1	mg	6/21/2013	7/30/2013	5	No	1
5	4	256	1	mg	1/10/2013	10/24/2013	2	Yes	1
6	5	398	1	mg	9/10/2012	9/12/2013	3	Yes	1
7	6	121	1	mg	4/26/2013	8/30/2013	4	Yes	1
8	7	932	1	ml	1/24/2013	9/22/2013	2	Yes	1
9	8	523	1	ml	1/29/2013	6/14/2013	3	No	1
10	9	311	1	ml	9/24/2012	11/25/2013	4	Yes	1
11	10	366	1	ml	3/14/2013	7/26/2013	3	Yes	1
12	11	444	1	mg	2/24/2012	1/20/2013	4	Yes	1
13	12	642	1	mg	4/12/2013	2/11/2013	3	Yes	1
14	13	878	1	mg	5/16/2013	12/12/2013	2	No	1
15	14	852	1	mg	4/11/2013	11/20/2013	3	Yes	1
16	15	654	1	mg	1/22/2012	1/8/2013	3	No	1
17	16	398	1	mg	4/15/2012	6/11/2013	4	Yes	1

Customers are listed only once in the Customers worksheet, and all prescriptions filled for those customers are listed in the Prescriptions worksheet. There is no longer a need to create daily worksheets to track the prescriptions filled each day. These worksheets could last for some time, and it seems that you have solved the problem. However, there is no indication of which customer purchased which prescription. The only way to distinguish customers is by name, and the worksheets do not share any common fields. Although pharmacists might be able to distinguish customers by name for the time being, what would happen if there were two customers named John Smith? You might suggest distinguishing the John Smiths by their addresses. But, what if the two people named John Smith are father and son, both sharing the same address, telephone number, and doctor? There would be no way to distinguish the customers and no way to know who ordered which prescriptions, as the worksheets lack a unique identifying value for each customer and prescription.

Professional relational database design requires that every table has a primary key field that stores unique values. To satisfy this requirement, a new column named CustID was added to the Customers worksheet. In Figure 1.21, Isabel Lopez has the CustID 27. No one else has this number, ever had this number, or ever will have this number, except for Isabel Lopez and her family. It uniquely identifies her record in the table. Therefore, the CustID field would be assigned to Isabel Lopez. And, once it is assigned, her CustID will be used with her prescriptions in another table.

Figure 1.21: Customer data with CustID column added

CustID values uniquely identify each customer

	A	B	C	D	E	F	G	H
1	CUSTID	First Name	Last Name	Birth Date	Address	City	State	ZIP
2	1 Anders	Aannestad	9/11/1974	623 South Hampton Way	Farmington	NM	87499
3	5 Geoffrey	Baaz	12/31/2001	1233 Myrna Place	Kirtland	NM	87417
4	5 Rose	Baaz	4/12/1970	1233 Myrna Place	Kirtland	NM	87417
5	12 Jonathan	Cardenas	8/22/2004	620 East Empire	Kayenta	AZ	86033
6	12 Danny	Cardenas	5/12/2002	620 East Empire	Kayenta	AZ	86033
7	12 Albert	Cardenas	10/14/1965	620 East Empire	Kayenta	AZ	86033
8	12 Sonia	Cardenas	4/12/1968	620 East Empire	Kayenta	AZ	86033
9	12 Daniel	Cardenas	5/12/2002	620 East Empire	Kayenta	AZ	86033
10	16 Dallas	Coats	10/31/1972	912 North Hampton Ave	Yellow Jacket	CO	81335
11	16 Octavia	Coats	6/30/1976	912 North Hampton Ave	Yellow Jacket	CO	81335
12	16 Dana	Coats	8/16/2002	912 North Hampton Ave	Yellow Jacket	CO	81335
13	27 Isabel	Lopez	8/30/1949	633 Empire Street	Flora Vista	NM	87415

Assigning a primary key to the Customers worksheet reduces the amount of data repetition and the number of errors. For example, a pharmacist could identify Daniel Cardenas and Danny Cardenas by sorting the records by customer ID number—both records have the CustID 12 Don could then remove the duplicate record and implement ways to avoid redundancy prior to entering customer data to prevent duplicate records from occurring. Thus, assigning a primary key to the Customers worksheet helps pharmacists distinguish customer records. Even so, problems will remain in this design because the customer and prescription worksheets do not share any common fields.

Although the Prescriptions worksheet includes a PrescriptionID (uniquely identifying each prescription) and the Customers worksheet includes a CustID (uniquely identifying each customer), there is no way to know which prescription belongs to which customer, or vice versa. A solution is to add the CustID field to the Prescriptions worksheet and assign each prescription to its customer. Figure 1.22 shows the Prescriptions worksheet with the CustID field added to it. Now it is possible to associate a customer with his prescriptions using the CustID. For example, CustID 27 was prescribed PrescriptionID 15.

Figure 1.22: Prescription data with CustID column added

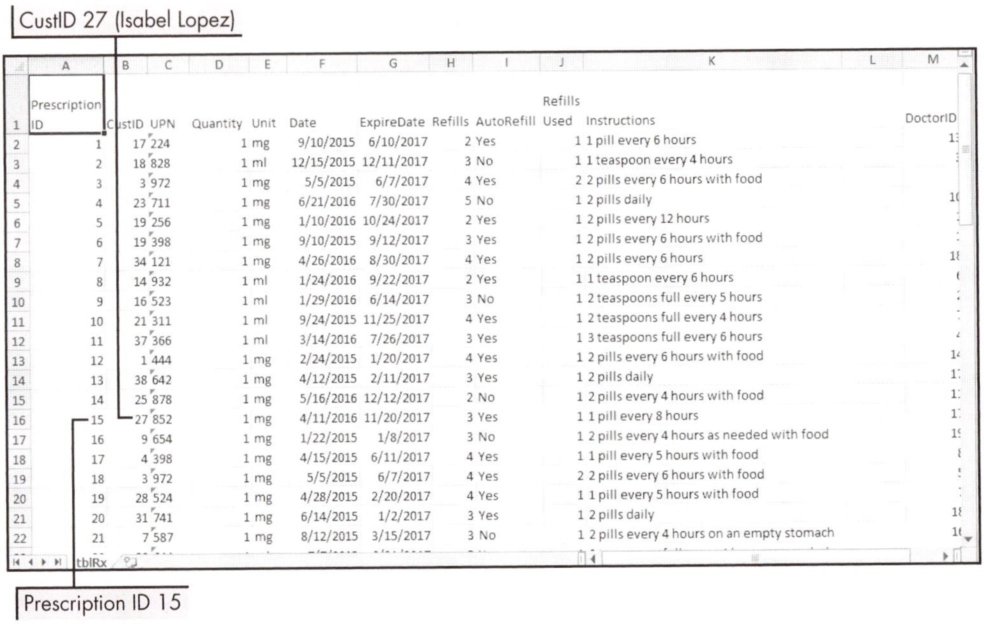

CustID 27 (Isabel Lopez)

	A	B	C	D	E	F	G	H	I	J	K	L	M
	Prescription									Refills			
1	ID	CustID	UPN	Quantity	Unit	Date	ExpireDate	Refills	AutoRefill	Used	Instructions		DoctorID
2	1	17	224	1	mg	9/10/2015	6/10/2017	2	Yes		1	1 pill every 6 hours	13
3	2	18	828	1	ml	12/15/2015	12/11/2017	3	No		1	1 teaspoon every 4 hours	
4	3	3	972	1	mg	5/5/2015	6/7/2017	4	Yes		2	2 pills every 6 hours with food	
5	4	23	711	1	mg	6/21/2016	7/30/2017	5	No		1	2 pills daily	10
6	5	19	256	1	mg	1/10/2016	10/24/2017	2	Yes		1	2 pills every 12 hours	
7	6	19	398	1	mg	9/10/2015	9/12/2017	3	Yes		1	2 pills every 6 hours with food	
8	7	34	121	1	mg	4/26/2016	8/30/2017	4	Yes		1	2 pills every 6 hours	18
9	8	14	932	1	ml	1/24/2016	9/22/2017	2	Yes		1	1 teaspoon every 6 hours	6
10	9	16	523	1	ml	1/29/2016	6/14/2017	3	No		1	2 teaspoons full every 5 hours	
11	10	21	311	1	ml	9/24/2015	11/25/2017	4	Yes		1	2 teaspoons full every 4 hours	
12	11	37	366	1	ml	3/14/2016	7/26/2017	3	Yes		1	3 teaspoons full every 6 hours	4
13	12	1	444	1	mg	2/24/2015	1/20/2017	4	Yes		1	2 pills every 6 hours with food	14
14	13	38	642	1	mg	4/12/2015	2/11/2017	3	Yes		1	2 pills daily	17
15	14	25	878	1	mg	5/16/2016	12/12/2017	2	No		1	2 pills every 4 hours with food	17
16	15	27	852	1	mg	4/11/2016	11/20/2017	3	Yes		1	1 pill every 8 hours	17
17	16	9	654	1	mg	1/22/2015	1/8/2017	3	No		1	2 pills every 4 hours as needed with food	19
18	17	4	398	1	mg	4/15/2015	6/11/2017	4	Yes		1	1 pill every 5 hours with food	8
19	18	3	972	1	mg	5/5/2015	6/7/2017	4	Yes		2	2 pills every 6 hours with food	5
20	19	28	524	1	mg	4/28/2015	2/20/2017	4	Yes		1	1 pill every 5 hours with food	
21	20	31	741	1	mg	6/14/2015	1/2/2017	3	Yes		1	2 pills daily	18
22	21	7	587	1	mg	8/12/2015	3/15/2017	3	No		1	2 pills every 4 hours on an empty stomach	16

tblRx

Prescription ID 15

Sorting the prescription data by CustID, rather than by PrescriptionID, reveals that CustID 9 had two prescriptions filled at 4Corners Pharmacy: Prescription IDs 15 and 60, filled on 1/22/2015 and 3/16/2015 respectively, as shown in Figure 1.23. The CustID field is called a common field in this case because it appears in the Customers and Prescriptions worksheets. A **common field** in an Access database is a field that appears in two or more tables and contains identical data to relate the tables. The common field is a primary key in the first table. The common field is called a **foreign key** in the second table.

Figure 1.23: Prescription data sorted by CustID column

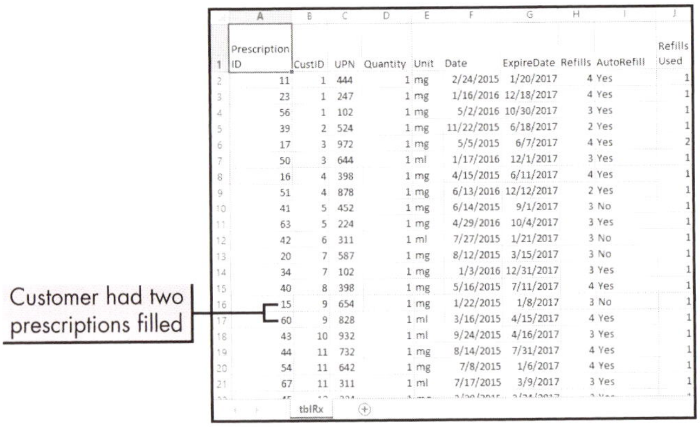

	A	B	C	D	E	F	G	H	I	J
	Prescription									Refills
1	ID	CustID	UPN	Quantity	Unit	Date	ExpireDate	Refills	AutoRefill	Used
2	11	1	444	1	mg	2/24/2015	1/20/2017	4	Yes	1
3	23	1	247	1	mg	1/16/2016	12/18/2017	4	Yes	1
4	56	1	102	1	mg	5/2/2016	10/30/2017	3	Yes	1
5	39	2	524	1	mg	11/22/2016	6/18/2017	2	Yes	1
6	17	3	972	1	mg	5/5/2015	6/7/2017	4	Yes	2
7	50	3	644	1	ml	1/17/2016	12/1/2017	3	Yes	1
8	16	4	398	1	mg	4/15/2015	6/11/2017	4	Yes	1
9	51	4	878	1	mg	6/13/2016	12/12/2017	2	Yes	1
10	41	5	452	1	mg	6/14/2015	9/1/2017	3	No	1
11	63	5	224	1	mg	4/29/2016	10/4/2017	3	Yes	1
12	42	6	311	1	ml	7/27/2015	1/21/2017	3	No	1
13	20	7	587	1	mg	8/12/2015	3/15/2017	3	No	1
14	34	7	102	1	mg	1/3/2016	12/31/2017	3	Yes	1
15	40	8	398	1	mg	5/16/2015	7/11/2017	4	Yes	1
16	15	9	654	1	mg	1/22/2015	1/8/2017	3	No	1
17	60	9	828	1	ml	3/16/2016	4/15/2017	4	Yes	1
18	43	10	932	1	ml	9/24/2015	4/16/2017	3	Yes	1
19	44	11	732	1	mg	8/14/2015	7/31/2017	4	Yes	1
20	54	11	642	1	mg	7/8/2015	1/6/2017	4	Yes	1
21	67	11	311	1	ml	7/17/2015	3/9/2017	3	Yes	1

Customer had two prescriptions filled

tblRx

To overcome the limitations of using worksheets for data management, use Access to do the following:

- Create separate tables for each entity.
- Assign a primary key to each table, using either a field that already uniquely identifies each record or an AutoNumber field that generates a unique number.
- Include a common field in the related table that identifies which records match.

Figure 1.23 shows that CustID 9 filled two prescriptions with the Prescription IDs 15 and 60. However, there's no easy way to determine the identity of CustID 9. Unless the pharmacist recalls the customer's name for this customer ID, they would not be able to identify this information. You cannot easily overcome this limitation in a spreadsheet. The solution is to create a relational database.

Creating Table Relationships

By now you see the limitations of using worksheets for data management and are familiar with the objects in a relational database. You also have a good idea of how these objects interact: Tables store the data, queries display subsets of data from the tables in response to a command that asks a question, forms present an interface to enter data into tables and view individual records, and reports produce aesthetically pleasing views and printouts of data pulled from tables or queries. Although a relational database might consist of just one table and several interrelated objects, a database usually consists of at least two related tables. You might wonder why you need to create table relationships. You need to create relationships between tables so that you can take advantage of benefits in doing so. Remember that the goal in good database design is to create separate tables for each entity, ensure that each table has a primary key, and use a common field to relate tables. If you relate two (or more) tables, you can query them as though they are one big table, pulling as much or as little data as you need from each table.

The question then arises: How do you know if tables are related? You know they are related if they share a common field and have joins between them. A **join** specifies a relationship between tables and the properties of that relationship. You can view how tables are joined and create joins between tables in the Relationship window in Access. When tables are joined, you will see a line that starts from the field in one table and then goes to the common field in the related table. The first step in creating table relationships is to decide which type of relationship you need to create: one-to-many, one-to-one, or many-to-many.

One-to-Many Relationships

Most tables have a **one-to-many relationship** (abbreviated as 1:∞), in which one record in the first table matches zero, one, or many records in the related table. For example, one customer can have zero, one, or many prescriptions at 4Corners Pharmacy; one teacher can have zero, one, or many students; and one realtor can list zero, one, or many homes for sale. In a one-to-many relationship, the **primary table** is on the "one" side of the relationship and the **related table** is on the "many" side of the relationship. For example, at 4Corners Pharmacy, tblCustomer is the "one" table and tblRx is the "many" table because one customer can have one or many prescriptions. Figure 1.24 illustrates the one-to-many relationship between customers and prescriptions.

Figure 1.24: One-to-many relationship between customers and prescriptions

CustID is the primary key in tblCustomer

CustID is the common field that relates the tables

tblCustomer

CustID	FirstName	LastName
18	Anders	Aannestad
27	Byron	Buescher
113	John	Kohlmetz

CustID is a foreign key in tblRx

tblRx

PrescriptionID	UPN	CustID
60	366	18
2	828	18
123	852	27

In Figure 1.24, CustID 18 (Anders Aannestad) has two prescriptions with the PrescriptionIDs 60 and 2, CustID 27 (Byron Buescher) has one prescription (PrescriptionID 123), and John Kohlmetz, a new customer at 4Corners Pharmacy, has not yet filled a prescription, and, therefore, has no related records in tblRx.

One-to-One Relationships

A **one-to-one relationship** (abbreviated as 1:1) exists when each record in one table matches exactly one record or no records in the related table. For example, Paul seeks to expand part of his business by selling large quantities of drugs to hospitals. Each hospital has a physical mailing address to use when delivering prescriptions. However, some hospital clients have their accounts payable operations off-site, with separate billing addresses. To store the physical and billing addresses of the hospitals, Don could create one table to store the name and physical address of each hospital and another table to store the billing address for each hospital. These two tables have a one-to-one relationship in which each hospital has one physical address that matches exactly one billing address and one billing address matches exactly one physical address, as shown in Figure 1.25.

Figure 1.25: One-to-one relationships between physical and billing addresses

tblHospital

HospitalID	Name	Address	City	State	ZIP
1	County	123 Main	Chinle	AZ	86547
2	St. John's	555 Maple	Blanding	UT	84512
3	Bellview	2121 Chestnut	Farmington	NM	87499

tblHospitalBilling

HospitalID	BillingAddress	City	State	ZIP
1	2727 Jefferson	Chinle	AZ	86544
2	8292 Brady	Blanding	UT	84518
3	3230 Bradford	Farmington	NM	87492

HospitalID 1 has exactly one matching record

One-to-one relationships are used infrequently because it is often possible to combine the data in the related tables into one table. As another example of a one-to-one relationship, suppose you have tblEmployees and tblSalariedEmployees. All employees are in tblEmployees, but only full-time, salaried employees are in tblSalariedEmployees, which contains fields that are specific to these types of employees, such as health insurance and retirement plan information. It is still a 1:1 relationship, just optional.

Many-to-Many Relationships

A **many-to-many relationship** (abbreviated as ∞:∞) occurs when each record in the first table matches many records in the second table, and each record in the second table matches many records in the first table. For example, Maria needs to print a class roster for the instructor of the CPR class so employees can sign it to verify their attendance. At the same time, Maria wants to print a report of all the classes that Richard Conlee has attended in the previous year so that she can evaluate Richard's certification status as a pharmacy technician for his next annual review. To be able to print Richard's certification records, Maria needs the database to have a relationship between tblEmployee and tblClass, but what is the nature of that relationship? The classes will go on perfectly fine if Richard never registers for one of them and Richard will be fine if he never takes a class. They are related, but neither is dependent on the other. Thus, there is no one-to-many or one-to-one relationship. The relationship is, instead, a many-to-many (∞:∞) relationship. Each class can be attended by many employees and each employee can attend many classes.

Maria needs a way to produce the class roster and Richard's attendance report, but a relational database cannot directly represent a ∞:∞ relationship using the same techniques we've discussed for 1:∞ or 1:1 relationships. You cannot put a single foreign key field in tblEmployee that lists all of the classes that Richard has taken. Nor can you add a single field to tblClass to store all of the employees who have taken a specific training class.

To represent a ∞:∞ relationship, Don must create a third, intermediary table, called a **junction table**, named tblEmployeeTraining, which contains the primary keys from tblEmployee and tblClass. The tblEmployeeTraining table lets you create two one-to-many relationships between the two primary tables (tblEmployee and tblClass) and the related table (tblEmployeeTraining). A record will be added to this table each time an employee takes a class and it will simply indicate which employee took which class. The tblEmployeeTraining table exists primarily as a conduit so that data can be retrieved from the primary tables. Figure 1.26 shows this many-to-many relationship. The result is the ability to query both tables as though they are one big table. Now, Maria can display only those classes that Richard or any other employee has taken, and she can display all employees who have taken a specific class, such as Child/Infant CPR.

Figure 1.26: Many-to-many relationship between employees and classes

tblEmployee

EmpID	EmpFirst	EmpLast
7	Brian	Cavillo
8	Cynthia	Jones
10	Tara	Kobrick

One-to-many relationship using the primary key (EmpID) in tblEmployee

tblClass

ClassID	Description	Cost
1	Adult CPR	$15.00
2	Child/Infant CPR	$15.00
3	Adult CPR Recertification	$10.00

One-to-many relationship using the primary key (ClassID) in tblClass

EmpID	Date	ClassID
10	4/10/2016	1
10	11/15/2016	2
8	11/21/2016	2

tblEmployeeTraining

Junction table created using the primary keys of tblEmployee and tblClass as foreign keys

Note that although the primary purpose of a junction table is to allow for a many-to-many relationship between two tables, it is also possible for this table to store additional information about this relationship. For example, if Maria wants to know when Richard took the Child/Infant CPR course, she would need to store this information somewhere. It cannot be stored in tblEmployee because the employee could take many different classes on many different dates. Likewise, it could not be stored in tblClass because a class could be taken by employees on many different dates. The date of attendance must be stored in the junction table as it is the date when the specific employee Richard took the specific class Child/Infant CPR.

Understanding Referential Integrity

Now that you know the three types of relationships that you can create in a relational database, it is important that you understand how to create them properly. By now you are familiar with the importance of including a primary key in each table to ensure that the table does not contain duplicate records. The database also prohibits users from failing to enter a value in the primary key field because doing so would risk data duplication. How would you differentiate customers if the CustID field contains no value? When a field does not contain a value, either because that value is unknown or inapplicable, it is called a **null value**. Including a primary key field in a table ensures **entity integrity**, a guarantee that there are no duplicate records in a table, that each record is unique, and that no primary key field contains null values.

Entity integrity specifies that the primary key value must not repeat in the primary table. For example, if Tara Kobrick is EmpID 10, no other employee can have EmpID 10. However, her EmpID can repeat in the related tblEmployeeTraining table. Indeed, you would expect to see Tara's EmpID number several times in tblEmployeeTraining because Tara has taken more than one training class. This common field, shared by both the primary and related tables, is the foreign key in the related tblEmployeeTraining table.

Referential integrity is a rule that states that if the foreign key in one table matches the primary key in a second table, the values in the foreign key must match the values in the primary key. When the database does not enforce referential integrity, certain problems occur that lead to inaccurate and inconsistent data. For example, in tblDrug the primary key is the UPN field, which is a universal drug identifier for prescription drugs. The record for the drug Phalastat has a UPN value of 366. No other record in tblDrug can have a UPN value of 366 because it is this record's primary key value and duplicate values are not allowed in the primary key field. When the pharmacy fills a prescription, no UPN can exist or be entered into tblCustomer that is not a valid UPN in tblDrug. Therefore, when the pharmacy fills prescriptions for Phalastat to CustIDs 18, 22, and 37, only the valid UPN of 366 may be used.

Referential Integrity Errors

Suppose that the drug manufacturer for Phalastat changes the drug formulation and issues a new UPN code of 367. The pharmacy would need to update its database to use the new code. This UPN doesn't exist in tblDrug, so it would be an allowable primary key value because it meets the requirement of being unique. At first, it might seem like this change is possible.

However, if the pharmacy changes Phalastat's UPN value from 366 to 367, then there no longer exists a drug with the UPN value 366 in the database. Yet Customers 18, 22, and 37 were prescribed drug 366 and remain in the database with that designation. Were they to seek a refill, or worse yet—become allergic to drug 366—there would be no way to identify which drug they were prescribed. The prescription records would become **orphaned** because the UPN primary key was changed in the primary table but the corresponding foreign keys in the related table were not. Enforcing referential integrity prevents this data loss. Figure 1.27 illustrates this referential integrity error.

Figure 1.27: Referential integrity errors

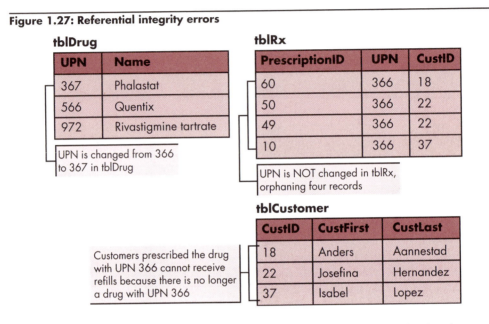

Another reason to enforce referential integrity is to prevent orphaned related records if the record in the primary table is deleted. For example, identity theft is discovered on occasion at 4Corners Pharmacy; in two cases, a customer used fake identification to obtain restricted prescription drugs. When Paul is informed of such occurrences— usually by the health plan that refuses to pay for such charges—he is obligated to turn over the prescription data to the FBI. After doing so, he no longer wants to retain this data in his database because he cannot collect on the accounts and does not want to keep the record of fictitious customers. Consequently, he is inclined to delete the customer's name, address, and entire record from the database. If he does so, however, the customer's corresponding prescriptions will remain in the database. These prescriptions will become orphaned, appear to belong to no one, and will confuse auditors trying to reconcile the pharmacy's accounts receivable.

A third reason to enforce referential integrity is to make it impossible to add records to a related table that does not have matching records in the primary table. An inexperienced or hurried technician might add prescriptions to tblRx for a new customer that she did not first enter into tblCustomer, resulting in orphaned records in tblRx because it would contain prescriptions that would not belong to a customer.

The results of all three scenarios lead to inconsistent data in the relational database. By enforcing referential integrity, however, you can avoid the following three errors:

- Changing the primary key of the records in the primary table if matching records exist in the related table
- Deleting records in the primary table if matching records exist in the related table
- Adding records to the related table if no matching record exists in the primary table

Overriding Referential Integrity

Referential integrity is the rule that makes it possible for a DBMS to prevent records from being orphaned if a user attempts to change a primary key or delete a record in a table that has matching records in another table. But there are times when you might want to override referential integrity. For example, you can choose the **Cascade Update Related Fields** option, which permits a user to change a primary key value so that the DBMS automatically updates the appropriate foreign key values in the related table. In this case, when the pharmacy changes the UPN value of 366 to 367, the records for the customers with CustIDs 18, 22, and 37 will still indicate that they were prescribed the drug because the DBMS will update the UPN value in the records for these customers by changing it from 366 to 367. Figure 1.28 shows how cascading updates works.

Figure 1.28: Update cascades to related fields

tblDrug

UPN	Name
367	Phalastat
566	Quentix
972	Rivastigmine tartrate

UPN is changed from 366 to 367 in tblDrug

tblRx

PrescriptionID	UPN	CustID
60	367	18
50	367	22
49	367	22
10	367	37

Cascade Update Related Fields option changes the UPN for matching records in tblRx from 366 to 367

What if the drug Phalastat is discontinued because a risk of heart attack has been identified? In this case, the pharmacy might want to delete the drug from the database to discontinue it. When the pharmacy tries to delete the record from tblDrug with the UPN 366, the DBMS will not permit the deletion because there are related records in tblRx. However, if you have chosen to enable the **Cascade Delete Related Records** option, the DBMS will permit the deletion of the record from tblDrug. In addition, the DBMS will also delete the related records from tblRx. Before you enable the Cascade Delete Related Records option, it is a good idea to verify that you really want to delete all data for this drug and all related data from the database. A better method might be to leave the drug in the database so the customer's prescription records are not deleted with it. If you delete Phalastat from the database, the database will show that CustIDs 18, 22, and 37 never received the drug. Figure 1.29 shows an example of how the Cascade Delete Related Records option works.

Figure 1.29: Delete cascades to related records

tblDrug

UPN	Name
~~366~~	~~Phalastat~~
566	Quentix
972	Rivastigmine tartrate

The record for UPN 366 is
deleted from tblDrug

tblRx

PrescriptionID	UPN	CustID
~~60~~	~~366~~	~~18~~
~~50~~	~~366~~	~~22~~
~~49~~	~~366~~	~~22~~
~~10~~	~~366~~	~~37~~

Cascade Delete Related Records option
deletes all matching records in tblRx

Steps To Success: Level 2

You have learned a great deal about database objects, concepts, and table relationships, all requisite knowledge for planning a relational database. Now it is time to consider which database objects are required for the 4Corners Pharmacy database and how to relate the tables.

On a piece of paper, complete the following:

1. Although the 4Corners Pharmacy database might ultimately include additional tables, it will include tables for the following entities: customers, prescriptions, drugs, doctors, clinics, employees, job titles, and training classes. Given these tables, describe five queries, two forms, and three reports that managers at the pharmacy might create and describe how they would use them in the pharmacy's day-to-day operations.

2. What are some examples of using worksheets instead of a database that you have used? How would a relational database simplify the work you needed to complete?

3. What primary keys might you assign to tables that store data about the following entities: customers, prescriptions, drugs, doctors, clinics, employees, job titles, and training classes? Describe why and how you chose the primary key for each table.

4. Suppose that tblDoctor includes the fields DoctorID, DoctorFirst, DoctorLast, and Phone; and tblClinic includes the fields ClinicID, ClinicName, Address, City, State, ZIP, and Phone. Is there a common field? Is there a foreign key? What kind of relationship might you create between these two tables?

   TROUBLESHOOTING: In order to successfully complete this task, begin by reviewing the tables, and then decide which fields can be related between the tables. If necessary, create any new field within the tables so that they can be related to other tables.

5. Paul wants to monitor prescription refills. He wants to use the UPN field to query which drugs are refilled most often. (For example, Paul wants to know how many times the drug Phalastat, with UPN 366, was refilled and by whom.) At the same time, he needs to determine which employees filled a given prescription. (For example, customer Marvin Gattis was prescribed Hyometadol on 7/7/2017, his doctor authorized five refills, and Cynthia Jones refilled the prescription for Mr. Gattis three times.) Suppose that tblRx lists every prescription that every customer has filled at 4Corners Pharmacy and contains the following fields: PrescriptionID, UPN, Quantity, Date, Refills, Instructions, CustID, and DoctorID. Also suppose that tblEmployee lists every employee working at 4Corners Pharmacy and contains the following fields: EmpID, FirstName, LastName, DOB, SSN, Address, City, State, and ZIP. What would you do to create a relationship between these two tables so that Paul can query them to answer his questions? Identify the primary and foreign keys necessary to create this relationship. Would you use the Cascade Update Related Fields and Cascade Delete Related Records options? Why or why not?

LEVEL 3

Identifying and Eliminating Database Anomalies by Normalizing Data

Normalizing the Tables in the Database

By now you are familiar with database concepts and how to create tables and relationships between them. You have learned that good database design seeks to avoid data redundancy and inconsistent data. Now you will learn the specific rules for ensuring good database design using a process called **normalization**. Figure 1.30 details the third step of the database design process and illustrates how normalization fits into the plan.

Normalization requires a series of steps, each one building on the previous. These steps are called normal forms, or first, second, and third normal forms, sometimes abbreviated as 1NF, 2NF, and 3NF. Notice in Figure 1.30 that 3NF is the final step necessary before the database is created and tested.

Figure 1.30: Database design process: normalizing the data

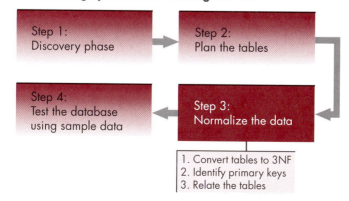

Normalization has three goals. First, normalization reduces the space required to store data by eliminating duplicate data in the database (with the exception of duplicate data in the foreign key fields). Second, normalization reduces inconsistent data in the database by storing data only once, thereby reducing the chance of typographical, spelling, and transposition errors and other inconsistent data, similar to the data in the worksheets you viewed in Level 2. Finally, normalization reduces the chance of anomalies. An **anomaly** is a deviation of a common rule. There are three types of anomalies in Access: deletion, update, and insertion. The data shown in Figure 1.31 is not normalized (also called **unnormalized data**) and exhibits all three anomalies.

Figure 1.31: Data with anomalies

Deleting Connie Nader's record creates two deletion anomalies because she is the only cashier and the only employee enrolled in the Yoga class; deleting her record also deletes the job title and class information

Adding a new job title or class creates an insertion anomaly because there must first be an employee with that title or taking the class, which is not possible until you add the title or class

EmpID	EmpFirst	EmpLast	SSN	Title	Description
15	Connie	Nader	705-19-1497	Cashier	Yoga
21	Dora	Langston	718-78-4111	Technician	Nutritional Supplements
21	Dora	Langston	718-78-4111	Technician	First Aid
3	Virginia	Sanchez	921-23-3333	Technician	Defibrillator Use
17	Rachel	Thompson	928-98-4165	Technician	Defibrillator Use
13	Paul	Ferrino	953-23-3639	Owner	Child/Infant CPR Recertification
27	Vincent	Ferrino	998-01-5466	Pharmacist	Child/Infant CPR Recertification
14	Richard	Conlee	968-96-3214	Technician	Child/Infant CPR Recertification
2	Marco	Farello	885-00-7777	Technician	Child/Infant CPR Recertification
3	Virginia	Sanchez	921-23-3333	Technician	Child/Infant CPR Recertification
8	Cynthia	Jones	000-23-3655	Pharmacist	Child/Infant CPR Dynamics
2	Marco	Farello	885-00-7777	Technician	Child/Infant CPR
10	Tara	Kobrick	728-12-3465	Technician	Child/Infant CPR
21	Dora	Langston	718-78-4111	Technician	Child/Infant CPR
13	Paul	Ferrino	953-23-3639	Owner	Adult CPR Recertification
27	Vincent	Ferrino	998-01-5466	Pharmacist	Adult CPR Recertification
27	Vincent	Ferrino	998-01-5466	Pharmacist	Adult CPR Recertification
27	Vincent	Ferrino	998-01-5466	Pharmacist	Adult CPR Recertification
12	Louis	Moreno	666-16-7892	Pharmacist	Adult CPR Recertification

Changing the Child/Infant CPR class description in the record for Cynthia Jones creates an update anomaly in three other records

A **deletion anomaly** occurs when a user deletes data from a database and unintentionally deletes the only occurrence of that data in the database. In Figure 1.31, Connie Nader is the only cashier at 4Corners Pharmacy and the only employee who took the Yoga class. Deleting her record also deletes the Cashier title and the Yoga class from the database, making it appear as though her title and the Yoga class never existed. An **update anomaly** occurs when, due to redundant data in a database, a user fails to update some records or updates records erroneously. For example, in Figure 1.31, changing the description for the course titled "Child/Infant CPR" in the record for Cynthia Jones leaves inconsistent data in the other records for employees who took this class and creates corrupted data. An **insertion anomaly** occurs when a user cannot add data to a database unless it is preceded by the entry of other data. In Figure 1.31, an insertion anomaly occurs if you try to add a new class. You cannot add a class unless an employee has registered for it, but how is this possible for a new class? As you can see, it is important to avoid creating anomalies in a database; normalization seeks to avoid these problems.

The goal of normalization is to split tables into smaller related tables to avoid creating anomalies. To understand more about normalization, you must first understand **functional dependency** because it will help you analyze fields within tables and help you decide if they need to be split into smaller tables. A field in a table is considered functionally dependent on another field if each value in the second field is associated with exactly one value in the first field. For example, as shown in Figure 1.31, Dora Langston's Social Security number (718-78-4111) is associated with exactly one EmpID, 21. Therefore the SSN field is functionally dependent on the EmpID field. So, both SSN and EmpID should be in the same table. The Title field, however, is not functionally dependent on the EmpID field because there are many employees that can have the title Technician. Consequently, the Title field becomes a prime candidate for its own table because many records can link to the same title. Therefore, creating a table with this information would prevent data redundancy. Use your knowledge of functional dependency to test the fields in the tables that you create, identify fields that are not functionally dependent, and consider moving them to their own tables.

Before doing this, however, you must be aware of a partial dependency. A **partial dependency** occurs when a field is dependent on only part of the primary key. Therefore, it is best to identify tables that might contain partial dependencies since it is best to avoid them. For example, the ClassID field cannot be the table's primary key because it will contain repeating data if more than one employee attends the same class. Neither the ClassName nor ClassProvider fields can be the table's primary key because they also contain repeating data.

The EmpID field cannot be the table's primary key because an employee can take many classes and, therefore, would have many records in the table. The Date field cannot be the table's primary key because it will contain repeating data if more than one class is taught on the same date or if more than one employee attends the same class on the same date—both of which are likely occurrences. Thus, you must create a composite key to create unique values for the records in this table. In some cases, a **composite primary key** consists of two fields, but this table requires the combination of three fields—EmpID, Date, and ClassID—to create unique records in the table.

When a primary key uses two or more fields to create unique records in a table, it is called a composite primary key (or a **composite key**). Figure 1.32 shows a conceptual diagram of the fields in a proposed tblClassesAttended that indicates which employee took which classes on which dates.

Figure 1.32: tblClassesAttended table design

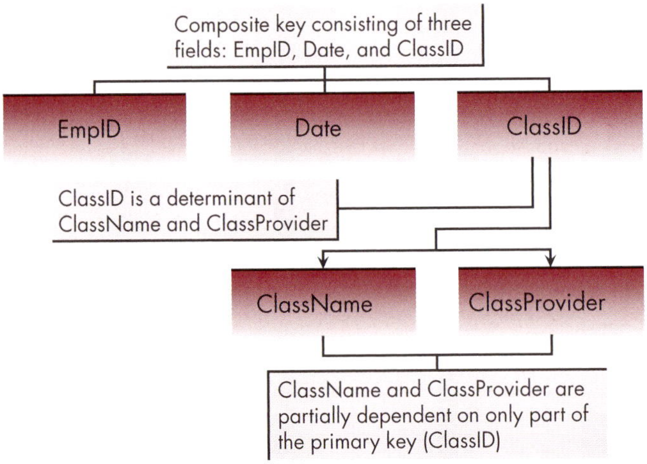

Notice the arrows pointing from ClassID to the ClassName and ClassProvider fields. This structure indicates that ClassID is a determinant of the other two fields. A **determinant** is a field or collection of fields whose value determines the value in another field. This determinant relationship between fields is the cause of dependency, as ClassName and ClassProvider are dependent on ClassID. However, this relationship exhibits a partial dependency because the two fields are dependent on only part of the composite key. Your goal should be to rid your tables of partial dependencies to avoid anomalies. Using this example, the solution would be to create a separate tblClass table and then create a relationship between tblClass and tblClassesAttended using the common field, ClassID.

A **natural key** is a primary key that details an obvious and innate trait of a record. For example, the UPN field in tblDrug is a unique value for each drug sold, and is, therefore, a natural key for the table. Other examples of natural keys include Social Security numbers for people and International Standard Book Numbers (ISBNs) for books. When a natural key exists, it is easy to identify and use as a primary key.

Sometimes, however, a table does not contain a natural key, and no field or combination of fields can be used as a primary key. In these cases, you can create an **artificial key**, a field whose sole purpose is to create a primary key. For example, if a Customer table does not have a field that uniquely identifies each customer, you can add a field that automatically assigns a number to a customer when a new customer is added.

Best Practice

Choosing a Primary Key

After completing data normalization, you must assign primary keys to your tables. This task is easy to do if a natural key, such as an SSN, PIN, or ISBN, exists in your table. If it does not, which field should be the primary key: an artificial key or a composite key? There is no definitive answer, but a best practice is to consider possible negative consequences of creating a composite key. If the composite key comprises more than two fields, as was shown in tblClassesAttended in Figure 1.32, you might want to choose an artificial key because three fields will be consumed in every table that includes the three-field composite key as a foreign key, wasting database space. In addition, primary keys cannot be null. This might prove frustrating if you are trying to enter a record, but lack the values to enter in one or more of the three fields that the composite key comprises. You will not be able to enter a record unless you have all three fields. Consequently, think twice before creating composite keys and consider using artificial keys instead.

Having a good grasp of the fundamental concepts of how fields interact as determinants, dependents, and in composite primary keys is essential to combating anomalies in relational table design. After you understand these concepts, you are prepared to normalize the tables.

First Normal Form

When a field contains more than one value, it is called a **repeating group**. A table is in **first normal form (1NF)** if it does not contain any repeating groups. Table 1.6 shows a "training classes attended" table that violates 1NF rules because the Description field contains more than one value in some cases, creating unnormalized data. Marco Farello, for instance, has taken three classes, all of which reside in the Description field. The repeating groups in this table would make it difficult to filter or query this table to determine which employees have taken which classes.

Table 1.6: Unnormalized data contains repeating groups

EmpID	EmpFirst	EmpLast	SSN	Description	DateAttended	Provider
14	Richard	Conlee	968-96-3214	Child/Infant CPR Recertification	11/15/2015	Red Cross
2	Marco	Farello	885-00-7777	Child/Infant CPR	1/30/2015	Red Cross
				Child/Infant CPR Recertification	1/15/2016	Red Cross
				Adult CPR Recertification	2/1/2016	Red Cross
13	Paul	Ferrino	953-23-3639	Adult CPR Recertification	2/5/2017	Red Cross
				Child/Infant CPR Recertification	6/15/2016	Red Cross
27	Vincent	Ferrino	998-01-5466	Adult CPR Recertification	2/2/2015	Red Cross

Table 1.6: Unnormalized data contains repeating groups (cont.)

EmpID	EmpFirst	EmpLast	SSN	Description	DateAttended	Provider
				Adult CPR Recertification	4/2/2017	Red Cross
				Adult CPR Recertification	4/5/2016	Red Cross
				Child/Infant CPR Recertification	5/21/2016	Red Cross
1	Joan	Gabel	901-88-3636	Adult CPR	2/6/2015	Red Cross
8	Cynthia	Jones	000-23-3655	Child/Infant CPR	11/21/2016	Red Cross

A seemingly good solution might be to remove the repeating groups and instead create new rows for each class attended, as shown in Table 1.7.

Table 1.7: Unnormalized data contains repeating rows

EmpID	EmpFirst	EmpLast	SSN	Class Description	DateAttended	Provider
14	Richard	Conlee	968-96-3214	Child/Infant CPR Recertification	11/15/2016	Red Cross
2	Marco	Farello	885-00-7777	Child/Infant CPR	1/30/2015	Red Cross
2	Marco	Farello	885-00-7777	Child/Infant CPR Recertification	1/15/2016	Red Cross
2	Marco	Farello	885-00-7777	Adult CPR Recertification	2/1/2016	Red Cross
13	Paul	Ferrino	953-23-3639	Adult CPR Recertification	2/5/2017	Red Cross
13	Paul	Ferrino	953-23-3639	Child/Infant CPR Recertification	6/15/2016	Red Cross
27	Vincent	Ferrino	998-01-5466	Adult CPR Recertification	2/2/2015	Red Cross
27	Vincent	Ferrino	998-01-5466	Adult CPR Recertification	4/2/2017	Red Cross
27	Vincent	Ferrino	998-01-5466	Adult CPR Recertification	4/5/2016	Red Cross
27	Vincent	Ferrino	998-01-5466	Child/Infant CPR Recertification	5/21/2016	Red Cross
1	Joan	Gabel	901-88-3636	Adult CPR	2/6/2015	Red Cross
8	Cynthia	Jones	000-23-3655	Child/Infant CPR	11/21/2016	Red Cross

© 2014 Cengage Learning

You already know, however, that repeating data by adding records in this fashion is called data redundancy and is inefficient, wastes space, and can lead to errors. Marco Farello now has three records, all of which repeat his EmpID, EmpFirst, EmpLast, and SSN. Table 1.7 violates normalization rules because of this repetition. What can be done, then, to make this table conform to 1NF? The answer is to create two tables: one for employees and one for classes. Examples of what these tables might look like are shown in Tables 1.8 and 1.9.

Table 1.8: Employee data in 1NF

EmpID	EmpFirst	EmpLast	SSN
1	Joan	Gabel	901-88-3636
2	Marco	Farello	885-00-7777
3	Virginia	Sanchez	921-23-3333
8	Cynthia	Jones	000-23-3655
10	Tara	Kobrick	728-12-3465
12	Louis	Moreno	666-16-7892
13	Paul	Ferrino	953-23-3639
14	Richard	Conlee	968-96-3214
15	Connie	Nader	705-19-1497
17	Rachel	Thompson	928-98-4165
19	Amy	Urquiza	728-65-6941
21	Dora	Langston	718-78-4111
27	Vincent	Ferrino	998-01-5466

© 2014 Cengage Learning

Table 1.9: Class data in 1NF

ClassID	Description	EmpID	DateAttended	Provider
1	Adult CPR	1	2/6/2017	Red Cross
1	Adult CRP	10	4/10/2017	Red Cross
1	Adult CPR	17	3/17/2017	Red Cross
1	Adult CPR	19	6/20/2017	Red Cross
2	Child/Infant CPR	2	1/30/2017	Red Cross
2	Child/Infant CPR	8	11/21/2016	Red Cross
2	Child/Infant CPR	10	11/15/2017	Red Cross
2	Child/Infant CPR	21	6/9/2017	Red Cross
3	Adult CPR Recertification	2	2/1/2016	Red Cross
3	Adult CPR Recertification	3	6/1/2017	Red Cross
3	Adult CPR Recertification	3	6/29/2015	Red Cross
3	Adult CPR Recertification	10	4/12/2015	Red Cross
3	Adult CPR Recertification	12	4/1/2016	Red Cross

© 2014 Cengage Learning

Table 1.9: Class data in 1NF (cont.)

ClassID	Description	EmpID	DateAttended	Provider
3	Adult CPR Recertification	13	2/5/2017	Red Cross
3	Adult CPR Recertification	17	3/16/2015	Red Cross
3	Adult CPR Recertification	19	6/21/2015	Red Cross
3	Adult CPR Recertification	19	3/10/2016	Red Cross
3	Adult CPR Recertification	21	6/15/2016	Red Cross
3	Adult CPR Recertification	21	3/5/2017	Red Cross
3	Adult CPR Recertification	27	2/2/2015	Red Cross
3	Adult CPR Recertification	27	4/2/2017	Red Cross
3	Adult CPR Recertification	27	4/5/2015	Red Cross
4	First Aid	21	6/12/2016	Red Cross
5	Defibrillator Use	3	1/25/2015	Johnston Health Systems
5	Defibrillator Use	17	5/2/2017	Johnston Health Systems
6	Child/Infant CPR Recertification	2	1/15/2016	Red Cross
6	Child/Infant CPR Recertification	3	5/15/2016	Red Cross
6	Child/Infant CPR Recertification	13	6/15/2015	Red Cross
6	Child/Infant CPR Recertification	14	11/15/2016	Red Cross
6	Child/Infant CPR Recertification	27	5/21/2016	Red Cross
7	Nutritional Supplements	21	9/1/2017	Food Co-op
8	Yoga	15	1/23/2017	Yoga Center

The employee training class data now satisfies the requirements for 1NF. This was accomplished by creating two tables—a primary Employee table and a related Class table. These tables share a common field, EmpID, which creates a relationship between them. Note that, while this table is in 1NF, it contains repetition that can be resolved by normalizing to 2NF.

Second Normal Form

To ensure that a table is in **second normal form (2NF)**, the table must be in 1NF and must not contain any partial dependencies if the table has a composite primary key. Tables that are in 1NF and contain a primary key and not a composite primary key are automatically in 2NF. The data shown in Table 1.9 violates 2NF rules because the description of the class is dependent not just on the ClassID, but also on the EmpID and DateAttended; the combination of ClassID, EmpID, and DateAttended is the table's composite primary key. If left as is, this table might include inconsistent data, such as the misspelling of "Adult CRP" in the second record. To convert this table to 2NF, it is necessary to break it into two tables: one table listing the classes offered and another table listing the classes taken. Tables 1.10 and 1.11 show these changes.

Table 1.10: ClassesOffered table in 2NF

ClassID	Description	Provider
1	Adult CPR	Red Cross
2	Child/Infant CPR	Red Cross
3	Adult CPR Recertification	Red Cross
4	First Aid	Red Cross
5	Defibrillator Use	Johnston Health Systems
6	Child/Infant CPR Recertification	Red Cross
7	Nutritional Supplements	Food Co-op
8	Yoga	Yoga Center

© 2014 Cengage Learning

Table 1.11: ClassesTaken table in 2NF

ClassID	EmpID	DateAttended
1	1	2/6/2017
1	10	4/10/2017
1	17	3/17/2017
1	19	6/20/2017
2	2	1/30/2017
2	8	11/21/2016
2	10	11/15/2017
2	21	6/9/2017
3	2	2/1/2016
3	3	6/1/2017
3	3	6/29/2016
3	10	4/12/2016
3	12	4/1/2016
3	13	2/5/2017
3	17	3/16/2016

© 2014 Cengage Learning

Table 1.11: ClassesTaken table in 2NF (cont.)

ClassID	EmpID	DateAttended
3	19	6/21/2016
3	19	3/10/2016
3	21	6/15/2016
3	21	3/5/2017
3	27	2/2/2016
3	27	4/2/2017
3	27	4/5/2016
4	21	6/12/2016
5	3	1/25/2016
5	17	5/2/2017
6	2	1/15/2016
6	3	5/15/2016
6	13	6/15/2016
6	14	11/15/2016
6	27	5/21/2016
7	21	9/1/2017
8	15	1/23/2017

The data shown in Tables 1.10 and 1.11 is in 2NF—notice that the ClassesTaken table is a junction table that creates a many-to-many relationship between the ClassesOffered table (Table 1.10) and the Employee table (Table 1.8). As a result, you can query these tables as though they are one big table and do so from two perspectives. You can list all the classes taken by a single employee, or produce a report for a single class, listing all those employees who attended a class on a given day.

Third Normal Form

For a table to be in **third normal form (3NF)**, it must be in 2NF and the only determinants it contains must be candidate keys. A **candidate key** is a field or collection of fields that could function as the primary key, but was not chosen to do so. Table 1.10 is in 2NF, but one problem remains. ClassID is the primary key, but Description and Provider are **nonkey fields**—fields that are not part of the primary key. A **transitive dependency** occurs between two nonkey fields that are both dependent on a third field; tables in 3NF should not have transitive dependencies. The Provider field gives more information about the Description field, so you might think that it is important to keep this field in this table. You might also think that Table 1.10 is pretty small as it is and appears to cause little harm other than having the Red Cross provider repeating a few times. The truth is, however, that this table is in jeopardy of a deletion anomaly. The Provider has a transitive dependency on the ClassID and Description fields. If you delete ClassID 5 (Defibrillator Use) from

this table, you would also delete Johnston Health Systems from the database. Johnston Health Systems might offer other classes that employees could attend in the future, but if the only occurrence of the Defibrillator Use class is removed from this database, Johnston Health Systems is also removed. Consequently, to put the data in 3NF, it is necessary to break it, once again, into two smaller tables. The result, as shown in Tables 1.12 and 1.13, is two tables: one solely for class titles and one solely for providers.

Table 1.12: ClassesOffered table in 3NF ClassID Description ProviderID

ClassID	Description	ProviderID
1	Adult CPR	3
2	Child/Infant CPR	3
3	Adult CPR Recertification	3
4	First Aid	3
5	Defibrillator Use	2
6	Child/Infant CPR Recertification	3
7	Nutritional Supplements	1
8	Yoga	4

© 2014 Cengage Learning

Table 1.13: Provider table in 3NF

ProviderID	Provider
1	Food Co-op
2	Johnston Health Systems
3	Red Cross
4	Yoga Center

© 2014 Cengage Learning

You can see that data normalization requires creating additional tables so that normalization rules are not violated. You should also be aware that determining the extent of normalization is, in some cases, a judgment call depending on the situation. It can be an art as much as a science.

Best Practice

Testing the Database Using Sample Data

After normalizing your data and assigning primary keys, you might think that your work is done in the database design process. Figure 1.33 shows that there is one major step left: testing the database using sample data.

You should, of course, test the database yourself, but as Figure 1.33 suggests, the best practice to follow is to recruit pilot testers, hold feedback sessions, modify the design and functionality using the recommendations given during feedback sessions, and then unveil the finished database. Getting criticism from third parties is invaluable; the more eyes and hands that scrutinize and investigate your database, the better it will perform after modifications are made from feedback.

Figure 1.33: Database design process: testing the database

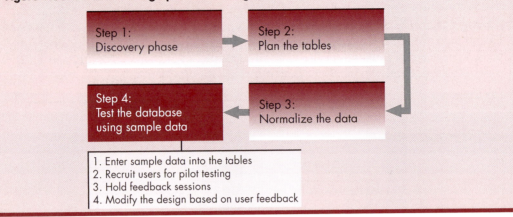

1. Enter sample data into the tables
2. Recruit users for pilot testing
3. Hold feedback sessions
4. Modify the design based on user feedback

Steps To Success: Level 3

After learning how Don will normalize the data in the 4Corners Pharmacy database, you have gained a deeper understanding of how to pare down tables so that anomalies do not occur. This process requires ensuring that groups do not repeat in fields, such as avoiding a Dependents field that stores the names of two people. Breaking the data into two tables—HeadOfHousehold and Dependent—satisfies the requirement for 1NF. After doing that, however, it is important to analyze the resultant tables for violations of 2NF. Does data repeat within the same field? For example, in the Dependent table, is the same doctor listed multiple times? Breaking the data into two tables—Dependent and Doctor—satisfies the requirement for 2NF. Converting tables to 3NF is also important and requires diligence to make sure that every field is dependent on the primary key and not on another field.

On a piece of paper, write any anomalies that are identified in Figure 1.34. And, create as many tables as necessary that you need to create to normalize this data to 3NF. Figure 1.34 contains potential anomalies.

Figure 1.34: Worksheet with potential anomalies

	A	B	C	D	E	F	G	H	I
1	PrescriptionID	RefillDate	CustID	CustFirst	CustLast	EmpID	EmpFirst	EmpLast	Title
2	2	4/14/2017	16	Samuel	Naylor	EmpFirst	Joan	Gabel	Owner
3	5	3/11/2017	20	Roliff	Purringtor	EmpFirst	Joan	Gabel	Owner
4	10	3/11/2017	2	Jerry	Jester	EmpFirst	Joan	Gabel	Owner
5	21	5/16/2017	31	Marla	Kennady	EmpFirst	Joan	Gabel	Owner
6	23	9/18/2017	20	Edward	Fowler	EmpFirst	Joan	Gabel	Owner
7	36	10/8/2016	38	Wyatt	Hardesty	EmpFirst	Joan	Gabel	Owner
8	59	6/14/2016	17	Samuel	Naylor	EmpFirst	Joan	Gabel	Owner
9	68	3/30/2017	18	Elizabeth	Callahan	EmpFirst	Joan	Gabel	Owner
10	6	6/3/2017	36	Mary Eller	Felps	EmpLast	Karl	Fujikawa	Pharmacist
11	14	6/10/2016	28	Emil	Angel	EmpLast	Karl	Fujikawa	Pharmacist
12	24	2/15/2017	22	Vijay	Iman	EmpLast	Karl	Fujikawa	Pharmacist
13	35	12/1/2016	37	Ethan	Oxford	EmpLast	Karl	Fujikawa	Pharmacist
14	40	11/30/2016	17	Sharon	Lockhart	EmpLast	Karl	Fujikawa	Pharmacist
15	41	2/2/2017	16	Craig	Lusk	EmpLast	Karl	Fujikawa	Pharmacist
16	42	9/19/2016	33	Pam	Lusk	EmpLast	Karl	Fujikawa	Pharmacist
17	44	5/15/2017	26	William	Gayner	EmpLast	Karl	Fujikawa	Pharmacist
18	45	1/3/2017	29	Sarah	Breed	EmpLast	Karl	Fujikawa	Pharmacist
19	47	5/23/2017	24	Mark	Callahan	EmpLast	Karl	Fujikawa	Pharmacist
20	51	12/1/2017	7	Lance	Holt	EmpLast	Karl	Fujikawa	Pharmacist
21	53	1/16/2017	4	Vijay	Iman	EmpLast	Karl	Fujikawa	Pharmacist
22	54	9/4/2016	5	William	Gayner	EmpLast	Karl	Fujikawa	Pharmacist
23	60	8/20/2016	10	Irlene	Zapalac	EmpLast	Karl	Fujikawa	Pharmacist

Figure_1_34

Chapter Summary

This chapter presented some of the fundamental concepts you need to understand when planning an Access database. In Level 1, you learned that the discovery phase of database planning takes a great deal of work and requires researching existing sources of data within an organization, researching sources of missing data, and interviewing users about desired output. The next step is to assimilate your findings by grouping fields into tables, assigning data types to fields, choosing appropriate field sizes, and assigning standardized names to the tables.

Level 2 covered database objects and concepts. You learned that there are seven types of objects in an Access database, four of which—tables, queries, forms, and reports—were discussed at length. Tables hold data. Queries display subsets of data in response to a question about the data. Forms provide an electronic interface for entering data into tables while at the same time allowing you to view records in the tables. Reports allow you to organize data in a custom or standard format for on-screen display or in a printout. After learning about database objects, you learned about how using several worksheets instead of a database leads to inconsistent and redundant data; the importance of creating primary keys, foreign keys, and common fields in tables; and the process of creating relationships between tables in a relational database, including one-to-many, one-to-one, and many-to-many. You also learned about referential integrity and how it works to prevent anomalies in the database.

In Level 3, you studied the process of normalizing data, which requires putting tables in first normal form by removing repeating groups, then putting tables in second normal form by eliminating partial dependencies, and finally putting tables in third normal form by eliminating transitive dependencies. You also learned that it is important to assign primary keys and how to distinguish between natural, artificial, and surrogate keys. Finally, you learned that testing a database before implementation and seeking feedback from pilot testers is the best way to make modifications to a database before implementing the final version.

Conceptual Review

1. Name and describe the four steps in the database design process.

2. What are data duplication and data redundancy, and how do you work to remove these problems from a database?

3. What is scope creep?

4. What are some of the considerations you must evaluate about the data before assigning it a field data type and size?

5. What is the difference between the Short Text and Long Text data types, and how would you use each one?

6. What is the difference between the Number and Currency data types, and how would you use each one?

7. Name and describe the Calculated data type available in Access 2013. Give an example, not already described in the book, of when you could use this data type.

8. Why and when should you use the Lookup data type? Give two specific examples not described in the book.

9. What are three general rules about naming objects in a database?

10. What are the four main database objects, and how is each one used?

11. What are the four types of queries you can use, and what does each one accomplish?

12. What are three limitations associated with using worksheets for data management?

13. What is a primary key? What is a foreign key? How do these keys work together in a database?

14. Which of the following pairs of entities would require a one-to-one, one-to-many, and many-to-many relationship? Describe your answer.

a. Customers and orders

b. States and state capitals

c. College students and classes

15. What is entity integrity? What is referential integrity? Should you enforce referential integrity in a database all the time? Why or why not?

16. Name and describe the three types of anomalies that can occur in a database.

17. What is the goal of normalization? Name and describe the three normal forms.

18. What is a determinant? A partial dependency? A transitive dependency?

Case Problems

Level 1 – Creating the Database Design for NHD Development Group Inc.

NHD Development Group Inc. builds, leases, and manages shopping centers, convenience stores, and other ventures throughout the country. Last year, NHD purchased several antique malls in the southeastern United States. The antique malls have shown potential for a good financial return over time. Tim Richards is the chief information officer for NHD. Tim's responsibility is to provide information to the board of directors so it can make strategic decisions about future development ventures.

Most of the antique malls do their bookkeeping on paper, and Tim is concerned that the data he needs from the antique malls will not be easy to obtain. Because of the paper-based systems, Tim expects it to be difficult to obtain items such as total sales, total commissions, dealer sales, and staff expenses such as salaries. Tim believes that by creating a specialized database for the antique mall managers to use, he can ensure that the data he needs will be easy for managers to create and maintain. The antique malls will be able to use the database to create the reports he needs so he can easily demonstrate the financial health of the malls to the board.

The antique malls are housed in large buildings that are owned by the parent company, NHD. The buildings are divided into booths that are rented to dealers, who then fill the booths with inventory that is sold to customers. A dealer might be a small company or an individual. It is each dealer's responsibility to manage its own inventory; the mall does not maintain an inventory list for the dealers. As the dealer sells items from its inventory, the mall records the dealer number and the price of each item using the information on the item's price tag. At the end of the month, the mall generates a list of total sales for each

Information Systems

dealer, computes the mall's commission, deducts the dealer's rent for booth space, and then issues the dealer a check for the remaining amount.

Tim determined that the database must manage sales, booths in the mall, dealers that rent the booths, and mall employees. At the end of each month, the database must be able to produce a complete list of sales by dealer. In addition, the database must calculate the commission on the sales, subtract the dealer's rent, and determine the profit amount for each dealer.

Some malls also offer classes to their customers. Because the classes provide customers with a reason to return to the mall, NHD will encourage all malls to offer classes. Tim suggests that the database should store information about the classes offered, their instructors, and the customers who enroll in the classes. Instructors are not employees of the mall; rather, they are freelance instructors who are paid from the fees customers pay to take the courses. Customers can sign up for more than one class; payments for course fees are collected at enrollment or on the first day of class. The database needs to manage data about the customers who take these courses, including their name, the course(s) in which they enroll, and the payment of course fees.

Tim has discussed his goals with the board and it has agreed to go forward with developing a database. Tim suggested selecting one mall to serve as a 6-month pilot for the project, allowing him to design and test the database before using it elsewhere. Tim selected the Memories Antique Mall in Cleveland, TN, for the pilot project. The mall's manager, Linda Sutherland, has managed the mall for many years and is excited about replacing the mall's manual systems with a database. After meeting with Linda to discuss the database, Tim asks her to provide him with all of the existing documents that she uses to run the mall, including any forms used for customer classes, so he can examine them and use them to better understand the data he needs to collect.

In this chapter, you will begin the discovery and planning phases of creating a database for NHD. You will use the documents that Linda provides to develop a database design. After completing the database design, Tim will review it and provide feedback that you will use to create the database in Chapter 2.

Complete the following:

1. Linda uses the form shown in Figure 1.35 to collect data about customers who enroll in classes. On paper, design a customer table based on this form. Notice that the form does not contain a place for a customer identification number. Rather, the paper documents are currently filed alphabetically according to the customer's name. You know that you will need an identification number to uniquely identify customers. Be certain to add this field to your table design. Your table design should include field names, data types, field properties (as necessary), and field descriptions.

Figure 1.35: Customer information form

**Memories Antique Mall
Customer Information Form**

Name: _Angela Sutherland_

Address: _7890 Grandview Dr_

City: _Cleveland_   State: _TN_ ZIP: _37364_

Phone: _423-396-1214_

Comments: _____

Do you want to receive our newsletter?   Yes ____ No _X_

2. Linda uses the form shown in Figure 1.36 to obtain information about dealers. On paper, design a dealer table based on this form. Your table design should include field names, data types, field properties (as necessary), and field descriptions. Be certain that each dealer is uniquely identified.

Figure 1.36: Dealer information form

**Memories Antique Mall
Dealer Information Form**

Name: _Marcia Tyler_

Address: _9800 Harbor Lane_

City: _Cleveland_   State: _TN_ ZIP: _37364_

Phone: _(423) 890-8788_   Cell Phone: _(423) 645-8900_

Tax ID: _34-5690654_

Comments: _Call cell phone first. Up to 15% discount is approved._

3. During her interview with you, Linda tells you that she needs to manage the dealer booths, their sizes, and their monthly rental amounts. She currently keeps this information on a piece of paper that she posts on the bulletin board in her office. Create the booth table using the information in the map shown in Figure 1.37. Linda also tells you that she needs to store data about the booth's location (outside perimeter, inside perimeter, or aisle), its color (green, tan, yellow, or white), which dealer rents the booth (or which booths are vacant), and whether the booth has rafters above it and carpeting.

Figure 1.37: Map of the Memories Antique Mall

A-16 12x8 $175	A-15 12x8 $175	A-14 12x10 $230	A-13 12x10 $230	A-12 12x18 $310	A-11 12x18 $310	A-10 12x10 $230	A-09 12x10 $230	A-08 12x10 $230	A-07 12x12 $290

A-17 12x8 $175

A-18 12x12 $290

A-19 12x18 $310

A-20 12x18 $310

B-12 8x12 $175   B-11 8x12 $175

B-13 8x12 $175   C-13 8x16 $150

B-14 8x10 $120   C-14 8x20 $200

B-15 8x10 $120   C-15 8x20 $200

B-10 8x10 $120   B-09 8x10 $120

C-12 8x16 $150

C-11 8x8 $90

Front Counter

C-06 8x8 $90
C-07 8x8 $90
C-08 8x8 $90
C-09 8x8 $90
C-10 8x8 $90

B-08 8x10 $120   B-07 8x8 $105   B-06 8x8 $105

C-05 8x8 $90   B-05 8x8 $105

C-04 8x8 $90   B-04 8x8 $105

C-03 8x8 $90   B-03 8x10 $120

C-02 8x8 $90   B-02 8x10 $120

C-01 8x8 $90   B-01 8x10 $120

A-06 12x18 $310

A-05 12x12 $290

A-04 12x12 $290

A-03 12x12 $290

A-02 12x18 $310

A-01 12x18 $310

4. Linda uses the spreadsheet shown in Figure 1.38 to collect personal data about the mall's employees.

She uses the spreadsheet shown in Figure 1.39 to collect other data about employees, including their hire date, last personnel review date, and salary. Use these spreadsheets to design an employee table. Your table design should include field names, data types, field properties (as necessary), and field descriptions. Be certain that each employee is uniquely identified and that you eliminate redundant data. Create any additional tables as necessary.

Figure 1.38: Personal data about employees

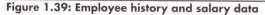

	Emp First	Emp Last	Last 4 Digits of SSN	DOB	Address	City	State	ZIP	Phone	Cell	Salary	Hourly Rate	Review
2	Linda	Sutherland	8987	8/15/1968	1102 Jackson Street	Cleveland	TN	37311	423-396-1777	423-644-1222	67,000.00		
3	Mary	Sanchez	7655	10/15/1968	633 Empire Street	Chattanooga	TN	37415	423-398-9898	423-665-1211	35,500.00		5/31/2016
4	William	Sullivan	4286	2/14/1975	12933 Road G	Cleveland	TN	37311	423-23-36321	423-651-2342		9.25	3/1/2016
5	Frances	Miller	2642	10/15/1968	755 Cherry Street	Cleveland	TN	37312	423-344-7212	423-985-3410		12.50	4/1/2016
6	Gretchen	Archibald	5070	12/22/1969	906 East Second Street	Athens	TN	37303	423-435-2648	423-751-2042		9.25	
7	Scott	Cox	4988	4/22/1969	1309 Mesa Avenue	Ooltewah	TN	37315	423-435-3147	423-952-0010		15.50	
8	Cheri	Greene	6322	4/12/1980	403 North Madison Street	Collegedale	TN	37311	423-396-6412	423-825-1643	35,500.00		1/15/2017
9	Angela	Scott	4257	5/4/1981	133 South Washington	Ooltewah	TN	37315	423-435-2616	423-844-1200		15.00	2/1/2016
10	Francois	Feliciano	3716	3/15/1980	307 Memorial Drive	Cleveland	TN	37311	423-233-1697	423-165-2974		16.00	5/1/2016
11	Robert	Toriano	1678	4/10/1974	9411 Clarkston Avenue	Chattanooga	TN	37401	423-344-4289	423-592-1352		15.50	6/1/2016
12	Adam	Jones	4632	6/21/1977	623 South Hampton Way	Knoxville	TN	37901	865-465-2122	423-241-5230		15.00	6/1/2016
13	Luke	Hoffman	6420	9/15/1968	1322 East Fairmont Street	Cleveland	TN	37312	423-398-1647	423-789-9552		15.50	
14	Frances	Gomez	6006	5/30/1981	912 North Hampton Avenue	Athens	TN	37303	423-398-5454	423-502-1200		12.00	11/1/2016
15	Hae Yeon	Choi	1876	12/12/1979	322 South Cripple Creek Avenue	Chattanooga	TN	37402	423-233-9745	423-583-2420		13.50	3/1/2017
16	Dawn	Young	100	6/20/1977	56 East Pioneer Road	Cleveland	TN	37323	423-344-8458	423-264-3213		15.50	12/15/2016

Figure 1.39: Employee history and salary data

	Emp First	Emp Last	Start Date	End Date	Cell	Salary	Hourly Rate	Review	Memo	Position
2	Linda	Sutherland	2/15/2007		423-644-1222	67,000.00				Manager
3	Mary	Sanchez	6/15/2010		423-665-1211	35,500.00		5/31/2016		Accounting
4	William	Sullivan	5/23/2009		423-651-2342		9.25	3/1/2016		Maintentance
5	Frances	Miller	3/22/2009		423-985-3410		12.50	4/1/2016		Sales
6	Gretchen	Archibald	1/5/2005	5/16/2009	423-751-2042		9.25			Maintentance
7	Scott	Cox	4/19/2008	4/22/2010	423-952-0010		15.50			Sales
8	Cheri	Greene	8/5/2010		423-825-1643	35,500.00		1/15/2017		Assistant Manager
9	Angela	Scott	9/22/2010		423-844-1200		15.00	2/1/2016		Sales
10	Francois	Feliciano	7/16/2009		423-165-2974		16.00	5/1/2016		Sales
11	Robert	Toriano	9/16/2009		423-592-1352		15.50	6/1/2016		Administrative Assistant
12	Adam	Jones	10/12/2010		423-241-5230		15.00	6/1/2016		Sales
13	Luke	Hoffman	11/16/2009	2/22/2012	423-789-9552		15.50			Sales
14	Frances	Gomez	5/31/2011		423-502-1200		12.00	11/1/2016	Speaks fluent Spanish	Administrative Assistant
15	Hae Yeon	Choi	12/15/2012		423-583-2420		13.50	3/1/2017		Administrative Assistant
16	Dawn	Young	1/16/2009		423-264-3213		15.50	12/15/2016		Sales

5. Linda also needs to maintain data about the instructors who teach the classes at the mall. For instructors, she needs to store the instructor's personal information (name, address, phone number, and cell phone number) and the fee that the instructor charges for teaching a class. Design a table that maintains information about instructors. Be certain that each instructor is uniquely identified.

6. Linda needs to maintain information about the classes that instructors teach at the mall. Currently, classes do not have an identification number, and, as such, Linda has a hard time distinguishing different classes with the same class name. For example, the mall offers three "Tattered Treasures" classes, all taught by the same instructor, but the only difference between the classes is the date they occur. Linda wants to distinguish the classes better, and store the class name, cost, classroom in which it is taught, date and time, and the instructor. Classrooms at the mall have a single-digit room number. Recently, the local community college approved some of the mall's classes for continuing education units (CEU) in certain fields, so Linda also needs to indicate whether the classes qualify for credit. Design a table to store this information for Linda.

7. Finally, you need a table that maintains data about class enrollments, including the customer, class, and payment information. Customers can sign up for more than one class. Customers can pay their class fees when they enroll in the class or on the first day of class. Be certain you have a way to indicate the customer's payment status (paid or not paid) for each class.

8. For each table you design, use a piece of paper to sketch the table design so that you can enter five sample records into it. After creating five records, determine whether you need to make any adjustments in your table designs so that each table is in third normal form. For example, is the job title repeated in the table that stores data about employees? What field will you use as the primary key in each table, or do you need to create a field to use as the primary key? If you need to make any changes to your table designs, do so on your paper and add the necessary documentation to the existing table designs.

9. Review each table design to ensure you have created all of the necessary fields and that they have the correct data type and field size. Be certain that you have designated a primary key field in each table and that your primary key field will contain unique values for each record.

10. Draw arrows to indicate the fields that will form the relationships in the database.

11. If your instructor asks you to turn in your database design, keep a copy for yourself as you will need it to develop the database in subsequent chapters.

Level 2 – Creating the Database Design for MovinOn Inc.

Information Systems

MovinOn Inc., is a moving company that provides moving and storage services in Washington, Oregon, and Wyoming. MovinOn provides a truck, driver, and one or more moving assistants to move residential and commercial items from one location to another within the defined coverage area. In addition to moving services, the company provides temporary and long-term storage in its warehouses. MovinOn's customers are commercial and residential. Some of the storage warehouses are climatically controlled for customers who need to store items that are sensitive to extreme temperatures.

The business started in 1995 with a single truck and a single warehouse in Oregon. Due to a very satisfied clientele, the company has grown over the years into a much larger business. Currently, MovinOn has one warehouse in each state it services and is working on a merger with another company that offers similar services in different service areas. When the merger is complete, MovinOn will acquire additional storage warehouses, trucks, and employees and will expand its operations into different states.

David Bowers is the CEO of MovinOn. In the past, David managed the business using a combination of spreadsheets and paper forms. However, with a merger in the company's future, David needs to expand his system to manage data better. David recently hired Robert Iko, an information systems specialist, to recommend and implement a new plan for managing the company's data.

Robert's first task is to understand the current system and its limitations by talking extensively with David about data management and user needs. David explains that the office in each state accepts reservations for moving and storage services by completing a job order form that includes the customer's name, address, phone number, and the job's details. Jobs that involve trucking items from one location to another or from an outside location to a storage unit in a warehouse are maintained in a filing cabinet that is organized by customer name. Leases for storage space are stored alphabetically in a separate filing cabinet for each warehouse. All of the forms are stored in the on-site offices at the warehouse from which they were purchased. Unfortunately, David admits that forms are often lost or misplaced and sometimes contain inaccurate or missing data. In addition, when a customer requires the services of another warehouse, a MovinOn employee has to copy the customer's record and send it to the second warehouse so that it is on file at the second location. David wants the new system to be capable of sharing data between the three warehouses and any warehouses that the company acquires in the future so that it is easy for the company to share and maintain data.

Each warehouse has its own manager, office staff, and moving assistants. Drivers are contract employees and may work for other companies. David wants the new system to manage employee data, including personal information, salary information, and work performance.

In addition to managing personnel data, David also wants to use the new system to manage information about drivers, including their personal information and driving records. The system also needs to store information about the trucks and vans that MovinOn owns and operates.

Finally, the system must maintain data about customers who utilize moving and storage services. Some customers might require storage in more than one location. When there is a request for services, the requests are recorded on forms. In addition to the job order form, a job detail form is created that shows the details about the job such as the driver, the van used, actual mileage, and actual weight.

Robert gathered a collection of documents during the discovery phase that will help you design the database. You need to be certain that every data item in the existing documents is also represented in the tables in your design. In this chapter, you will begin the discovery and planning phases of creating a database for MovinOn. You will use the documents that Robert provides to develop a database design. After completing the database design, Robert will review it and provide feedback that you will use to create the database in Chapter 2.

Complete the following:

1. Robert uses the form shown in Figure 1.40 to collect data about employees. In addition to storing the data shown in Figure 1.40, Robert also needs to identify the warehouse in which the employee works. On paper, design an employee table and any other necessary tables based on this form. The table design for all tables that you create should include field names, data types, field properties (as necessary), and field descriptions. Remember that each table must have a primary key field.

2. The database must manage data about drivers, who are hired on a contract basis. Design a table that stores information about drivers. The table should include the same information stored for employees, except for an indication about the warehouse in which the driver works, in addition to storing the following additional information:

   - Drivers are not paid an hourly rate or salary; they are paid based on the number of miles driven for any job. The payment for a job is determined by multiplying the rate per mile by the number of miles for the job.
   - MovinOn rates drivers based on their safety records, successful on-time deliveries, and other factors. The company's rating system uses the values A, B, C, D, and F to rate drivers, with A being the highest rating and F being the lowest rating. (You do not need to worry about how MovinOn assigns ratings to drivers; you only need to store the driver's rating.)

3. Design a table that stores data about the trucks and vans owned by MovinOn. Each vehicle has a unique identification number appearing on the vehicle in the format TRK-001 for trucks or VAN-009 for vans. David wants to store the vehicle's license plate number, number of axles, and color.

4. Design a table that stores data about warehouses using the data shown in Figure 1.41. The warehouse identification number is the two-letter state abbreviation in which the warehouse is located followed by a dash and then a number. For example, the warehouse in Wyoming is WY-1.

Figure 1.40: Employee information form

mOvinOn Inc.

Employee Information Form

Name: David Bowers

Address: 10124 Metropolitan Drive

City: Seattle   State: WA ZIP: 98117

Phone: (206) 246-5132   Cell Phone: (206) 575-4321

SSN: 154-00-3785   Date of Birth: 9/12/1958

(The following information to be filled out by MovinOn human resources manager)

Hire Date: 1/22/1998   Termination Date: _____

Position: General Manager

Annual Salary: $72,000   or Hourly Rate: _____

Date of last personnel review: _____

Notes about this employee:

_____

_____

_____

_____

Figure 1.41: Data about warehouses

	A	B	C	D	E	F	G	H
1	WarehouseID	Address	City	State	ZIP	Phone	Climate Control	Security Gate
2	OR-1	#3 Industrial Park Way	Portland	OR	97212	5035512432	No	Yes
3	WA-1	8798 Warehouse Rd	Seattle	WA	98121	2063242312	Yes	Yes
4	WY-1	54781 Hixson Pike	Jackson Hole	WY	83001	3075413571	Yes	No

5. Currently, information about storage units is stored in an Excel worksheet; a portion of this data is shown in Figure 1.42. Use this information to help you design a table that manages data about the storage units.

Figure 1.42: Data about storage units

	A	B	C	D	E
1	UnitID	WarehouseID	Unit Size	Rent	
2	1	OR-1	8 x 8	25.00	
3	1	WA-1	12 x 12	35.00	
4	1	WY-1	12 x 12	45.00	
5	2	OR-1	8 x 12	30.00	
6	2	WA-1	12 x 12	35.00	
7	2	WY-1	12 x 12	45.00	
8	3	OR-1	8 x 8	25.00	
9	3	WA-1	9 x 12	30.00	
10	3	WY-1	12 x 12	45.00	
11	4	OR-1	8 x 12	30.00	
12	4	WA-1	9 x 12	30.00	
13	4	WY-1	12 x 18	70.00	
14	5	OR-1	8 x 8	25.00	
15	5	WA-1	12 x 12	85.00	
16	5	WY-1	12 x 18	70.00	
17	6	OR-1	8 x 12	30.00	
18	6	WA-1	12 x 12	85.00	
19	6	WY-1	12 x 12	45.00	
20	7	OR-1	8 x 10	25.00	
21	7	WA-1	12 x 10	80.00	
22	7	WY-1	12 x 12	85.00	
23	8	OR-1	15 x 15	95.00	

tblStorageUnit

6. You also need to manage data to indicate which customer rents which unit. David wants to store the date the lease started and ended on each unit in each warehouse. For current customers, the ending lease date will be null. Design a table that manages data about unit rentals.

7. You have learned that data pertaining to moving jobs is actually accumulated in two steps. When the customer requests a job, the administrative assistant from the warehouse that will perform the services fills out the form shown in Figure 1.43. This form is considered a "job order." Design a table that manages the job order data.

8. David needs to store the following data about customers: company name (for commercial customers only), the job contact's name, and the address, city, state, ZIP code, phone number, and balance. Design a customer table using this information.

9. The administrative assistant uses a scheduling program to manage and assign vehicles and drivers for moving jobs, and then this information is entered into the database. Upon completion of a job, the database must store the details about the job, including the customer, truck or van used, driver, actual mileage, and actual weight. This step is considered to be the "job detail." David wants to store job detail data separately from job order data. Design a table that manages the job detail information.

Figure 1.43: Job order information form

mOvinOn Inc.

Job Order Information Form

Customer: *Piazza Real Estate*

Move Date: *9/15/2017*

Address Moving **FROM**:   *1789 Eighth Avenue*

Spokane, WA

Address Moving **TO**:   *7899 Grandview Apt #5*

Pullman, WA

Estimated Mileage: *60*   Estimated Weight: *1250 lbs*

Do you need packing service?   Yes _*X*_ No _____

Do you need us to move any heavy items (such as a piano or freezer)?

Yes _*X*_ No _____

Do you need to store any items?   Yes _____ No _*X*_

10. For each table you design, use a piece of paper to sketch the table design so that you can enter five sample records into it. After creating five records, determine whether you need to make any adjustments in your table designs so that each table is in third normal form. If you need to make any changes to your table designs, do so on your paper and add the necessary documentation to the existing table designs.

11. Review each table design to ensure you have created all of the necessary fields. Be certain that you have designated a primary key field in each table and that your primary key field will contain unique values for each record.

12. Draw arrows to indicate the fields that will form the relationships in the database.

13. If your instructor asks you to turn in your database design, keep a copy for yourself as you will need it to develop your database in subsequent chapters.

Level 3 – Creating the Database Design for Hershey College

Information Systems

Hershey College is a small liberal arts college in Hershey, Pennsylvania. Because student enrollment at Hershey College is small, the college participates competitively only in football and basketball. However, the Athletic Department has been encouraging the college for the past several years to develop an Intramural Department. The Athletic Department has conducted research showing that people who exercise regularly have fewer instances of heart disease, osteoporosis, and other illnesses. After receiving a large cash endowment for the development of the Intramural Department, the college's board of directors agreed to its creation. The board also met with student leadership at the college and by mutual agreement implemented a small activity fee that all students will pay with their tuition to provide funding for the Intramural Department's activities.

The primary goal of the Intramural Department is to encourage students to participate in sports and activities that promote good health and strong bodies. In addition, many studies have shown that students who are actively involved in sports or other extracurricular activities are less likely to participate in undesirable activities.

The Intramural Department will offer organized sports leagues for interested students. The department will create schedules for each sport, assign players to teams, provide a coach and a student captain, and manage the team's playing locations. The department will also offer sports equipment that teams can check out and use for practice and games. The sports that will be offered by Hershey College are shown in Figure 1.44.

Figure 1.44: Hershey College's sports offerings

Basketball	Football
Ping Pong	Soccer
Softball	Swimming
Tennis	Track
Wrestling	Pool

Part of the mandate set by the board for the Intramural Department is to demonstrate that students are using its services by participating on teams and using equipment. The Intramural Department must provide reports each semester documenting which sports were offered, how many students participated in them, and other information as requested by the board. Admission counselors will also use these reports to show prospective students that there are many opportunities to participate in sports at the college.

The college has appointed Marianna Fuentes as the director of the Intramural Department. Marianna has hired you to develop and maintain the database that will manage the departmental activities and produce the required reports. Because the Intramural Department is new, Marianna is not yet certain of the data the department needs to collect and manage. Initially, she wants the database to manage data about each sport offered by the Intramural Department (including team assignments, coaches, and scheduling), the students who sign up for sports teams, and the equipment.

Because you are the only person working on the database, there is a lot of responsibility on your shoulders to provide a database that works well for the department. In this chapter, you will begin the discovery and planning phases of creating a database for the Intramural Department. You will use the information that Marianna provides to develop a database design. After completing the database design, Marianna will review it and provide feedback that you will use to create the database in Chapter 2.

Complete the following:

1. Marianna decides that the best way to get started planning the database is to prepare a list of all the data items that are needed to support the department. Table 1.14 shows her list, which she asks you to use when planning the database. You will need to identify the data to collect, group fields into tables, normalize the data, and relate the tables.

Table 1.14: Intramural Department information needs

Item	Description
Students: We need to store information about students who participate on teams and the sports in which they participate, including the team. Students can sign up for more than one sport.	
ID number	Student and faculty IDs at Hershey are five digits.
Name	First and last names.
Phone	Home phone number, cell phone number.
Waiver	Students must sign a waiver to play on a team; we must have this document on file.
Academic eligibility	Students must be academically eligible to play sports by maintaining a C or better grade point average; we must check eligibility at registration.
Sports	
Name	Sports include basketball, football, ping pong, pool, soccer, softball, swimming, tennis, track, and wrestling.

Table 1.14: Intramural Department information needs (cont.)

Item	Description
Coach	Each sport has an assigned coach. We need to know the coach's name, office number (such as G-18), phone number, and cell phone number. A person can coach one or more teams over one or more seasons.
Minimum and maximum players	Each sport has a designated minimum and maximum number of players.
Begin date	The date each sport begins.
Notes	A place to record notes about each sport.
Equipment: Teams or coaches check out the equipment they need for their sport's practice sessions. Some sports, such as wrestling, do not have equipment.	
ID number	Equipment is assigned an ID number using a sport abbreviation and a number (BAS = basketball, FTB = football, PNG = ping pong, POL = pool table, SOC = soccer, SOF = softball, TEN = tennis, and WRS = wrestling). For example, BAS-1 is a basketball. Some equipment ID numbers indicate a collection of items. For example, BAS-3 is three basketballs.
Description	A description of the equipment.
Storage building	The building where the equipment is stored, such as SB-1.
Fields: Different courts, fields, and tables are available for practice and games.	
ID number	Courts, fields, and tables are assigned ID numbers. For example, CRT-1 is a basketball court, FLD-2 is a soccer field, and TBL-2 is a pool table.
Type	Identify the court, field, or table type (basketball, softball, and so on).
Maintenance contact	Each court, field, and table has an assigned maintenance person who manages and resolves problems with the court, field, or location. We will need to know the maintenance person's name, phone number, and office number.
Season	The seasons each field is available for use by a team (some fields are unavailable off-season for maintenance purposes). The seasons are fall and spring; some sports run year-round, in which case the season is "always."
Teams: For each team, we need to know the team number, captain, sport name, location games are played, and the equipment needed for the game.	

2. For each table you identified, determine the data type to assign to each field and which fields to use as the primary key.

3. For each table you designed, use a piece of paper to sketch the table design so that you can enter five sample records into it. After creating five records, determine whether you need to make any adjustments in your table designs so that each table is in third normal form. If you need to make any changes to your table designs, do so on your paper and add the necessary documentation to the existing table designs.

4. Use arrows to indicate the relationships between tables and the relationship types. Indicate which fields are involved in the relationship and determine how to maintain data integrity.

5. If your instructor asks you to turn in your database design, keep a copy for yourself as you will need it to develop your database in subsequent chapters.

1

SAM: Skills Assessment Manager

For current SAM information, including versions and content details, visit SAM Central (http://samcentral.course.com). If you have a SAM user profile, you may have access to hands-on instruction, practice, and assessment of the skills covered in this chapter. Since various versions of SAM are supported throughout the life of this text, check with your instructor for the correct instructions and URL/Web site for accessing assignments.

Building the Database
Information Systems: Creating, Populating, Relating, and Maintaining the Tables in a Database

LEARNING OBJECTIVES

Level 1

Review the database design
Create the database tables using the database design
Work in Design view

Level 2

Create additional tables for the database
Import data into the database tables
Work with primary and foreign keys
Create one-to-many and many-to-many relationships between tables
Use a subdatasheet to view related records

Level 3

Learn about the role of the database administrator
Compact, repair, and back up a database
Document the database design using the Database Documenter
Secure the database from unauthorized use

TOOLS COVERED IN THIS CHAPTER

Database Documenter

Database security

Datasheet view

Design view

Import Spreadsheet Wizard

Input Mask Wizard

Lookup Wizard

Relationships window

Subdatasheet

Chapter Introduction

In Chapter 1, Don Linebarger, the Information Systems Director at 4Corners Pharmacy, interviewed the pharmacy's owner, pharmacists, managers, and key employees to learn more about the data needs of the pharmacy and to understand the existing systems the pharmacy uses to conduct business. Don's work resulted in a plan that identifies the tables he needs to create, the fields for those tables, the data types and field sizes needed to store the data, and the relationships between the tables. With his plan approved by management, Don is ready to begin building the database using Access 2013.

In this chapter, you will learn different techniques for creating tables, entering data, verifying data, relating tables, documenting the database objects, backing up the database, repairing the database, and securing data.

Case Scenario

Don needs to begin work on the database for 4Corners Pharmacy by creating the database in Access and then creating the tables that will store the data the pharmacy needs to track customers, prescriptions, drugs, employees, training classes, health insurance companies, doctors, and clinics. The pharmacy's owner, Paul Ferrino, worked as a cashier, pharmacy technician, and pharmacist in his father's pharmacy before purchasing the pharmacy upon his father's retirement. Vincent Ferrino still works part time at the pharmacy as a pharmacist. Although Vincent's business was successful for more than two decades, his system for managing data about the pharmacy is obsolete. Paul wants to automate many of the processes at the pharmacy so he can better evaluate and operate the business.

Paul's top priority was hiring Don, who will create the system for the pharmacy, train users (that is, the employees) to use the system, and maintain and expand the system over time.

LEVEL 1

Creating the Database Tables

Reviewing the Database Design

Throughout the database design process, Don researched and evaluated existing and missing sources of data at the pharmacy. He also interviewed the owner, pharmacists, managers, and key employees to learn about how they plan to use the database so he can better understand the needs of the business. One of Don's most important roles is to make sure that the database he develops stores the pharmacy's data in the correct format and outputs the correct queries, forms, and reports for Paul and the managers.

You learned in Chapter 1 that a relational database is a collection of related tables. As an information systems professional, Don knows the importance of properly planning and designing the database so that it meets users' needs and expectations. Paul already knows that Vincent's system for tracking prescriptions, refills, and customer information does not work because it is prone to data entry errors and inconsistent data. In addition, Paul has limited tools available to him in Microsoft Excel to search a large worksheet to find related records and other information.

After careful analysis and preparation, Don formulated the database design for Paul's approval. Don reviews the database design with Paul to ensure that it is correct and meets the needs of the pharmacy. To make the design easier to understand, Don begins by presenting some of the table designs to Paul. Figure 2.1 shows the table that stores customer data, including each customer's name, address, phone number, date of birth, gender, account balance, preference for childproof caps, health plan, household information, and allergies. The table that stores customer information is linked to the table that stores details about the customer's prescriptions, to the table that stores details about the customer's health plan, and to the table that stores the details about the customer's household. These links are made by creating foreign keys in the related tables.

Figure 2.1: Data stored about customers

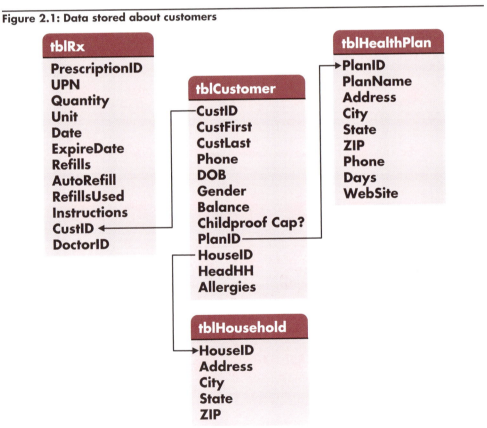

© 2014 Cengage Learning

Don used the Leszynski/Reddick guidelines for naming database objects and created four tables: tblCustomer, tblRx, tblHousehold, and tblHealthPlan. Because tblCustomer is linked to the related tables tblRx, tblHousehold, and tblHealthPlan, Don can retrieve detailed information about each customer and the prescriptions they have filled, the household to which they belong, and the health plan that covers them. These related tables will also enable him to list all the customers within a household and determine which drugs are being prescribed to which customers.

Figure 2.2 shows the table that stores prescription data, including the prescription's identification number, UPN, quantity ordered, unit of measurement, fill date, expiration date, refills authorization, preference for automatic refills, number of refills used, and the prescribing instructions. In addition, tblRx stores the identification numbers of the customer and the prescribing doctor. The table that stores prescription information is linked to the table that stores the details about the prescribing doctor, to the table that stores details about the customer, to the table that stores details about the drug, and to the table that stores information about refills using foreign keys in the related tables.

Figure 2.2: Data stored about prescriptions

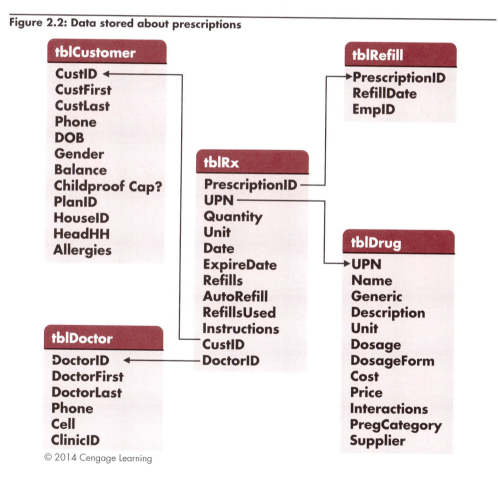

© 2014 Cengage Learning

Figure 2.3 shows the table that stores data about employees at the pharmacy, including the employee's identification number, first name, middle initial, last name, Social Security number, date of birth, start date, termination date (if applicable), address, city, state, ZIP code, job identification number, phone number, cell phone number, salary or hourly rate of compensation, and next personnel review date. In addition, there is a field named Memo to store miscellaneous information about the employee, such as being part time or bilingual. The table that stores employee information is linked to the table that stores the details about the employee's training, to the table that stores information about the refills that the employee has filled, and to the table that identifies the different job titles at the pharmacy.

Figure 2.3: Data stored about employees

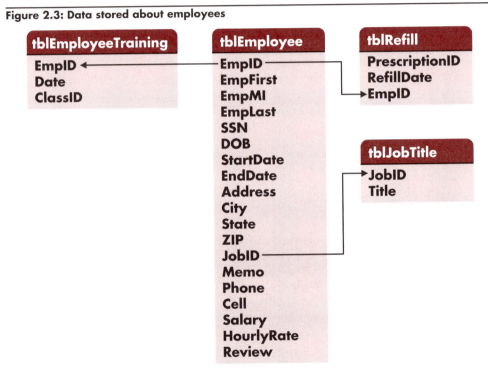

© 2014 Cengage Learning

Figure 2.4 shows the table that stores data about doctors, including the doctor's identification number, first and last names, phone number, cell phone number, and the identification number of the clinic at which the doctor works. The table that stores doctor data is linked to the table that stores details about the clinic at which the doctor works and to the table that stores details about prescriptions the doctor has written.

Figure 2.4: Data stored about doctors

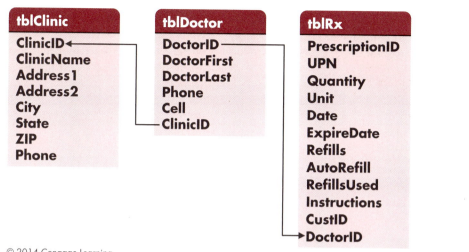

© 2014 Cengage Learning

Figure 2.5 shows the table that stores data about the classes that pharmacy employees must take to maintain their professional certifications and other classes of interest. The table stores data about classes, including the class identification number, description, cost, renewal requirement (in years), and provider. In addition, there is a field to indicate whether the class is required. The table that stores data about classes is linked to the table that stores details about the employees who took the classes.

Figure 2.5: Data stored about classes

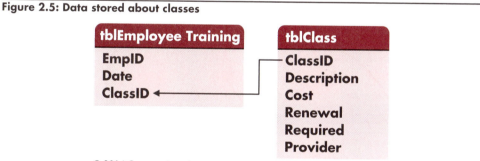

© 2014 Cengage Learning

As is customary in the design process, Paul and Don agreed to limit the scope of the new system to managing data about customers, prescriptions, drugs, employees, training classes, doctors, and clinics. As the pharmacy's staff and managers begin using the system, Paul and Don might reevaluate it and add additional functionality, such as managing the inventory of nonprescription items. If Paul opens additional pharmacy locations in the future, he and Don might plan for the system to go on a network so it is possible for employees and managers at each location to share data and other resources across a network. The entire database design appears in Figure 2.6.

Figure 2.6: Database design for 4Corners Pharmacy

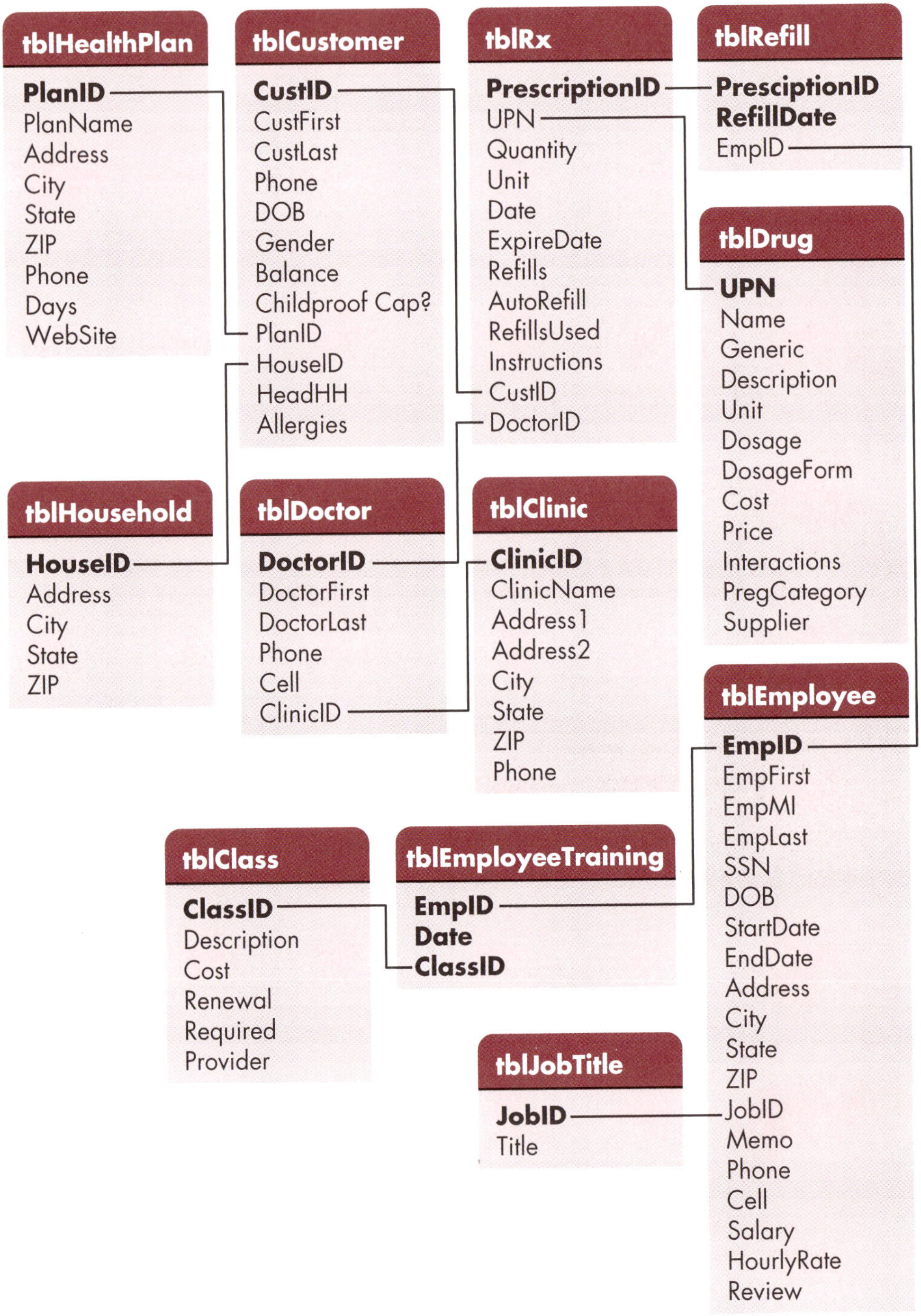

tblHealthPlan

PlanID
PlanName
Address
City
State
ZIP
Phone
Days
WebSite

tblCustomer

CustID
CustFirst
CustLast
Phone
DOB
Gender
Balance
Childproof Cap?
PlanID
HouseID
HeadHH
Allergies

tblRx

PrescriptionID
UPN
Quantity
Unit
Date
ExpireDate
Refills
AutoRefill
RefillsUsed
Instructions
CustID
DoctorID

tblRefill

PresciptionID
RefillDate
EmpID

tblDrug

UPN
Name
Generic
Description
Unit
Dosage
DosageForm
Cost
Price
Interactions
PregCategory
Supplier

tblHousehold

HouseID
Address
City
State
ZIP

tblDoctor

DoctorID
DoctorFirst
DoctorLast
Phone
Cell
ClinicID

tblClinic

ClinicID
ClinicName
Address1
Address2
City
State
ZIP
Phone

tblEmployee

EmpID
EmpFirst
EmpMI
EmpLast
SSN
DOB
StartDate
EndDate
Address
City
State
ZIP
JobID
Memo
Phone
Cell
Salary
HourlyRate
Review

tblClass

ClassID
Description
Cost
Renewal
Required
Provider

tblEmployeeTraining

EmpID
Date
ClassID

tblJobTitle

JobID
Title

Paul is satisfied that the database will collect and manage the correct data, so he gives his final approval to the design. Don begins by starting Access and creating a new database.

Creating the Database Using the Database Design

After receiving Paul's approval on the database design, Don's first task is to create the database in Access. After starting Access, Don clicks Blank desktop database, as shown in Figure 2.7.

Figure 2.7: Choosing Blank desktop database

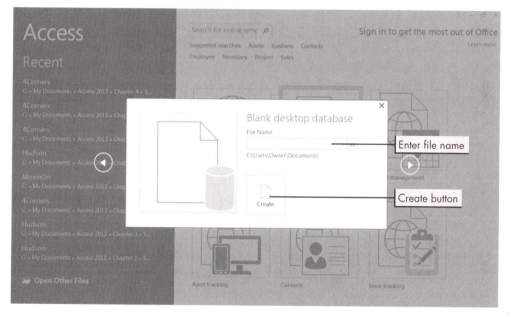

In the Blank desktop database dialog box, Don types **4Corners** in the File Name text box, chooses a file location in which to save the database, and then clicks the Create button. The 4Corners database automatically opens in the Database window, as shown in Figure 2.8.

Figure 2.8: 4Corners database in the Database window

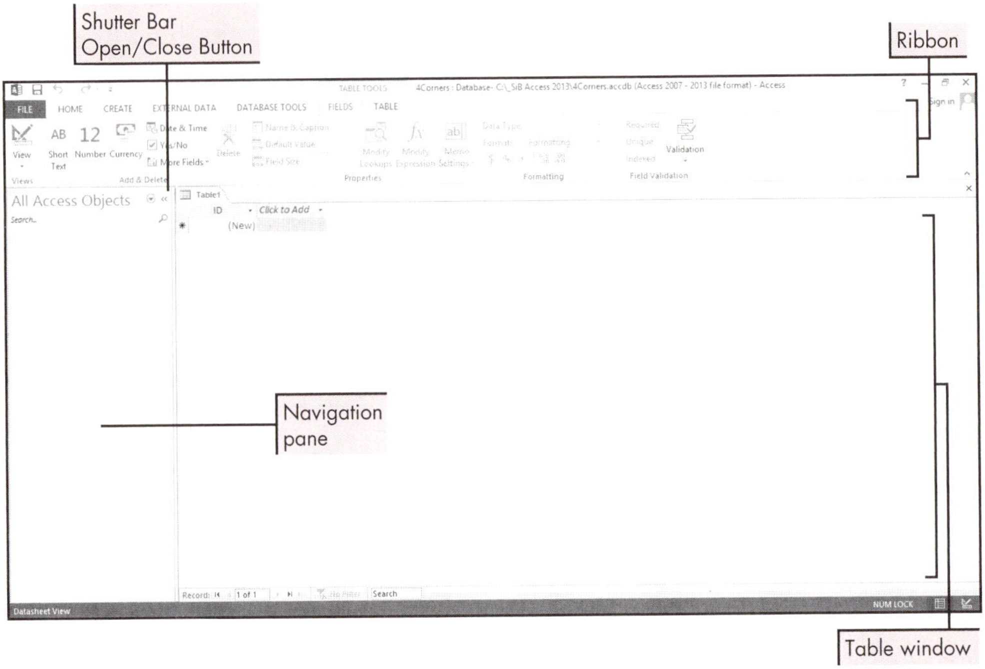

The **Database window** is the main control panel for the database. The **Navigation pane**, located on the left side of the window, lists all objects (tables, reports, etc.) in the database so you have easy access to them. If you need additional room on your screen, you can click the Shutter Bar Open/Close Button to open or close the Navigation pane. The first database object you must create is a table because tables store all of the data in a database. You can create a table by entering data in Datasheet view or designing a table in Design view. The method that you select depends on the type of data that you are entering or need to organize in a table and on your own work preferences. Don will use both methods to create the tables in the 4Corners database. The first table that Don wants to create is the one that will store the details about the different health plans to which customers subscribe. Because he already has a printout with the data for several health plans, he decides to create this table by entering data in the table in Datasheet view.

Creating a Table by Entering Data in Datasheet View

When you first create a database, it appears in the Database window. To the right of the Navigation pane is the Table window which displays an empty table in Datasheet view. The contextual TABLE TOOLS tabs, FIELDS and TABLE, also appear, providing table-specific commands and options. Datasheet View appears in the status bar reminding you of which view you are in. Make a note that while you are in Datasheet view, the Design view icon appears on the Ribbon and vice versa. Rely on the status bar to indicate which view you are in.

The **Datasheet view** displays a table's records in rows and the table's fields in columns. The **Table window** indicates the table's name; in this case, the table name is given a default name, Table1, because Don hasn't saved it yet. Whenever you work in a table, the Table window automatically opens, so you can enter data directly in the table or modify existing data easily. See Figure 2.9.

Figure 2.9: Table in Datasheet view

As Don begins to enter data in the database, the table will display default field names, such as Field1, Field2, and so on. Don can rename the field names after he has entered the data. After you enter the data into the first field, you can either press the Enter key or the Tab key, which enters the data in the field and moves you to the next field to enter more data. Figure 2.10 shows the datasheet after Don entered the data for six health plans. Some fields had text that was cut off because it was too long. To fix this, Don resized the fields by double-clicking the borders of the field names.

Figure 2.10: Records for six health plans entered

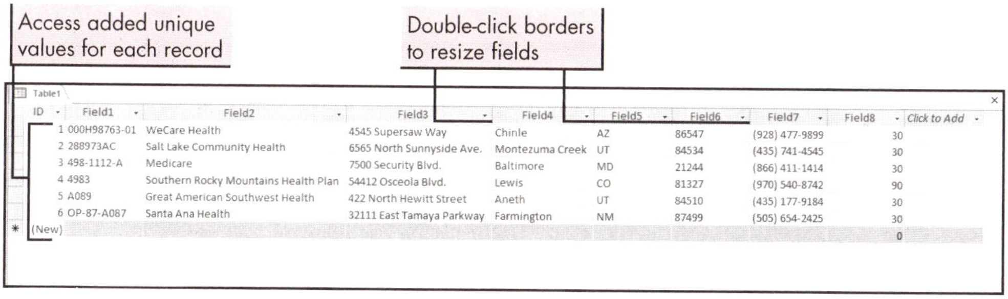

Access added unique values for each record

Double-click borders to resize fields

ID	Field1	Field2	Field3	Field4	Field5	Field6	Field7	Field8
1	000H98763-01	WeCare Health	4545 Supersaw Way	Chinle	AZ	86547	(928) 477-9899	30
2	288973AC	Salt Lake Community Health	6565 North Sunnyside Ave.	Montezuma Creek	UT	84534	(435) 741-4545	30
3	498-1112-A	Medicare	7500 Security Blvd.	Baltimore	MD	21244	(866) 411-1414	30
4	4983	Southern Rocky Mountains Health Plan	54412 Osceola Blvd.	Lewis	CO	81327	(970) 540-8742	90
5	A089	Great American Southwest Health	422 North Hewitt Street	Aneth	UT	84510	(435) 177-9184	30
6	OP-87-A087	Santa Ana Health	32111 East Tamaya Parkway	Farmington	NM	87499	(505) 654-2425	30

As Don was entering records, Access added an AutoNumber field to the datasheet. Each record that Don entered has a unique value in the ID field. The datasheet has blank rows for additional records.

Now that Don has entered the data for the health plans, he needs to save the table as an object in the 4Corners database and define the fields. Don clicks the Save button on the Quick Access Toolbar, types "tblHealthPlan" in the Table Name text box in the Save As dialog box, and then clicks the OK button.

To define the fields in a table, Don changes to Design view by clicking the View button in the Views group on the HOME tab on the Ribbon. See Figure 2.11.

Figure 2.11: Table design for tblHealthPlan

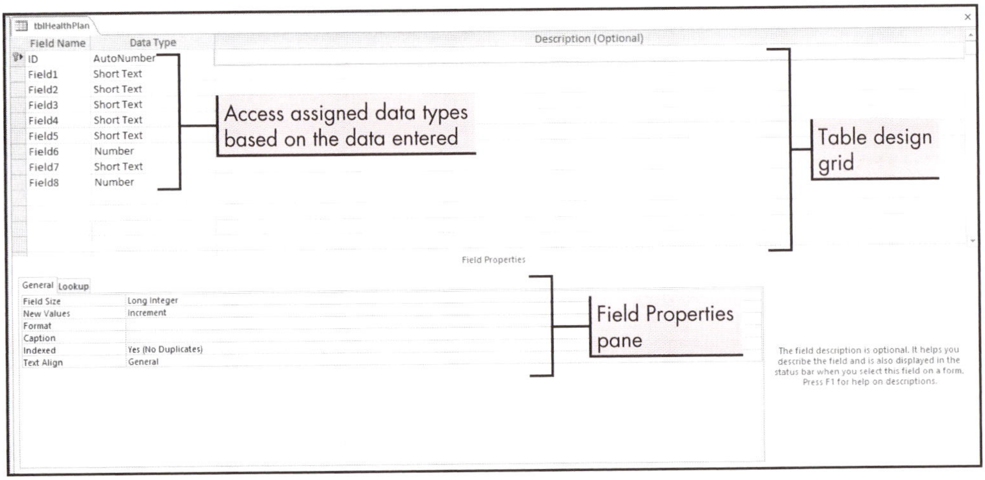

Working in Design View

Don uses **Design view** to define the table's fields and the field properties and rearrange the order of fields as necessary. The top part of Design view is called the **Table Design grid** (or the **design grid**); this area includes the Field Name, Data Type, and Description columns. If you need to change the order of fields, you would do it in the Table Design grid. Each row in the Table Design grid is a field in the table. The bottom part of Design view is called the **Field Properties pane**; this area displays the field properties for the selected field. You can select a field by clicking the field in the Table Design grid. When a field is selected, a highlighted border appears around the field. In Figure 2.11, the ID field (an AutoNumber field) added by Access appears as the first field. Don decides that since he has a field that shows each plan ID, he can delete the AutoNumber field.

Next, Don needs to rename the default field names to match the ones in his table design by selecting each field name and typing the new value. Most DBMSs, including Access, have specific rules that you must follow when naming fields and database objects. The following rules apply to naming Access objects:

- Names can contain up to 64 characters.
- Names can contain any combination of letters, numbers, spaces, and special characters, except a period (.), an exclamation point (!), an accent grave (`), and square brackets ([and]).
- Names cannot begin with a space.

In addition to these rules, some organizations establish standards for naming objects and fields. Some organizations might include acronyms or abbreviations in field names to make them shorter. At 4Corners Pharmacy, for example, the field that stores a person's date of birth is abbreviated as "DOB," and field and object names that contain multiple words are capitalized but do not contain any spaces (such as the table name tblHealthPlan or the field name ClinicName).

After changing the default field names, he decides to add a field so that the Web sites for insurance companies can be entered. By adding Web site addresses, they may be quickly accessed. Next, Don defines the data type and field properties for each field. To change the data type, he clicks the right side of the Data Type box for the field to display a list of all the data types for Access, and then he clicks the desired data type. When Don selects a data type, the Field Properties pane changes to display properties associated with the selected data type. Don knows that Short Text fields can contain a maximum of 255 characters and that there are different field sizes for numeric fields. To save space in the database and improve its performance, Don can use the **Field Size property** to limit the number of characters to store in a Short Text field or the type of numeric data to store in a Number field.

Best Practice

Setting the Field Size Property for Text and Number Fields Correctly

Choosing the correct Field Size property for a Text or Number field is easy when you have sample data to examine. For Short Text fields, you can examine the existing data and count the number of characters in the longest field value. For example, the longest address in the sample data might be 29 characters. In this case, you can set the Field Size property for the Address field to 30 or 40 characters to provide enough room for even longer addresses. You can increase the size of a field after designing it, but it is always better to set the field size correctly from the start. If the field size is too small, users might not be able to enter complete data into a field without resizing it in Design view. Depending on the database configuration, users might not be able to make this type of change, in which case the field entry will be incomplete.

Another problem with resizing fields later occurs when the field is involved in one or more relationships. For example, if an EmployeeID number is originally set as a Short Text field that stores three digits and the company hires 1,000 people, necessitating a four-digit EmployeeID, then the field isn't long enough to store the employee with EmployeeID 1000. If the EmployeeID field is a primary key field with a foreign key in a related table, Access prohibits you from changing the field size unless you delete the relationship. In this case, you would need to change the field size in the primary and foreign keys and then re-create the relationship.

The same problem can occur with Number fields. The values that Access can store in a Number field with the Byte field size are different from the values it can store in a Number field with the Double field size. AutoNumber fields store data using the Long Integer field size. Relationships between fields with the AutoNumber and Number data types must have the same field type, such as Long Integer, to create the relationship.

When setting field sizes, be certain to consider the data you have from the discovery phase, and then to create a reasonable margin of error to avoid setting the field size so it cannot store values in the future.

Although he can change field options after creating them, Don knows that if the field size is too small, data might be truncated (or cut off) after a certain number of characters, and if set too long, valuable space might be wasted. The default field size for a Short Text field is 255 characters; a Short Text field can store 0 to 255 characters. Don changes the default field size for Short Text fields to match his table design: 50 characters for the PlanName field and 40 characters for the Address and City fields. The State and ZIP fields are changed to 2 and 10 characters, respectively. He sets the Phone field to 15 characters. For the Days field, which is a Number field, Don changes the field size from the default of Long Integer to Byte because this field will store whole numbers, such as 30 and 90.

Adding Descriptions to Fields in Table Design View

Some developers like to use the optional **Description property** for a field to document its contents, such as identifying a field as a primary or foreign key or providing users with instructions about entering values into the field, for example, adding a description of "Must be M or F" in a Description property that requests a person's gender. When a database is being developed by a team, using the Description property is an important part of documenting the table designs and providing clear instructions for users. Don knows that the Description property is important and adds descriptions to each field in the table to document their contents.

The last thing that Don does is delete the AutoNumber field because he plans to use the PlanID field as the primary key field. He selects the PlanID field and clicks the Primary Key button in the Tools group on the DESIGN tab. Access adds a key symbol to the PlanID row to indicate this field as the table's primary key. He then clicks the box next to AutoNumber to select the field, then he presses Delete so that the field is deleted. Figure 2.12 shows the completed table design for tblHealthPlan.

Figure 2.12: Table design for tblHealthPlan

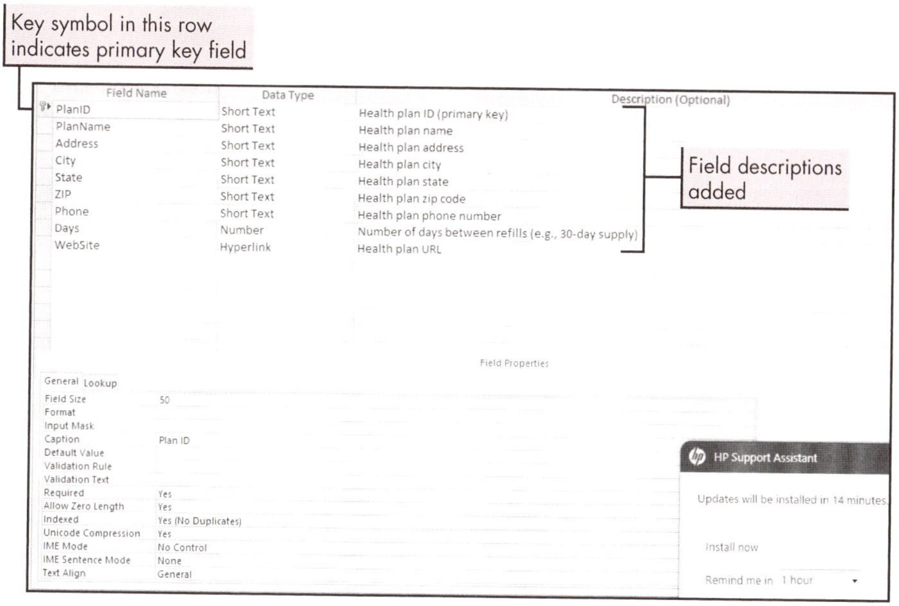

Key symbol in this row
indicates primary key field

Field Name	Data Type	Description (Optional)
PlanID	Short Text	Health plan ID (primary key)
PlanName	Short Text	Health plan name
Address	Short Text	Health plan address
City	Short Text	Health plan city
State	Short Text	Health plan state
ZIP	Short Text	Health plan zip code
Phone	Short Text	Health plan phone number
Days	Number	Number of days between refills (e.g., 30-day supply)
WebSite	Hyperlink	Health plan URL

Field descriptions
added

Field Properties

General Lookup

Field Size	50
Format	
Input Mask	
Caption	Plan ID
Default Value	
Validation Rule	
Validation Text	
Required	Yes
Allow Zero Length	Yes
Indexed	Yes (No Duplicates)
Unicode Compression	Yes
IME Mode	No Control
IME Sentence Mode	None
Text Align	General

HP Support Assistant

Updates will be installed in 14 minutes

Install now

Remind me in 1 hour

Don finished the first table's design and entered data into it. To view the table in the Navigation pane, he clicks the down arrow Navigation pane title bar and clicks the Tables option. See Figure 2.13.

Figure 2.13: Show Objects in database window

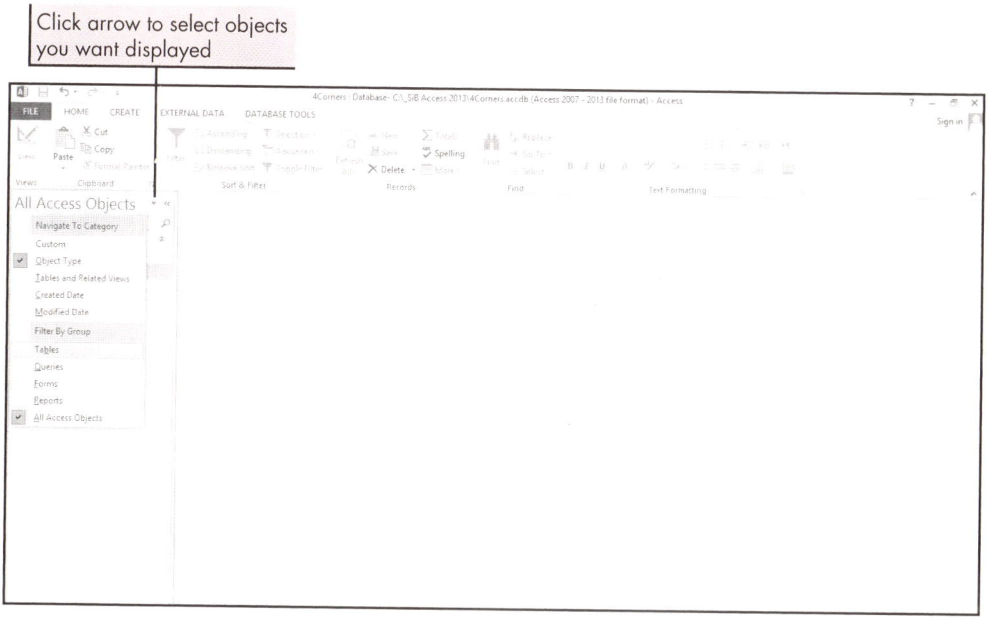

Click arrow to select objects
you want displayed

4Corners : Database- C:_SiB Access 2013\4Corners.accdb (Access 2007 - 2013 file format) - Access

FILE   HOME   CREATE   EXTERNAL DATA   DATABASE TOOLS

Sign in

Cut
Copy
Paste
Format Painter
Views   Clipboard   Sort & Filter   Records   Find   Text Formatting

All Access Objects

Navigate To Category
Custom
Object Type
Tables and Related Views
Created Date
Modified Date
Filter By Group
Tables
Queries
Forms
Reports
All Access Objects

Creating a Table in Design View

Another way to create a table is in Design view. This will work well for the remaining tables that Don needs to create as they all have specific requirements that would make it difficult for him to create them in Datasheet view. To create a table in Design view, click the CREATE tab on the Ribbon, and then click the Table Design button in the Tables group. The Table window opens in Design view. The table's default name is Table1, just like it would be if created in Datasheet view. The next step for Don will be to define the fields by entering the field names, data types, and properties.

Don uses Design view to create the next table, which stores data about the classes that employees must take to maintain their professional certifications. He begins by entering the first field name, ClassID, and then he moves to the Data Type box. Short Text appears automatically and since the ClassID field is a Number data type Don makes the change and then presses the Tab key to move to the Description box. Making the ClassID a Number field ensures that only numbers will be entered into this field, which is how the course preparers have stated they will identify the classes. Don clicks the Primary Key button in the Tools group on the DESIGN tab, which adds a key symbol to the left of the ClassID field indicating that it is the table's primary key. Don does not need to make any other changes to this field, so he moves to the Field Name box for the next field. Don creates the other fields in the table and sets their properties. When he is finished, he saves the table using the name tblClass. Figure 2.14 shows the table design.

Figure 2.14: Table design for tblClass

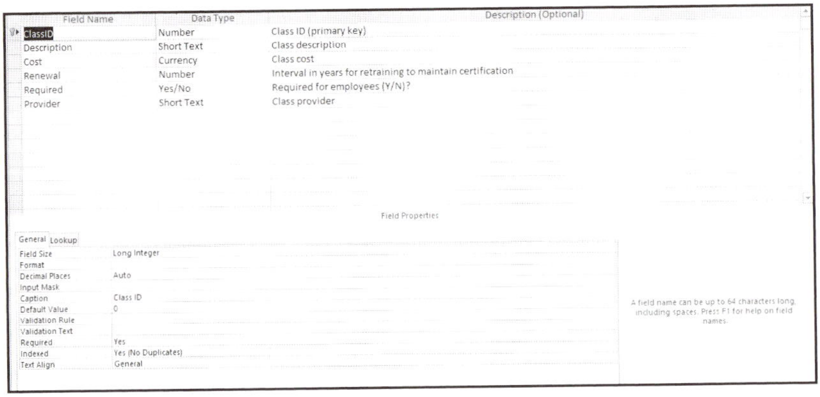

Evaluating and Testing the Table Design

After creating and saving the table design for tblClass, Don clicks the View button in the Views group to switch to Datasheet view. He begins entering the data for this table using the information provided to him by Maria Garcia, the Human Resources manager. Don enters the first value in the ClassID field, enters text in the Description field, and then enters 15 in the Cost field. Because the Cost field uses the Currency data type, Access changes the value to $15.00 when Don presses the Enter (or Tab) key to move to the next field. He enters "0" in the Renewal field since the initial certification class only needs to be taken one time. Therefore, zero would indicate that it does not need to be renewed.

To enter a value for the Required field, which is a Yes/No data type, you can either press the Tab key to leave the box unchecked or press the Spacebar to enter a check mark into the field. If you press the Tab key, you bypass the field without selecting it so the default value of No remains. Don enters "Red Cross" in the final field for the first record, and then moves to the next record. As Don moves to the next record, Access automatically saves the record in the table. If Don decided against the data he had entered, he could cancel the record by pressing the Esc key. Don enters the rest of the records for tblClass. The completed tblClass is shown in Figure 2.15.

Figure 2.15: Table tblClass with records

tblClass

	Class II	Description	Cost	Renewal	Required?	Provider	Click to Add
	1	Adult CPR	$15.00	0	☑	Red Cross	
	2	Child/Infant CPR	$15.00	0	☑	Red Cross	
	3	Adult CPR Recertification	$10.00	1	☑	Red Cross	
	4	First Aid	$15.00	2	☐	Red Cross	
	5	Defibrillator Use	$25.00	1	☑	Johnston Health Systems	
	6	Child/Infant CPR Recertificatio	$10.00	1	☑	Red Cross	
	7	Nutritional Supplements	$25.00	0	☐	Food Co-op	
	8	Yoga	$50.00	0	☐	Yoga Center	
*	0		$0.00	0	▣		

After saving the table for the first time, Don needs to save the table again only whenever he makes changes to its design (such as changing a field property in Design view) or to its layout (such as increasing or decreasing a field's width in the datasheet). If you make these kinds of changes to a table and try to close it, Access prompts you to save the layout of the table, not the records in the table because they are saved automatically.

Recall from Chapter 1 that data types are necessary to ensure that each field in a table collects the correct values. In theory, you could use the Short Text data type for any field, but then you would lose the capability to perform calculations on numbers, the flexibility that a Yes/No field provides, the ability to include hyperlinks in a table, and so on.

Now the database contains two tables. Don continues working by creating the table that stores data about customers. He creates the table in Design view and enters the field names, data types, and descriptions for each field in the table's design. He also uses the Field Properties pane to set the properties for fields that do not use the default settings. To make his work go faster, he presses the F6 key to move between the design grid and the Field Properties pane. Don sets the field properties for tblCustomer, as shown in Table 2.1.

Table 2.1: Table design for tblCustomer

Field Name	Data Type	Description	Field Size
CustID	AutoNumber	Customer ID (primary key)	
CustFirst	Short Text	Customer first name	30
CustLast	Short Text	Customer last name	30
Phone	Short Text	Customer home phone	15
DOB	Date/Time	Customer date of birth	
Gender	Short Text	Customer gender (M/F)	1
Balance	Currency	Outstanding balance	
Childproof Cap?	Yes/No	Does the customer require childproof caps (Y/N)?	
PlanID	Short Text	ID of the health plan covering this individual (foreign key)	50
HouseID	Number	Household ID (foreign key)	Long Integer
HeadHH	Yes/No	Head of household (Y/N)?	
Allergies	Long Text	Customer allergies	

© 2014 Cengage Learning

After creating all of the fields and defining their properties, Don selects the CustID field and sets it as the table's primary key, and then saves the table as tblCustomer. Figure 2.16 shows the table's design.

Figure 2.16: Table design for tblCustomer

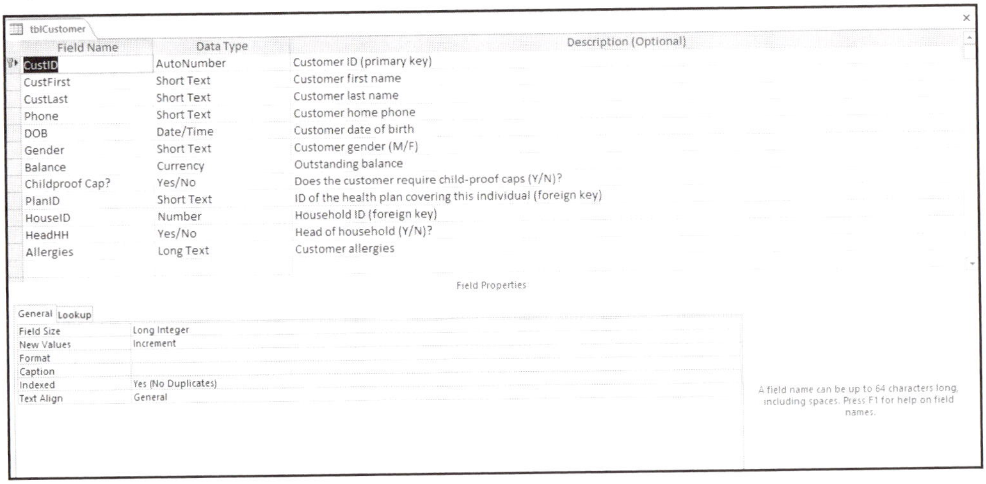

Don changes to Datasheet view and begins entering the data for the first customer, shown in Figure 2.17. (Some of the record has scrolled to the left side of the screen.)

Figure 2.17: tblCustomer with one record entered

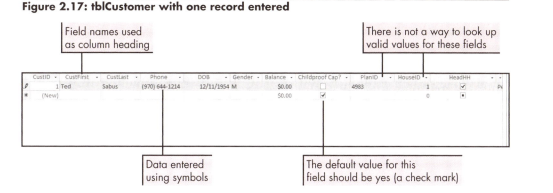

As Don enters the data, he notices several potential problems with the current field properties. All of these can be fixed by using the tools available in Design view to set the fields' properties. This will ensure that the data entered is clearly labeled, accurate, and consistent.

Problem #1: Field Names are Not Descriptive

The field names are used as the column heading names in the datasheet; for example, "CustFirst" and "CustLast" are the column headings for the fields a pharmacy technician or pharmacist uses to enter the customer's first and last names. However, these field names are not as descriptive as they could be for users who enter data. These users might be delayed when entering data because they would need to mentally translate that CustLast is the customer's last name field. Don considers the fact that these field names, although correct, will not be the best ways to identify the information in each field, especially when this data is used in a query, form, or report.

Solution: Display Descriptive Field Names Using the Caption Property

The first item on Don's list is to ensure that the field names are displayed in clear, simple language so their function is obvious in a table's datasheet and in queries, forms, and reports. Don could edit the field names in Design view, but the naming conventions for field names might prevent him from being able to use the field identifiers that he wants. Instead of changing the field names, Don can use the **Caption property** for a field to change the way the field name is displayed. The Caption property specifies how a field name will appear in different database objects; the default Caption property is the field name for all data types unless you change it. For example, instead of seeing "CustFirst" in a table datasheet, Don wants users to see "First Name." Setting the Caption property properly can turn abbreviated field names into meaningful identifiers that make data entry easier.

How To

Change a Field's Caption Property

1. Change to Design view, and then select the field that you want to change.
2. Click the Caption box in the Field Properties pane.
3. Type the caption. An example is shown in Figure 2.18.
4. Save the table design.

Figure 2.18: Caption property changed for the CustID field

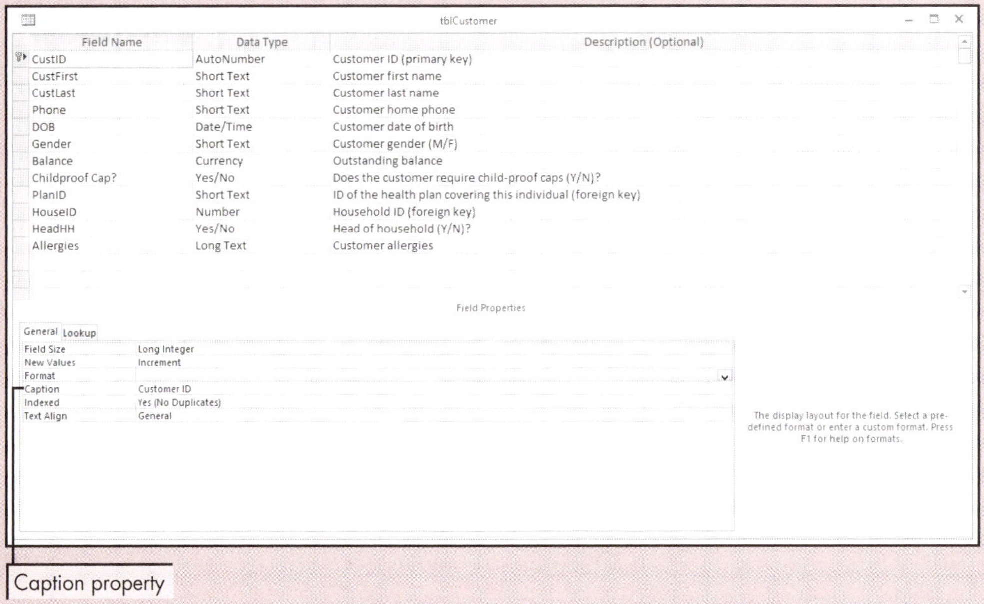

Caption property

Figure 2.19 shows part of the datasheet for tblCustomer after Don changed the Caption property for several of the fields from the default field names to more meaningful descriptions.

Figure 2.19: Datasheet with new captions and resized columns

Captions

Problem #2: Users Might Use Different Punctuation when Entering Telephone Numbers

The Phone field values include telephone numbers. Don entered the phone number using a common format for displaying phone numbers in which the area code appears in parentheses, followed by a space and the seven-digit phone number. He entered the phone number in this way so that it would be displayed with this format each time it appears in a query, form, or report. However, he is concerned that other users won't follow this approach, resulting in inconsistently formatted data. In addition, there is no way to ensure that users enter all 10 digits of the customer's phone number.

Solution: Format Field Values Using an Input Mask

Formatting Field Values Using an Input Mask

Don wants the phone number and date of birth for each customer to be formatted the same way: He wants phone numbers in the format (970) 644-1214 and dates of birth in the format 12/11/1954. When Don entered the first record in tblCustomer, he typed the parentheses, space, and dash character in the phone number and the slashes in the date of birth. However, he realizes that other users might not enter these values using the same characters, which could result in inconsistently formatted data. In addition, Don knows that by typing parentheses, spaces, dashes, and slash characters in these fields, these characters must be stored in the database, which requires additional space. The amount of space needed to store these characters in one record isn't significant, but the amount of space required for hundreds or thousands of records is significant.

In Access, you can control the format of a value by creating an input mask. An **input mask** dictates how you enter the data by determining how it is stored in a predefined format. For example, a user might enter a customer's phone number as 9706441214 and this value is stored in tblCustomer. However, when you view the table datasheet or a query, form, or report that includes this value, you see it with the input mask that you defined, such as (970) 644-1214 or 970-644-1214 or 970.644.1214. The input mask supplies these characters, called **literal characters**, but the literal characters need not be stored in the database, nor does a user need to type them. An input mask not only works to format data correctly, but also ensures that all of the necessary data is entered. If a user tries to enter the phone number 6441214 without the area code 970 or 970kajfjfjf, he receives an error message when trying to move to the next field because the input mask only accepts 10-digit numbers. In Access, you can create an input mask for fields by using the **Input Mask Wizard**, which guides you through the necessary steps for creating an input mask and lets you enter sample values to ensure the correct results.

Don changes to Design view for tblCustomer. He then selects the Phone field in the design grid and then clicks in the Input Mask box in the Field Properties pane. To create an input mask, Don can type it directly into the Input Mask box, or he can click the Build button [...], which appears on the right side of the Input Mask box to activate the Input Mask Wizard. Because using the Input Mask Wizard is easier, he clicks the Build button [...], and then clicks the Yes button to save the table design. The Input Mask Wizard dialog box opens, as shown in Figure 2-20.

Figure 2.20: Input Mask Wizard dialog box

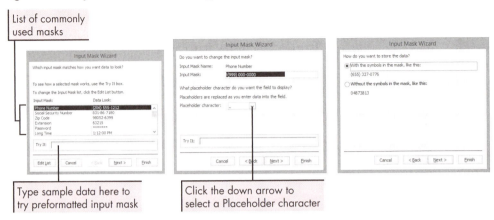

List of commonly used masks

Type sample data here to try preformatted input mask

Click the down arrow to select a Placeholder character

Don selects the top option, which is the default format for phone numbers. He then clicks Next to move to the next dialog box, which is also shown in Figure 2-20. He chooses the underscore as the placeholder that will appear in the cell when the user is entering a value into this field in Datasheet view. And, then he clicks Next to go to the third dialog box. He selects the first option so users can see the symbols as they enter data. The phone number will be stored with these characters as well. Don then selects Finish.

There might be occasions when you need to create an input mask from scratch, rather than using a wizard. Table 2.2 lists some characters that you can use in an input mask.

Table 2.2: Input mask characters and descriptions

Character	Description
0	Required entry of a digit from 0 to 9
9	Optional entry of a digit from 0 to 9 or a space
L	Letter entry required
?	Letter entry optional
>	Entry that converts all characters following the > to uppercase
<	Entry that converts all characters following the < to lowercase
!	Entry that causes the input mask to display from right to left. And, the characters typed into the mask always fill from left to right.
\	Entry that causes the character following this character to be displayed as a literal character
" "	Entry that causes text and characters enclosed in quotation marks to appear as literal characters

© 2014 Cengage Learning

How To

Create an Input Mask Using the Input Mask Wizard

1. In Design view, click the field for which you want to create the input mask, click the Input Mask box in the Field Properties pane, and then click the Build button to the right of the Input Mask property to start the Input Mask Wizard.

2. Select the input mask that is best suited for the field, and then if you want, use the Try It box to test the input mask using your own data. Click the Next button.

3. If necessary, change the input mask shown in the Input Mask box and change the placeholder character to use. (Note: You do not need to add quotation marks, semicolons, or backslashes to the input mask at this time; Access adds them for you.) If you want, use the Try It box to test the revised input mask using your own data. Click the Next button.

4. If necessary, choose the option that specifies how you want to store literal characters and then click the Next button.

5. Click the Finish button.

6. Save the table design.

The input mask !\(000")"000\-0000;;_ shown in Figure 2.21 includes other characters that indicate how to store the input mask in the table, how to display the input mask when a user enters a value into it, and the identification of literal characters. The first character of the input mask ! indicates that when data is entered into this field, it will appear from left to right. Following the exclamation point is a \, which indicates that the (needs to be included before the area code when it is entered. The 000 following the open parenthesis require that a three-character area code be entered. Next, the) enclosed in quotation marks places the closing parenthesis after the area code. Also, because 000 appear next, three more characters of the phone number must be entered. Because the - appears after the slash, the dash will be entered automatically as a character when data is entered. The 0000 that appear next require the final four characters of the phone number to be entered.

Figure 2.21: Input mask for the Phone field

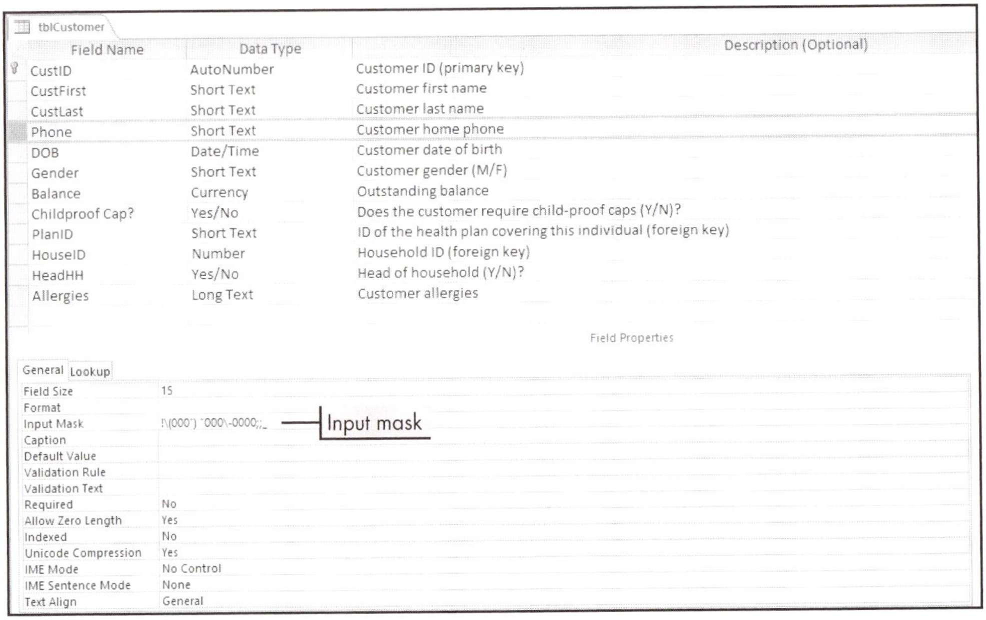

The characters ;; near the end of the input mask specify that the literal characters, such as the parentheses and dashes in the telephone number, will be stored with the data. Literal characters are used to enhance the readability of the information, and they should be stored if they are an essential part of the data.

The _ at the end of the input mask specifies that an underscore be displayed when the user is entering a value into the input mask to indicate the current character and total number of characters that the user must enter. You can also display other characters for the user to see as placeholders such as #, @, !, $, %, and *. Other characters in the input mask, such as the backslashes (\), indicate the literal characters displayed by the input mask.

Because customers can live in multiple states and have different area codes, Don wants to ensure that employees always enter the customer's seven-digit phone number and the three-digit area code. To ensure this data entry, Don changes the default placeholders in the input mask, which specifies an optional data entry, to 000, which ensures that employees must enter the area code. Now users must enter 10 digits in the Phone field. Attempts to store letters, symbols, and incomplete phone numbers will be rejected.

Problem #3: Possibility of Inconsistent Data Entry

Don entered the DOB (date of birth) field value in a common date format in which the month, date, and year are separated by slash characters. He also entered the year as four digits. However, there is no way to ensure that users enter birth dates in this format, nor is there a way to ensure that users enter four-digit years. He wants the data entered in the same format so if he wants to use a query to find customers born in 1997, he would know that he should use 1997 for the criteria and not 97. Also, if users enter two-digit years, there might be problems later if it becomes necessary to perform calculations with dates, such as determining whether a customer is 18 years old.

Solution: Format Fields Using an Input Mask

To ensure that customers' birth dates are formatted consistently and entered properly, Don uses the Input Mask Wizard to create an input mask for the DOB field so that it only accepts digits and displays slashes and four-digit years. The input mask he created for the DOB field is 00/00/0000;_. This input mask accepts only digits and ensures that users enter two-digit months and days, four-digit years, and complete dates. Because all digits are required, users must enter single-digit months and single-digit days using the leading zero (for example, entering "01" for January and "07" to indicate the seventh day of the month). Requiring input in this manner ensures that all digits are entered into the DOB field for each customer.

Problem #4: Data Entry for Uppercase and Lowercase Letters May Not be Consistent

Don entered the uppercase letter M in the Gender field to indicate that this customer is a male. Don wants to ensure that the Gender field can contain only the uppercase letter M (for male) or the uppercase letter F (for female). He defined the Gender field using the Short Text data type and a field size of one character. However, he realizes that he or another person entering data could type inaccurate data, such as a q or a 9 in this field, either accidentally or on purpose. This problem can lead to inaccurate data.

Solution: Validate Fields to Ensure Accurate and Consistent Data

In Access, you can specify restrictions on the data that users can enter into a field by creating a validation rule. A **validation rule** compares the data entered by the user against one or more valid values that the database developer specified using the Validation Rule property for the field. The **Validation Rule property** specifies the valid values that users can enter into the field. If a user attempts to enter an invalid value, the **Validation Text property** for the field opens a dialog box with a predefined message that explains the valid values.

For the Gender field, the only valid values are M and F. Don selects the Gender field's Validation Rule property and enters the validation rule as "M" or "F." Access changes the validation rule to "M" Or "F" because the values are stored in a Short Text field and text values must be enclosed within quotation marks. To help users understand the valid values for the Gender field, Don clicks the Validation Text property box, and then types "Value must be M or F." to specify the valid values. Don also uses the Input Mask property to convert all letters entered in this field to uppercase by entering the input mask >L. Regardless of how the data is entered, it will display as an uppercase letter. Figure 2.22 shows the completed validation rule, validation text, and input mask for the Gender field. When a user enters an "m" or "f" into the Gender field, Access stores the value as M or F. However, if a user enters any other value, Access opens a dialog box with the message specified in the Validation Text property. After reading the message, the user clicks the OK button to close the message and then can enter a valid value in the Gender field before continuing data entry for the customer.

Figure 2.22: Validation rule and validation text entered for the Gender field

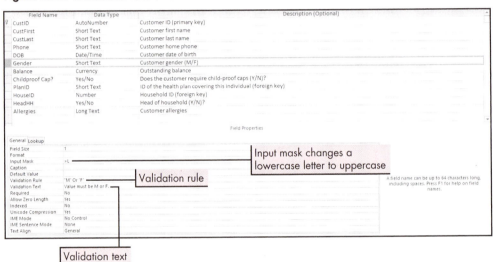

Table 2.3 describes some of the validation rules and validation text that you can specify for a field. In the first example, valid values are specified using the In operator and typing valid values within parentheses and separated by commas. The second example uses "Is Not Null" to specify that the field cannot accept null values. The third and fourth examples use comparison operators to specify valid date and numeric values. (You will learn more about operators in Chapter 3.)

Table 2.3: Sample validation rules and validation text

Sample Validation Rule	Sample Validation Text
In('CO', 'AZ', 'NM', 'UT')	The state must be CO, AZ, NM, or UT.
Is Not Null	You must enter a value in this field.
>#01/01/1980#	The date must be later than January 1, 1980.
>=21 And <100	The value must be greater than or equal to 21 and less than 100.

© 2014 Cengage Learning

Problem #5: Default Value Needed in Field

The pharmacy's policy about childproof caps is to give them to all customers unless they specifically request regular caps, so the default value for the Childproof Cap? field should be "Yes." Don needs to implement a way to set the default value for using childproof caps on prescription bottles to "Yes." To order regular caps for prescription bottles, the user would click the check box or press the spacebar to remove the check mark and change the value to "No."

Solution: Add a Default Value in the Field Properties

According to the pharmacy's policy, all prescriptions are dispensed with childproof caps unless the customer requests regular caps. Therefore, the value of the Childproof Cap? field should be set to "Yes" for all prescriptions and changed to "No" only when the client requests a regular cap. By specifying a default value for the Childproof Cap? field, Don can save data entry time for the user and ensure that all customers receive childproof caps unless they do not want them. The **Default Value property** enters a default value into any type of field except for an AutoNumber field. To accept the default value specified in the Default Value property, the user simply tabs through the field during data entry. To change the default value, a user can simply type the new value. Because the Childproof Cap? field is a Yes/No field, Don needs to specify "Yes" as the field's default value. He clicks the Childproof Cap? field in the design grid, clicks the Default Value property box in the Field Properties pane, and then types "Yes," as shown in Figure 2.23.

Figure 2.23: Default value entered for the Childproof Cap? field

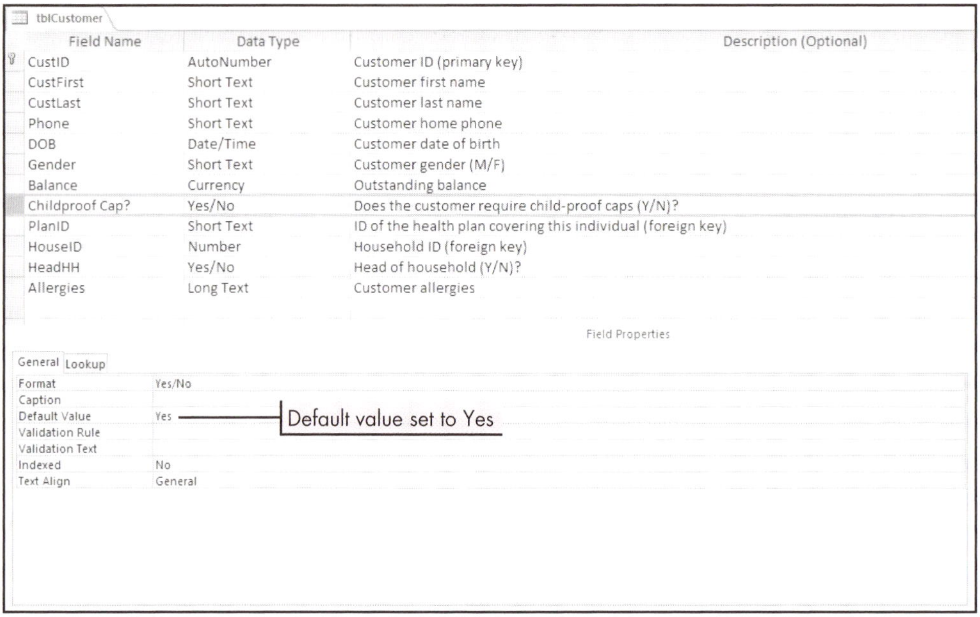

Field Name	Data Type	Description (Optional)
tblCustomer		
CustID	AutoNumber	Customer ID (primary key)
CustFirst	Short Text	Customer first name
CustLast	Short Text	Customer last name
Phone	Short Text	Customer home phone
DOB	Date/Time	Customer date of birth
Gender	Short Text	Customer gender (M/F)
Balance	Currency	Outstanding balance
Childproof Cap?	Yes/No	Does the customer require child-proof caps (Y/N)?
PlanID	Short Text	ID of the health plan covering this individual (foreign key)
HouseID	Number	Household ID (foreign key)
HeadHH	Yes/No	Head of household (Y/N)?
Allergies	Long Text	Customer allergies

Field Properties

General Lookup

Format	Yes/No
Caption	
Default Value	Yes ———— Default value set to Yes
Validation Rule	
Validation Text	
Indexed	No
Text Align	General

Problem #6: Potential Data Entry Errors for PlanID and HouseID

Don entered the plan ID 4983 in the PlanID field to indicate that this customer is insured by Southern Rocky Mountains Health Plan. Knowing that plan ID numbers are often complicated, Don determines that he needs a way to ensure that the plan ID is accurate. For example, a plan ID number might contain commonly mistyped characters, such as reading a zero and typing an uppercase letter O or reading a lowercase letter l and typing the digit 1. In these cases, the health plan would reject the plan ID number and reject the prescription, causing inconvenience to the customer and the pharmacist who would have to spend time to discover and correct the error.

Don assigned the HouseID value of 1 to this customer, but realizes that there is no way to determine which HouseIDs correlate with which households without reviewing the data in another table. Don needs to ensure that the health plan ID and house ID values for customers are accurate and easy to enter.

Solution: Automate Data Entry by Using a Lookup Field

As Don was entering the first record in tblCustomer, he realized that it would be possible for a user to enter a plan ID number for the customer's health plan that is not in tblHealthPlan. He also realized that the user would need a separate method to determine whether the customer belongs to an existing household in the database. Don can solve both of these potential problems by creating a **lookup field** that lets the user select a field value from a list of existing field values stored in the database or from a list of values that he specifies when he creates the lookup field. For example, instead of entering the

PlanID 4983 for a customer, Don could select this PlanID from a list of PlanIDs stored in tblHealthPlan. Instead of entering the HouseID, Don could select this household's address by matching it to a list of addresses stored in tblHousehold. Both of these changes to the table design require that the tables on which the lookup will be performed should already exist. For example, if the customer resides at a new household that is not yet stored in tblHousehold, the user would need to enter the household information before entering the customer's information so that the household would already exist.

To add a lookup field to a table, you change the field's data type to Lookup. For the first lookup field, Don selects the PlanID field in the design grid of tblCustomer, clicks the Data Type arrow, and then clicks Lookup Wizard in the list that appears. The **Lookup Wizard** starts, as shown in Figure 2.24.

Figure 2.24: Using the Lookup Wizard to specify the lookup column

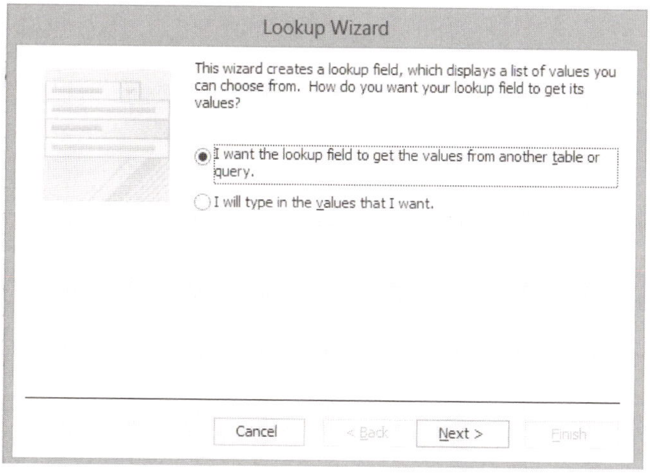

Two types of lookup fields are available. The first type lets you look up field values in another table or query; use this method when the data you want to look up already exists in the database. The second type lets you enter a list of values that you want to permit in the field; use this method when you want to supply a list of valid values for the data entered into the field that are not stored elsewhere in the database.

Don selects the option to look up the data in an existing table or query and clicks the Next button. The Lookup Wizard shows the tables that Don can choose, so he needs to select one of these tables as the source of the values he wants to look up. The lookup data for the PlanID field is stored in tblHealthPlan, so he selects this table, as shown in Figure 2.25.

Figure 2.25: Selecting tblHealthPlan as the data source for the lookup field

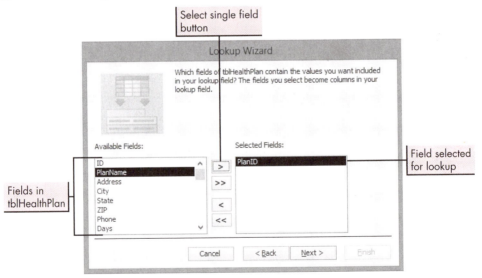

Don clicks the Next button to display the next dialog box where he will select the field or fields in the data source (tblHealthPlan) that he wants to include in the lookup field. Don wants to display the PlanID values in the lookup field, so he selects this field in the Available Fields box and then clicks the select single field button to move the PlanID field to the Selected Fields box, as shown in Figure 2.26.

Figure 2.26: Selecting the PlanID field as the lookup field

Don could select additional fields to be displayed in the lookup column, but because he only needs to display the PlanID values, he clicks the Next button, which opens the dialog box that lets him sort the values displayed in the lookup field. Selecting a sort order is optional, but as more health plans are added to tblHealthPlan, data entry will be easier if the health plans are sorted in ascending order by PlanID. Don clicks the arrow for the

first box and then clicks PlanID to select this field. The button to the right of the first box displays the label "Ascending," which indicates that the values in the lookup field will be displayed in alphabetical (A to Z) or numerical (lowest to highest) order. You can also display values in descending order by clicking this button, in which case the label changes to "Descending." Figure 2.27 shows the PlanID field will be sorted in ascending order.

Figure 2.27: PlanID specified to sort in ascending order

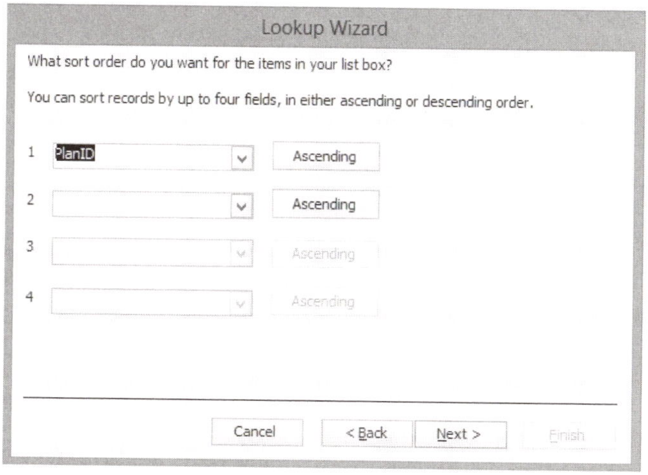

	Lookup Wizard

What sort order do you want for the items in your list box?

You can sort records by up to four fields, in either ascending or descending order.

1 PlanID ⌄ Ascending

2 ⌄ Ascending

3 ⌄ Ascending

4 ⌄ Ascending

Cancel   < Back   Next >   Finish

Don clicks the Next button and sees how the lookup field will display existing values in the PlanID field in tblHealthPlan. In some cases, you might need to click and drag the right side of the column to increase or decrease its width so that the data in the lookup field is displayed correctly and completely. The default field size is acceptable, as shown in Figure 2.28, so Don clicks the Next button.

Figure 2.28: Setting the lookup field size

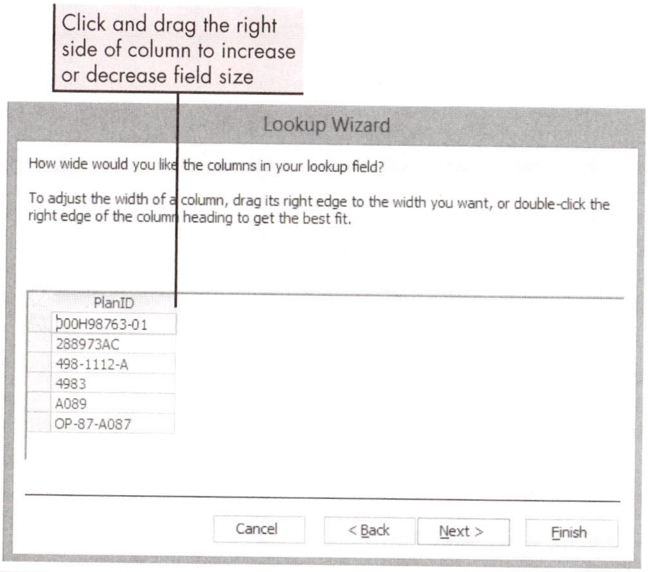

Click and drag the right side of column to increase or decrease field size

Lookup Wizard

How wide would you like the columns in your lookup field?

To adjust the width of a column, drag its right edge to the width you want, or double-click the right edge of the column heading to get the best fit.

PlanID
000H98763-01
288973AC
498-1112-A
4983
A089
OP-87-A087

Cancel   < Back   Next >   Finish

In the final dialog box, you can accept the default label for the lookup field (which is the lookup field's name) or specify a new one. Don clicks the Finish button to accept the default name, PlanID, and the Lookup Wizard closes. Don is prompted to save the table design and the lookup field he created in tblCustomer, which he does. Don knows that the data type will not be Lookup, but instead will be the data type of the primary key of the referenced table. The only way Don can tell that it is a lookup field from Design view is to select the field and click the Lookup tab in the Field Properties pane. If the Display Control is set to something other than a Text Box, it is a lookup field.

Don changes to Datasheet view for tblCustomer, and then clicks the PlanID field arrow for the first record. The lookup field displays the PlanID values from tblHealthPlan, as shown in Figure 2.29.

Figure 2.29: Lookup field values for the PlanID field

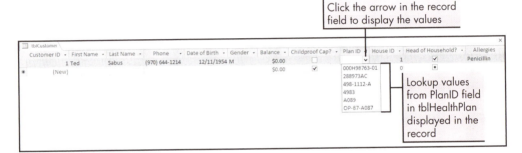

Now users can select the correct PlanID from this list by clicking the arrow in the field when they are entering or changing a record. Don will create a Lookup field for the HouseID field after he creates the table in Level 2.

Change a Lookup Field Back to a Text Box Field

1. In the Design view for the table, click the field with the lookup you want to delete.
2. Click the Lookup tab in the Field Properties pane.
3. Click the Display Control property and then click the arrow that appears on the right.
4. Click Text Box in the list to remove the lookup feature.
5. Save the table.

Steps To Success: Level 1

Don just received a request from Paul to develop a database for a new pharmacy that Paul is opening in Edmonton, Alberta, Canada. Because the data collected about customers, employees, and drugs is slightly different in Canada, Don decides to create the databases simultaneously, but separately, so he can account for the individual differences in each version. Don wants you to create the database for Hudson Bay Pharmacy. (You will create nine tables in this exercise using the skills you have learned so far. You will create three more tables in the Level 2 Steps To Success exercises.) He will provide you additional information so you know how to account for the differences in the Canadian version of the database.

Complete the following:

1. Start Access and create a new database named **Hudson.accdb** and save it in the Level 1 STS folder.

2. Create the following tables in the Hudson database using the method you prefer: tblClass, tblCustomer, tblHealthPlan, and tblHousehold. Be certain that each table includes a primary key and the necessary fields. Also, be certain to set the field properties as necessary to collect the correct data. Fields should include appropriate captions and field descriptions. These tables have the same requirements as the ones in the 4Corners database, with the following exceptions:

   - Canadian addresses include a street address, city, province, and postal code. Provinces are abbreviated using two uppercase letters. Add properties to the Prov field so that the data entered by the user is converted to uppercase letters. Also, make sure that users cannot enter digits or any other characters except letters into the Prov field, such as an input mask of >L>L.
   - Postal codes in Canada have the following format: uppercase letter, number, uppercase letter, space, number, uppercase letter, number (for example, T6H 8U7). Add properties to the PostalCode field to ensure that data entry into this field is accurate and correctly formatted. You might want to consider an input mask, such as >L0>L\0>L0.

3. Change the PlanID field in tblCustomer to a lookup field that displays the PlanID and PlanName values from tblHealthPlan but stores only the PlanID values. Sort values in ascending order by PlanID and adjust the lookup column widths as necessary to display the values that will be stored in these fields.

   TROUBLESHOOTING: In order to complete this task, you need to think about the record(s) that might already be entered in the table and decide whether it is okay to change the data integrity. Typically, you would want the data integrity to be updated. After you create a lookup field with the Lookup Wizard, a dialog box might appear letting you know that data integrity rules have been changed. Click the OK button.

4. Change the HouseID field in tblCustomer to a lookup field that displays the HouseID and Address values from tblHousehold but stores only the HouseID values. Sort the values in ascending order by Address.

5. Use Datasheet view and the data shown in Table 2.4 to create tblJobTitle. JobIDs are whole numbers and the Title field stores 30 characters. Use the Description property to document each field.

Table 2.4: Data for tblJobTitle

JobID	Title
1	Owner
2	Pharmacist
3	Technician
4	Cashier
5	Manager

© 2014 Cengage Learning

6. Examine the 4Corners database tblDoctor table shown in Figure 2.2, and then create a table in Design view in the Hudson database. The tblDoctor table is not related to any other database table yet (you will create relationships in the next level). The fields for the doctor's first name and last name should store 30 characters each. The fields that store phone numbers should store 15 characters each and format values with an input mask that formats values with the following format: (###) ###-####. Note that these pound signs simply indicate numeric values, not a valid Access input mask. The ClinicID field is a foreign key to tblClinic, which you will create in the next level. (*Hint:* Create this field in Design view.) Store ClinicID values as long integers. Use the Description property to document each field and enter appropriate captions to fields that require them.

7. Use Design view and the following information to create tblDrug shown in Figure 2.2. Make sure that the table includes a primary key and the necessary fields. Also, make sure that you set the field properties as indicated in the following list to collect the correct data. Fields should include appropriate captions and field descriptions.

   - Canadian drugs do not have UPNs. Instead, drugs are uniquely identified using a Drug Identification Number (DIN). The DIN is a unique, eight-digit value that identifies each drug sold in Canada. DINs are not used in calculations.
   - Drug names do not exceed 30 characters.
   - Generic drugs are indicated by selecting a check box.
   - Descriptions are alphanumeric values that might exceed 255 characters. The Description field collects data about the drug, such as countraindications, generic equivalents, and recommended dosage.
   - The Unit field stores information about the unit of measure for a drug, such as pill or bottle, and requires 10 characters.
   - The Dosage field stores information about the drug's strength and requires 10 characters. The Dosage field is not used in calculations.
   - The DosageForm field stores information about the unit of measure for the drug strength, such as mg (for milligrams) or mcg (for micrograms). Dosage abbreviations do not exceed 20 characters.

- The Cost and Price fields store the cost and price, respectively, for one unit of the drug. The Canadian government regulates the prices that pharmacies can charge for drugs so pharmacies cover their overhead costs by charging a separate dispensing fee of $10 to $12 per prescription. Dispensing fees are determined by the pharmacy and set individually for each drug.
- The Interactions field stores information about possible drug interactions and possible reactions. This field's data might exceed 255 characters.
- Canada does not track pregnancy risk categories like pharmacies in the United States.
- The Supplier field identifies the drug company or manufacturer from which a drug was purchased. Supplier names do not exceed 50 characters.

8. Use Design view and the following information to create tblEmployee shown in Figure 2.3. Make sure that the table includes a primary key and the necessary fields. Also, make sure that you set the field properties where indicated in the following list to collect the correct data. Fields should include appropriate captions and field descriptions.

- EmpIDs are assigned by the pharmacy using unique numbers. EmpIDs are used to relate tables in the database.
- The EmpFirst and EmpLast fields do not exceed 30 characters each. The EmpMI field stores up to two characters.
- Canada issues Social Insurance numbers (SINs) instead of Social Security numbers. An SIN is a nine-digit number displayed with the following format: ###-###-###.
- The DOB (date of birth), StartDate, EndDate, and Review fields should store two-digit months and days and four-digit years in the format ##/##/####.
- Make sure that the table stores a province (Prov) and postal code (PostalCode) for employees instead of a state and ZIP code.
- JobID is a foreign key in tblJobTitle. This field stores values as numbers.
- Memo field stores other information about employees that might exceed 255 characters.
- The Phone and Cell fields should store 15 characters in the format of (###) ###-####. Area code entry is required.
- Employees are paid an annual salary or an hourly rate.
- There is an annual review date for each employee based on his or her hire date.

9. Use Design view and the following information to create tblRx shown in Figure 2.2. Make sure that the table includes a primary key and the necessary fields. Also, make sure that you set the field properties as indicated in the following list to collect the correct data. Fields should include appropriate captions and field descriptions.

- PrescriptionIDs are assigned by Access as records are added to the table.
- The DIN is a unique, eight-digit value that identifies each drug sold in Canada. DINs are not used in calculations.

- The Quantity field stores the amount of medication dispensed and it is a numeric field that might contain decimal places.
- The Unit field stores information about the unit of measure for a drug, such as mg or ml, and requires 10 characters.
- The Date and ExpireDate fields store the date of the prescription and the prescription's expiration date, respectively. Both fields should store two-digit months and days and four-digit years in the format ##/##/####.
- The Refills field indicates the number of refills authorized by the prescribing doctor.
- The AutoRefill field indicates the customer's preference (yes or no) for automatic refills. The default value is not to order auto refills unless requested by the customer.
- The RefillsUsed field stores the number of refills a customer has used.
- The Instructions field stores medication directions and does not exceed 50 characters.
- The CustID field is a foreign key in tblCustomer and the DoctorID field is a foreign key in tblDoctor. Both fields store numbers.

10. You will enter data into these tables and create the relationships between tables in the next level. Close the Hudson.accdb database.

LEVEL 2

Populating and Relating the Database Tables

Creating Additional Tables for 4Corners Pharmacy

While you were working on creating the database and tables for the Hudson Bay Pharmacy, Don created the tblJobTitle, tblDoctor, tblDrug, tblEmployee, and tblRx tables in the 4Corners database. The table designs and properties he used in these tables appear in Tables 2.5 through 2.9. These table designs are necessary to set up the tables correctly.

Table 2.5: Table design for tblJobTitle

Field Name	Data Type	Description	Field Size	Properties
JobID	Long Integer	Job ID (primary key)	30	Caption: Job ID
Title	Short Text	Job title (e.g., owner, pharmacist, technician, cashier, manager)	30	

© 2014 Cengage Learning

Table 2.6: Table design for tblDoctor

Field Name	Data Type	Description	Field Size	Properties
DoctorID	Long Integer	ID of prescribing doctor (primary key)	30	Caption: Doctor ID
DoctorFirst	Short Text	Doctor first name	30	Caption: First Name
DoctorLast	Short Text	Doctor last name	30	Caption: Last Name
Phone	Short Text	Doctor phone number	15	Input mask: !\(000") "000\-0000;;_
Cell	Short Text	Doctor cell phone number	15	Input mask: !\(000") "000\-0000;;_
ClinicID	Number	Clinic ID (foreign key)	Long Integer	Caption: Clinic ID

© 2014 Cengage Learning

Table 2.7: Table design for tblDrug

Field Name	Data Type	Description	Field Size	Properties
UPN	Short Text	Drug ID (primary key)	3	Input mask: 000
Name	Short Text	Drug name	30	
Generic	Yes/No	Is this the generic (Y/N)?		Caption: Generic?
Description	Long Text	Description of drug, contraindications, generic equivalent, and recommended dosage		
Unit	Short Text	Unit of measure of drug (pill, bottle)	10	
Dosage	Short Text	Strength of drug (e.g., 30 mg)	10	
DosageForm	Short Text	Unit of measure	20	Caption: Dosage Form
Cost	Currency	Cost per unit		
Price	Currency	Retail price per unit		
Interactions	Long Text	Interactions of drugs and possible reactions		
PregCategory	Short Text	Pregnancy risks	1	Input mask: >L Caption: Pregnancy Category Validation rule: In ('A','B','C','D','X') Validation text: Invalid pregnancy category. Valid values are A, B, C, D, or X.
Supplier	Short Text	Name of drug supplier	50	

© 2014 Cengage Learning

Table 2.8: Table design for tblEmployee

Field Name	Data Type	Description	Field Size	Properties
EmpID	Number	Employee ID (primary key)	Long Integer	Caption: Employee ID
EmpFirst	Short Text	Employee first name	30	Caption: First Name
EmpMI	Short Text	Employee middle initial	2	Caption: Middle Initial
EmpLast	Short Text	Employee last name	30	Caption: Last Name
SSN	Short Text	Employee Social Security number	9	Input mask: 000\-00\-0000;;_
DOB	Date/Time	Employee date of birth		Input mask: 00/00/0000;;_ Caption: Date of Birth
StartDate	Date/Time	Employee hire date		Input mask: 00/00/0000;;_ Caption: Start Date
EndDate	Date/Time	Employee termination date		Input mask: 00/00/0000;;_ Caption: End Date
Address	Short Text	Employee address	30	
City	Short Text	Employee city	30	
State	Short Text	Employee state	2	
ZIP	Number	Employee ZIP code	10	
JobID	Long Integer	Employee job ID (foreign key)	30	Caption: Job ID
Memo	Long Text	Other information about the employee		
Phone	Short Text	Employee home phone	15	Input mask: !\(000") "000\-0000;;_
Cell	Short Text	Employee cell phone	15	Input mask: !\(000") "000\-0000;;_
Salary	Currency	Employee salary		
HourlyRate	Currency	Employee hourly rate (for nonsalaried employees)		Caption: Hourly Rate
Review	Date/Time	Date of next review		Input mask: 00/00/0000;;_

© 2014 Cengage Learning

Table 2.9: Table design for tblRx

Field Name	Data Type	Description	Field Size	Properties
PrescriptionID	AutoNumber	Prescription number (primary key)		Caption: Prescription ID
UPN	Short Text	Drug ID (foreign key)	3	Input mask: 000
Quantity	Number	Prescription quantity	Long Integer	Default value: 0

Table 2.9: Table design for tblRx (cont.)

Field Name	Data Type	Description	Field Size	Properties
Unit	Short Text	Unit of measure	10	
Date	Date/Time	Date prescription was written		Input mask: 00/00/0000;;_
ExpireDate	Date/Time	Date prescription expires		Input mask: 00/00/0000;;_ Caption: Expire Date
Refills	Number	Number of refills allowed	Integer	Caption: Refills Authorized Default value: 0
AutoRefill	Yes/No	Does customer want auto refills (Y/N)?		Caption: Auto Refill?
RefillsUsed	Number	Number of refills used	Integer	Caption: Refills Used
Instructions	Short Text	Instructions for prescription	50	
CustID	Number	Customer ID (foreign key)	Long Integer	Caption: Customer ID Default value: 0
DoctorID	Long Integer	Doctor ID (foreign key)	30	Caption: Doctor ID Default value: 0

© 2014 Cengage Learning

Populating the Database Tables

The 4Corners database now contains eight tables. The next step is to load the tables with data, also known as populating the database. Don could enter records into each table by typing in Datasheet view. However, because much of the data he needs to load is stored in sources found during the discovery phase, Don can import this data into the tables. There are several ways to import data into a database. Don will use two of them, which includes copying and pasting records from another database table and importing data from an Excel workbook.

Importing and Copying Records from One Table to Another

Before he hired Don, Paul started working on a database and entered his customer data into a Customer table. Don knows that he can import Paul's existing data into tblCustomer as long as the structures of the two tables are identical. Tables have identical structures if they have the same number of fields and those fields have the same data types and field sizes. For example, you cannot copy the contents of a Short Text field with a field size of 50 into a Short Text field with a field size of 10, nor can you copy a Number field with the Long Integer field size into a Number field with the Byte field size. Similarly, you cannot copy Short Text fields into Number fields, and so on.

If tblCustomer did not already exist in the 4Corners database, Don could import Paul's table design and the data it contains in one step. When you import a table from another database, instead of just the records it contains, you have the option of importing the table's structure (called the table definition) and the data stored in the table. You can also choose to import the relationships for the imported table.

How To

Import an Existing Access Table into an Access Database

1. Open the database into which you will import the existing table.
2. Click the EXTERNAL DATA tab on the Ribbon. In the Import & Link group, select the import button associated with the program (in this case Access) or type of file that you are importing.
3. Specify the source and location of the data.
4. Click the table or tables that you want to import. If you want to import more than one table, press and hold the Ctrl key, click each table to import, and then release the Ctrl key. To select all of the tables, choose the Select All button.
5. Click the Options button. The Import Objects dialog box expands to include options for importing tables.
6. To import the tables and their relationships, select the Relationships check box in the Import section.
7. To import the table definition and data, click the Definition and Data option button in the Import Tables section. To import only the table definition, click the Definition Only option button.
8. Click the OK button.

Because tblCustomer already exists in the 4Corners database, Don just needs to import the data stored in Paul's table, and not the table definition. Don opens Paul's Customer.accdb database, opens the tblCustomer table in Datasheet view, and then confirms that the structures of the two tables are exactly the same. Next, he selects all of the records except for the one with CustomerID 1 because he already entered this record into the table. Don clicks the Copy button in the Clipboard group on the HOME tab, closes the Customer database, clicks the Yes button to keep the data he copied on the Clipboard, and then opens tblCustomer in the 4Corners database in Datasheet view. He clicks the second record in the datasheet and clicks the Paste button in the Clipboard group on the HOME tab. When he changes to Datasheet view, the numbers are listed in sequential order from 1 to 41, which matches the original numbering in Paul's tblCustomer table; see Figure 2.30. The tblCustomer table is now populated with data.

Figure 2.30: Imported data in tblCustomer

Customer ID	First Name	Last Name	Phone	Date of Birth	Gender	Balance	Childproof Cap?	Plan ID
1	Ted	Sabus	(970) 644-1214	12/11/1954	M	$0.00	☐	4983
2	Tabitha	Sabus	(970) 644-1214	10/14/1956	F	$0.00	☐	4983
3	Shannon	Sabus	(970) 644-2100	9/10/1990	F	$0.00	☐	4983
4	Steven	Nguyen	(435) 122-4545	10/12/1976	M	$30.00	☐	498-1112-A
5	Rose	Baaz	(505) 477-8989	4/12/1970	F	$0.00	☑	OP-87-A087
6	Geoffrey	Baaz	(505) 477-8989	12/31/2001	M	$0.00	☑	OP-87-A087
7	Albert	Cardenas	(928) 551-5547	10/14/1965	M	$0.00	☑	498-1112-A
8	Sonia	Cardenas	(928) 551-5547	4/12/1968	F	$0.00	☑	498-1112-A
9	Daniel	Cardenas	(928) 551-5547	5/12/2002	M	$0.00	☑	498-1112-A
10	Jonathan	Cardenas	(928) 551-5547	8/22/2004	M	$0.00	☑	498-1112-A
11	Paula	Hargus	(505) 744-1889	6/11/1970	F	$24.00	☑	OP-87-A087
12	Steven	Hargus	(505) 744-1889	8/14/2000	M	$0.00	☑	OP-87-A087
13	Christina	Hargus	(505) 744-1889	2/14/1998	F	$0.00	☑	OP-87-A087
14	Malena	D'Ambrosio	(435) 444-1233	4/15/1980	F	$0.00	☐	2B8973AC
15	Gina	Mercado	(970) 514-3212	6/17/1979	F	$12.00	☐	4983
16	William	Gabel	(970) 223-4156	7/4/1980	M	$0.00	☐	4983
17	Maria	Gabel	(970) 223-4157	8/12/1980	F	$0.00	☐	4983
18	Anders	Aannestad	(505) 499-6541	9/11/1974	M	$35.00	☐	498-1112-A
19	Dusty	Alkier	(435) 693-1212	4/5/1940	M	$0.00	☐	A089
20	Kevin	Wachter	(435) 477-8989	6/22/1972	M	$40.00	☐	A089
21	Cesar	Lopez	(970) 631-2222	1/14/1977	M	$0.00	☐	4983
22	Josefina	Hernandez	(505) 498-6478	6/30/1978	F	$0.00	☐	OP-87-A087
23	Jennifer	Ramsey	(928) 888-3545	11/21/1980	F	$0.00	☐	498-1112-A
24	Kimberley	Schultz	(928) 647-2477	1/16/1969	F	$0.00	☐	498-1112-A
25	Adriane	Walters	(970) 436-6398	4/22/1952	F	$15.00	☐	4983
26	Jessica	Cortez	(928) 644-1674	8/13/1978	F	$0.00	☐	498-1112-A

Record: ◄ ◄ 1 ► ►► ► No Filter Search

Best Practice

Importing Records with AutoNumber Fields or Input Masks into a Table

When you import data from another database into a table that contains an AutoNumber field, you should be aware of two potential problems.

First, when you use an AutoNumber field to create primary key values in a table, Access uses each incremented value only once. For example, if you delete a record with the value 11 in an AutoNumber field, record 11 is deleted permanently from the table. To the user, record 11 does not exist after you delete it and there is no way to reenter a record with that AutoNumber value. However, if you import data into another table that also contains an AutoNumber field, Access creates a record 11 in the new table because AutoNumber 11 is an available record number in the new table. This difference can cause problems when the AutoNumber field has matching foreign key values with referential integrity enforced in the relationship. In this case, record 11 does not exist in the primary table. However, when you import the data into a new table, record 11 does exist, and all subsequently imported records are renumbered. If you try to relate data using the AutoNumber field, the foreign key values in the related table might not match.

Second, after importing data into a new or existing table, you cannot change a field's data type to AutoNumber because Access will not create AutoNumber values in a table that contains data. You can, however, add a new field with an AutoNumber data type. You can also use a Number data type and the Long Integer data type to relate the field to an AutoNumber field. If your table design does include an AutoNumber field, create the table structure prior to importing data into it so you can keep the AutoNumber field.

An input mask in a field's properties can also cause an issue. For example, you might receive an error message when copying records into a table if the field property for a field contains an input mask and the data you are copying does not comply with the input mask. If an error message does appear, you can cancel pasting the records. Then, change back to Design view for the table, delete the input mask from the field temporarily to be able to copy and paste the customer records. After saving the table, change back to Datasheet view and paste the records. Once the records are pasted, Don needs to check the data in the field with the input mask. When the mask is reapplied, only those entries that comply will be masked. The data that did not comply and has not been corrected will appear without the mask. After Don checks the data, he changes back to Design view for the table and adds the input mask back into the field's properties.

Importing Data from an Excel Workbook

In some cases, you might need to import data stored in an Excel workbook into a table. If you have not yet created the table in the database, you can import the data and create the table at the same time. In the discovery phase, Don received some Excel files from Paul containing data that he needs to store in the database. One of those files, tblClinic.xlsx, contains data about the clinics that employ the doctors who write prescriptions for 4Corners Pharmacy customers. Don decides to create tblClinic by importing the data from the Excel file.

When you import data stored in an Excel workbook into a database, you need to review the contents of the workbook to understand how it is arranged. In most worksheets, the first row of data contains column headings that define the data in each column. If the column heading names comply with the rules for naming fields in Access, Access uses them as field names when you import the data. Figure 2.31 shows the tblClinic.xlsx workbook in Excel. Paul inserted column headings that are valid Access field names, so these column headings will become the field names in tblClinic. If Don wanted to change any existing column headings to different names or to make them comply with the field naming rules in Access, he would make these changes in the worksheet before importing the data into Access.

Figure 2.31: Clinic worksheet data in Excel

	A	B		C	D	E	F	G	H	I
1	ClinicID	ClinicName		Address1	Address2	City	State	ZIP	Phone	
2	1	Southern Colorado Area Clinic		8989 Highway 16	P.O. Box 2311	Cortez	CO	81321	970-322-5747	
3	2	Chinle Memorial Clinic		1255 State Street	Suite 101	Chinle	AZ	86538	928-888-4178	
4	3	St. Thomas Clinic		477 Gund Avenue	Suite 400	Yellow Jacket	CO	81335	970-898-4788	
5	4	Connley Memorial Clinic		1245 Marville Drive	P.O. Box 14447	Kayenta	AZ	86033	928-488-1741	
6	5	Blanding City Clinic		9030 Preston Road		Blanding	UT	84511	435-887-1818	
7	6	Sodt Memorial Clinic		7910 Treehouse Lane	P.O. Box 1245	Aneth	UT	84510	435-189-9874	
8	7	Northwest New Mexico Area Clinic		4039 Midrose Avenue		Farmington	NM	87402	505-545-1879	
9	8	San Juan County Clinic		14879 Southwestern Boulevard		Flora Vista	NM	87415	505-884-0542	
10	9	University of Northern Arizona Clinic		84569 Holly Hill Circle	P.O. Box 98994	Chinle	AZ	86556	928-449-4174	
11	10	Dolores LaPlata Memorial Clinic		419 Lupton Drive	Building 200	Pleasant View	CO	81331	970-429-7475	
12	11	Southeastern State Clinic & Hospital		4577 East Gunnison Parkway		Montezuma Creek	UT	84534	435-321-4789	
13	12	Kirtland Community Clinic		84111 North Alamosa Avenue	P.O. Box 7456	Kirtland	NM	87417	505-744-1684	
14										

If the worksheet does not contain any column headings or if the existing column headings violate Access field naming rules, Access assigns generic field names.

Access can import most data from a worksheet, with a few exceptions. It cannot import graphics, such as chart objects. Cells that contain formulas are imported as numbers, without the formulas, and hyperlinks are imported as text data. Access automatically assigns a data type to each column of data it imports by evaluating the data in the first 25 rows of the worksheet. For example, if the data in a column contains text values, Access assigns the Short Text data type to the field.

Access imports data in columns exactly as they are arranged in the worksheet. If you want to arrange the fields in a different way, you can rearrange the columns in the worksheet to meet your requirements. For example, the worksheet might list a customer's last name first. If you want the database to organize the fields so that the customer's first name comes first, you would need to move the FirstName column in the worksheet so it appears to the left of the LastName column. However, after importing the data, you can always rearrange the fields in the Table Design grid of Design view as you would for any other table.

You can use Access to import specific data saved in a workbook. In most cases, you will import the data stored in a single worksheet, but you can also import named ranges of data. For example, if you only want to import the records in the range A2:H3 of the Clinic worksheet, you could specify a name for this range in the worksheet and specify it when you import the data. Access then would import the column headings as field names and the data in rows 2 and 3 and columns A through H of the worksheet.

After examining the worksheet, Don determines that it is properly organized with appropriate field names. He closes the workbook, clicks the EXTERNAL DATA tab on the Ribbon, and then clicks the Excel button in the Import & Link group. The Get External Data – Excel Spreadsheet dialog box opens. The default option—Import the source data into a new table in the current database—is selected, so Don only needs to specify the location that contains the workbook. He browses to and double-clicks tblClinic.xlsx to select it and then clicks the OK button to start the Import Spreadsheet Wizard, as shown in Figure 2.32.

Figure 2.32: Import Spreadsheet Wizard

Clinic worksheet data appears in columns

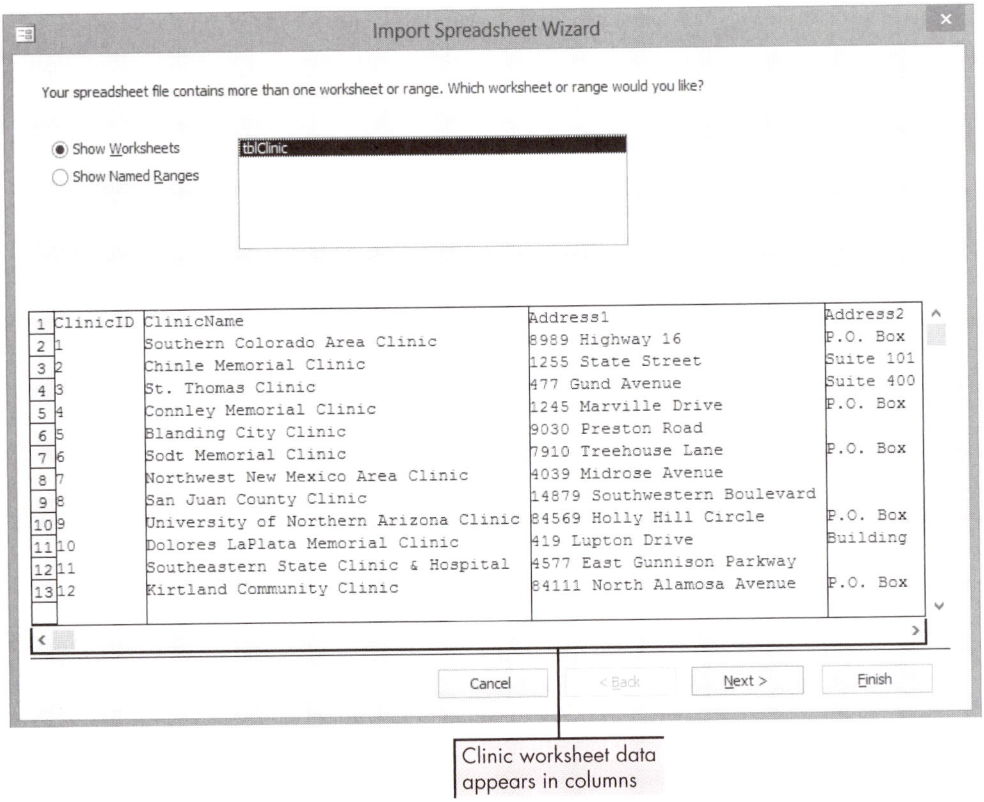

Don wants to import the data stored in the tblClinic worksheet, which is the selected option. (If the workbook contained other worksheets, they would be listed in the box.) If Don wanted to select a named range in the worksheet, he would click the Show Named Ranges option button to display the ranges. Don clicks the Next button to accept these settings, and the second wizard dialog box opens, as shown in Figure 2.33.

Figure 2.33: Identifying column headings in the worksheet

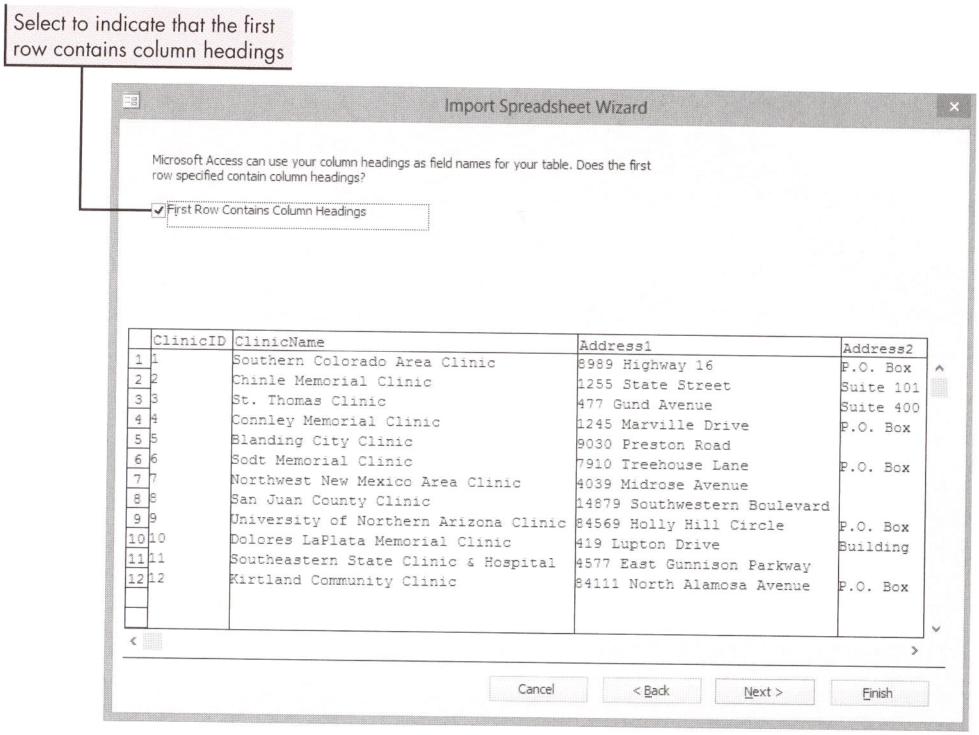

Select to indicate that the first
row contains column headings

In this dialog box, you specify whether the first row of the worksheet contains column headings. Don clicks the First Row Contains Column Headings check box to select it, indicating that the data in the first row should become the field names in the imported table. He clicks the Next button to display the next wizard dialog box in which you can specify options that you want to apply to the field you are importing. See Figure 2.34.

Figure 2.34: Field options for the imported data

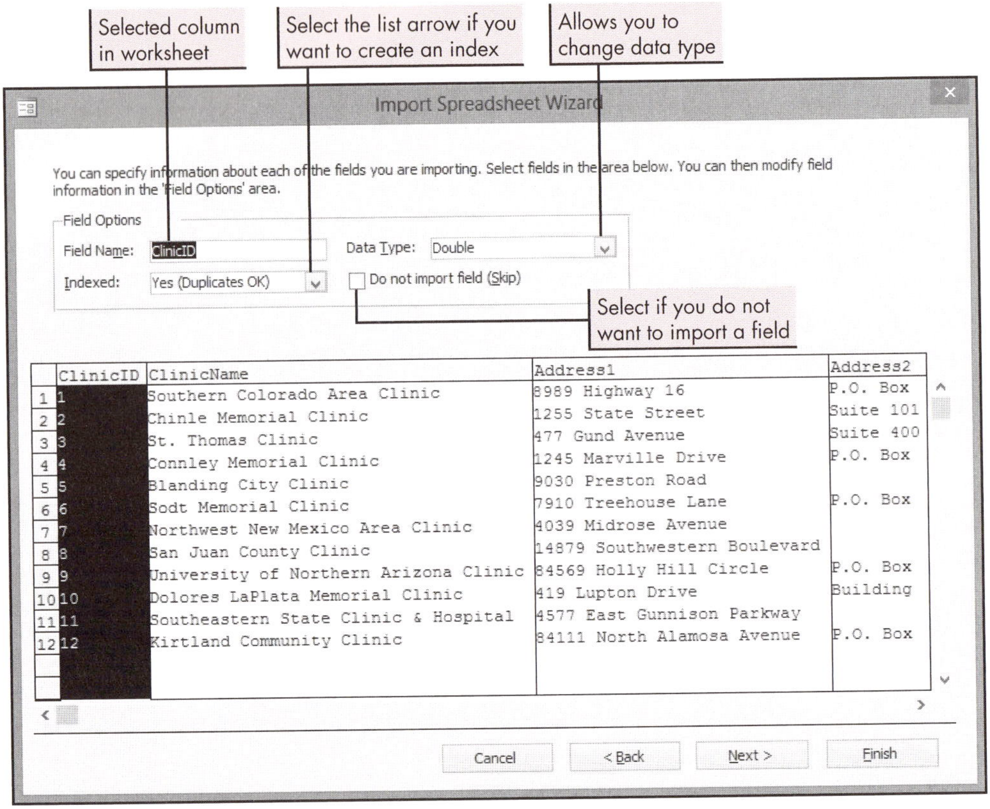

In this dialog box, you can change the default field names, indexing requirements, and data types for each field by selecting the field in the table (in this case, the ClinicID field). (You can use the scroll bars to examine fields to the right and below the default values.) If the worksheet from which you are importing data is set up correctly, you usually will not need to make any changes in this dialog box. Don accepts the default settings, and then clicks the Next button to open the next wizard dialog box, shown in Figure 2.35.

Figure 2.35: Setting a primary key field

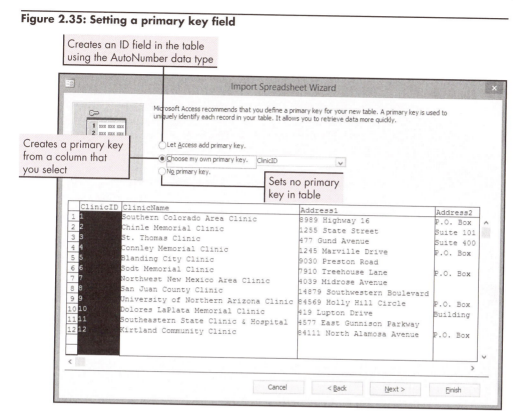

Creates an ID field in the table using the AutoNumber data type

Creates a primary key from a column that you select

Sets no primary key in table

In this dialog box, you can let Access select a primary key (by adding an AutoNumber field to the imported table), choose a primary key field from the existing worksheet columns, or specify that the data contains no primary key. The default option adds an ID field to the table design. Because the worksheet already contains unique values in the ClinicID field, Don clicks the Choose my own primary key option button, and then selects ClinicID using the arrow to the right of this option button. He clicks the Next button to open the final dialog box, verifies the table name is tblClinic, and then clicks the Finish button. Access creates tblClinic in the 4Corners database and loads it with data. He chooses not to save the import steps and closes the Get External Data – Excel Spreadsheet dialog box.

Don was able to use the tblClinic worksheet because it contained a valid table structure and data. However, the table design that Access created from the imported data most likely does not match the exact table design that Don prepared for this table. To finish creating the table, Don opens tblClinic in Design view so he can verify the field properties for each field in the table and make any necessary changes. The first field, ClinicID, has the Number data type, which is correct. Most of the other fields are Short Text fields. Access will set the Short Text field sizes to 255 characters. Because Don knows that the Short Text field sizes are too long, he changes the field sizes to match his table design. In addition, he adds field descriptions to all fields, captions to the ClinicID, ClinicName, Address1, and Address2 fields, and an input mask to the Phone field. If the table needs to contain any foreign keys, Don would need to add those fields to the table design. He saves the table and closes it. Because he decreased the field sizes for all of the Short Text fields, a dialog box opens and warns him about potential data loss in one or more fields. Don clicks the Yes button to finish saving the table, knowing that none of the existing data will be truncated by the new field sizes.

Don uses these same steps with the Import Spreadsheet Wizard to create a table and import the data for tblHouseHold. After he completes these steps, he uses the Lookup Wizard in the HouseID field in tblCustomer so that he can select the HouseID from a list. However, in this case, Don wants to display two fields in the lookup field, not just one like in the PlanID field. Displaying only the HouseID field values won't provide enough information for the user entering a record in tblCustomer to determine which household to select because the HouseID stores values in the format 1, 2, 3, and so on. The user needs to enter the HouseID value from tblHousehold, but the user determines the correct HouseID based on the complete street address. Because households are unique, displaying the street address will be sufficient information to select the correct household for a new customer. To select more than one field's values in the lookup field, Don adds the HouseID and Address fields from a list of available fields from tblHousehold to the Selected Fields box in the Lookup Wizard, as shown in Figure 2.36.

Figure 2.36: HouseID and Address fields added to the Selected Fields box

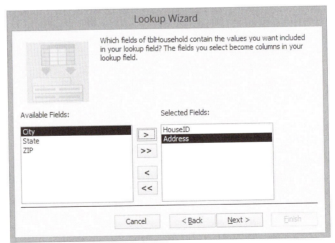

To make values easier to find, Don sorts the lookup field values in ascending order by address, and then removes the check mark from the Hide key column (recommended) check box to display the HouseID and Address values in the lookup field so users entering customer records can select the correct household using either value. Don increases the size of the Address field and decreases the size of the HouseID field so the lookup field will display the complete field values. He then selects the HouseID as the value to store in the HouseID field in tblCustomer (see Figure 2.37) and then accepts the default lookup field name of HouseID.

Figure 2.37: Selecting HouseID values for the HouseID field in tblCustomer

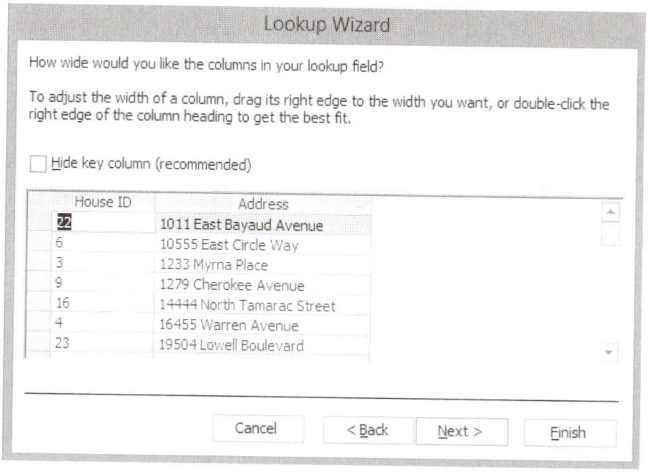

Once tblCustomer is saved, the lookup field will display data from the HouseID and Address fields stored in tblHousehold. Figure 2.38 shows the lookup field for the HouseID field. Note that this list will appear as shown when the table tblHousehold is created. To select a household for the customer, the user clicks the correct one from the list, based on a known HouseID field value or the street address. The values are sorted in ascending order by street address and users can scroll the values using the scroll bar on the lookup field. When the user selects a value in the lookup column, the HouseID value is stored in the HouseID field in tblCustomer.

Figure 2.38: Lookup field values for HouseID

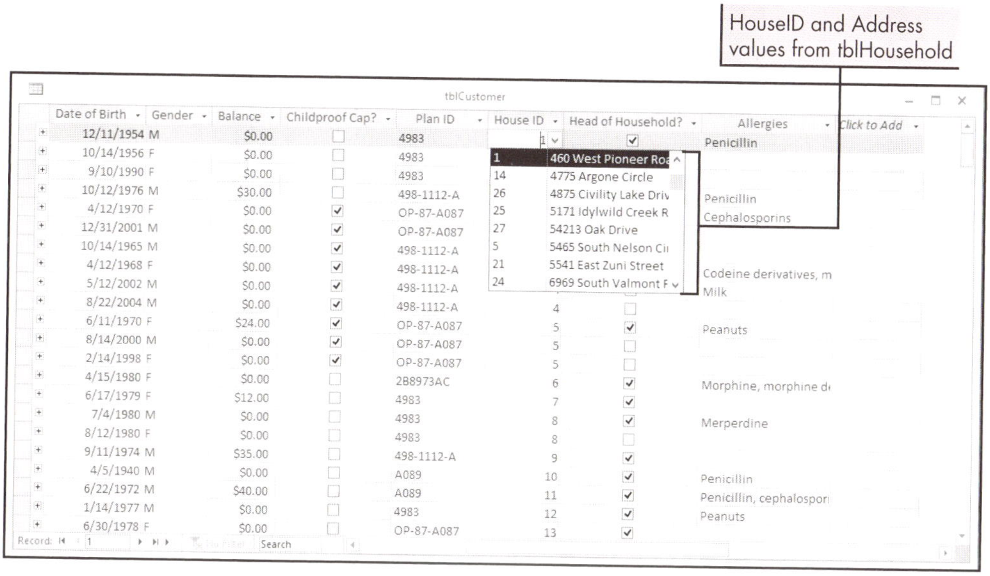

Don now uses the Import Spreadsheet Wizard to import data into the tblDoctor, tblDrug, tblEmployee, tblJobTitle, and tblRx tables. He uses the option called Append a copy of the records to a table.

How To

Import Spreadsheet Data into an Existing Table

1. Create and save the table in Access and then close it.
2. Examine the source data and make sure that the columns are arranged in the same order as the fields in the table, make any necessary changes, and then close the spreadsheet file.
3. In the Access Database window, click the EXTERNAL DATA tab on the Ribbon and then click the Excel button in the Import & Link group. The Get External Data – Excel Spreadsheet dialog box opens.
4. Browse to the folder or drive that contains the file to import, select the source file, click the Open button, click the Append a copy of the records to the table tblDoctor option, if necessary, and then click the OK button to start the Import Spreadsheet Wizard.
5. If necessary, select the worksheet or named range that contains the data to import and then click the Next button.
6. If necessary, click the First Row Contains Column Headings check box to indicate that the first row in the source file contains headings, and then click the Next button.
7. Verify that the table name to import is correct, and then click the Finish button.
8. Click the Close button to close the wizard.

Working with Primary and Foreign Keys

Don's table designs include primary key fields that will contain values that uniquely identify each record in the tables. The table designs also include foreign key fields as necessary to join tables to each other to create the relationships in the database. A primary key and its foreign key counterparts must have the same data type and field size and the fields must contain identical values—you cannot relate fields that have different data types, field sizes, and values. Also, if referential integrity is set, a primary key value must exist before entering a corresponding record. For example, you must enter a new household into tblHousehold before you can add a new customer who lives in that household to tblCustomer.

The main objective of creating a primary key field in a table is to prevent users from entering duplicate records into the table, but it also has other advantages. When a field has no value—a value that is unknown or unavailable or just missing—it is called a **null value**. A user cannot enter a null value into a primary key field because the primary key field is required for data entry. For example, if a user enters a drug into tblDrug but does not specify a UPN field value, Access has no way to uniquely identify each record in tblDrug. However, in some cases, you might want *nonprimary* key fields to store null values. For example, in tblDrug, the PregCategory field indicates the risk of using the drug during pregnancy; "A" indicates safe usage and "X" indicates a strong likelihood that the drug

will cause birth defects. Most drug manufacturers assess their products for risk during pregnancy, but some drugs have unknown drug risks. In this case, the pharmacist doesn't enter a value in the PregCategory field—the risk is simply unknown.

You don't need to specify that primary key values are required in a table; this occurs automatically by setting a field as a table's primary key. By default, nonprimary key fields can store null values. You can, however, use the **Required property** for a nonprimary key field to ensure that users enter a value into the field. For example, Don could set the CustFirst and CustLast fields in tblCustomer so that users must enter values into these fields to add a customer's record to the table. To set the Required property, select the field in Design view and then change its value in the Required property box from "No" to "Yes" (without the quotation marks). You must be careful about requiring data entry into a field, however. What if you require data entry in the Address field in tblHousehold, but the customer has just moved and doesn't yet have an address to give? If you require data entry in the Address field, you cannot enter the customer's information in tblHousehold.

The primary key field also works to make data retrieval faster. When you specify a field as a table's primary key, Access creates an index for the primary key field. An index in a database is similar to an index that you find in a published book. When you need to find a specific topic in a book, you can find the topic in the book's index and obtain a list of the page numbers on which the topic appears so you can find them quickly. In a database, an **index** is a list maintained by the database (but hidden from users) that associates the field values in the indexed field with the records that contain the field values. You might think of a database index as a small table containing values from a table and record numbers that reference those values. An index does not contain an entire record—it only contains the field from the record and a pointer to the record number.

As the pharmacy grows, more records will be added to the tables and additional tables might be added to the database structure. As the number of records and the complexity of the database increase, the efficiency of the database might decrease if proper procedures are not added in the beginning. Don knows that employees will use certain tables and fields more often than others. For example, the pharmacy staff will use tblCustomer on a regular basis to manage data about the pharmacy's customers. In the first year alone, tblCustomer might grow in size to include hundreds of records. Don also knows that the data in tblCustomer will be used many times by other tables, queries, and reports. Don decides to change the table structure to increase the performance of tblCustomer, which, in turn, will increase the speed of the entire database.

Creating an Index

Don anticipates that the pharmacy staff might need to search tblCustomer frequently to find customers by using their last names. To increase the speed at which Access searches tblCustomer, Don can create an index on the CustLast field. To create an index in a table, open the table in Design view, select the field to index, and then click the Indexed property arrow. You can create an index for any field, except for fields with the Calculated, Attachment, and OLE Object data types. When you click the Indexed property for a field, three options appear in a menu, as shown in Figure 2.39.

Figure 2.39: Creating an index for a nonprimary key field

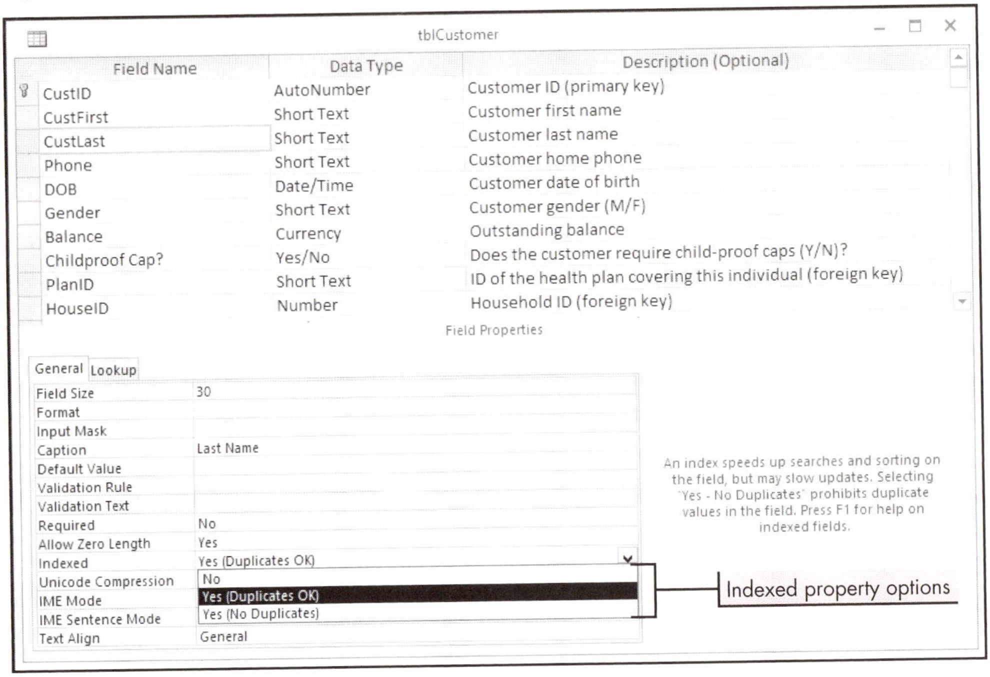

The first option, which is the default option for nonprimary key fields, is No. The No option means that there is no index for the field. The second option, Yes (Duplicates OK), creates an index for the field that accepts and stores duplicate values. Because it is likely that some customers of the pharmacy will have the same last names, using the Yes (Duplicates OK) option permits users to enter duplicate last names into this field. The third option is Yes (No Duplicates), which is the default option for primary key fields. You can set this option for nonprimary key fields to control data entry. For example, because U.S. citizens have unique Social Security numbers, two employees in tblEmployee cannot have duplicate Social Security numbers. By setting the SSN field to Yes (No Duplicates), Access prevents duplicate values from being stored in the SSN field.

To view the indexes created in a table, click the Indexes button in the Show/Hide group on the DESIGN tab. Don sets the Indexed property to Yes (Duplicates OK). Figure 2.40 shows the Indexes window for tblCustomer. There are five indexes in this table—two for CustID (the table's primary key), one each for the HouseID and PlanID fields, which are foreign keys, and the one Don just set for the CustLast field. You can add indexes to the Indexes window by typing an index name, field name, and the sort order. Note that you can delete an index by right-clicking the index name and then clicking Delete Rows on the shortcut menu.

Figure 2.40: Indexes window for tblCustomer

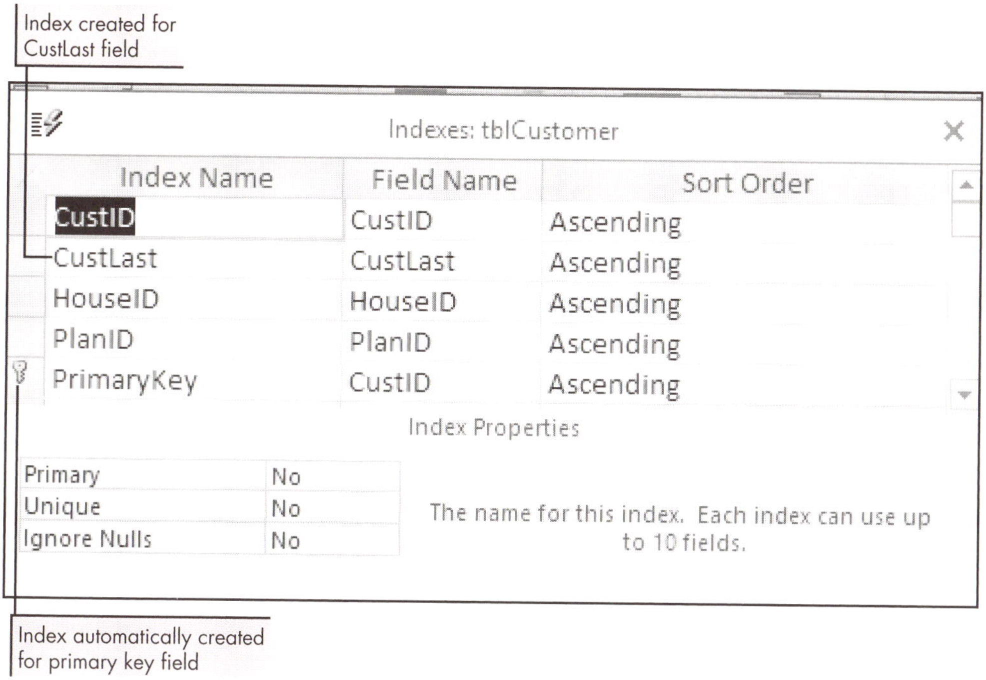

Index created for
CustLast field

Index Name	Field Name	Sort Order	
CustID	CustID	Ascending	▲
CustLast	CustLast	Ascending	
HouseID	HouseID	Ascending	
PlanID	PlanID	Ascending	
PrimaryKey	CustID	Ascending	▼

Indexes: tblCustomer   ✕

Index Properties

Primary	No
Unique	No
Ignore Nulls	No

The name for this index. Each index can use up
to 10 fields.

Index automatically created
for primary key field

Don can create indexes for as many fields as necessary to optimize searches in the database. When you create an index, the records are indexed when you save the table. The index is updated automatically as records are added, deleted, or changed in the table. A disadvantage of creating an index on a nonprimary key field is that it increases the size of the database and slows down the database because it must update the index as users add, change, and delete records. To overcome these drawbacks, you can add indexes as needed when improved search or query performance is necessary, and then delete indexes to increase the speed of creating, modifying, and deleting records. For example, Don could add an index prior to running a query or report and then remove the index to reduce the size of the database and to improve efficiency when updating.

Creating One-to-Many Relationships Between Tables

In Chapter 1, you learned how to relate tables in a database using primary key and foreign key fields. In Access, you define table relationships in the Relationships window or when you create a lookup field that searches the records in another table. To open the Relationships window, click the Relationships button on the DATABASE TOOLS tab on the Ribbon. Figure 2.41 shows the Relationships window for the 4Corners database.

Figure 2.41: Relationships window

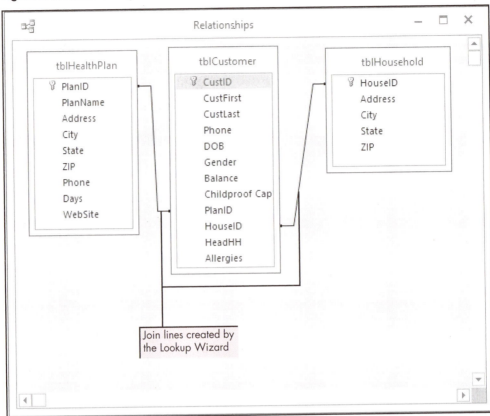

The Relationships window contains the field lists for three tables—tblHealthPlan, tblCustomer, and tblHousehold. Don can use the mouse pointer to resize the field lists to display all of the fields in each table. He can also drag the field lists to new positions to better illustrate the relationships. Because Don created lookup fields in tblCustomer to look up fields in tblHealthPlan and tblHousehold, there are two existing relationships in the database. These relationships appear as join lines that connect the tables to each other. The other tables in the database do not appear in the Relationships window because they do not contain any lookup fields and because Don has not added them to the window yet.

You also learned that a relationship has certain properties associated with it. The relationship has a certain type, such as one-to-many, one-to-one, or many-to-many, and certain attributes that specify how to manage changes when records are updated or deleted. To view the properties for a relationship, you can right-click the join line, and then click Edit Relationship on the shortcut menu. Don right-clicks the join line between tblHealthPlan and tblCustomer and opens the Edit Relationships dialog box shown in Figure 2.42.

Figure 2.42: Edit Relationships dialog box

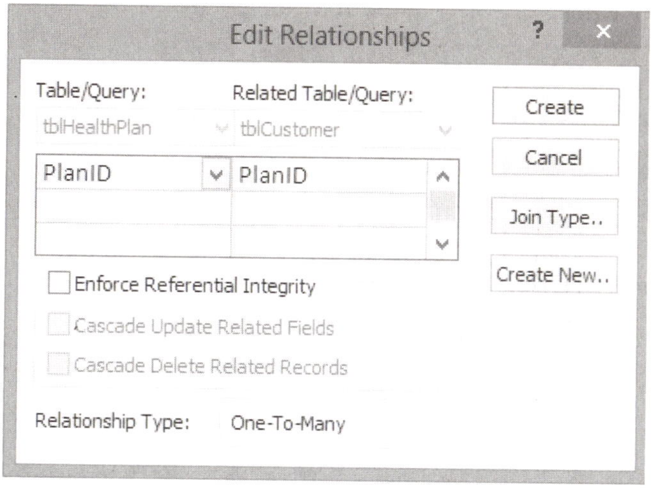

The Edit Relationships dialog box shows the relationship between the primary table tblHealthPlan and the related table tblCustomer, which resulted when Don created the lookup field for PlanID. The relationship type, one-to-many, indicates that one PlanID in the primary table is related to zero, one, or many PlanIDs in the related table (tblCustomer). Don enforces this rule by clicking the Enforce Referential Integrity check box to add a check mark to it. Because a PlanID value in tblHealthPlan might change as a result of a new plan number from an insurance company, Don needs to make sure that changes to the PlanIDs in tblHealthPlan are updated in the related records, so he clicks the Cascade Update Related Fields check box to select it. Don does not, however, want to delete all related records if a PlanID is deleted from tblHealthPlan, so he does not select the Cascade Delete Related Records check box. Don knows that a novice database user might unintentionally delete records if the Cascade Delete Related Records is checked. After making these changes, Don clicks the OK button. If he receives an error message, Don knows that he will need to correct the table data and repeat this procedure. To save the changes, he clicks the Save button on the Quick Access toolbar.

The Relationships window shows a one-to-many relationship between the PlanID field in tblHealthPlan to the PlanID field in tblCustomer. A "1" appears on the "one" side of the relationship and an infinity symbol (∞) appears on the "many" side of the relationship. Don edits the relationship created by the lookup field between tblHousehold and tblCustomer to enforce referential integrity and cascade updates as well. The Relationships window appears in Figure 2.43.

Figure 2.43: Relationships window after creating two 1: ∞ relationships

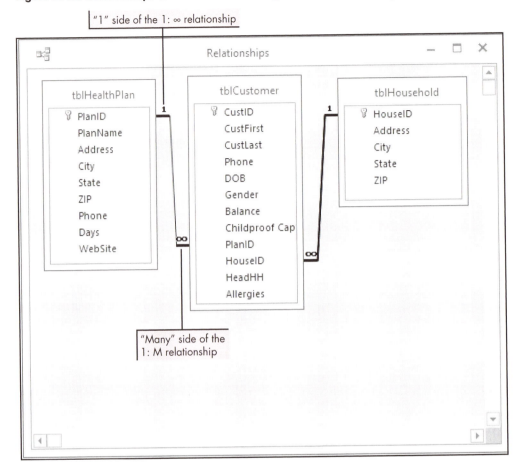

"1" side of the 1: ∞ relationship

"Many" side of the 1: M relationship

Now Don needs to add the remaining tables to the Relationships window and create the relationships between the appropriate tables using his database design. He clicks the Show Table button in the Relationships group to open the Show Table dialog box, clicks tblClass in the Tables list, and then clicks the Add button. The tblClass table is added to the Relationships window. He repeats this process to add tblClinic, tblDoctor, tblDrug, tblEmployee, tblJobTitle, and tblRx to the Relationships window, and then clicks the Close button to close the Show Table dialog box. He resizes the field lists to display all fields in each added table and rearranges the field lists so that related tables are next to each other, as shown in Figure 2.44, to make it easier to create the relationships.

Figure 2.44: Relationships window after adding, resizing, and repositioning the database tables

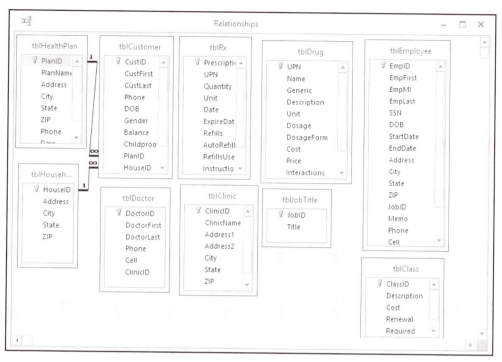

Now Don can start creating the relationships between tables. The first one that Don creates is the one-to-many relationship between tblDoctor and tblRx. A primary key field and the corresponding foreign key field are not required to have the same field name, but the values in the primary key and foreign key fields must match exactly, including data types and properties, to create the relationship. You can create the relationships by dragging the primary key field from the primary table to the foreign key field in the related table. When you release the mouse button, the Edit Relationships dialog box opens, into which you specify the relationship properties. Don drags the DoctorID field from tblDoctor to the DoctorID field in tblRx, and then releases the mouse button. The Edit Relationships dialog box opens, and he clicks the check boxes to enforce referential integrity and cascade updates. After clicking the Create button, the one-to-many relationship between doctors and prescriptions is created. Don also creates one-to-many relationships between the tblJobTitle and tblEmployee tables, between the tblDrug and tblRx tables, and between the tblCustomer and tblRx tables and then selects the options to enforce referential integrity and cascade updates. The Relationships window now looks like Figure 2.45.

Figure 2.45: Relationships window after creating 1: ∞ relationships

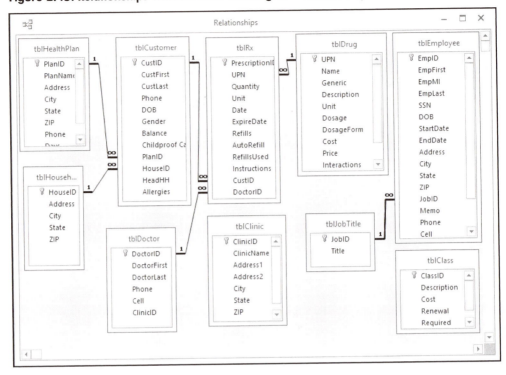

Don sees that he has not yet related the tblClinic and tblDoctor tables. He drags the ClinicID field from tblClinic to the ClinicID field in tblDoctor, and selects the options to enforce referential integrity and to cascade updates. This time, however, instead of creating the one-to-many relationship, Don receives an error message. Don knows that this error message indicates that he is trying to join tables with fields that do not have the same data type or field size. He clicks the OK button to close the message box, clicks the Cancel button to close the Edit Relationships dialog box, and then saves the Relationships window and closes it. He opens tblClinic in Design view and sees that the primary key field, ClinicID, has the Number data type and the Double field size. He then remembers how this problem occurred—when he created the table by importing data, Access assigned this field a data type and field size based on the data he imported. He accepted the default field size, Double, and saved the table. However, the ClinicID field in tblDoctor uses the Long Integer field size. The different field sizes caused the error message, so Don changes the field size of ClinicID field in tblClinic to Long Integer and saves tblClinic. A message box appears, informing him that some data might be lost. He clicks the Yes button to acknowledge and close the message, and then returns to the Relationships window. This time, he is able to create the one-to-many relationship between tblClinic and tblDoctor.

Don looks at the Relationships window and sees that he has no way to relate employees to the classes they take because there are no common fields between tblEmployee and tblClass. To create this relationship, he needs to create another table in the database that he can use to create a many-to-many relationship.

Troubleshooting Referential Integrity Errors

Relating tables in the Relationships window is usually a smooth process, but you might encounter a few potential problems, especially when you have imported existing table designs and data into your database.

You might receive an error message when creating relationships, as discussed previously. Another error message you might see when attempting to relate tables in the Relationships window is shown in Figure 2.46.

Figure 2.46: Error message about referential integrity violation

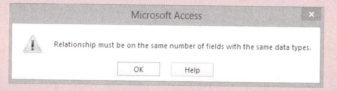

This error message shows another error that you might see when attempting to relate tables in the Relationships window. In this case, Access cannot create the relationship because it would create orphaned records in the primary or related table. If you receive this error message, it is more difficult to correct the problem because you must compare the primary key values in the primary table with the foreign key values in the related table and identify values in the first table that do not match the second table. To enforce referential integrity and create the relationship, there must be a primary key value in the primary table for every foreign key value in the related table. Correcting this error usually involves adding a missing record to the primary table that matches an existing record in the related table.

Creating a Many-To-Many Relationship Between Tables

Don's database design includes creating tblEmployeeTraining, which is a junction table to create the many-to-many relationship between employees and classes. Don creates this table in Design view, as shown in Figure 2.47. Notice that the primary key of tblEmployeeTraining is the combination of all three fields in the table, which is also referred to as a composite primary key.

Figure 2.47: Table design for tblEmployeeTraining

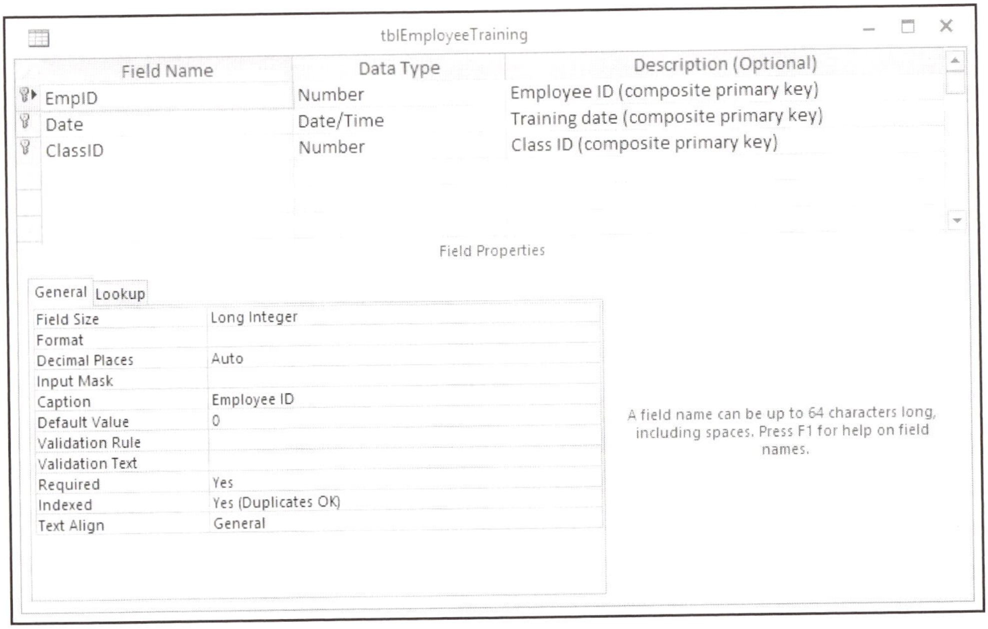

	tblEmployeeTraining	— □ ✕

Field Name	Data Type	Description (Optional)
🔑▸ EmpID	Number	Employee ID (composite primary key)
🔑 Date	Date/Time	Training date (composite primary key)
🔑 ClassID	Number	Class ID (composite primary key)

Field Properties

General | Lookup

Field Size	Long Integer
Format	
Decimal Places	Auto
Input Mask	
Caption	Employee ID
Default Value	0
Validation Rule	
Validation Text	
Required	Yes
Indexed	Yes (Duplicates OK)
Text Align	General

A field name can be up to 64 characters long, including spaces. Press F1 for help on field names.

How To

Create a Composite Primary Key

1. In Design view, click the row selector for the first field that will become the composite key.
2. Press and hold the Ctrl key, and then click the second field that will become the composite key. If necessary, continue holding the Ctrl key and click any other fields that will become the composite key.
3. When all fields in the composite key are selected, release the Ctrl key.
4. Click the Primary Key button in the Tools group on the contextual TABLE TOOLS DESIGN tab.
5. Save the table.

An employee can take any class on any date—the combination of the EmpID, Date, and ClassID creates a unique record in this table. Don adds tblEmployeeTraining to the Relationships window and rearranges the field lists so he can see all of the fields in each table and so that related tables are arranged next to each other. To create the many-to-many relationship between employees and classes, he starts by creating the one-to-many relationship between tblClass and tblEmployeeTraining, via the ClassID field, and enforces referential integrity and cascades updates. Then he creates the one-to-many relationship between tblEmployee and tblEmployeeTraining. The result is a many-to-many relationship between employees and classes, as shown in Figure 2.48.

Figure 2.48: Relationships window after creating ∞:∞ relationship

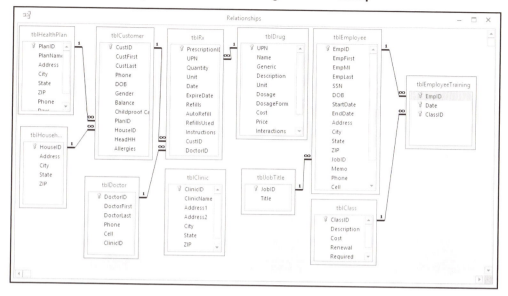

Don needs to add one more table to the database, tblRefill, which will store data about prescription number (ID), refill date, and the employees who fill the order. He returns to Design view and creates tblRefill, as shown in Figure 2.49.

Figure 2.49: Table design for tblRefill

Field Name	Data Type	Description (Optional)
PrescriptionID	Number	Prescription ID (composite primary key)
RefillDate	Date/Time	Refill date (composite primary key)
EmpID	Number	Employee ID who filled the prescription (foreign key)

Field Properties

General | Lookup

Field Size	Long Integer
Format	
Decimal Places	Auto
Input Mask	
Caption	Prescription ID
Default Value	0
Validation Rule	
Validation Text	
Required	Yes
Indexed	Yes (Duplicates OK)
Text Align	General

A field name can be up to 64 characters long, including spaces. Press F1 for help on field names.

After creating and saving tblRefill, Don adds it to the Relationships window and creates the one-to-many relationship between tblRx and tblRefill, via the PrescriptionID field, and the one-to-many relationship between tblEmployee and tblRefill, via the EmpID field. Now there is a many-to-many relationship between employees and prescriptions. The final Relationships window is displayed in Figure 2.50.

Figure 2.50: Completed Relationships window

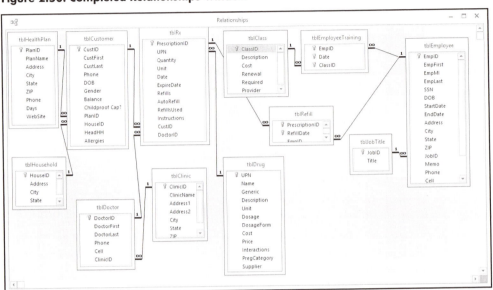

Now that Don has created all of the relationships in the database, he imports the existing data he has from the discovery phase into tblEmployeeTraining and tblRefill. The database is now fully populated.

Using a Subdatasheet to View Related Records

After importing data into a database, it is a good idea to open each table in Datasheet view and check the data for any problems. Don checks each table, including tblHousehold, by opening it in Datasheet view. Because of the relationship Don created between the tblHousehold and tblCustomer tables, an expand indicator (box with the plus sign) appears to the left of each record in the HouseID field, as shown in Figure 2.51, to show that the field has related records in other tables. When you click the expand indicator, a subdatasheet with the related records appears.

Figure 2.51: tblHousehold in Datasheet view

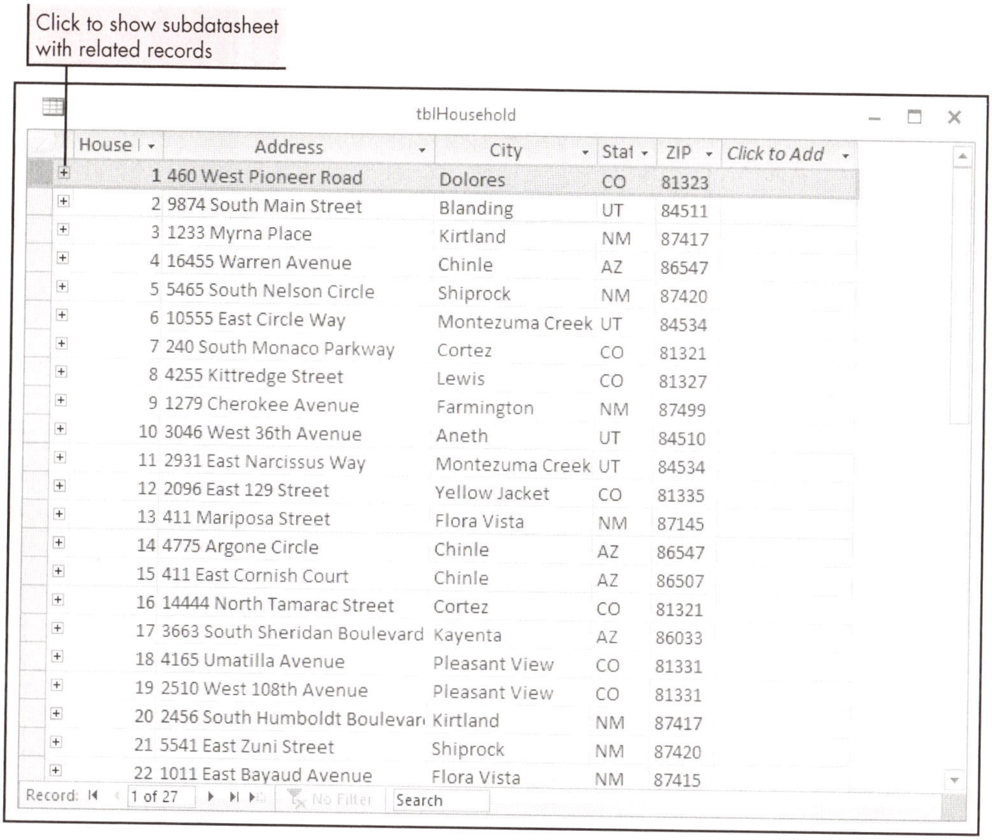

Click to show subdatasheet
with related records

House ⁞	Address	City	Stat	ZIP	Click to Add
⊞	1 460 West Pioneer Road	Dolores	CO	81323	
⊞	2 9874 South Main Street	Blanding	UT	84511	
⊞	3 1233 Myrna Place	Kirtland	NM	87417	
⊞	4 16455 Warren Avenue	Chinle	AZ	86547	
⊞	5 5465 South Nelson Circle	Shiprock	NM	87420	
⊞	6 10555 East Circle Way	Montezuma Creek	UT	84534	
⊞	7 240 South Monaco Parkway	Cortez	CO	81321	
⊞	8 4255 Kittredge Street	Lewis	CO	81327	
⊞	9 1279 Cherokee Avenue	Farmington	NM	87499	
⊞	10 3046 West 36th Avenue	Aneth	UT	84510	
⊞	11 2931 East Narcissus Way	Montezuma Creek	UT	84534	
⊞	12 2096 East 129 Street	Yellow Jacket	CO	81335	
⊞	13 411 Mariposa Street	Flora Vista	NM	87145	
⊞	14 4775 Argone Circle	Chinle	AZ	86547	
⊞	15 411 East Cornish Court	Chinle	AZ	86507	
⊞	16 14444 North Tamarac Street	Cortez	CO	81321	
⊞	17 3663 South Sheridan Boulevard	Kayenta	AZ	86033	
⊞	18 4165 Umatilla Avenue	Pleasant View	CO	81331	
⊞	19 2510 West 108th Avenue	Pleasant View	CO	81331	
⊞	20 2456 South Humboldt Boulevard	Kirtland	NM	87417	
⊞	21 5541 East Zuni Street	Shiprock	NM	87420	
⊞	22 1011 East Bayaud Avenue	Flora Vista	NM	87415	

Record: I◄ ◄ 1 of 27 ► ►I ►▸ 🇹x No Filter   Search

A **subdatasheet** lets you view and edit joined data in the relationship when you click the plus sign. After you click the expand indicator, it then becomes a collapse indicator (box with the minus sign). Clicking this box closes the subdatasheet. Don clicks the expand indicator for the first record to open the subdatasheet shown in Figure 2.52.

Figure 2.52: tblHousehold with subdatasheet displayed

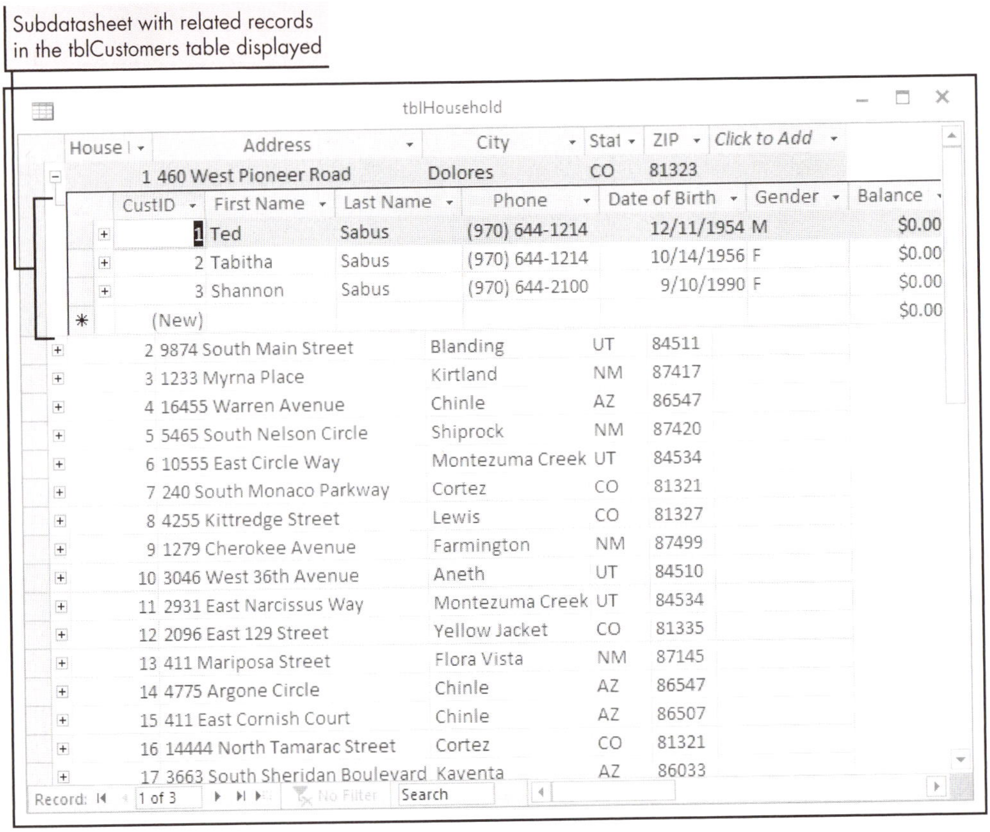

Subdatasheet with related records
in the tblCustomers table displayed

House I ▾	Address	▾	City	▾	Stat ▾	ZIP ▾	Click to Add ▾
	1 460 West Pioneer Road		Dolores		CO	81323	

CustID ▾	First Name ▾	Last Name ▾	Phone ▾	Date of Birth ▾	Gender ▾	Balance ▾
1 Ted		Sabus	(970) 644-1214	12/11/1954	M	$0.00
2 Tabitha		Sabus	(970) 644-1214	10/14/1956	F	$0.00
3 Shannon		Sabus	(970) 644-2100	9/10/1990	F	$0.00
(New)						$0.00

2	9874 South Main Street	Blanding	UT	84511
3	1233 Myrna Place	Kirtland	NM	87417
4	16455 Warren Avenue	Chinle	AZ	86547
5	5465 South Nelson Circle	Shiprock	NM	87420
6	10555 East Circle Way	Montezuma Creek	UT	84534
7	240 South Monaco Parkway	Cortez	CO	81321
8	4255 Kittredge Street	Lewis	CO	81327
9	1279 Cherokee Avenue	Farmington	NM	87499
10	3046 West 36th Avenue	Aneth	UT	84510
11	2931 East Narcissus Way	Montezuma Creek	UT	84534
12	2096 East 129 Street	Yellow Jacket	CO	81335
13	411 Mariposa Street	Flora Vista	NM	87145
14	4775 Argone Circle	Chinle	AZ	86547
15	411 East Cornish Court	Chinle	AZ	86507
16	14444 North Tamarac Street	Cortez	CO	81321
17	3663 South Sheridan Boulevard	Kaventa	AZ	86033

Record: I◄ ◄ 1 of 3 ► ►I ► No Filter Search

When Don clicks the plus box for a record in a table that has a one-to-many relationship, the subdatasheet displays records from the related table. In Figure 2.52, Don uses the subdatasheet to see that the customers living in HouseID 1 are Ted, Tabitha, and Shannon Sabus. You can display or hide the subdatasheet for any record in the primary table by clicking the expand or collapse indicator, respectively. In addition, you can use the subdatasheet to make changes to the related records, and the subdatasheet will display those changes. The changes are also made in the related table.

The tblCustomer subdatasheet also displays with plus signs. Even though tblHousehold is the primary table and the related field in tblCustomer is displayed as the subdatasheet, there are plus signs in this subdatasheet as well. These plus signs indicate that tblCustomer is related to an additional table, which is tblRx. Clicking the plus sign in the tblCustomer subdatasheet displays additional related records from tblRx that can be viewed or edited. See Figure 2.53.

Figure 2.53: tblCustomer with subdatasheet from tblRx displayed

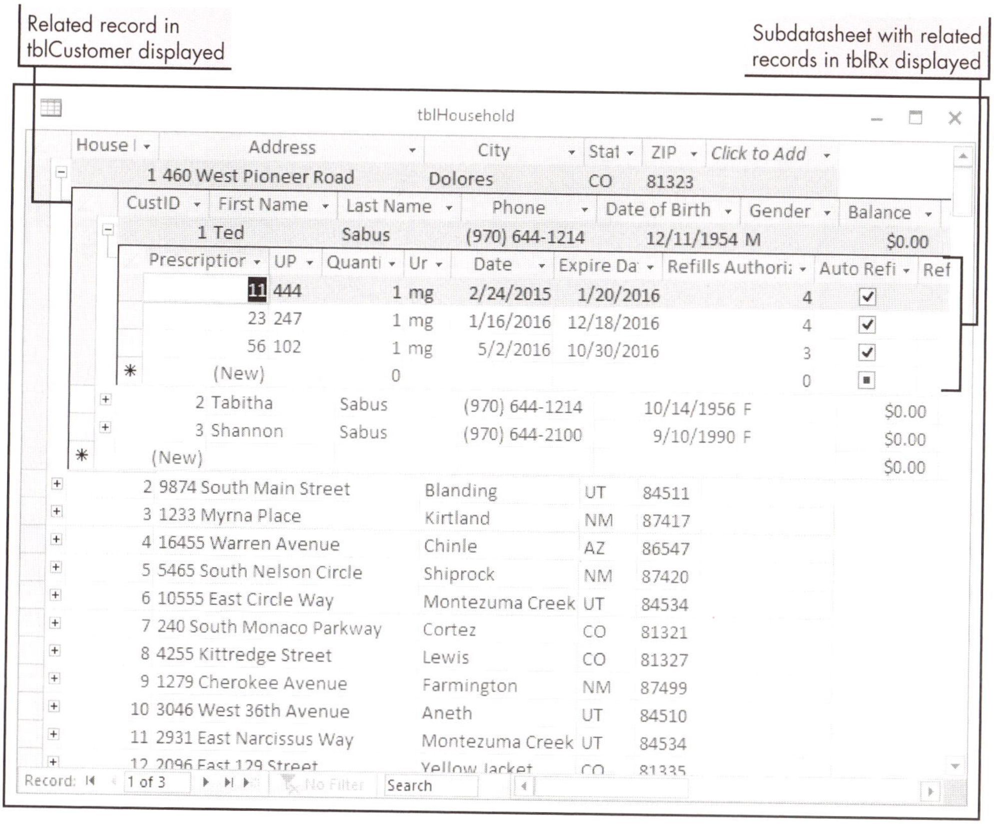

Related record in
tblCustomer displayed

Subdatasheet with related
records in tblRx displayed

Don knows that using these subdatasheets allows for quick viewing and editing of related records. He will certainly show other 4Corners employees the benefits of using subdatasheets.

Steps To Success: Level 2

In the Steps To Success for Level 1, you created the database for Hudson Bay Pharmacy and created the nine tables: tblClass, tblCustomer, tblDoctor, tblDrug, tblEmployee, tblHealthPlan, tblHousehold, tblJobTitle, and tblRx. The only table that contains data at this point is tblJobTitle. Don asks you to create the remaining tables in the database (tblClinic, tblEmployeeTraining, and tblRefill) and to populate the database with data using various sources that he has provided to you. You also need to relate the appropriate tables to each other.

Complete the following:

1. Start Access and open the Hudson.accdb database from the STS folder.

2. Populate the existing database tables. The files you need are saved in the STS folder. Remember that you might need to delete input masks and make other adjustments as necessary for importing to work.

   a. Use the file hbpClass.xlsx to populate tblClass.

   b. Use the file hbpHhold.xlsx to populate tblHousehold.

   c. Use the file hbpCust.xlsx to populate tblCustomer.

   d. Use the file hbpHPlan.xlsx to populate tblHealthPlan.

   e. Use the file hbpDrug.xlsx to populate tblDrug.

   f. Use the file hbpRx.xlsx to populate tblRx.

   g. Use the file hbpEmp.xlsx to populate tblEmployee.

   h. Copy and paste the records in the Doctor table in the hbpDoc.accdb database into tblDoctor in the Hudson.accdb database.

3. Create tblClinic by importing data from the file hbpClin.xlsx. Be certain the table meets the following requirements:

   - Add a ClinicID field and make it the table's primary key.
   - The ClinicName cannot exceed 50 characters.
   - The Address1, Address2, and City fields cannot exceed 40 characters.
   - The default value for the Prov field is "AB" and all values entered into this field must be uppercase and two characters in length.
   - Values in the PostalCode field must appear in the following format: uppercase letter, number, uppercase letter, space, number, uppercase letter, number (for example, T6H 8U7).
   - The Phone field stores 15 characters, displays values in the format of (###) ###-####, and area code entry is required.
   - All fields must have appropriate captions and field descriptions.

4. Create tblEmployeeTraining using the following information:

   - The EmpID and ClassID fields store numbers with no decimal places and are foreign keys.
   - The Date field stores the date of the training session. Display the date using the format ##/##/####.
   - Set the composite primary key, add captions to appropriate fields, and add appropriate field descriptions to all fields.
   - Use the hbpEmpTr.xlsx file to populate the table.

5. Create tblRefill using the following information:

- The PrescriptionID and the EmpID fields store numbers with no decimal places and are foreign keys.
- The RefillDate field stores the date the prescription was refilled. Display the date using the format ##/##/####.
- Set the composite primary key, add captions to appropriate fields, and add appropriate field descriptions to all fields.
- Use the hbpRefl.xlsx file to populate the table.

6. Create an index on the CustLast field in tblCustomer and on the Name field in tblDrug.

7. Create the appropriate relationships in the database.

8. Close the Hudson.accdb database.

LEVEL 3

Maintaining and Securing a Database

The Database Administrator Role

The 4Corners database now contains 12 related tables that store the data needed to dispense prescriptions to customers of the pharmacy. Don populated the tables with the existing data he gathered during the discovery phase. It might be tempting to think that the database is "finished" at this point, but it is not. Don knows that there are other tasks he needs to complete before bringing the database online for users. These tasks include securing the database, backing up and restoring the database, archiving data, and compacting and repairing the database. He also needs to document the database design for himself and other database users. Collectively, these tasks are known as maintaining a database. Most organizations assign these tasks to **database administration**, also known as **DBA**. In many organizations, DBA is a group that is responsible for designing, maintaining, and securing the database. In other organizations, DBA is assigned to an individual who is charged with these tasks; sometimes, this individual is called the **database administrator**. At 4Corners Pharmacy, Don is the database administrator. The database administrator sets the security and other features of a database in addition to setting options for individual users and groups of users.

When you open an Access database, the default option is to open it so that it is available to other users should they choose to open the same database at the same time. To change the way you open a database, click the FILE tab, select the Open command, and then choose the location and file you want to open. In the lower-right corner of the Open dialog box, click the Open button arrow to display the available open options, as shown in Figure 2.54.

Figure 2.54: Open dialog box in Access

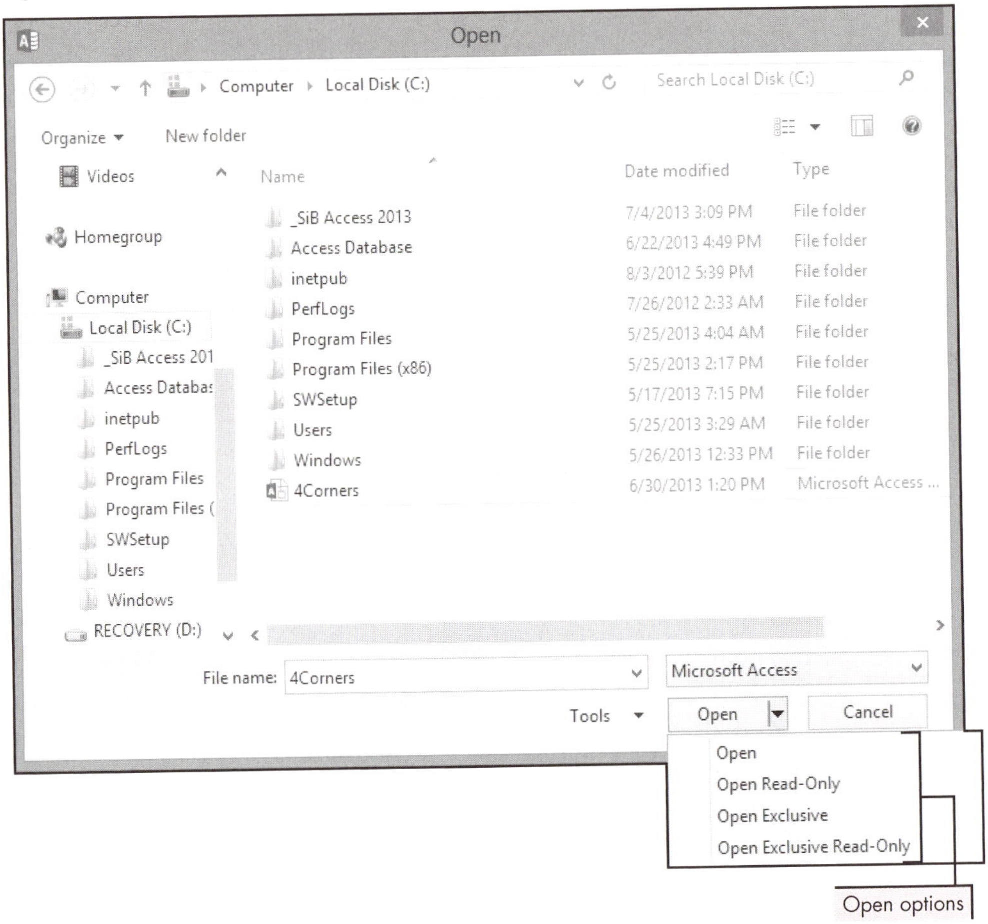

You can open an Access database in several ways:

- **Open mode** allows multiple users to open and use the database at the same time. This is the default option for opening a database.
- **Open Read-Only mode** allows multiple users to open a database, but they cannot write any information to the database, such as adding or changing records or creating new objects. Users are limited to viewing existing data only.
- **Open Exclusive mode** opens the database so that all users except for the current user are locked out from opening and using the database at the same time. A database administrator uses this option to open the database prior to setting a password or database security.
- **Open Exclusive Read-Only mode** opens the database so that all users except for the current user are locked out, but the current user can only view the data in the database.

As the database administrator, Don must have exclusive access to the database to perform database maintenance and set security options without other users having access to it. Don knows that there are no other users accessing the database, so he can perform some of these tasks now. He begins by opening the database in exclusive mode.

How To

Open a Database in Exclusive Mode

1. Start Access, click the FILE tab on the Ribbon, and then click the Open command. Choose a location, then click Browse. The Open dialog box opens.
2. Navigate to the file location and select the database you want to open.
3. Click the Open button arrow to display the options.
4. Click Open Exclusive.

With all other users locked out from the 4Corners database, Don can maintain the database and set the security options. First, he will compact, repair, and back up the database.

Compacting and Repairing a Database

As users work in a database by adding and deleting records and objects, the size of the database increases and decreases. However, the space created by deleting a record or object is not automatically recovered for use by records and objects that users add to the database. Just like any other computer file, a database becomes large with blocks of unused space. These unused areas can ultimately increase the database size and make it inefficient. The process of recovering unused space in a database is known as compacting the database. When you **compact** a database, the data and objects in the database are reorganized and unused spaces are reassigned and deleted. The end result is usually a database with a decreased file size and improved efficiency.

Don knows that it is extremely important to maintain the integrity of the database by doing such procedures as compacting and repairing the database. He also knows from previous experience that backing up the database at regular intervals before compacting and repairing the database is a good procedure. There are two options for compacting the database: You can compact the database manually when you feel it is needed, or you can set the database to compact automatically each time it closes.

When the database is open, you can manually compact a database. You click the FILE tab, select the Info command, and then click the Compact & Repair Database utility, as shown in Figure 2.55.

Figure 2.55: Compact & Repair Database utility in Backstage view

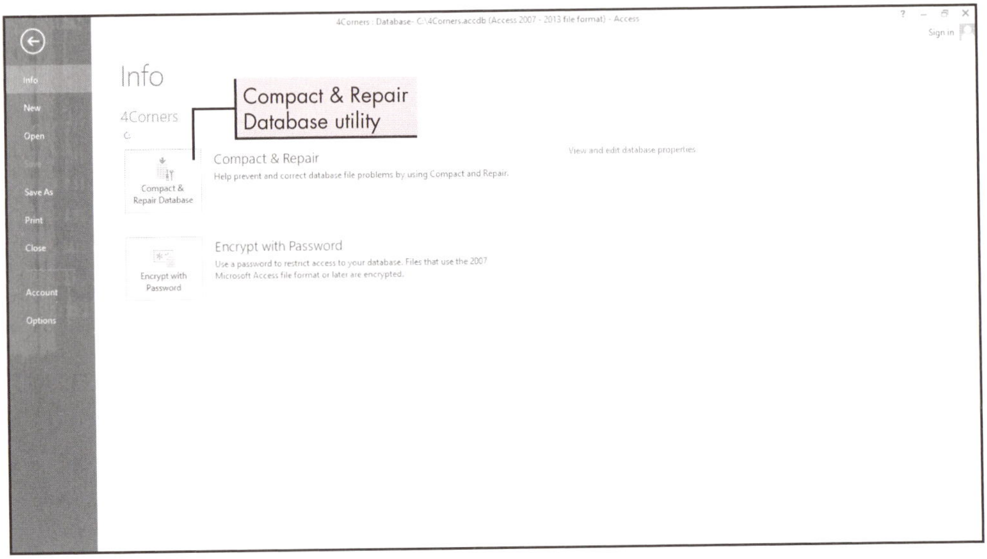

You can also set an option so the database automatically compacts and repairs each time it is closed. To set the database to compact each time it closes, Don clicks the FILE tab, selects the Options command to open the Access Options dialog box, and then selects Current Database in the list of Access options. See Figure 2.56.

Figure 2.56: Compact on Close option in Current Database settings

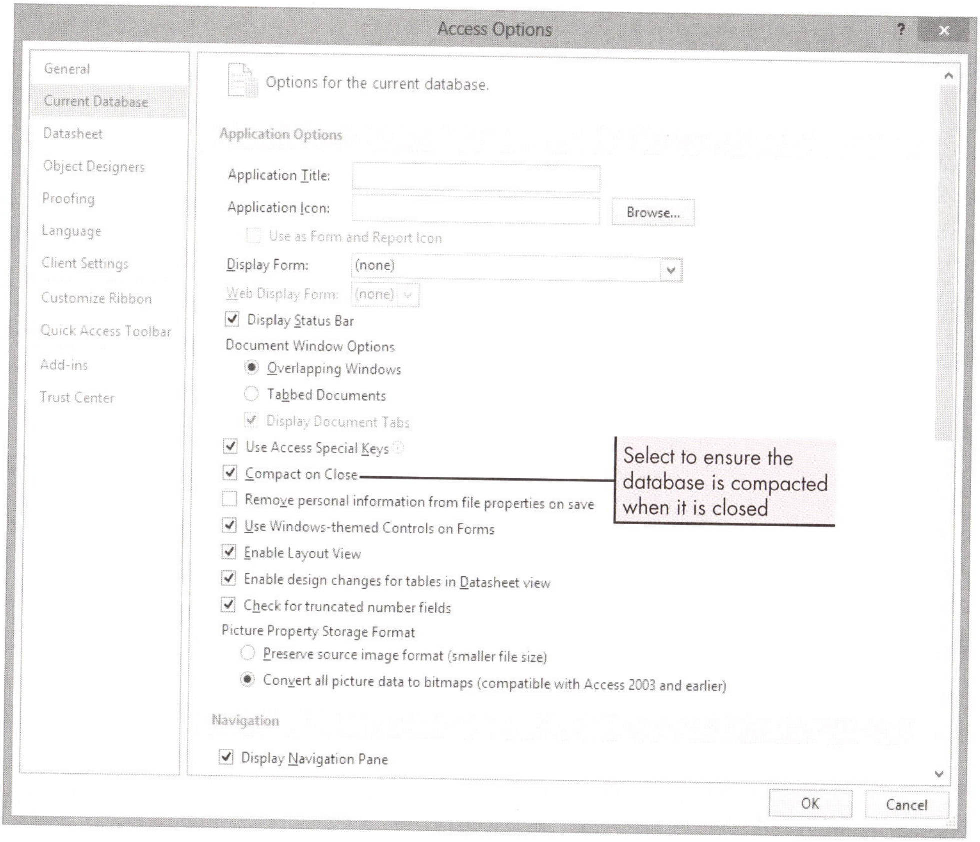

Don clicks the Compact on Close check box to select it. After clicking the OK button, Access compacts the database each time it is closed. It is important to note that setting the Compact on Close option does not repair the database. Even when the Compact on Close option has been set, you can run the Compact & Repair Database utility periodically to repair any problems in the database. Don notices that the 4Corners database was just over 1 MB in size before he compacted it manually. After compacting, the database size decreased to about 432 KB, which is less than half the original size. Don's next task is to back up the database so he has another copy of it in case of damage or loss.

Best Practice

Compacting a Database Before Backing Up a Database

Even if you have been compacting a database on a regular basis, either by running the Compact & Repair Database utility or by setting the Compact on Close option, it is a good idea to compact the database immediately prior to performing a backup. When you back up a database, any unused areas become a part of the backup file. By compacting the database first, you might reduce the size of the backup file because unused spaces will not be included.

Backing Up a Database

Now that Don has compacted the database, he wants to create a backup copy. **Backing up** a database creates a copy of the database that you can restore in the event of a loss. A loss might be caused by a power failure or hard disk crash, a user who maliciously or accidentally deletes database objects, or any other situation that affects the records and objects in the database. Most database administrators perform regular database backups for each day the database is used. A good rule of thumb is to schedule database backups based on the amount of data loss that you can manage. If you cannot manage reentering all of the transactions completed in a week's time, you should schedule backups more frequently than once a week. It is not uncommon for an organization to back up a database nightly, after all users have completed their work.

After creating a backup copy of the database, it is important to store the copy in a fireproof location, preferably at a location outside the pharmacy. In most cases, a backup is created on external media, such as a CD, DVD, USB Flash Drive, or external hard drive. Many organizations store multiple backup copies of their databases in multiple locations. This protects them from losing their business data in the event that a fire or other disaster destroys their company headquarters.

To back up the database, Don clicks the FILE tab, clicks the Save As command, selects the Back Up Database option, and then clicks the Save As button, as shown in Figure 2.57. The Save As dialog box opens.

Figure 2.57: Back Up Database option in Backstage view

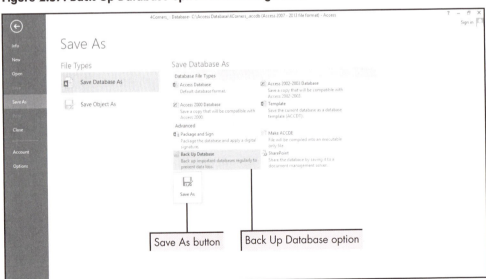

The default backup database name is the original database name followed by the current date. You can accept this default filename or create a new one. To start the backup process, Don clicks the Save button. Depending on the size of the database, it might take anywhere from a few minutes to several hours to complete the task. When the backup utility is complete, Access reopens the database.

The backup copy of the database is a copy that you can open just like any other Access database. In the event of loss in the master copy of the database, Don could copy the backup copy to the computer. In this case, he would need to identify any changes that were made between the time of the loss in the original database and the time he installed the backup copy because the backup might not contain all of the data he needs to restore.

The next task Don wants to complete is to document the database objects so he has a record of each table, including the fields in the table and their properties.

Documenting the Database Design

After you finish the initial database design, it is a good idea to document the design so you have it for future reference. In Access, the **Database Documenter** tool produces a report of every object or just selected objects in a database. Don wants to document all of his table designs. Because tables are the only objects in the current database, he will select the option to document every object using the Database Documenter. To run the Database Documenter, Don clicks the DATABASE TOOLS tab and then clicks the Database Documenter button in the Analyze group. The Documenter dialog box opens, as shown in Figure 2.58.

Figure 2.58: Documenter dialog box

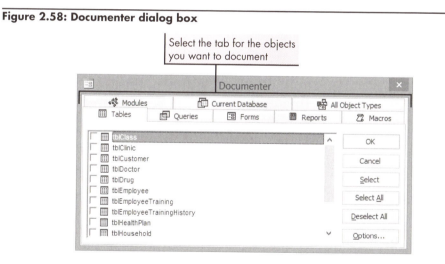

The tabs at the top of the Documenter dialog box let you select objects by type. The All Object Types tab includes all objects in the current database. Selecting the Current Database tab lets you document the properties of objects or the relationships of objects that you select. Because the 4Corners database contains only tables, Don clicks the Tables tab and then clicks the Select All button, which adds a check mark to each table's check box. Clicking the Options button on this tab opens the Print Table Definition dialog box shown in Figure 2.59.

Figure 2.59: Print Table Definition dialog box

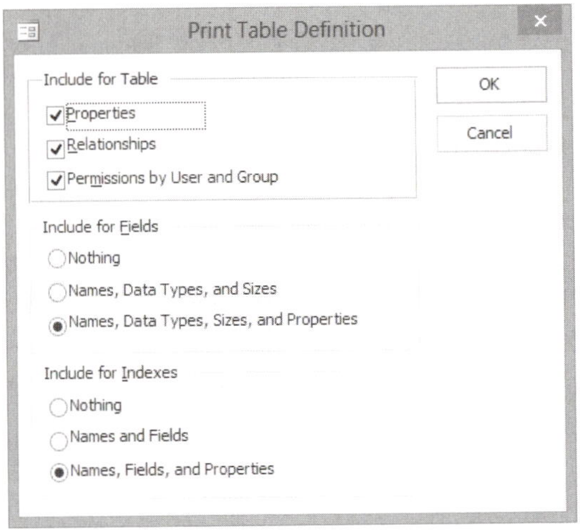

The options in the Print Table Definition dialog box let you specify what to document for each table. You can include table properties, relationships, and permissions; names, data types, field sizes, and field properties for fields; and names, fields, and properties for indexes. Don wants to include the table relationships, names and data types, so he selects these options. When he clicks the OK button in the Documenter dialog box, Access creates an **Object Definition report**. The first page of this report appears in Figure 2.60.

Figure 2.60: Page 1 of the Object Definition report

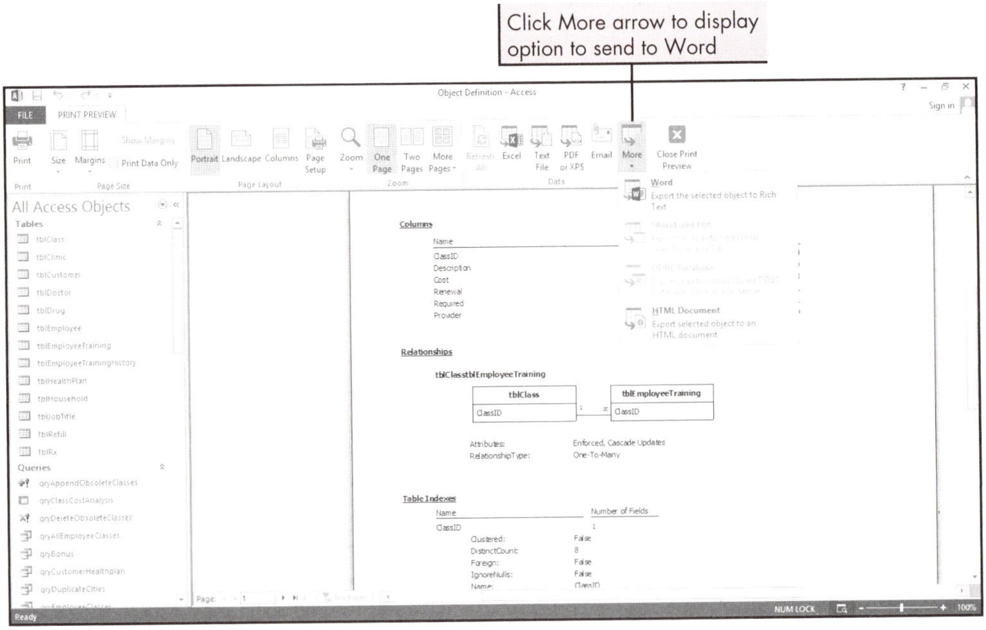

Don can use the Print button in the Print group on the PRINT PREVIEW tab to print the report so he can file it away in a safe place. He can also export the file as a Rich Text Format (RTF) file by clicking the More button arrow in the Data group on the PRINT PREVIEW tab and selecting the Word option. After printing the report, Don clicks the Close Print Preview button.

Securing a Database from Unauthorized Use

Even though Don will create regular backup copies of the database, it is still very important to plan for and prevent data loss in the first place. One of Don's most important tasks is to protect the database from unintentional or malicious damage. Access includes several features that let you control access to a database. These features include setting a database password, encrypting a database, and hiding database objects. In most cases, the database administrator will open the database with exclusive access in order to set these protection features.

Using Database Encryption

In addition to protecting the pharmacy's data, Don is responsible for making sure the pharmacy protects its customer and employee data. The 4Corners database stores personal information about customers and employees, such as Social Security numbers, phone and address information, salary data, and prescription information. The potential exists for an employee to use information in the database inappropriately or for a hacker to gain access to the database and use it in an identity theft scheme. Don knows that the pharmacy is responsible for maintaining and protecting private information and customers must feel confident that the pharmacy is taking steps to protect their data from fraud and abuse.

The easiest way to secure a database from unauthorized use is to set a password. A **password** is a collection of characters that a user types to gain access to a file. When a database administrator sets a database password, users cannot open the database file in Access unless they provide the correct password. As long as the database administrator and users who know the password protect it from being known by unauthorized users, the password can adequately protect the database.

Access 2013 combines two tools for database security: encryption and database passwords. When you **encrypt** a database with a password, the data is made unreadable by other tools. This combined safety feature provides a stronger algorithm, or protection, than previous versions of Access.

Don might want to set a password for the 4Corners database. Because the database is already open in Exclusive mode, the Encrypt with Password option appears when Don clicks the FILE tab and then clicks the Info command. When he clicks the Encrypt with Password option, the Set Database Password dialog box opens, as shown in Figure 2.61.

Figure 2.61: Set Database Password dialog box

To set a database password, Don would type a password in the Password box, press the Tab key, and then type the same password in the Verify box. When he clicks the OK button, Access requests the password from the next user who attempts to open the database. If the user fails to provide the correct password in the Password Required dialog box that opens, Access does not open the database. Don can give the password to users as necessary to provide them with the ability to open the database.

If Don decides to remove the password, he could click the Decrypt Database option that appears in place of the Encrypt with Password option. He would then enter the password and click the OK button.

At this time, Don decides not to set a password until he brings the database online for employee use. The password will prevent customers and vendors who are in the store from being able to access the database. He is confident that the password will protect the pharmacy's data.

Best Practice

Choosing a Strong Password

When creating a password for a database, it is important to select a password that is easy to remember so it is easy to use. However, some users choose passwords that are easy to remember but are also very easy for another person to guess, such as the name of a pet, child, or spouse, or a date of birth or anniversary. Security experts suggest that users create *strong passwords*, which are character strings that contain at least seven characters consisting of combinations of uppercase and lowercase letters, numbers, and symbols. Random collections of characters are much harder to guess or break because the combination of characters is not a word. In any program that requests a password, choose a strong password over one that is a simple word. Even if your password is 5&uJK#8, you will learn it quickly if you type it frequently. It is always best with sensitive databases to require logins and passwords to access them or perhaps keep the databases on separate workstations.

Hiding Database Objects from Users

Don designed the 4Corners database so that all objects in a database are accessible to all users through the Navigation pane. As the database administrator, Don is skilled at manipulating database objects for the benefit of users. Novice users who do not have Don's experience can damage the database by unintentionally altering an object's design or by deleting an object entirely. Another simple technique to add some security to the database is to hide objects from being displayed in the Navigation pane. These objects are still part of the database and interact with other objects but are not visible to the novice user. The advantage of hiding objects is that the user will not be able to accidentally or intentionally damage the database. Unfortunately, revealing a hidden object is not difficult and a user who knows Access or how to use the Access Help system could learn how to reveal hidden objects.

Don might protect the data in tblEmployee, which contains employees' Social Security numbers and salary information, from being viewed by the pharmacy's staff. To hide tblEmployee, Don right-clicks the table in the Navigation pane and clicks Table Properties on the shortcut menu to open the Properties dialog box for tblEmployee, as shown in Figure 2.62.

Figure 2.62: Properties dialog box for tblEmployee

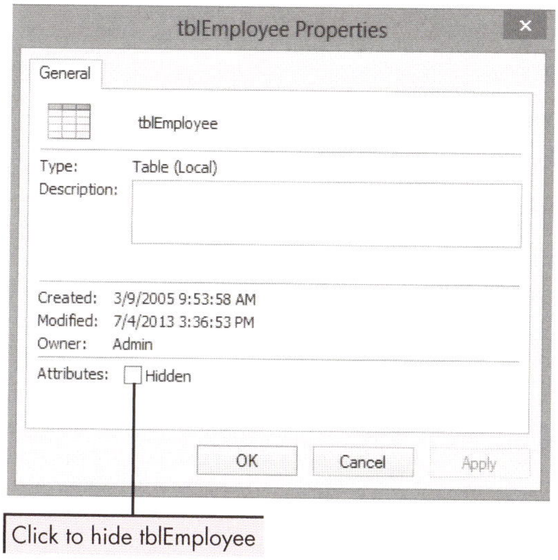

Click to hide tblEmployee

To hide tblEmployee, Don would click the Hidden check box to select it. When he clicks the OK button, tblEmployee will no longer appear in the Navigation pane. Maria Garcia, the pharmacy's Human Resources manager, will need to access this table. Don can show her how to reveal hidden objects by right-clicking the Tables bar at the top of the Navigation pane and selecting Navigation Options. If Maria clicks the Show Hidden Objects check box to select it, tblEmployee will be visible in the Navigation pane again. Figure 2.63 shows the Navigation Options dialog box.

Figure 2.63: Navigation Options dialog box

Click to display
hidden objects

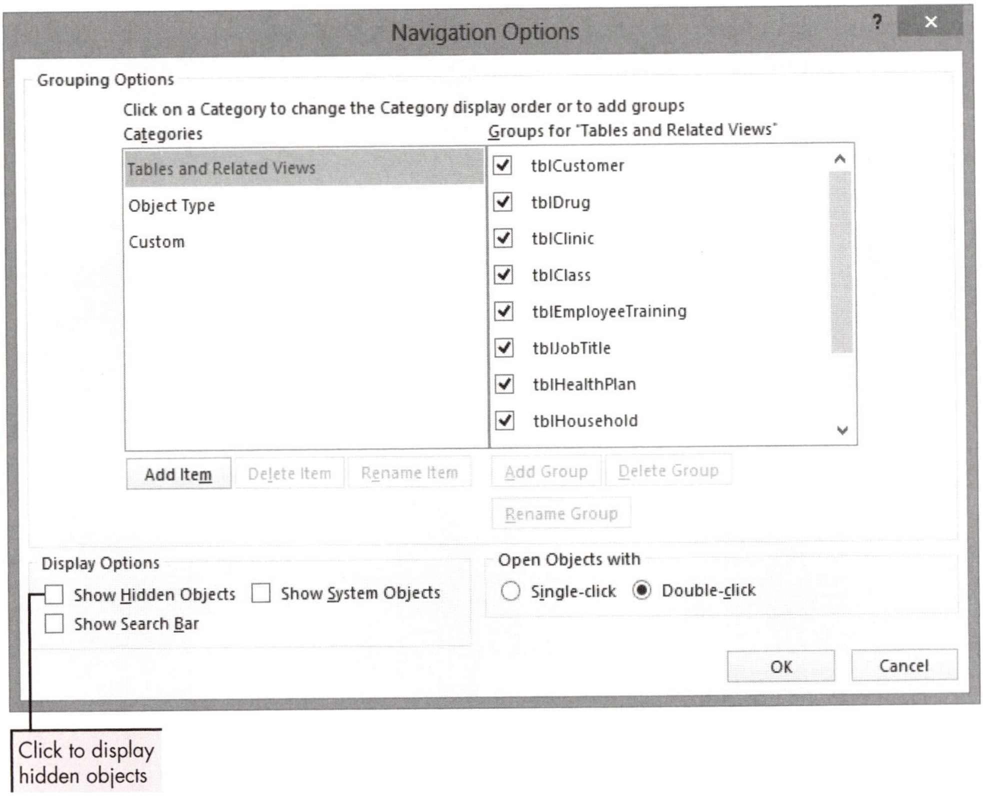

Hidden database objects remain visible unless you remove the check mark from the Show Hidden Objects check box in the Navigation Options dialog box. To permanently restore a hidden object, open the Properties dialog box for the object, and then clear the Hidden check box.

Don decides not to hide database objects because Access has better and more secure techniques for hiding objects from users. In Chapter 6, you will learn more about hiding objects from users.

Steps To Success: Level 3

With the tables created, Don wants to protect the Hudson database and improve its operation.

1. Start Access and open the Hudson.accdb database in Exclusive mode from the STS folder.

2. Run the Compact & Repair Database utility, and then set the option to compact the database when you close it.

3. Create a backup copy of the Hudson database and save it using the default filename in the STS folder.

4. Document the designs for all tables in the database. Include the table relationships and the field names, data types, and field sizes in the report. Export the report as an RTF file using the default filename and save it in the STS folder.

5. Suggest three strong passwords that you could use to secure the Hudson database, but do not set any passwords.

6. Close the Hudson.accdb database.

Chapter Summary

This chapter presented the different ways to transform a database design into a collection of related tables in an Access database. In Level 1, you learned how to use Datasheet view and Design view to create tables. You also learned how to create fields in a table, how to set their data types, and how to set properties that format data and ensure its accuracy. These properties included setting a field's caption, formatting values using an input mask, validating fields to ensure accurate and consistent data, and entering a default value in a field. You also learned how to create a lookup field to automate data entry in a field.

In Level 2, you learned how to populate the tables in the database by copying records from one table to another and by importing data from another Access database or from an Excel workbook. Copying or importing existing data into a database saves data entry time and reduces the risk of incorrect data, but it also is subject to problems. You learned how to troubleshoot problems, such as importing data with mismatched data types and nonmatching values into a related table's foreign key field when there are no matching values in the primary table's primary key field. You also learned how to create relationships in a database, how to create an index on a nonprimary key field, how to set a field's properties to require data entry, and how to create a composite primary key. Finally, you learned how to view related records using a subdatasheet.

In Level 3, you examined the role of the database administrator and his duties of securing and maintaining a database. The database administrator provides database maintenance, including compacting and repairing a database, creating and storing database backups, and documenting the database design. The database administrator is also charged with securing the database by setting a password and encrypting the database and hiding database objects.

Conceptual Review

1. Describe the two methods presented in this chapter for creating a table in Access.

2. What are the rules for naming objects in Access?

3. Write the input mask to control data entry in a field so that users can enter only three uppercase letters followed by three digits.

4. How do you validate a field and inform users of the validation rule?

5. Give three examples not presented in this chapter of how you might use a lookup field to control data entry into a table.

6. Describe how to import data from an Access table into an existing table.

7. Can you set a primary key field so it accepts null values? Why or why not?

8. Can you set a nonprimary key field to accept null values? If so, give three examples not presented in this chapter of fields that might contain null values.

9. Name one advantage and one disadvantage for setting a field's Required property to Yes.

10. What are the three values for the Indexed property? Give one example not presented in this chapter of how you might use each Index value for a field in a table that stores data about employees.

11. How do you create a many-to-many relationship between two tables in Access?

12. What is a subdatasheet? Can you change the values in the records displayed by the subdatasheet?

13. What is DBA?

14. Describe the four Open modes available when opening an Access database.

15. What happens to a database's size and content when you compact it?

16. What is the Database Documenter?

17. How does encrypting a database provide security?

Case Problems

Level 1 – Creating the Database for NHD Development Group Inc.

In Chapter 1, you created the database design for NHD Development Group to use at the Memories Antique Mall in Cleveland, TN. Tim Richards, the company's chief information officer, reviewed your database design and did some additional work to finalize it. Now you will use Access to create the database. Figure 2.64 shows the database design that Tim approved.

Tim is confident that the design will satisfy all of the user requirements and output the data he needs to manage the mall. With the design approved, you can begin developing the database.

Information Systems

Figure 2.64: Database design for NHD

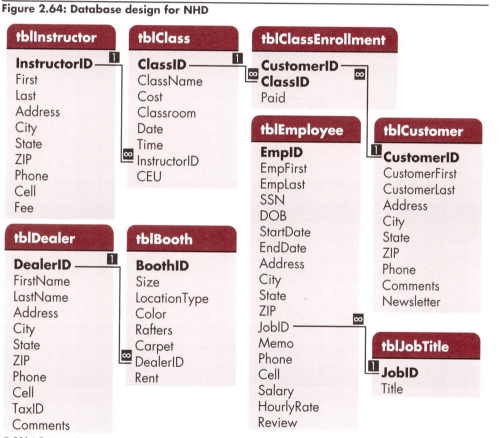

© 2014 Cengage Learning

Complete the following:

1. Compare the database design you developed in Chapter 1 with the one shown in Figure 2.64. If necessary, change your database and table designs to match the ones shown in the figure. If necessary, add or change fields in your table designs, setting the properties that will support the data being stored in those fields.

2. Start Access and create a new database named **Antiques.accdb** in the Case 1 folder.

3. While Tim was working with your design, he learned that the mall's manager, Linda Sutherland, already built the portion of the database related to classes using Excel worksheets. He opens each of the worksheets to determine if the data will import correctly into the tables he created. All the data pertaining to classes is stored in the Excel files located in the Case 1 folder.

4. Follow your database design to create the remaining tables in the Antiques database using any method you choose. Be certain to specify the field names, data types, field descriptions, and field sizes as you create each table. Create validation rules and validation text, input masks, field captions, default values, and lookup fields as necessary to ensure that users enter consistent, complete, and accurate data in the tables. From the discovery phase, Tim and Linda gathered the following information that you need to consider in your table designs:

   - Tax ID numbers for dealers are unique.
   - The valid booth locations at the mall are Inside Perimeter, Outside Perimeter, and Aisle. (On Linda's map—see Figure 1.37 in Chapter 1—booths that line the outside edge of the mall are outside perimeter booths, booths across from outside perimeter booths are inside perimeter booths, and booths on the inside rows are aisle booths.)
   - Valid booth sizes are 8×8, 8×10, 8×12, 8×16, 8×20, 12×8, 12×10, 12×12, and 12×18.

5. After creating all of the tables in the database, create the relationships between the tables, as shown in Figure 2.64. Enforce referential integrity in each relationship and cascade updates.

6. Now that you have all the tables set up, you can import the existing data Tim and Linda provided during the discovery phase into your tables. Prior to importing this data, open the files and carefully review the data to identify and correct any compatibility errors between your table and the imported data. If you encounter errors, make the appropriate adjustments in your database, and then populate the existing database tables. The files you need are located in the Case 1 folder.

7. Use Table 2.10 to enter data into tblJobTitle.

Table 2.10: Data for tblJobTitle

JobID	Title
1	Manager
2	Assistant Manager
3	Sales
4	Maintenance
5	Accounting
6	Administrative Assistant

© 2014 Cengage Learning

8. Check all your tables for accuracy and ensure that all your relationships have been established according to the design shown in Figure 2.64.

9. Set the option to compact the database when you close it.

10. Close the Antiques.accdb database.

Level 2 – Creating the Database for MovinOn Inc.

In Chapter 1, you created the database design for MovinOn Inc. The database will be used to manage data about the company and its operations. David Powers, the company's general manager, and Robert Iko, the company's information systems specialist, reviewed your database design and worked to finalize it. Figure 2.65 shows the database design that David and Robert approved.

Information Systems

Figure 2.65: Database design for MovinOn

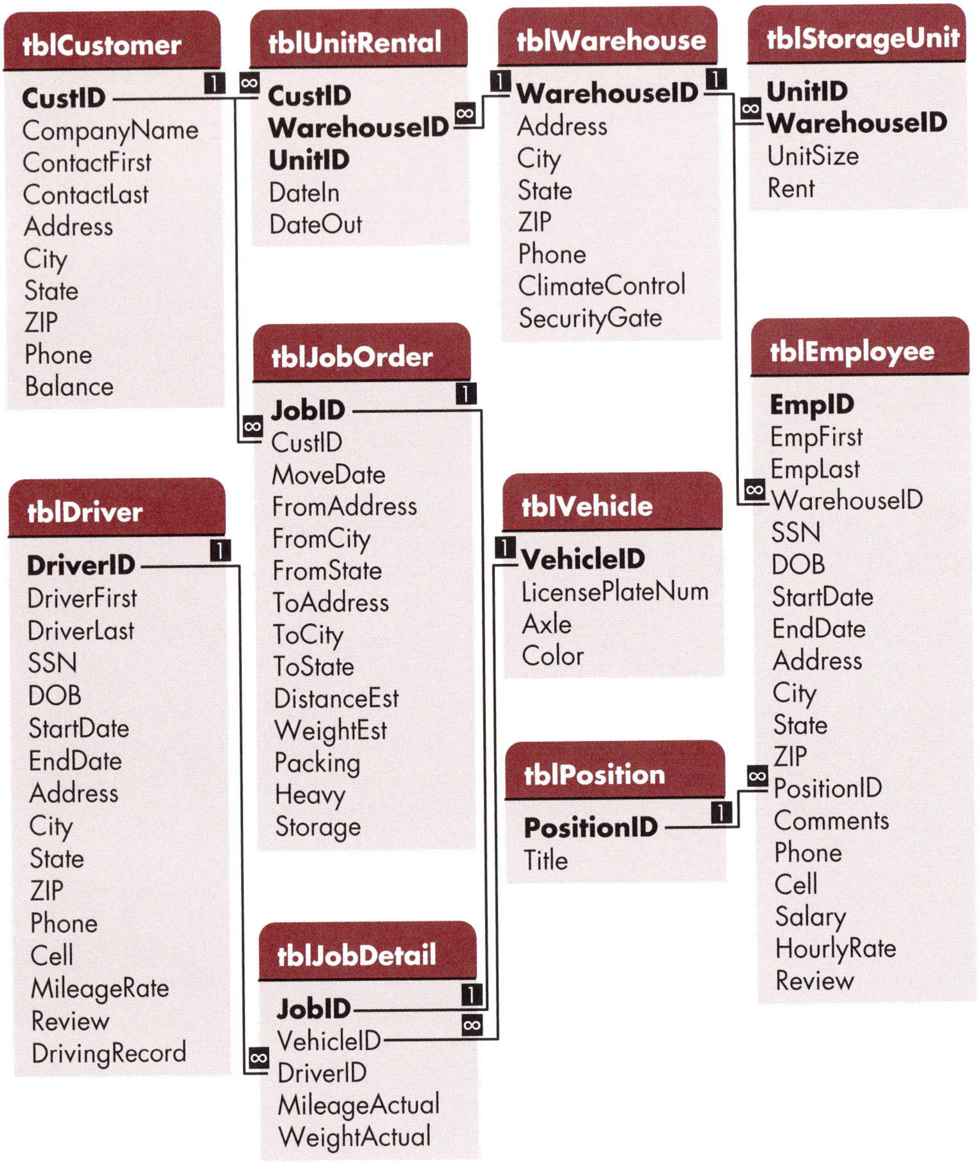

tblCustomer

CustID
CompanyName
ContactFirst
ContactLast
Address
City
State
ZIP
Phone
Balance

tblUnitRental

CustID
WarehouseID
UnitID
DateIn
DateOut

tblWarehouse

WarehouseID
Address
City
State
ZIP
Phone
ClimateControl
SecurityGate

tblStorageUnit

UnitID
WarehouseID
UnitSize
Rent

tblJobOrder

JobID
CustID
MoveDate
FromAddress
FromCity
FromState
ToAddress
ToCity
ToState
DistanceEst
WeightEst
Packing
Heavy
Storage

tblEmployee

EmpID
EmpFirst
EmpLast
WarehouseID
SSN
DOB
StartDate
EndDate
Address
City
State
ZIP
PositionID
Comments
Phone
Cell
Salary
HourlyRate
Review

tblDriver

DriverID
DriverFirst
DriverLast
SSN
DOB
StartDate
EndDate
Address
City
State
ZIP
Phone
Cell
MileageRate
Review
DrivingRecord

tblVehicle

VehicleID
LicensePlateNum
Axle
Color

tblPosition

PositionID
Title

tblJobDetail

JobID
VehicleID
DriverID
MileageActual
WeightActual

© 2014 Cengage Learning

David and Robert are satisfied that the design shown in Figure 2.65 will satisfy all of the user requirements and output the data needed to manage the business. With the design approved, you can begin developing the database.

Complete the following:

1. Compare the database design you developed in Chapter 1 with the one shown in Figure 2.65. If necessary, change your database and table designs to match the ones shown in the figure. If you determine that you need to add or change fields in your table designs, be certain to carefully consider and then set the properties that will support the data being stored in those fields.

2. Start Access and create a new database named MovinOn.accdb in the Case 2 folder.

3. Use the database design shown in Figure 2.65 as a guide to help you develop the database. Be certain to specify the field names, data types, field descriptions, and field sizes as you create each table. Create validation rules and validation text, input masks, field captions, default values, and lookup fields as necessary to ensure that users enter consistent, complete, and accurate data in the tables. From the discovery phase, David and Robert gathered the following information that you must consider in your table designs:

   • Driving records for drivers are rated using the following values: A, B, C, D, or F. A user should input these values from a list.
   • A user should be able to select the warehouse in which an employee works and the employee's position from a list of values.
   • In tblJobDetail, a user should select the JobID, VehicleID, and DriverID from a list of values.
   • In tblJobOrder and tblUnitRental, a user should select the CustID from a list of values.
   • In tblStorageUnit, a user should select the WarehouseID from a list of values.

4. Check your database carefully to ensure that you have created all the tables, that you have created all the fields and set their properties, and that you have created all the necessary relationships.

5. Use the data shown in Table 2.11 to populate tblPosition.

Table 2.11: Data for tblPosition

PositionID	Title
1	General Manager
2	Warehouse Manager
3	Administrative Assistant
4	Accountant
5	Maintenance
6	Moving Assistant
7	Information Systems

© 2014 Cengage Learning

6. Use the data shown in Table 2.12 to populate tblWarehouse.

Table 2.12: Data for tblWarehouse

Warehouse ID	Address	City	State	ZIP	Phone	Climate Controlled?	Security Gate?
OR-1	#3 Industrial Park Way	Portland	OR	97212	(503) 551-2432	No	Yes
WA-1	8798 Warehouse Rd	Seattle	WA	98121	(206) 324-2312	Yes	Yes
WY-1	54781 Hixson Pike	Jackson Hole	WY	83001	(307) 541-3571	Yes	No

© 2014 Cengage Learning

7. Populate the tables in your database using the data stored in the files located in the Case 2 folder. Before importing the data, review each worksheet in the file and confirm that your table designs are set up correctly.

8. Set the option to compact the database when you close it.

9. Close the MovinOn.accdb database.

Level 3 – Creating the Database for Hershey College

Information Systems

In Chapter 1, you created the initial database design for the new Intramural Department at Hershey College. The department's manager, Marianna Fuentes, provided you with a list of data needs that you used to create the database design. Figure 2.66 shows the database design that Marianna approved.

Figure 2.66: Database design for Hershey College

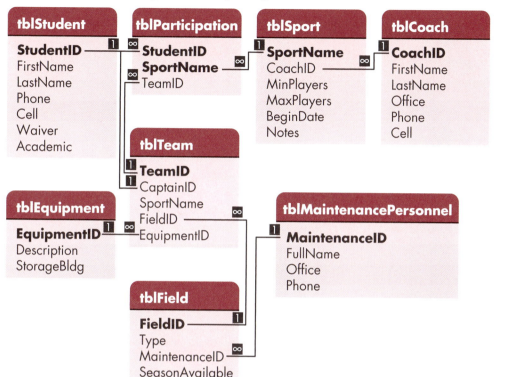

© 2014 Cengage Learning

Marianna is confident that the database design will satisfy all user requirements and output the data needed to manage the department. With the design approved, you can begin developing the database.

Complete the following:

1. Compare the database design you developed in Chapter 1 with the one shown in Figure 2.66. If necessary, change your database and table designs to match the ones shown in the figure. If you determine that you need to add or change fields in your table designs, be certain to carefully consider and then set the properties that will support the data being stored in those fields.

2. Start Access and create a new database named **Hershey.accdb** in the Case 3 folder.

3. Follow your database design to create the tables using any method you choose. Be certain to specify the field names, data types, field descriptions, and field sizes for each table. Create validation rules and validation text, input masks, field captions, default values, and lookup fields as necessary to ensure that users enter consistent, complete, and accurate data in the tables. From the discovery phase, Marianna gathered the following information that you must consider in your table designs:

- There are four storage buildings (SB-1, SB-2, SB-3, and SB-4) in which equipment is stored. In tblEquipment, a user should select equipment locations from a list of values.

- In tblTeam, a user needs to specify the court or field and equipment assigned to the team. Set up the table so that a user can select Storage Bldg and CoachIDs from a list of values, as shown in Figure 2.67.

- Team captains are assigned from the pool of students. Set up the Captain field so that students are selected from a list of valid students. Store the StudentID in the Captain field.

- In tblSport, a user should select the CoachID from a list of values.

Figure 2.67: List of available values for the Storage Bldg field and the CoachID field

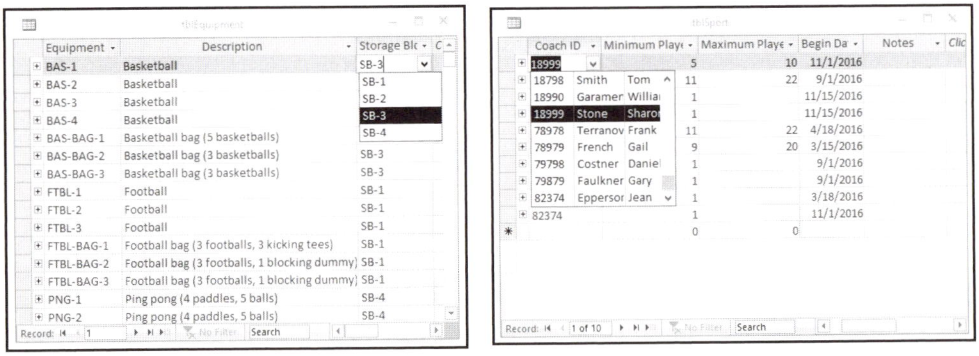

4. Create the relationships between all the tables, as shown in Figure 2.66. Enforce referential integrity in each relationship and cascade updates.

5. With all the tables set up, you can import the existing data you found during the discovery phase into your tables. Prior to importing this data, open the files and carefully review the data to identify and correct any compatibility errors between the tables and the imported data. Make the appropriate adjustments in your database, and then populate the database tables using the files located in the Case 3 folder.

6. Use Table 2.13 to enter the data into tblSport.

Table 2.13: Data for tblSport

Sport Name	Coach ID	Minimum Players	Maximum Players	Begin Date	Notes
Basketball	18999	5	10	11/1/2016	
Football	79798	11	22	9/1/2016	
Ping Pong	18990	1		11/15/2016	
Pool	18990	1		11/15/2016	
Soccer	17893	11	22	4/18/2016	
Softball	18797	9	20	3/15/2016	
Swimming	78979	1		9/1/2016	
Tennis	78979	1		9/1/2016	
Track	79879	1		3/18/2016	
Wrestling	82374	1		11/1/2016	

© 2014 Cengage Learning

7. Run the Compact &Repair Database utility, and then set the option to compact the database when you close it.

8. Create a backup copy of the Hershey database and save it using the default filename.

9. Close the Hershey.accdb database.

SAM: Skills Assessment Manager

For current SAM information, including versions and content details, visit SAM Central (http://samcentral.course.com). If you have a SAM user profile, you may have access to hands-on instruction, practice, and assessment of the skills covered in this chapter. Since various versions of SAM are supported throughout the life of this text, check with your instructor for the correct instructions and URL/Web site for accessing assignments.

Analyzing Data for Effective Decision Making
Human Resources: Managing Employees at 4Corners Pharmacy

"The human problems which I deal with every day—concerning employees as well as customers—are the problems that fascinate me, that seem important to me."
—Hortense Odlum

LEARNING OBJECTIVES

Level 1

Filter and sort data to make it more meaningful
Create simple queries to answer business questions
Develop queries using comparison criteria and wildcards
Display and print query results

Level 2

Design queries that compare data from more than one table
Refine table relationships by specifying the join type
Perform calculations in queries
Customize queries and their results

Level 3

Calculate and restructure data to improve analysis
Examine and create advanced types of queries
Make decisions in a query using the immediate IF (IIF) function
Develop queries using SQL

TOOLS COVERED IN THIS CHAPTER

Action queries (update, append, delete, crosstab, and make-table)
Aggregate functions (Avg, Max, Min, Sum)
Calculated field
Comparison and logical operators
Crosstab query
Filter by Form and Filter by Selection
Find duplicates query
Find unmatched records query
Immediate IF (IIF) function
Parameter query
Design view
Select query
Simple Query Wizard
SQL commands (AS, FROM, GROUP BY, HAVING, ORDER BY, SELECT, WHERE)
Top Values query
Wildcard character

Chapter Introduction

As you add data to a database, it can become increasingly difficult to find the information you need. This chapter begins by showing you how to filter data in a Microsoft Office Access 2013 database so you can retrieve and examine only the records you need. You will also learn how to sort data to rearrange records in a specified order. Next, the chapter focuses on queries, which provide quick answers to business questions, such as which employees earn the highest pay rate, which employees have completed their occupational training requirements, and whether a company should continue to reimburse employees for job-related training. In Level 1, you will learn how to perform simple select queries, which specify only the fields and records Access should select. Level 2 explains how to increase the complexity of queries by using multiple tables and adding options to prepare data for forms and reports. It also explores how to make your queries interactive. Level 3 covers advanced types of queries such as those that update and add records to a table, and explains how to use the Immediate IF function to make decisions in a query and Structured Query Language (SQL) to retrieve data from an Access database.

Case Scenario

Human Resources

Maria Garcia is the human resources manager for 4Corners Pharmacy. Her responsibilities involve hiring and firing employees and making sure they complete the necessary employment paperwork. In addition, she manages employee training, schedules periodic job reviews, and helps analyze compensation and other employee information.

Human Resources

Most of the training sessions that employees of 4Corners Pharmacy attend involve mandatory certification for cardiopulmonary resuscitation (CPR) and the use of defibrillators. Maria needs a way to make sure all employees attend required classes and receive annual certification, as necessary.

Until now, Maria has maintained employee and training information on printed forms that she stores in a filing cabinet. However, it is often inconvenient and time consuming to access and update these forms, especially to answer management questions that require her to analyze data. Maria plans to automate the records by using the 4Corners.accdb database to track employee and training information.

LEVEL 1

Organizing and Retrieving Information From a Database

Filtering and Sorting Data

Paul Ferrino, the owner of 4Corners Pharmacy, periodically reviews the wages he pays to his employees so he can budget for upcoming pay raises. He has recently increased the salaries of the two pharmacists at 4Corners, but he needs to check the hourly rates he pays to the other employees. He asks Maria to list the wages for pharmacy technicians and cashiers, ranked from highest to lowest so he can quickly see the full range of pay for nonsalaried employees.

Four tables in the 4Corners.accdb database contain employee information that Maria needs to perform her management tasks. These tables and their relationships are shown in Figure 3.1 and are described in the following list.

Figure 3.1: Relationships in the 4Corners Pharmacy database

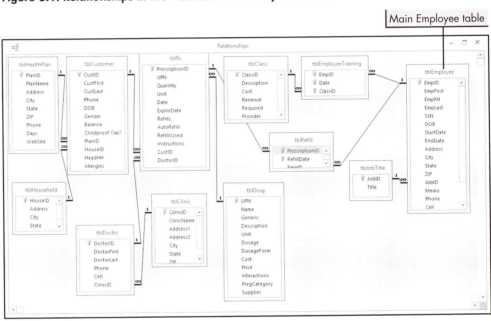

Microsoft product screenshots used with permission from Microsoft Corporation.

- **tblEmployee**—This table contains information about employees, including identifying information such as their ID number, name, Social Security number, contact information such as their address and phone numbers, and employment information such as their starting date, salary or hourly rate, and job ID.
- **tblJobTitle**—This table lists the five job categories at 4Corners Pharmacy by ID number: 1—Owner, 2—Pharmacist, 3—Technician, 4—Cashier, and 5—Manager.
- **tblEmployeeTraining**—This table tracks the training classes that employees attend.
- **tblClass**—This table lists the classes employees can attend to receive required certifications or other professional training.

Maria thinks she can find the information she needs by using a filter and then sorting the results. A filter restricts data in a single table to create a temporary subset of records. A filter allows you to see only certain records in a table based on criteria you specify. Sorting records involves organizing them in a particular order or sequence. You can sort records in a table regardless of whether it's filtered.

Filtering by Selection

Access has two tools for filtering data. They are Filter by Selection and Filter by Form. Filter by Selection lets you select a particular field in a datasheet and then display only data that matches the contents of that field. When you filter by selection, you specify only one criterion for the filter.

Maria first wants to review employment information for pharmacy technicians only. She opens the tblEmployee table, which currently contains 24 records, and clicks the first JobID field that contains a "3." (Recall that pharmacy technicians have a JobID of 3.) Then she clicks the Selection button ▼ located in the Sort & Filter group on the HOME tab and selects Equals 3. Access filters the data by selecting only those records with a "3" in the JobID field, and then displays the filtered results—the employment records for the eight pharmacy technicians. See Figure 3.2.

Figure 3.2: Using Filter by Selection to display a temporary subset of records

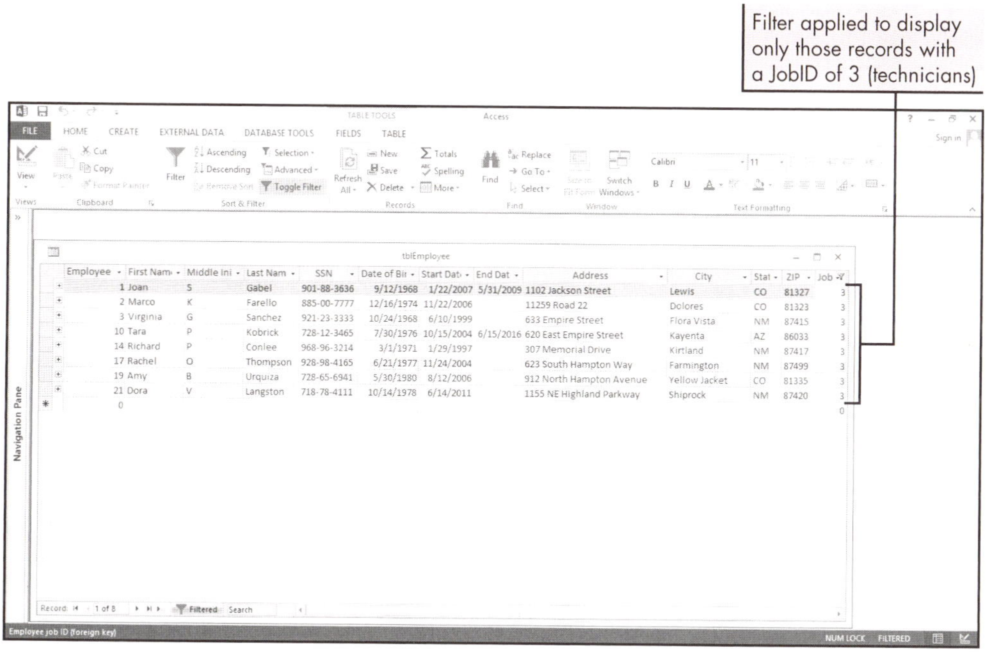

Filter applied to display only those records with a JobID of 3 (technicians)

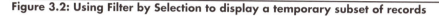

Now Maria can focus on the employment information for technicians, including their hourly rate of pay. After she prints this datasheet, she could remove the filter for displaying technician records and apply a different filter for displaying cashier records. She can also use the Filter by Form tool to display the hourly pay rates for technicians and cashiers at the same time.

Filtering by Form

When you use Filter by Selection you only specify one criterion. When you want to specify two or more criteria, you use Filter by Form. In addition, Filter by Selection filters for records that exactly match the criterion, such as those that contain "3" in the JobID field, while Filter by Form can filter for comparative data, such as those records in which the HourlyRate field value is greater than or equal to $8.00. To enter comparative data, you use comparison operators, such as >= for greater than or equal to. You specify these criteria in a blank version of the datasheet by entering or selecting the data in one or more fields that you want to match. Access displays only those records that contain the data you selected.

Maria wants to view hourly pay rates for employees whose records contain a "3" (for technicians) or "4" (for cashiers) in the JobID field. Because she needs to specify more than one criterion, she will use the Filter by Form tool. Before doing so, however, she notes that a filter is still applied to tblEmployee because Filtered appears in the status bar (shown earlier in Figure 3.2). Maria redisplays all the records in tblEmployee by clicking the Remove Filter button ▼ in the Sort & Filter group in the HOME tab. She could also have clicked the Filtered button next to the record navigation buttons to remove the filter and redisplay all of the records.

Next, she clicks the Advanced Filter Options button 🗐 in the Sort & Filter group and then clicks Filter By Form. A blank version of the tblEmployee datasheet appears in the Filter by Form window. See Figure 3.3.

Figure 3.3: Using Filter by Form to specify more than one criterion

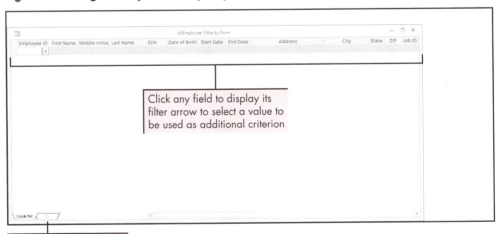

Click any field to display its filter arrow to select a value to be used as additional criterion

Use the Or tab to display additional criteria

To specify the first criterion, she clicks the list arrow in the JobID field to display all of its values, and then clicks 3 (for technician). This means that Access will display records in tblEmployee that contain a "3" in the JobID field. If Maria wanted to display a list of technicians who live in Colorado, she could also click the list arrow in the State field and then click CO. This type of criteria is called AND criteria—it selects records that contain *all* specified values.

However, Maria wants to view records that contain a "3" (technicians) or "4" (cashiers) in the JobID field. This type of criteria is called OR criteria—it selects records that contain *any* of the specified values. To enter an OR criterion, Maria clicks the Or tab at the bottom of the window. Another version of the blank tblEmployee datasheet appears in the Filter by Form window. She clicks the list arrow in the JobID field, and then clicks 4. When she clicks the Advanced Filter Options button in the Sort & Filter group and selects Apply Filter/Sort, Access displays the records that satisfy any of her criteria—records that contain a "3" or a "4" in the JobID field. This list is what Maria wants—information about the current 4Corners technicians and cashiers, including their rate of pay.

Now that Maria has filtered the tblEmployee datasheet, she needs to sort the records to rank the hourly rates of pay for technicians and cashiers.

Sorting Data to Increase Information Content

Recall that sorting records means organizing them in a particular order or sequence. Table 3.1 describes how Access sorts different types of data.

Table 3.1: Sorting types of data

Data Type	Ascending Sort Order	Descending Sort Order
Text	Alphabetic order from A to Z	Reverse alphabetic order from Z to A
Numbers and Currency	From lowest to highest	From highest to lowest
Date/Time	From earliest to latest	From latest to earliest
Yes/No	Yes values appear first	No values appear first

© 2014 Cengage Learning

Sorting the data in a table or datasheet organizes the data and lets you view the information in a variety of ways. When you designate one or more fields as the primary key, Access sorts the records based on the primary key values. To change the order of the records in the field, you can sort the records. For example, you could sort a list of customers by state or a list of vendors in alphabetic order.

When you sort records, you select a sort field, the one Access uses first to reorder the records. For example, if you are sorting an employer list, you might choose LastName as the sort field and sort it in ascending or descending order since it is a Text data type.

You can select more than one sort fields, such as when you want to sort records first by last name and then by first name. If two or more employees have the same last name, you can then have Access list those employee records in alphabetic order according to their first name. Therefore, to sort on multiple fields, you must be in Datasheet view so that the fields are adjacent. The leftmost field becomes the primary sort field, meaning that Access sorts the records by this field first. For example, you could move a LastName field to the left of a FirstName field in an employee table, select both columns, and then sort in ascending order. Access would list the records in alphabetical order by last name.

Now that Maria has filtered tblEmployee to show records only for technicians and cashiers, she can sort the records in descending order by the HourlyRate field so that the employee with the highest hourly wage appears first and the one with the lowest hourly wage appears last. To do so, she clicks in the HourlyRate field, and then clicks Descending in the Sort & Filter group.

Although it took Maria several steps, she produced the results she needs. She prints the sorted datasheet, clicks the Advanced Filter Options button 🔲 in the Sort & Filter group, and selects Clear All Filters to turn off the filter.

Filtering Using the Filter Arrow

Another method Maria can use to filter data is to select the filter arrow located next to a field name. Doing so displays a filter list from which she can make selections. She now wants to view the employees who work in either Colorado or Utah, so she clicks the filter arrow next to the State field name. A list of selection options appears, as shown in Figure 3.4.

Figure 3.4: Using the filter arrow to specify more than one criterion

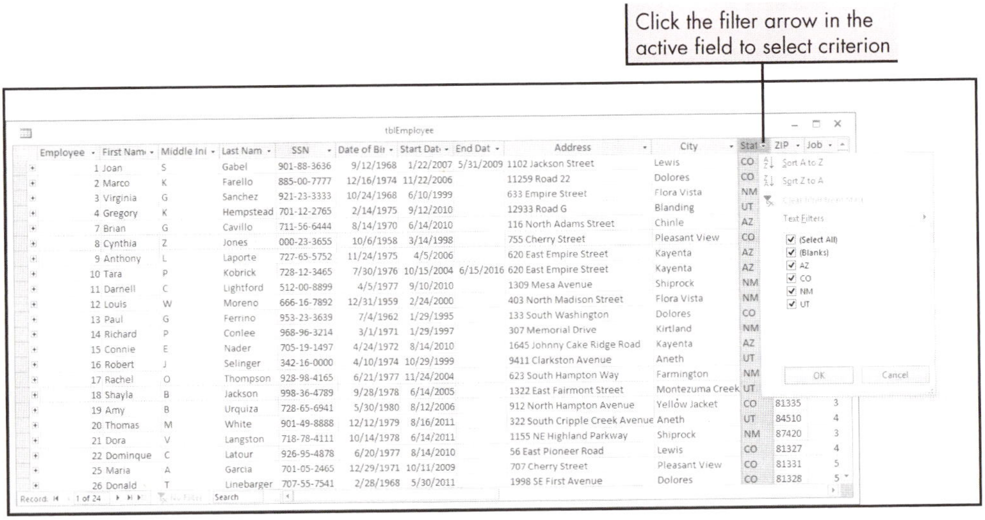

Click the filter arrow in the active field to select criterion

Maria first clicks the Select All check box to deselect all of the check boxes, then she clicks the CO and UT check boxes to place a checkmark in them, and then clicks OK. She then sorts the records in ascending order by selecting Ascending in the Sort & Filter group before printing the results.

After reviewing the list, Maria removes the filter by clicking the filter arrow in the State field and selecting Clear filter from State, and then closes tblEmployee without saving any of the changes. Now Maria wants to explore an easier way to produce the same results using queries.

Using Queries to Answer Business Questions

If you need a quick way to filter table data, the Filter by Selection tool, Filter by Form tool, and the filter arrow are appropriate. However, recall that a filter creates a *temporary* subset of records in a single table. An easier approach is to create a query. A query is a database object that stores criteria for selecting records from one or more tables based on conditions you specify. You can save a query and use it again when you want to see the results of its criteria. Queries are often used as the basis for forms and reports and they can add, update, and delete records in tables. A special kind of query can even create a table based on criteria you supply.

Although queries and filters both display records based on specified criteria, a query is more powerful than a filter. Besides saving the criteria and letting you select records from more than one table, you can also use a query to display only some of the fields in a table. (When you use a filter, you must display all of the fields.) In addition, you can create fields in a query that perform calculations, such as sums and averages.

The following list summarizes the capabilities of Access queries:

- Display selected fields and records from a table.
- Sort records on one or multiple fields.
- Perform calculations.
- Generate data for forms, reports, and other queries.
- Update data in the tables of a database.
- Find and display data from two or more tables.
- Create new tables.
- Delete records in a table based on one or more criteria.

The most common type of query is called a select query. Select queries allow you to ask a question based on one or more tables in a database. Access responds by displaying a datasheet containing the set of records that answers your question. You can select only the fields you want in your result. To analyze the data that you retrieve, you can also use a select query to group records and calculate sums, counts, averages, and other kinds of totals. When you save a query, you are saving the criteria that select the records you want to display. Each time you open, or run, the query, it retrieves the records that meet the criteria you specified and displays them in a recordset, a datasheet that contains the results of a query. Running a typical select query does not affect the records and fields in the underlying tables; it only selects records to make your data more useful.

Maria determines that she can use a select query to provide the list of hourly wages for the technicians and cashiers. Because she is still getting acquainted with the 4Corners database, the easiest way for her to create a select query is to use the Simple Query Wizard.

Using the Simple Query Wizard to Create a Query

Access provides a number of query wizards, which guide you through the steps of creating a query. The Simple Query Wizard presents a list of tables and queries in your database and the fields that they contain. You select the fields you want from one or more tables, and the wizard creates and displays the results. For example, if an employee table contains 20 fields of information, including name, address, phone number, and Social Security number, you can use the Simple Query Wizard to create a phone list that contains only the name and phone number for each employee. Although the Simple Query Wizard provides a quick way to retrieve selected records, it does have some limitations. Table 3.2 lists the advantages and limitations of the Simple Query Wizard.

Table 3.2: Advantages and limitations of the Simple Query Wizard

You Can Use the Simple Query Wizard to	You Cannot Use the Simple Query Wizard to
Display selected fields and records from one or more tables and queries	Update data, create tables, or delete records
Produce summary data if one or more of the selected fields are of the numeric or currency data type	Add selection criteria
Include a count of the records	Choose the sort order of the query
Specify summary grouping by day, month, quarter, or year if one or more of your fields is a Date/Time field	Change the order of the fields in a query; fields appear in the order they are added to the Selected Fields list in the first wizard dialog box

© 2014 Cengage Learning

To start the Simple Query Wizard, Maria clicks the Query Wizard button in the Queries group on the CREATE tab, and then double-clicks Simple Query Wizard in the New Query dialog box. The Simple Query Wizard dialog box opens, which Maria can use to select the fields she wants to display in the query results. All of the fields she needs are included in tblEmployee, so she clicks the Tables/Queries list arrow, and then clicks tblEmployee. See Figure 3.5.

To make the results easy to read, Maria decides to list only the employee's name, job ID, and hourly rate. She double-clicks the EmpLast, EmpFirst, JobID, and HourlyRate fields in that order to move them to the Selected Fields list. These are the fields Access will include in the query results. Then she clicks the Next button to open the next dialog box in the wizard, which asks if she wants to create a detail or summary query. A detail query shows every selected field of every record. A summary query groups records and can calculate the sum, average, minimum, or maximum value in each selected field. It can also provide a count of the records in a table. Maria wants to show every field of every record, so she selects the Detail option button, and then clicks Next.

Figure 3.5: The Simple Query Wizard dialog box

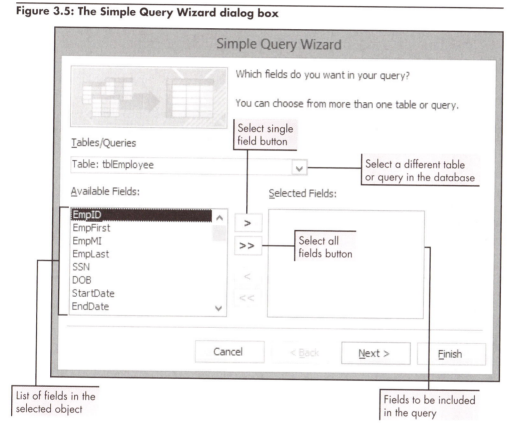

The next dialog box in the wizard opens, where Maria can enter a name for the query. She types qryHourlyRate as the name, and then clicks the Finish button. Access displays the results—a list of 4Corners employees showing only the employee name, job ID, and hourly pay rate.

Best Practice

Using Prefixes in Database Object Names

When prompted to save a query, be certain to use the "qry" prefix in the query name. Naming objects with a prefix that identifies the object type is particularly important with queries because it distinguishes those objects from tables. (A query recordset looks exactly like a table datasheet.) The query wizards, however, usually suggest using a table name as the start of the query name, even if the table name uses the "tbl" prefix. Using the "qry" prefix helps you distinguish queries from tables, which is especially helpful when you are using one or the other as the basis for a new form or report.

How To

Create a Detail Query with the Simple Query Wizard

1. To create a query with the Simple Query Wizard, click Query Wizard on the CREATE tab, and then double-click the Simple Query Wizard option.
2. Click the Tables/Queries list arrow and then select the table or query you want to use as the basis for the query. From the Available Fields list, select the fields you want to include in the query. Use the Select Single Field button ⟩ to select the fields one by one; use the Select All Fields button ⟩⟩ to select them all at once. If you want to include fields from more than one table or query, click the Tables/Queries list arrow again, select another table or query, and then select the fields you want to include. Click the Next button. If a selected field contains a numeric value, the next dialog box asks if you want a detail or summary query.
3. Click the Detail option button to show all the records. Click the Next button.
4. Name the query using the "qry" prefix, and then click the Finish button.

Maria can now achieve the results she wants by sorting the results of the query. She selects the HourlyRate field and then clicks the Descending button on the HOME tab, then selects the JobID field and clicks the Descending button again. The records with a JobID of 5 appear first, followed by the records with a JobID of 4. The records with a JobID of 3 appear next, also sorted from highest to lowest by HourlyRate. The records with no HourlyRate value appear at the top and bottom of the list because employees with a JobID of 5, 2, and 1 are the owner, managers, and pharmacists who receive a salary instead of hourly wages. See Figure 3.6.

Figure 3.6: The sorted results of the qryHourlyRate query

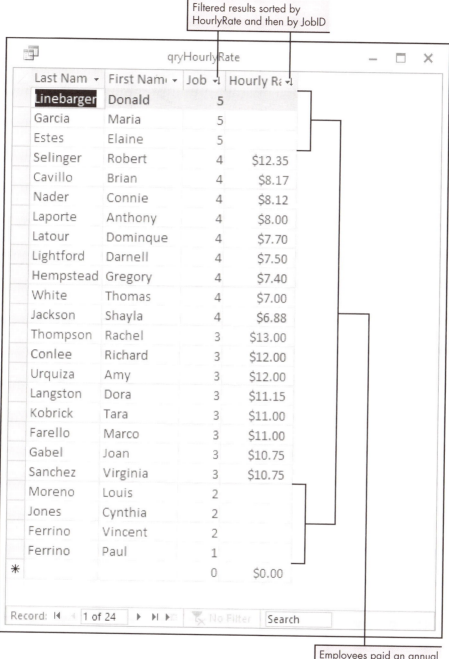

Filtered results sorted by HourlyRate and then by JobID

Employees paid an annual rate have no value in Hourly Rate field

Although using the Detail option with the Simple Query Wizard displays all the employee records, even for employees other than technicians and cashiers, creating a query allows Maria to increase the information content of the results by displaying only relevant fields and sorting the records. She shows the query results to Paul Ferrino, noting that the records at the top and bottom of the list are for salaried employees. Paul looks over the list, mentioning that he appreciates the sort order because he can quickly analyze the range of pay for nonsalaried employees. He wonders if she could provide this information in a more accessible format, listing only the highest and lowest hourly pay rates. Including the average pay rate would also help him analyze the wages. Maria decides to explore the summary option in the Simple Query Wizard to produce the results Paul requests.

Including Summary Statistics in a Query for Data Analysis

Recall that a summary query groups records and can calculate the sum, average, minimum, or maximum value in each selected field. It can also count the records in a table or query.

Maria starts the Simple Query Wizard again so she can use it to create a summary query. In the first dialog box (shown earlier in Figure 3.5), she clicks the Tables/Queries list arrow and then selects qryHourlyRate. She can create the new query by modifying qryHourlyRate and then saving it with a different name. Instead of listing the employee name and job ID for each record, she only wants to summarize the hourly pay rate data. She double-clicks HourlyRate so it becomes the only field in the Selected Fields list. When she clicks the Next button, the next dialog box asks if she wants to create a detail or summary query. This time, she chooses to create a summary query, and clicks the Summary Options button to select the statistics she wants Access to calculate for the HourlyRate field. See Figure 3.7.

Figure 3.7: Creating a summary query with the Simple Query Wizard

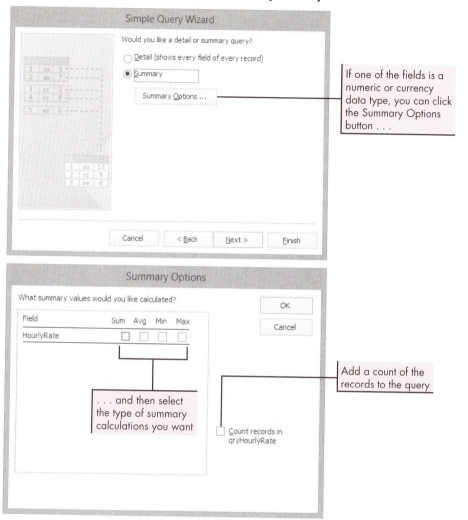

Maria selects the Avg, Min, and Max options because Paul wants to analyze the pharmacy's pay structure by examining the average, lowest, and highest hourly wages, and then she completes the wizard, naming the new query qryHourlyRateSummary. The results, shown in Figure 3.8, include the average, minimum, and maximum calculations for the values in the HourlyRate field.

Figure 3.8: Summary statistics in the qryHourlyRateSummary query

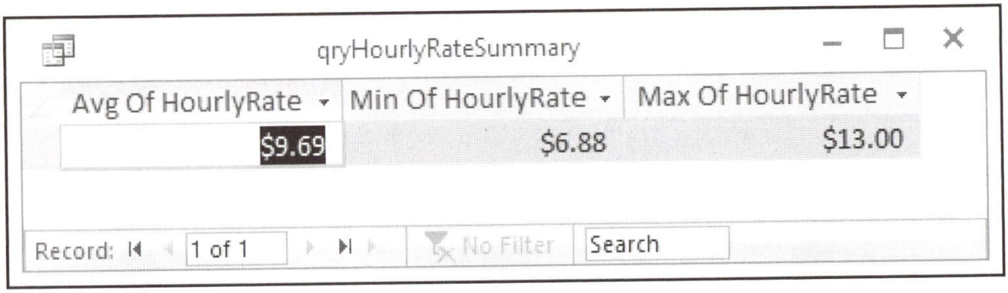

Avg Of HourlyRate ▾	Min Of HourlyRate ▾	Max Of HourlyRate ▾
$9.69	$6.88	$13.00

Record: ◄ ◄ 1 of 1 ► ►► ▾ No Filter Search

How To

Create a Summary Query with the Simple Query Wizard

1. To create a summary query with the Simple Query Wizard, click Query Wizard on the CREATE tab, and then double-click Simple Query Wizard.

2. Click the Tables/Queries list arrow and then select the table or query you want to use as the basis for the query. From the Available Fields list, select the fields you want to include in the query. Use the Select Single Field button to select the fields one by one; use the Select All Fields button to select them all at once. If you want to include fields from more than one table or query, click the Tables/Queries list arrow again, select another table or query, and then select the fields you want to include. Click the Next button. If a selected field contains a numeric value, the next dialog box asks if you want a detail or summary query.

3. Click the Summary option, and then click the Summary Options button to open the Summary Options dialog box.

4. Click the check boxes for the summary values you want to calculate on each field that contains numeric data. Click the Count records in check box to count records in the table or query that contains numeric data. Click the OK button and then click the Next button.

5. Name the query using the "qry" prefix, and then click the Finish button.

As she examines the results, Maria becomes concerned about the average value, recalling that in the records for salaried employees, the HourlyRate field is blank. She is not sure if qryHourlyRateSummary is using these blank fields as zero or null values. (Recall that nulls have no value.) The average is calculated by summing all the values in the HourlyRate field and then dividing that by the number of records (24, as shown earlier in Figure 3.6). However, the calculation should include only those fields that are not blank—these fields belong to records for technicians and cashiers, the employees who receive hourly wages. Therefore, the average should be calculated by summing only the nonblank values in the HourlyRate field and then dividing that by the number of records for employees who receive hourly wages (17). If the HourlyRate field contains zero, instead of null values, the AvgOfHourlyRate fields in qryHourlyRateSummary will not reflect the average pay rate for employees who receive hourly wages—it will erroneously include the zero values for salaried employees. Maria wants to make sure that the query does not include the records for salaried employees, and realizes she needs to create a query using a method that allows her more options than the Simple Query Wizard. She needs to use selection criteria to display only records for technicians and cashiers, and then calculate summary statistics using those records. To accomplish this, she must work in Design view.

Best Practice

Verifying Calculation Results

After Access calculates a value, examine the results to make sure the value makes sense in the context of the data. Many database developers use a calculator to check the results by hand to make sure the calculations they use in queries are working correctly. For this reason, most developers prefer to test their queries and other objects with only a few sample records and simple data so they can easily determine whether their results are correct.

Creating a Query in Design View

Recall from Table 3.1 that the Simple Query Wizard does not allow you to use selection criteria when creating a query, set the sort order of the results, or change the order of the fields displayed in the results. If you need to perform any of these tasks, create a query in Design view instead of using a wizard. In Design view, you can still create queries that accomplish the same goals as the Simple Query Wizard, such as displaying selected fields and records from one or more tables and calculating summary statistics.

When you create a query in Design view, you work in a window similar to the one shown in Figure 3.9.

Figure 3.9: The Select Query window in Design view

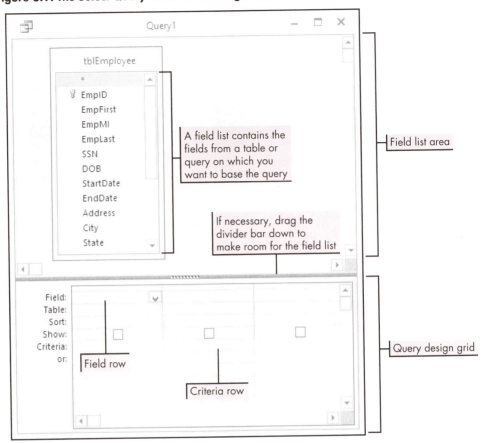

The Select Query window in Design view has two sections: an area for field lists at the top of the window and the design grid below it. You can add the tables you need for the query to the top part of the window; they appear as field lists. You can resize the field lists as necessary to display all the fields and the complete field names. You can add the fields you want in the query to the design grid by dragging the field from the field list to the design grid or by double-clicking the field name.

For each field you add to the design grid, you can specify criteria by typing an expression in the Criteria row. For example, to select only employees with a JobID of 3, type 3 in the Criteria row for the JobID field. Typing the value you are looking for as a criterion is why Access calls this approach query by example (QBE).

Table 3.3 describes the tools and features of Design view.

Table 3.3: Design view tools

Feature or Tool	Description
Field list	Contains the fields for a selected table or query
Design grid	Provides a grid for the fields and record selection criteria you want to use in the query
Field row	Displays the field name in the design grid
Table row	Displays the name of the table that contains the current field
Sort row	Specifies ascending or descending sort order for the field; sorting is from left to right, and fields do not need to be next to each other to be included in the sort
Show row	When the Show box is checked, the field displays in the results; when the Show box is unchecked, the query uses the field to establish criteria, but does not display the field in the results
Criteria row	Specifies the criteria for including or eliminating the record for the field; when one or more criteria are specified in this row, all criteria must be true for the query to display a record in the results
Or row	Specifies OR criteria for including or eliminating the record for the field; when one or more criteria are specified in this row and the Criteria row, any criteria can be true for the query to display a record in the results
Datasheet View button	Click to display the query results
Design View button	Displays the design of the query where you can make changes to the query
Run button	Click to run the query and display the results
Show Table button	Click to select tables and add them to the field list area
Totals button Σ	Click to add a Total row to the design grid and perform calculations with the values in a field

© 2014 Cengage Learning

Maria is ready to design a query that will display the names of 4Corners technicians and cashiers, their job IDs, and their hourly pay rates. The query will also sort the list in descending order first by the JobID field and then by HourlyRate.

To create this query, Maria clicks the Query Design button on the CREATE tab. The Show Table dialog box opens listing the tables in the 4Corners database in the Query window. All of the fields Maria needs are in the tblEmployee table, so she double-clicks tblEmployee to display its field list in the field list area, and then she clicks the Close button to close the Show Table dialog box.

Next, she adds the four fields she needs to the design grid. In the tblEmployee field list, she double-clicks EmpLast, EmpFirst, JobID, and HourlyRate in that order to add them to the design grid.

Her next task is to specify the criteria for displaying records only for technicians and cashiers. To do so, she must use multiple criteria, as she did when she used Filter by Form.

Creating Queries with Multiple Criteria

Most queries involve more than one criterion. You can represent AND criteria—multiple conditions that must all be true—by entering the conditions in the same Criteria row in the query design grid. For a record to be included in the results of the query, it must meet all criteria specified in the Criteria row. For example, if you want to display information about cashiers who live in Colorado, you enter *4* in the Criteria row for the JobID field and *CO* in the Criteria row for the State field.

To specify OR criteria—conditions that allow more than one alternative condition to be true—you use the "or" row of the query design grid. If the conditions apply to the same field, you enter the first condition in the Criteria row for the field, and then enter each additional condition in an "or" row for that field. The query selects records that meet all the criteria in the Criteria row, or those that meet all of the criteria in an "or" row. For example, if you want to display information about employees who live in Arizona or New Mexico, you can enter "AZ" in the Criteria row and "NM" in the "or" row for the State field. You can also type all the conditions separated by the Or operator in the same Criteria cell, as in "AZ" Or "NM".

If the conditions apply to different fields, you also enter the first condition in the Criteria row for one field, and then enter each additional condition in an "or" row for the other fields. For example, if you want to display information about employees who live in Colorado or Phoenix, you can enter "CO" in the Criteria row for the State field and "Phoenix" in the "or" row for the City field.

Best Practice

Understanding OR Criteria

In querying, "or means more." A query with criteria in more than one row of the query design grid is likely to return more results than the more restrictive AND criteria, in which two or more conditions in the same row must be true.

Now, Maria can specify the criteria for displaying records only for technicians and cashiers. Because she wants to display records that include 3 or 4 in the JobID field, she will use OR criteria. Recall that Maria could do this earlier when she used Filter by Form, but not when she used the Simple Query Wizard. She clicks in the Criteria row of the JobID field and then types 3 to set the criteria for displaying records only for technicians. To include an OR criterion, she clicks in the "or" row of the JobID field and then types 4 to set the criterion for also displaying cashier records. See Figure 3.10.

Figure 3.10: Setting criteria for the query in Design view

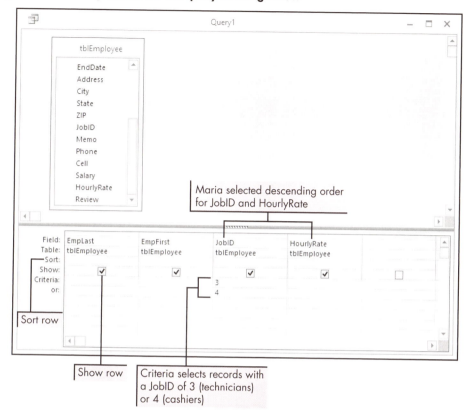

Maria's only remaining task is to sort the records the query displays so that the records for cashiers appear first, sorted from highest to lowest by hourly pay rate. Then she wants the records for technicians to also appear sorted from highest to lowest by hourly pay rate.

Specifying Sort Order in Queries

Query results appear in the same order as the data from the underlying tables unless you specify a sort order when you design the query. Sort order is determined from left to right, so the primary sort field must appear to the left of any other sort field on the grid. You might want to sort on one or more additional fields to determine the order of records that all have the same primary sort order value. Fields do not need to be next to each other to be included in a sort within a query. You can choose ascending or descending sort order.

For example, to sort employee records alphabetically by name, you could place the EmpLast field to the left of the EmpFirst field in the query design grid. If you specify an ascending sort order for both fields, Access sorts the records in alphabetic order by last name. If two employees have the same last name, Access sorts those records according to the names in the EmpFirst field. For example, if one employee is named Arthur Johnson and another is named Tyrone Johnson, Access sorts Arthur before Tyrone.

The main reason to specify a sort order for a query is that it is saved as part of the design with the other query settings. After you run a query, you might decide to sort the data in one or more columns as you examine the data in Datasheet view. This sort order is not saved as part of the query design. Recall also that multiple columns must be adjacent to sort on more than one field in Datasheet view. In Design view, you can sort on more than one field even if they are not adjacent—the sort order is determined by their left-to-right placement in the design grid.

To sort the records first by JobID and then by HourlyRate, Maria must make sure that the JobID field appears in any column to the left of the HourlyRate field in the design grid. Maria clicks in the Sort row of the JobID field, clicks the list arrow, and then clicks Descending. She does the same for the HourlyRate field. She reviews her selections before she runs the query.

Running a Query

After you establish the criteria you want for a query, you click the Run button in the Results group on the DESIGN tab to display the results. Access displays a datasheet of records that meet the criteria you specified in the design grid. Note that although the datasheet looks like a set of records in a table, and you can often enter and change data from the query datasheet, the data is still actually stored in the underlying tables that were used to create the query. When you save a query, you save only the design, not the values from the tables displayed in the results. When you run the query again, Access reapplies the criteria saved in the design grid to the data in the underlying tables to produce the query results. If the data in the query fields has changed, these changes appear when you rerun the query.

Maria saves the query as qryHourlyRateAnalysis. She is ready to run her query, so she clicks the Run button on the DESIGN tab. Access runs the query and displays the results in Datasheet view. See Figure 3.11.

Figure 3.11: Results of the query in Datasheet view

The four selected fields are displayed

Last Nam ⁻	First Nam ⁻	Job ⁻	Hourly Ra ⁻
Selinger	Robert	4	$12.35
Cavillo	Brian	4	$8.17
Nader	Connie	4	$8.12
Laporte	Anthony	4	$8.00
Latour	Dominque	4	$7.70
Lightford	Darnell	4	$7.50
Hempstead	Gregory	4	$7.40
White	Thomas	4	$7.00
Jackson	Shayla	4	$6.88
Thompson	Rachel	3	$13.00
Urquiza	Amy	3	$12.00
Conlee	Richard	3	$12.00
Langston	Dora	3	$11.15
Kobrick	Tara	3	$11.00
Farello	Marco	3	$11.00
Gabel	Joan	3	$10.75
Sanchez	Virginia	3	$10.75
*		0	$0.00

qryHourlyRateAnalysis

Results are sorted first by JobID in descending order and then by HourlyRate in descending order

Only records for technicians and cashiers are displayed

Record: ◄ ◄ 1 of 17 ► ►I ►⁜ No Filter Sear⁝

Referring to Query Results

Results from a query are not new tables. The original tables and queries used to create the query do not change when you run a select query. A query recordset contains "columns" and "rows" to display the query results. As you will see later, you can create a new column with a calculated value that does not appear in the underlying tables in the database.

Working with Query Datasheets

Avoid entering or editing data in the query results. It is generally considered best practice to enter data directly into a table (or form, as you will see in Chapter 4) to make sure you enter data for all fields, not only those in the query results.

Under certain conditions, you can edit the values in the query datasheet to update the records in the underlying tables. Access lets you update table records from a query datasheet if the query is based on only one table or on tables that have a one-to-one relationship (which is rare), or if the query results contain a Comments, Hyperlink, or OLE Object field. Editing records from query results saves you a few steps if you need to correct a typographical error, for example, because you don't need to close the query datasheet and then open the table datasheet to make a change.

Access might also let you update table records from a query datasheet if the query is based on two or more tables that have a one-to-many relationship. You cannot update the primary key field for the table on the "one" side of the relationship, unless you've enabled cascading updates when you set referential integrity for the relationship.

You can add records using the query datasheet only if you include a primary key or foreign key field in the query. One exception is a summary query—because it displays calculations based on the contents of the underlying tables, you cannot enter or change the data itself. If you try to enter a record or change data in a query that does not include a primary or foreign key for the under-lying tables, you will receive an error message similar to the one shown in Figure 3.12, which indicates a data integrity error.

Figure 3.12: Error message received when trying to add records to query

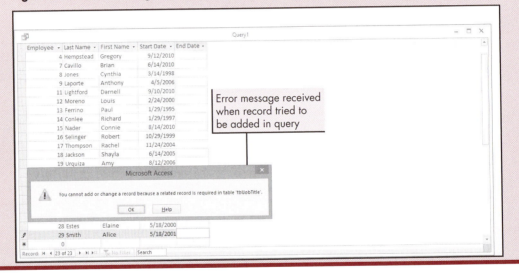

Now that Maria knows how to work in Design view, she can modify the qryHourlyRateSummary query so it uses only hourly pay rates for technicians and cashiers in its average calculation. She opens the query in Design view, adds the JobID field to the design grid, and enters the same criteria she used to select records only for technicians and cashiers in qryHourlyRateSummary—she enters 3 in the Criteria row of the JobID field and 4 in the "or" row.

If Maria runs the query now, she will probably receive an error—the three fields that calculate the average, minimum, and maximum values summarize the values in all the selected employee records, while the JobID field selects each employee record that matches the criteria. Access can't run a query that shows summary values in one row of the query results, and then uses two or more rows to display detail information. To solve this problem, Maria can use the JobID field in the query design grid to specify criteria, but not show the JobID field in the query results. She can remove the check mark from the Show box in the JobID field to indicate that it should not appear in the query results. Figure 3.13 shows the modified query design for qryHourlyRateSummary and the results, which verify that the original query calculated the average hourly rate correctly.

Figure 3.13: Revised qryHourlyRateSummary

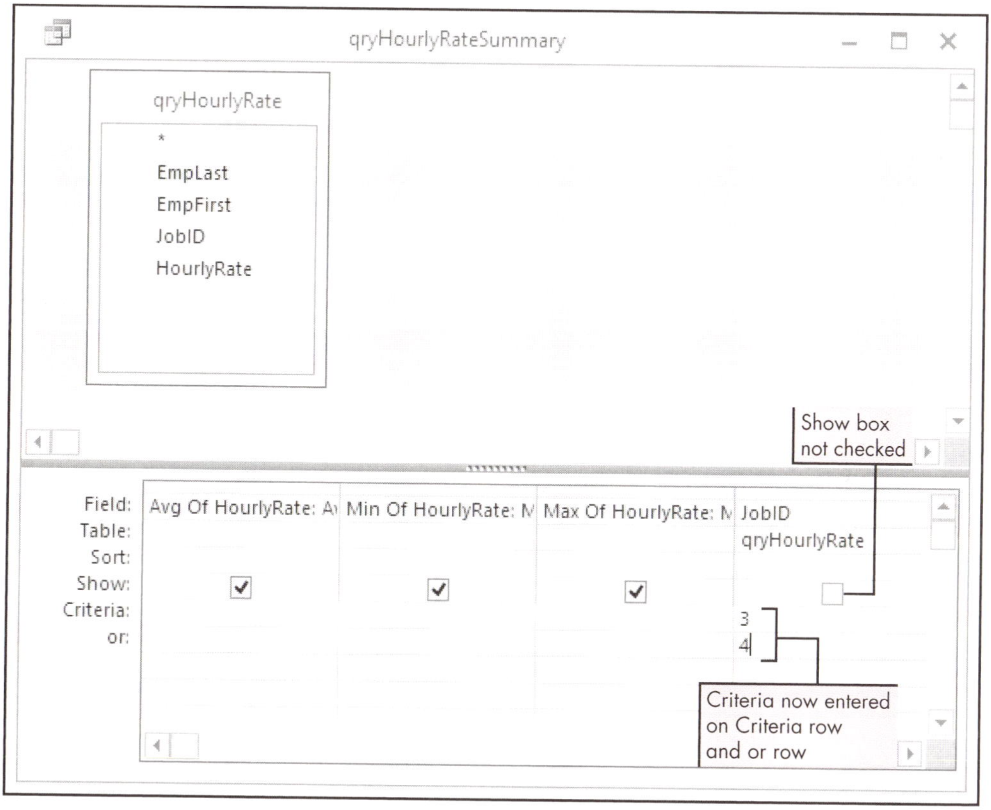

Maria has another problem she wants to work on next. Paul asked Maria to look into the possibility of scheduling at least one employee in the pharmacy who is fluent in Spanish for all shifts. She thinks she can create a query that uses broader criteria than the exact match criteria she's used so far to help with Paul's scheduling request.

Enhancing Query Criteria to Improve Data Analysis

When you specify the criteria for a query, you are setting conditions that determine which records Access should display in the query results. Recall that to define a condition for a query, you enter the criterion in the Criteria row of the query design grid. If you enter a value, Access displays records that have an exact match of that value in the appropriate field. For example, when Maria entered 3 in the Criteria row of the JobID field, Access selected records in tblEmployee with the value 3 in the JobID field. Specifying a single criterion that Access must match exactly means you can pinpoint the records you want to select. However, suppose you want to select records for employees who earn between $8.00 and $9.00 per hour. If you know that the wages range from $8.00 to $9.00 in $.10 increments, for example, you could specify "8.00" as the first criterion, "8.10" as the next OR criterion, "8.20" as the next OR criterion, and so on, up to "8.90." Specifying 10 OR criteria is inefficient and can slow the query if the data source contains many records. In addition, this method of specifying multiple OR criteria is only possible if you are already familiar with the data in the database. If you don't know all the wage values, the criteria you specify will only retrieve some of the appropriate records. Instead of specifying exact criteria in such a case, you can expand the criteria by using wildcards or comparison operators so that you only need to enter one criterion to find all the employees who earn $8 up to $9.

Using Wildcards for Inexact Query Matches

Suppose you want to use a criterion such as a name, but do not know the spelling, or want to display records with values that match a pattern, such as phone numbers that all begin with a certain area code. In these cases, you cannot specify an exact match. Instead, you can use a wildcard character, a placeholder that stands for one or more characters. Use wildcard characters in query criteria when you know only part of the criteria, want to search for a value based on some of its characters, or want to match a pattern. Table 3.4 summarizes the wildcards you can use in queries.

Table 3.4: Wildcard characters used in queries

Symbol	Purpose	Example
*	Match any number of characters	Ab* to locate any word starting with Ab
?	Match any single alphabetic character	J?n finds Jan, Jon, and Jen
#	Match any single digit in a numeric field	(970) ###-#### finds phone numbers that have 970 area codes; 1/##/16 finds dates during January 2016
[ ]	Match any single character listed within the brackets	J[eo]n finds Jen and Jon but not Jan
!	Match any character not within the brackets	J[!eo] finds Jan but not Jen or Jon
-	Match any one of a range of characters within the brackets; letters must be in ascending order	A[d-p] finds aft, ant, and apt, but not act and art

© 2014 Cengage Learning

Wildcards can help you match a pattern. For example, if you want to display the employees who started working in 2016, you could use */*/2016 or *2016 as the criterion in the StartDate field. Wildcards can also help you overcome data-entry errors. For example, if you want to retrieve records for employees who live in Dolores, Colorado, which is often misspelled as Delores, you could specify D?lores as the criterion in the City field. In these ways, using wildcards can make your queries more powerful, allowing you to retrieve data without using criteria that demand an exact match.

Access inserts the word "Like" for criteria with wildcards, quotation marks around text, and pound signs around dates you enter, as in Like "*Spanish*" or Like #12/*/2016#.

Maria is ready to turn to Paul's scheduling request. Because many of the pharmacy's clientele speak Spanish, he wants to schedule at least one Spanish-speaking employee for each shift. If an employee speaks Spanish (or any other language besides English), it is noted in the Comments field of tblEmployee. Because the Comments data type allows for lengthy text or combinations of text and numbers, it is often best using wildcards in criteria that involve Comments fields.

As you enter data in Comments fields, try to use the same keywords throughout the comments so that you can easily retrieve records later. Be certain to use wildcards when you specify the keyword as a query criterion to select records that contain characters before and after the keyword. For example, to discover how many employees speak Spanish at 4Corners Pharmacy, Maria could type *Spanish* in the Criteria row of the Comments field. The asterisk (*) wildcard character on either side of the criterion means Access selects records that contain text or other values before and after "Spanish" in the Comments field, such as those that include "Speaks Spanish fluently" and "Knows some Spanish." If Maria specifies Spanish without the asterisks, Access selects records that contain only the word Spanish in the Comments field.

To create this query, Maria clicks the Query Design button on the CREATE tab. The Query window opens in Design view, with the Show Table dialog box open in front of it. All the fields she needs are in tblEmployee, so she double-clicks tblEmployee to display its field list, and then closes the Show Table dialog box. She adds the EmpLast, EmpFirst, JobID, and Comments fields to the design grid by double-clicking each one in that order. She selects EmpLast before EmpFirst because she plans to sort the records alphabetically by last name; the sort order will then be clear to anyone viewing the query results. She types *spanish* in the Criteria row for the Comments field. The asterisks are necessary so that Access selects records that contain Spanish anywhere in the field. When she presses the Enter key, she notices that Access adds the word Like and inserts quotation marks around Spanish. See Figure 3.14.

Figure 3.14: Entering a query criterion using wildcards

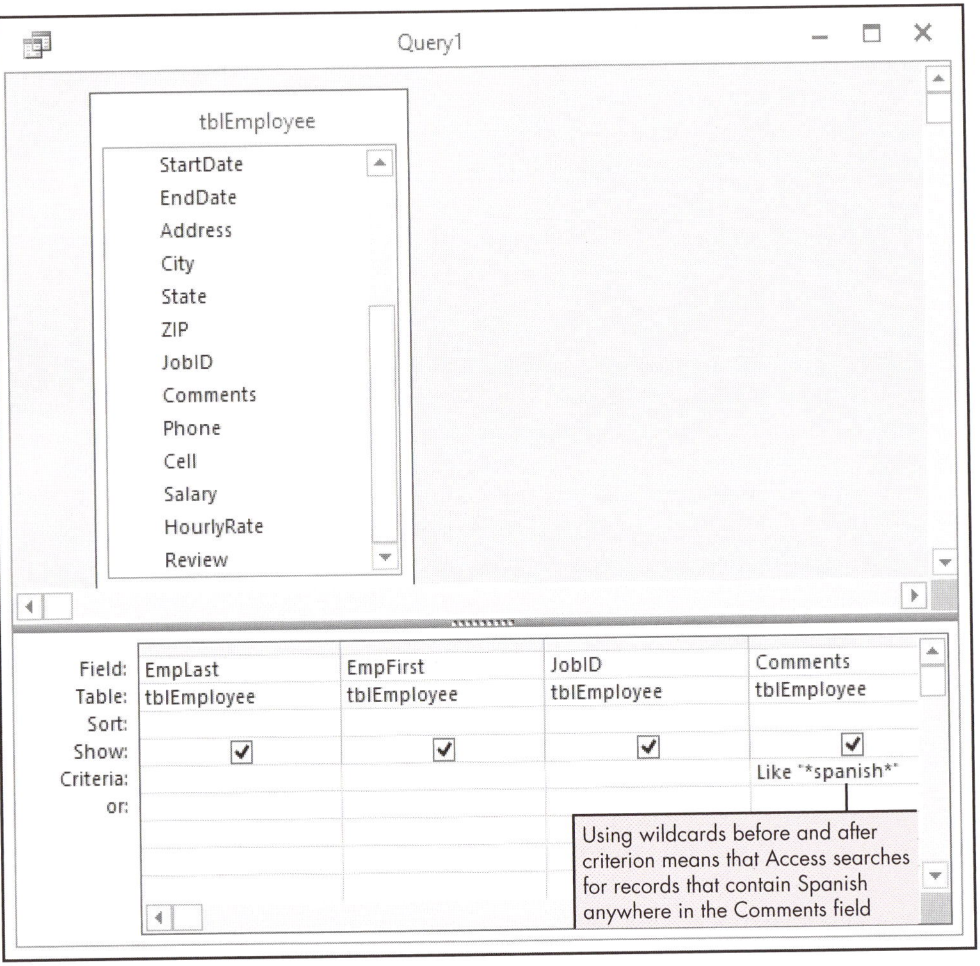

Maria saves the query as qrySpeakSpanish, runs the query, and finds three employees who speak Spanish, noting that none of them are pharmacists and that one no longer works at 4Corners. See Figure 3.15. She plans to talk to Paul Ferrino about hiring more Spanish-speaking employees; she cannot currently meet the goal of scheduling a Spanish-speaking employee for each shift. Maria can use this query in the future to periodically update the list since the query will save the design, criteria, and sort order.

Figure 3.15: Results of a wildcard search for Spanish-speaking employees

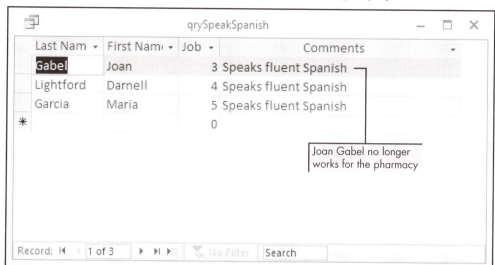

Joan Gabel is listed as an employee who speaks Spanish, however, she no longer works at 4Corners Pharmacy. Therefore, Maria needs to add a field in the query that will have criteria to exclude employees who are no longer working at the pharmacy.

Maria also needs to solve the problem of keeping data about employees who no longer work for the pharmacy. In the 4Corners database, she included records for past employees so she wouldn't lose the data about them. Eventually, the pharmacy will discard or archive printed information about previous employees, and the database will contain only current records. Maria needs a way to exclude the past employees from her queries.

Using Comparison Operators to Refine Query Criteria

In addition to entering a criterion that exactly matches a single value or using wildcards to match a pattern, you can use criteria that match a range of values. In this case, you use comparison operators, which compare the value in a field with a range of values in a criterion. If the value is within the range, data from the record is included. For example, you might want to know if an employee was hired after a particular date, such as June 1, 2016. Using a date as the criterion would only display those employees hired on that date. Instead, you can use a comparison operator to specify a range of dates, such as >= #6/1/2016# in the StartDate field to display employees who started working on June 1, 2016 or later. (Recall that Access requires pound signs around date values used in query criteria.) Table 3.5 shows the comparison operators used to specify a range of values.

Table 3.5: Comparison operators

Operator	Description	Examples
<	Less than	<500 <12.75
<=	Less than or equal to	<=500 <=#12/31/2016#
=	Equal to	=500 ="CO"
>=	Greater than or equal to	>=500 >=12.75
>	Greater than	>500 >#12/31/2016#
<>	Not equal to	<>500 <>"CO"
Between… And	Include values within the specified range (inclusive); always use with dates	Between #1/01/2016# And #1/31/2016# Between 5000 And 10000
In	Include values within the specified list	In("CO","AZ")
Is	Include records in which the field contains a null, not null, true, or false value, as specified	Is Null, Is Not Null, Is True, Is False
Like	Include values matching the specified pattern	Like "*Spanish*"

© 2014 Cengage Learning

When Maria queries the 4Corners database for employee information, she needs to use a comparison operator in the criteria so that the query excludes employees who no longer work for 4Corners Pharmacy. These are employees whose records include a value in the EndDate field. For example, Joan Gabel stopped working for 4Corners in 2009. The EndDate field in her employee record contains the date value 5/31/2009, the last date of her employment. Maria considers using the Not comparison operator because it excludes records that contain a specified value. However, if she uses Not #5/31/2009# as the criterion in the EndDate field, the query excludes only Joan Gabel's record, and not those of other past employees. She could use the In operator with Not to list the EndDate values of all the past employees, as in Not In(#5/31/2009#,#6/15/2016#), but that requires her to find and possibly update these values each time she runs the query.

Maria reexamines the fields in the tblEmployee field list, trying to find a fresh approach to solve her problem. Instead of excluding employees with a value in the EndDate field, perhaps she could focus on selecting only those employees who do not have a value in the EndDate field. Instead of a value, the EndDate field for current employees is blank, or null. She could use the Is operator with null, as in Is Null, in the EndDate field to select current employees only.

Best Practice

Understanding Null Fields

Access has a special character called a null that indicates a field contains no value, or is blank. Nulls are different from a space or zero character, and can be used in expressions to check whether a field contains a value. To do so, you can use Is Null or *Is Not Null* as a criterion. Is Null selects records in which the specified field does not contain a value. Is Not Null selects records in which the specified field contains any type of value.

Maria modifies qrySpeakSpanish by adding the EndDate field to the design grid. Then she enters Is Null as its criterion to select only those records in which the EndDate field is blank, effectively eliminating former employees from the query results. She also clears the Show check box for the EndDate field because she does not want to display this field in the query results. She saves the modified query, and then runs it. Figure 3.16 shows the design and results of this query.

Figure 3.16: Only EndDate fields with null values displayed

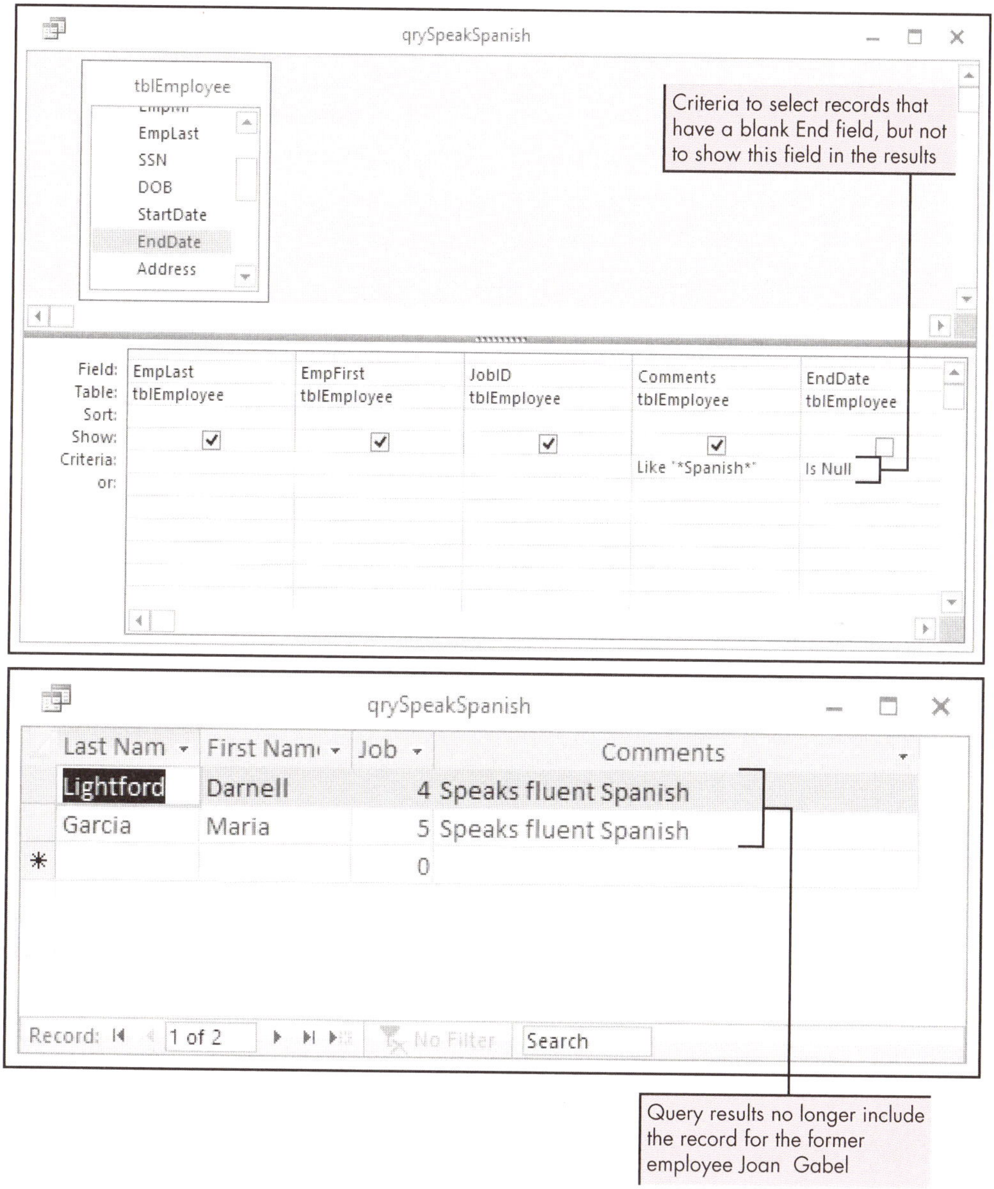

Now that Maria has refined her query for displaying current Spanish-speaking employees, she can turn her attention to solving a different problem. Paul Ferrino wants to reward long-term employees because he knows that they increase the efficiency, consistency, and quality of the pharmacy and its services. He also knows that hiring and training employees is expensive and employee turnover can erode morale. He is considering presenting substantial bonuses to each employee who has worked at the pharmacy for more than five years. In addition, he has asked Maria to schedule a celebration later this year to acknowledge these employees and their contributions to the pharmacy. Maria needs to produce a list of employees who have worked at 4Corners Pharmacy for at least five years, or since January 1, 2015.

To produce this list, Maria can create a query that includes the StartDate field and uses the less than or equal to comparison operator (<=) to select records in which the start date is January 1, 2015 or earlier.

Because she needs to use the same tblEmployee field list as in qrySpeakSpanish, which is still open in Datasheet view, Maria switches to Design view to start with the same field list. To remove the fields in the Query grid, Maria selects the columns by dragging her mouse pointer across the gray bar above the field names and selecting the Delete Columns button in the Query Setup group on the DESIGN tab. She adds the EmpLast, EmpFirst, StartDate, and EndDate fields, and uses <=#1/1/2015# as the criterion in the StartDate field. She also decides to sort the records in ascending order by the values in the StartDate field so she and Paul can easily see who has worked for the pharmacy the longest. Finally, Maria uses the Is Null criterion in the EndDate field. As she is entering the Is Null criterion, she notices a list of available expressions appears to the right of the criterion she is typing as shown in Figure 3.17.

Figure 3.17: IntelliSense appears when typing criterion

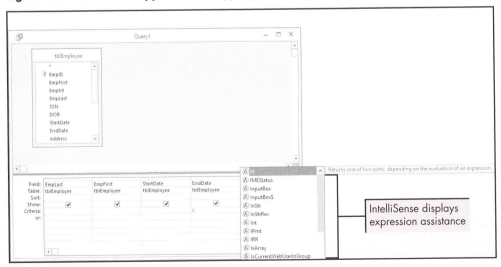

This list is the IntelliSense feature at work. As you enter expressions, Access assists you by offering a list of possible expressions. In this case Maria does not need the list of expressions, so she enters the Is Null criterion. After she types the criterion, she removes the check from the Show check box so this field does not appear in the query results. She saves the query as qryStartDate, and then runs it. Figure 3.18 shows the design and results of this query.

Figure 3.18: Using comparison operators with dates

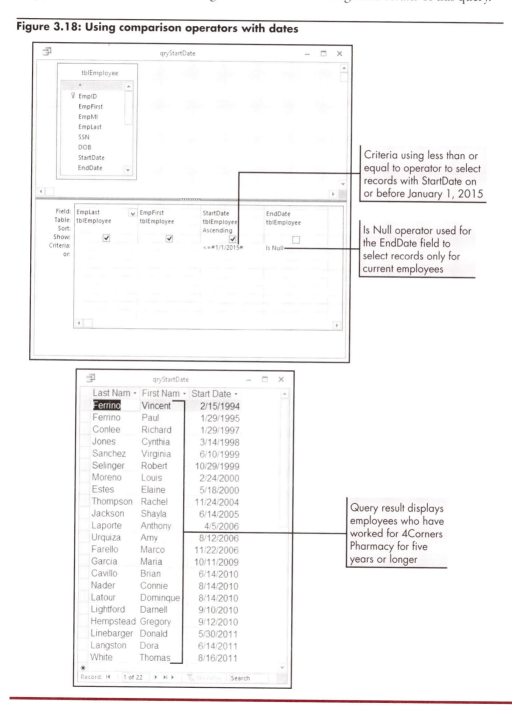

Criteria using less than or equal to operator to select records with StartDate on or before January 1, 2015

Is Null operator used for the EndDate field to select records only for current employees

Query result displays employees who have worked for 4Corners Pharmacy for five years or longer

Best Practice

Clearing the Design Grid to Create or Modify a Query

When you are working with a query in Design view, you can clear the design grid by selecting the thin gray bar above the field names (your mouse pointer will appear as a downward arrow), and clicking the Delete Columns button in the Query Setup group on the DESIGN tab. You can then create a query using the field lists that are already open in the field list area. Be certain to save the new query with a different name. The copied query will be pasted with the previous queries name with the words Copy. If you want to continue working in Design view and don't plan on saving the current query, you might want to clear the grid. If the query is not producing the results you expect, try clearing it and using different criteria.

Before continuing her work with queries, Maria decides to print the results of all the queries she's created so far so that she can show them to Paul later.

Verifying and Printing Query Results

Before you distribute a query to others or use it as the basis for decisions, verify its results. Use your business knowledge to determine whether the results adequately answer the question you intended to answer. For example, if you want to list all the employees who have worked for your company for at least five years, but the query displays those who were hired within the last five years, you probably used the wrong comparison operator in the query criteria, such as the greater than operator (>) instead of the less than or equal to operator (<=).

Best Practice

Correcting Errors in Queries

If your query does not return any results, it might have a number of problems. Perhaps the underlying tables do not contain any matching data. Perhaps you have entered the criteria incorrectly. If you run a complex query that does not return any results when you know it should, revise the query so it specifies only one condition, and then run the query. If that works, add another condition and run the query again. As you build your query, you will probably see which additional condition is causing the problem.

If you receive an error similar to "Can't evaluate expression," look for a typographical error in the query criteria. An error similar to "Type mismatch" probably indicates that you have tried to perform mathematical operations on a Text or Date/Time data type value. An error similar to "Enter Parameter Value" usually indicates that you have misspelled a field name or have modified the table structure without changing the query to reflect the changes.

After you verify the query results, you can print the query datasheet. Printing query results in the form of a report is more attractive and accessible than a datasheet, however, printing a query datasheet can help you and others review the query results and verify their accuracy or answer a quick question. It is good practice to check the format of the datasheet in Print Preview before printing so you can modify column widths and orientation for best results.

Modifying Query Datasheets

Access provides a number of formatting options to help you improve the appearance of a query or table datasheet. You set these formatting options when you are working in Datasheet view. (They are not available in Design view.) Table 3.6 describes the most common options you can use to format datasheets you print or view. You can view most of the options noted in Table 3.6 by clicking the HOME tab on the Ribbon and then clicking the appropriate option.

Table 3.6: Formatting options for query and table datasheets

Format Option	Effect	Access Buttons on the HOME Tab
Font	Change font and font size	Font, Font Size buttons in the Font group
	Change font formats such as bold, italics, underline, font color, and alignment	Bold, Italics, Underline, Font Color, Align Text Left, Center, and Align Text Right buttons in the Font group
Datasheet	Change cell effects to flat, sunken, or raised, gridline colors, datasheet border	Datasheet Formatting dialog box (displayed by clicking the Font dialog box launcher)
	Change background colors	Fill/Back Color, Alternate Fill/Back Color in the Font group
	Show or hide gridlines	Gridlines button in the Font group

© 2014 Cengage Learning

Note that you can resize the column widths in any datasheet by double-clicking the line between field names to resize the columns to their best fit. If you have too many columns or they are too wide to fit on a single page in portrait orientation, you can select the Print option on the FILE menu, click Print Preview, and then select Landscape in the Page Layout group on the PRINT PREVIEW tab.

Maria formats qryStartDate by increasing the size of the font and resizing the columns so that each is wide enough to display all the data it contains. She clicks the FILE menu, selects Print, and then clicks Print Preview to view the effects of her changes. To print the results, she clicks the Print button on the PRINT PREVIEW tab.

Steps To Success: Level 1

Kim Siemers, human resources manager at Hudson Bay Pharmacy, is ready to use the Hudson database to extract information that will help her manage employees. She asks for your help in filtering table data and creating queries, especially those that use criteria to select the information they need. As you create and save new queries, be certain to use the "qry" prefix as part of the naming convention. Also consult your instructor for instructions about submitting your results.

Note: To complete the following steps, you must have completed the Steps To Success for Levels 1, 2, and 3 in Chapter 2.

Complete the following:

1. Start Access and open the **Hudson.accdb** database from the STS folder.

2. Kim needs quick answers to three questions. First, she needs to know how many pharmacists are listed in the tblEmployee table. Filter the data in the tblEmployee table to answer Kim's question. How many records are displayed?

3. Next, Kim wants to know how many records in tblEmployee are for pharmacists, owners, or managers. Refilter the data in tblEmployee to answer Kim's second question. How many records are displayed?

4. Finally, Kim wants to know who was the first employee hired by Hudson Bay Pharmacy, and who was the most recent. Organize the data in tblEmployee so that you can easily answer Kim's question. Who was the first employee hired by the pharmacy? Who was the most recent employee hired by the pharmacy?

5. To help Kim call employees when she needs a substitute, create an alphabetical phone list of Hudson Bay employees and their phone numbers. Save the query as **qryEmpPhoneList**.

6. Kim is planning to meet with Mai Yan the manager of Hudson Bay Pharmacy, to review the wages paid to employees so they can budget for upcoming pay raises. Kim wants to check the hourly rates paid to employees. List the wages for employees who are paid according to their hourly rate, ranked from highest to lowest, to display the full range of pay for current, nonsalaried employees. Also include information that clearly identifies each employee. Save the query as **qryHourlyRate**.

7. Kim mentions that a summary of the hourly rate information would also be helpful as she prepares for her meeting. List only the highest, lowest, and average pay rates for nonsalaried employees. Make sure that the average calculation does not include zero values for salaried employees. Save the query as **qryHourlyRateAnalysis**.

8. Kim wants to schedule employees so that at least one Spanish-speaking employee is working each shift. Produce a list of current employees at Hudson Bay Pharmacy who speak Spanish. Save the query as **qrySpeakSpanish**.

9. To prepare for employee reviews, Kim asks you to produce a list of all employees who have been reprimanded at least once. (*Hint:* Look for keywords in the Comments field.) Save the query as **qryReprimand**.

10. Kim has analyzed employment data and discovered that those who have been working for one to three years are most likely to accept employment elsewhere. Kim asks you to identify employees who started working between January 1, 2012 and January 1, 2016, ranked so the most recent start date is first. Save the query as **qryStartDate**.

11. Format one of the queries you created for Hudson Bay Pharmacy to make it easier to read, and then print one page of the results.

12. Close the **Hudson.accdb** database and then close Access.

LEVEL 2
Creating More Complex Queries

Evaluating Data Using Special Types of Queries

In addition to the Simple Query Wizard, Access provides other query wizards that help you evaluate and verify the data stored in a database. For example, you can use the Find Duplicates Query Wizard to retrieve duplicate records in a table. This is especially useful if the table contains data for a mailing list or if you have imported records from another source. Table 3.7 lists query wizards other than the Simple Query Wizard and describes their purpose.

Table 3.7: Wizards for specialized queries

Query Type	Purpose	Example
Crosstab	Displays data in a compact, spreadsheet-like format	Identify training costs over time
Find Duplicates	Locate duplicate records in a table or query	Identify the same employee who is entered multiple times with different IDs
Find Unmatched	Locate records with no related records in a second table or query	Identify employees who have not taken any training classes

© 2014 Cengage Learning

In this section, you will learn how to use the Find Duplicates and Find Unmatched query wizards to answer complex business questions, analyze data, and maintain the integrity of your database. You will learn about Crosstab queries in Level 3.

Now that Maria Garcia is familiar with the 4Corners database, she wants to use it to automate many of her human resources tasks. To conserve gasoline and other vehicle maintenance costs, employees have asked Maria to help them coordinate car pools. One of her tasks will be to help employees determine how they can share rides to work. She will create a car pool list identifying those employees who live in the same city.

Using Queries to Find Duplicate Records

The Find Duplicates Query Wizard searches for duplicate values in the fields you select. For example, you might have accidentally entered the same employee or customer name twice with two different IDs. Newly transferred data from a spreadsheet or other source to an Access table also often contains duplicate information, as does a database that was not set up correctly. In these cases, you can use the Find Duplicates Query Wizard to identify duplicate records. Be certain to examine the records the wizard identifies to determine if they indeed contain duplicate data. You can then edit the data in the table as necessary.

In addition to finding errors, you can use the Find Duplicates Query Wizard to improve business operations. For example, you can find customers who live in the same city so you can coordinate sales calls, compare costs of vendors who supply the same products, or alert employees enrolled in the same training session of a schedule change.

The Find Duplicates Query Wizard is designed to identify records that contain the same information in a particular field, even if you don't know all or part of the duplicated values. If a table of employee data contains five records with "Springfield" and three records with "Ashton" in the City field, the wizard selects all eight records. To select records containing the same value that you specify, you can set criteria to select those records. For example, if you want to retrieve the records for employees who live in Springfield, use "Springfield" as the criterion in the City field. The query then selects five employee records.

Maria wants to identify employees who live in the same city so they can create car pools and share rides to work. Because 4Corners Pharmacy is located in southwestern Colorado and borders four states (Arizona, Colorado, New Mexico, and Utah), employees live in many surrounding cities. Maria can use the Find Duplicates Query Wizard to create a list of employees who live in the same city. She can post this list so that employees can form car pools.

To accomplish this task, Maria clicks the Query Wizard button on the CREATE tab and then double-clicks the Find Duplicates Query Wizard. The first dialog box in the wizard opens, as shown in Figure 3.19.

Because the tblEmployee table contains employee addresses, she clicks tblEmployee and then clicks the Next button.

The next wizard dialog box asks her to identify the fields that might contain duplicate information. Maria double-clicks City and State in the Available fields box to add them to the Duplicate-value fields box. She includes State because cities with the same name might be located in more than one state. See Figure 3.20.

Figure 3.19: First dialog box in Find Duplicates Query Wizard

Find Duplicates Query Wizard

Which table or query do you want to search for duplicate field values?

For example, to find cities with more than one customer you would choose a Customer table below.

Table: tblClass
Table: tblClinic
Table: tblCustomer
Table: tblDoctor
Table: tblDrug
Table: tblEmployee
Table: tblEmployeeTraining
Table: tblHealthPlan

View

● Tables   ○ Queries   ○ Both

Cancel   < Back   Next >   Finish

> Choose a table to search for duplicate field values

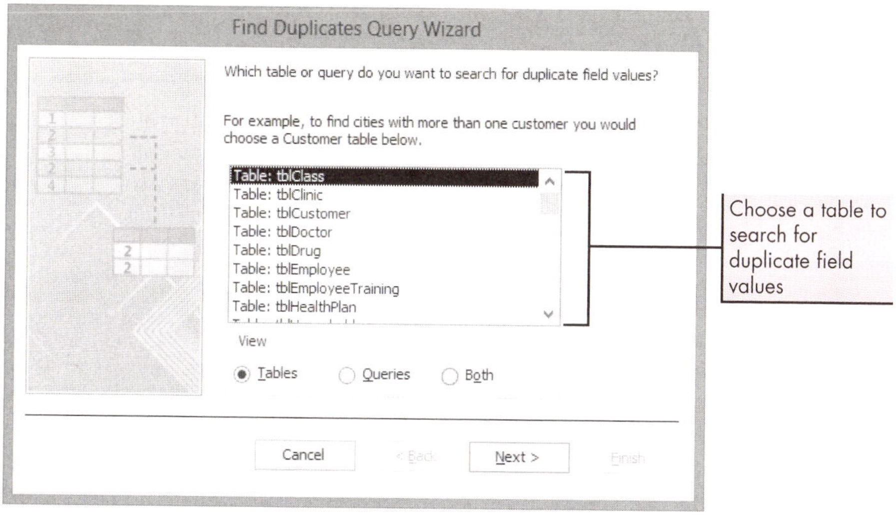

Figure 3.20: Select field or fields that might contain duplicate information

> Select fields that might contain duplicate values

Find Duplicates Query Wizard

Which fields might contain duplicate information?

For example, if you are looking for cities with more than one customer, you would choose City and Region fields here.

Available fields:

DOB
StartDate
EndDate
Address
ZIP
JobID
Phone
Cell

Duplicate-value fields:

City
State

Cancel   < Back   Next >   Finish

> Field list of possible duplicate values

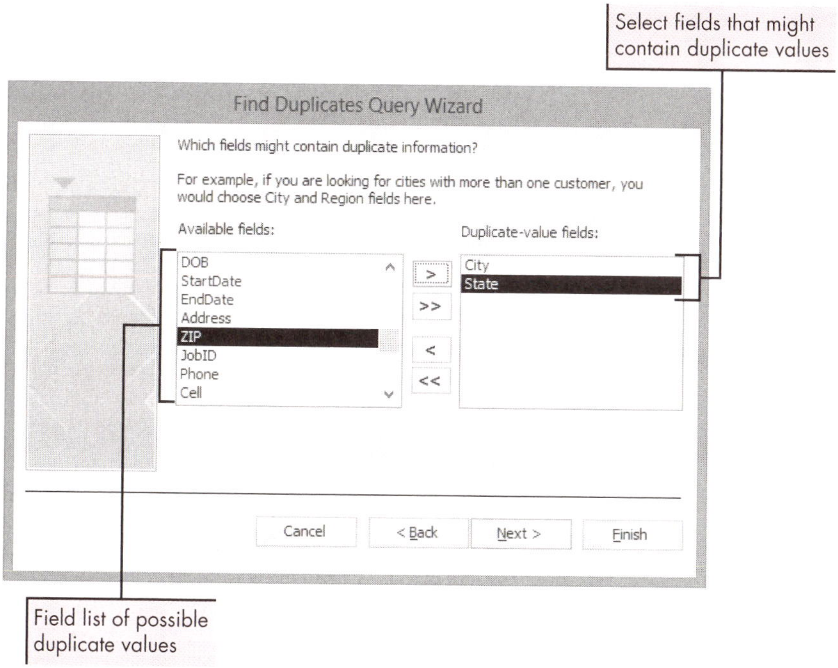

When she clicks the Next button, the third dialog box in the wizard opens, asking if she wants the query to show fields in addition to those with duplicate values. Maria selects the EmpFirst, EmpLast, Address, Phone, and Cell fields so the list will have all the information employees need to contact each other, and then clicks the Next button. She names the query qryDuplicateCities, and clicks Finish. The results are shown in Figure 3.21.

Figure 3.21: Results of the Find Duplicates Query Wizard

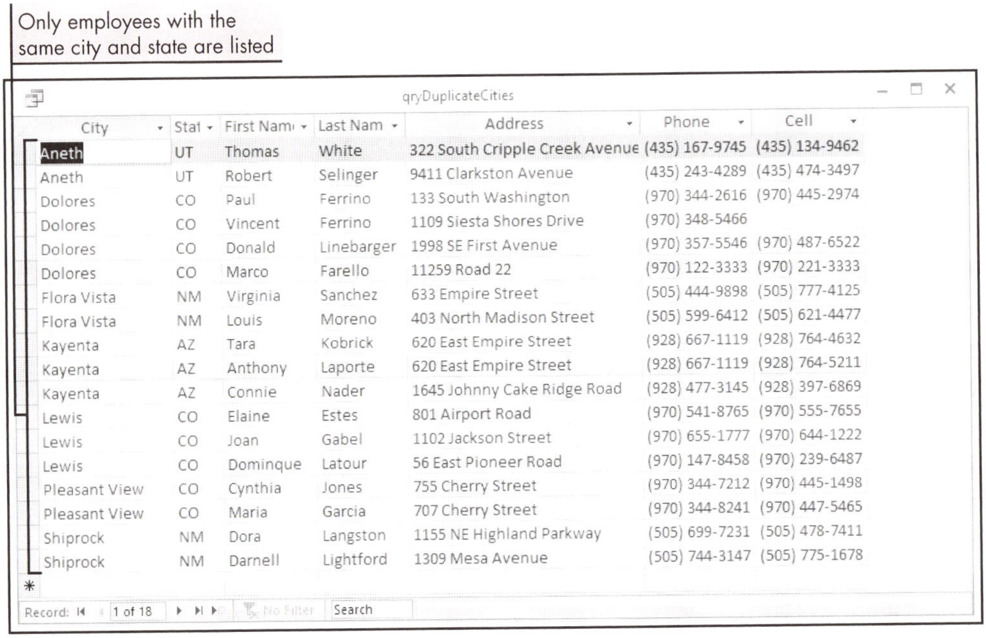

Only employees with the
same city and state are listed

City	Stat	First Nam	Last Nam	Address	Phone	Cell
Aneth	UT	Thomas	White	322 South Cripple Creek Avenue	(435) 167-9745	(435) 134-9462
Aneth	UT	Robert	Selinger	9411 Clarkston Avenue	(435) 243-4289	(435) 474-3497
Dolores	CO	Paul	Ferrino	133 South Washington	(970) 344-2616	(970) 445-2974
Dolores	CO	Vincent	Ferrino	1109 Siesta Shores Drive	(970) 348-5466	
Dolores	CO	Donald	Linebarger	1998 SE First Avenue	(970) 357-5546	(970) 487-6522
Dolores	CO	Marco	Farello	11259 Road 22	(970) 122-3333	(970) 221-3333
Flora Vista	NM	Virginia	Sanchez	633 Empire Street	(505) 444-9898	(505) 777-4125
Flora Vista	NM	Louis	Moreno	403 North Madison Street	(505) 599-6412	(505) 621-4477
Kayenta	AZ	Tara	Kobrick	620 East Empire Street	(928) 667-1119	(928) 764-4632
Kayenta	AZ	Anthony	Laporte	620 East Empire Street	(928) 667-1119	(928) 764-5211
Kayenta	AZ	Connie	Nader	1645 Johnny Cake Ridge Road	(928) 477-3145	(928) 397-6869
Lewis	CO	Elaine	Estes	801 Airport Road	(970) 541-8765	(970) 555-7655
Lewis	CO	Joan	Gabel	1102 Jackson Street	(970) 655-1777	(970) 644-1222
Lewis	CO	Dominque	Latour	56 East Pioneer Road	(970) 147-8458	(970) 239-6487
Pleasant View	CO	Cynthia	Jones	755 Cherry Street	(970) 344-7212	(970) 445-1498
Pleasant View	CO	Maria	Garcia	707 Cherry Street	(970) 344-8241	(970) 447-5465
Shiprock	NM	Dora	Langston	1155 NE Highland Parkway	(505) 699-7231	(505) 478-7411
Shiprock	NM	Darnell	Lightford	1309 Mesa Avenue	(505) 744-3147	(505) 775-1678

Record: 14 ◀ 1 of 18 ▶ ▶I ▶ No Filter Search

Best Practice

Avoiding Duplicate Records

If you expect duplicates to be a problem, the best way to solve the problem is to use good database design. For example, the 4Corners database allows only one person to be listed as the head of household in the HeadHH field in tblCustomer, and addresses are listed only once in a separate table named tblHousehold. The tblCustomer and tblHousehold tables share a common field, HeadHH which allows the two tables to be used in queries. By setting a criterion that HeadHH must be Yes, the problem of duplicates is eliminated.

Using Queries to Find Unmatched Records

Another useful query wizard is the Find Unmatched Query Wizard. This type of select query compares the records in two specified tables or recordsets, and finds all the records in one table or query that have no related records in a second table or query. For example, you could find all customers who have not ordered any products, or vendors who provide services you no longer use. Identifying these unmatched records means you can then contact inactive customers to solicit business or delete records for vendors who no longer serve your needs. Remember that the Find Unmatched Query Wizard requires that the two tables being compared have a common field.

At 4Corners Pharmacy, Paul Ferrino has set a store policy that all employees must maintain certifications in adult, infant, and child CPR and in defibrillator use. One of Maria's new responsibilities is to monitor training to make sure employees are enrolling in the required certification classes. This information is stored in the tblEmployeeTraining table. However, Maria is concerned that some employees may not have completed any training, and therefore would not have a record in tblEmployeeTraining. To identify these employees, she can use the Find Unmatched Query Wizard.

To start the query, Maria clicks the Query Wizard button on the CREATE tab. Then, she double-clicks Find Unmatched Query Wizard. The first dialog box opens, as shown in Figure 3.22.

Figure 3.22: Find Unmatched Query Wizard opening dialog box

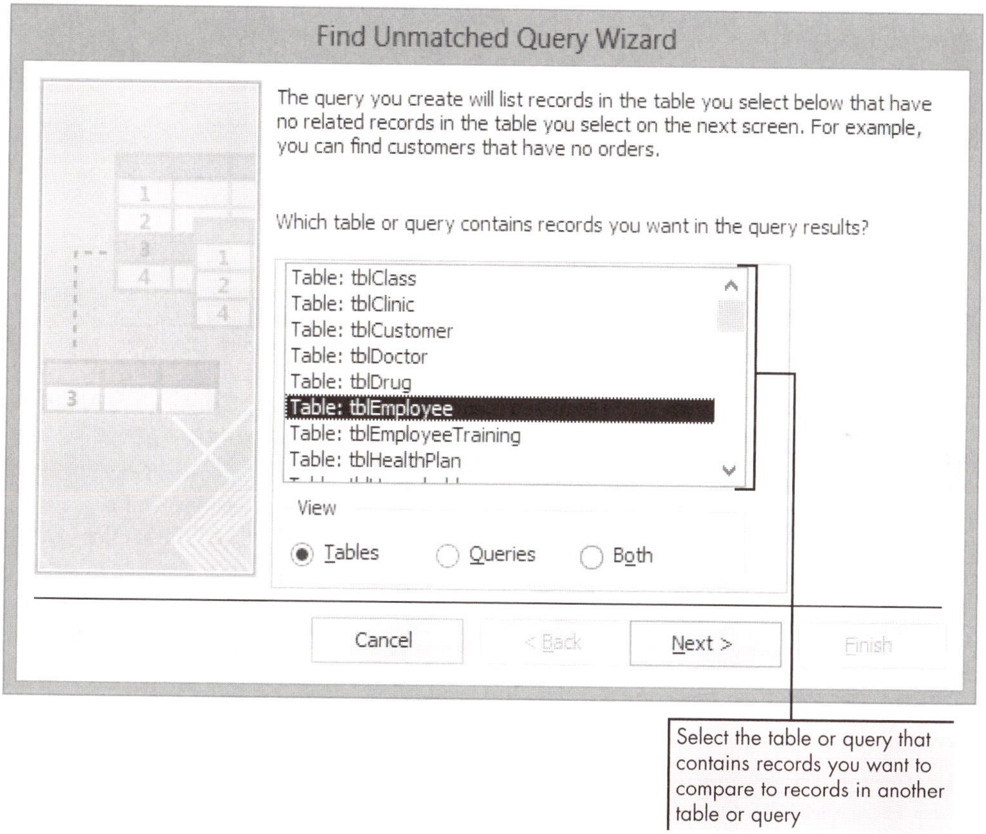

Select the table or query that contains records you want to compare to records in another table or query

Maria wants to produce the names of employees who have not enrolled in any training classes. She selects tblEmployee because it contains the employee records, which include employee names. She clicks the Next button, and the dialog box shown in Figure 3.23 opens.

Figure 3.23: Selecting the related tables to compare records

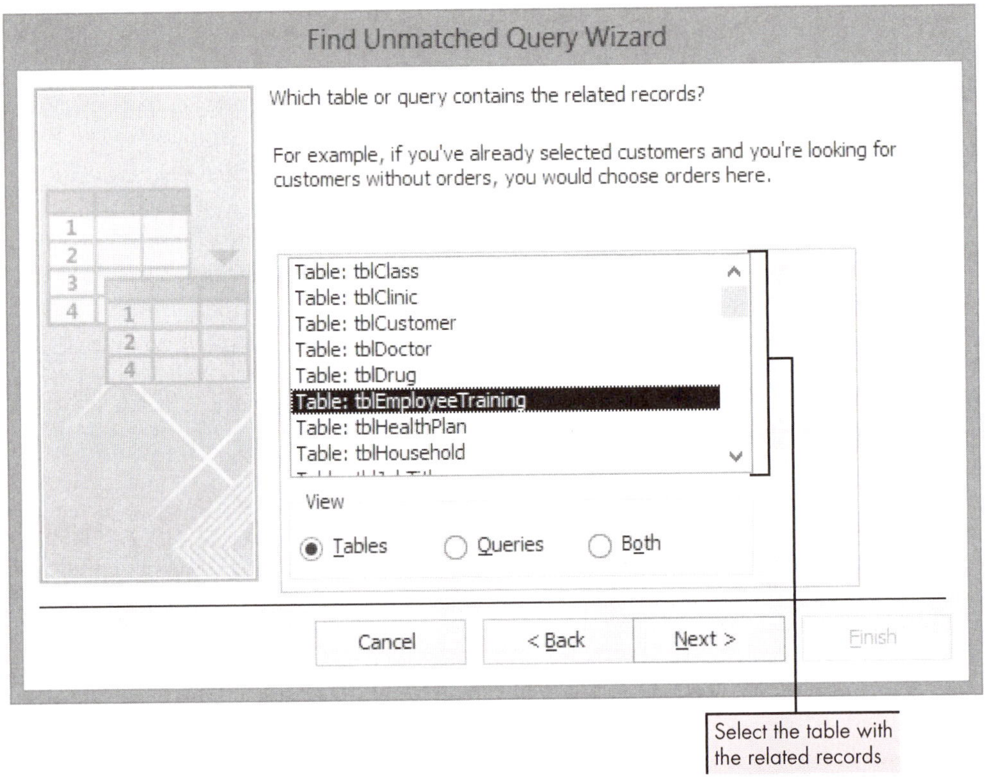

Maria selects tblEmployeeTraining and clicks the Next button because she suspects that this table might not contain records for all the employees in tblEmployee. She knows that both tables must have a common field so that the query can compare the records; tblEmployee and tblEmployeeTraining share the common field EmpID. Maria clicks the <=> button to link the two EmpID fields. See Figure 3.24.

Figure 3.24: Identifying the field to relate the two tables or queries

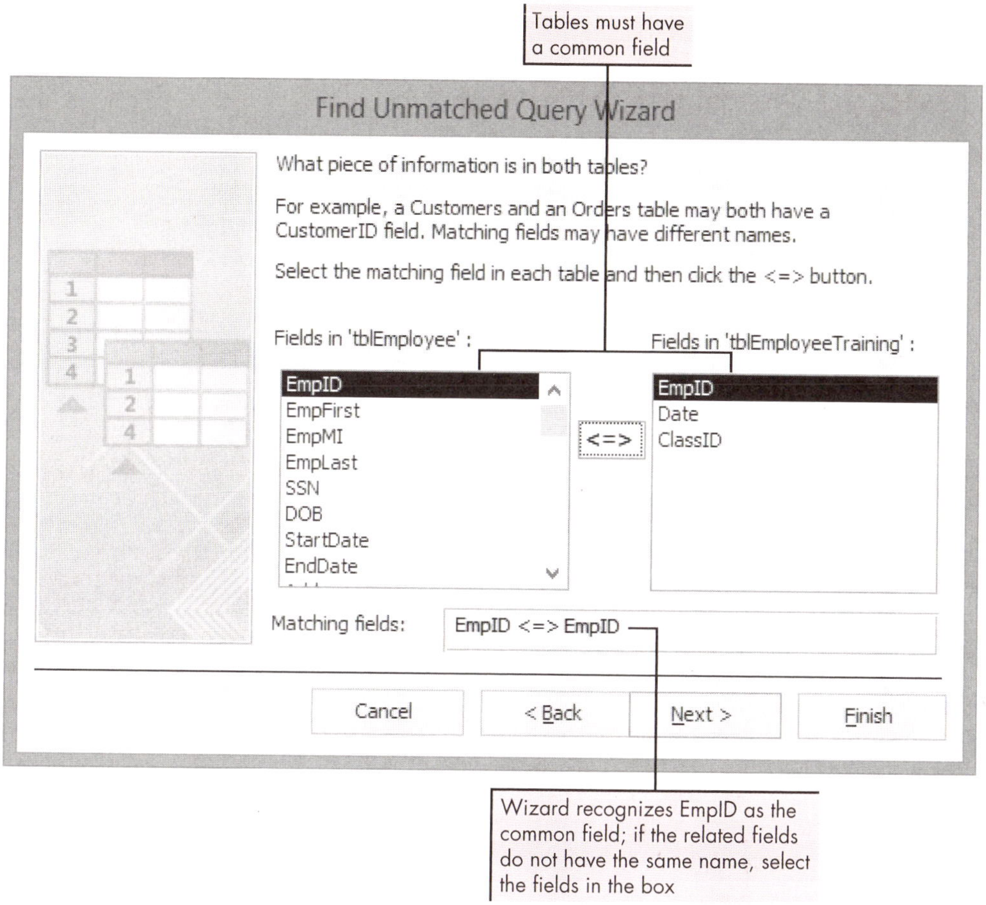

Tables must have a common field

Find Unmatched Query Wizard

What piece of information is in both tables?

For example, a Customers and an Orders table may both have a CustomerID field. Matching fields may have different names.

Select the matching field in each table and then click the <=> button.

Fields in 'tblEmployee' :

EmpID
EmpFirst
EmpMI
EmpLast
SSN
DOB
StartDate
EndDate

<=>

Fields in 'tblEmployeeTraining' :

EmpID
Date
ClassID

Matching fields: EmpID <=> EmpID

Cancel	< Back	Next >	Finish

Wizard recognizes EmpID as the common field; if the related fields do not have the same name, select the fields in the box

She clicks the Next button, and the next dialog box asks what other fields she wants to see in the query results. She decides to include EmpLast and EmpFirst in the results so she can easily identify the employees. Then she clicks the Next button, names the query qryNoTraining, and clicks the Finish button. The results are shown in Figure 3.25.

Figure 3.25: Results of the Find Unmatched Query Wizard

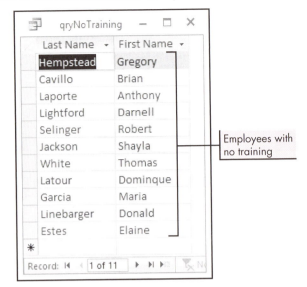

How To

Create a Query Using the Find Unmatched Query Wizard

1. Click Query Wizard on the CREATE tab of the Ribbon.
2. Double-click Find Unmatched Query Wizard.
3. Click to select the table or query that has the records you want in your query results. Click the Next button.
4. Click to select the table or query with the related records. Click the Next button.
5. If necessary, click the matching field in each table. Access identifies the common field if the fields have the same name in each table. Click the Next button.
6. Double-click the fields you want to display in the query results, and then click the Next button.
7. Name the query and then click the Finish button.

Maria finds 11 employees who have no matching records, meaning these employees have never received certification. Now she can contact these employees and tell them to schedule certification training as soon as possible. In the meantime, Paul Ferrino has asked her to perform another task for him. He wants to identify the five best nonsalaried employees; those who have been rewarded for extraordinary customer service or other contributions to the pharmacy. He is considering developing a program that encourages employee excellence, and he might start by recognizing these five employees. Maria considers how to provide this information. She could pull out the file folders for all nonsalaried employees and scan the printed employee reviews to find citations for special service. However, this would be time consuming and error-prone; she would have to read carefully to make sure she doesn't overlook relevant information. She recalls that Paul regularly rewards employees for their performance by increasing their wages. Maria can use the 4Corners database to identify the top five wage earners—these are the same employees who provide the best service to the pharmacy.

Limiting the Records in the Query Results

Sometimes, showing all the data in a query provides more detail than you need, especially if the query selects many records that match your criteria. Limiting the results to only a few records often aids analysis. For example, schools need to identify students in the top 5% of their class. A bookstore might want to list the top 10 best-selling books, while a national business might want to increase advertising in the three regions with the fewest sales. To limit the number of records in the query results, you can indicate the number of records you want the query to display by entering or selecting an integer, such as 10 (to display the top or bottom 10 records), or a percentage, such as 25% (to display the top or bottom 25% of records). To indicate whether you want to select records with the top or bottom values, set a sort order for the field—Descending to display the records with the highest values, or Ascending to display the records with the smallest values.

Maria wants to identify the top five current wage earners at 4Corners Pharmacy in tblEmployee. She creates a query in Design view using the EmpFirst, EmpLast, HourlyRate, and EndDate fields from tblEmployee. She uses the Is Null criterion in the EndDate field to select records only for current employees, and then removes the check mark from the Show check box so the EndDate field doesn't appear in the results. Then she clicks in the Sort row of the HourlyRate field and specifies a Descending sort order. To limit the records to the top five values in that field, she clicks the Return list arrow in the Query Setup group on the DESIGN tab, and then clicks 5. She saves the query as qryTop5HourlyRates, and then runs the query. Figure 3.26 shows the design and results of qryTop5HourlyRates.

Figure 3.26: qryTop5HourlyRates results

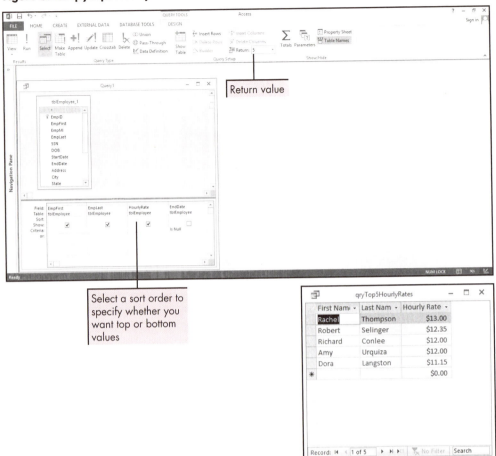

Return value

Select a sort order to specify whether you want top or bottom values

Maria will give the results of qryTop5HourlyRates to Paul to support his plans for an employee excellence program. Before she can return to notifying employees about certification training, a pharmacy technician calls in sick. Maria needs to find another pharmacy technician who can work for him. Instead of pulling out an employee phone list and searching for technicians as she's done in the past, Maria decides to create a query that will help her schedule employees when someone else cannot work. She'd like a way to generate a list of employees using a job category so she can quickly call others with the same job and find a substitute. She can create a query that selects employee information, including name and phone number, and uses the job ID as the criterion for selection. The problem she faces, however, is that the job ID will change depending on who is missing work. If a cashier calls in sick, for example, Maria needs to run the query using 4 as the criterion. If she needs a substitute for a pharmacy technician, she'll use 3 as the criterion. She needs to create a query that requests the criterion before it runs—then she can enter 3 or 4 as appropriate, and generate a list of employees in a particular job category.

Using Parameter Values in Queries

When you need to run a query multiple times with changes to the criteria, you can enter a parameter value. A parameter value is a phrase, usually in the form of a question or instruction, enclosed in square brackets, such as [Enter a job ID:] or [What job category do you want to select?]. The parameter value serves as a prompt to the user to enter a value. To create a parameter query, you enter a parameter value as the criterion for a field, such as the JobID field. When you run the query, it opens a dialog box displaying the prompt you specified and asks you to enter a value. After you enter the value and click OK or press Enter, the query continues. Your response is then used as a criterion for the query. The benefit of a parameter query is that it is interactive—you can run the same query many times and specify different values each time.

Maria decides to create a parameter query by specifying a parameter value in the JobID field of tblEmployee. She begins creating the query in Design view using tblEmployee. She chooses EmpLast, EmpFirst, Phone, Cell, JobID, and EndDate as fields for the query. In the Criteria row for JobID, she types the prompt [What job classification do you want?], including the required square brackets. She sorts the data in alphabetical order by last name, and removes the check mark in the Show check box for the JobID field because all employees in the results will have the same JobID. She remembers to include the EndDate criterion Is Null and to remove the check mark in its Show check box. She saves the query as qrySubstituteList, and then runs it to make sure the Enter Parameter Value dialog box appears. Figure 3.27 shows the design of qrySubstituteList, the dialog box that appears when running the query, and the results.

Figure 3.27: Parameter query to allow user input when the query is run

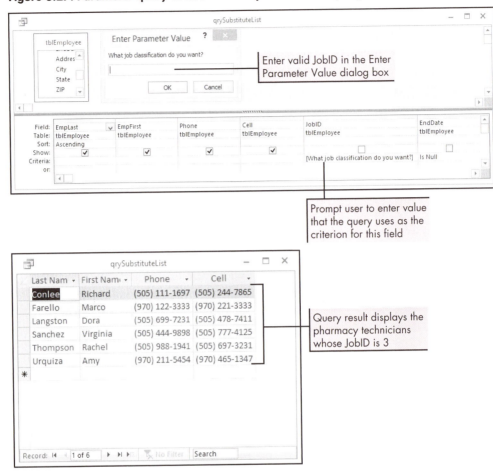

When Maria runs the query, the Enter Parameter Value dialog box appears first. In this dialog box, she can enter the job ID of the job for which she needs a substitute. When she clicks OK, the results will display a list of employees in that job category.

When you enter the parameter value prompt as a criterion in Design view, Access assumes you want users to enter a value with the default data type, which is Short Text. If the required value is of a different data type, you can click the Parameters button in the Show/Hide group on the DESIGN tab, and use the Query Parameters dialog box to specify the parameter's data type. Because many parameter queries work without specifying the data type, you should try the query first without specifying the data type to see if it runs correctly.

3

How To

Specify the Parameter's Data Type

1. Open a query in Design view. In the Criteria row for the field whose criterion will change each time the query runs, type the prompt you want to appear in the Enter Parameter Value dialog box. Be certain to type the prompt within square brackets.

2. Copy the text of the parameter prompt without including the square brackets. (Select the text and then press Ctrl+C to copy it.)

3. Click Parameters in the Show/Hide group on the DESIGN tab; the Query Parameters dialog box opens.

4. Click in the first open line of the Query Parameters dialog box, and then press Ctrl+V to paste the prompt. You can also type the prompt instead.

5. Click in the corresponding Data Type text box, click the list arrow, and then click the appropriate data type. See Figure 3.28.

6. Click the OK button.

Figure 3.28: Changing the data type of a parameter value

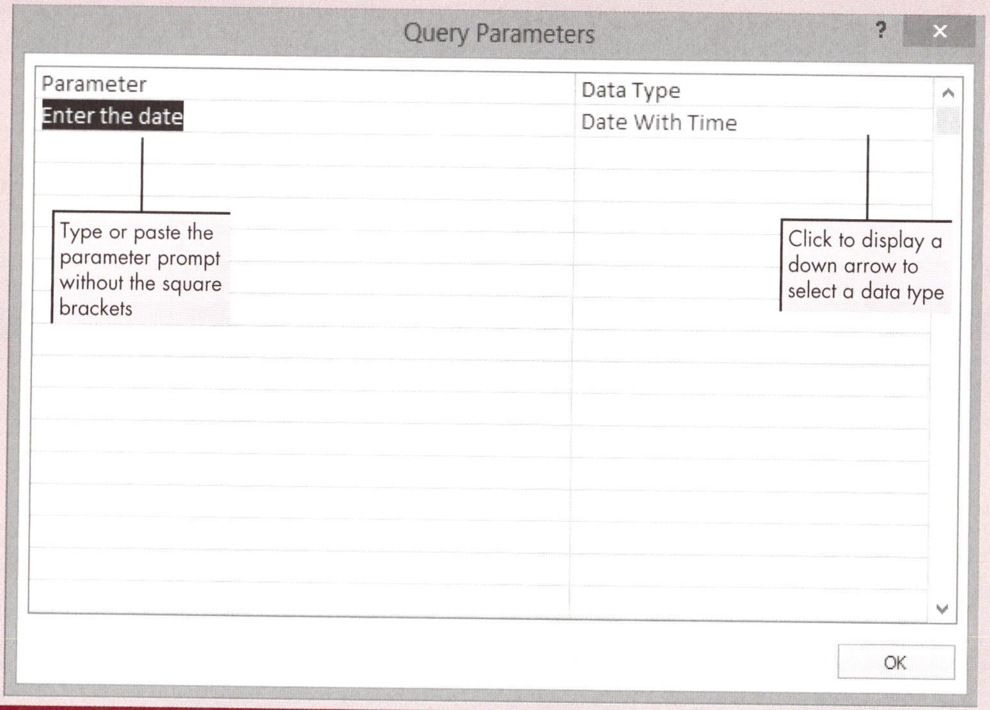

Query Parameters

Parameter	Data Type
Enter the date	Date With Time

Type or paste the parameter prompt without the square brackets

Click to display a down arrow to select a data type

OK

Best Practice

Testing a Parameter Query

As you create a parameter query, test it by using fixed criteria and then add the parameter prompts. You can then switch between Design view and Datasheet view without stopping to enter one or more parameters. After you have tested the query, replace the fixed criteria with the prompt for the Enter Parameter Value dialog box.

Maria is now ready to revisit the training issues for the pharmacy's employees. She needs to know which employees need to attend training classes to keep their certifications up to date. To investigate this problem fully, she needs to analyze data from tblEmployee and tblEmployeeTraining.

Analyzing Data from More Than One Table

Often, data from more than one table is required to answer a question. In fact, the most powerful advantage of creating queries is that they let you combine records from two or more tables to display only the information you need. For example, Maria needs data from both tblEmployee and tblEmployeeTraining to answer questions about employee certification training. Although you can use the Simple Query Wizard to select fields from more than one table or query, you must work in Design view to specify criteria for selecting records from multiple tables. Figure 3.29 shows the field lists for two tables in Design view for a select query.

Figure 3.29: Field lists for two tables in Design view

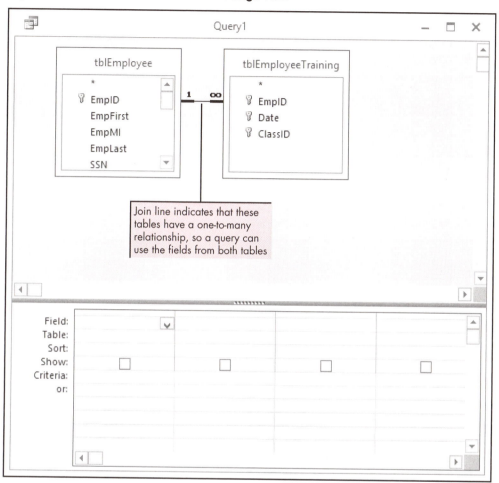

Join line indicates that these tables have a one-to-many relationship, so a query can use the fields from both tables

Notice the join line that connects the EmpID fields in the two tables. Recall that the join line represents the relationship between the primary key in tblEmployee and a foreign key in tblEmployeeTraining. This was created when you established referential integrity in Chapter 2. If tables are related, you can select fields from those tables and use them together in queries. The lines between tables link the primary key, the field designated with a "1," in a table called the primary table to the foreign key, the field designated with an infinity symbol (∞), in a table called a related table. The primary table is on the "one" side of the relationship, and the related table with the foreign key is on the "many" side of the relationship. For example, in tblEmployee, the EmpID field is the primary key. Each employee has only one ID and only one record in tblEmployee, but the employee can take many classes. By including the EmpID in the tblEmployeeTraining table, the two tables are linked by EmpID, and fields from both tables can therefore be used in a query. This linking of tables using their primary and foreign keys is called a join of the tables.

If you have not already established a relationship between two tables, Access creates a join under the following conditions: each table shares a field with the same or compatible data type and one of the join fields is a primary key. In this case, Access does not display the "1" and "many" symbols because referential integrity is not enforced.

If the tables you want to use in a query do not include fields that can be joined, you must add one or more extra tables or queries to link the tables that contain the data you want to use. For example, suppose Maria needs to display a list of classes taken by pharmacists only, and wants to include the ClassID and Date fields from tblEmployeeTraining and use the JobID field from tblJobTitle to set the criterion. The tblEmployeeTraining and tblJobTitle tables are not related and do not share any common fields. She must add a table to the query that is related to tblEmployeeTraining and tblJobTitle, which is tblEmployee. Then tblEmployee serves as a bridge between the two unrelated tables so that Maria can produce a list of classes taken by pharmacists.

Note that if your query includes related tables, the values you specify in criteria for fields from the related tables are case sensitive—they must match the case of the values in the underlying table.

Maria wants to start investigating employee training by producing a list of employees who have taken certification classes, including the date and class ID. To do so, she needs fields from two tables: tblEmployee and tblEmployeeTraining. She starts creating a query in Design view, selecting the field lists for tblEmployee and tblEmployeeTraining. To the query design grid, she adds the EmpLast and EmpFirst fields from tblEmployee and the Date and ClassID fields from tblEmployeeTraining. She notes that the tables have a one-to-many relationship, and that they are linked by the common EmpID field. Maria saves the query as qryEmployeeClasses, and then runs it. The results list employees who have attended training classes. Because some employees have taken more than one class, they are listed more than once. See Figure 3.30.

Figure 3.30: Query using fields from two tables

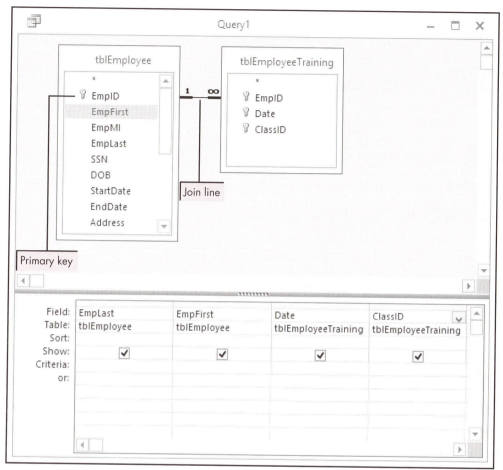

Maria can use this list herself, but she needs a similar list that includes the class description instead of the class ID. She'll post this list on the employee bulletin board as a reminder about the certification classes. Now that she's created qryEmployeeClasses, she can save time by using it as the basis for a new query that lists class descriptions. The qryEmployeeClasses query already has fields from tblEmployee and tblEmployeeTraining, including ClassID. However, neither table contains the Description field, which provides a description or title of each class. Because only tblClass contains that field, she needs to include the tblClass table in the new query to list class descriptions instead of class IDs.

You can use queries as the source of the underlying data for another query in place of one or more tables. For example, you might want to restrict the records you select by using a Top Values query or you might have already saved a query with the fields and criteria you want as the start for a new query. When you use the Show Table dialog box to select the objects to query, you can click the Queries tab or the Both tab to choose queries as well as tables for field lists. Queries do not have primary keys or defined relationships the way tables do, but a line connects a field in a query used as a field list if the field names are the same in the other table or query.

Maria starts creating a query in Design view. When the Show Table dialog box opens, she clicks the Both tab to show tables and queries, and then adds qryEmployeeClasses and tblClass to the query. Because she wants to list employee names, the date they attended a class, and the class description, she double-clicks EmpLast, EmpFirst, and Date in the qryEmployeeClasses field list and Description in the tblClass field list to add these fields to the query design grid, and sorts the EmpLast field in ascending order. She saves the query as qryEmployeeClassesDescription, and then runs it. The results now include the descriptions of the classes instead of the ClassIDs, which is more meaningful to the employees who will view the list. See Figure 3.31.

Figure 3.31: Joining a query and a table

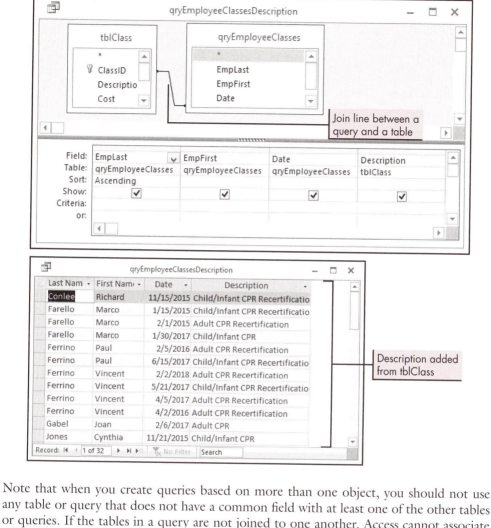

Note that when you create queries based on more than one object, you should not use any table or query that does not have a common field with at least one of the other tables or queries. If the tables in a query are not joined to one another, Access cannot associate one record with another, so it displays every combination of records between the two tables. The data from a query created with unrelated tables therefore contains many extra records, often producing meaningless results. For example, suppose Maria tried to produce a list of employee names and class descriptions by including EmpLast and EmpFirst from tblEmployee and Description from tblClass. The tblEmployee and tblClass tables are not related and contain no common fields. When Maria runs the query, Access would simply list the 24 current employees in the EmpLast and EmpFirst columns of the results, and the descriptions for all eight classes contained in tblClass in the Description column. The results would contain 192 rows of information, or 8 × 24—each employee name listed eight times for each class, regardless of whether the employee attended the class. See Figure 3.32.

Figure 3.32: Unrelated tables show no join line and give meaningless results when queried

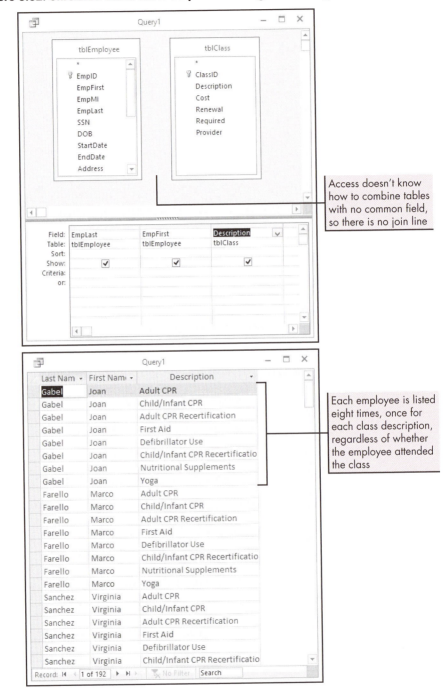

Access doesn't know how to combine tables with no common field, so there is no join line

Each employee is listed eight times, once for each class description, regardless of whether the employee attended the class

Best Practice

Verifying that Your Query Results Make Sense

When you examine the results of a query, be certain to verify that they make sense for your data and your business. One quick check is to note the number of rows in the query datasheet. Queries created using unrelated tables often contain many more rows than you expect. If you combine a large customer list of 100 customers, for example, with many purchases for each customer, you expect hundreds of rows in the results. However, if you list customers who live in a few specified cities, you expect the list to contain fewer than 100 customers. As a general rule, when the query results include a high number of rows, check to make sure the field lists have join lines and that the results seem plausible.

As Maria examines the results of qryEmployeeClassesDescription, she realizes it would provide more information if she could include the employees who have not attended any training classes—these are the employees who need to schedule training as soon as possible. She already used the Find Unmatched Query Wizard to create qryNoTraining, which identified employees who have not attended any training classes. Ideally, the list she posts on the employee bulletin board will include these employees and those who have attended training—some might need to update their certification. She decides to find out if she can refine the query to list all employees and their training information, even if they have not attended a class.

Refining Relationships with Appropriate Join Types

Tables with a relationship (and a common field) can be joined in two ways, and each affects the records a query selects. Double-clicking the join line opens the Join Properties dialog box, so you can view or change the join type.

The most common type of relationship for select queries is an inner join. This type of join displays all records in one table that have corresponding values in the common field in another table. Usually, this joins the records of the primary table to the records of a related table (one with a foreign key). Records must match before they are displayed in the query results. For example, in the 4Corners database, the tblEmployee table is on the "one" side of a one-to-many relationship with the tblEmployeeTraining table. The primary key for tblEmployee is EmpID. In the tblEmployeeTraining table, EmpID is a foreign key. When these tables are related with an inner join, a query displays only those records that have a matching EmpID value—all the records in tblEmployee that have a matching record in tblEmployeeTraining, or all the employees who have attended training classes.

If you want to display all the records of one table regardless of whether a corresponding record is stored in a related table, use an outer join. With this type of join, an employee record in tblEmployee might not have a corresponding record in tblEmployeeTraining because not every employee has attended a training class. Figure 3.33 is a Venn diagram illustrating outer join queries.

Figure 3.33 Venn diagram illustrating outer join query

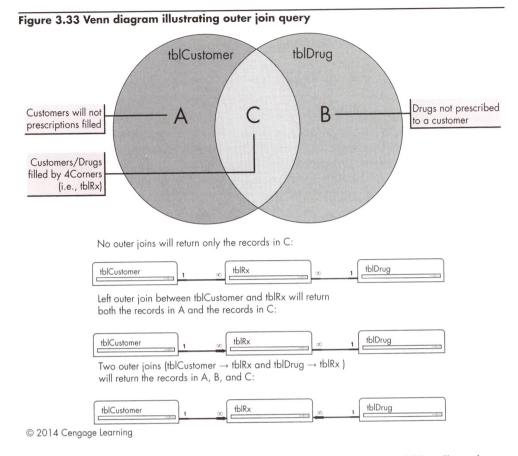

No outer joins will return only the records in C:

Left outer join between tblCustomer and tblRx will return
both the records in A and the records in C:

Two outer joins (tblCustomer → tblRx and tblDrug → tblRx)
will return the records in A, B, and C:

© 2014 Cengage Learning

An outer join query using tblEmployee and tblEmployeeTraining would list all employees regardless of whether they have attended a training class. This type of outer join applies when you want to show all the records from the primary table and only data that matches in the related table. Another type of outer join shows all the records from the related table and only data that matches in the primary table. Figure 3.34 shows an inner join, while Figures 3.35 and 3.36 show the two types of outer joins.

Figure 3.34: Inner join

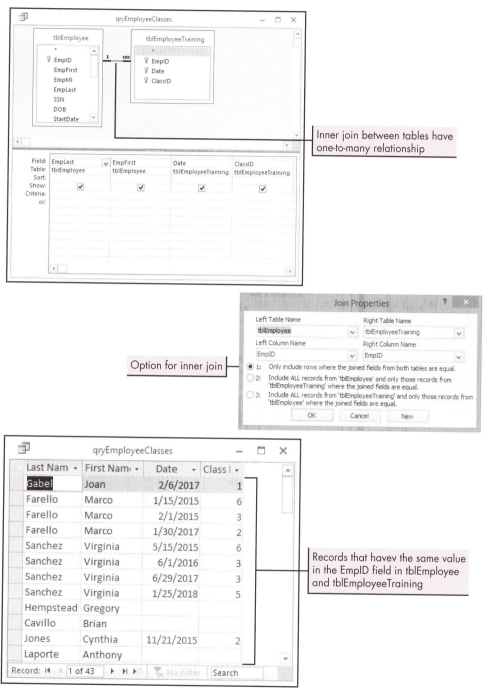

Inner join between tables have one-to-many relationship

Option for inner join

Records that havev the same value in the EmpID field in tblEmployee and tblEmployeeTraining

Figure 3.35: Left outer join

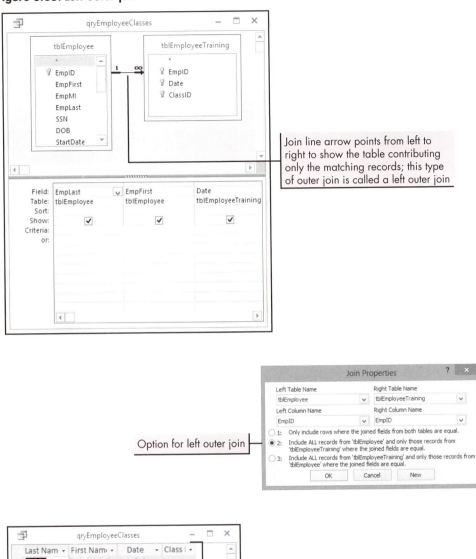

Join line arrow points from left to right to show the table contributing only the matching records; this type of outer join is called a left outer join

Option for left outer join

All records from tblEmployee and only those records from tblEmployeeTraining that have a matching value in the EmpID field

Figure 3.36: Right outer join

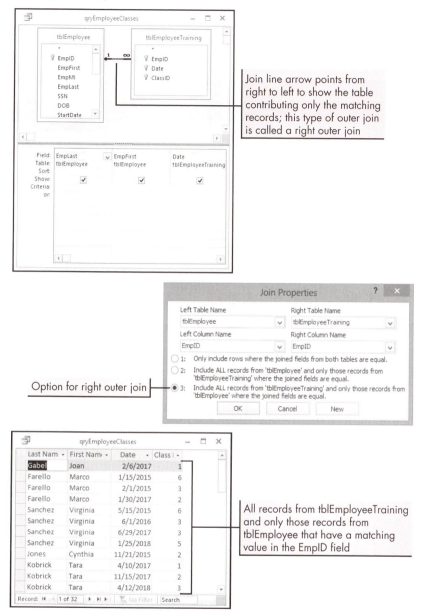

Join line arrow points from right to left to show the table contributing only the matching records; this type of outer join is called a right outer join

Option for right outer join

All records from tblEmployeeTraining and only those records from tblEmployee that have a matching value in the EmpID field

The two types of outer joins are often designated as left or right, depending on the placement of the field lists in Design view for the query and whether you want the one on the right or the left to show all its records. Left outer joins include all of the records from the table on the left, even if there are no matching values for records in the table on the right. Right outer joins include all of the records from the table on the right, even if there are no matching values for records in the table on the left. Changing the position of the field lists in the query reverses the right/left designation for the join.

To produce a list of all employees and their training information, even if they have not attended a class, Maria needs fields from tblEmployee and tblEmployeeTraining, the same fields she used to create qryEmployeeClasses. She opens qryEmployeeClasses in Design view so she can modify it, and saves it as qryAllEmployeeClasses. By default, this query uses an inner join between tblEmployee and tblEmployeeTraining. To change the join type, she double-clicks the join line. The Join Properties dialog box opens, shown in Figure 3.37.

Figure 3.37: Changing the join type using the Join Properties dialog box

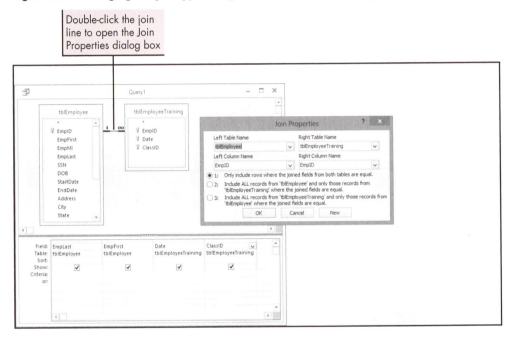

The first option, "Only include rows where the joined fields from both tables are equal," is for an inner join. The second option, "Include ALL records from 'tblEmployee' and only those records from 'tblEmployeeTraining' where the joined fields are equal," is exactly what Maria wants. This type of outer join selects all the records from tblEmployee, even if there are no matching records in tblEmployeeTraining. In other words, it lists all the employees and the classes they've taken. If an employee has not attended a class, this outer join query would list the employee name, but leave the Date and ClassID fields blank. The third option, "Include ALL records from 'tblEmployeeTraining' and only those records from 'tblEmployee' where the joined fields are equal," would select all the records from tblEmployeeTraining, even if there are no matching records in tblEmployee. If a class was scheduled, for example, but no employees were recorded as attending it, the results would include the Date and ClassID of that class, but no data in the EmpLast and EmpFirst fields.

Maria clicks second option button to create a left outer join, runs the query, and then saves it using the same name. The results are shown earlier in Figure 3.35.

This query, however, has the same problem as qryEmployeeClasses—it lists classes by ID number, not by the class description. Maria wants to display the Description column in the query results, not the ClassID column. Recall that tblClass contains the Description field, not tblEmployeeTraining. If she starts creating a query and uses fields from tblEmployee and tblClass, the query will not produce the results she wants because the tables are not related—they contain no common field. That means a query cannot retrieve records from these two tables as if they were one larger table, and will not produce meaningful results. Instead, she can use a third table to link tblEmployee and tblClass. The tblEmployeeTraining table is linked to tblEmployee by the common EmpID field, and is also linked to tblClass by the common ClassID field. She starts creating a query in Design view, adds the field lists for tblEmployee, tblEmployeeTraining, and tblClass to the query window, and then adds the EmpLast, EmpFirst, and Description fields to the design grid so she can list all employees and any classes they have attended. She decides to sort the records in ascending order by last name.

By default, the tables are related using inner joins. She double-clicks the join line between tblEmployee and tblEmployeeTraining to open the Join Properties dialog box, and then reviews the options for joining the two tables:

- Option 1 for an inner join is selected by default. It only includes records that contain the same value in the common field that links the tables.
- Option 2 is for an outer join that selects all records from the tblEmployee table and only those records from tblEmployeeTraining that contain matching EmpID fields.
- Option 3 is for an outer join that selects all records from the tblEmployeeTraining table and only those records from tblEmployee that contain matching EmpID fields.

Given that she wants to list all employees in the query results, she selects Option 2 to include all records from tblEmployee. The join line now includes an arrowhead pointing from tblEmployee to tblEmployeeTraining. She tries running the query, but receives an error message indicating that the query contains an ambiguous outer join. She also needs to specify the properties for the join line between tblEmployeeTraining and tblClass.

She double-clicks the join line between tblEmployeeTraining and tblClass, rereads the options in the Join Properties dialog box, and realizes that she needs to select Option 3 to include all records from tblEmployeeTraining and only those records from tblClass that contain matching ClassID fields. The join line includes an arrowhead pointing from tblEmployeeTraining to tblClass. She saves the query as qryEmployeeTraining, and then runs it. The query with outer joins produces the results she wants, shown in Figure 3.38.

Figure 3.38: Query results showing all employees and descriptions of classes

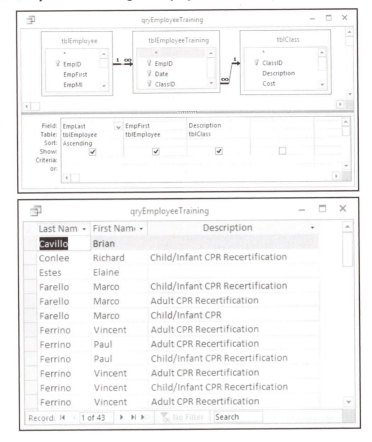

Now that Maria has produced the list she wants, she needs to review the classes that employees have attended. 4Corners requires a few classes, such as Defibrillator Use and CPR, and she wants to determine how many employees are complying with the policy. All required classes must be completed annually. Until now, it has been difficult for Maria to track compliance with the certification policy—employees postpone classes when they are busy, and she suspects that many certifications have lapsed.

Using Logical Operators to Specify Multiple Conditions

Some queries require one or more logical operators, which are used to test values that can only be true or false. You have already used the logical AND and OR in filters and queries when you want to combine criteria by comparing conditions. Figure 3.39 shows how the logical AND and OR operators work in the query design grid.

Figure 3.39: Using the logical operators AND and OR in query selection criteria

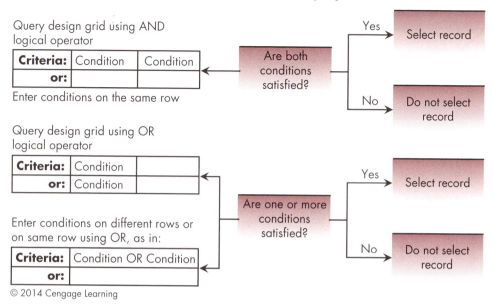

© 2014 Cengage Learning

Recall that if you place conditions in separate fields in the same Criteria row of the design grid, all conditions in that row must be met to select a record. For example, if you want to select pharmacy technicians (JobID 3) who live in Colorado, enter "3" in the Criteria row for the JobID field, and "CO" in the Criteria row for the State field. You can combine the AND logical operator with the Like comparison operator to set conditions for the same field. For example, if you want to identify all the employees who are scheduled for a review in October 2016, enter the following condition in the Criteria row for the Review field: Like "10*" And Like "*2016".

If you place conditions in different Criteria rows in the query design grid, at least one of the conditions must be met to select a record. If the conditions apply to the same field, you can enter each condition separated by OR in the Criteria row. For example, if you want to select employees who live in Colorado or those who live in Utah, enter the following condition in the Criteria row for the State field: "CO" OR "UT".

The NOT logical operator excludes values that don't meet the criterion. For example, if you enter NOT 3 in the Criteria row for the JobID field, the query results show all employees except for pharmacy technicians. The NOT logical operator is often combined with the In comparison operator, as in NOT In("CO","UT"), which selects employees who do not live in Colorado or Utah. (Table 3.5 describes the comparison operators, including In and Like.)

Table 3.8 lists the logical operators you can use in an Access query and the results they return.

Table 3.8: Logical operators

Operator	Description	Examples	Results
AND	Logical AND	A AND B	Record selected only if both criteria are true
OR	Inclusive OR	A OR B	Record selected if any one of the rows of criteria is true
NOT	Logical NOT	NOT A	Record selected if it does not meet the condition

© 2014 Cengage Learning

You can combine the logical and comparison operators to retrieve the records you need. For example, if you want to identify all the technicians and cashiers (JobIDs 3 and 4) who are scheduled for a review in October 2016, enter the following conditions in the query design grid:

	JobID	Review
Criteria:	3	Like "10*" And Like "*2016"
or:	4	Like "10*" And Like "*2016"

The qryEmployeeTraining query produces a list that includes employees and the classes they've attended and employees who have not attended any classes. Maria wants to base a new query on qryEmployeeTraining to see if employees taking required classes are up to date on their certifications in Adult CPR, Child/Infant CPR, and Defibrillator Use. Each type of certification needs to be renewed at different intervals, so she needs to set the criteria carefully to produce the results she needs.

Maria decides to save qryEmployeeTraining as qryUpToDate and then modify it in Design view. The query already includes field lists for tblEmployee, tblEmployeeTraining, and tblClass, with outer joins specified so that all employees are listed in the results, even if they have not attended a class. The EmpLast and EmpFirst fields from tblEmployee and the Description field from tblClass already appear in the query design grid. To determine whether an employee's certification is up to date, she needs the Date field from tblEmployeeTraining and she puts this field between the EmpFirst and Description fields. To determine whether a particular class is required for certification, she needs to include the Required field from tblClass. She also decides to include the ClassID field from tblClass to make setting up the criteria easier—all she will have to do is specify the ID of the class rather than the long description. She adds the three fields—Date, Required, and ClassID—to the design grid. She clears the Show check boxes for ClassID and Required because she doesn't need to see the contents of these fields in the results.

Next, she will specify the criteria for selecting information about only the classes required for certification. Pharmacy employees must take the five classes listed in Table 3.9.

Table 3.9: Required classes for pharmacy employees

ClassID	Description	Renewal in Years
1	Adult CPR	0
2	Child/Infant CPR	0
3	Adult CPR Recertification	1
5	Defibrillator Use	1
6	Child/Infant CPR Recertification	1

© 2014 Cengage Learning

The first two classes—Adult CPR and Child/Infant CPR—are the comprehensive classes employees take to receive CPR certification for the first time. Employees complete these comprehensive classes only once, and do not need to renew them. Instead, they need to complete classes with IDs 3 and 6, which are refresher courses for recertification. ClassID 5 provides certification for defibrillator use, and must be taken every year.

First, Maria adds a criterion to determine which employees are current in their Adult CPR certification. These employees would have completed the Adult CPR or the Adult CPR Recertification classes (ClassIDs 1 or 3) in the past year. She can use the logical operator OR to select employees who have completed ClassID 1 or 3, so she types "1 Or 3" in the Criteria row for the ClassID field (remember that the quotes do not need to be typed in with the criteria).

To narrow the criteria and select only those employees who have taken these courses in the past year, Maria can use the Between…And comparison operator, which you use to specify two Date fields. She needs to specify the time period from January 1, 2016 to December 31, 2016, so she types "Between #1/1/2016# And #12/31/2016#" in the Criteria row for the Date field. (Recall that you use pound signs on either side of date values entered as criteria, but no quote marks.)

Finally, she enters "Yes" as the criterion for the Required field to make sure the class is required. And, she includes the EndDate field and enters Is Null for the criteria. She runs qryUpToDate to test the results. See Figure 3.40.

Figure 3.40: Multiple criteria for listing employees who are up to date in their Adult CPR certification

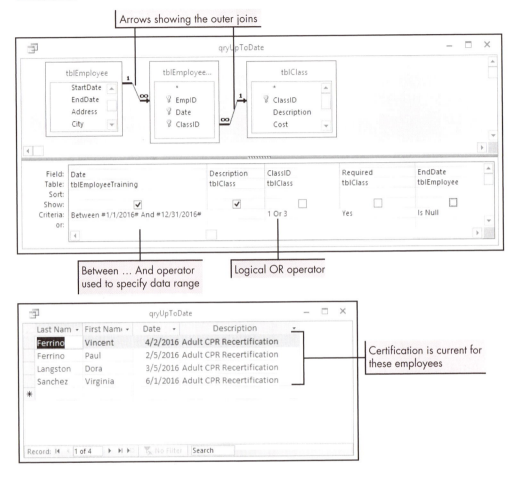

The results show that only two employees are currently certified in Adult CPR. Because these results seem accurate, Maria can continue adding criteria to the query for the other classes, starting with Child/Infant CPR. She knows that data on a second criteria row means that as long as all criteria on either line are true, records that satisfy one or the other line of criteria will be included. She types "2 Or 6" as the second criterion for the ClassID field to identify employees who have current Child/Infant CPR certification. Now, the results will include any employee who has completed Adult or Child/Infant CPR classes.

She also needs to specify the time period for the second ClassID criterion. If she doesn't, the results will include employees who have completed Adult CPR certification this year and those who have completed Child/Infant CPR certification at any time. To select only employees who have completed Child/Infant CPR in the past year, she copies the Between #1/1/2016# And #12/31/2016# criterion from the first criteria row to the second. She also enters "Yes" as the second criterion for the Required field. The three conditions on the second Criteria row are three AND conditions—a record must contain all of the criteria to appear in the query results. See Figure 3.41.

Figure 3.41: Results of modified qryUpToDate query with two rows of criteria

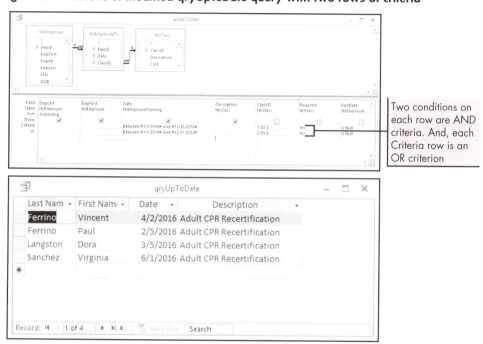

Two conditions on each row are AND criteria. And, each Criteria row is an OR criterion

She enters the third criteria for the Defibrillator Use class—Between #1/1/2016# And #12/31/2016# as the criterion for the Date field, "5" as the criterion for the ClassID field, and "Yes" as the criterion for the Required field. Maria saves the query with the same name— qryUpToDate—and then runs it. As Maria suspected, employees have been postponing certification classes, and many no longer have current CPR certifications. The results now include two records, but only Vincent Ferrino is completely up to date on CPR certifications. He needs to take the Defibrillator Use class again.

As she examines qryUpToDate in Design and Datasheet view, Maria realizes that using specific dates in the Date field criteria can cause problems. The query shows who has up-to-date certifications now, but if employees complete their requirements in the next three months, the query won't reflect that information. To allow her to enter a range of dates when she runs the query instead of changing the criteria in Design view each time she runs the query, she can change the fixed dates to parameter values. She replaces the fixed dates in the Date field with prompts for beginning and ending dates, so that Between #1/1/2016# And #12/31/2016# becomes Between [Beginning date?] And [Ending date?]. When she runs the query, it stops to ask for beginning and ending dates and waits for user input. This will make the query much more flexible in the future. See Figure 3.42.

Figure 3.42: Prompts for parameter values instead of fixed dates

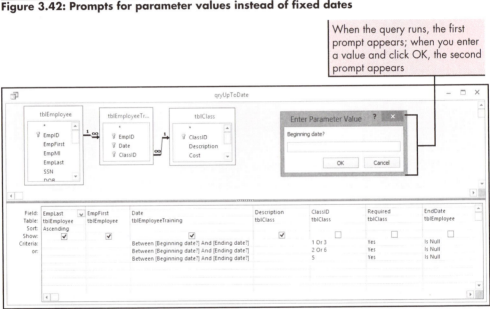

When the query runs, the first prompt appears; when you enter a value and click OK, the second prompt appears

As Maria finishes qryUpToDate, Paul Ferrino returns and asks her to take another look at the hourly rate analysis. The two queries she created list the hourly rates paid to part-time employees (qryHourlyRateAnalysis) and the minimum, maximum, and average hourly rates (qryHourlyRateSummary). Paul wants to improve these results so they list these statistics by job ID, not by employee name. He also wants to know how many years each employee has worked at 4Corners Pharmacy—he is reviewing plans for retirement accounts and needs to set eligibility rules if he decides to offer a plan.

Performing Calculations with Queries

So far, you have worked with queries that retrieve and sort records based on criteria. More complex queries often need to include statistical information or calculations based on fields in the query. For example, you can calculate the sum or average of the values in one field, multiply the values in two fields, or calculate the date three months from the current date. Any information that can be derived from fields in a table or query should be calculated in a query rather than included as data in a table. For example, if you want to know the age of an employee or customer, calculate the age in a query rather than include the age as a field in a table. Over time, the age would become obsolete; calculating it each time you need it ensures that the age is current.

The types of calculations you can perform in a query fall into two categories: predefined and custom calculations. Predefined calculations, also called totals, compute amounts for groups of records or for all the records combined in the query. The amounts predefined calculations compute are sum, average, count, minimum, maximum, standard deviation, and variance. You select one totals calculation for each field you want to calculate.

A custom calculation performs numeric, date, and text computations on each record using data from one or more fields. For example, you can multiply each value in one field by 100. To complete a custom calculation, you need to create a calculated field in the query design grid.

When you display the results of a calculation in a field, the results aren't actually stored in the underlying table. Instead, Access performs the calculation each time you run the query so that the results are always based on the most current data in the database.

Calculating Statistical Information

Recall that you can use the Summary options in the Simple Query Wizard to calculate statistical information such as totals and averages in query results. You can also use Design view to set up these calculations. To do so, you use aggregate functions, which are mathematic and statistical operations you apply to records that meet a query's selection criteria. You can group, or aggregate, the records so that your results are for records in each group that meet the selection criteria. Table 3.10 lists the aggregate functions available in Access.

Table 3.10: Aggregate functions

Aggregate Function	Operation
Avg	Average of the field values for records meeting the criteria within each group
Count	Number of records meeting the criteria in each group
Max	Highest field value for selected records in each group
Min	Lowest field value for selected records in each group
Sum	Total of the field values for the selected records
StDev	Standard deviation for the selected records
Var	Statistical variance for the selected records
First	Returns the value from the first row encountered in the group; results may be unpredictable because the result depends on the physical sequence of the stored data
Last	Returns the value for the last row encountered for the group; results may be unpredictable because the result depends on the physical sequence of the stored data

© 2014 Cengage Learning

You can calculate all types of totals by using the Total row in the query design grid. You add this row to the grid by clicking the Totals button on the DESIGN tab. You can then click the Totals list arrow in a field to select an aggregate function for the calculation you want to perform on the field. To show the calculation results for a particular field, you select Group By in the Total row. For example, because Maria wants to calculate statistics for each job ID, she can group the records on the JobID field.

Maria needs to calculate the minimum, maximum, and average hourly rates for each job ID. She creates a query in Design view, adding the JobID and HourlyRate fields from the tblEmployee table to the query design grid and setting criteria to display only records for technicians and cashiers, so she adds the criteria 3 or 4 in the Criteria row in the JobID field. Because she wants to calculate three types of statistics on the HourlyRate field, she adds that field to the design grid two more times. Then she clicks the Totals button in the Show/Hide group on the DESIGN tab to specify the aggregate functions and group options she wants to use—Max for the first HourlyRate field, Min for the second, and Avg for the third. She names the query qryMaxMinAvgHourlyRate, and then runs it. See Figure 3.43.

Figure 3.43: Using aggregate functions in a query

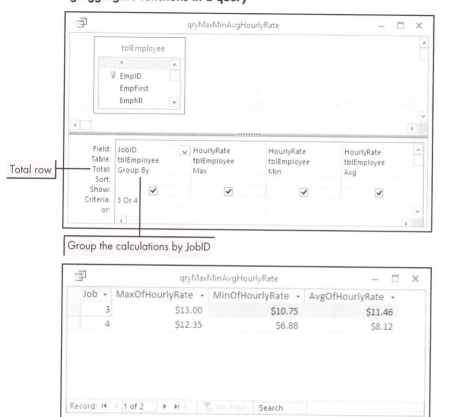

Total row

Group the calculations by JobID

As hourly rates change, Maria can run this query again to recalculate the statistics and produce updated results for Paul.

Next, Maria can determine how long each employee has worked at 4Corners Pharmacy. She knows that she can calculate the number of days of service by subtracting the current date from the value in the StartDate field. Then she can convert the number of days to years. The aggregate functions do not perform this type of calculation. Instead, she needs to create a calculated field in a query.

Creating Calculated Fields in a Query

You can use a query to perform a calculation for immediate use or to include the calculation later when you create a report or form based on the query. You specify the calculation by defining an expression that contains a combination of database fields, constants, and operators. An expression is an arithmetic formula used to make the calculation. You can use the standard arithmetic operators (+, -, *, and /) in the expression. If an expression is complex, use parentheses to indicate which operation should be performed first. Access follows the order of operations precedence: multiplication and division before addition and subtraction. If the precedence is equal, Access works from left to right. For example, if you use 5 + 6 * 100, the result is 605. If you use (5 + 6) * 100, the result is 1100. It's a good idea to check your formula with a calculator to make sure it is working correctly.

To perform a calculation in a query, you add a field to the query design grid called a calculated field. Where you would normally insert the field name from a table or query, you type an expression. For example, suppose you want to calculate the wages employees earn if all hourly rate employees receive a 10% bonus based on their hourly rate. In the query design grid, you could enter an expression in a blank field such as the following:

Wage with Bonus: ([HourlyRate]* 1.10)

In this expression, Wage with Bonus is the name you specify for the field. Field names in the expression are enclosed in square brackets. The calculation ([HourlyRate]*1.10) computes the bonus as 10% of the value in the HourlyRate field. This bonus is added to the value in the HourlyRate field to calculate the total wages including bonus. When the query is run, the expression uses values from the records that meet the criteria you specify to make the calculation.

To type a complete expression, you often need more space than is provided by the field box in the query design grid. In this case, you can open the Zoom dialog box, which provides a large text box for entering expressions or other values.

Some database developers use the Expression Builder when they need to build complex expressions or when they are not familiar with the field, table, and query names in the database. This database tool, shown in Figure 3.44, allows you to work with lists of objects such as tables and queries as well as constants, functions, and common operators to help you construct the expression for your calculation. You can click a field name or operator and then paste it into the expression you are building. You type any constant values that need to be part of the expression.

Figure 3.44: Using the Expression Builder to create an expression for a calculated field

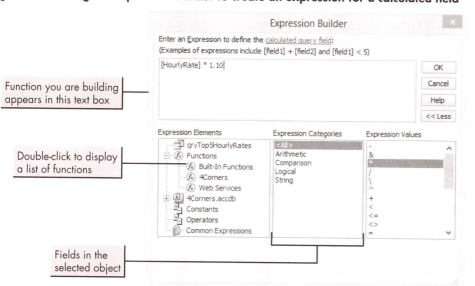

Maria needs to calculate how long each employee has worked for 4Corners Pharmacy. Paul will use this information as he reviews retirement account plans and sets eligibility rules. Maria needs to calculate the years of service each employee has provided 4Corners, and decides to use a calculated field in a query to do so. In the calculation, she needs to subtract the value in the StartDate field from today's date. She could create a parameter query that prompts her to enter today's date and then uses that value in the calculation. However, that means she would enter today's date 24 times, which seems unnecessarily repetitive. Instead, she can use the Date function to retrieve today's date.

When you are creating expressions, you can use a function to perform a standard calculation and return a value. The Date function is a built-in function, meaning it is provided with Access, and has the following form: Date(). To use today's date in an expression, type Date() instead of a fixed date value. The calculation then stays current no matter when you run the query. The Date function can also be used in query criteria.

Maria creates a query in Design view, using the EmpFirst, EmpLast, and StartDate fields from tblEmployee. Even former employees might be eligible for the retirement plan, so Maria does not include the EndDate field and criteria to eliminate former employees from the query results. She right-clicks the Field row in the first empty column, and then clicks Zoom on the shortcut menu to open the Zoom dialog box. This provides room for typing an expression and creating a calculated field. She types "Years of Service:" as the name for the calculated field. The expression should subtract the value in the StartDate field from today's date to calculate the number of days of service. Then the expression should divide that result by 365 to calculate the years of service. Rather than using a fixed date for today's date, she will substitute Date() so that Access retrieves this value each time the query runs. She types the following expression into the Zoom box:

```
Years of Service: (Date() - [StartDate]) / 365
```

"Years of Service" is the name that will appear as the datasheet column heading. The colon (:) separates the name from the calculated expression. The first part of the expression—Date()—is the Access function for calculating today's date. Next comes the subtraction operator followed by [StartDate], which is the name of the StartDate field enclosed in square brackets. You use square brackets around field names to distinguish them from function names or other types of values. Including Date() – [StartDate] in parentheses means that Access subtracts the value in the StartDate field from today's date before performing the second part of the calculation, which is to divide that value by 365, the approximate number of days in a year. (This number is approximate because it doesn't account for leap years.) Dividing by 365 converts the days to years.

She clicks the OK button to close the Zoom dialog box, sorts the calculated field in descending order, saves the query as qryYearsOfService, and then runs it. Maria knows that depending on the current date, her results will differ. Therefore, if she runs this same query several months from now, her results would be different because the current date will be different. The results calculate the approximate years of service, but display a number with many digits after the decimal point. See Figure 3.45.

Figure 3.45: Using a calculated field in a query

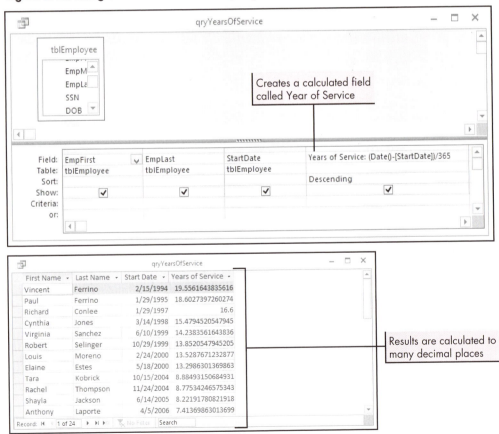

To change the format and number of decimal places for the calculated field, Maria switches to Design view, right-clicks the Years of Service field, and then clicks Properties on the shortcut menu to display the Property Sheet pane. The Property Sheet pane lists the properties for the selected field. Table 3.11 describes the common properties you can set for fields in a query.

Table 3.11: Field properties

Property	Description
Description	Provides information about the field
Format	Specifies how numbers, dates, times, and text are displayed and printed; you can select a predefined format, which varies according to data type, or create a custom format
Decimal Places	Specifies the number of decimal places Access uses to display numbers
Input Mask	Specifies an input mask to simplify data entry and control the values users can enter in a field as you do when designing a table
Caption	Enter the text that appears as a column heading for the field in Query Datasheet view
Smart Tags	Assigns an available Smart Tag to the field

© 2014 Cengage Learning

Maria uses the Format and Decimal Places properties to specify the format of the field values. She selects Standard as the Format and 1 for Decimal Places. She closes the Property Sheet pane, and then saves and runs the query again. She resizes each column in the resulting datasheet to its best fit. See Figure 3.46. (Your results will vary depending on the current date.)

Figure 3.46: Formatting a calculated field

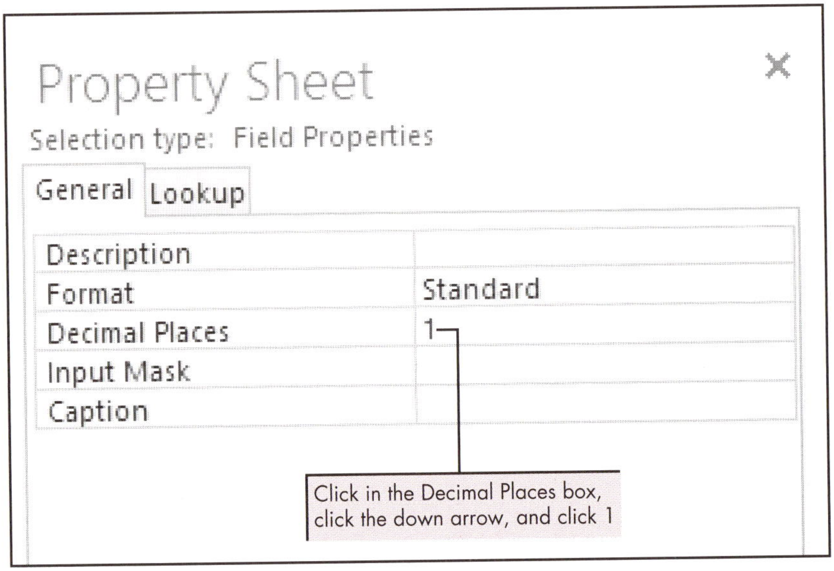

Property Sheet   ✕

Selection type: Field Properties

General Lookup

Description	
Format	Standard
Decimal Places	1
Input Mask	
Caption	

Click in the Decimal Places box,
click the down arrow, and click 1

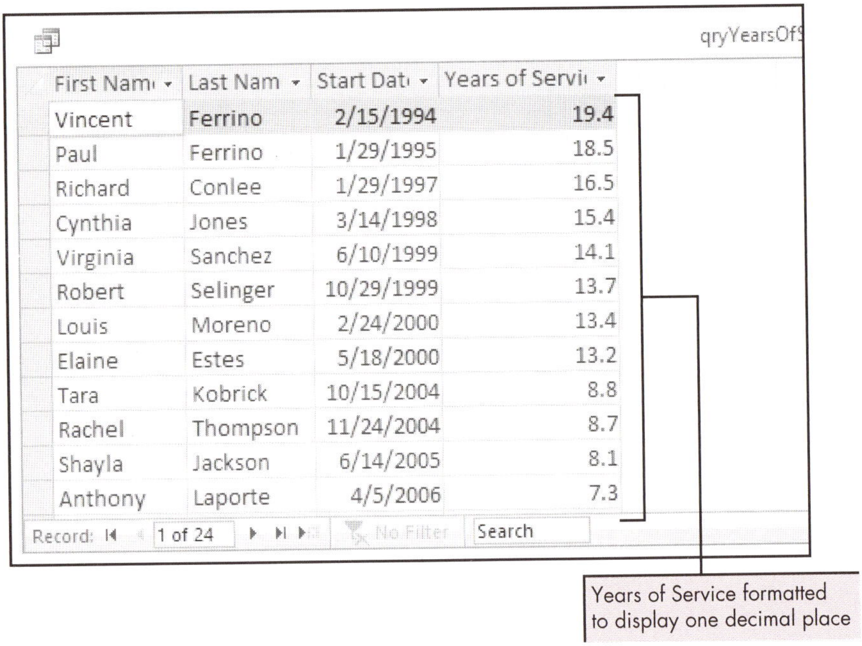

qryYearsOfS

First Nam ▾	Last Nam ▾	Start Dat ▾	Years of Servi ▾
Vincent	Ferrino	2/15/1994	19.4
Paul	Ferrino	1/29/1995	18.5
Richard	Conlee	1/29/1997	16.5
Cynthia	Jones	3/14/1998	15.4
Virginia	Sanchez	6/10/1999	14.1
Robert	Selinger	10/29/1999	13.7
Louis	Moreno	2/24/2000	13.4
Elaine	Estes	5/18/2000	13.2
Tara	Kobrick	10/15/2004	8.8
Rachel	Thompson	11/24/2004	8.7
Shayla	Jackson	6/14/2005	8.1
Anthony	Laporte	4/5/2006	7.3

Record: I◀ ◀ 1 of 24   ▶ ▶I ▶⧵   ⧸ No Filter   Search

Years of Service formatted
to display one decimal place

As she looks over the results of qryYearsOfService, she considers fine-tuning the results to display employee names as full names instead of as separate last name and first name values. Doing so will make the printed datasheet more appealing and easy to use for Paul. Furthermore, if Paul decides to institute a retirement plan, a report based on qryYearsOfService, using full names, would be very helpful.

Best Practice

Using Calculated Fields

Values that can be derived from other fields generally should not be stored as separate fields in a database. If you plan to use a calculation in a form or report, you should create a query to perform the calculation and then use the query as the basis for the form or report. For example, in a table of product orders, rather than store the quantity ordered, unit price, and total price in three fields, you should use a calculated field to derive the total price from the quantity and unit price (Quantity*UnitPrice, for example).

Concatenating in Queries

When you create field names for a table, you usually want to store data in separate fields for common values such as first name, last name, city, state, and ZIP code. Sorting or querying on a field containing a last name value is faster than on a field containing first and last name. However, when using the data in a mailing label or report, you might want to present these common values together to save space and improve readability. In the same way that you can add two or more numbers to obtain a result, you can also add text data, such as first name and last name, to display the full name. To do this, you create a calculated field that combines the values in other fields. Combining the contents of two or more fields is called concatenation.

You use the concatenation operator (&) for concatenating. Specify spaces that naturally fall between words or other characters by enclosing the spaces in quotation marks. For example, you could use the following expression to concatenate the EmpFirst and EmpLast fields, displaying the first name and last name separated by a space:

<code>[EmpFirst]& " " & [EmpLast]</code>

Maria wants to combine the contents of the EmpFirst and EmpLast fields in qryYearsOfService so that a single field displays the first and last name. She opens qryYearsOfService in Design view, deletes the contents of the EmpLast field so that the column is blank, and then deletes the EmpFirst field. In the first column, she types the following expression to specify "Name" as the field name and displays the first name and last name separated by a space:

<code>Name: [EmpFirst]& " " & [EmpLast]</code>

She saves her changes and runs the query. Figure 3.47 shows the final design and results of qryYearsOfService.

Figure 3.47: Concatenated field for employee names

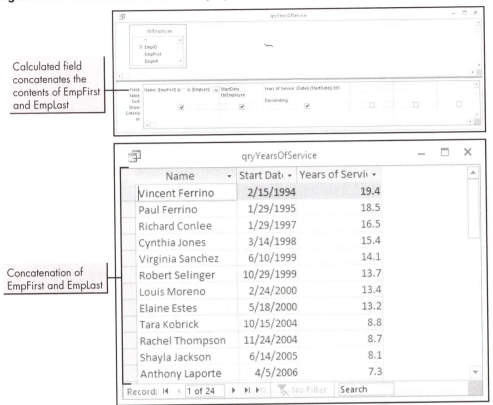

Calculated field concatenates the contents of EmpFirst and EmpLast

Concatenation of EmpFirst and EmpLast

Steps To Success: Level 2

Hudson Bay Pharmacy is ready to create more complex queries to analyze employee data. Kim Siemers, human resources manager for Hudson Bay, asks for your help in creating queries that extract the employee information she needs from their database. As you create and save the new queries, be certain to use the "qry" prefix as part of the naming convention. Also consult your instructor for instructions about submitting your results.

Complete the following:

1. Start Access and open the **Hudson.accdb** database from the STS folder.

2. Kim wants to identify employees who live in the same neighborhood in Edmonton so they can create car pools and share rides to work. In Edmonton, the postal codes roughly correspond to neighborhood. Prepare a list of employees who live in the same neighborhood so that Kim can create a list of employees who can share rides to work. Name the query qryDuplicatePostalCodes.

3. A new policy at Hudson Bay Pharmacy is that all employees must acquire and maintain certifications in adult, infant, and child CPR and in using defibrillators. Kim asks you to identify employees who have not completed any certification training. Save the query as qryNoTraining.

4. Kim also needs to list all employees and the classes they have taken. The results should include current employees who have not attended training as well as those who have. Save the query as qryEmployeeTraining.

5. Kim also needs to identify employees whose CPR or defibrillator certification has expired, depending on the time period she specifies. Show all employees whose Adult CPR, Child/Infant CPR, or Defibrillator Use certification has expired in any specified time period. Save the query as qryUpToDate.

6. Mai Yan, manager of Hudson Bay Pharmacy, wants to identify the five current nonsalaried employees who are earning the highest wages per hour. These are the five employees who have been working for the pharmacy the longest or who have regularly received raises for their work. List the top five wage earners of all the current nonsalaried employees. Save the query as qryTop5HourlyRates.

7. To prepare for employee reviews, Kim needs to calculate the minimum, maximum, and average hourly rates for each job category. Provide this information for her, saving the query as qryMaxMinAvgHourlyRate.

8. Mai is considering offering life insurance as an employee benefit, and needs to know the current age of all employees. Provide this information for her. Be certain to provide an appropriate name for the column with the result and to show the ages in descending order. Include the job title and format the results so that they include one decimal place. Also show the first name and last name together. Save the query as qryEmployeeAge.

9. Kim asks you to provide one other statistical analysis. Show the average age of employees by job title. Save this query as qryAvgEmployeeAge.

10. Close the **Hudson.accdb** database and Access.

LEVEL 3

Exploring Advanced Queries and Queries Written in Structured Query Language

Analyzing Query Calculations

In this level, you will learn about more advanced queries. You will learn how to use the Crosstab Wizard to create a crosstab query, one of the most useful queries for preparing data for further analysis. You will also learn how to create action queries, which are those that change or move many records in one operation. There are four types of action queries: append, update, delete, and make-table. You use these types of queries to add records to one table from another, change values in a field based on criteria, delete records based on criteria, or make a new table. You will also learn how to use the IIF function to make decisions in a query and to write queries in Structured Query Language (SQL), which is the language Access uses to query, update, and manage its databases.

A crosstab query is a special type of Totals query that performs aggregate function calculations on the values of one database field and allows you to determine exactly how your summary data appears in the results. You use crosstab queries to calculate and restructure data so that you can analyze it more easily. Crosstab queries calculate a sum, average, count, or other type of total for data that is grouped by two types of information—one as a column on the left of a datasheet and another as a row across the top. It might help to think of a crosstab query rotating the data to present repeating fields as columns so your data appears in a spreadsheet-like format. Figure 3.48 compares a select query and a crosstab query.

Figure 3.48: Comparing a select and crosstab query

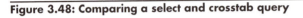

Date	Description	Cost
11/21/2016	Child/Infant CPR	$15.00
2/1/2016	Adult CPR Recertification	$10.00
6/1/2018	Adult CPR Recertification	$10.00
6/29/2015	Adult CPR Recertification	$10.00
4/12/2016	Adult CPR Recertification	$10.00
4/1/2016	Adult CPR Recertification	$10.00
2/5/2018	Adult CPR Recertification	$10.00
3/16/2016	Adult CPR Recertification	$10.00
6/21/2016	Adult CPR Recertification	$10.00
3/10/2016	Adult CPR Recertification	$10.00
6/15/2016	Adult CPR Recertification	$10.00
3/5/2018	Adult CPR Recertification	$10.00

The select query only groups the totals vertically by year and class, resulting in more records

qryClassCostAnalysis

Description	Total Of Cost	2015	2016	2018
Adult CPR Recertification	$140.00	$20.00	$80.00	$40.00
Child/Infant CPR	$15.00		$15.00	
Child/Infant CPR Recertification	$50.00	$20.00	$30.00	
Defibrillator Use	$25.00		$25.00	
First Aid	$15.00		$15.00	
Nutritional Supplements	$25.00			$25.00
Yoga	$50.00			$50.00

Record: 1 of 7   No Filter   Search

The Crosstab query displays the same information, but groups it both horizontally and vertically so the results are easier to analyze

Crosstab queries have the following benefits:

1. You can display a large amount of summary data in columns that are similar to a spreadsheet. The results can be easily exported for further analysis in a program such as Microsoft Office Excel 2013.

2. You can view the summary data in a datasheet that is ideal for creating charts automatically using the Chart Wizard.

3. You can easily design queries to include multiple levels of detail.

4. Crosstab queries work especially well with time-series data, which is data that shows performance over time for periods such as years, quarters, or months.

Creating a Crosstab Query

You create a crosstab query using a wizard to guide you through the steps, or on your own in Design view. If you want to work in Design view, it's best to start with a select query that includes numeric values or summary calculations. You can then create a crosstab query manually by clicking Crosstab in the Query Type group on the DESIGN tab. This method adds a Crosstab row to the design grid. Each field in a crosstab query can have one of four settings: Row Heading, Column Heading, Value, or (not shown). Table 3.12 explains the four settings, which also help you answer the questions the Crosstab Query Wizard asks, if you choose to use the wizard.

Table 3.12: Crosstab field settings

Crosstab Field Setting	Explanation
Row Heading	You must have at least one row heading, and you can specify more than one field as a row heading. Each row heading must be a grouped value or expression, with the expression containing one or more of the aggregate functions (such as Count, Min, Max, or Sum). The row heading fields form the first column on the left side of the crosstab.
Column Heading	Only one field can be defined as the column heading, and this must also be a grouped or totaled value. These values become the headings of the columns across the crosstab datasheet.
Value	Only one field is designated as the value. This field must be a totaled value or expression that contains one of the aggregate functions. The value field appears in the cells that are the intersections of each row heading value and each column heading value.
(not shown)	You can use other fields to limit the results. If you include a field in the query design grid, and then click the (not shown) option in the Crosstab cell and Group By in the Total cell, Access groups on the field as a Row Heading, but doesn't display the row in the query's results.

© 2014 Cengage Learning

In addition to creating crosstab queries manually, you can also use the Crosstab Query Wizard if you want Access to guide you through the steps and show samples of how the crosstab results will look based on your selections.

Although the Crosstab Query Wizard can generate a crosstab query from a single table, a single table usually doesn't contain the data necessary for the Crosstab Wizard. For instance, you might want to analyze employee training costs over time. You can retrieve cost data from tblClass, but you need tblEmployeeTraining to include the dates of the training. To prepare the data for the Crosstab Query Wizard, you often need to create a query first. This query should contain data that you want to include as the row headings column headings, and values in the crosstab query. For example, each row might be a class available to employees. The column headings would be dates grouped by years. And, the values the sum of the class costs per year.

In 2013 Maria, Vincent, and Paul established a policy that all health-related training would be reimbursed by 4Corners Pharmacy. In preparation for this year's training budget, Maria wants to analyze the annual cost of training to determine whether Paul should continue the policy. She could create a Totals query that would calculate the total cost of training, but that would not display the cost per year. She decides to create a crosstab query to help with this analysis.

Maria starts by creating a select query with only the fields she needs in the crosstab query—Description and Cost from tblClass and Date from tblEmployeeTraining. She does not need any fields from tblEmployee because she is only interested in summary data for the costs by year for classes. She saves this query as qryTrainingCostAndDate.

She then starts the Crosstab Query Wizard by clicking the Query Wizard button on the CREATE tab and then double-clicking Crosstab Query Wizard, and selects qryTrainingCostAndDate as the basis for the Crosstab query. See Figure 3.49.

Figure 3.49: First dialog box of the Crosstab Query Wizard

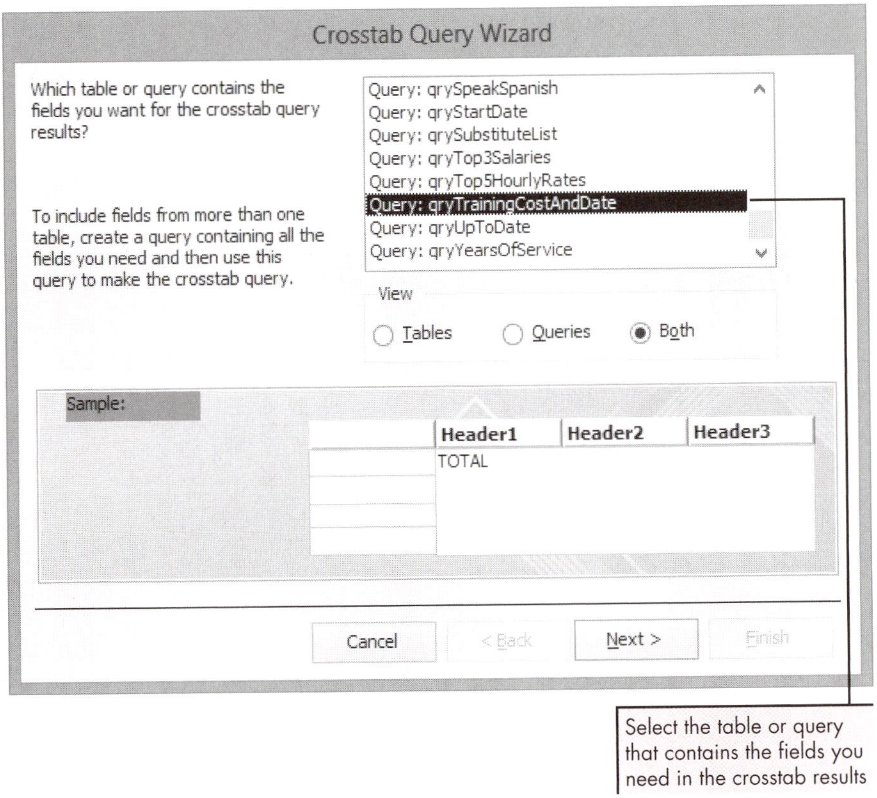

For the row headings, she selects Description because she wants to see the costs for each class. See Figure 3.50.

Figure 3.50: Selecting Description for row heading

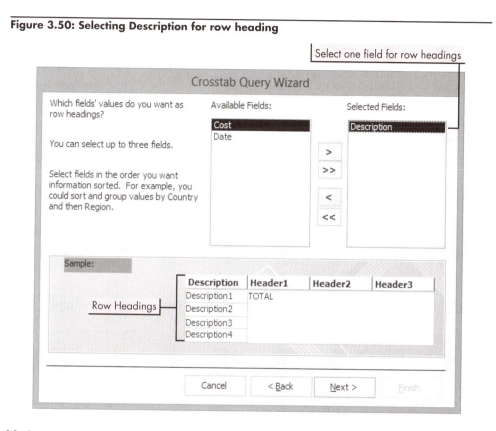

Maria wants to analyze the data by year, so she chooses Date for column headings. Because she is interested in annual cost, she chooses Year as the interval. See Figure 3.51.

Figure 3.51: Selecting the column headings

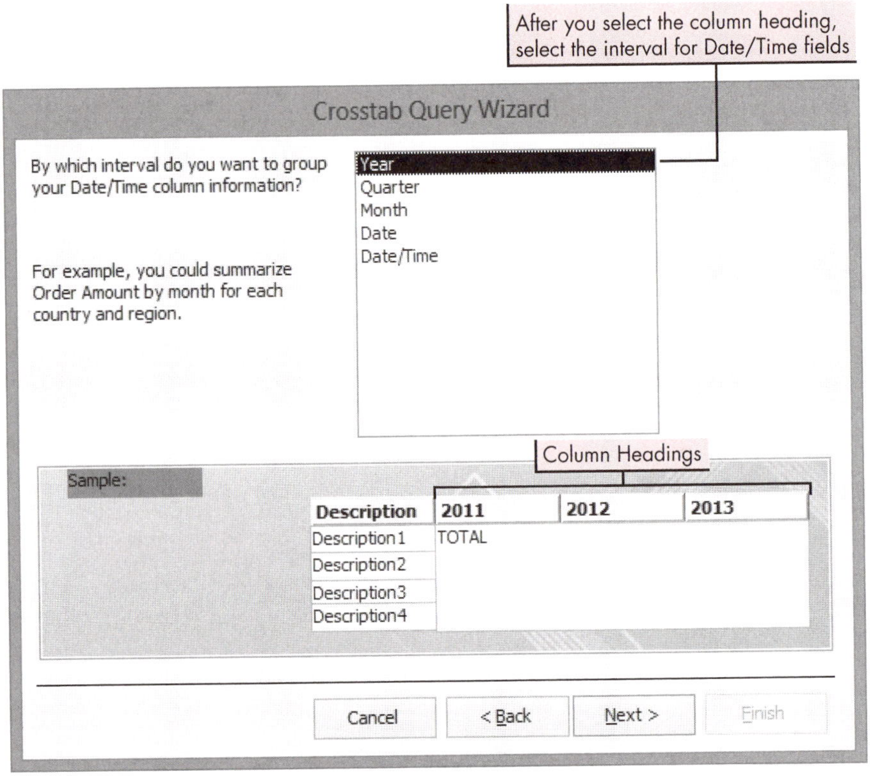

After you select the column heading, select the interval for Date/Time fields

Crosstab Query Wizard

By which interval do you want to group your Date/Time column information?

- Year
- Quarter
- Month
- Date
- Date/Time

For example, you could summarize Order Amount by month for each country and region.

Column Headings

Sample:

Description	2011	2012	2013
Description1	TOTAL		
Description2			
Description3			
Description4			

Cancel   < Back   Next >   Finish

She wants the total cost for classes as the value, so she chooses Cost as the field and Sum as the function. See Figure 3.52.

Figure 3.52: Selecting the value to calculate

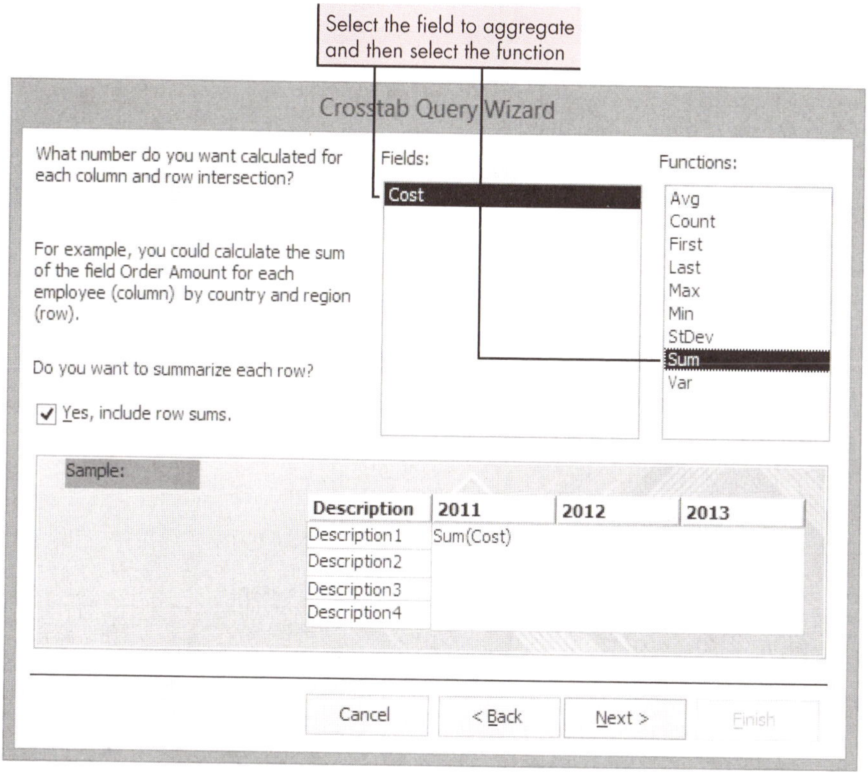

Select the field to aggregate and then select the function

Crosstab Query Wizard

What number do you want calculated for each column and row intersection?

For example, you could calculate the sum of the field Order Amount for each employee (column) by country and region (row).

Do you want to summarize each row?

☑ Yes, include row sums.

Fields:

Cost

Functions:

Avg
Count
First
Last
Max
Min
StDev
Sum
Var

Sample:

Description	2011	2012	2013
Description1	Sum(Cost)		
Description2			
Description3			
Description4			

Cancel   < Back   Next >   Finish

She names the query qryClassCostAnalysis, clicks Finish, and then runs the query. See Figure 3.53. The results clearly compare the total annual costs of training classes and the annual costs per class.

Figure 3.53: Results of the crosstab query

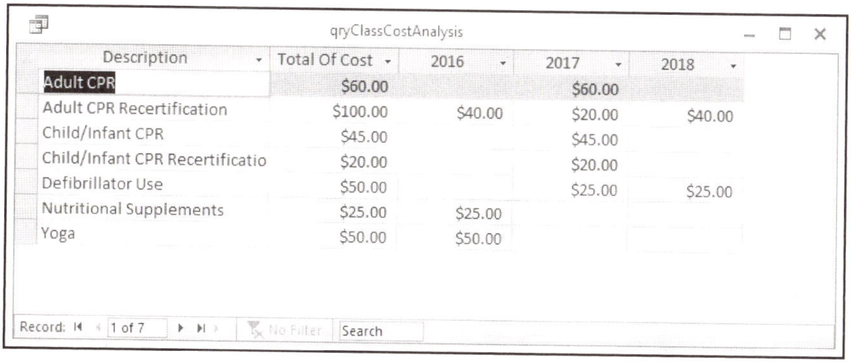

qryClassCostAnalysis

Description	Total Of Cost	2016	2017	2018
Adult CPR	$60.00		$60.00	
Adult CPR Recertification	$100.00	$40.00	$20.00	$40.00
Child/Infant CPR	$45.00		$45.00	
Child/Infant CPR Recertificatio	$20.00		$20.00	
Defibrillator Use	$50.00		$25.00	$25.00
Nutritional Supplements	$25.00	$25.00		
Yoga	$50.00	$50.00		

Record: 14 ◄ 1 of 7 ► ►I No Filter   Search

Next, Maria needs to remove obsolete data from the database. She is interested in removing records for classes that employees have completed and for which their certification has already been updated. In addition, she must currently remember to exclude previous employees when she is querying the 4Corners database, and wants to archive those employee records in a table separate from tblEmployee. Rather than manually deleting out-of-date class records and reentering previous employee data in a new table, she plans to use action queries to automate these tasks.

Modifying Data Using Queries

In addition to the select and crosstab queries, Access provides a number of query types that perform an action on the data in a database: the update, append, delete, and make-table queries. These action queries let you modify data in a table, add records to or delete records from a table, or create a new table based on expressions you enter and criteria you set. Table 3.13 lists the purpose of each type of action query and provides an example of how it might be used.

Table 3.13: Access action queries

Query Type	Purpose	Example
Append	Adds records from one table to another table with the same structure based on a criterion	Adding records of employees no longer with the pharmacy to a separate employee history table to archive the records while removing them from a table of current employees
Delete	Deletes records from a table based on a criterion	Deleting the employees from the current employee table after the records of past employees have been appended to an employee history table
Make-table	Creates a table from the results of a query	Creating the history table of past employees the first time you decide to remove past employees from tblEmployee
Update	Changes the contents of a field based on a criterion	Changing values for hourly wage of all hourly employees to reflect a negotiated raise in a job category

© 2014 Cengage Learning

Best Practice

Backing Up Your Database Before Using Action Queries

Because action queries permanently change the data in a database, you should always back up the database before performing an action query. To do so, open the database you want to back up, click the FILE tab, click Save As, scroll in the Save Database As section, if necessary, and then click Back Up Database. Then, click Save As again. If you are working in a network environment that allows multiple users to work in the database simultaneously, the other users should close the database while you create the backup. Note that you can also make a copy of the database and place it in a secure location before you perform that action queries.

Maria wants to delete old classes for employees after the certification time has expired. She needs to set criteria that select only obsolete class records in tblEmployeeTraining, and then wants Access to delete the records. While discussing her problem with Donald Linebarger, database developer, he suggests that she archive the obsolete data in a new table before she deletes it from tblEmployeeTraining. If she later needs the data for another query or report, she can retrieve it from the archived table. He suggests the general procedure shown in Figure 3.54 for archiving obsolete data.

Figure 3.54: Process for archiving data

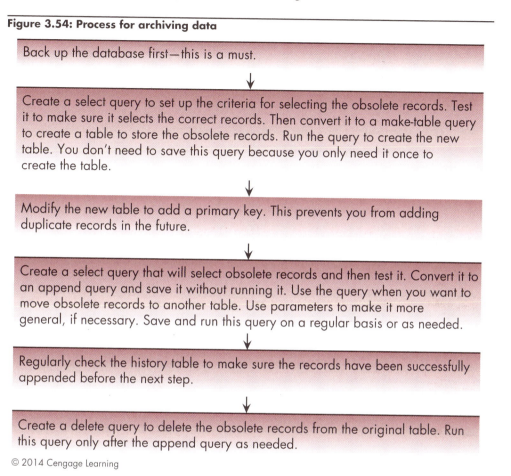

Back up the database first—this is a must.

Create a select query to set up the criteria for selecting the obsolete records. Test it to make sure it selects the correct records. Then convert it to a make-table query to create a table to store the obsolete records. Run the query to create the new table. You don't need to save this query because you only need it once to create the table.

Modify the new table to add a primary key. This prevents you from adding duplicate records in the future.

Create a select query that will select obsolete records and then test it. Convert it to an append query and save it without running it. Use the query when you want to move obsolete records to another table. Use parameters to make it more general, if necessary. Save and run this query on a regular basis or as needed.

Regularly check the history table to make sure the records have been successfully appended before the next step.

Create a delete query to delete the obsolete records from the original table. Run this query only after the append query as needed.

© 2014 Cengage Learning

Archiving Data with Make-Table Queries

As its name suggests, a make-table query creates a table from some or all of the fields and records in an existing table or query. When you create a new table based on an existing one, Access does not delete the selected fields and records from the existing table. Keep in mind that the new table reflects the data as it appeared when you created the table; changes you subsequently make to the original table are not reflected in the new table.

When you use a make-table query, you usually create a select query first that contains the necessary fields and selection criteria, and then run the query to make sure the results contain the data you want. When you are sure that the query is working properly, you can change the query type to make-table. When you run the make-table query, Access creates a table containing the table structure and records that meet the criteria you established. Access asks for a new table name and adds this table to the list of available tables in the database. Be sure to change the default name of any table created with a make-table query to include the tbl prefix.

Best Practice

Using Make-Table Queries

Make-table queries are often used to create history tables for accounting applications. These tables contain records that need to be saved or archived, but are no longer needed in the tables used for current activities in the database. Make-table queries are also frequently used by developers who inherit poorly designed tables in a database. The developer can choose those fields that should be part of new and well-designed tables as the fields in the make-table queries. If necessary, fields from multiple tables can be combined in a query first, and then the new table can be created from the fields in the query. This way, the developer doesn't need to reenter data, but the data from the tables and queries used in the make-table queries remain in the database until they are removed manually or with a delete query.

You can also use a make-table query to create a table to export to other Access databases. For example, you could create a table that contains several fields from tblEmployee, and then export that table to a database used by the accounting or payroll personnel.

Maria backs up the database before beginning the tasks that Donald outlined. She plans her next task—creating a select query—by considering the goals of her query and the criteria she should use. She wants to select the following classes in which employees earn certification: Adult CPR (class ID 1), Child/Infant CPR (class ID 2), Adult CPR Recertification (class ID 3), or Child/Infant CPR Recertification (class ID 6). In addition to classes 1, 2, 3, or 6, Maria wants to select all of the classes attended on or before January 1, 2016 because certification achieved in these classes is now out of date. She briefly considers setting parameters so that she can specify the date each time she runs the query. However, she realizes that she does not need to save the make-table query—after she runs it to create a table of obsolete employee training records, she can add subsequent obsolete records to it using an append query, not a make-table query.

Maria creates a select query that contains all of the fields in tblEmployeeTraining. She adds all the fields by double-clicking the field list title bar, and then dragging the selection to the design grid. She types <=#1/1/2016# in the Criteria row for the Date field and then types In(1,2,3,4,6) as the criteria for the ClassID field. Before converting the query to a make-table query, she runs the query to make sure it selects the correct data—it selects nine records from tblEmployeeTraining, all containing obsolete data.

To convert the select query to a make-table query, she returns to Design view, then clicks the Make Table button in the Query Type group on the DESIGN tab. The Make Table dialog box opens, in which Maria enters tblEmployeeTrainingHistory as the name of the new table, and specifies that Access should save it in the current database.

She clicks the OK button, and then clicks the Run button in the Results group on the DESIGN tab to run the query. Access displays a message indicating that she is about to paste nine rows into a new table. She clicks the Yes button to confirm that she wants to create the table. To verify that the query created the table as she planned, she closes the make-table query without saving it, opens tblEmployeeTrainingHistory in Datasheet view, and sees the nine records for obsolete classes as she expected. However, when she opens the table in Design view, she notices that the new table doesn't have a primary key. She also notices that the captions are missing, as are other property settings for the fields.

Best Practice

Modifying Tables Created with Make-Table Queries

When you use a make-table query to create a new table, only the field name and data type are included in the new table. You lose other property settings, such as captions, formats, and decimal places. Furthermore, the new table doesn't inherit the primary key from the original table. If you plan to use the data for reports or queries in the future, you should add a primary key and correct any important field properties such as default formats for Date/Time fields. Adding the primary key also prevents you from adding duplicate rows.

Maria creates the composite primary keys for the new table and adds captions to match the old table. Her next step is to create an append query to continue to archive obsolete training records in tblEmployeeTrainingHistory.

Adding Records to Tables with Append Queries

An append query is another type of action query that allows you to select records from one or more tables by setting criteria and then add those records to the end of another table. The selected records also remain in the original tables. Because the table to which you add records must already exist (as opposed to a make-table action query that creates a table), you can define field properties and primary keys in advance. You can also use an append query to bring data from another source into your database, even if some of the fields in one table don't exist in the other table. For example, the tblEmployee table has 19 fields. If you import a table named tblPersonnel, for example, and it includes only 10 fields that match the 19 in tblEmployee, you could use an append query to add the data from tblPersonnel in the fields that match those in tblEmployee and ignore the others.

Maria remembers that she needs to add obsolete records for the Defibrillator Use class to tblEmployeeTrainingHistory. She can create an append query for adding obsolete training records from tblEmployeeTraining to tblEmployeeTrainingHistory. Again, she considers the goals of her query and the criteria she should use. As with the make-table query, she can use all of the fields in tblEmployeeTraining and similar criteria. However, because she will continue to use this query, she can use parameter values that prompt for the Date and ClassID field values. For the Date field, she uses the following criterion:

```
<=[Enter the date before which certification is out of date:]
```

If she were entering a fixed criterion for the ClassID field, she would enter "In(1,2,3,4,6)" to select the required certification classes. To convert this criterion to a parameter prompt, she can still use the In comparison operator and substitute a parameter value for each ClassID value, as follows:

```
In([Enter the ID of the first certification class:],
     [Enter the ID of the second certification class:],
       [Enter the ID of the third certification class:],
         [Enter the ID of the fifth certification class:],
           [Enter the ID of the sixth certification class:])
```

This criterion will work even if she wants to select fewer than five classes—she can specify "4," for example, and then click the OK button in the Enter Parameter Value dialog box without entering a value the next four times it opens.

When she runs the select query, a dialog box opens and prompts her for the date. After she enters 1/1/2016 to test the query, five other dialog boxes open and prompt her for the five class IDs. When she is sure her query returns the results she wants, she saves it as qryAppendObsoleteClasses. She then converts it to an append query by clicking Append in the Query Type group on the DESIGN tab. The Append dialog box opens, in which Maria enters tblEmployeeTrainingHistory as the name of the table to which she wants to append the data, and specifies that this table should be appended to the current database. See Figure 3.55.

Maria meets with Paul Ferrino to review all of the hourly rate analyses. Paul has been reviewing the results, and decides to give all technicians a 3% raise effective immediately. Maria could calculate the new hourly rates by hand and then update the table, but she can use an update query instead to automatically change the HourlyRate value for pharmacy technicians.

Updating Data with an Update Query

An update query changes the values of data in one or more existing tables. It is very useful when you must change the values of a field or fields in many records, such as raising salaries by 3% for all employees within a particular job category. Rather than change each value by editing the individual records, you can create an expression to update all the values based on a criterion you set.

How To

Create an Update Query

1. Back up the database before creating and running an action query.

2. Create a select query that includes only the field or fields you want to update and any fields necessary to determine the criteria for the update.

3. Enter the criteria and run the query to verify that the results contain the appropriate records and values and that the criteria are correct.

4. Click the Update button ![Update] in the Query Type group on the DESIGN tab to convert the select query to an update query.

5. In the Update To row for the fields you want to update, enter the expression or value you want to use to change the fields. If necessary, right-click the cell and then click Zoom on the shortcut menu to use the Zoom dialog box to enter the expression.

6. Run the query. Accept the modifications by clicking the Yes button.

Maria needs to change the values in the HourlyRate field for pharmacy technicians so they reflect the 3% raise Paul Ferrino has approved. She needs to update the records in the tblEmployee table to reflect these pay increases, and knows that an update query is the easiest way to change a number of records at the same time based on criteria. First, she backs up the 4Corners database to protect its data before performing an action query. She also notes a few wage rates for technicians so she can check the results with her calculator. For example, Virginia Sanchez currently earns $10.75 per hour. Three percent of $10.75 is about $.32, so Virginia's salary after the raise should be $11.07.

In the 4Corners database, Maria creates a query in Design view using tblEmployee and its JobID, EndDate, and HourlyRate fields. She specifies "3" as the criterion for JobID to select only pharmacy technicians, and Is Null as the criterion for EndDate so that the query selects only current employees. She also unchecks the Show check box so the EndDate field does not appear in the results.

After she runs this query to make sure it selects only current pharmacy technicians, she clicks the Update button in the Query Type group on the DESIGN tab to convert the select query to an update query. A new row named Update To appears in the design grid, in which Maria enters the following expression to increase the technicians' HourlyRate by 3%:

`[HourlyRate]*1.03`

When she enters this expression, her Query window looks like Figure 3.56.

Figure 3.56: Creating and running an update query

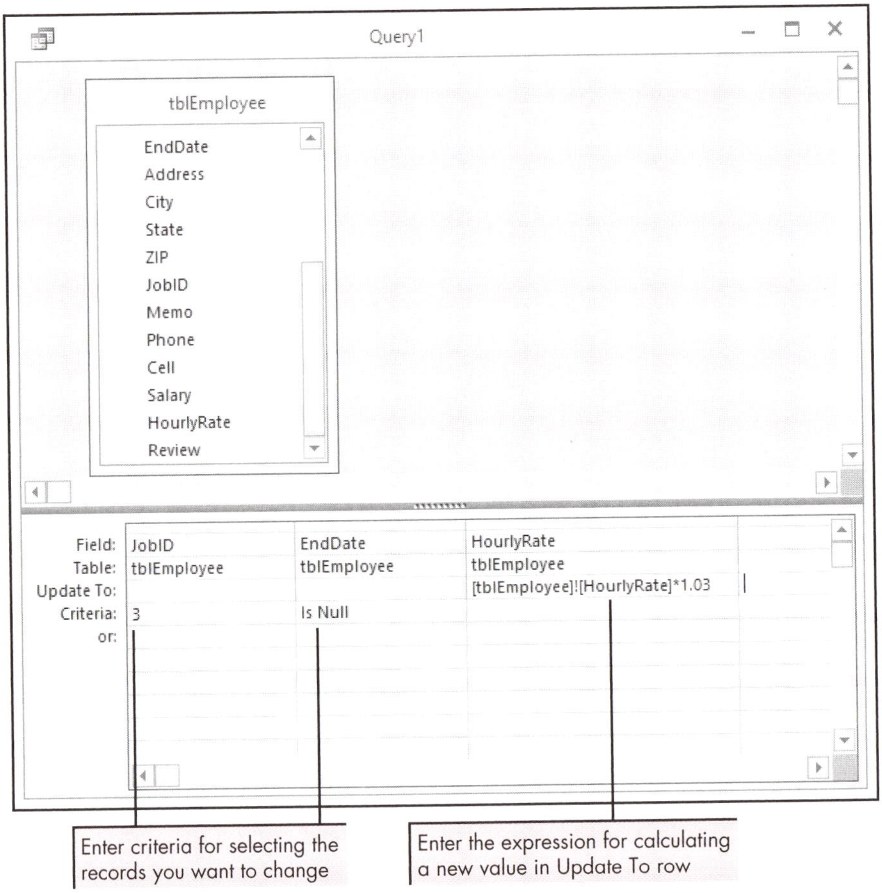

Enter criteria for selecting the records you want to change

Enter the expression for calculating a new value in Update To row

When she clicks the Run button on the DESIGN tab, a warning appears, reminding her that action queries are not reversible. She clicks the Yes button to update the records. Maria closes the update query without saving it, checks the new rate for Virginia Sanchez, and verifies that she now makes $11.07 per hour—a 3% raise. She doesn't save the query because she doesn't want to run it by accident and give the technicians another 3% raise.

Paul also wants to encourage employees to maintain their employment at 4Corners—low employee turnover saves the pharmacy training time and costs and is strongly associated with excellent service. He has decided to award a $500 bonus to employees who have worked at 4Corners for at least five years, and a $1,000 bonus to employees who have worked at 4Corners for least 10 years. How can Maria set up criteria that display a $1,000 bonus for some records that meet one condition and a $500 bonus for other records that meet a different condition? To do so, she needs an expression that assigns one of two values to a field based on a condition, one that, in effect, makes a decision and takes different actions depending on the outcome.

Making Decisions in Queries

One of the most powerful tools available in programming languages is the ability to make a decision based on more than one condition. You do so using an IF statement, a programming statement that tests a condition and takes one action if the condition is true and another action if the condition is false. In Access, you can use the IIF function, also called an Immediate IF, Instant IF, and Inline IF, to perform the same task. The format for an IIF function statement is as follows:

IIF(*condition to test, what to do if true, what to do if false*)

For example, to determine which employees receive a $1,000 bonus, you can use an IIF function that tests the following condition:

IIF(you've worked for the pharmacy for 10 or more years, get $1,000 bonus, get no bonus)

You can interpret this expression as "If you've worked for the pharmacy for 10 or more years, you receive a $1,000 bonus; otherwise, you do not receive a bonus." You can also nest IIF functions by using a second IIF statement to test another condition if the first condition is false. For example, to determine which employees receive a bonus and how much the bonus should be, you can use a nested IIF function that tests the following conditions:

IIF(you've worked for the pharmacy for 10 or more years, get $1,000 bonus, IIF(you've worked for the pharmacy for more than 5 years, get $500 bonus, get no bonus))

You can interpret this expression as "If you've worked for the pharmacy for 10 or more years, you receive a $1,000 bonus; if you've worked for the pharmacy for five or more years, you receive a $500 bonus; otherwise, you do not receive a bonus."

You can use an IIF function to return a value or text. Enclose the text in quotation marks. For example, the following IIF statement checks to see if the value in the OrderAmt field is greater than 1,000. If it is, it displays "Large." If the value is not greater than 1,000, it displays "Small."

`IIF(OrderAmt > 1000, "Large", "Small")`

How To

Use the Immediate IF Function in Expressions

1. Create or open a query in Design view.
2. In a calculated field, as criteria, or in the Update To row of an update query, enter an expression beginning with IIF.
3. Within parentheses, enter the condition to test, the action to take if the condition is true, and the action to take if the condition is false.
4. As you type the expression, remember that each left parenthesis must have a right parenthesis to match. If you have one IIF, you need one set of parentheses. If you nest IIF statements, count the IIFs and make sure the parentheses on the right match the number of IIFs.
5. Test your results by clicking the Datasheet view button.

Maria writes the expression that assigns a bonus to an employee depending on their years of service. She can use this expression in a query that includes a calculated field for determining an employee's years of service to 4Corners Pharmacy. The first condition selects employees who have worked for the pharmacy for 10 or more years and assigns a $1,000 bonus to those employees. The IIF statement for this part of the expression is as follows:

`IIF([Years of Service]>=10,1000,`

This statement can be interpreted as "If the value in the Years of Service field is greater than or equal to 10, return the value 1,000." After the second comma in that statement, Maria inserts an expression that the query should perform if the first condition is false—in other words, if the value in the Years of Service field is not greater than or equal to 10. The second condition is as follows:

`IIF([Years of Service]>=5,500,`

This statement can be interpreted as "If the value in the Years of Service field is greater than or equal to 5, return the value 500." After the second comma in that statement, Maria inserts an expression that the query should perform if the first and second conditions are false—in other words, if the value in the Years of Service field is not greater than or equal to 5: 500,0)).

This part of the expression returns the value 0 if the first and second conditions are false—if employees have worked at 4Corners Pharmacy for less than five years. The two parentheses complete the first and second condition. Maria will include the complete expression in a new calculated field named Bonus. The complete entry is as follows:

Bonus: IIF([Years of Service]>=10,1000,IIF([Years of Service]>=5,500,0))

Maria is ready to create the query that includes employees who are eligible for a bonus and lists the bonus they should receive. In Design view, she opens qryYearsOfService, the query she created earlier to calculate years of service for each employee. She saves the new query as qryBonus, and adds a calculated field named Bonus to the query. She then enters the IIF statement, shown in Figure 3.57.

Figure 3.57: Using an IIF in an expression

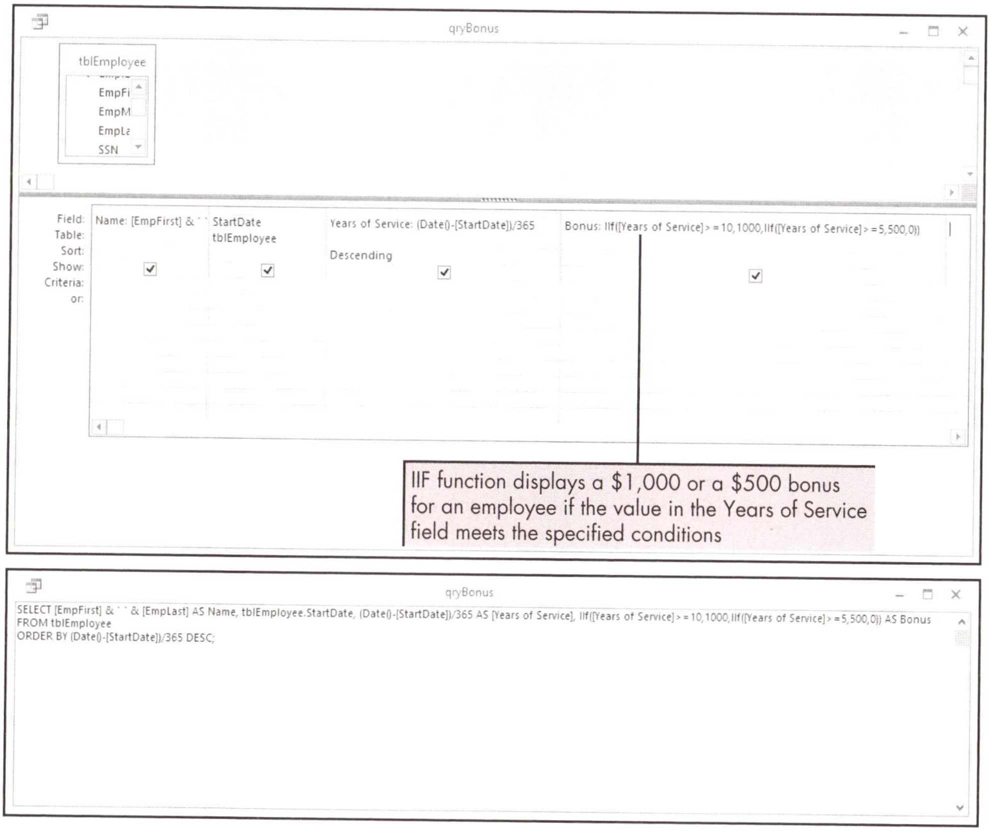

IIF function displays a $1,000 or a $500 bonus for an employee if the value in the Years of Service field meets the specified conditions

When she runs the query, the results include many employees who are not eligible for bonuses and two who no longer work for 4Corners. She realizes that she only wants to display employees who are eligible for bonuses, so she adds the criterion >=5 to the Years of Service field. Then she adds the EndDate field to the query design grid, enters Is Null as the criterion, and unchecks the Show check box. Figure 3.58 shows the results—current employees who are eligible for a bonus.

Figure 3.58: Employees who are eligible to receive a $500 or $1,000 bonus

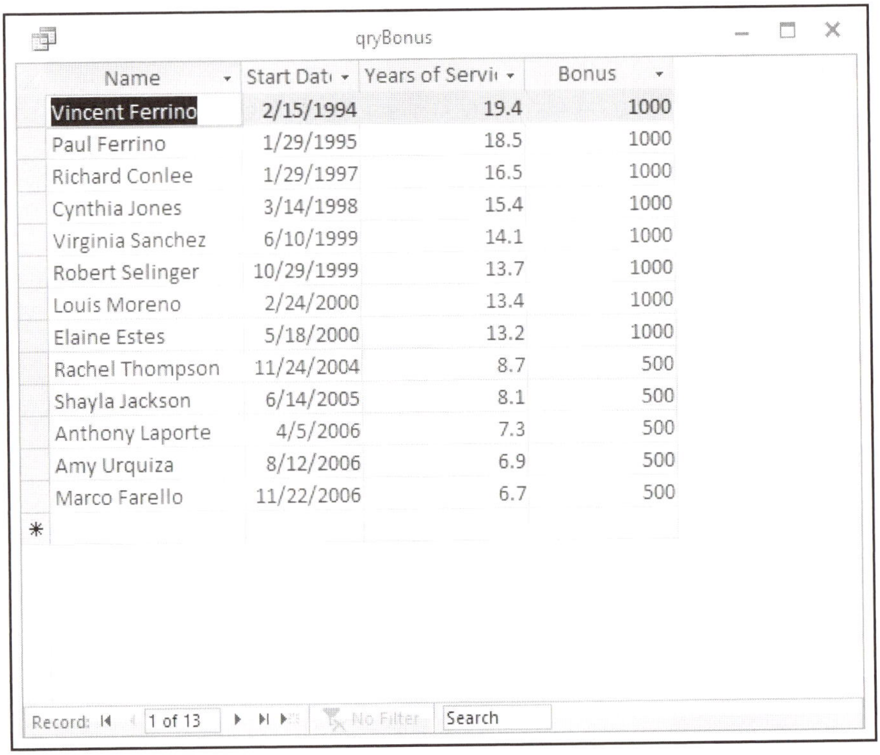

Name	Start Date	Years of Service	Bonus
Vincent Ferrino	2/15/1994	19.4	1000
Paul Ferrino	1/29/1995	18.5	1000
Richard Conlee	1/29/1997	16.5	1000
Cynthia Jones	3/14/1998	15.4	1000
Virginia Sanchez	6/10/1999	14.1	1000
Robert Selinger	10/29/1999	13.7	1000
Louis Moreno	2/24/2000	13.4	1000
Elaine Estes	5/18/2000	13.2	1000
Rachel Thompson	11/24/2004	8.7	500
Shayla Jackson	6/14/2005	8.1	500
Anthony Laporte	4/5/2006	7.3	500
Amy Urquiza	8/12/2006	6.9	500
Marco Farello	11/22/2006	6.7	500

Record: 1 of 13   No Filter   Search

Customizing Queries Using Structured Query Language

Access was designed as a database management system (DBMS) for small businesses or departments within large businesses, not a DBMS for large, enterprise systems that must run at high performance levels. Creating basic database objects such as queries, forms, and reports is easy for Access users, but users of enterprise DBMSs generally do not have the same access to database objects. Their interaction is usually to query the enterprise system and import the data to a program such as Access for further analysis. To do so, they must use a common query language that their DBMS and Access can both interpret.

Structured Query Language (SQL—usually pronounced "sequel" but more properly pronounced "ess-cue-ell") is the common query language of most DBMSs, including Access. You can use SQL to query, update, and manage relational databases such as Access.

When you create a query in Design view, Access translates the entries and criteria into SQL statements. You can view these statements by switching from Design view to SQL view. Parts of the SQL statements are the same as the entries you make in Design view. For example, when you use a field name in a calculation, you enclose it in square brackets in Design view or SQL view. The two views are similar enough that some SQL developers use the query design grid in Access to develop the basic SQL code before adding specialized features.

For example, Figure 3.59 shows the qryHourlyRate query in Design view and SQL view. Recall that this query lists all nonsalaried employees and their hourly pay rates.

Figure 3.59: qryHourlyRate in Design view and SQL view

qryHourlyRate   — □ ✕

Last Name ▾	First Name ▾	Job ID ↴	Hourly Rate ↴
Linebarger	Donald	5	
Garcia	Maria	5	
Estes	Elaine	5	
Selinger	Robert	4	$12.35
Cavillo	Brian	4	$8.17
Nader	Connie	4	$8.12
Laporte	Anthony	4	$8.00
Latour	Dominque	4	$7.70
Lightford	Darnell	4	$7.50
Hempstead	Gregory	4	$7.40
White	Thomas	4	$7.00
Jackson	Shayla	4	$6.88

Record: I◀ ◀ 1 of 24 ▶ ▶I ▶ ▓ No Filter | Search

qryHourlyRate   — □ ✕

```
SELECT tblEmployee.EmpLast, tblEmployee.EmpFirst, tblEmployee.JobID, tblEmployee.HourlyRate
FROM tblEmployee;
```

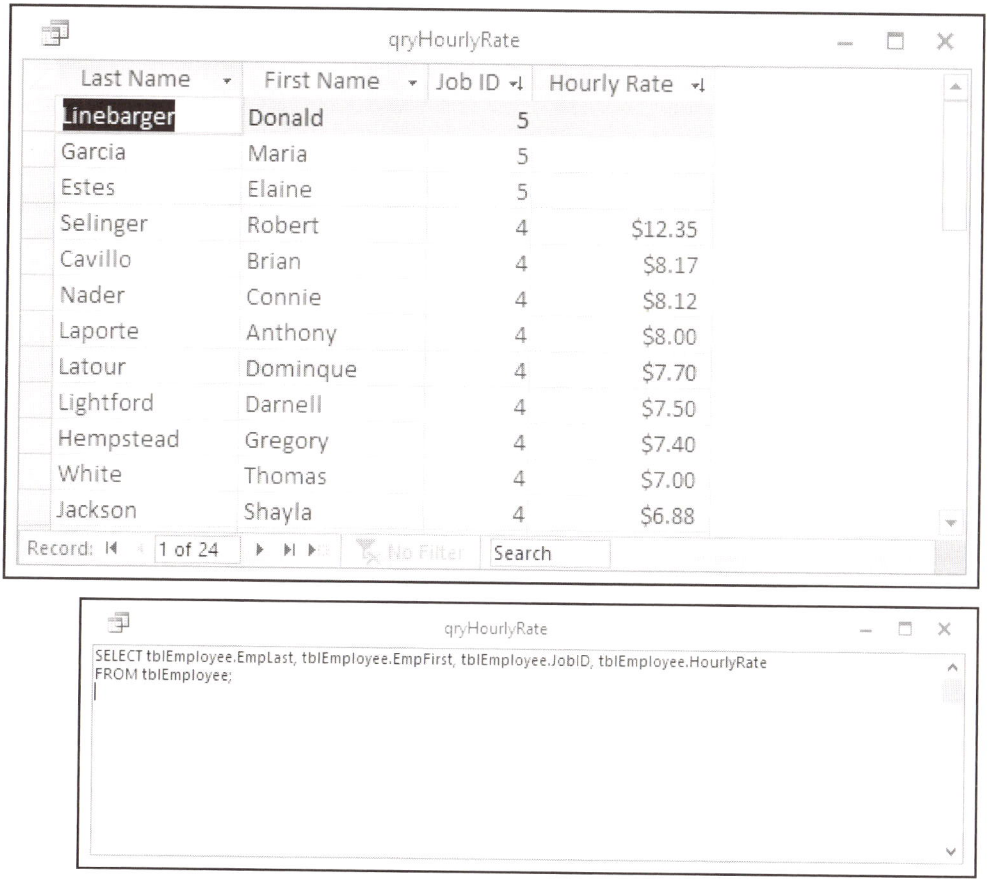

The SELECT statement defines what data the query should retrieve from the database and how it should present the data. For example, SELECT tblEmployee.EmpLast indicates that the query should select data from the EmpLast field in the tblEmployee table. The FROM statement defines the database objects that contain this data. For example, FROM tblEmployee indicates that all the data is stored in tblEmployee. SELECT and FROM are keywords in SQL; they have special meaning in SQL. To make it easy to identify the keywords in SQL code, Access displays them in all uppercase letters. An SQL statement usually begins with a keyword, which serves to define a command or clause in the expression.

Exploring the Components of an SQL Query

Table 3.14 lists the common keywords you can use to construct SQL statements. SQL code isn't required to follow a particular format, but Access and most developers place each statement on a separate line to make the SQL code easy to read. All of the wildcards, comparison operators, and logical operators you learned about in this chapter are also available in SQL.

Table 3.14: Common SQL keywords

SQL Term	What Follows the Term	Example
SELECT	List the fields you want to display. They will appear in the results in the order you list them. Note that field names with no spaces or special symbols do not require square brackets around them, but it is good practice to use the square brackets for consistency. Separate the field names with commas.	SELECT tblEmployee.EmpLast Display the EmpLast field from tblEmployee
FROM	List the table or tables involved in the query. Separate the table names with commas, and use square brackets around table names that include a space or special symbol.	FROM tblEmployee Use the tblEmployee table in the query
WHERE	List the criteria that apply. If more than one table has a field with the same name, you need to "qualify" your conditions with the name of the table followed by a period.	WHERE ((tblEmployee.JobID)=3) AND ((tblEmployee.EndDate) Is Null)) Select records in which the value in the JobID field of tblEmployee is 3 and the value in the EndDate field is null or does not have a date in this field.
GROUP BY	Group records with identical values in the specified fields into a single record, usually to calculate summary statistics.	GROUP BY tblEmployee.JobID Group the results by records in the JobID field
HAVING	List the conditions for selecting grouped records, connected by AND, OR, or NOT.	HAVING ((tblEmployee.JobID)=3 Or (tblEmployee.JobID)=4)) Select records that have the value 3 or 4 in the JobID field of tblEmployee
ORDER BY	Specify sorting specifications; for descending order, insert DESC after a sort field.	ORDER BY tblEmployee.EmpLast Sort the records by the EmpLast field in tblEmployee
AS	Use with calculated columns to specify the name of the resulting calculation.	[EmpFirst] & " " & [EmpLast] AS Name Concatenate the contents of the EmpFirst and EmpLast fields and display the results as the Name field
; (semicolon)	Use to end every SQL command, because it is required in some versions of SQL.	N/A

© 2014 Cengage Learning

Maria wants to explore SQL view in case she needs to modify queries to include more flexibility or power than Design view can offer. One task Paul asked her to complete is to create a query similar to qryTop5HourlyRates that displays the top three salaries paid to employees. She can open qryTop5HourlyRates in SQL view and then modify it so that it selects the three records that have the highest values in the Salary field instead of the five records that have the highest values in the HourlyRate field.

Maria opens qryTop5HourlyRates in Design view, clicks the View button arrow on the RESULTS tab, and then clicks SQL View. The query appears in SQL view. See Figure 3.60.

Figure 3.60: SQL view of qryTop5HourlyRates

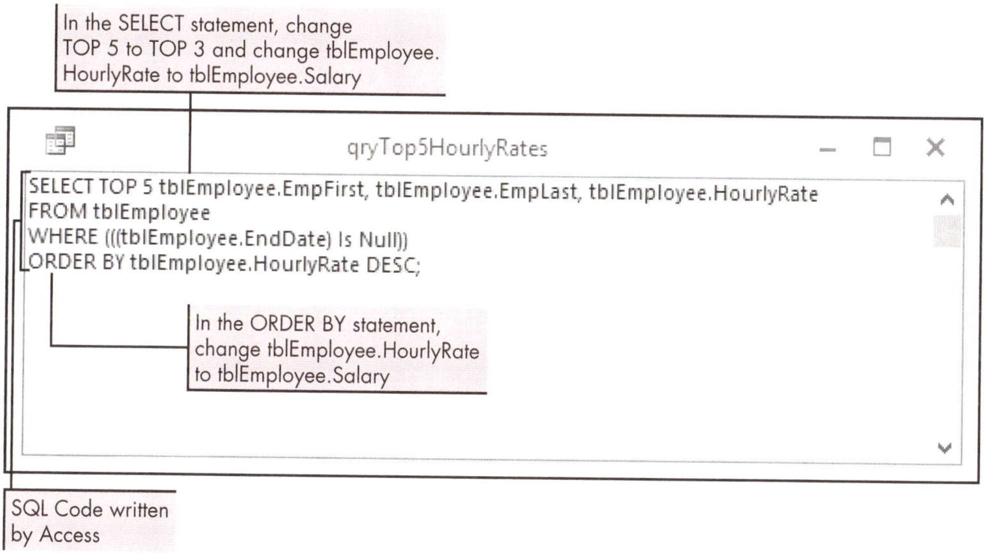

In the SELECT statement, change TOP 5 to TOP 3 and change tblEmployee.HourlyRate to tblEmployee.Salary

```
qryTop5HourlyRates                                          —  □  ×

SELECT TOP 5 tblEmployee.EmpFirst, tblEmployee.EmpLast, tblEmployee.HourlyRate
FROM tblEmployee
WHERE (((tblEmployee.EndDate) Is Null))
ORDER BY tblEmployee.HourlyRate DESC;
```

In the ORDER BY statement, change tblEmployee.HourlyRate to tblEmployee.Salary

SQL Code written by Access

Maria takes some time to interpret the SQL statements in this view:

- **SELECT TOP 5 tblEmployee.EmpFirst, tblEmployee.EmpLast, tblEmployee.HourlyRate**—Display the EmpFirst, EmpLast, and HourlyRate fields from tblEmployee, and select the top five records in the field specified in the ORDER BY clause.
- **FROM tblEmployee**—Use only the tblEmployee table in the query.
- **WHERE ((tblEmployee.EndDate) Is Null))**—Select only those records in which the value in the EndDate field is null.
- **ORDER BY tblEmployee.HourlyRate DESC;**—Sort the results in descending order by the values in the HourlyRate field, and then end the query.

To change this query to select the records with the top three values in the Salary field, Maria changes "TOP 5" in the SELECT statement to "TOP 3". She also changes "tblEmployee.HourlyRate" in the SELECT statement to "tblEmployee.Salary." She doesn't need to change the FROM statement because she still wants to select records only from the tblEmployee table, nor does she need to change the WHERE statement—she only wants to display salaries of current employees. However, she does need to change the ORDER BY statement so that it sorts records by the Salary field instead of HourlyRate. That change also means the query selects the three records with the highest values in the Salary field. She completes these changes, saves the query as qryTop3Salaries, and switches to Design view, which reflects the changes she made in SQL view. Finally, she runs the query to view the results. See Figure 3.61.

Figure 3.61: Three views of qryTop3Salaries

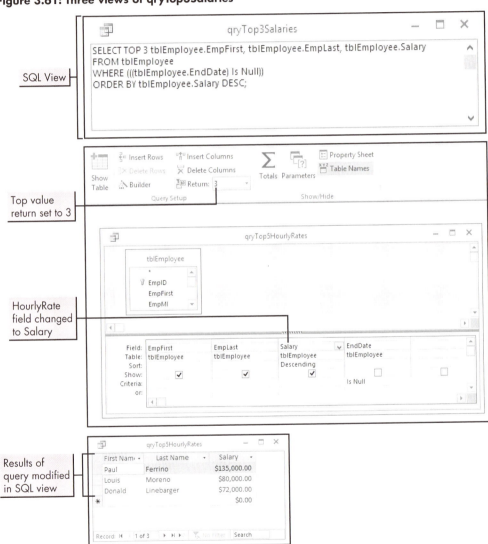

As you create or modify SQL statements in SQL view, Access makes corresponding changes in the query design grid in Design view. After you create a query in SQL view, you can modify it in Design view. Access reformats your SQL code so it looks like an Access-generated SQL command. Access SQL code always uses the qualified field names even if you only have one table in your query, not all fields will be enclosed in square brackets, and there might be extra parentheses in the criteria. While you are learning how to create SQL queries, you can change from SQL view to Design view to Datasheet view to gauge the effect of your SQL statements in the other views.

Creating a Union Query Using SQL

Maria would like to create a list of employees and customers for holiday cards. She realizes that tblEmployee has the employee names and addresses, but tblCustomer only has customer names and its related table tblHousehold has the customer addresses. Now that she is more confident using SQL, she decides to use a union query to bring this data together. A union query lets you combine, or unite, the results from two or more select queries. So, Maria creates two select queries: one based on tblEmployee that has the fields First Name, Last Name, Address, City, State, and ZIP. The second query is based on tblCustomer and tblHousehold and also has the First Name, Last Name, Address, City, State, and ZIP fields. She knows that the two queries need to have the same number of fields and that the order of the fields must be identical. She does not save either query. However, Maria changes the view for both of these queries to SQL view. Her queries appear as shown in Figure 3.62.

Figure 3.62: SQL view of Query1 and Query2

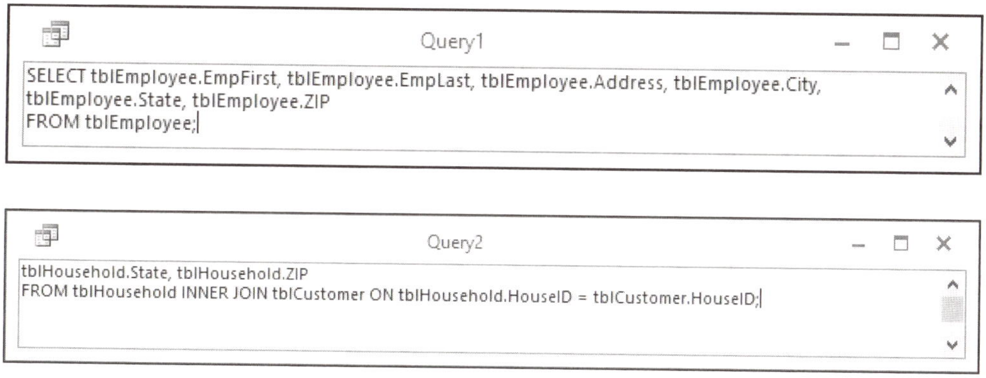

```
Query1                                                        —  □  ✕
SELECT tblEmployee.EmpFirst, tblEmployee.EmpLast, tblEmployee.Address, tblEmployee.City,
tblEmployee.State, tblEmployee.ZIP
FROM tblEmployee;
```

```
Query2                                                        —  □  ✕
tblHousehold.State, tblHousehold.ZIP
FROM tblHousehold INNER JOIN tblCustomer ON tblHousehold.HouseID = tblCustomer.HouseID;
```

Maria then clicks Query Design on the CREATE tab. She wants to create a union query. A **union query** lets you combine the result sets of two or more **SQL SELECT statements**. Because she does not want a table in this query, she closes the Show Table dialog box. She then clicks the DESIGN tab and selects the Union Query button. Query3 displays a blank window, referred to as the Query Designer window, into which Maria can copy the SQL code from the other two queries.

She then minimizes Query3 and maximizes Query1 to select and copy the SQL code. After minimizing Query1 and maximizing Query3, she pastes the code into the Query3 window. Maria then deletes the final semicolon at the end of the code and presses the Enter key. On the new row, she types "UNION" and presses the Enter key to move to the next line. See Figure 3.63.

Figure 3.63: SQL view of Query3 with Query1 SQL code pasted

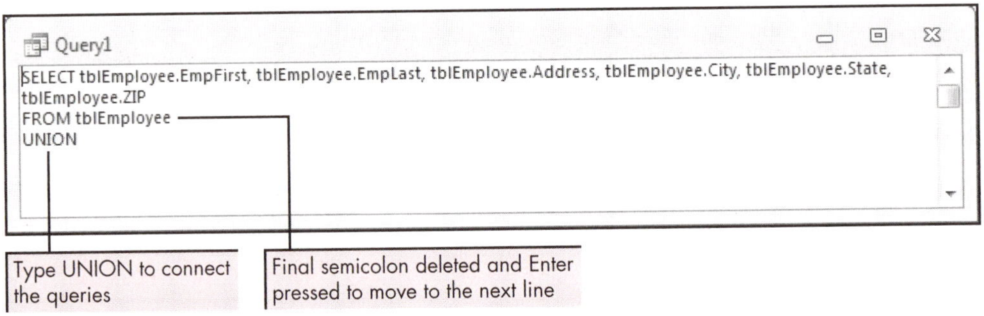

```
Query1

SELECT tblEmployee.EmpFirst, tblEmployee.EmpLast, tblEmployee.Address, tblEmployee.City, tblEmployee.State,
tblEmployee.ZIP
FROM tblEmployee
UNION
```

Type UNION to connect the queries

Final semicolon deleted and Enter pressed to move to the next line

Maria then copies the SQL code from Query2 and pastes it into Query3, as shown in Figure 3.64. She then saves the query as qryHolidayAddressesUnion.

Figure 3.64: SQL view of Query3 with both Query1 and Query2 SQL code pasted

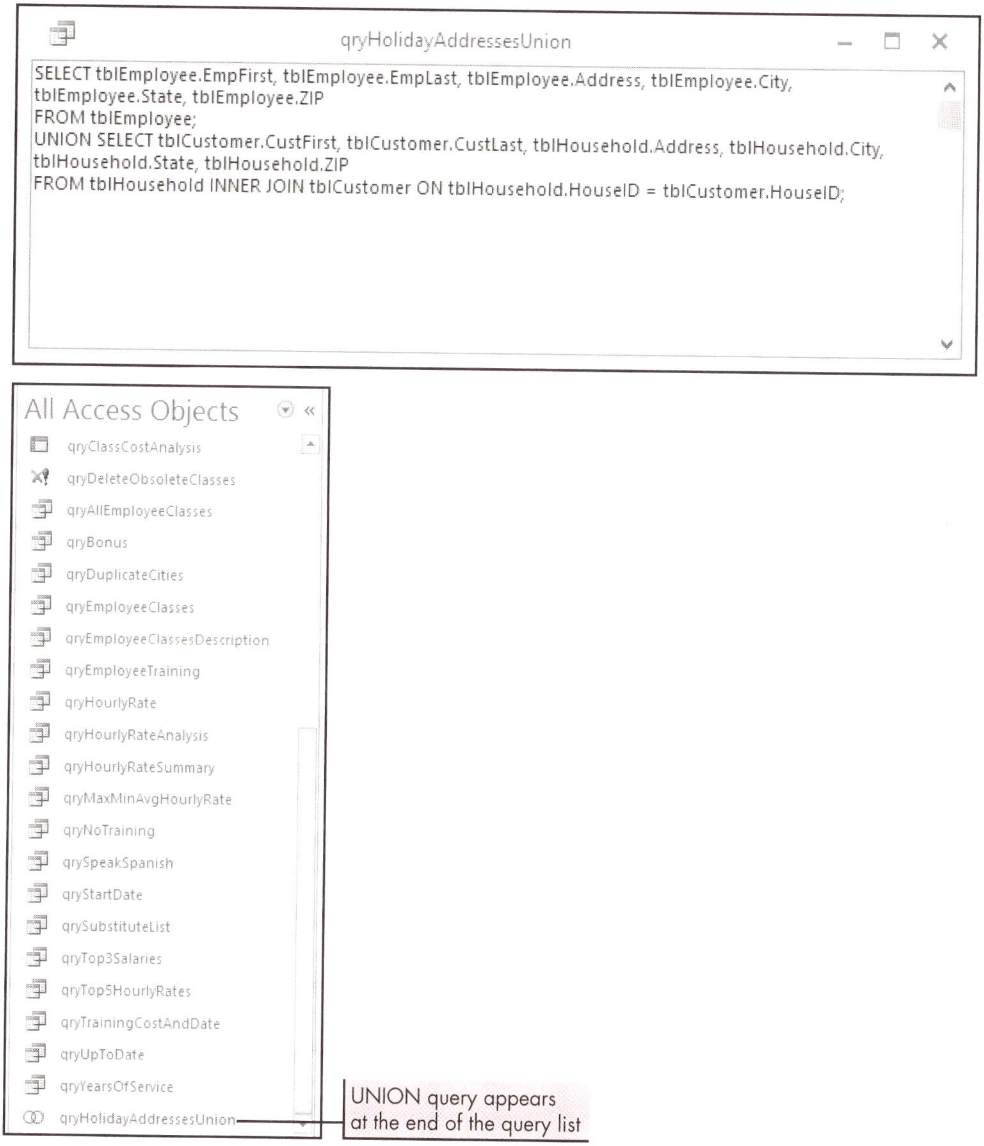

```
qryHolidayAddressesUnion                          —   ☐   ✕

SELECT tblEmployee.EmpFirst, tblEmployee.EmpLast, tblEmployee.Address, tblEmployee.City,
tblEmployee.State, tblEmployee.ZIP
FROM tblEmployee;
UNION SELECT tblCustomer.CustFirst, tblCustomer.CustLast, tblHousehold.Address, tblHousehold.City,
tblHousehold.State, tblHousehold.ZIP
FROM tblHousehold INNER JOIN tblCustomer ON tblHousehold.HouseID = tblCustomer.HouseID;
```

All Access Objects ⊙ «

- 🔲 qryClassCostAnalysis
- ✖ qryDeleteObsoleteClasses
- 🗒 qryAllEmployeeClasses
- 🗒 qryBonus
- 🗒 qryDuplicateCities
- 🗒 qryEmployeeClasses
- 🗒 qryEmployeeClassesDescription
- 🗒 qryEmployeeTraining
- 🗒 qryHourlyRate
- 🗒 qryHourlyRateAnalysis
- 🗒 qryHourlyRateSummary
- 🗒 qryMaxMinAvgHourlyRate
- 🗒 qryNoTraining
- 🗒 qrySpeakSpanish
- 🗒 qryStartDate
- 🗒 qrySubstituteList
- 🗒 qryTop3Salaries
- 🗒 qryTop5HourlyRates
- 🗒 qryTrainingCostAndDate
- 🗒 qryUpToDate
- 🗒 qryYearsOfService
- ∞ qryHolidayAddressesUnion ——

UNION query appears
at the end of the query list

To review the results, she clicks the View button to switch to Datasheet view. She is satisfied that all 24 employee records and 41 customer records are included in this query for a total of 65 records. She then closes qryHolidayAddressesUnion. She also closes Query1 and Query2 without saving them. Maria knows that she cannot modify the qryHolidayAddressesUnion query any more using the Query Designer as it doesn't have a way of visualizing a union query.

Don Linebarger explains to Maria that there are two additional SQL queries in Access, the pass-through query and the data-definition query. He tells her that pass-through queries can be used when you have an external database such as Microsoft SQL or Oracle.

The pass-through query can then directly access the data on these servers. Data-definition queries use DDL (data definition language), which is a part of SQL. These queries are used to create, modify, or delete database objects. However, caution is needed when these queries are run because there are not any confirmation dialog boxes. If you make a mistake, you could accidentally change the design of a table.

Maria decides to keep these queries in mind in the event that 4Corners acquires a server. But, for now, she is confident with the existing information and experience she has with queries.

Steps To Success: Level 3

Kim Siemers, human resources manager for Hudson Bay Pharmacy, needs to analyze statistical data for the pharmacy and to archive obsolete records. She asks for your help creating crosstab queries and action queries that modify the data in the Hudson database. As you create and save the new queries, be certain to use the "qry" prefix as part of the naming convention. Also consult your instructor for instructions about submitting your results.

Complete the following:

1. Start Access and open the **Hudson.accdb** database from the STS folder.

2. Kim is preparing the human resources budget for Hudson Bay Pharmacy, and needs to analyze the annual cost of training to determine how much to budget for training classes. She asks you to provide summary data for the costs by year for classes. The results you create should clearly compare the total annual costs of training classes and the annual costs per class. Save the query as **qryClassCostAnalysis**.

3. Kim needs to remove obsolete data from the Hudson database. First, she asks you to identify all employees who no longer work for Hudson Bay Pharmacy. She then wants you to create a new history table with that data. Name the history table **tblEmployeeHistory**. Save the query as **qryEmpHistory**.

4. Kim also wants to remove records for classes that employees have completed and for which their certification has already been updated. She asks you to select classes in which employees earn certification—Adult CPR, Adult CPR Recertification, Child/Infant CPR, and Child/Infant CPR Recertification—and that they attended before January 1, 2015 because certification achieved in these classes is now out of date in Canada. Create a history table that contains this data, and name the table **tblEmployeeTrainingHistory**. Name the query **qryEmployeeTrainingHistory**.

5. Kim checked your results, and realizes that tblEmployeeTrainingHistory should also include obsolete data for Defibrillator Use classes. Add the obsolete training records for Defibrillator Use classes to tblEmployeeTrainingHistory. Because Kim will continue to use this query for other classes as they become outdated, set up the query so that it prompts her for the necessary criteria before running. Defibrillator Use certifications before 1/1/2016 are no longer valid. Save the query as **qryObsoleteClasses**.

6. Verify that tblEmployeeTrainingHistory includes all the obsolete classes. Delete the now archived records from tblEmployeeTraining. As with qryObsoleteClasses, Kim will continue to use this query to remove obsolete records after they've been archived. Set up the query so that it prompts her for the necessary criteria before running. Save the query as **qryDeleteClasses**. Make sure the total number of records you deleted is the same as the number of records in tblEmployeeTrainingHistory.

7. Kim recently met with Mai Yan, manager of Hudson Bay Pharmacy, who authorized a 5% raise for all current pharmacy technicians. Update the employee records for pharmacy technicians so that their pay rate includes this 5% raise. Save the query as **qryTechnicianRaise**.

8. Current Hudson Bay Pharmacy employees are eligible for participation in a 401(k) retirement plan after one year. Identify each employee by full name and show whether they are eligible for the plan with a column stating "Eligible" or "Not Eligible" in the results. Save the query as **qryRetirement**.

9. Kim is meeting with Mai later today, and needs to report which salaried employees earn the top three salaries. Create a query in SQL view that lists all employees who earn the top three salaries. Be certain to separate the SQL terms to make it more readable. Save the query as **qryTop3Salaries**.

10. Close the **Hudson.accdb** database and then close Access.

Chapter Summary

In this chapter, you learned how to retrieve data from a database so that you can examine only the information you need. Level 1 showed you how to filter data by form and by selection to create a temporary subset of records, and how to sort data to rearrange records in a specified order. Level 1 also introduced queries, explaining how to create select queries using the Simple Query Wizard, including those that provide summary statistics, or Design view, which is necessary when you need to use multiple criteria. In addition to multiple criteria, queries you create in Design view can include wildcards and comparison operators.

Level 2 focused on more complex queries and specialized query wizards. You learned how to create special types of queries that find duplicate records or unmatched records. You also learned how to create Top Value queries that limit the records in query results and parameter queries that pause before running so that users can enter values that the query uses as criteria. In addition, Level 2 explored refining relationships with appropriate join types and using logical operators to specify multiple conditions. It also explained how to perform calculations in a query by using aggregate functions and by creating calculated fields.

Level 3 covered advanced types of queries, including crosstab queries, which present data to facilitate statistical analysis. In addition, it showed you how to create action queries, including those that create tables, and add, update, or delete records in a table.

Level 3 also explained how to create a calculated field with an Immediate IF function that makes decisions in a query. Finally, Level 3 introduced Structured Query Language (SQL), the language Access uses to query its databases.

Conceptual Review

1. When is it appropriate to use Filter by Selection and Filter by Form?

2. What restrictions does the Simple Query Wizard have for creating queries?

3. Why is it important to use the naming prefix "qry" for all saved queries?

4. Why is it not a good idea to add records to a table from a query datasheet?

5. What is the difference between entering multiple criteria for a query on one line of the design grid versus entering criteria on two or more lines?

6. What query wizards are available other than the Simple Query Wizard? For what do you use these types of queries?

7. What is the purpose of an outer join?

8. What role does "null" play in a field?

9. When should you use the Expression Builder?

10. What is a history table and why would a database designer include one or more in the design?

11. What is the difference between a query written in the query design grid and one written directly in SQL?

12. Describe a situation in which the IIF function would be appropriate.

13. What is the difference between an update query and an append query?

14. Why do many people run a delete query after running a make-table or append query?

15. Name an advantage that crosstab queries offer that other types of queries do not.

Case Problems

Case 1—Managing Customer Information for NHD Development Group Inc.

Marketing

After creating the tables and relationships for the Antiques database, you meet with Tim Richards, the chief information officer for the NHD Development Group, and Linda Sutherland, the manager of the antique mall. As you review the database, Linda makes a few requests. When she tracked sales for a month, she found that repeat customers accounted for 60% of her revenue. She therefore wants to use the Antiques database to increase marketing efforts to her current customer base. First, she wants to extract information about her customers, such as a list that organizes customers by city and another that provides customer names and phone numbers. She also needs to retrieve information about the antique and restoration classes the mall offers to determine which customers enroll in the classes. Then she could provide information in the classes about items that might interest those customers. She asks for your help filtering data and creating queries that extract the information she needs.

Complete the following:

1. Open the **Antiques.accdb** database from the Case 1 folder.

2. Many of the mall's customers live in Cleveland or Collegedale, Tennessee, and Linda is debating whether to place an ad in their community newspapers or to send postcards advising these customers about upcoming sales. If she sends more than 50 postcards, mailing costs will exceed advertising rates.

   Show Linda a quick way she can produce a temporary list of customers who live in Cleveland or Collegedale, with all the customers in Cleveland listed first. Is it more economical to send these customers postcards or to advertise in the community newspapers?

3. To increase repeat business, Linda wants to call customers and let them know when new collectibles arrive at the mall. She wants to produce a list of her customers and their phone numbers. To track the customers effectively, this telephone list should also include the customer's ID number.

   a.   Create a list that includes the ID numbers, last names, first names, and phone numbers of all the customers.

   b.   Because Linda expects to refer to this list by customer name, sort the list by last name.

   c.   Save the query as **qryPhoneList**.

4. Linda is planning to create a brochure for the mall, and wants to highlight the number of booths within the mall. She wants to advertise that the mall has fifteen 8 × 8 booths, five 12 × 10 booths, and so on. Because Linda has recently reworked the booth divisions and expects to make additional changes in the future, she wants to list how many booths of each size the mall currently has. Name the query **qryBoothSize**.

5. Linda wants to promote the classes that will be offered in February. She will be placing an ad in the local newspaper, and wants to include the class list in the ad. She asks you to create a list of all the February classes sorted by date and by time. Be sure the list includes information readers are most interested in, such as the name of the class, the date and time, and the class fee. Name the query **qryFebruaryClasses**.

6. When Linda reviews the list of February classes, she thinks that the dates would be more meaningful if they spelled out the day of the week, using a format such as "Saturday, February 5, 2016." Linda asks you to modify the class list to display long dates. (*Hint*: In Design view, right-click the date field, click Properties, and in the Property Sheet pane, click the Format property's list arrow, and then click Long Date.)

7. Linda also needs a list of classes that she can use in the mall when customers and others inquire about the classes. When people call for information about the classes, they often want to know when the classes will be held. Linda also wants to use this list to call enrollees in case of a cancellation. Linda considers a person officially enrolled only when they have paid for the class.

    a. Create a list that includes the class ID and other information that callers want to know about the classes. Test your results.

    b. Modify the list so that it also includes information Linda needs to call customers and determine whether a customer is enrolled in a class. To help her find the information she needs, sort the list first by class and then by whether the customer has paid.

    c. Save the query as **qryClassListing**.

8. To manage the classes and instructors, Linda needs a summary of class enrollment. In addition to the names of the class and instructor, she needs to know the number of students enrolled in each class and the total of the class fees that have been paid. Save this query as **qryClassEnrollment**.

9. Unless at least five people are enrolled in a class, the class will be canceled. However, Linda wants to review the list of classes that are likely to be canceled to see if she can encourage some of her customers to take these classes. Modify qryClassEnrollment to include only those classes that have fewer than five customers enrolled. Save this query as **qryClassDeletions**.

10. Linda explains that the primary reason she offers the classes is to have people visit the mall. She has observed that most people come early for the classes and wander around the mall before the class begins. The classes are, therefore, part of her marketing strategy for the mall and she wants to protect this endeavor. One problem she wants to solve is that customers sometimes sign up for classes, but do not attend them. If class attendance is low, instructors will move their classes to a different antiques mall. Classes with high fees seem to have the lowest attendance. Linda asks you to create a list that shows customers who have signed up for classes with a fee greater than $25 but have not paid. Provide information Linda needs so she can call the customers and request their payment, and sort the list so she can easily find customers by name. Name the query **qryUnpaidClassesOver25**.

11. Linda often receives calls asking whether any of the dealers carry military memorabilia. She asks you to create a list of the dealers who sell such items. She will use this list to call dealers and to find other information about the memorabilia, such as discounts offered. Name this query **qryMilitaryMemorabilia**.

12. Close the **Antiques.accdb** database and then close Access.

Case 2—Retrieving Employee Information for MovinOn Inc.

Now that you have worked with Robert Iko at the MovinOn moving and storage company to develop the design for the MovinOn database, he explains that their most pressing task is to serve the needs of the Human Resources department. Darnell Colmenero is an administrative assistant responsible for many human resources tasks, and asks for your help extracting information from the MovinOn database. Although an outside company processes payroll for MovinOn, Darnell and others maintain all employment information and strive to meet management's goal of recruiting and retaining skilled, qualified employees who are well trained in customer service. Having employees working in three warehouses in three states has made it difficult to track employee information, and the potential merger and expansion means that human resources must take advantage of the MovinOn database to maintain and retrieve employee information. Darnell asks for your help in filtering data and creating queries that provide the information that he needs.

Human Resources

Complete the following:

1. Open the **MovinOn.accdb** database from the Case 2 folder.

2. The truck drivers for MovinOn are a special type of employee, and their data is stored in a table separate from the rest of the employees because of driving certification requirements. Drivers are certified to drive trucks with a specified number of axles, and MovinOn must be certain that a driver is certified to drive a particular truck.

a. When Darnell meets with David Bower, the general manager, he learns that only drivers who have a driving record of "A" or "B" are allowed to drive the large trucks (those with four axles or more). He asks you to identify the drivers qualified to drive the four-axle trucks. Because he will use the list you create to call drivers when he needs a substitute, include the phone numbers and driving record for each driver. Save the query as **qry4AxleDrivers**.

b. Darnell also learns that he must immediately review drivers who have a driving record lower than "A" or "B." Those drivers who have a record of "C" will be put on notice, and those with a record "D" or "F" can be terminated immediately. List the drivers with these low driving records, and sort the list so that Darnell can easily determine the driving record of each driver. Because he can enroll long-term drivers in a training program, he also needs to know when each driver started working for MovinOn and whether the driver is still employed. Save the query as **qryDriversWithLowRecords**.

    c. If drivers are to be terminated because of their driving record, Darnell wants to include them in an additional list. Create this list for Darnell, and include all relevant employment information. Save this query as **qryDriversForTermination**.

3. Darnell is completing a small business certification form for the U.S. Department of Labor, and needs quick answers to some basic questions about employees. Answer the following questions:

    a. In what states do the MovinOn employees reside?

    b. How many employees live in each state?

    c. Who is the oldest employee? Who is the youngest?

    d. Who makes the highest salary?

    e. Who is paid by salary? Who is paid by hourly rate?

    f. Who is paid the lowest hourly rate?

    g. Are there any positions for which there are no employees?

    h. How many types of jobs are offered at MovinOn? How many people are employed in each type of job?

4. When MovinOn hires employees, Darnell must process the employees by informing them about company policies and making sure they complete required printed forms. Darnell sometimes spends an entire day with a new employee. He wants to make this process more efficient. So, he looks over the forms and his training notes to discover how he can work more effectively. He asks you to produce a list of employees who were processed on the same day so that he can review it by Social Security number. Name the query **qryDuplicateStartDates**.

5. David Bowers is considering providing bonuses to long-term employees. Darnell asks you to list the 10 employees who have worked for MovinOn the longest. Name the query **qryLongestEmployment**.

6. To prepare for a payroll, Darnell must provide a list of employees that includes their salary or hourly pay rate. The list must also include Social Security numbers and employee IDs so that an outside firm can properly process the payroll. Produce an employee list that provides this information, and sort it so that it's easy to find an employee by name. For those employees who are on a salary, the list should show their monthly wage. Save the query as **qryPayroll**.

7. Darnell sometimes needs to contact the warehouse managers, accountants, administrative assistants, and other employees at the warehouse where they work. Create a contact list that he can use to phone employees, and that contains enough information to identify employees, their positions, and their warehouses along with the warehouse phone number. Because Darnell might eventually use this list as the basis for a report, the employee's name should appear as one full name, with the last name first. Save the query as **qryEmployeeContact**.

8. When you show qryEmployeeContact to Darnell, he realizes that it would be more helpful if he could specify a particular warehouse before producing the list, and then see the contact information only for the employees who work in that warehouse. Create a query that meets these needs, saving it as **qryEmployeeContactByWarehouse**. Test this query with valid and invalid warehouse information.

9. MovinOn knows that having a workforce of long-term employees improves customer service and avoids the high expense of training new employees. Darnell wants to know if one warehouse is more effective at retaining employees than another. He asks you to do the following:

   a. Create an employee list that calculates the number of years each employee has worked for MovinOn.

   b. Organize the list by job title within each warehouse.

   c. Save the query as **qryEmployeeLongevity**.

10. MovinOn wants to offer hourly pay rates that are competitive with other moving companies in the Pacific Northwest. To identify nonsalaried employees who might be eligible for a raise in pay, Darnell asks you to do the following:

    a. Identify employees at each warehouse who earn less than $12.00 per hour. Do not include salaried employees in the list.

    b. Let users specify a particular warehouse, and then see information only for the employees who work in that warehouse.

    c. Save the query as **qryEmployeeLowWage**.

11. Darnell learns that the manager of the Oregon warehouse has decided to give his hourly employees a 10% raise. He asks you to list all the employees who work in the Oregon warehouse, and show the old hourly rate along with the new hourly rate after a 10% increase to their hourly pay rate. The increase applies only to hourly employees. Save the query as **qryOregonRateIncrease**.

12. Close the **MovinOn.accdb** database and then close Access.

Case 3—Managing Equipment and Preparing for Games in the Hershey College Intramural Department

Recall that you are working on a database for the intramural department at Hershey College, under the direction of Marianna Fuentes. The department is preparing for its first semester of operation and needs to set up teams for each sport, manage the equipment and fields for each sport, keep track of coaches and team captains, and allow students to sign up for the sports offerings.

Marianna has interviewed the intramural staff to determine the data needs of the department. She has prepared a list of those needs. Your next task is to create lists that meet the operational needs of the department. For each list, Marianna asks you to give the columns a descriptive name so that it is clear what each column contains.

Complete the following:

1. Open the **Hershey.accdb** database from the Case 3 folder.

2. Review the tables that you created in Chapter 2. Keep in mind that you will use the existing data to test the database. When the database has been fully designed, the department staff will enter real data in place of the test data you have provided.

3. The intramural staff often needs to contact students who have enrolled in an intramural sport. Create a phone list the staff can use. Marianna states that they usually use the cell phone number to contact students, but they want to have both the landline and the cell phone numbers on the contact list. The list should be ordered so that it is easy to find a student by name. Name the query **qryStudentContact**.

4. Because the intramural department staff members serve as coaches in addition to their other responsibilities, the staff needs to schedule their time carefully. In particular, they need to monitor people who coach more than one sport. Marianna asks you to list coaches who are assigned to more than one sport and to identify the sports to which each coach is assigned. Name the query **qryCoachesWithMultipleSports**.

5. Before students can participate in a sport, they must provide a liability waiver and academic approval form. One staff member is assigned to calling students who are missing a required form. Marianna asks you to create a list, including all phone numbers, of students who are missing one or both of the required forms. The list should also identify the missing form. Name the query **qryMissingApprovals**.

6. For the next staff meeting, the department needs a list of coaching assignments. Coaches often want a quick reference to their sport, the maximum and minimum numbers of players on each team, and the date the teams start playing. Name the query **qryCoachingAssignments**.

7. Recall that students must sign a waiver of liability and maintain academic approval before they can play an intramural sport. The department wants to have a list showing students and these two ratings. If a student has submitted a signed waiver and academic approval forms, indicate that they are approved to play. If the student has not submitted both forms, indicate that they are not approved to play. Organize the list so that those with approval are grouped at the beginning. Save the query as **qryApprovalStatus**.

8. In some cases, students who have academic approval but not a signed liability form can play intramural sports. However, students who do not have academic approval cannot participate in intramural sports. At the beginning of each semester, the department receives a list of students who are not approved to play sports. The staff records that information in the student table. They want to remove the students

who do not have academic approval from the table. Marianna asks you to identify students who do not have academic approval, isolate them in a separate table named **tblUnapprovedStudents**, and then remove them from the student table, which should contain only those students who have been academically approved. Name the queries **qryUnapprovedStudents** and **qryDeleteUnapprovedStudents** as appropriate.

9. All of the students who have signed up to play a sport have been assigned to a team. Provide a list of teams and the students assigned to those teams. Name the query **qryTeamAssignments**.

10. The staff also needs a way to track students in the future in case someone signs up for a sport and is not assigned to a team. Provide a way for the staff to track these students. Name the query **qryStudentWithoutTeam**.

11. To manage the teams, the coaches need a list of teams and their student captains. The captain names for this list are most useful as full names, with the last name appearing first. Name the query **qryTeamCaptainAssignments**.

12. If a sports field is available in the spring, it is also available in the summer. In other words, a field that is recorded as available only in the spring is actually available in the spring and summer, and a field that is recorded as available in the fall and spring is actually available in the fall, spring, and summer. Marianna wants to know if you can easily update the data to reflect this information. Name the query **qrySeasonChange**.

13. Provide at least two additional lists that would be helpful to the intramural staff, such as students who are in multiple sports or teams where players are needed. Create at least one by modifying an existing query in SQL view.

14. Close the **Hershey.accdb** database and then close Access.

Collecting Data
with Well-Designed Forms
Operations Management: Managing Daily Operations at 4Corners Pharmacy

LEARNING OBJECTIVES

Level 1

Design forms for efficient data entry
Create simple forms for data entry and editing
Develop a consistent user interface

Level 2

Create multitable forms
Improve navigation on forms
Add controls to forms

Level 3

Improve usability of forms
Place calculations on forms
Develop advanced forms

TOOLS COVERED IN THIS CHAPTER

Themes
Calculated field
Combo box (for locating a record)
Command button
Control Wizards
Find tool
Form properties
Form Wizard
Subform control
Tab control
Tab order

4

Chapter Introduction

This chapter focuses on automating the important process of acquiring the data needed for the day-to-day operation of a business. Although developers often add data to databases by importing it from other sources, most users of database applications enter and edit data using custom forms. In contrast to a datasheet, forms typically show only one record at a time and provide many advantages to database users. You can design electronic forms to match familiar paper ones, grouping fields to facilitate rapid data entry. You can also show related records on the same form by using a main form and one or more subforms, making it easy for users to view and enter related data.

Forms also offer flexibility for users and designers. You can create forms from a single table, multiple tables with a common field, or a query. Because forms can contain all the fields from a table or just a few, they can consist of one or many pages (or screens), depending on the number of fields you choose. You can design all the forms in a database to create a consistent look and feel, and include buttons that facilitate navigation, allowing the user to move from one form to another, or print the current record. To provide security, you can restrict each user to work with data in a particular view, such as one that allows users to view but not change the data.

Throughout this chapter, you will learn how to use forms to enter and view data. Level 1 examines the data-entry process and explores creating simple forms. Level 2 explains how to create forms with subforms, improve navigation, and modify forms to facilitate rapid and accurate data entry. Level 3 covers more complex forms that contain data from multiple tables and provide additional navigation options. You will also learn to customize forms by modifying their properties.

Case Scenario

Of all employees at 4Corners Pharmacy, technicians will interact with the new database application the most frequently. Rachel Thompson, a pharmacy technician, will work with the 4Corners database to create custom electronic forms so that the technicians can enter information directly into the database. To facilitate a smooth transition to the new system, she wants to make the forms easy to use and, if appropriate, similar to the paper forms they now use. Rachel has been working for 4Corners Pharmacy for many years and is very familiar with how the pharmacy operates. Naturally, her main interests are to automate the process of registering new customers and their prescriptions and processing refills.

Operations Management

Rachel also plans to develop custom forms so that they allow data entry and editing for every table in the database and so that they share a similar look and feel. Because the pharmacy can be very busy with phone orders and walk-in traffic, she must make sure that the forms facilitate rapid and accurate data entry.

LEVEL 1

Developing Simple Forms To Facilitate Data Entry

Designing Forms for Efficient Data Entry

An electronic **form** is an object you use to enter, update, and print records in a database. Although you can perform these same tasks in tables, forms present records in a format that makes data easy to enter and retrieve. Most database users interact with a database solely through its forms. They use forms to enter and update all the data in the database because forms provide better readability and control than tables and queries. In this way, the forms become the user interface of the database. Their design should, therefore, suit the way users enter or view data.

Well-designed forms let people use a database quickly, guiding them to find what they need. They should be easy to read and understand. Visually appealing forms make working with the database more pleasant and effective. The following are generally accepted guidelines for designing electronic forms:

- **Provide a meaningful title**—The title of a form should clearly state its purpose or content.
- **Organize fields logically**—Group related fields and position them in an order that is meaningful and logical for the database users. Users will feel familiar with electronic forms that matches its printed counterpart.
- **Use an appealing form layout**—Use few colors, fonts, and graphics to maintain a clean design that focuses on the data. Align fields and labels for readability. Use a consistent style for all forms in a database.
- **Include familiar field labels**—Assign descriptive names to each field for clarity.
- **Be consistent with terminology and abbreviations**—Be consistent with terms, instructions, and abbreviations that appear more than once in a form and in other forms.
- **Allow for convenient cursor movement**—Set up fields in a form so that users can enter data in a logical and convenient order and easily find information later.
- **Prevent and correct errors**—Use techniques such as providing default values or list boxes to reduce user errors by minimizing keystrokes and limiting entries. Prevent users from changing and updating fields, and allow them to correct data entered in other fields.
- **Include explanatory messages for fields**—If a field is optional, clearly mark it as such.

Figure 4.1 compares a well-designed form with a poorly designed one.

Figure 4.1: Comparing a well-designed form with a poorly designed form

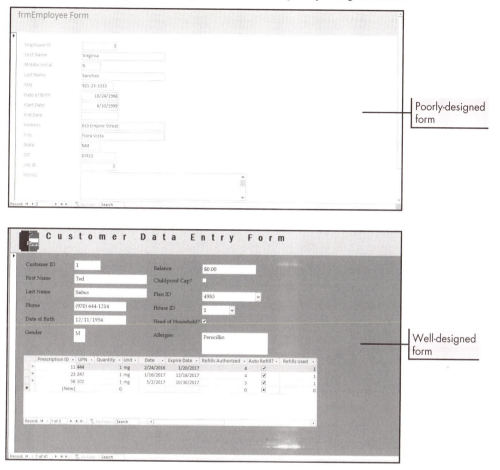

The top form is clearly difficult to use. It looks cluttered, disorganized, and unappealing. The form on the bottom is well-designed, attractive, and logically organized, enhancing the user experience of working with the form.

Before you create forms using Access, you should sketch the form design on paper, then meet with users and other database developers as necessary to determine content and an effective design. You should also verify database integrity, test tables and relationships, and examine and enter sample data.

Verifying Database Integrity

Paul Ferrino, the owner of 4Corners Pharmacy, is very aware of the potential problems with accuracy in databases. Because the purpose of the new 4Corners database is to provide timely data for decision making and to increase productivity in the pharmacy, he wants to make sure that employees can enter data accurately and efficiently. He also wants to make sure that it will be well received by the employees and, that after a short training period, it will speed up the daily operations of the pharmacy. He asks Rachel Thompson, a pharmacy technician, to design the data-entry forms so that they are complete, consistent, appealing, and easy to use.

Rachel starts by examining all 12 tables in the 4Corners database. These tables and their relationships are shown in Figure 4.2 and are described in the following list.

Figure 4.2: Tables and relationships for the pharmacy database

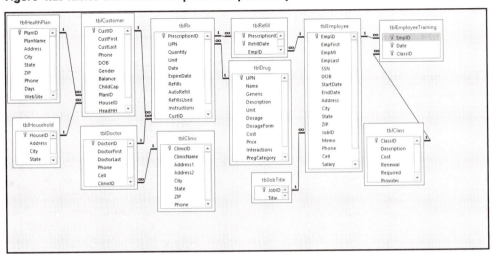

- **tblEmployee**—This table contains information about employees, including identifying information such as their ID number, name, and Social Security number, contact information such as their address and phone numbers, and employment information such as their starting date, salary or hourly rate, and job ID.
- **tblJobTitle**—This table lists the five jobs performed at 4Corners Pharmacy by ID number: 1—Owner, 2—Pharmacist, 3—Technician, 4—Cashier, and 5—Manager.
- **tblEmployeeTraining**—This table tracks the training classes that employees attend.
- **tblClass**—This table lists the classes employees can attend to receive required certifications or other professional training.
- **tblRefill**—This table tracks which employee refills a particular prescription and when.
- **tblCustomer**—This table contains information about the customers, including their ID number, name, phone, birth date, gender, and health plan ID. Each customer is assigned a household ID and information about whether they are the designated head of household. The table also contains information for the pharmacist, including known allergies and preference for childproof caps on prescription bottles, and indicates any unpaid balance on the customer's account.
- **tblHealthPlan**—This table lists the ID and name of the customer's health plan as well as the address and phone number. Also included is the number of days allowed per prescription and a hyperlink to the plan's Web site in case the pharmacy needs additional information.

- **tblHousehold**—Each customer is assigned to a household. This table includes the household ID and address so it is entered only once for each household. Unrelated customers with the same address, such as roommates, are assigned their own household ID.
- **tblDoctor**—This table contains information about doctors who write prescriptions that 4Corners Pharmacy fills. The table includes the name, phone numbers, additional phone contact (often a nurse or secretary), and the ID of the clinic with which the doctor is affiliated.
- **tblClinic**—Doctors are affiliated with one clinic. This table contains the clinic name, address, and phone number.
- **tblRx**—This table lists each prescription that the pharmacy fills, including the prescription number (called an ID), the UPN (a numeric code assigned by the drug companies), and other details about the prescription.
- **tblDrug**—This table contains information about the drugs used in the prescriptions, such as the UPN, drug name, dosage and dosage form, cost and price, and any known interactions.

Accurate data is a major goal in every database. Unintentional data-entry errors range from a typo in an address to an incorrect customer ID. Some errors can be prevented by the design of the database itself, such as entering job titles only once in the tblJobTitle table and relating this table to the tblEmployee table. By relating these tables, the job title does not need to be entered for each employee in tblEmployee. Typing the job title many times into a table can lead to incorrectly spelled job titles. These are the types of errors that Rachel tests first. For example, she notes that addresses are entered only once for each customer in the tblHousehold table. Employees can verify the address with the customer when they enter this data to ensure its accuracy.

Rachel examines each table in Design view to verify that field properties, such as input masks and validation rules, are in place to allow entry of data in the proper format and within appropriate ranges. In the table datasheets, she enters test dates and phone numbers to make sure that all formats, input masks, and validation rules are working properly. She also tests referential integrity rules by trying to enter the same ID number for two records. For example, the medications listed in the tblDrug table are identified by UPN number, such as 102 for ampicillin. When Rachel tries to use 102 in the UPN field for a different drug, she receives an error message explaining that she cannot make that change because it would create duplicate values in the primary key. This ensures that each drug in tblDrug has a unique UPN.

She also tries to enter mismatching data on the many side of one-to-many relationships. For example, the tblEmployee and tblRefill tables have a one-to-many relationship—one employee can refill many prescriptions. The EmpID field in tblEmployee contains values 1–28. When Rachel enters a new refill in the tblRefill table and uses "30" as the EmpID, she receives an error indicating that she cannot add that record because a related record is required in tblEmployee. This indicates that the tables are maintaining referential integrity—only a valid employee can enter a prescription refill. After Rachel verifies that the database is designed to prevent critical data-entry errors, she deletes the test data.

Best Practice

Testing Tables and Relationships

It is much easier to test all relationships, data integrity rules, input masks, and other field proper-ties before creating forms. If you import data from a spreadsheet, edit the data in table Datasheet view to make it compatible with your new application. For example, you might need to adjust the customer and prescription ID numbers to match the new scheme. If your database design needs further modification, complete the redesign before spending substantial time developing forms (and reports). Modifying forms (and reports) to accommodate a change in database design involves a considerable amount of work. For example, changing data types of fields and adding or removing fields from tables all require changing the forms that include those fields.

Examining and Entering Data

You can enter data into records using a table's Datasheet view or using a form that includes fields from one or more tables. Datasheet entry is efficient when you need to enter many records at the same time, especially if you routinely work with the same documents. You might also use a datasheet to quickly enter sample data for testing, especially in a table on the "one" side of a one-to-many relationship. The primary table must contain data before you can enter data in the related table, the one on the "many" side of the one-to-many relationship. However, most Access database applications use forms for data entry after the database is released for regular business use. Activities such as taking telephone orders or looking up product or customer information are more efficient and accurate with forms. For example, forms can include calculations so you can provide grand totals and they can include list boxes so you can select correct items. You can also use forms to enhance the appearance of your data, making it easier to find the information you need.

When the 4Corners database is used in everyday business operations, employees will use forms to enter data. For example, when customers order prescriptions by phone or walk-in customers request prescription refills, a pharmacy technician will open a prescription or refill form as appropriate to enter the necessary data.

When she examines the tblCustomer table, Rachel sees an expand indicator to the left of the records. When she clicks the expand indicator next to Ted Sabus, the prescriptions Ted received appear in a subdatasheet containing records from tblRx. (Recall that a subdatasheet is a datasheet nested in another datasheet that displays records from a related table.) If necessary, Rachel could edit or enter data in the subdatasheet to update prescription data in tblRx. The subdatasheet appears because tblCustomer is on the "one" side of a one-to-many relationship with tblRx established in the Relationships window. Records for a particular customer in tblRx are linked to that customer in tblCustomer by their common field, CustID. See Figure 4.3.

Figure 4.3: Examining data before creating forms

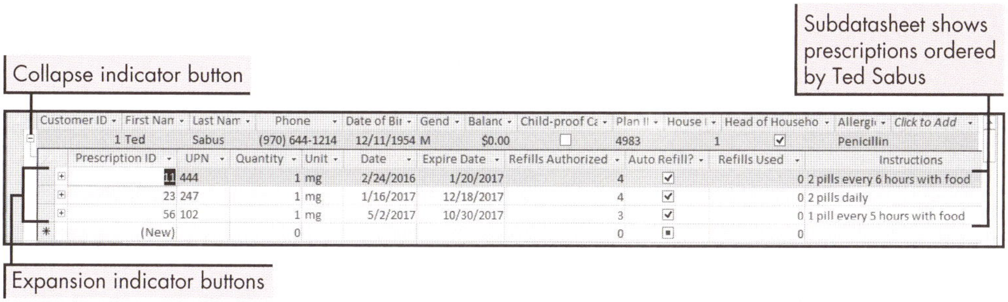

Collapse indicator button

Subdatasheet shows prescriptions ordered by Ted Sabus

Expansion indicator buttons

Rachel also notices that when she clicks the PlanID field, a list arrow appears so she can select the health plan ID. The HouseID field also has a list arrow that lets her display a list of valid household IDs and their corresponding addresses. When Rachel opens tblCustomer in Design view and examines the PlanID and HouseID fields, she finds that these are both defined as lookup fields, which streamline data entry by listing only valid choices for a field.

Creating Simple Forms for Data Entry and Editing

As with other database objects such as tables and queries, Access provides many ways to create a form, including options for creating simple forms. Use a form tool in the Forms group on the CREATE tab to create a form that contains all the fields from a table or query arranged in a common format. Choices in the Forms group include Form, Form Design, and Blank Form. The More Forms list arrow lets you choose Multiple Items, Datasheet, Split Form, and Modal Dialog. These forms are described in Table 4.1.

Table 4.1: Form tools in the Forms group

Form tools	Purpose
Form	Creates a form that allows you to enter information for one record at a time.
Multiple Items	Produces a form similar to a datasheet that shows one record per row.
Datasheet	A form that contains a datasheet typically displays different data sources. The data in the datasheet is usually related to data in the form. For example, a form might show employees and the datasheet in the form might show certification classes that the employee has taken.
Split Form	Generates a split form with the datasheet in the top section and a form in the lower section where you can enter information about the selected record in the top section.
Modal Dialog	Requires a response from the user before they can continue in the form. An example could be that a dialog box opens and requires the CustomerID be entered before the customer information is displayed.

You can also use the Form Wizard to guide you through the steps of creating a form, letting you select options such as including some or all of the fields in a table or query, including fields from more than one table, and using a particular layout and style.

Best Practice

Determining User Screen Resolutions

Before you begin creating forms, find out from your users which screen resolution they typically use on their computer monitors. When designing forms, you should set the display properties on your computer to match the lowest resolution that your users are using. A screen resolution of 800 × 600 is the safest. If all users of the database have screen resolutions of 1024 × 768 or higher, it would be OK to design forms at this higher resolution. Designing forms at the proper resolution ensures that users don't need to scroll from left to right to work with the complete form. If scrolling from left to right is unavoidable, you can split the form into multiple pages, as you will learn to do later in this chapter.

Creating a Form Using the Form Tool

Rachel is ready to create a form based on the tblCustomer table. She will use the 800 × 600 screen resolution because that is the resolution that everyone in the pharmacy uses. Rachel clicks once on tblCustomer in the Navigation pane, clicks the CREATE tab and then clicks the Form tool in the Forms group. Access creates a form by arranging all the fields in tblCustomer in a columnar format, and displays the first record in the form window. The form is displayed in Layout view, which allows you to make changes to the form while viewing live data. Access also converts the subdatasheet into a **subform**, which contains the fields from tblRx just as the subdatasheet does. Note that the structure of the data in the table is reflected in the structure of the form. For example, the fields appear in the same order and the field names in the form match those in the table's datasheet. See Figure 4.4.

Figure 4.4: tblCustomer form in Layout view

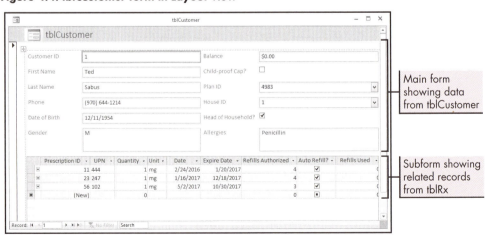

To move from one field to the next, Rachel switches to Form View and presses the Tab key. To move from one record to another, she clicks the buttons on the navigation bar at the bottom of the main form. As she moves to another record, the data in the subform changes. For example, when she clicks the Next record button 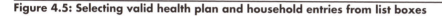 on the navigation bar to view the next customer record (Tabitha Sabus), the subform displays information about the prescriptions Tabitha has received.

Rachel can also use the Tab key in the subform to move from one field to the next, and the buttons in the subform's navigation bar to move from one record to another. She also knows that the column widths in the subform can be increased or decreased by dragging the border next to the field name. The subform provides the solution Rachel needed to link related tables on a form.

Rachel notices that the PlanID and HouseID fields have list arrows in the form, just as they do in the tblCustomer table. As before, Rachel can click the arrow on the View button arrow and select Form View to leave Layout View, and she can click the list arrows to select a valid health plan ID or house ID. See Figure 4.5.

Figure 4.5: Selecting valid health plan and household entries from list boxes

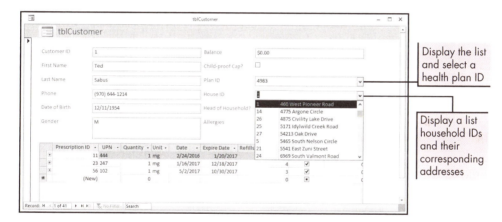

Rachel closes the form, saving it as frmCustomer. She uses "frm" as the prefix to identify the object as a form.

How To

Create a Form Using a Form Tool
1. Click the table name in the Navigation pane.
2. Click the CREATE tab on the Ribbon.
3. Click the Form tool in the Forms group.
4. Click the Save button and enter a name for the form.

OR

1. Open a table in Datasheet view. This table provides the fields and data for the form.
2. Click the CREATE tab on the Ribbon.
3. Click the Form tool in the Forms group.
4. Click the Save button and enter a name for the form.

Now Rachel is ready to create forms for other tables in the 4Corners database.

Using the Form Wizard

Next, Rachel wants to create a form for the tblDoctor table. When she examines tblDoctor, she finds it includes the DoctorID, DoctorFirst, DoctorLast, Phone, Cell, and ClinicID fields, in that order. She thinks it would be more helpful to list the ClinicID field right after the DoctorID field on the form—technicians often associate doctors with clinics. Because she wants to change the order of the fields on the form, she can't use a form tool because the form tools place fields from a selected table (or query) on a form in the same order as they appear in the table. Instead, Rachel can use the Form Wizard, which will let her specify the field order and an attractive layout and style for the form.

Rachel clicks the Form Wizard button in the Forms group on the CREATE tab. She then selects tblDoctor as the table containing the source data for the form. See Figure 4.6.

Figure 4.6: Starting the Form Wizard

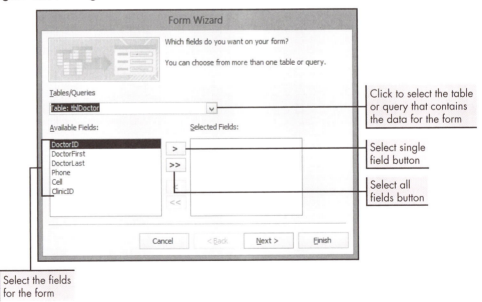

Select the fields for the form

Click to select the table or query that contains the data for the form

Select single field button

Select all fields button

She then selects the DoctorID, ClinicID, DoctorFirst, DoctorLast, Phone, and Cell fields from the tblDoctor table in that order using the select single field button. See Figure 4.7.

Figure 4.7: Select the fields you want to show on the form

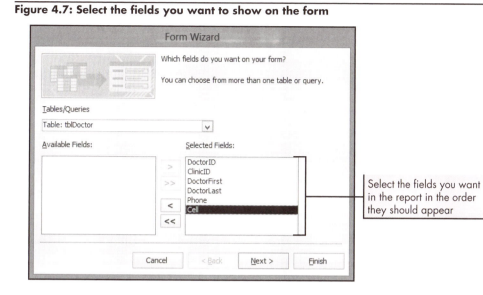

Rachel selects the Columnar layout. Then she saves the form as frmDoctor and opens it in Form view.

The completed form contains all the fields in tblDoctor listed in the order she selected them in the Form Wizard. See Figure 4.8.

Figure 4.8: Form for the tblDoctor table

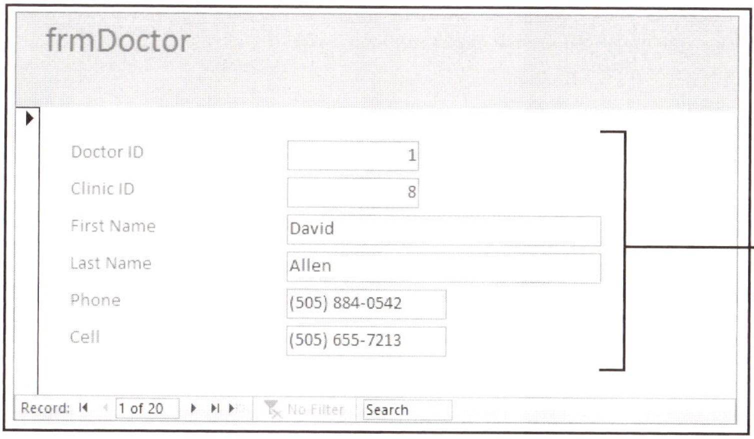

Create a Form Using the Form Wizard

1. Click the Form Wizard button in the Forms group on the CREATE tab.
2. Click the list arrow, and then select the table (or query) you want to use as the source of data for the form.
3. From the Available Fields list, select the fields you want to include in the form. (When you are creating data-entry forms for adding data to a table, add all fields to the form.) Use the Select Single Field button to select the fields one by one; use the Select All Fields button to select them all at once. Click the Next button.
4. Select a layout for the form. A sample of the selected layout appears in the preview box of the dialog box. Click the Next button.
5. Select a style for the form. A sample of the selected style appears in the preview box. Click the Next button.
6. Type the name of the form, using "frm" as the prefix to identify the object as a form. Click the Finish button. The completed form opens in Form view.

Rachel has now created two forms—one based on tblCustomer and another on tblDoctor—that look different from each other. Before she creates other forms for the 4Corners database, she wants to make some changes to these forms so that the size and layout of the fields is appropriate for the forms.

Understanding the Importance of Consistent Style and Layout for Forms

Most developers design their forms so they share a color scheme, fonts, and general layout. Because users expect to find similar features in the same location on each form, consistency in design simplifies data entry. Follow the guidelines for designing effective electronic forms, listed earlier in this chapter in the "Designing Forms for Efficient Data Entry" section, and apply them consistently to your forms to present a unified, professional interface.

The data in most forms comes from the tables and queries in the database. A form's **record source** is the underlying object that provides the fields and data in the form.

A data-entry form is usually a **bound form** that displays data from the fields in its record source. (**Unbound forms** do not have a record source; they are usually designed to help users navigate through a database.) Other information on the form, such as the title, page number, calculations, and graphics, are stored in the form's design.

You link a form to its record source by using design elements called **controls**, which are small objects such as text boxes, buttons, and labels that let users interact with the form. When you work with a form in Design view, you manipulate its controls. These controls are described in Table 4.2. Understanding when to use the various types of controls makes it easier to create and modify forms.

Table 4.2: Important controls on the DESIGN tab

Tool or Control	Name	Function
	Attachment	Inserts an attachment control in the form design grid that allows you to attach and view multiple files stored in the underlying field.
	Bound Object Frame	Creates a bound OLE object stored in an Access database table such as a picture stored in an OLE Object data type field.
	Check Box	Creates a check box control that holds on/off, yes/no, or true/false data.
	Combo Box	Creates a combo box control that contains a list of potential values for the control and lets you type text or select a table or query as the source of the values in the list. You can also use the combo box to find a record.
	Button	Creates a control that users can click to take an action, such as record navigation to move to another record, record operation to do such items as print a record, or form operation such as close a form.
	Date and Time	Displays the date and/or time control to the form header section.
	Image	Displays a static graphic image on the form. This object becomes part of the form, not part of the data from an underlying table or query.
	Chart	Inserts a chart into a form to display data graphically.
	Insert Image	Allows you to browse to locate the desired image and then places the selected image into the form.
	Hyperlink	Creates a link to a Web page, program, or e-mail address.
	Label	Displays text, such as titles or instructions; an unbound control.
	Line	Draws a line to enhance the appearance of the form.
	List Box	Creates a list of values for the control either by typing values or specifying a table or query for the source.
	Logo	Inserts a picture into the form that will be used as a logo in an image control.
	Navigation Control	Allows you to add an additional navigation tab in a navigation form.
	Option Button	Display an option button control bound to a yes/no field.
	Option Group	Groups toggle buttons, option buttons, or check boxes, so the user can only select one button or check box in a group.
	Insert or Remove Page Break	Adds or removes a page break between the pages of a multipage form.
	Rectangle	Draws a rectangle to enhance the form's appearance.
	Subform/ Subreport	Embeds another form in the current form. If the forms have a related field, Access maintains the link between the two forms.
	Tab Control	Creates a series of tab pages on a form. Each tab page can contain a number of other controls that display information from another table or query.

4

Level 1

Table 4.2: Important controls on the DESIGN tab (cont.)

Tool or Control	Name	Function
`ab|`	Text Box	Displays a label attached to a text box that is bound to a field in an underlying table or query or contains a calculated value.
▦	Toggle Button	Displays a toggle button control bound to a yes/no field. Similar to a check box.
🖼	Unbound Object Frame	Adds an object from another application such as a Microsoft Excel spreadsheet. The object becomes part of the form, not part of the data from an underlying table or query. You can add pictures, sounds, charts, or slides to your form.
▣	Web Browser Control	Allows you to add web pages to a form.

© 2014 Cengage Learning

Because Rachel wants to make additional changes to frmCustomer, she needs to work in Design view. In the Database window, she switches to Design view by right-clicking frmCustomer and then clicking Design View. The Form window in Design view includes a **Detail** section for the main body of a form, which displays records and usually contains all the bound controls. In the form Rachel is creating, the Detail section contains all the fields in the tblCustomer table, with one record per page.

All forms have a Detail section, but some also include a form header, form footer, page header, and page footer. Figure 4.9 shows a blank form with these sections.

Figure 4.9: Blank form in Design view

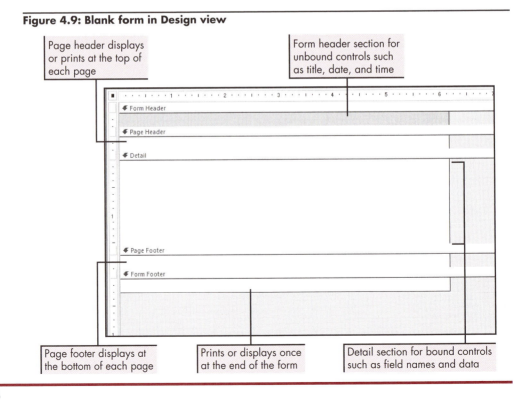

Page header displays or prints at the top of each page

Form header section for unbound controls such as title, date, and time

Page footer displays at the bottom of each page

Prints or displays once at the end of the form

Detail section for bound controls such as field names and data

A **form header** displays information that always appears on the form, even when the records change. Form headers appear at the top of the screen in Form view and at the top of the first page when the form is printed. If you want to include a title on your form, you usually place it in the form header. A **form footer** also displays information that always appears on a form, but at the bottom of the screen in Form view and the bottom of the last page when the form is printed. Form footers often contain instructions for using the form or a button to perform an action, such as printing the form.

Page headers and **footers** display information at the top or bottom of every page, respectively, and appear only when you print the form by default. However, you can change the form properties to display the page header or footer, only in Form view, or only in Print Preview and when printed. (The same is true for form headers and footers.) Page headers are useful for column headings, dates, and page numbers. Page footers are often used to display summaries and page numbers.

Forms created with the Form Wizard or the Form tool have a form header and footer by default. The titles that Access includes by default can be easily edited to add or remove text. The gray area called the **grid** (the form background) has gridlines and dots. This grid is useful for aligning controls and other items on the form.

If you need to add a field to the form, you can drag it from the field list and position it anywhere in the Detail section of the form. To open the field list, you click the Add Existing Fields button in the Tools group on the DESIGN tab. You can add more than one field to a form by selecting the fields you want in the field list or by using the Shift key to select adjacent fields or the Ctrl key to select nonadjacent fields. You can then drag the selection to the form. When you drag a field to the form, Access creates the appropriate type of control for the field based on its data type. For example, a field with a Number data type appears as a text box with a label, and a Yes/No field appears as a check box.

Examining a Form in Design View

Rachel first decides to change some of the form features. For example, she notices that some of the fields are too large for the field data that is displayed. In order to make these changes, she needs to open the form in Design view. She opens frmCustomer in Design view as shown in Figure 4-10. She knows that the fields in the Detail section have two parts. The right side of the field, called the **label**, describes the information found in the field. The left side is called the **text box** where the field data from the table is displayed.

Figure 4.10: Form for the tblCustomer in Design view

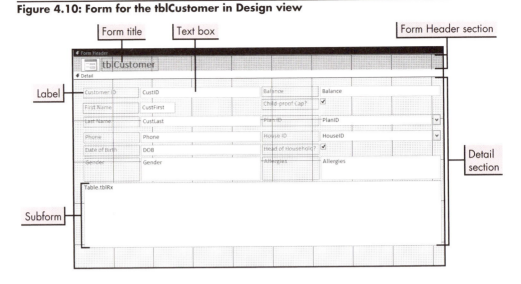

She decides to change the size of the text box controls so they display all the table information, but do not take up too much room in the form. Rachel knows that in Design view she can resize and move all the controls together unless the grouping for the controls is removed from the fields.

Rachel then selects all the controls in the Detail section by dragging and holding down the mouse button along the ruler to the left of the Detail section. She then clicks the ARRANGE tab and clicks the Remove Layout button in the Table group to remove the control grouping.

When you select a control, eight handles appear on its corners and edges. The larger handle in a control's upper-left corner is its **move handle**, which you use to move the control. You use the other seven handles, called **sizing handles**, to resize the control. To move a text box and its attached label together, you place the mouse pointer anywhere on the label or text box border except over its move or sizing handle. When the pointer changes to a four-headed arrow shape, you can drag the text box and its attached label to the new location.

Rachel resizes each of the fields on the left side of the form starting with Customer ID and ending with Gender. She moves between the Form view and Design view to see how the fields are displayed.

Rachel moves the fields on the right side of the form closer to the center since she now has more room. She selects the fields by placing the mouse pointer above the first field on the right and then, with the mouse button pressed, drags in a downward direction until all of the fields on the right are selected. Now she can drag all of them at once by placing the mouse pointer on one of the field borders so that a four-sided arrow appears. Finally, she resizes the fields so that the data fits. She changes the title of the form to Customers. She then saves the form. Her completed form appears as shown in Figure 4.11.

Figure 4.11: Completed form for tblCustomer

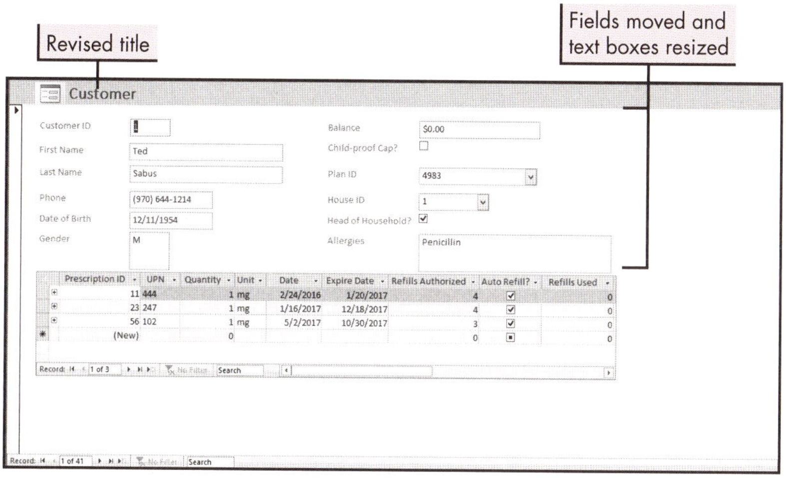

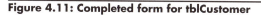

Modify a Form in Design View

1. Select the controls in the section that you wish to modify by clicking on any control to display the Layout Selector.
2. Click the Layout Selector to select all items in the section.
3. Click the ARRANGE tab and click the Remove Layout button in the Table group.
4. Move and resize the fields as necessary.
5. Save the form.

Before Rachel creates more forms for the 4Corners database, she wants to determine an appropriate design for the forms and then make sure that all the forms share this design.

Developing a Consistent User Interface

Recall that forms serve as the user interface of a database because most people use forms to enter and retrieve data. If all the forms in your database share the same design, they present a consistent user interface. This means users only need to learn how to use the forms once to apply what they learn to all the forms in the database.

Rachel knows that if she applies font and background colors in the form, she will need to apply the same formats to each item or control in each form, which will be very time consuming. Therefore, for design consistency, Rachel decides to use themes. Themes are a simple way to make your forms and reports appear more professional. Themes are a set of formats including borders, background colors, shading, and graphic effects.

Once you apply a theme to a form, you can change it to another theme by just selecting a new theme. The form is automatically updated with the new theme settings.

Before themes can be applied in Access, you must apply theme colors to the background and text areas. After that, when you apply a theme, Access will apply the new theme colors to the already-formatted areas. Rachel opens frmCustomer in Design view. She then clicks in the Form Header section, clicks the FORMAT tab on the Ribbon, and then clicks Shape Fill in the Control Formatting group to display the shape fill colors as shown in Figure 4.12.

Figure 4.12: Shape Fill colors gallery

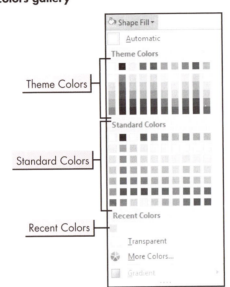

The Theme Colors group is at the top of the Shape Fill colors gallery. However, any color may be selected and used in a theme. She decides that she wants a professional theme with desert style colors. So, Rachel chooses Maroon 2 in the Standard Colors. Next, she clicks in the Detail section and selects Maroon 4.

Rachel decides to change the font colors. She selects the title text box, clicks the FORMAT tab and then clicks the Font Color arrow to display the Font Color gallery. This gallery also shows three groups of font colors (Theme Colors, Standard Colors, and Recent Colors). She chooses the theme color Black, Text 1. She then selects all the labels in the Detail section by holding down the Shift key and clicking on each label. Rachel applies the same theme color to the labels.

Now that the theme colors are applied to the form, Access knows where themes should be applied in the form. Rachel is ready to save this theme, so she selects the DESIGN tab and clicks Themes in the Themes group to display the Themes gallery. Then, she clicks the Save Current Theme option to open the Save Current Theme dialog box. She types Corners for the theme File name and then clicks Save to save the theme for use for other objects in the database. As shown in Figure 4.13, the Corners theme appears in the Custom and the In this Database categories of the Themes gallery.

Figure 4.13: Themes gallery

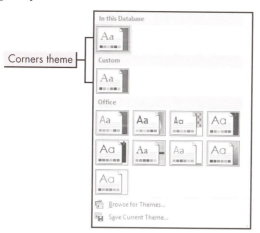

Rachel reviews the form and she decides to use the Corners theme for the remainder of the forms. A completed form appears as shown in Figure 4.14.

Figure 4.14: frmCustomer with Corners theme applied

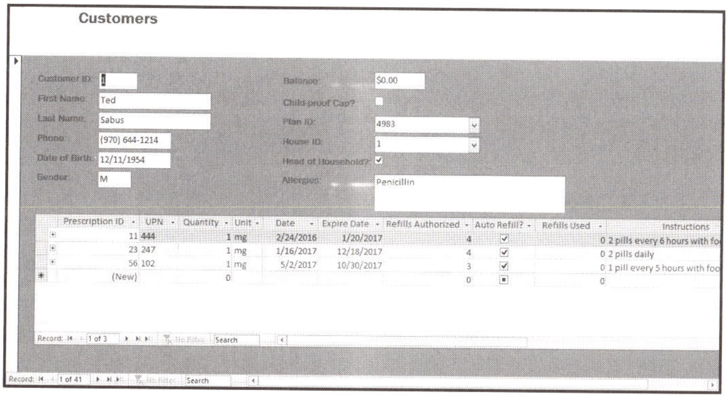

How To

Apply Themes to Forms

1. Select the Form Header section, click the FORMAT tab, click the Shape Fill button arrow, and then choose a shape fill theme color.
2. Click in the background of the Detail section, click Shape Fill, click the Shape Fill button arrow, and then choose a shape fill theme color.
3. Select the form title, click the FORMAT tab, click the Font Color button arrow, and then choose a color from the Theme Colors group.
4. Select any label in the Detail section, hold down the Shift key and click on each of the remaining labels.
5. Click the Font Color button arrow, and then choose a color from the Theme Colors group.
6. Click the DESIGN tab, click Themes, and then select a theme of your choice.

Besides using the same colors and fonts on each form, Rachel also wants to include an informative title. To do so, she'll work with the Label control in the Controls group.

Changing Label Properties in a Form

Rachel wants to add a custom title to the Form Header section so that the title always appears at the top of the form. She needs a more descriptive title so that users will understand the purpose of the form. She clicks in the title text box and deletes the current text. She then types "Customer Data Entry Form". When she views this label in Form view, she discovers that the text is a bit small, so she returns to Design view to change the font size. She right-clicks the new label and then clicks Form Properties on the shortcut menu. The label's Property Sheet opens on the right as shown in Figure 4.15.

Figure 4.15: Properties of a label

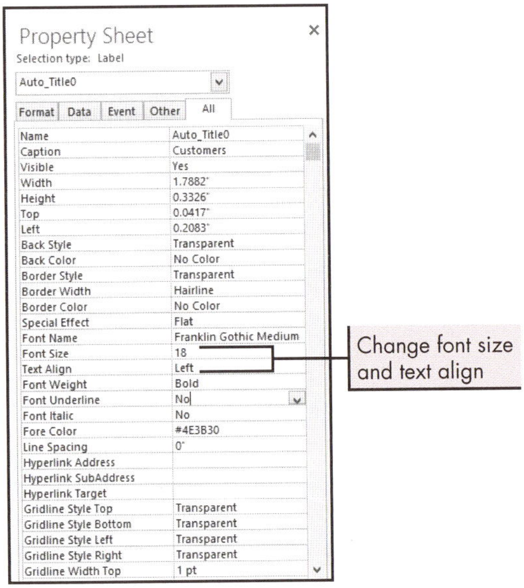

The Property Sheet lists all of the possible settings to modify the appearance and behavior of the label. You can view a description of each property by clicking the property and then pressing the F1 key. Table 4.4 lists some common properties for labels.

Table 4.4: Common label properties

Property	Description
Back Style	Select Transparent (default) to make the background of the label transparent; in other words, the color of the form behind the control is visible. Select Normal and then set a background color if you want to change the color of the label background.
Back Color	If you want a background color for the label, specify the numeric value of the color or click the Build button to use the Color Builder to select a color from a palette.
Special Effect	Specify whether the label should appear as flat (default), raised, sunken, etched, shadowed, or chiseled.

Table 4.4: Common label properties (cont.)

Property	Description
Border Style	Specify whether the label's border should appear as transparent (default), solid, dashes, short dashes, dots, sparse dots, dash dot, dash dot dot, or double solid.
Border Color	If you set a nontransparent border style, set the border color of the label by specifying the numeric value of the color or clicking the Build button to use the Color Builder to select a color from a palette.
Border Width	If you set a nontransparent border style, set the width of the border to hairline (default) or to 1–6 points.
Font Size	Specify the point size of the label text.
Font Weight	Specify the font weight of the label text, such as normal or bold.
Font Underline	Specify whether the label text appears as underlined.
Text Align	Specify the alignment of the text within the label.

© 2014 Cengage Learning

Although Rachel could use the tools on the DESIGN tab to change the font, she also wants to use a special alignment only available in the Property Sheet. She uses the Property Sheet to increase the font size to 20 and to set the Text Align property to Distribute to space the characters evenly across the width of the label. Rachel realizes that the title does not need to be the entire width of the form. She closes the Property Sheet and decreases the width of the label. Her revised form appears in Figure 4.16.

Figure 4.16: New formats applied to frmCustomer

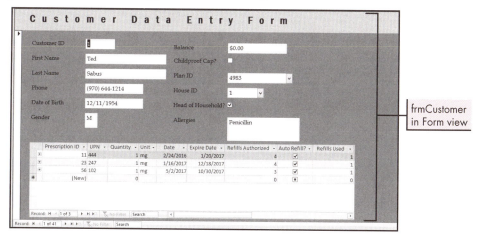

frmCustomer in Form view

Using Undo to Reverse Changes

The Undo button ↺ on the Quick Access toolbar remembers the last 20 changes you make to a form. When you click the list arrow on the Undo button, you can scroll down the list of actions you recently performed. If you select an action in the list, you undo all the actions since you performed that action. As you modify a form, make liberal use of the Undo button and switch between Design view and Form view often to view the changes.

To complete her changes to frmCustomer, Rachel widens the background of the form and then widens the tblRx subform so that it shows as many fields as possible. In Form view, she resizes the subform's columns to their best fit. She switches between Design and Layout views and uses the Undo button on the Quick Access toolbar as necessary until she is satisfied with the result.

Best Practice

Using Unbound Controls for Titles

The label that contains the title for the form is an unbound control, so it only shows the title text—it is not bound to data in the record source. A common mistake for new database developers is to use the Text Box button instead of the Label button to create a title. If you add a text box to the form header, for example, and then enter the title in the text box, an error message such as #Name? appears in the text box in Form view. This is because a text box is a bound control and Access expects that it is bound to data in the underlying table.

Adding an Unbound Graphic to a Form

Rachel wants to identify the forms as belonging to 4Corners Pharmacy, so she wants to add the 4Corners logo to the forms. She'll add the logo to frmCustomer and then circulate that form so the managers can approve it. She opens frmCustomer in Design view and resizes the form header. To add the logo, she clicks the FORM DESIGN TOOLS DESIGN tab and then clicks the Logo button in the Header/Footer group, and then inserts the 4Corners.jpg graphic into the form header. See Figure 4.17. (The 4Corners.jpg graphic is located in the Level 1 folder in the Data Files folder for this chapter.)

Figure 4.17: Adding the logo to frmCustomer

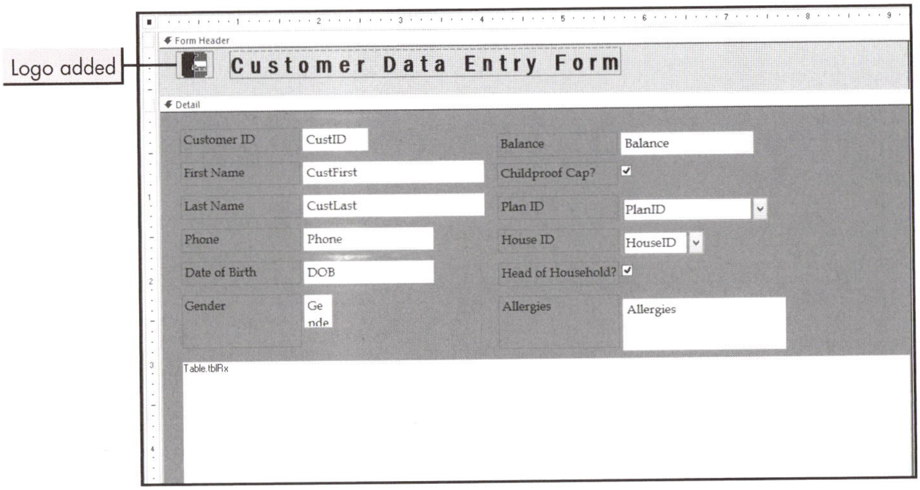

The logo needs to be larger and moved to a better location. Rachel clicks the image and points to the sizing handle in the lower-left corner, and then drags to make the image larger. She can't see the entire image so she checks the Size Mode property in the Property Sheet on the Format tab to see if it is set to Clip, Stretch, or Zoom. Clip sets the picture to its actual size; Stretch lets the picture be stretched horizontally and vertically to fit the form; and Zoom enlarges the picture to fit within the form, but maintains the original height to width ratio. She chooses the Zoom option so the height to width ratios are maintained and the picture will appear as it did when originally created and allows her to resize it to fit in any location. See Figure 4.18. Now she will show frmCustomer with the logo added to the managers to get their feedback before continuing to place it on other forms.

Figure 4.18: frmCustomer with resized graphic

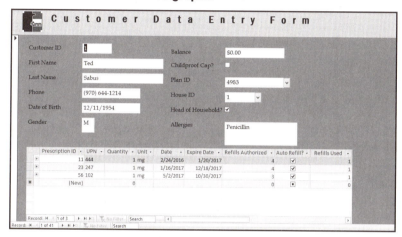

Rachel uses the Form Wizard to create a form for the tblHousehold table and applies theme font and background colors and the Corners theme to the form. She also creates forms based on tblClinic, tblDrug, tblEmployee, tblEmployeeTraining, tblClass, and tblJobTitle, using all the fields from each table. She includes a descriptive title for each form and then applies the themes. She replaces the "tbl" prefix with the "frm" prefix when naming the forms. For example, she saves the form based on tblClinic as frmClinic. Now she is ready to develop more complex forms.

Steps To Success: Level 1

Anne Lessard is an experienced pharmacy technician at Hudson Bay Pharmacy, and is coordinating efforts to develop the automated forms in the Hudson database. To ease data entry, she wants to create a form for each table in the Hudson database. She asks for your help in creating the forms and developing a consistent form design. As you save the new forms, be certain to use the "frm" prefix as part of the naming convention. Also consult your instructor for instructions about submitting your results.

Complete the following:

1. Start Access and open the **Hudson.accdb** database from the STS folder.

2. Anne asks you to prepare for creating forms by examining the tables and relationships in the database, noting any subdatasheets and lookup fields used in the tables. Then test the relationships and verify that the field sizes and data types are appropriate. Enter test dates and phone numbers to make sure that all formats, input masks, and validation rules are working properly.

3. Anne's goal is to create a data-entry form for each table in the Hudson Bay Pharmacy database. She asks you to start by creating a form that contains all the fields from tblCustomer. Navigate through the records in the main form and note the changes in the subform. Also navigate the records in the subform. Then save the form as **frmCustomer**.

4. Next, create a form based on the tblDoctor table that lists the ClinicID field right after the DoctorID field. Select a layout and style that make the form easy to read and use. Add an appropriate title, and save the form as **frmDoctor**.

5. Anne wants to use a consistent form design so that the look and feel of the Hudson Bay Pharmacy database provides a uniform user interface. She approves of the design, style, and contents of frmDoctor, and suggests that you use them as the basis for creating and formatting the other forms. First, you need to modify frmCustomer so that it is similar to frmDoctor. Add an appropriate title to frmCustomer and then format and resize it as necessary.

6. Apply the same theme to frmCustomer that you used for frmDoctor.

7. To identify the forms as belonging to Hudson Bay Pharmacy, Anne asks you to add the **HudsonBay.jpg** logo in the Chapter 4\Level 1 STS folder to frmCustomer. She'll add logos to the other forms later. Make other changes to frmCustomer to make it more informative and easier to use.

8. Create forms that Hudson Bay Pharmacy employees can use to enter data in the following tables:

   - tblClass
   - tblClinic
   - tblDrug
   - tblEmployee
   - tblEmployeeTraining
   - tblHousehold
   - tblJobTitle

   Save each new form with a name that replaces the "tbl" prefix with the "frm" prefix. Make sure the forms present a consistent user interface along with the other forms you've created for Hudson Bay Pharmacy.

9. Close the **Hudson.accdb** database and then close Access.

LEVEL 2

Creating Forms That Use Fields From More Than One Table

Adding a Subform to an Existing Form

As you have already seen, a subform is a form embedded in another form. The primary form is called the **main form**, and its underlying table usually has a one-to-many relationship with the table underlying the subform. The main form and subform are linked so that the subform displays only records that are related to the current record in the main form. For example, when the main form displays the record for a particular customer in the 4Corners database, the subform displays only the prescriptions for that customer.

If you use a wizard to create a subform, Access automatically synchronizes the main form with the subform only if the tables containing the fields for the form are related. The relationship can be one-to-one, one-to-many, or many-to-many. If you are using queries as the record source for the forms, the tables underlying the queries must be related. The subform must also have a field with the same name or compatible data type and field size as the primary key in the table underlying the main form.

A main form can have more than one subform. A subform can also contain another subform. This means you can have a subform within a main form, and you can have another subform within that subform, and so on. For example, you could have a main form that displays customers, a subform that displays prescriptions, and another subform that displays refill information.

Rachel examines and tests the frmHousehold form, which includes the HouseID, Address, City, State, and ZIP fields from tblHousehold. This form is helpful because 4Corners considers that related people residing at the same address are part of a household, and designates one customer as the head of the household. Rachel wants frmHousehold to display only the names and phone numbers of the customers in each household.

Because tblHousehold and tblCustomer are linked by a common HouseID field, each record in tblHousehold includes a subdatasheet that displays related records from tblCustomer. However, the subdatasheet includes all the fields in tblCustomer, and Rachel only wants to display the fields related to the customer's name and phone number. If she re-creates frmHousehold using the Form tool, she'll create a main form with a subform that contains all the fields from tblCustomer.

How can she create a subform that includes only some of the fields from tblCustomer? Because tblHousehold and tblCustomer share a common field, one way to do this is to use the Subform Wizard to add a subform to frmHousehold and include only selected fields from tblCustomer.

How To

Add a Subform to a Form

1. In Design view, open the form you want to modify.
2. Resize the form as necessary to make room for the subform.
3. Click the Subform/Subreport button in the Controls group on the DESIGN tab, and then click the form where you want to place the subform. The Subform Wizard dialog box opens.
4. To use selected fields from a table or query in the subform, select the Use existing Tables and Queries option button. To use a form as the subform, select the Use an existing form option button and then select the form you want to use. Then click the Next button.
5. If you are using an existing table or query, select the one you want to use as the record source, and then select the fields to include in the subform. Then click the Next button.
6. Choose which fields to link your main form to the subform or define the fields yourself. Click the Next button.

   In most cases, Access determines the relationship between the main form and the new subform so you can choose from a list. If Access does not recognize the relationship, you can specify your own as long as there is a common field.
7. Enter a name for the subform using "frm" as the prefix for the name and "subform" as part of the name to identify it as part of another form.

Rachel opens frmHousehold in Design view and drags the Form Footer bar down to make room for the subform in the Detail section. Then she uses the Subform Wizard to add the CustID, CustFirst, CustLast, Phone, and HeadHH fields from tblCustomer to the subform. When the wizard asks if she wants to define her own fields that link the main form to the subform, or choose from a list, she selects the Choose from a list option button. Show tblCustomer for each record in tblHousehold using HouseID should be selected as shown in Figure 4.19.

Figure 4.19: Defining the fields that link frmHousehold with a subform

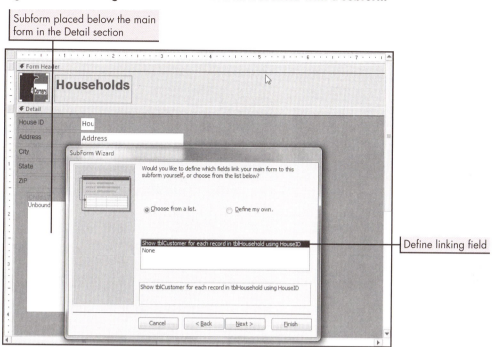

Subform placed below the main form in the Detail section

Define linking field

She names the subform frmCustomer subform, and then she examines the results in Form view. See Figure 4.20.

Figure 4.20: frmHousehold after adding a subform

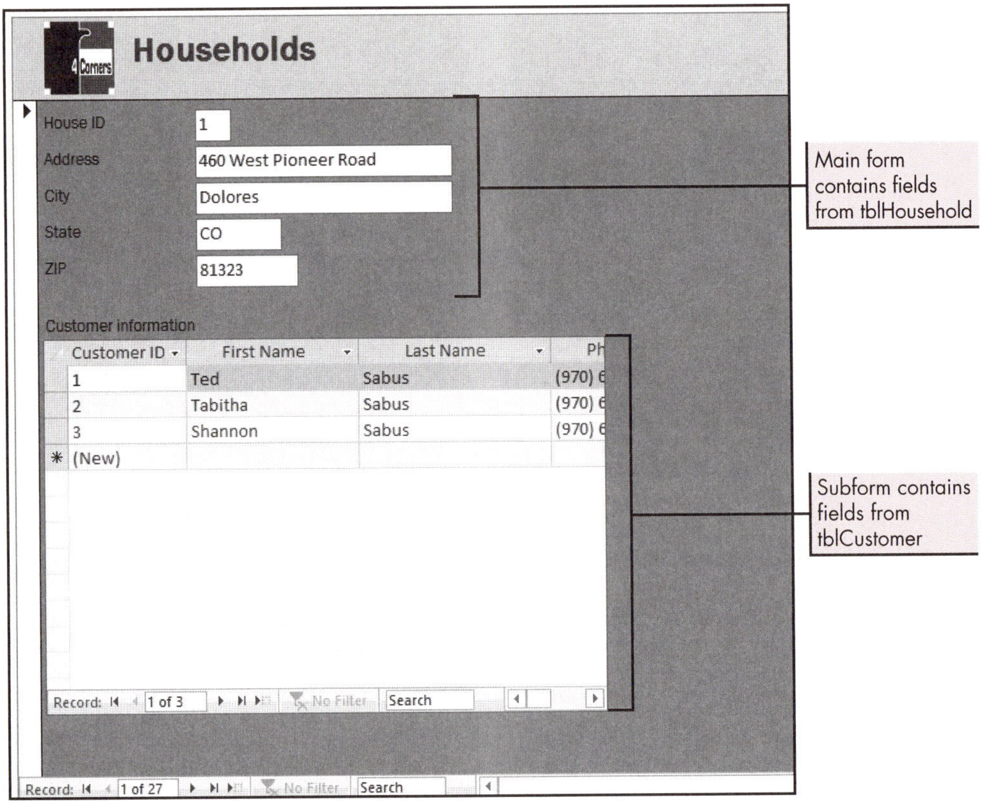

Because she needs to widen the subform so it displays all of the fields, she returns to Design view.

Modifying the Form Layout

To modify a form's layout, you can move and resize its controls, including a subform. Rachel is ready to widen the subform in frmHousehold. In Design view, she notes that she must first widen the entire form to accommodate the wider subform. First, she points to the right edge of the form until the pointer changes to a four-sided arrow. Then she drags the form so that it is 12.5-inches wide. To widen the subform, she clicks its border until sizing handles appear. She points to the middle-right handle until the pointer changes to a double-sided arrow, and then she drags the subform border until it is 7-inches wide. She switches to Form view to check the results, and resizes the columns in the subform to their best fit.

Next, Rachel adds the logo, theme background and font colors, and the Corners theme. Finally, she clicks in the subform label and changes tblCustomer subform to "Customer Information". Figure 4.21 shows the form in Design and Form view.

Figure 4.21: Modified frmHousehold in Design and Form views

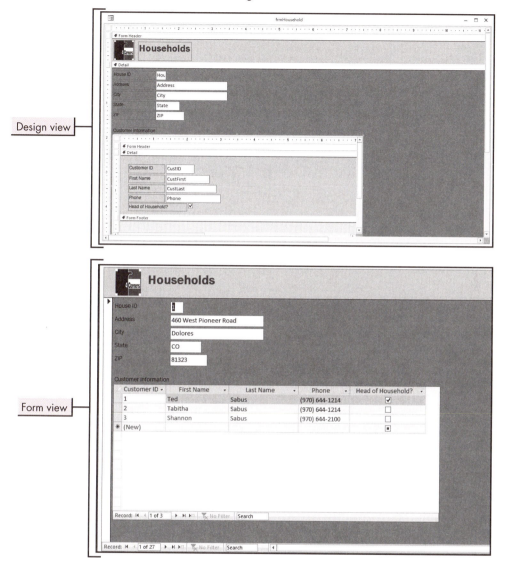

Now that Rachel is satisfied with the layout of frmHousehold, she opens frmCustomer to review its layout. She decides to move some controls so the form looks more like the paper form the pharmacy used for recordkeeping—this will help users adapt to the electronic form more quickly. She opens frmCustomer in Design view, and moves the Last Name text box and label to the right of the other controls. Then she does the same for the Date of Birth and Balance controls. See Figure 4.22.

Figure 4.22: Moving controls on a form

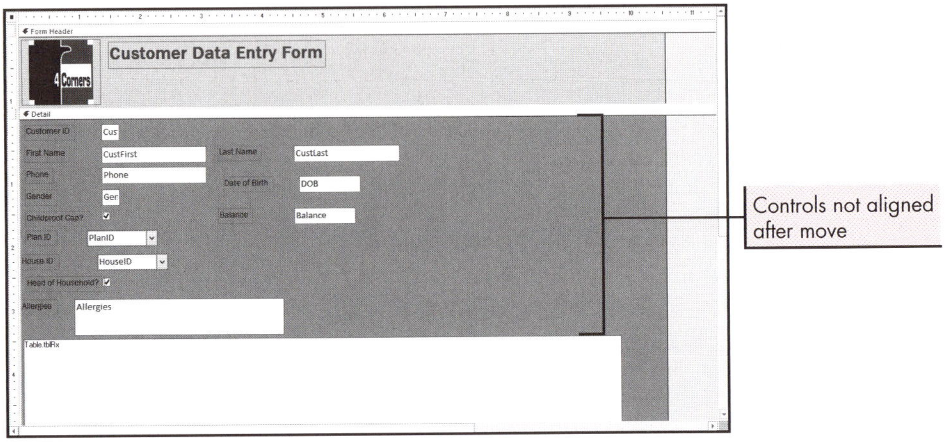

Because she moved the controls one at a time, they are not aligned. She needs to select the three controls, and then move them together so that they maintain their alignment.

How To

Move and Align Controls as a Group

1. In Design view, click a control you want to move.
2. Press and hold the Shift key and then click the additional controls you want to move. When all the controls are selected, release the Shift key.
3. Move the pointer over a selected control until it changes to a four-headed arrow shape.
4. Drag the group of controls to a new location.
5. To align the selected controls, click the ARRANGE tab, and in the Sizing & Ordering group click the Align button arrow, and the select To Grid, Left, Right, Top, or Bottom.

Best Practice

Arranging Controls for Logical Data Entry

A well-designed form makes it easier to add data quickly and minimizes data-entry errors by grouping similar fields together in logical arrangements. For example, first name and last name are often grouped on the same line. The next logical line is for address, and then city, state, and ZIP code on another line. Designing forms to match traditional paper forms makes it easier for users to adapt to them. See Figure 4.23.

Figure 4.23: Designing the customer form to be similar to the paper form

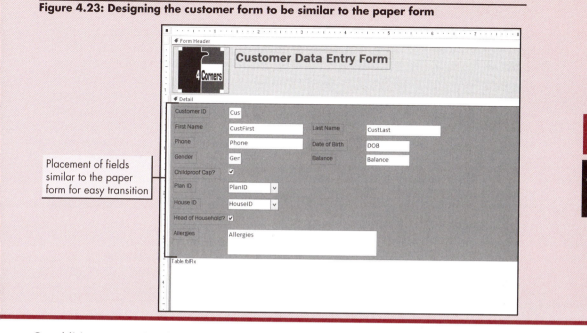

Placement of fields similar to the paper form for easy transition

4

Level 2

In addition to moving labels along with their text boxes, you can move them on their own. You can also modify labels in other ways, such as by editing the text they contain and resizing them. You can use any of the following techniques to modify a label:

- To edit a label's text, double-click the label to highlight the text and then type the new text.
- To resize a label, click the label and then drag a sizing handle to make the label larger or smaller.
- To move the label without its text box, click the label to select it, point to its move handle, and when the pointer changes to a four-headed arrow shape, drag the label to the new location. (Note that you can do the same for moving a text box without moving its label.)
- To modify more than one label at the same time, Shift+click to select a group of labels, and then make the changes.

Rachel moves and aligns the remaining controls on frmCustomer, checking the changes in Form view. She also needs to resize some controls on the frmDoctor form—the Phone and Cell text boxes need to just be wide enough to display the complete phone numbers. She saves frmCustomer, opens frmDoctor in Design view, and then widens the two text boxes. Finally, she opens frmDrug in Design view, and uses good design principles to modify the form.

Now that she has modified the forms she created, she's ready to develop other forms for the database.

Creating a Form from a Query

Maria Garcia asks Rachel if she would create a form that lists the training classes 4Corners Pharmacy provides, and shows which employees have taken them. She has to schedule a number of classes and thinks this form will serve as a helpful reference. She shows Rachel the query named qryEmployeeClassesDescription, which displays the class and employee information that Maria wants, and contains fields from three tables: tblEmployee, tblEmployeeTraining, and tblClass. Rachel can use this query as the basis for the form that will be a **user view** for Maria. A user view is a custom form that shows only the fields a particular user wants; it might or might not be used for data entry and, in some cases, the fields may be locked so that the user can only view them and not edit them.

Best Practice

Using a Query as the Basis for a Form

If you need data from multiple tables and do not want to create a complex form with a subform embedded in another subform, a query is a good way to create the necessary field list for a form. If you plan to use the form for data entry, you must include the primary keys from each table in the query. The tables must also have some common fields for the query to make sense.

Rachel uses the Form Wizard to create a form based on qryEmployeeClassesDescription. She selects all the query fields to include in the form—these are the EmpFirst and EmpLast fields from tblEmployee, Date from tblEmployeeTraining, and Description from tblClass. Because the fields come from three tables, Access asks whether she wants to view the data by tblEmployee, tblEmployeeTraining, or tblClass as shown in Figure 4.24.

Figure 4.24: Form Wizard view data question

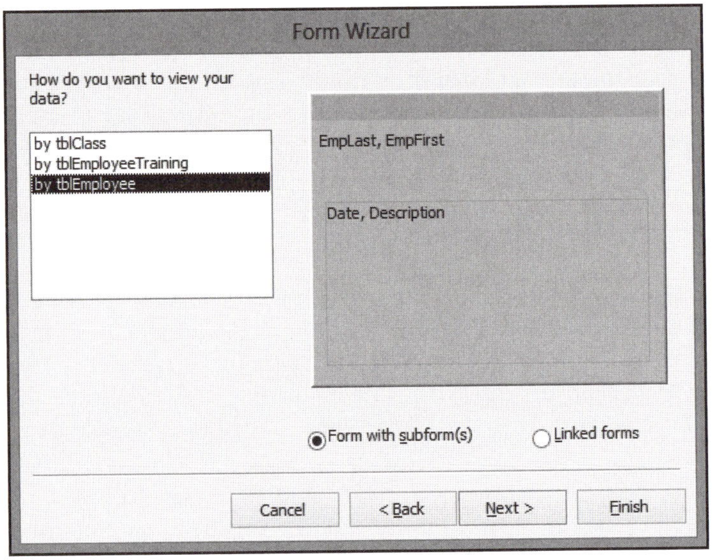

Rachel pauses to think this over. If she chooses to view the data by tblEmployee, the wizard shows that EmpFirst and EmpLast will appear in the main form and Date and Description will be in the subform. If she chooses to view the data by tblEmployeeTraining, all the fields will be in the main form; Access will not create a subform. If Maria chooses tblClass, Description will appear in the main form and EmpLast, EmpFirst, and Date will appear in the subform. Because Maria will need to be able to filter the data in various ways, she decides to select tblEmployeeTraining and view the data from all three tables in the query in a single form. She chooses Datasheet for the layout and names the form frmClassView. She goes into Design view and changes the title to Classes Taken. Then, she adds the logo, theme background and font colors and the Corners theme. She then views the completed form, as shown in Figure 4-25. If she needs to filter the data, she will switch to Datasheet view.

Figure 4.25: User view of classes and employees

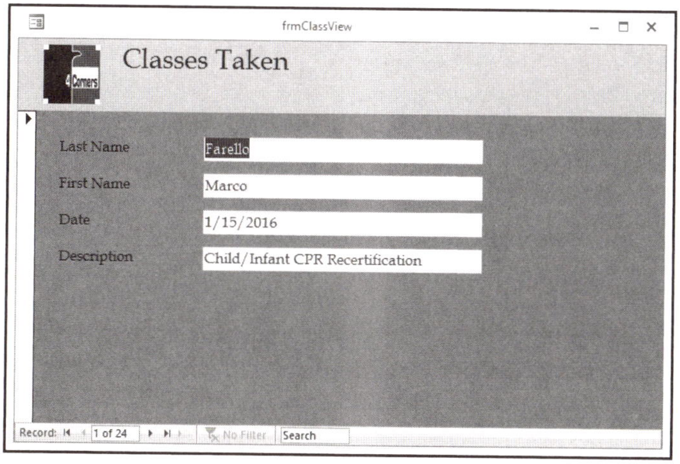

Creating a Form for Each Table

Every table should either have a form of its own or serve as a subform in another form. In some cases, such as to save space, you might not want to display all the fields in a table, especially on a subform. Creating a user view that contains only part of the data serves the purpose of showing only the important fields for a particular user. If you create a user view based on one or more tables, the database should still provide forms so that users can add and modify data in all the fields of all the tables.

Rachel tests the frmClassView form by trying to add a new record. However, because this user view does not include the EmpID field, the primary key in tblEmployeeTraining, Access does not allow her to add new records to tblEmployeeTraining from this form. Next, she tries to enter a new record to tblClass, which she cannot do because frmClassView does not include the primary key field (ClassID) in tblClass. She can, however, edit the value in the Description field, which could cause problems. Maria only wants to view data from this form, so Rachel modifies the form to prevent adding, editing, or deleting data by changing the Allow Edits, Allow Deletions, Allow Additions, and Data Entry form properties from Yes to No. See Figure 4.26.

Figure 4.26: Preventing additions, deletions, and editing in a user view

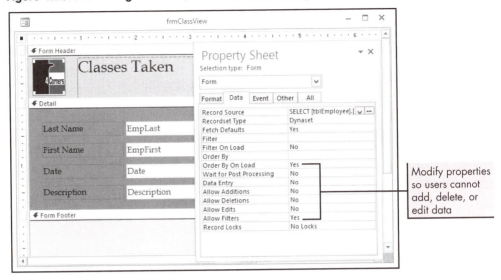

She then changes to Form view and tries to make changes to the data. Rachel realizes that she is not able to make any changes and that the New Record button is not available. She now believes this form is secure.

Rachel also creates a user view so that technicians can quickly view employees and their job titles without changing any employee or job information. She adds a subform to frmJobTitle that includes only the EmpID, EmpFirst, EmpLast, and Phone fields from tblEmployee, and names the subform frmEmployee subform and the completed form frmEmployeeView.

She changes the title of the main form to Employees and Positions and adds theme colors and the Corners theme. Finally, she changes the text label for the subform to "Employees." Next, Rachel wants to explore how to make the forms easier to use for all the pharmacy employees.

Adding Command Buttons to a Form

Rachel is becoming proficient in using Access, but not all technicians and pharmacists are. She is looking for ways to make the forms easier to use and to simplify the training process for new and existing employees so they can begin using the new application as soon as possible. She's planning to conduct a short training session and then introduce the database into the pharmacy for daily use.

One way to make the forms easier to use is to include **command buttons** that users can click to perform common tasks. Access provides a collection of command buttons that are associated with actions such as moving to the next record in the form, adding a record, or printing a form. Command buttons can contain text, standard icons available from

Access, or your own graphics. You can create a command button in Design view in two ways: by using the Button control which launches the Command Button Wizard or by adding a button to a form and then setting its properties. Table 4.5 lists the categories of command buttons Access provides and their actions.

Table 4.5: Command button options

Category	Actions
Record Navigation	Move from one record to another and find a record using Find.
Record Operations	Add, delete, duplicate, print, save, and undo a record.
Form Operations	Open and close form, print form, apply and edit form filter, print current form, refresh form data.
Report Operations	Mail report, open report, preview report, print report, send report to file.
Application	Quit application.
Miscellaneous	Auto Dialer, print table, run macro, run query.

© 2014 Cengage Learning

Rachel concludes that when a form is open, users will frequently want to move to the next or previous record, add or delete a record, and close the form. She can add these five command buttons to frmCustomer to perform these tasks. After she adds the buttons to frmCustomer, she can add the same five command buttons to all the forms in the 4Corners database. She'll use the Command Button Wizard to guide her through the steps of creating the buttons on the form.

She opens frmCustomer in Design view and determines that the best place to include five command buttons is along the right side of the form. She clicks Button in the Controls group, and then clicks the right side of the form. The Command Button Wizard dialog box opens. See Figure 4.27.

Figure 4.27: First dialog box in the Command Button Wizard

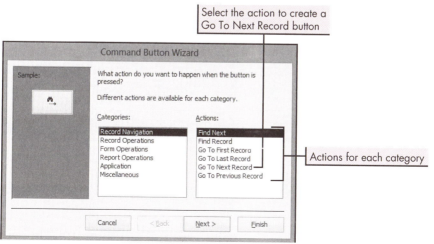

With the Record Navigation category selected on the left, she selects the Go To Next Record action on the right, and then clicks Next. She then selects the Text option button and enters Next Record as the name for the button, and then clicks Finish. She adds a name to this object so that she can locate it quickly. Default names for objects such as buttons do not help identify the object. For example, the default name could be something like Control316. But, if she gives it a meaningful name, such as NextRecord, when she looks at the object properties, she will easily be able to recognize the purpose of the object. She uses the Command Button Wizard again to add the four other buttons to the form—the Previous Record, Add Record, Delete Record, and Close Form buttons. All the buttons perform the actions that correspond to their labels.

Rachel selects all the buttons and aligns them. However, she notices that the buttons are not equally spaced. So, she decides to use the Size/Spacing option. First, she selects each of the buttons using Shift+click. Then, she selects the ARRANGE tab and in the Sizing & Ordering group, she clicks the Size/Space button arrow. Since she wants the buttons to be equally spaced from the top button to the bottom button, she selects Equal Vertical. She also wants the buttons to be the same size. So with the buttons still selected she clicks the Size/Space button arrow and chooses To Widest in the Size section and then To Tallest. Choosing both of these options makes the buttons equally tall and equally wide. The buttons are now aligned and spaced evenly. See Figure 4.28.

Figure 4.28: Command buttons for typical form tasks

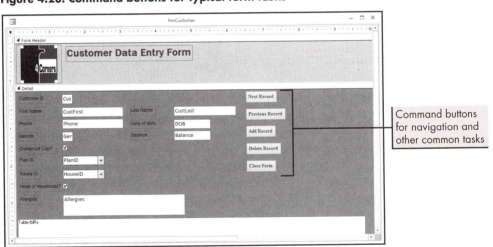

Command buttons for navigation and other common tasks

How To

Create a Command Button on a Form

1. Open a form in Design view.
2. Decide where you want to place the command buttons and move the form footer or widen the form, if necessary, to make room for the buttons.
3. Click Button in the Controls group on the DESIGN tab, and click where you want to place the command button. The Command Button Wizard dialog box opens.

4. Click a category on the left and then click the action you want to perform when the button is clicked. Click the Next button.

5. Click the Text option button and then type the text that should appear on the button, or click the Picture option button and then select a picture for the button. Click the Next button.

6. Enter a name for the button. This name will not appear on the form, but it should be unique. If you decide to delete the button for any reason, Access will not let you reuse the name of the deleted button. Click the Finish button. The new button appears on the form.

Best Practice

Being Consistent When Placing Command Buttons

When you are placing command buttons on forms, be certain to place them in the same order and location on all forms. Users will expect to find the buttons in the same location; inconsistency in button placement is interpreted as poor design. The goal is for all employees to be able to add or edit data quickly, not to hunt around for the appropriate button. It is especially dangerous to move the location of the Delete Record button because users might click it in error and delete records inadvertently.

Rachel also adds command buttons to frmEmployee, frmJobTitle, and frmDrug so that users can move to the next record, move to the previous record, add a record, delete a record, and close the form. To maintain a consistent user interface, she places the buttons in the same location on all the forms.

Exploring Other Form Properties

Each form has properties that affect the entire form and other properties that affect a section of the form. To open the Property Sheet for a form, right-click the item you wish to modify the properties for and then click Properties on the shortcut menu. Also, when you open the form in Design view, the Property Sheet button appears on the DESIGN tab in the Tools group. Table 4.6 lists frequently used properties for forms, and Table 4.7 lists frequently used properties for form sections. A common reason to use form properties is when you decide to base a form on a record source different from the one used to create the form. Making that simple change can prevent you from needing to start over on a new form.

Table 4.6: Common form properties

Form Property	Description
Record Source	Enter or select a table, query, or SQL statement that you want to use as the source of the data for the form.
Caption	Enter the text that you want to appear in the title bar in Form view.
Allow Edits	Select Yes or No to specify whether a user can edit saved records when using the form. You can use this property to prevent changes to existing data displayed by a form.

Table 4.6: Common form properties (cont.)

Form Property	Description
Allow Deletions	Select Yes or No to specify whether a user can delete saved records when using the form. You can use this property to prevent users from deleting existing data displayed by a form.
Allow Additions	Select Yes or No to specify whether a user can add records when using the form.
Navigation Buttons	Specify whether navigation buttons and a record number box are displayed on the form. You can use this property to remove the standard navigation buttons and restrict users to command buttons that you add to the form.
Height and Width	Specify the dimensions of a form.
Cycle	Specify what happens when you press the Tab key and the focus is in the last control on a bound form. The All Records option is designed for data entry, and allows the user to move to a new record by pressing the Tab key.

© 2014 Cengage Learning

Table 4.7: Common form section properties

Form Section Property	Description
Force New Page	Specify whether the Detail or footer form sections print on a separate page, rather than on the current page.
Keep Together	Select Yes or No to specify whether to print a form section all on one page.
Back Color	Specify the background color for the section by entering the numeric value of the color or clicking the Build button to use the Color Builder to select a color from a palette.
Special Effect	Specify whether the section should appear as flat (default), raised, sunken, etched, shadowed, or chiseled.
Display When	Select Always to display the section in Form view and when printed. Select Print Only to hide the section in Form view but display it when you print the form. Select Screen Only to display the section in Form view but not print it.

© 2014 Cengage Learning

Best Practice

Including Primary Keys in Forms

If you want to use a form to add data to the underlying tables, be sure to include the primary and foreign key(s) fields in the form. Without the primary key, Access does not allow you to add new records. You can edit existing nonkey fields, however. If you do not want users to add, edit, or delete records from a form, change the properties so this is not allowed.

Some of the forms that Rachel has created so far display the form object name in the title bar in Form view. For example, "frmDoctor" appears in the title bar of the frmDoctor form. Users generally appreciate more descriptive text in the title bar, such as the title displayed in the form header. Rachel uses the Property Sheet for each form to change the Caption property as listed in Table 4.8.

Table 4.8: Caption properties set for 4Corners Pharmacy forms

Form Name	Caption Property
frmCustomer	Customer Data Entry Form
frmClassView	Classes Taken
frmHousehold	Households and Customers
frmDoctor	Doctor Data Entry Form
frmClinic	Clinic Data Entry Form
frmEmployee	Employee Data Entry Form
frmEmployeeTraining	Employee Training Form
frmClass	Class Data Entry Form
frmJobTitle	4Corners Pharmacy Job Titles

© 2014 Cengage Learning

Controlling Form Printing

Rachel suspects that other employees will want to print forms and records for reference until they become familiar with the database. She therefore wants to control the form's vertical spacing on the printed page and include a date and page number on the form. Instead of using one of the forms she has already created, she uses the Form Wizard to create a sample form to test printing options based on tblEmployee, and names the form frmTestPrinting. By creating a sample form, she can avoid making changes to existing forms that might cause problems for users.

After creating the frmTestPrinting form, Rachel opens it in Design view, right-clicks a blank spot on the grid, and then clicks Page Header/Footer on the shortcut menu. The page header and footer sections open in the form. You can specify different header and footer information for the printed form and for the on-screen form. Recall that page headers and footers are a good place to display the date and page numbers on a form. You can also use the page header to include a different title in the printed version of a form, such as an invoice or order confirmation.

Access provides functions to add a date or a page number to a form. Where the date is placed depends on whether the date should be visible on the form while viewing it on the screen or only when it is printed. Keep in mind that information in the form header and footer will appear on screen and when printed, and information in the page header and footer appears in the same manner.

Rachel wants to include the date and page numbers in the page footer. She clicks the page footer section, clicks the Date and Time button in the Header/Footer group on the DESIGN tab. She specifies that the date should print in a dd/mm/yy format, such as 13-02-16. Rachel then deselects the Include Time option. She also adds sample text to the form header and footer sections to verify that their contents appear only in Form view and does not print. Then, she adds an Alternate Back Color so she can see when records change when printed. She brings up the Property Sheet for the Detail section and clicks the Alternate Back Color arrow and selects Access Theme 1. See Figure 4.29.

Figure 4.29: Section formats in Property Sheet

Rachel feels comfortable that an employee who uses this form for a test print will be able to see the form features both in Design view and in Print Preview. She saves the form and reviews it in Print Preview. See Figure 4.30

Figure 4.30: Contents in the page header and footer sections

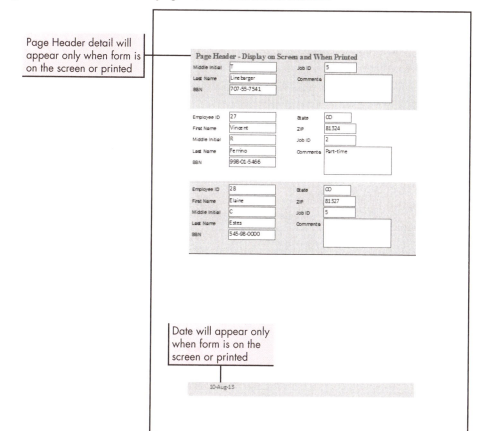

Page Header detail will appear only when form is on the screen or printed

Date will appear only when form is on the screen or printed

How To

Insert the Date and Time

For Date and Time

1. In Design view, click the Date and Time button in the Header/Footer group on the DESIGN tab. The Date and Time dialog box opens.
2. Make sure the Include Date and Include Time check boxes are selected; otherwise, click to remove the check mark if you do not want to include the date or time.
3. Select the date and time formats you want to use. A sample appears at the bottom of the dialog box.
4. Click the OK button. A label containing the code =Date() appears in the page footer to display the date, and a label containing the code =Time() appears to display the time.
5. Reposition the date and time label controls as necessary.

Rachel needs to see if the header and footer sections she added appear when the form is printed. Now she's ready to try printing a form.

Printing a Selected Record in Form View

Rachel decides to print one record of frmTestPrinting. After clicking the FILE tab, and then Print, she clicks the Print Preview button to preview how the form will print. She notices that when one record changes to another record, the background color changes just as she specified. When she clicks Print, she can choose to print just one record or all of the records using the options in the Print Range section of the Print dialog box, as shown in Figure 4-31. She prints one record of the form.

Figure 4.31: Print dialog box

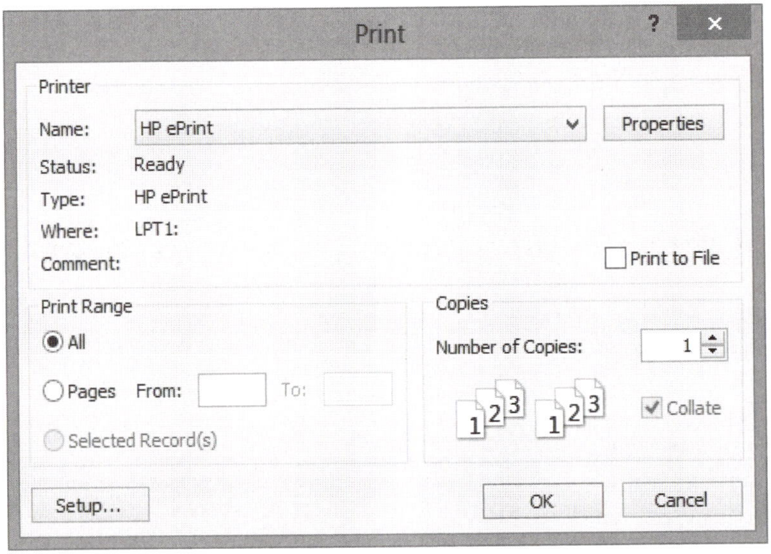

Rachel reviews the printed record, and verifies that the page number and date are included on the printed page. Next, she will create the more complex forms that the pharmacists and technicians will use every day.

Steps To Success: Level 2

Now that you have created basic data-entry forms for Hudson Bay Pharmacy, Anne asks you to create and modify other forms to improve their appearance and ease of use. As you save the new forms, be certain to use the "frm" prefix as part of the naming convention. Also consult your instructor for instructions about submitting your results.

Complete the following:

1. Start Access and open the **Hudson.accdb** database from the STS folder.

2. As Anne and the other pharmacy technicians at Hudson Bay Pharmacy enter household information, they want to see which customers belong to a household. Knowing this information can help them make sure they have the correct address information for a customer. Modify the frmHousehold form as necessary to show the customers

who belong to each household and include their phone numbers. Change the title to reflect your changes to the form.

3. Anne also requests a quick way to view employee names and job titles in one form. She only needs to reference the employee's name and phone number, and doesn't want to enter or change any employee or job information. She'll reference this information by job title. Create a form and subform that meet this request, and name them **frmEmployeeView** and **frmEmployee subform**. Make sure that users cannot add, delete, or modify data on the form.

4. Anne suggests that you fine-tune the form to make it more appealing and easy to use. Modify the frmEmployeeView form and its controls as necessary to display all the fields in Form view. Provide descriptive or more meaningful text labels for all the controls in the form, including the title bar.

5. Anne asks you to revise the frmEmployee form to meet the same goals. Organize the controls in frmEmployee in logical data-entry order. Make sure the controls are aligned and attractive.

6. Modify the frmDrug form using good design principles so that it matches the design of the other Hudson Bay forms.

7. Anne also wants to make the forms easy to use, even for employees new to the Hudson Bay Pharmacy database. She asks you to include command buttons on frmEmployee, frmJobTitle, and frmDrug to allow users to move to the next record, move to the previous record, add a record, delete a record, and close the form. Be sure to place the buttons in the same location on all forms.

8. Anne says she knows that Kim in human resources often wants to print selected records in frmEmployee, and needs to include the date on the printed copies so she can track the information. Anne asks you to modify frmEmployee to display the date, time, and page numbers in the printed form. Make sure the title for the form shows only in Form view. Preview the form to verify that the correct information prints, but the title does not.

9. Close the **Hudson.accdb** database and then close Access.

LEVEL 3

Creating Forms for Completing Daily Business Tasks

Improving the Usability of Forms

In this level, you explore using form controls as a way to speed up the process of locating a particular record. In addition, you will learn how to include a calculated control in a form, and how to create multiple-page forms and forms with multiple subforms. You will also learn about tab order, and how to control the focus in a form to skip unbound controls.

Rachel knows that the pharmacy gets very busy at certain times during the day. Anything she can do to decrease waiting time for customers is appreciated. One task that is currently inefficient for technicians is finding customer records—customers call for prescriptions and refills or make the request in person, and before technicians can enter prescription information, they need to find the appropriate customer record. Access provides a Find feature for finding records, but Rachel wants to see if she can develop a more-efficient alternative.

Another time-consuming task is looking up the cost of a drug and its selling price. 4 Corners Pharmacy keeps track of its drug costs and periodically compares them to the selling price to make sure they are maintaining their targeted profit margin. When Rachel creates the form the pharmacists and technicians use to record prescriptions and refills, she wants to display the difference between cost and selling price for each drug. Doing so will save time for the technicians and will provide valuable tracking information for management.

Locating a Record Quickly

When a customer requests a refill, the technicians want to locate the correct customer quickly so they can enter a new prescription or process a refill. Besides navigating one record at a time, Rachel knows that Access provides two other ways to locate a record: the Find tool and the Combo Box control. When you click the Find button, the Find and Replace dialog box opens. Click the field in which you want to search for a particular value, and then enter the value you want Access to match. Access searches for records that contain the same value in the selected field.

A combo box displays a list of values and lets users select one from the list. As with a command button, you can use a control wizard to add a combo box to a form. Like other wizards, a control wizard asks a series of questions and then uses your answers to create a control in a form (or report). Access offers control wizards for many controls, including Combo Box, List Box, Option Group, Check Box, and Subform/Subreport controls.

In the first Combo Box Wizard dialog box, you can specify that the combo box lists values for finding a record in the form. If you list the values in the CustID, CustLast, and CustFirst fields, for example, you can select a particular customer ID from the combo box to find the record for that customer. Table 4.9 compares using the Find tool and a combo box as ways to locate a record.

Table 4.9: Ways to locate a record

Method	Advantages	Disadvantages
Find button	Easy to use	Can be confusing for novice users
	Finds the first instance of a record containing a value that matches the criterion	Time-consuming with a large number of records
	The Find and Replace dialog box includes a Find Next button, which locates the next record that matches the specified value	May have to use the Find Next button many times to locate the record you want
	Searches the entire database or only one field	
	Matches only part of the contents of a field if you do not know the correct spelling or complete contents	
	Starts searching with any record in the form	
	Does not require working in Design view	
	Searches well for a nonunique value in a field	
	Replaces values if necessary	
Combo box on a form	Easy to use	Requires you to work in Design view of the form to create the combo box
	Looks for a unique record based on its primary key	
	Creates a list using additional fields to help identify a record	
	Allows you to sort the list of values alphabetically to help you find a record quickly	

© 2014 Cengage Learning

Rachel first explores using the Find button to locate a record. She opens the frmCustomer form in Form view and clicks the Last Name text box. This gives Last Name the **focus**, which indicates the control that is currently active and ready for user action. She clicks the Find button 🔍 in the Find group on the HOME tab to open the Find and Replace dialog box. The dialog box requires her to type at least part of the last name she wants to locate, such as Cardenas. Because many of the customers are part of families, she might have to click the Find Next button several times to locate the record she wants. See Figure 4.32.

Figure 4.32: Using the Find button to locate a record

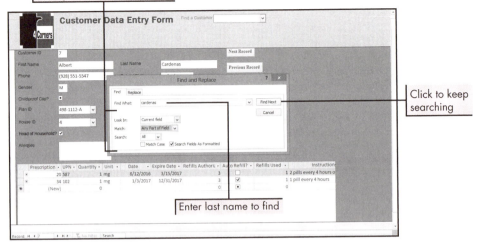

Modify conditions if necessary

Click to keep searching

Enter last name to find

Rachel thinks the technicians and other employees will prefer using a combo box that lets them select a customer name rather than a dialog box in which they must enter a name. With frmCustomer still open, she switches to Design view and considers where to include the combo box. If she places it in the Detail section, it might be hard to find among the text boxes and command buttons. Finding a customer is probably the first task a technician will perform when adding a new prescription or a request for a refill, so the combo box needs to be easy to locate. She decides to place the combo box in the form header where it is prominent and appears to be separate from a particular record. To be consistent and use good design principles, Rachel plans to place similar combo boxes on other forms in the same place.

She clicks the Combo Box button in the Controls group, and then clicks the right side of the Form Header section. The first dialog box in the wizard opens, as shown in Figure 4.33.

Figure 4.33: Creating a combo box to locate a unique record

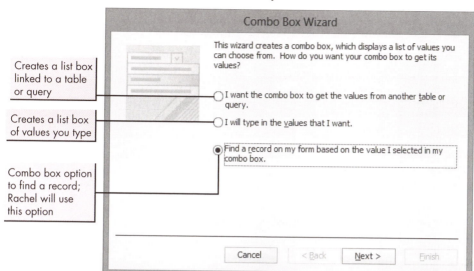

Creates a list box linked to a table or query

Creates a list box of values you type

Combo box option to find a record; Rachel will use this option

Combo Box Wizard

This wizard creates a combo box, which displays a list of values you can choose from. How do you want your combo box to get its values?

○ I want the combo box to get the values from another table or query.

○ I will type in the values that I want.

◉ Find a record on my form based on the value I selected in my combo box.

Cancel   < Back   Next >   Finish

This dialog box provides three options for listing values in the combo box: it can look up values in a table or query, let users type a value, or let users select a value that Access matches to find a record. Rachel selects the third option to use the combo box for finding a record in the form.

Next, she selects the fields that contain the values she will use to find records. One of the fields must be a primary key field in the record source for this form, which is tblCustomer. She selects the CustID, CustLast, and CustFirst fields so that employees can easily find customer records.

Rachel completes the wizard by specifying a width for the columns of field values in the combo box list and hiding the primary key field, which does not contain information that technicians need when finding customer records. She also uses "Find a Customer" as a name for the combo box control. After she clicks the Finish button, she adjusts the width and position of the combo box control on the form. Then she tests the control in Form view. See Figure 4.34.

Figure 4.34: Using a combo box to locate a customer record

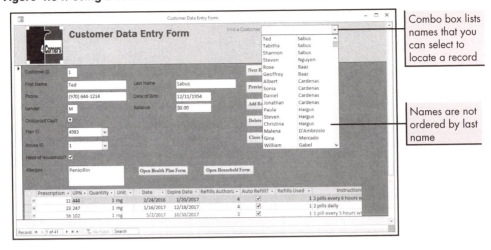

Rachel tests the combo box by selecting a few names to make sure Access finds the appropriate records. The Find a Customer combo box is working well, but she notices that the order of the customer names is not logical. She wants to investigate how to sort the contents of a combo box.

How To

Create a Combo Box to Locate a Record

1. Open a form in Design view.
2. Click the Combo Box button in the Controls group.
3. Click the form where you want to position the combo box. The Combo Box Wizard starts. Be sure to leave room for the text box identifying the unbound control.
4. Click the third option button to find a record, and then click the Next button.
5. Select the primary key field and two or three other fields that will help a user to identify a record. Note that the fields should be in sort order from left to right (sort on CustLast, then on CustFirst if two or more customers have the same last name). Click the Next button.
6. Modify the width of the columns of the combo box by double-clicking between the columns if necessary. Make sure the Hide key column (recommended) check box is selected if you do not want to display the primary key field values. Click the Next button.
7. Name the combo box. Because this name appears on the form, provide a name that identifies the purpose of the control, such as "Find a Customer." Click the Finish button.
8. Modify the position of the combo box and widen the text box to display all the text, if necessary.

Best Practice

Including the Primary Key Field in a Combo Box List

Although you usually do not need to show the primary key field in a combo box list, you should always include this field when you are selecting fields to list in a combo box that locates a record. Access refers to the primary key as the unique identifier to use when locating the record. However, be sure also to include enough descriptive data to identify each record—arbitrary ID numbers by themselves are not helpful when your database contains many records. When you want to find records based on names, include last and first names.

Adding a Calculation to a Form

Recall that you can create forms from tables or queries, and that queries can include calculated fields, which display the results of an expression that is recalculated each time a value in the expression changes. To include a calculated field on a form, most database developers create the field in a query, and then use that query as the record source for a form. In Chapter 3, you learned how to build the expression in the Field row in a new column of a query. Although most database developers recommend that you create calculated fields in a query, you can also add an unbound control that contains a calculation directly to a form.

Paul Ferrino asks Rachel to calculate the difference between the cost of a drug and its selling price. This is called **gross margin**. Paul wants to track the gross margin for the drugs to make sure they are maintaining their targeted profit margin.

Rachel opens the frmDrug form in Design view and moves the Cost field below the Price field on the form. She moves other fields in the form so that the form is easier to use. She adjusts the width of the controls until the numbers align vertically. She inserts a horizontal line using the Line button on the Controls group. While the line is selected, she uses the Shape Outline button arrow in the Control Formatting group on the FORMAT tab to select Black, Text 1 in the Theme Colors group. Then she uses the Text Box button to add an unbound control to calculate the gross margin value. For the calculation, she uses the following formula: =**[Price]**-**[Cost]**

Note that she uses square brackets around the field names, although the brackets are not required if the field names have no spaces. She changes the label for the text box to Margin and aligns the label. She uses the Property Sheet for the text box to change its Format property to Currency and the Decimal Places property to 2. See Figure 4.35.

Figure 4.35: Text box with Property Sheet displayed

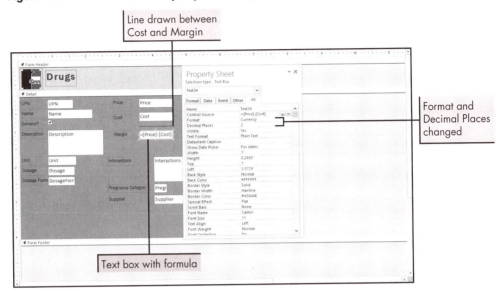

Line drawn between Cost and Margin

Format and Decimal Places changed

Text box with formula

Rachel switches to Form view to see if the text box is aligned correctly under the Price and Cost fields. Finally, she makes other changes that make the form appealing and easy to use as shown in Figure 4.36.

Figure 4.36: Calculated field in the form

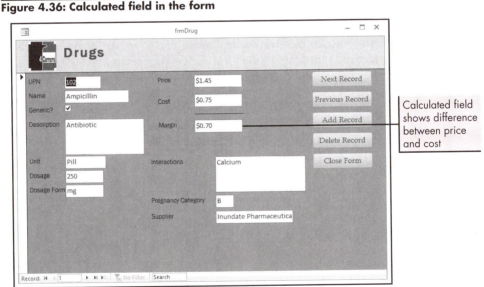

Calculated field shows difference between price and cost

How To

Place a Calculated Field on a Form

1. Open the form in Design view.
2. Click the Text Box button in the Controls group on the DESIGN tab.
3. Click the form where you want to place the unbound control.
4. Click again to edit the contents of the empty control.
5. Type the formula preceded by an equal sign (=).
6. Click on the label for the control and click in the control where the label is located to type a new label name to make it more descriptive than the default name.
7. To format the result of a calculation, right-click the calculated field and then click Properties to open the Property Sheet. If necessary, change the format property to Currency, for example, and change the alignment of the text to Right-align, for example.

4

Level 3

Now that Rachel has some experience developing forms, she can work on the form that includes the main activities of the pharmacy in one central location.

Streamlining the Main Pharmacy Processes in a Complex Form

The main purpose of the 4Corners database application is to streamline the main function of the pharmacy—filling prescriptions. Paul Ferrino has placed priority on automating this business process and, if possible, making changes to the procedures in the pharmacy. Rachel expects that including multiple processes on a single form is part of the solution. When Donald Linebarger was developing the database, he worked with the technicians and pharmacists to understand the process necessary to fill a prescription for a new customer and a current customer. He created a process analysis by listing the steps and substeps employees perform and indicating which database objects they use to complete each task. Rachel reviews that analysis before starting to develop the necessary form. The steps a technician and pharmacist perform are summarized in Table 4.10.

Table 4.10: Steps to filling a prescription

Step	Tables Requiring Data Input
Step 1: Register Customer	
Register customer	tblCustomer, tblHousehold, tblHealthPlan
Record prescription	tblRx
Step 2: Fill/Refill Prescription	
Check allergies and drug interactions	tblCustomer, tblDrug
Determine in-stock availability of drug	Manual at this point because database does not yet include inventory management
Fill prescription	tblRx, tblDoctor, tblRefill, tblEmployee

© 2014 Cengage Learning

Rachel develops the main pharmacy form by following the steps in the process analysis. First, however, she creates a data-entry form for tblHealthPlan and a query that displays customer and health plan information, which she names qryCustomerHealthplan. She also uses the Form Wizard to create a form that contains all the fields in tblRx, and names this form frmRx.

Step 1: Registering New Customers or Confirming Customer Identity

Step 1 in the process is usually completed by a technician. Each time a customer requests a refill for a prescription, the technician needs to enter data for a new customer or confirm the identity of the existing customer and verify that their information has not changed. From her analysis, Rachel decides to modify frmCustomer by adding two command buttons that allow the technician to quickly open frmHousehold and frmHealthPlan if needed. She does not need to add a button to open frmRx because data from tblRx is already included in a subform in frmCustomer. The frmCustomer form also already includes the HouseID and PlanID fields as list boxes, and employees can use these list boxes to verify household and health plan membership as necessary. They only need to open frmHousehold or frmHealthPlan if the customer is part of a new household or health plan. Rachel notices that tblHealthPlan has no form, so she creates a form and calls it frmHealthPlan. Then she uses the Command Button Wizard to add two command buttons to frmCustomer—one to open frmHousehold and another to open frmHealthPlan—choosing the Form Operations category and the Open Form action in the wizard. See Figure 4.37. She also adds Command buttons in frmHealthPlan and frmHousehold to close the form.

Figure 4.37: Adding command buttons to open frmHealthPlan and frmHousehold

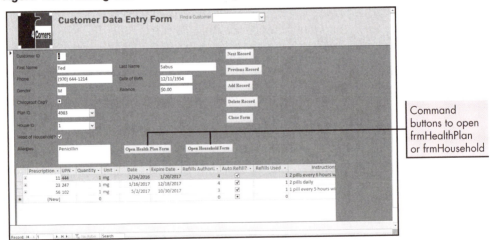

Step 2: Filling and Refilling Prescriptions

Step 2 is started by the technicians, but a pharmacist must check for drug interactions and confirm instructions and dosages for each prescription. The pharmacist gives the prescription to the customer, and encourages the customer to ask questions about the prescription. Rachel consults with the pharmacists and decides that it would be most efficient to include all the prescription information on one form if possible. She decides to create the main part of the form in Design view so she can place the fields exactly where she wants them and to save space for the rest of the data. If she decides to add subforms to include data from tblDrug, tblRx, tblRefill, and tblEmployee, she'll need to do so manually. Her analysis of the necessary fields is summarized in Table 4.11.

Table 4.11: Tables and fields necessary to automate Step 2

Table	Fields to Include
tblCustomer	CustID, CustFirst, CustLast, Phone, BirthDate, Childproof Cap?, Allergies
tblHealthPlan	PlanID, PlanName, Days
tblRx	PrescriptionID, Quantity, Unit, Date, ExpireDate, Refills, AutoRefill, RefillsUsed, Instructions
tblDoctor	DoctorID, DoctorFirst, DoctorLast
tblDrug	UPN, Name, Interactions, PregCategory
tblRefill	RefillDate, EmpID
tblEmployee	EmpFirst, EmpLast

© 2014 Cengage Learning

Creating Forms with Many Subforms

The focus of the form for Step 2 is the prescription to be filled, so Rachel starts by opening a blank form in Design view with tblRx as the source of the data. Rachel decides to add all the fields to the form and then to move them as necessary. The form will be crowded, so she needs to minimize the space the prescription part of the form requires. She double-clicks the title bar of the field list to select all the fields, and then drags them to the form. She arranges the fields in logical groups, according to how employees most often use them, keeping refill information together in one place and drug information together in another. She also creates a calculated field to show the refills remaining by adding a text box and then entering the following expression:

$$\texttt{=[Refills]-[RefillsUsed]}$$

She right-aligns the result and also right-aligns the UPN and Unit fields for improved appearance. She adds a title to the form, applies the 4Corners Pharmacy format to the entire form, and adds the 4Corners logo. She saves the form and names it frmPrimaryActivity to reflect its importance to the pharmacy. See Figure 4.38.

Figure 4.38: The initial frmPrimaryActivity

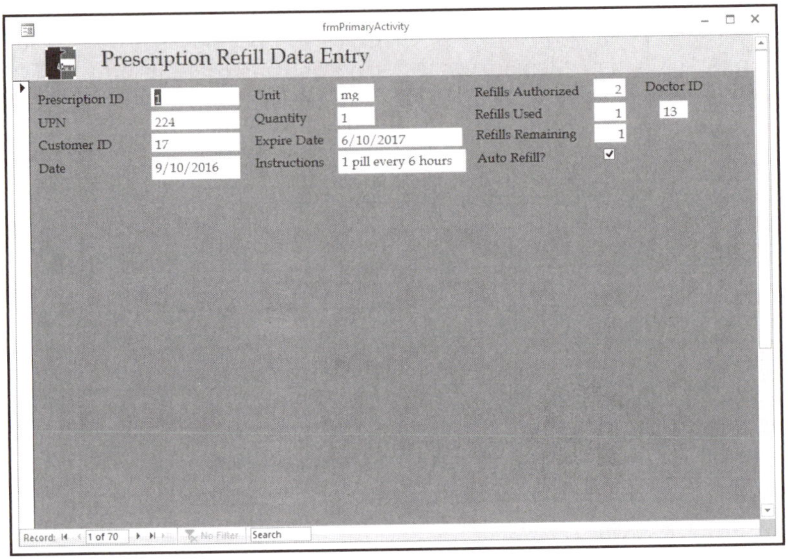

Next, Rachel wants to include a subform with the form that shows the refill history. To do this, she first creates a query named qryCustomerHealthplan. The query includes the tblCustomer and tblHealthPlan tables. These tables are related with the PlanID field. She adds the CustID, CustLast, CustFirst, Phone, Childproof Cap?, Allergies, and PlanName fields to the query grid and saves the query.

To create a subform for this query, she clicks the Subform/Subreport button to start the Subform Wizard, which guides her through the steps of adding a subform to the form. First, she selects qryCustomerHealthplan as the data for the subform because it has both customer and health plan fields the pharmacists want to reference. (She created this query as part of her preparation for creating the main pharmacy form.) She selects all the fields in this query. The wizard recognizes the common CustID field that links the subform to the main form. (To link a subform to a main form, the underlying record sources must be related.)

She names the form frmCustomerHealthplan subform. To save space, she switches to Design view, opens the Property Sheet for the subform and changes the Default View to Datasheet. See Figure 4.39.

Figure 4.39: Property Sheet for frmCustomerHealthplan subform

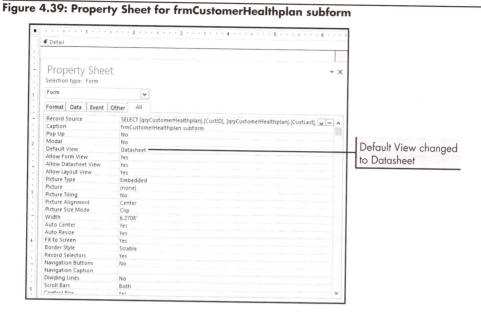

Default View changed to Datasheet

She then switches to Layout view and decreases the height of the subform to about one inch. To prevent data errors, she changes the properties of the subform so it does not allow edits, deletions, or additions. Because each prescription has only one customer record, the subform displays only one record and, without the ability to add a new record, the new blank record does not show, which saves a line on the form. Rachel switches between Design, Layout, and Form views until she positions the subform perfectly. She also changes the caption of the subform to "Customer and Health Plans." Figure 4.40 shows her progress on the form so far.

Figure 4.40: The frmPrimaryActivity form with first subform

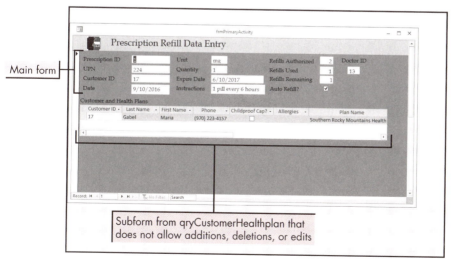

Main form

Subform from qryCustomerHealthplan that does not allow additions, deletions, or edits

Next, Rachel uses the Subform/Subreport Wizard to add the subform for the refills, using all the fields in tblRefill as the data source. Access recognizes that PrescriptionID is the related field between tblRefill and tblRx. She saves the subform as frmRefill subform, changes the caption to Refills, and aligns the subform. Technicians need to add each refill, so this subform must have adding and editing capabilities.

Then she adds a subform for the data in tblDrug including all fields except Cost, Price, and Supplier. When the wizard asks her to identify the linking field, she selects UPN, which is the common field in the main form and the subform for drug data, and she names the subform frmDrug subform. She changes the caption to Drug Information and modifies the properties for the subform so it does not allow additions, edits, or deletions. Because the drug information is so important, she decides to change the Default View property to Single Form, which displays all the fields in the subform using the same layout and style of the main form. Rachel adjusts and aligns the form until all fields are visible on the form, and saves the form. Figure 4.41 shows the completed form.

Figure 4.41: Completed frmPrimaryActivity form with three subforms

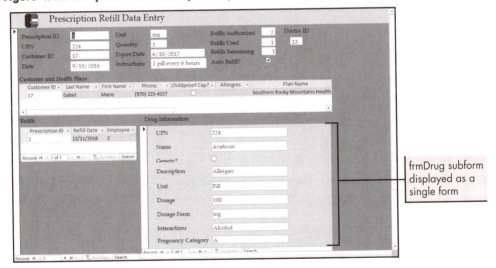

frmDrug subform displayed as a single form

Creating Multipage Forms Using Page Break

In some applications, you might have too many fields to fit comfortably on one screen. You can continue a form onto an additional page (or pages) by placing a page break in the form. A Page Up or Page Down key moves you from page to page.

Best Practice

Using Identifiers on Each Page of a Multipage Form

If you decide to break a form into two or more pages using a page break, users will find it easier to know where they are if the pages are numbered and include identifier fields on the additional pages of the forms. For example, if you are working with a form about customers, you would put bound controls for the customer first and last names on each page of the control. To keep from modifying the customer name, you can set its property to Display Only.

Creating Forms Using Tab Controls for Multiple Subforms

A **tab control** is another way to add multiple subforms to a form in a compact way. Each subform has a tab at the top and they are layered one on top of the other. The tabs are similar to the tabs in many Microsoft Office applications. They are an efficient alternative to creating multipage forms using the page break control because they conserve space on the screen and allow you to add or edit data with a single form open.

Rachel and the pharmacists review frmPrimaryActivity and decide that they want more information on the form. It is not unusual for the pharmacist to call a doctor before refilling a prescription because of illegible handwriting or an expired prescription. They agree that Rachel should create a new form that includes all the subforms already created but that also has a subform from tblDoctor.

Rather than start again from scratch, she will make a copy of frmPrimaryActivity. Then she will delete the subforms and replace them with tab control subforms. She will have tabs for the customer and household query data, refills, drugs, and doctors. Then pharmacists and technicians can evaluate both and decide which form is more functional. After the form closes, she wants to see at least partial data from these tables and queries:

- **qryCustomerHealthplan**—To determine any allergies and preference for a childproof cap as well as the days allowed for the prescription under the health plan
- **tblDoctor**—To facilitate contacting the doctor who wrote the prescription in case of questions
- **tblDrug**—To make sure the right drug, dosage, and any interactions are noted
- **tblRefill**—To add the refill date and employee information

Rachel begins by copying the frmPrimaryActivity. She right-clicks the form in the database window and clicks Copy. Then she right-clicks anywhere in the window and clicks Paste. She names the form frmPrimaryActivity2 to distinguish it from frmPrimaryActivity. She opens the form in Design view and deletes each subform by clicking it and pressing the Delete key. Next, she adds the first tab control by clicking the Tab Control button. She positions the tab control cursor under the main form and clicks. Two tabs appear. She right-clicks the left tab, clicks Properties, and types Refills as the caption in the Property Sheet. She then names the next tab Customers/Health Plans. She knows she will need two more tabs, so she right-clicks a blank spot in the tab control, and then clicks Insert Page. She does this again to create all four tabs. She names the third tab Doctors, and the fourth tab Drugs.

4

Level 3

To place the first subform, she clicks the Refills tab. Then she clicks the Subform/Subreport button. When she places the cursor over the tab, the page below the tab turns black. She clicks the black area and a square box appears which will be the subform. She selects the tblRefill for the subform in the Subform Wizard and selects all the fields. The link between the main form and the refill subform is PrescriptionID. She names the form frmPrimaryActivity2Refills subform.

Next, Rachel clicks the Customers/Health Plans tab and clicks the Subform/Subreport button. She selects qryCustomerHealthplan as the data source and adds all the fields. She selects CustID as the link between the subform and the main form. She names this subform frmPrimaryActivity2CustomerHealthplan subform.

To add the doctor information, Rachel follows the same procedure to select tblDoctor as the source and includes all but the ClinicID field. She links this subform on DoctorID and names the subform frmPrimaryActivity2Doctor subform. Finally, she adds the subform for drugs using tblDrug as the data source. She selects all but the Cost, Price, and Supplier fields and links on UPN. She names this subform frmPrimaryActivity2Drug subform.

Rachel needs to modify the subform on each tab next. She decides to move each subform to the left of the tab and to change the captions to the same names as the tabs. Except for the Refills subform, she makes sure the Default View property is Single Form and sets other properties not to allow additions, edits, or deletions. She moves and aligns the controls. See Figure 4.42.

Figure 4.42: Form with tab controls

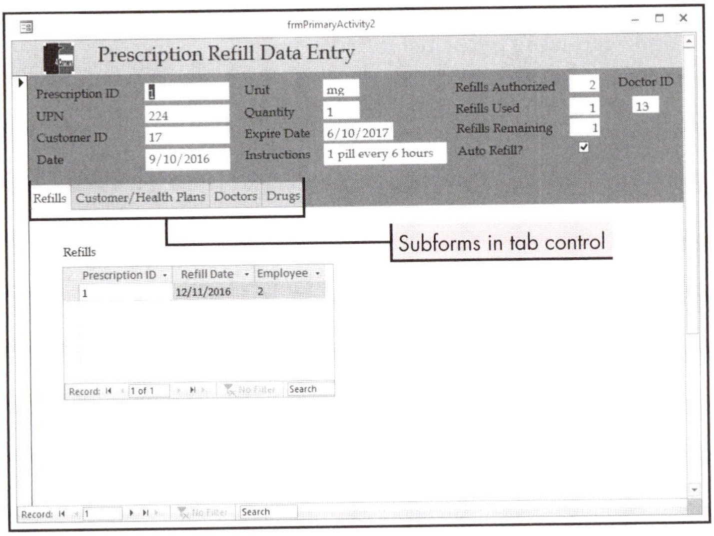

The pharmacists are delighted with the functionality of the new form. Rachel can add other tabs as they begin using the form, if necessary. Now she needs to complete a number of steps before the form is finished. She must arrange fields in logical groups, widen subforms to show all fields, and add a Find a Prescription combo box.

Changing Tab Order and Tab Stop

A form created with a form tool or the Form Wizard places the fields in the order they appear in the table design. In many cases, that is sufficient. However, after the fields are rearranged for more logical data entry, the form needs modification to arrange the order of movement through the fields. This order is called the **tab order**.

Typically, as you press Tab in a form, the cursor is moved from one control to the next control in the tab order. However, there may be a time when you do not want a control selected when you press Tab. For example, you may have a control that is only rarely used, but you still want it available when it is needed. So, in order to have the tab not stop on the control, you can set the Tab Stop property to No.

Rachel tests each form as she modifies it by opening the form and pressing the Tab key to see if the cursor stops in each field in an appropriate order. If not, she will change the tab order until the flow from field to field is an order that facilitates data entry.

How To

Change the Tab Order on a Form

1. Open the form in Design view.
2. Right-click the form and select Tab Order on the shortcut menu. The Tab Order dialog box opens.
3. Click Auto Order. Access attempts to redo the tab order based on the location of the fields on the form. Click OK.
4. Switch to Form view to test the result. If the order is satisfactory, you are done.
5. If the order is still not satisfactory, switch to Design view, open the Tab Order dialog box again, click to select a row, and then drag it to a new position in the dialog box.
6. For any field that should not have the focus, right-click the field, click Properties, and change the Tab Stop setting to No.

Rachel has completed a full set of forms for the 4Corners database, including a complex form for daily use.

Steps To Success: Level 3

Anne asks you to create the primary forms that the Hudson Bay Pharmacy technicians and pharmacists will use to perform their daily activities. As you save the new forms, be certain to use the "frm" prefix as part of the naming convention. Also consult your instructor for instructions about submitting your results.

Complete the following:

1. Start Access and open the **Hudson.accdb** database.

2. In the frmEmployee form, add a combo box to locate an employee.

3. Sort the employee names in the combo box.

4. Add a calculated control to frmEmployee to calculate the employees' ages.

5. Modify the tab order as needed.

6. Do not allow a tab stop on the calculated field.

7. Create the main form for frmPrimaryActivity using the fields from the tblRx table. Add a calculated field that subtracts the refills used from refills to show the number of refills remaining. Add the **HudsonBay.jpg** logo from the Chapter 4\Level 3 STS folder to frmPrimaryActivity.

8. Make sure that the controls and subforms are aligned and attractive on the form.

9. Change the tab order to make data entry flow logically.

10. Create a tab control for frmPrimaryActivity2, as shown in Figure 4.43.

Figure 4.43: frmPrimaryActivity2

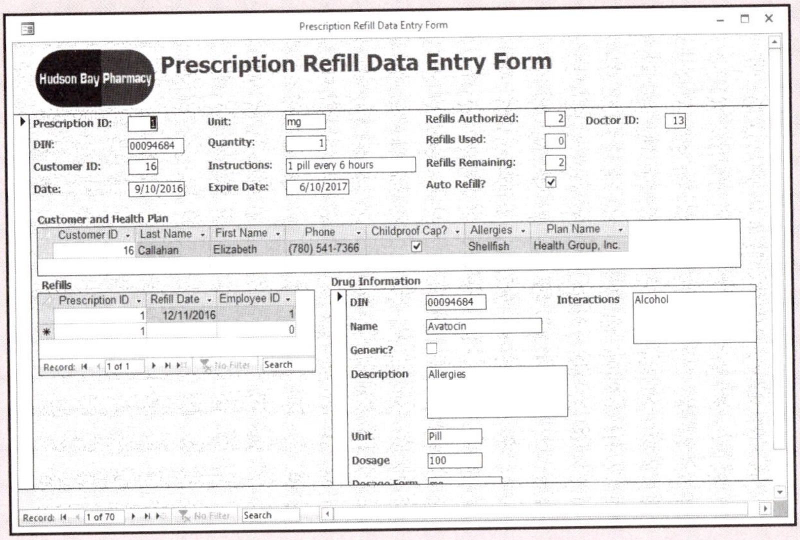

11. Add subforms to each tab and modify to show all the fields. Create the following subforms: Refills tab—frmRefillSubform, Customers/Health Plans tab—frmCustomerHealthplanSubform, Doctors tab—frmDoctorSubform, and Drugs tab—frmPrimaryActivity2DrugsSubform.

12. Add command buttons for next record, previous record, add a record, delete a record, and close the form.

13. Add a command button to open frmCustomer in case the pharmacists need more information about other prescriptions for a customer.

14. Add the **HudsonBay.jpg** logo from the Chapter 4\Level 3 STS folder to frmEmployee. Size it and make sure you can see the entire image.

15. Close the **Hudson.accdb** database and Access.

Chapter Summary

This chapter presented many techniques for creating forms that can be used in data entry and editing. Although data can be directly entered in tables, forms are especially useful when the relationships between tables are complex and users need to have access to data from several related tables at a time. In Level 1, you learned about the Form tools to create forms. You also found out how to use theme background colors, theme font colors, and themes. You learned about the importance of a consistent user interface and how it is best achieved. You also examined properties of forms and ways to create your own custom style and format for forms.

Level 2 moved into coverage of forms that use data from more than one table. You learned how to modify the layout of forms and how to add subforms to an existing form. You also learned about user views created with only portions of the data for specific applications. You learned how command buttons can perform many actions and how they help with user navigation. In addition, properties of forms and printing options were discussed.

Level 3 expanded the discussion of how forms might be involved in automating and streamlining business processes for the primary activities of a business by focusing on the usability and functionality of forms. You learned how to add calculations to forms. You saw how multitable forms could be created using multiple subforms. You also learned that you could add subforms to a main form using tab controls.

Conceptual Review

1. Why is it important to test your database before beginning the process of developing forms and reports?

2. When is it more appropriate to enter data in Datasheet view?

3. What are the differences between forms created with the Form Wizard and the Form tools?

4. What is the reason for working to have a consistent style and layout, especially of command buttons?

5. Explain the difference between a bound control and an unbound control.

6. What is a user view and why would you create one?

7. Name two ways to locate a record rather than just moving from record to record.

8. Why would you create a calculated field on a form?

9. Why would you choose to use a tab control for various subforms rather than multiple pages on the form?

10. What's the difference between a tab order and a tab stop? Why use a tab stop at all?

Case Problems

Case 1—Providing Efficient Data-Entry Forms for NHD Development Group Inc.

Operations Management

In this project, you continue working on the database for an antique mall, Memories Antiques in Cleveland, Tennessee. You have been working with Linda Sutherland, the manager of the mall, and with Tim Richards, CIO of the NHD development group, which owns this mall and several other malls across the country. Their main concern is that the database includes forms that make data entry easy and efficient.

Complete the following:

1. Start Access and open the **Antiques.accdb** database from the Case 1 folder in the EOC folder.

2. Linda has requested an easy way to browse customer data along with the classes in which customers have enrolled, so she will create a form for this purpose. She wants to also use this form to quickly mark the record when the customer has paid for a particular class. Create the requested form and save it as **frmCustomersAndClasses.**

3. Linda has just given you a list of three customers who have paid for one or more classes. Use your frmCustomersAndClasses form to record these payments according to Table 4.12 (that is, mark them as paid).

Table 4.12: Customers who have paid

Customer	Class ID
Angela Sutherland	5
Chloe Chastaine	10
Dianne Taylor	8

© 2014 Cengage Learning

4. Linda likes the form you created and asks that you create a similar form for entering all data in the database. As you discuss this task with Tim, he suggests that you provide a form for every table except the Class Enrollment table. Save each new form with a name that replaces the "tbl" prefix with the "frm" prefix. Make sure the forms present a consistent user interface along with the other forms you've created for the antiques mall.

As you build the forms, consider the design, arrangement of fields, and general attractiveness of the form. Select the layout and style that provides the best "look" for this application. Be sure to review your work and make any modifications necessary to create an attractive and simple way to work with the data in each of the existing tables.

5. Tim suggests that you add an appropriate title to each form and also add the NHD company logo. In Design view, open each of the forms you created and add an appropriate title to the header section of the form. For example, on the customer form, you might add "Customer Data Entry Form". Make the label text large (minimum of 18 points) and bold. Also add the company logo to the form (**NHD-logo.jpg** located in the Chapter 4\EOC\Case 1 folder). Resize the graphic as necessary to fit.

6. Use each form to browse the records of the form, making sure that all the data is fully displayed in the text boxes. Make any changes that are necessary to the form.

7. Close the **Antiques.accdb** database and then close Access.

Case 2—Providing Data-Entry Forms for MovinOn Inc.

In this project, you continue working with Robert Iko, the information manager for MovinOn. Robert asks you to begin building forms that let users view and enter data. He suggests that you start by building some simple forms that will be used for entering data into the customers, drivers, employees, trucks, and warehouses tables. He also needs a few more sophisticated forms that you can base on queries or multiple tables.

Complete the following:

1. Open the **MovinOn.accdb** database from the Case 2 folder.

2. Robert states that he wants to have simple data-entry forms for each of the following tables: customers (frmCustomerData), drivers (frmDriverData), employees (frmEmployeeData), vehicles (frmVehicleData), and warehouses (frmWarehouse-Data). Create those forms and save them in the database using appropriate form names. As you create the forms, consider the design and layout of the form. Make selections that you feel are most appropriate for this application.

3. Open each form and view it from the perspective of the user. As you observe the form, make decisions as to what fields need to be rearranged, sized, aligned, and so on. You might even decide that a particular field doesn't need to be on the data-entry form. For example, when you are entering a customer's records, would you need the balance field for that customer? Be sure each form is attractive.

4. While you have been working, Robert located the logo for MovinOn (**MovinOn-logo.jpg** located in the Chapter 4\EOC\Case 2 folder). He asks you to include the logo as well as a title on each of your forms, and continue including them on all forms you create in the future.

5. When Robert reviews the employee data form, he notices a modification that would improve the look of the form. Robert thinks it would look better to remove the comments field from the form and replace it with a button that will bring up a separate form where the user can record notes about the employee. The form should display

the employee's name as Last, First in a single text box along with the comments field. The form does not need to contain the company logo, but it should give the user the instruction to enter notes about the employee. Robert cautions you that the user should not be able to navigate this form and should not be able to change the name of the employee from the form.

6. The Human Resources department has asked that you create a form with which they can view the warehouses and the employees who work in each warehouse. This form is not to be used for data entry, rather the HR department will use it to view the employee assignments and review the salaries by warehouse. Robert has assigned you to create this form. In the main form, Robert asks that you place the pertinent data from the warehouse table. In this case, you do not need to add all the fields from the table. In the subform, Robert asks that you place data from the employees table that shows the employees for each warehouse, their position title, and what they are paid. (*Note*: Remember that some of the employees are paid a salary and some are paid an hourly rate. For this form, you will need both fields included.) As always, check your work carefully and make any adjustments you feel are necessary. Name this form **frmWarehouseAndEmployees**.

7. When you present the form to Robert, he suggests that you add a command button that will open the form used for entering new employees. You should already have a form for entering employees. Create the necessary command button, making sure that it properly opens the employees form.

8. Robert tells you that the Human Resources department has made another request. As they reviewed employee data, they noticed that employee reviews have not been recorded in the database. Prior to the creation of this database, employee reviews were done on paper and stored in a file cabinet. Human Resources plans to record their reviews directly into the database. They have requested a form they can use to enter the results of their employee review. The information will be recorded in the Comments field with a free format (that is, the HR representative who does the review will simply write notes into this comments field). Reviews are done every three years. Your form should display only those employees who have been employed more than three years. Create a query that will limit the data to employees who fit this specification, and then create a form that will properly display the employee data (all fields). Robert suggests that you use the same technique as you used on the employee form to open the form in which HR can record their notes about the employee. Name the form **frmEmployee3YearReviews**, and use a similar name for the corresponding query.

9. Close the **MovinOn.accdb** database and then close Access.

Case 3—Creating Data-Entry Forms for the Hershey College Intramural Department

Operations Management

In this project, you continue your work for Carla Stockman, assistant director of the intramural department at Hershey College. You have already created several tables and queries for the intramural department database. In this project, you will create some forms that will be used to enter and update data. Carla has requested that you create forms for each of the tables in the database. This will allow the department staff and student workers to enter data easily and efficiently.

After you create the simple forms, Carla asks that you create some forms that will be used to assign students to teams in their chosen sport. Carla states that it would be best to show the teams at the top of the form and that it would be helpful if the teams can be browsed by sport (for example, first you see the basketball teams, then the baseball teams, and so on). She has asked that the lower portion of the form contain information related to the students who are assigned to that team.

Complete the following:

1. Open the **Hershey.accdb** database from the Case 3 folder.

2. As Carla requested, create some simple forms for entering and modifying data related to coaches, equipment, fields, maintenance personnel, sports, students, and teams. Be sure each form has an appropriate title and the Hershey College logo (**HC-logo.jpg** located in the Chapter 4\EOC\Case 3). Make sure that the fields are attractively arranged and the data is fully displayed when browsing records. Carla has stated that she does not want to see just an ID on the forms. Rather, she wants to see the pertinent information related to that ID. For an example, she cites the form that will display field data. There is an ID for the maintenance personnel. Carla wants to see the name of the maintenance personnel as well as their contact information. Carla wants you to carry out this suggestion throughout the forms you create. You should decide how much additional information is important to include on each form.

3. Carla has reviewed the forms you created and is pleased with the way they look. However, she found it difficult to locate specific records. Carla has asked if you could provide a simple way for her to select the specific records she wants to view. If you can do this, she asks that you add this feature to the student, coach, and maintenance personnel forms.

4. Carla has expressed a need to see the details related to the team assignments. She asks you to separate the data somehow so that she can view each category of detail separately. The team details would include the identity of the team (Team ID and Sport Name) along with the following categories of information:

- The coach of the team, along with the coach's contact information
- The field assigned to the team, along with the contact information for the maintenance person responsible for that field
- Equipment, description of the equipment, and storage building where the equipment is located; the players on the team, along with their contact information

5. Carla is very pleased with what you have provided so far. She has asked for one more form that will help the staff review the coaching assignments. Carla wants to have a form that will display the coaches in one part of the form and the teams they coach in another part. She also asks you to provide a command button that the staff can click to add coaches to the database.

6. Review all your work and make appropriate changes where necessary.

7. Save your work, close the database, and then close Access.

Developing Effective Reports
Accounting: Supporting Sales and Managerial Decision Making

"Nothing succeeds like reports of success."
—Sue Sanders

LEARNING OBJECTIVES

Level 1

Create and modify basic reports
Improve the information content of reports by sorting and summarizing
Create labels using the Label Wizard

Level 2

Create a custom report
Add calculations to a report
Look at Design view and properties

Level 3

Define conditional formatting rules in a report
Develop reports with subreports
Develop graphs

TOOLS COVERED IN THIS CHAPTER

Conditional formatting

Label Wizard

Page breaks

Queries

Report button

Report Wizard

Sorting and Grouping

Subreports

Microsoft product screenshots used with permission from Microsoft Corporation.

Chapter Introduction

So far, you have learned how to create a database with related tables, develop queries that can be used as the basis for forms and reports or for ad hoc decision making, and design forms for data entry and editing. This chapter examines another important part of database development—reports that reflect the information in the database, summarize business activities, or provide details about your data. You can use reports to format your data in an attractive and informative layout for printing, though you can also view reports on-screen. Reports are often used by managers and others to determine whether their business is meeting its objectives. Reports also provide information that supports strategic decision making for the future.

Many of the skills you learned in previous chapters will prove useful as you begin creating reports, especially when developing queries and designing forms. Because reports are often based on data in multiple tables, database designers frequently use queries as the basis of the reports. Your proficiency with queries will therefore help you create effective reports. In addition, many form concepts and techniques apply to reports. For example, you use the same DESIGN tab for designing forms and designing reports.

In Level 1, you will learn three ways to create a report: using the Report button, using the Report Wizard, and basing a report on a query. You will also learn how to sort and group data in reports and create and modify mailing labels and other types of labels. In Level 2, you will create more complicated reports, such as those that summarize performance with subtotals and percentages on grouped data. You will learn how to add controls to reports, including those that calculate subtotals and use other aggregate functions. In Level 3, you will learn how to define conditional formatting rules in a report to highlight important performance results and add subreports and graphs to reports.

Case Scenario

Elaine Estes is the store manager for 4Corners Pharmacy. She watched with interest as Rachel Thompson created forms for the pharmacy. Elaine can see that many of the problems Rachel solved when designing forms are similar to those she will have as she develops reports. As the pharmacy becomes busier and the customers and managers require more feedback about their transactions, Elaine will need to prepare a number of reports to reduce response time for refills and assist in decision making and customer relations. One of Elaine's job responsibilities is to monitor the growth of the pharmacy and to report to Paul Ferrino, the owner, about how well the pharmacy is meeting its monthly and annual objectives and long-term strategic goals. Elaine decides to poll Paul and the employees to discover what reports would be the most helpful to them. Then she can begin creating simple reports and designing more comprehensive ones with Microsoft Access 2013.

Accounting

LEVEL 1
Creating Simple Reports and Labels

Understanding Reports

A **report** presents the information from one or more database tables in a printed format. Although you can print other Access objects, such as forms and table datasheets, reports provide the most options and advantages for printing database content—you can organize and format information to create a professional presentation, include numeric and textual data, and maintain flexibility when displaying summary information. For example, in a report that shows sales by employee, you can display the total goods sold by each employee and highlight each total as a percentage of the grand total. Typical business reports include sales summaries, purchase orders, mailing labels, invoices, and phone lists.

Access reports can include many design elements, though all should contribute to the purpose of the report and serve its audience. For example, you can combine text, calculations, and graphic elements to create a report that appeals to financial managers, sales personnel, stockholders, or employees and communicates the data clearly and effectively.

Like queries and forms, reports extract information from your database. Where a query retrieves records according to criteria you specify and a form provides an easy-to-use interface for viewing and editing database information, a report lets you precisely control and organize the appearance of information that you distribute to others, usually within your organization. The power and flexibility of a report is related to its design—after you create and save a report design, you can use it again to update the contents every time you print the report.

Use a report to accomplish the following goals:

- Create a printed copy of information that you use regularly.
- Distribute information to others.
- Customize the organization and appearance of printed information, presenting data in an appealing format with graphics, lines, charts, and meaningful colors.
- Group or summarize information for reporting to others, calculating running totals, group totals, grand totals, and percentages of totals.

Many of the methods you have learned for creating forms also work for creating reports. Table 5.1 summarizes the similarities and differences between forms and reports.

Table 5.1: Comparing forms and reports

Task	Applies to Forms	Applies to Reports
Use a wizard to quickly create a report or form based on the data in tables or queries.	X	X
Create a form or report using fields from more than one table without creating a query first.	X	X
Work in Design view to place controls in sections such as the detail, page header, and page footer sections.	X	X
Insert subforms or subreports that link to a common field in the main part of the form or report.	X	X
Include calculated fields to perform calculations with the values in fields.	X	X
Move, resize, and format controls.	X	X
Provide customized formats and styles.	X	X
Modify the data underlying a form or report.	X	
Group data to increase information content by showing detail and summary data together.		X

© 2014 Cengage Learning

Overall, reports are primarily designed to be printed, while forms are designed to be viewed on-screen. In addition, reports usually have more calculations, such as subtotals and totals. Also, although you can create reports in Design view, you view the results in Print Preview. Finally, layout and alignment are more critical with reports because variations in alignment are more obvious when printed.

Choosing the Appropriate Type of Report

Before you develop a report, determine its purpose and audience in order to select the appropriate type of report. For example, sales staff might use a detailed report to determine product availability, whereas management might need a summary or grouped report to analyze annual performance. Figure 5.1 shows common types of reports you can create in Access.

A **detailed report** lists data from a table or query, such as the tblEmployees table. A **grouped report** organizes data into groups, such as prescriptions by customer or sales by date. A **summary report** is a grouped report that calculates totals for each group and a grand total for the entire report, and doesn't necessarily include details. In a **mailing labels report**, you print names and addresses in a format suited for your mailing labels. A **multiple-column report** displays information in several columns, such as a telephone listing.

Figure 5.1: Examples of Access reports

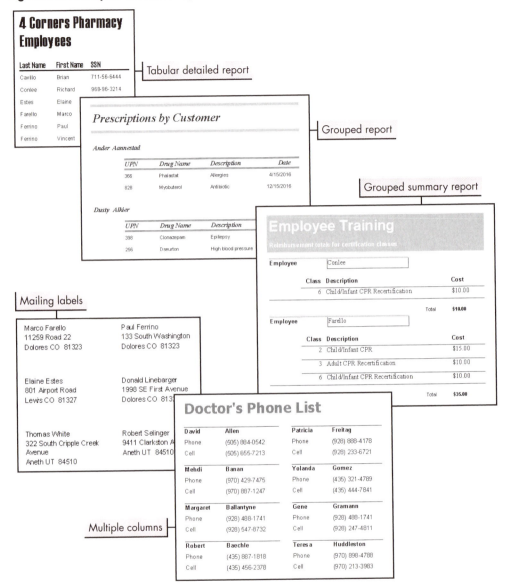

Any of these types of reports can contain other reports, called subreports, though they are most common in detailed and grouped reports. As you do with forms and subforms, you usually include a subreport when you need to display data from tables that have a one-to-many relationship. For example, a main report might take its data from tblEmployees and show the name and phone number of each employee. A subreport might take its data from tblRefill and show the prescriptions each employee refilled. Table 5.2 describes the types of reports available in Access.

Table 5.2: Types of reports available in Access

Type of Report	Description	Example
Detailed single column or columnar	• Lists field names in one column on the left side of the page with the corresponding data to the right • Can be quickly created using the Report Wizard option • Seldom used for long reports because it wastes paper	Doctor report that lists the ID, name, phone numbers, and clinic for one doctor, then the ID, name, phone numbers, and clinic for the next doctor, and so on
Detailed tabular	• Lists field names in a row across the page with the corresponding data below • Can be quickly created using the Report Wizard option, but might require modification to create an appealing and useful format • Best for reports with 10 or fewer fields due to space limitations on standard paper sizes • A common report format	Prescription drug report that lists the drug name, description, price, and supplier as column headings, with the data listed for each drug below the headings
Multiple columns	• Organizes field names and data in newspaper-style columns • Fits a lot of information on a single page • Used for mailing and other types of labels designed for printing on label stock • Can be quickly created using the Label Wizard, but might require modification to create an appealing and useful format	Phone list or address directory
Grouped or Summary	• Increases information content by organizing data into groups • Summarizes data within subgroups • Often has subtotals and totals for the data • Might have percentages for subgroups • Most common type of report • Can create simple grouped reports with the Report Wizard, but might require modification to create an appealing and useful format • Should use Design view to design more complex reports with multiple grouping levels from scratch	Employee report that lists employees by job type or a sales report that sums sales by employee
Mailing labels	• Special kind of multicolumn report • Uses preset label formats from well-known label manufacturers • Can be quickly created using the Label Wizard if data matches preset label requirements • Number of labels per page and size determined by preset label settings or a custom design	Address labels that print on a sheet containing 12 labels
Unbound	• Unbound main report serves as a container for one or more subreports from unrelated data sources • Likely to be created from scratch using Design view to meet specific presentation requirements	Main report containing a title and two subreports, one summarizing sales by employee and the other summarizing sales by product
Chart	• Compares one or more sets of data graphically • Often added as a subreport • Can use data from a crosstab or other type of advanced query • Can be created using a form or report Chart Wizard	Main report containing pharmacist information, and chart comparing the number of prescriptions filled

5

Level 1

After you identify the purpose and audience of the report and select the appropriate type, you determine which object in your database contains the information you want to display in the report. As in a form, this object is called the record source, and can be one or more tables or queries. After you identify the record source, you are ready to create the report.

Planning Basic Reports

As store manager, Elaine Estes needs to develop reports for herself and for other managers in the pharmacy. Some of the reports provide accounting information to help Paul Ferrino, the pharmacy owner, and the other pharmacy managers. Other reports provide information to help employees perform their jobs efficiently, such as a printed directory of employees and their phone numbers for human resources. Elaine decides to start by creating reports for various functions within the pharmacy so the managers of these areas can review the reports and comment on their usefulness and appearance. Table 5.3 lists the reports that Elaine plans to create first.

Table 5.3: First reports for the pharmacy

Category	Reports Needed
Customer relations	• Directory with information about drugs and possible interactions to post near the pharmacy counter
Daily operations	• List of health plans and the number of days allowed in each refill
Human resource management	• List of classes approved by the pharmacy for reimbursement • Alphabetical phone list of employees • Mailing labels for employees • Employee name tags
Management decision support and long-range planning	• Physical count of drugs and their manufacturers for inventory control • Outstanding credit balances

© 2014 Cengage Learning

Creating and Modifying Basic Reports

Similar to forms, you can create a basic report using the Report button or the Report Wizard. Use the Report button to create an instant report that displays all the fields and records in a single table or query. For more flexibility, you can use a **Report Wizard**, which guides you through the steps of creating a report based on one or more tables or queries by asking you questions about the record sources, fields, layout, and format you want to use. You will likely use one technique or the other to create a basic report, which you can customize by modifying the layout or adding features, for example, to meet your needs.

Creating a Report Using the Report Button

When Elaine polls the 4Corners Pharmacy employees and asks what types of reports they need, Maria Garcia is the first to respond. Maria mentions that she needs a report to post on the employee bulletin board advising employees about the classes that have been approved for reimbursement. Because the report should have all the fields and records in the tblClass table, Elaine starts with this table.

Elaine clicks the tblClass table in the Navigation pane, clicks the CREATE tab, and then clicks the Report button in the Reports group. Access creates a report that looks similar to a datasheet and includes all the fields from the record source, tblClass. See Figure 5.2.

Figure 5.2: Report created using Report button

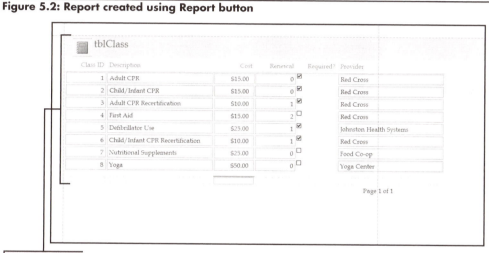

Data displays in tabular format

After creating a report with the Report button, Elaine knows that she can use Design view to make changes to the report. Elaine saves the report as rptClassList.

How To

Create a Report Using the Report Button

1. In the Navigation pane, click the table on which you want to base the report.
2. Click the CREATE tab on the Ribbon and click the Report button in the Reports group. Access creates a report that includes all the fields from the record source.
3. Save the report.

Best Practice

Naming Reports

Most database applications have many reports; distinguishing one from another can be difficult. In addition to using the "rpt" prefix for each report, use meaningful names that describe the contents of the reports. Although you can include spaces in field, control, and object names, most developers do not use spaces in field and control names because doing so can produce naming conflicts in some circumstances in Microsoft Visual Basic for Applications (VBA), a macro-language version of Microsoft Visual Basic that is used to program Windows applications, including Access.

In a report name, you can use an uppercase letter to start a new word, as in rptDrugList, to help make the names more readable. By default, Access uses the report name as its title, which might not be meaningful to readers of the printed report. So in Design view, you can change the label containing the report title so that a more readable name appears at the beginning of the report in Print Preview. You can use the report properties to specify the report caption—this changes the text that appears in the report's title bar. For example, you could change the caption of rptDrugList to Drug List in the report properties and make the same change to the title label in Design view.

Some database developers recommend using a more readable name for the report when you create it because this determines the title of the report. If you elect to use this approach, you can then change the name of the report in the Database window to reflect the best practices for naming objects. (In the Navigation pane right-click the report and then click Rename on the shortcut menu.)

Next, Elaine wants to create a report that serves as a directory of information about drugs and possible interactions. She'll post this directory near the pharmacy counter for employee and customer reference. Although she can base this report on a single table, tblDrug, the report is not a candidate for the Report button because she doesn't want to include all the fields in tblDrug, such as the Cost or Supplier fields. To take advantage of its greater flexibility, she decides to use the Report Wizard to create this report.

Creating a Report Using the Report Wizard

The Report Wizard provides a quick way to select only the fields you want to display in a report based on one or more tables or queries. You can also select one of several layouts and styles for the report. Even experienced Access users frequently create a report with the Report Wizard and then customize the report in Design view.

When customers pick up prescriptions at 4Corners Pharmacy, they often have questions about the medication, such as whether it's a generic drug or if it interacts with other drugs such as sedatives or alcohol. In a three-ring binder, Elaine plans to include an alphabetical listing of all drugs stocked at the pharmacy. Customers can consult this binder while they are waiting for their prescriptions, and employees can use it to answer questions.

All of the drug information is contained in the tblDrug table, but Elaine doesn't want to list the UPN (an internal drug ID), the selling price, the cost (to the pharmacy) of each drug, or the name of the supplier. Because the Report Wizard provides options for selecting fields, she decides to use it for this report. She selects tblDrug in the Navigation pane, clicks the CREATE tab on the Ribbon, and then clicks Report Wizard. The first dialog box in the Report Wizard opens. See Figure 5.3.

Figure 5.3: Selecting fields in the first Report Wizard dialog box

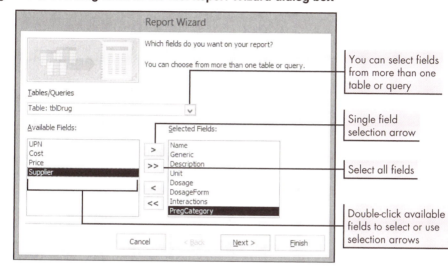

Elaine double-clicks all the tblDrug fields except the ones she does not want to include: UPN, Cost, Price, and Supplier. Then she clicks the Next button. She has the option of grouping on one of the fields but only wants to list the drugs in alphabetical order by name. See Figure 5.4. She clicks the Next button without specifying a grouping level.

Figure 5.4: Report Wizard grouping options

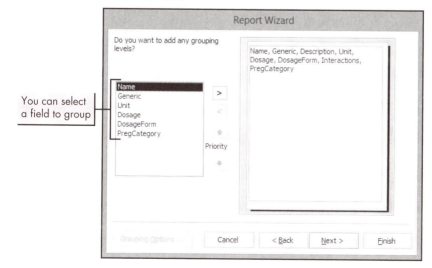

The next wizard dialog box asks if she wants to sort the records in the report. See Figure 5.5. Because she wants to sort the records alphabetically by drug name, she selects Name as the sort field. Then she clicks the Next button.

Figure 5.5: Selecting sorting options

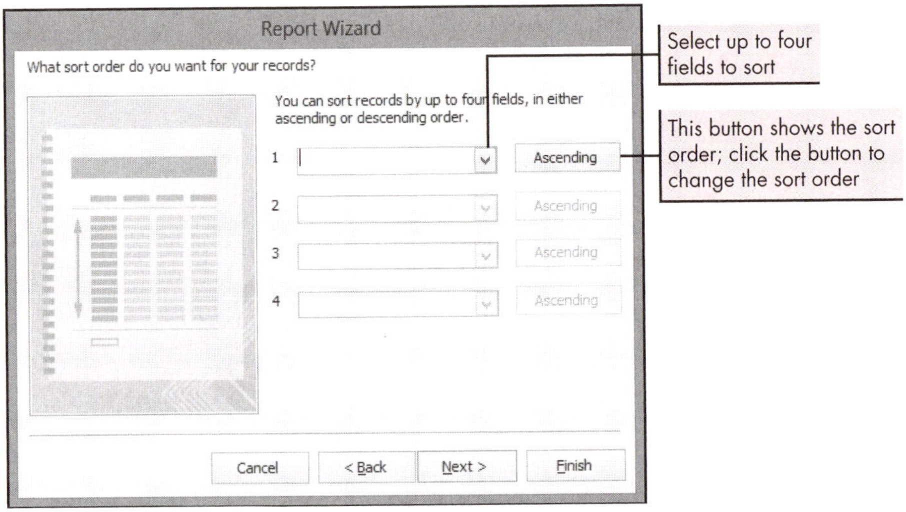

The next wizard dialog box displays layout options. Elaine selects Tabular as the Layout option and Portrait as the Orientation option. She makes sure that the Adjust the field width so all fields fit on a page check box is checked so the report includes all the fields she selected on a single page. See Figure 5.6. Then she clicks the Next button.

Figure 5.6: Choosing the report layout and orientation

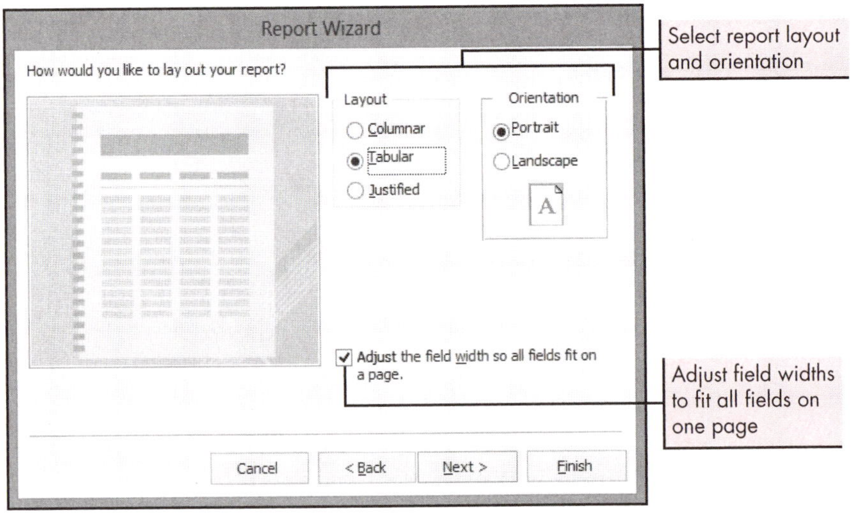

The next wizard dialog box displays and Elaine decides that she is ready to preview the report. She verifies that the Preview the report option button is selected, as shown in Figure 5.7, and then clicks the Finish button.

Figure 5.7: Final Report Wizard dialog box

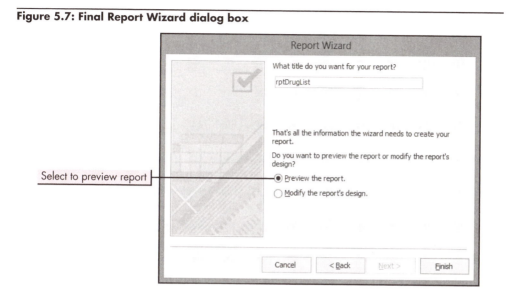

Select to preview report

Finally, Elaine names the report rptDrugList, maintaining the naming convention for all Access objects that Donald Linebarger, IS manager, suggested. She clicks the Finish button and Access displays the completed report in Print Preview, as shown in Figure 5.8.

Figure 5.8: Report created with the Report Wizard

rptDrugList appears as the report title

Field needs to be widened to show complete data

rptDrugList

Name	Gen	Description	Unit	Dosa	Dosage F	Interactions	Pregn
Acebutolol hy ☐		Arthritis	Pill	400	mg		A
Albuterol Sulf ☑		Asthma	Pill	2	mg		B
Almotriptan ☑		Conjunctivitis	Pill	6.25	mg		B
Ampicillin ☑		Antibiotic	Pill	250	mg	Calcium	B
Avatocin ☐		Allergies	Pill	100	mg	Alcohol	A
Cefixime ☑		Antihistamine	Pill	400	mg	Sedatives	A
Clonazepam ☐		Epilepsy	Pill	4	mcg		A
Diazapam ☑		Anxiety	Pill	5	mg		D
Didanosine ☑		Sinus infection	Pill	200	mg		C
Dseurton ☑		High blood pressure	Pill	175	mg	Sedatives	C
Dyotex ☐		Tonsillitis	Bottl	2	tsp		D
Epronix ☐		Pain	Pill	500	mg	Grapefruit	C

How To

Create a Report Using the Report Wizard

1. In the Navigation pane, click the table for the report.
2. Click the CREATE tab on the Ribbon.
3. Click the Report Wizard button in the Reports group. The first dialog box in the Report Wizard opens, asking which fields you want in your report.
4. From the Available Fields list, select the fields you want to include in the report. Use the select single field button to select the fields one by one; use the select all fields button to select them all at once. If you want to include fields from a different table or query, click the Tables/Queries list arrow, select a table or query, and then select the fields you want. Click the Next button.
5. If you want to add grouping levels to the report, click the field on the left by which you want to group records, and then click the select single field button. If you use grouping levels, you can click the Grouping Options button to select a grouping interval. Click the Next button.
6. If you want to sort the records in the report, click the list arrow and then select the field on which to sort. By default, Access sorts in ascending order. To change this to descending order, click the Ascending button. You can sort on up to four fields. Click the Next button.
7. Select a layout and orientation for the report. A sample of the selected layout appears in the preview box of the dialog box. Make sure the Adjust the field width so all fields fit on a page check box is selected if you want to fit all fields on a page, even if the fields must be shortened to fit. If you do not want to adjust the field widths, clear this check box. Click the Next button.
8. Type the name of the report, using "rpt" as the prefix to identify the object as a report. Click the Finish button. The completed report opens in Print Preview.

The title of the report that Elaine created—rptDrugList—reflects the name of the report object, but could be confusing to the customers who will refer to the report at the pharmacy counter. Some fields and labels are not wide enough to show all of the text they contain. To change the title of the report and make other revisions, Elaine must work in Design view.

Best Practice

Creating a Report from a Query

When you create a report, you can use a query as the record source. Many reports are created from queries because a query lets you retrieve information from more than one table and restrict the data by using criteria. Any data not meeting the criteria is not included in the report detail. If you use a parameter query as the record source, users who open the report to view or print it must first enter criteria, such as a range of dates. The report then includes only the records that meet the criteria the user entered.

All the steps in the Report Wizard work the same whether you choose multiple tables or queries as the record sources. Note that if you select fields from multiple tables, Access uses relationships you defined to build a hidden query. Access won't let you continue if you select fields from unrelated tables.

Modifying a Report in Design View

Access users often use the Report Wizard to quickly generate a report that contains the basic data they want to include. Then they modify the report in Design view to customize its appearance and contents. As with forms, you can also create reports from scratch in Design view. Experienced Access users might prefer to start in Design view to place fields and other controls precisely where they want them.

As in a form, a control is a small object such as a text box that displays data or a line that separates one record from another. Table 5.4 describes the three types of controls you can add to an Access report.

Table 5.4: Report controls

Type of Control	Description	Example
Bound control	A control whose source of data is a field in the report's record source. Bound controls display values from fields in the database. The values can be any data type, such as text, dates, numbers, Yes/No values, pictures, or hyperlinks.	A text box that displays an employee's last name stored in the EmpLast field in the tblEmployee table
Unbound control	A control that doesn't have a source of data, such as a field or mathematical expression. Unbound controls are often used to display report titles, informational text, lines, rectangles, and graphics not stored in an underlying table.	A label that displays the title of a report
Calculated control	A control whose source of data is a mathematical expression rather than a field. The results of a calculated control are updated when any of the values in the expression change.	A text box that calculates the total of the values in the Price field

© 2014 Cengage Learning

In Chapter 4, Table 4.2 describes the tools and controls you use to create form controls; you can use the same tools to create report controls.

Elaine wants to change the title of rptDrugList to one that is more meaningful to its users. With the report open in Print Preview, Elaine clicks the Close Print Preview button. She then clicks the View button arrow and notices it lists four report views: Report View, Print Preview, Layout View, and Design View. Table 5.5 summarizes the options available in each view. See Figure 5.9 for examples of each view of rptDrugList.

5

Level 1

Table 5.5: Four report views

View	Description
Report	• View the report as it would look if printed. • Follow a link by clicking an active hyperlink. • Filter for specific records and print only those records.
Print Preview	• View the report as it would look if printed. • Display one, two, or more pages at once. • Use the Page Setup button in the Page Layout group to launch the Page Setup dialog box to change the margins, page settings such as orientation, and column settings. • Use the navigation buttons to move from page to page. • Use the Zoom button or the Zoom slider to show the report using a larger or smaller magnification.
Layout	• Create and modify report designs. • Change control elements while accessing the data.
Design	• Modify any part of the report using the controls in Design view. • Use settings, controls, and other options similar to Design view for forms.

© 2014 Cengage Learning

Figure 5.9: Four views of rptDrugList

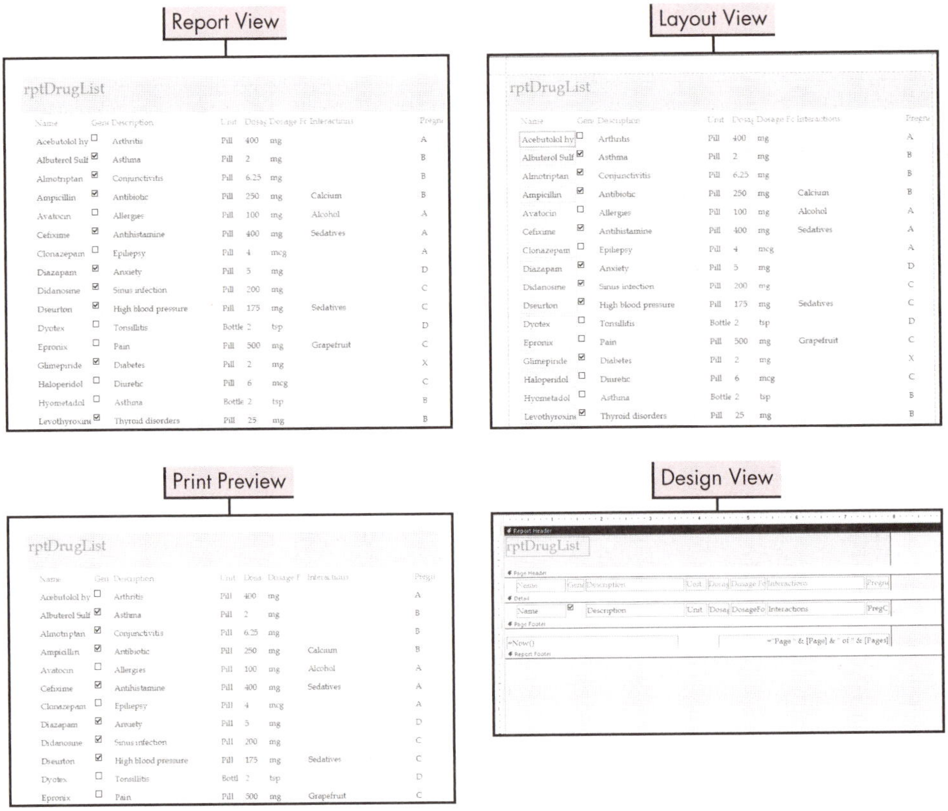

Report View

Layout View

Print Preview

Design View

Elaine will spend most of her time modifying the report in Layout view and Design view, and then switch to Print Preview to see the effects of changes. When she opens the report in Design view, she sees that it is divided into sections similar to those in forms. The rptDrugList report has Report Header, Page Header, Detail, Page Footer, and Report Footer sections. See Figure 5.10.

Figure 5.10: Sections of a report in Design view

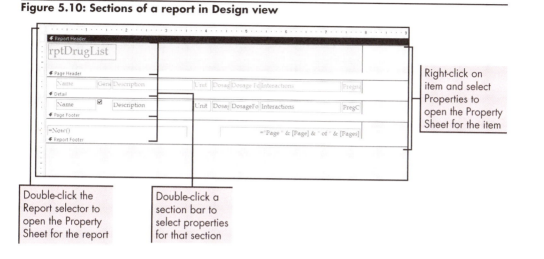

Right-click on item and select Properties to open the Property Sheet for the item

Double-click the Report selector to open the Property Sheet for the report

Double-click a section bar to select properties for that section

To create useful reports, you need to understand the purpose of each section. The section in which you place a control determines where and how often it appears in the printed report. An Access report can contain the following sections:

- **Report header**—Printed once at the beginning of the report. Use the report header for information that might normally appear on a cover page, such as a logo or a title and date. The report header is printed before the page header.
- **Page header**—Printed at the top of every page. For example, use a page header to repeat the report title on every page.
- **Group header**—Printed at the beginning of each new group of records. Use the group header to print the group name. For example, in a report that is grouped by product, use the group header to print the product name.
- **Detail**—Printed once for every row in the record source and includes the controls that make up the main body of the report.
- **Group footer**—Printed at the end of each group of records. Use a group footer to print summary information for a group.
- **Page footer**—Printed at the end of every page. For example, use a page footer to print page numbers.
- **Report footer**—Printed once at the end of the report. Use the report footer to print report totals or other summary information for the entire report. The report footer appears last in the report design, but is printed before the final page footer.

You can customize the appearance and behavior of report sections by changing their properties. To view a property sheet for a section, double-click the section bar, such as the Report Header bar. Table 5.6 lists common properties for sections. (You can view a description of each property by clicking a property and then pressing the F1 key.)

Table 5.6: Common section properties

Property	Description
Force New Page	Specify whether the Report Header, Detail, or Report Footer section prints on a separate page, rather than on the current page.
Keep Together	Select Yes to print a form or report section all on one page; select No to print as much of the section as possible on the current page and continue printing on the next page.
Back Color	If you want to include a background color for the section, specify the numeric value of the color or click the Build button to use the Color Builder to select a color from a palette.
Special Effect	Specify whether the section should appear as flat (default), raised, sunken, etched, shadowed, or chiseled when printed.
Can Grow	Select Yes to allow the section to expand in order to accommodate fields that might expand, such as memo fields.

The report itself also has properties that you can modify to customize the report. Table 5.7 lists common report properties that are discussed throughout the chapter.

Table 5.7: Common report properties

Property	Description
Record Source	Specify the source of the data for the report, which can be a table name, a query name, or an SQL statement.
Caption	Set the title for the report.
Width	Set the width for the report.
Picture	Select a graphic to display as the background for the report.
Picture Type	Select Embedded to store the graphic specified in the Picture property as part of the report. Select Linked to link the picture to the report. Access then stores a pointer to the location of the picture on the disk.

© 2014 Cengage Learning

Best Practice

The Importance of Previewing Reports During Report Development

Because printed reports show even minor misalignments of controls or problems with truncated data due to control width, switch from Design view to Print Preview regularly as you are creating reports. As you work on a report, also save it frequently to preserve your changes. If necessary, you can revert to a saved version of a report if you don't like your modifications. Also make liberal use of the Undo button as you work to undo your recent changes.

Because Elaine named the report rptDrugList, she has to change two properties in the report. The first is the report caption. This changes the name of the report in the title bar in Print Preview. The report header contains the title of the report in a label control, which has the same properties in Design view for a report as for a form. (See Table 4.4 in Chapter 4 for descriptions of common label properties.) To change the caption property for the report, Elaine opens the report in Design view, and then double-clicks the report selector button to open the Property Sheet for the entire report. She selects the rptDrugList label below the report selector button and then changes the Caption property to Drug List. The text in the label changes accordingly. See Figure 5.11. She also changes the Text Align property to Distribute, and then checks the report in Print Preview.

In Print Preview, some of the column headings seem crowded. To make room for the headings, Elaine can decrease the left and right margins of the page to provide more room for the column headings in the report. She makes these changes by clicking the Page Setup button on the PRINT PREVIEW tab.

Figure 5.11: Changing the label caption

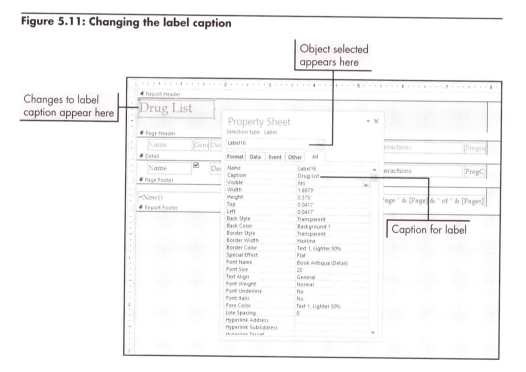

How To

Change Margins and Report Width

1. In Print Preview, click the Page Setup button. The Page Setup dialog box opens, shown in Figure 5.12.

Figure 5.12: Page Setup dialog box

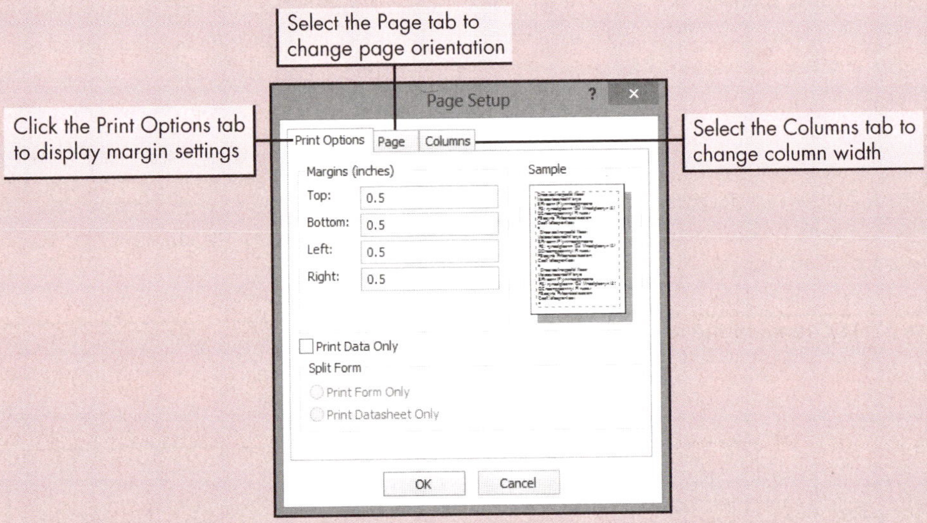

Select the Page tab to change page orientation

Click the Print Options tab to display margin settings

Select the Columns tab to change column width

Page Setup

Print Options | Page | Columns

Margins (inches)

Top: 0.5
Bottom: 0.5
Left: 0.5
Right: 0.5

Sample

☐ Print Data Only
Split Form
○ Print Form Only
○ Print Datasheet Only

OK   Cancel

2. To change the margins, click the Print Options tab. Most printers use minimum left and right margins of .5 inches for reports, and .25 inches for labels.

3. To change the page orientation from portrait to landscape, click the Page tab and then click the Portrait or Landscape option button.

4. To change the width of the report, click the Columns tab. Modify the width as desired, but remember that the total of margins and report width must equal the width of the paper for the report, which is usually 8.5 inches. If you exceed the combined width, Access displays an error message.

In rptDrugList, Elaine checks to see if the left and right margins are set to .25 inches to create more room for the column headings. She clicks the Columns tab to change the width of the report to 8 inches, if necessary. She uses the Width text box in the Page Setup dialog box, instead of manually dragging the report border in Design view, to prevent accidentally widening the report beyond the edge of the paper.

Best Practice

Developing a Report Design Checklist

A common error made by report developers is to set the width of the report plus the page margins wider than the actual width of the paper in the printer. When this happens, a blank page prints after each page of the report. Use the settings in the Page Setup dialog box and in the report's Property Sheet to make the total width of the report and the margins equal to the actual paper width. In Print Preview, you can also choose to view two or four pages at the same time. If doing so reveals blank pages, you know that your report is too wide for the paper.

Because a report is designed to be printed, the alignment of the headings and the spacing between lines and columns are very important. Minor variations in alignment are obvious when the report is printed, and can affect the report's readability. Incomplete field values can make the report meaningless.

If you are developing a series of reports for a database application, you should develop a checklist for the modifications you plan to make so the reports have a similar look and professional appearance. Answer the following questions as you develop your plan:

- Is the same format applied to all reports?
- Does the title label caption need to be modified?
- Have I changed the report caption?
- Can I read the complete column headings or are they truncated?
- Does all the data in the detail area appear or is some truncated?
- Is the report so wide that it should use landscape orientation?
- Is the vertical spacing too spread out or too close?
- If the report has many numbers, does it use gridlines to make reading it easier?
- Do any extra items on the report detract from its appearance?
- Do any errors or blank pages appear when the report is printed?
- Would the data have more information content if it were grouped?
- Would summary data add value to the information content of the report?

Elaine uses the checklist as she creates each report to see if there are any modifications that she should make. She wants each report to reflect the professionalism of the pharmacy and to use a standard format. She re-examines the report using her checklist to evaluate its format and sees a few modifications she needs to make. See Figure 5.13.

5

Level 1

Figure 5.13: Additional changes to make to rptDrugList

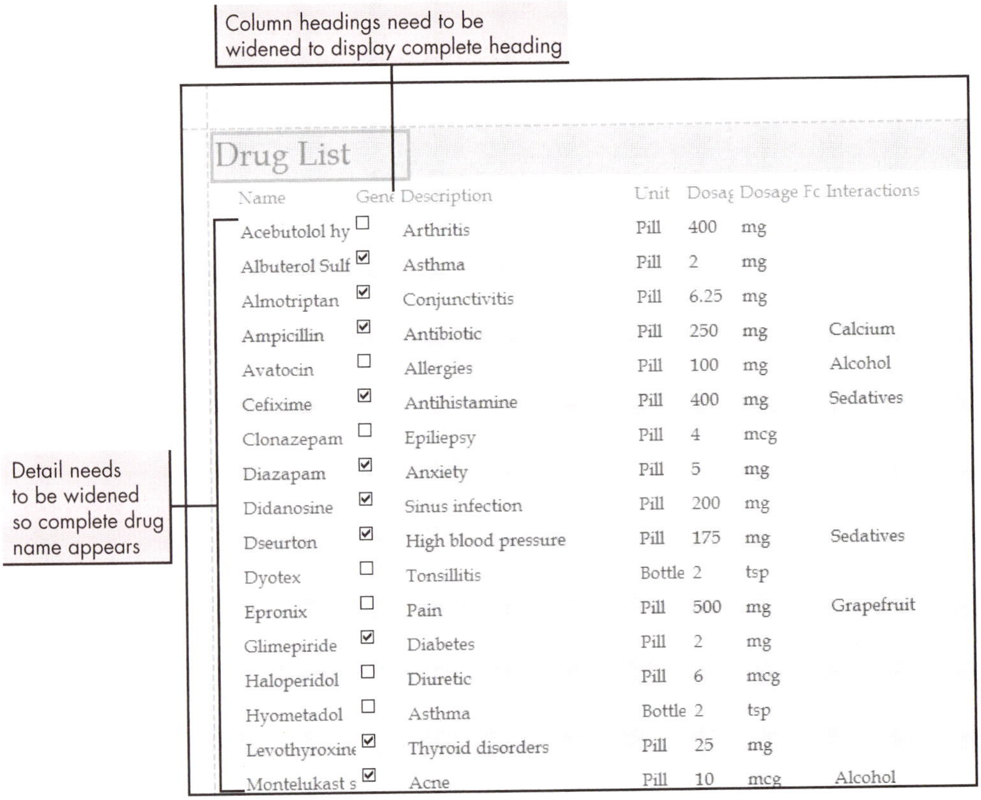

Column headings need to be
widened to display complete heading

Detail needs
to be widened
so complete drug
name appears

Drug List

Name	Gene	Description	Unit	Dosag	Dosage Fc	Interactions
Acebutolol hy	☐	Arthritis	Pill	400	mg	
Albuterol Sulf	☑	Asthma	Pill	2	mg	
Almotriptan	☑	Conjunctivitis	Pill	6.25	mg	
Ampicillin	☑	Antibiotic	Pill	250	mg	Calcium
Avatocin	☐	Allergies	Pill	100	mg	Alcohol
Cefixime	☑	Antihistamine	Pill	400	mg	Sedatives
Clonazepam	☐	Epiliepsy	Pill	4	mcg	
Diazapam	☑	Anxiety	Pill	5	mg	
Didanosine	☑	Sinus infection	Pill	200	mg	
Dseurton	☑	High blood pressure	Pill	175	mg	Sedatives
Dyotex	☐	Tonsillitis	Bottle	2	tsp	
Epronix	☐	Pain	Pill	500	mg	Grapefruit
Glimepiride	☑	Diabetes	Pill	2	mg	
Haloperidol	☐	Diuretic	Pill	6	mcg	
Hyometadol	☐	Asthma	Bottle	2	tsp	
Levothyroxine	☑	Thyroid disorders	Pill	25	mg	
Montelukast s	☑	Acne	Pill	10	mcg	Alcohol

Elaine begins to modify the format of the report in Design view by clicking the label control for the Pregnancy Category label and widening it to display the complete field name. She moves the label and its text box by holding down the Shift key as she clicks to select more than one control. She also widens the Dosage Form label to display its entire text. Moving from right to left, she moves each label with its associated text box, using the Undo button on the Quick Access toolbar as necessary to correct errors, and switching between Print Preview and Design view to see the effect of her changes. She decides to split the Pregnancy Category label text over two lines because the label is so much longer than the category text listed below it. She clicks after the word Pregnancy in the heading. By holding down the Shift key and pressing the Enter key, she splits the words over two lines.

Elaine moves the labels in the Page Header section and the text boxes for the fields in the Detail section so they are distributed evenly across the form, widening text boxes as necessary. She will need to remove these controls before she can resize an individual field. Rachel selects all the controls in the Detail section, then presses the Delete key. She can now make the desired changes to individual controls. When necessary, she uses the Align and Size commands on the ARRANGE tab of the Ribbon. Figure 5.14 shows the modified report.

Figure 5.14: Drug List report after modifications

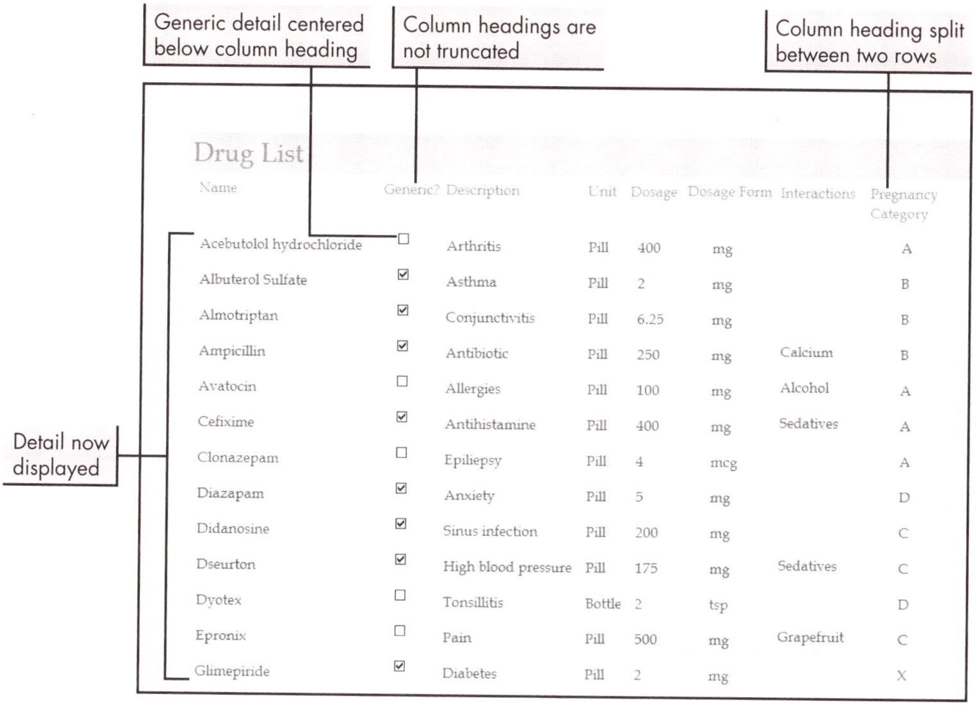

Generic detail centered below column heading

Column headings are not truncated

Column heading split between two rows

Detail now displayed

Drug List

Name	Generic?	Description	Unit	Dosage	Dosage Form	Interactions	Pregnancy Category
Acebutolol hydrochloride	☐	Arthritis	Pill	400	mg		A
Albuterol Sulfate	☑	Asthma	Pill	2	mg		B
Almotriptan	☑	Conjunctivitis	Pill	6.25	mg		B
Ampicillin	☑	Antibiotic	Pill	250	mg	Calcium	B
Avatocin	☐	Allergies	Pill	100	mg	Alcohol	A
Cefixime	☑	Antihistamine	Pill	400	mg	Sedatives	A
Clonazepam	☐	Epilepsy	Pill	4	mcg		A
Diazapam	☑	Anxiety	Pill	5	mg		D
Didanosine	☑	Sinus infection	Pill	200	mg		C
Dseurton	☑	High blood pressure	Pill	175	mg	Sedatives	C
Dyotex	☐	Tonsillitis	Bottle	2	tsp		D
Epronix	☐	Pain	Pill	500	mg	Grapefruit	C
Glimepiride	☑	Diabetes	Pill	2	mg		X

5

Level 1

Best Practice

Modifying the Format of a Report

As you work in Layout view or Design view to modify a report, keep the following suggestions in mind to enhance the format of the report:

- Decrease the left and right margins and widen the report in Print Preview using the Page Setup dialog box.
- Start modifying the layout by adjusting the rightmost label and text box. If they are readable, move both to align them with the new right margin.
- Modify the next label and text box as necessary and move them to the right.
- Continue to move labels and their text boxes to the right, making use of Print Preview and the Undo button to check and reverse your changes as necessary.
- If the report does not provide enough room for the labels in the Page Header section, click between two words in a label. Hold down the Shift key, and then press the Enter key to split the text into two lines. Increase the height of the Page Header section to accommodate the two lines.
- If your report has horizontal lines, they might need to be manually widened (or shortened) if you adjust the layout of the other controls. Shift+click the lines of the report to select them and then drag a selection handle to increase their length. If it is difficult to select the lines, press the Ctrl+A keys to select all the controls on the report, and then click to deselect all but the lines.
- If the labels and text boxes do not fit in portrait orientation, use the Page Setup dialog box to change the orientation to Landscape.

Moving Detail Fields to Multiple Lines on a Report

Because the rptDrugList report is designed for customers, Elaine wants to make sure it is easy to read, especially for the elderly customers. She decides to move some of the fields to a second detail line to improve spacing and to change the font for the drug names.

She increases the length of the Detail section to make room for a second row of text by dragging the Page Footer section bar down about another inch. Then she moves Dosage, Unit, and Dosage Form fields in the Detail section under the Name field. These are commonly associated with drugs, so she deletes their labels in the Page Header section. She adjusts the size and font of the Name field to make it easier to read in the field report properties, and then adds space in the Detail section to separate each drug for readability. Rachel also moves individual labels using Ctrl plus the arrow keys to make slight movement changes. See Figure 5.15.

Figure 5.15: Revising report and graphics

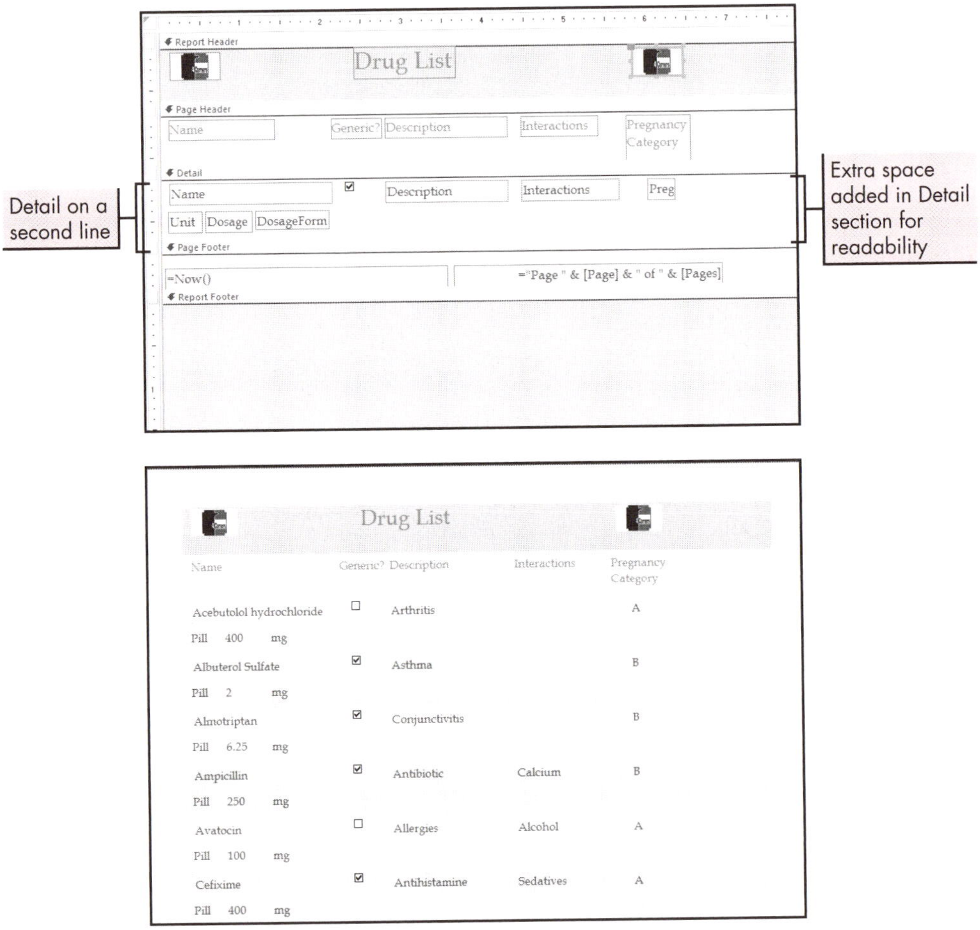

5
Level 1

How To

Move Detail Fields to Make More Space

1. In Design view, make room for additional lines in the Detail section.
2. Drag the text box for a field below another text box. For example, you could list a name on one line, move the address to a second line, and city, state, and ZIP to a third line. This is such a familiar format that column names are not necessary.
3. Delete the labels associated with the text boxes you moved.
4. Select the remaining labels and text boxes on the first two lines, and then move or resize them all at the same time.
5. Click the ARRANGE tab on the Ribbon and then click an alignment option as necessary to align the labels and text boxes vertically and horizontally.
6. Switch between Design or Layout view and Print Preview to check your work, making adjustments as necessary.

Elaine centers the report title and shows rptDrugList to Paul Ferrino, who suggests she include the pharmacy logo at the top of the report. He gives her a copy of the logo in an electronic file named 4Corners.jpg, and Elaine uses the Logo button on the DESIGN tab to add the pharmacy's logo. To add another logo on the other side of the report title, she copies and pastes the logo and drags it to the right side of the report title.

How To

Add a Picture to a Report

1. Save the picture or image you want to use in an electronic file on your system (preferably in the same folder where the database is located).
2. In Design view, click the Logo button on the DESIGN tab of the Ribbon. The Insert Picture dialog box opens.
3. Navigate to where you stored the picture file, and then double-click the file. Access inserts the picture in the report.
4. If necessary, move the image to your desired location and resize it by dragging a corner handle. Using the corner handles maintains the proportions of the image.
5. To change the properties of the image, double-click the image. For example, change the Size Mode property to Zoom to display the entire image.

Applying Themes to Reports

Elaine recalls the custom format that Rachel created to standardize the look of all 4Corners Pharmacy forms using the Corners theme. Although Rachel standardized the forms to create a consistent user interface, Elaine could standardize the reports to create consistency in the material the pharmacy prints. Employees could then save time when developing new reports, and customers would associate a particular report format with 4Corners Pharmacy, increasing customer recognition. When Paul Ferrino shares accounting and other management reports with his banker and other investors, he will also appreciate having a set of reports with a uniform design. Elaine meets with Rachel to determine how the forms were designed and then she implements these features into the reports.

First, Elaine will add theme colors to the background and theme font colors, so that Access knows where the theme formats should be applied. Elaine switches to Design view, saves her changes to rptDrugList. She clicks on the Report Header bar and then clicks the FORMAT tab. In the Control Formatting group, she clicks Shape Fill button arrow to display the Shape Fill gallery as shown in Figure 5.16.

Figure 5.16 Shape Fill gallery

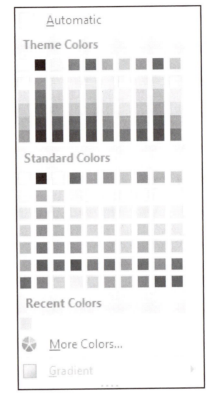

She selects Maroon 2 for the Report Header. Then, she clicks the Detail bar and applies the Maroon 4 color. Elaine decides to change the font colors. She selects the title label, clicks the FORMAT tab and then clicks the Font Color button arrow in the Font group to display the Font Color gallery. This gallery also shows groups of font colors. The Theme Colors are located at the top of the gallery and Standard Colors are displayed in the next section. Recently selected colors are shown at the bottom. She chooses the theme color Black, Text 1. She then selects all the labels in the Page Header section by placing the pointer in the ruler area to the left of the Page Header labels. When the pointer becomes an arrow that points to the right 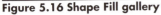, she clicks to select all of the Page Header labels at one time. Elaine applies the same theme color to these labels. She then applies this same font color to the Detail and Page Footer sections.

Now that the theme colors are applied, Access knows where the theme colors should be applied in the report. Elaine selects the DESIGN tab and clicks the Themes button in the Themes group to display the Themes gallery. As she moves her pointer over the different themes, she notices that the theme effects display in the report via Live Preview. She chooses the Corners theme because this is the theme Rachel used in her forms. When Elaine clicks the Themes button again, she notices that the theme she selected is now showing at the top of the Themes gallery in the In this Database section, as shown in Figure 5.17.

Figure 5.17 Themes gallery in the In this Database section

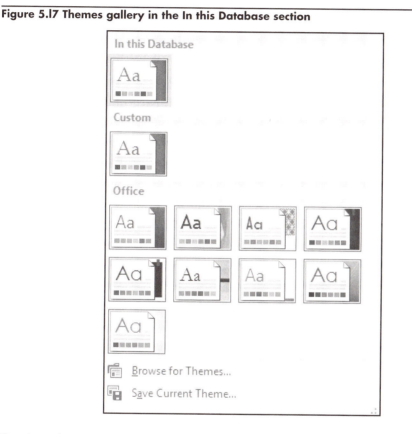

She views the report in Print Preview and notices that the right side of the report is wider than the left. She clicks the Page Setup button in the Page Layout group on the PRINT PREVIEW tab, clicks the Columns tab, and changes the column width to 6. Next, she clicks the Print Options tab and changes the left margin to 1.25. She clicks the OK button to close the Page Setup dialog box and then clicks the Close Print Preview button. Elaine saves the changes and then views her completed report, as shown in Figure 5.18.

Figure 5.18: Completed report rptDrugList displayed in Report view

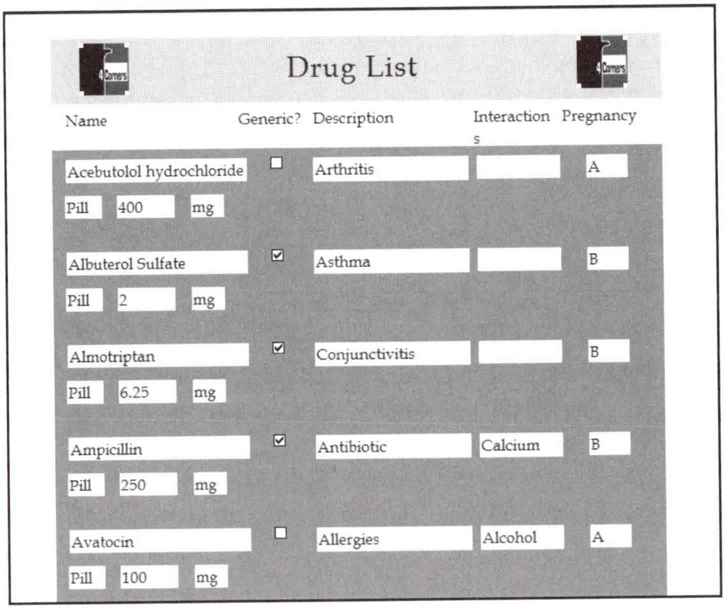

Apply Themes and Colors to Reports

1. Display the report in Design view.
2. Click the DESIGN tab on the Ribbon, click the Themes button in the Themes group, and then select the theme you want to apply to your report.
3. Select the Report Header section, click the FORMAT tab on the Ribbon, click the Shape Fill button in the Control Formatting group, and choose a shape fill color from the Theme Colors.
4. Select the title control in the report header, click the Font Color button arrow in the Font group, and choose a font color from the Theme Colors.
5. Select the labels in the Detail section, click the Font Color button arrow, and choose a font color from the Theme Colors.

Elaine is now confident that she will be able to apply formats and use the Corners theme for future reports. She now needs to create two other basic reports. The first one is an alphabetical phone list of all employees' last and first names with phone and cell numbers, which she creates using the Report Wizard, naming the report rptEmployeePhoneList and applying the theme formats. She also creates a report that shows the number of days that each health plan allows for each prescription refill. She creates this report using the Report Wizard, basing it on tblHealthPlan, and names the report rptRefillDays.

Finally, Elaine needs to create an accounts receivable report that identifies customers who have not paid in full for their prescriptions. These customers have a value in the Balance field in tblCustomer that is greater than zero. To produce this report, Elaine first creates a query called qryBalance that includes only the CustID, CustFirst, CustLast, and Balance fields from tblCustomer and enters ">0" as the criterion for the Balance field. Then she uses the Report Wizard to create a report named rptBalance based on qryBalance with the records sorted in descending order on the Balance field. She makes this report consistent with the others by applying the formats and theme.

Creating a Grouped Report Using a Single Table

Now that Elaine has created a number of basic reports, she can concentrate on other reports. The pharmacy has not yet created a database for inventory, so the technicians take a physical count of drugs on a monthly basis. They have asked Elaine to create a report that would help them with this task and facilitate ordering drugs as needed. She decides to create a report that lists each supplier and then all the drugs alphabetically for that supplier. She plans to leave a space for the technicians to write their physical count quantity for each drug on the report.

All of the drug information she needs is contained in tblDrug, as was the information for rptDrugList. However, this time she wants to arrange the data so that each supplier is listed once along with the drugs they supply. She could create a basic report based on tblDrug using the Report Wizard again and then sort the data first by supplier and then by drug name. However, this approach could create a cluttered report, and Elaine wants to find a way to organize the data but make the report easy to read.

Instead of sorting the report on two fields, Elaine can create a **grouped report**, which groups records based on the values in one or more fields. For example, to view all the drugs provided by a particular supplier, Elaine can group tblDrug records on the values in the Supplier field. See Figure 5.19.

5

Level 1

Figure 5.19: Using the Report Wizard to create a grouped report

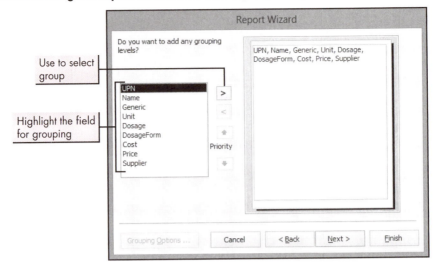

Although this report might contain the same fields and values as in a standard tabular report, grouping the records makes the report more informative—she can then skim the report to find the drugs provided by a supplier. The other advantage of grouped reports is that they can calculate totals and other values for each group. For example, Elaine can calculate the number of different drugs provided by one supplier.

You can create a grouped report by using the Report Wizard to group records at the same time you create the report. You can also group records after you create a report by using the Group & Sort button in the Grouping & Totals group on the DESIGN tab. The Group, Sort, and Total Panel appears at the bottom of the report. The Report Wizard only allows four grouping levels, but when working in Design view, you can create up to 10 grouping levels. For example, you could produce a report of doctors grouped first by their clinic and then by their specialty. To set up such a grouped report, you would assign the Clinic field to group level 1 and the Specialty field to group level 2. In other words, when you group on more than one field, the group level determines how the groups are nested.

To produce a drug physical count report, Elaine decides to create a grouped report using the Report Wizard. She bases the report on tblDrug, and selects the UPN, Name, Generic, Unit, Dosage, DosageForm, Cost, Price, and Supplier fields. By choosing to group by Supplier, all the drugs provided by a supplier will be listed under that supplier's name, as shown in Figure 5.20. She sorts each group on Name and selects Stepped as the Layout type. See Figure 5.21. She then applies the Corners theme and names the report rptPhysicalCount.

Figure 5.20: Report grouped by Supplier

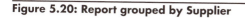

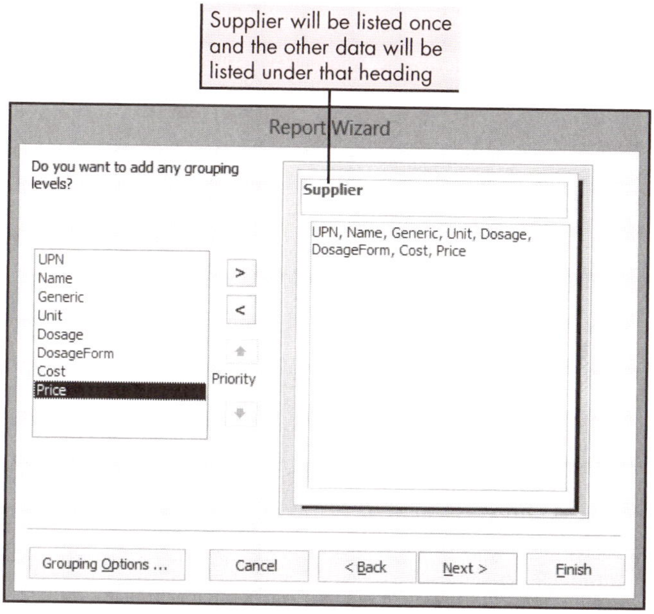

Figure 5.21: Choosing Stepped as the Layout type

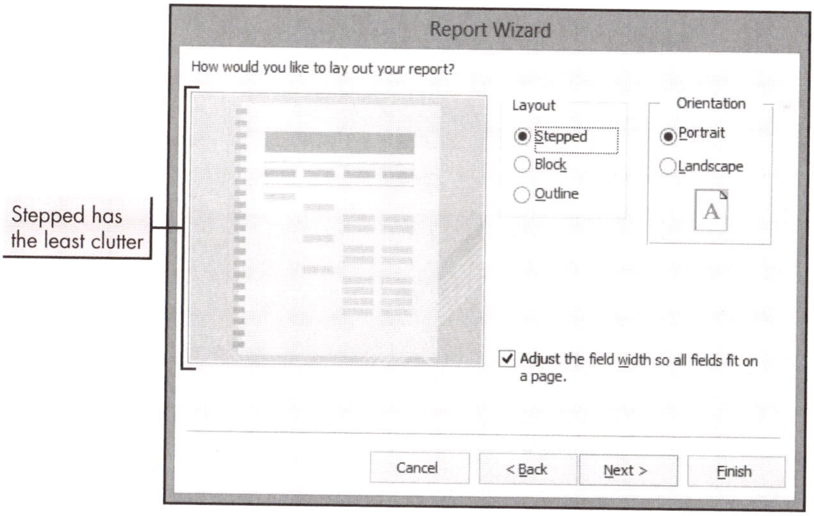

Elaine modifies the report to meet the standards she adopted and to add the unbound label control for the physical count. She uses the Line button on the DESIGN tab to draw a line that indicates where the technicians should write their inventory count. She also changes the report caption and title to Physical Count. Figure 5.22 shows the finished report in Design view and Print Preview. Elaine notes that the only difference between a simple tabular report and one with grouping is the way the data is organized.

Figure 5.22: The Physical Count report in Design view and Print Preview

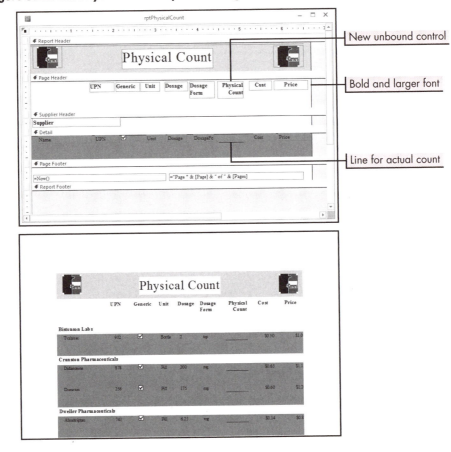

New unbound control

Bold and larger font

Line for actual count

Formatting Groups of Alphabetic Listings

Long alphabetic listings in a report can be difficult to read. You can break up a listing into subgroups based on up to five letters of the initial word in the field. For example, in the report rptPhysicalCount, you could group on the first letter and then on Supplier. To do so using the Report Wizard, click the Grouping Options button in the second dialog box in the wizard. The Grouping Intervals dialog box opens. Click the Grouping intervals list arrow, and change the setting from Normal to 1st Letter. See Figure 5.23. You can also sort codes that are part alphabetic and part numeric using the grouping options in the Grouping Intervals dialog box.

Figure 5.23: Modifying grouping options

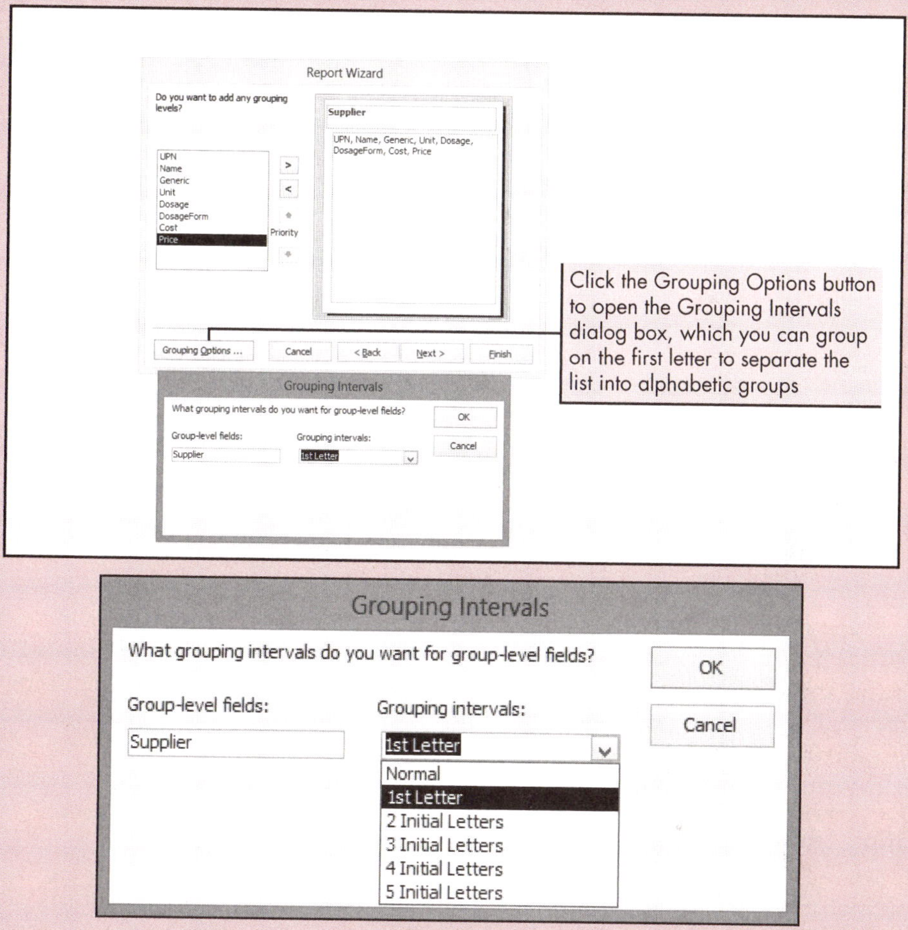

Click the Grouping Options button to open the Grouping Intervals dialog box, which you can group on the first letter to separate the list into alphabetic groups

In the finished report, Access inserts an "A" before all the group names that start with A, a "B" before all the group names that start with B, and so on, as shown in Figure 5.24.

Figure 5.24: Suppliers grouped by first letter and then by supplier

Supplier	UPN	Name	Generic?	Unit	Dosage	Cost	Price
Physical Count							
B							
Bistonson Labs	932	Tvalaxec	☑	Bottle	2	$0.50	$1.00
C							
Cranston Pharmaceuticals	256	Dseurton	☑	Pill	175	$0.60	$1.20
Cranston Pharmaceuticals	878	Didanosine	☑	Pill	200	$0.65	$1.12
D							
Dweller Pharmaceuticals	741	Almotriptan	☑	Pill	6.25	$0.14	$0.87
E							
Esterman Pharmaceuticals	452	Diazapam	☑	Pill	5	$0.45	$1.12
Esterman Pharmaceuticals	566	Quentix	☑	Pill	50	$0.50	$1.25
F							
Frankmeir Pharmaceuticals	311	Dyotex	☐	Bottle	2	$0.25	$1.05
G							
Gilman Labs	642	Montelukast sodium	☑	Pill	10	$0.32	$0.90
Gilman Labs	987	Rizatriptan Benzoate	☐	Pill	6	$0.47	$1.10

Next, Elaine needs to prepare mailing labels for the pharmacy. She occasionally needs to send tax forms to employees, and Maria also mails material to employees. Instead of re-creating the employee name and addresses in a word-processing program and using a mail merge, Elaine can extract this information already stored in tblEmployee and develop a report formatted for mailing labels.

Creating Labels Using the Label Wizard

As you probably know, blank mailing labels are available in dozens of stock formats with or without adhesive backing and they can be used for such diverse applications as rotary cards, calling cards, shipping labels, name tags, and file folder labels. A typical mailing label looks like this:

```
Name
Address
City, State ZIP
```

If you store name and address information in an Access database, you can create a simple report that is formatted to look like a mailing label. The report extracts the address data from the table or query that stores the addresses, and organizes it to print a label for each address in the record source. The simplest way to create mailing labels is to use the Label Wizard. As with other types of reports, you can customize the mailing labels using Design view, changing the font, color, and layout of the label text, for example.

When you use the Label Wizard, you specify the record source for the mailing label report, and then select the type of label on which you want to print mailing information.

The Label Wizard lists the most common mailing label formats. One prominent label manufacturer is Avery Dennison. They developed a numbering system for each of their labels that other companies in the United States often note as an equivalent for their products. The Label Wizard includes hundreds of sizes and styles, as well as many of the common product numbers from Avery Dennison and prominent overseas manufacturers. When you specify label size, you have the option of using the English system of inches or the Metric system for all measurements. You can also choose labels that are sheet fed (common today on laser and ink-jet printers) or continuous (common on "tractor-fed" printers that are often used for printing small quantities of labels at a time). If you need to use a label that is not included in the Label Wizard, you can also create a custom label of any size. Create a custom label when you want to print names and addresses directly on an envelope. Table 5.8 summarizes examples of label numbers, sizes and their usage.

Table 5.8: Examples of label sizes and uses

Number	Common Usage	Width in Inches
Clip Badge	Insert for clip-on name badge	2 1/4 × 3 1/2
5160	White permanent laser labels, 30 per sheet, used for most bulk mailings in the United States	1 × 2 5/8
5824	CD label	2 per sheet
5385	Rotary cards for Rolodex card holders	2 1/6 × 4
5889	Postcards for color laser printers	4 × 6

© 2014 Cengage Learning

Elaine needs mailing labels for all employees so she and other 4Corners managers can send out occasional mailings. She selects tblEmployee in the Navigation pane, clicks the CREATE tab, and then clicks the Labels button in the Reports group to start the Label Wizard. She chooses the Avery 5160 sheet feed type because the pharmacy has these in stock. This label stock is the most common for bulk mailings because it contains 30 labels per sheet—more than most other label stock. See Figure 5.25.

Figure 5.25: Selecting the label size in the Label Wizard

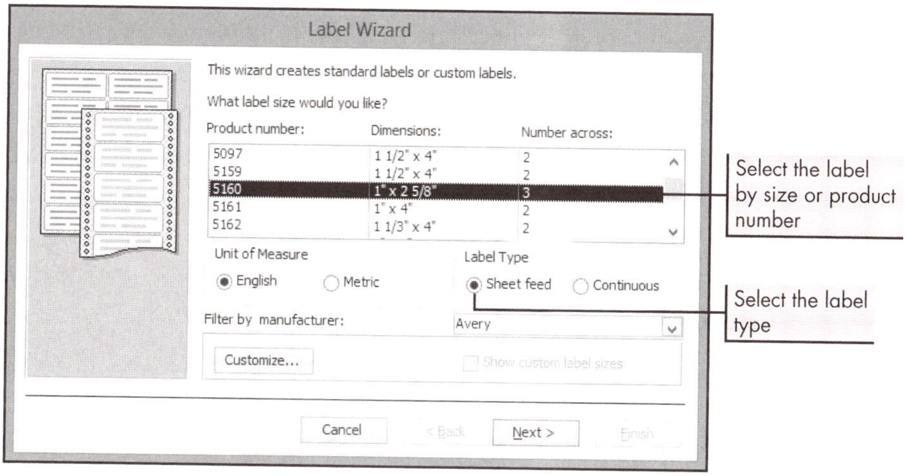

When you preview or print Avery 5160 labels, an error message often appears indicating that some data might not be displayed. If you don't change the font, you should be able to print all of the text on the labels without modifying the label report, so you can ignore this message. Level 2 explains how to modify the label properties to avoid this message.

Next, Elaine selects the font and font weight for the label text. Although it is tempting to increase the font size to improve readability, the label stock they have won't show the entire name and address if the font is too big. She changes the font weight to Medium. See Figure 5.26.

Figure 5.26: Label text and appearance selection

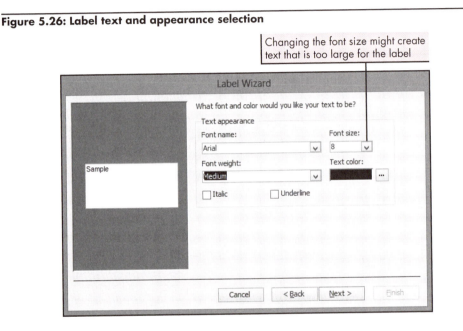

The Label Wizard lets you build a prototype of the label by selecting the necessary fields one at a time. Elaine selects the first name and then inserts a space before selecting the last name. Then she presses the Enter key to move to the next line. She selects the address and then presses Enter again. The last line of the label has city, state, and ZIP information. She inserts one space between each of these. See Figure 5.27.

Figure 5.27: Label prototype

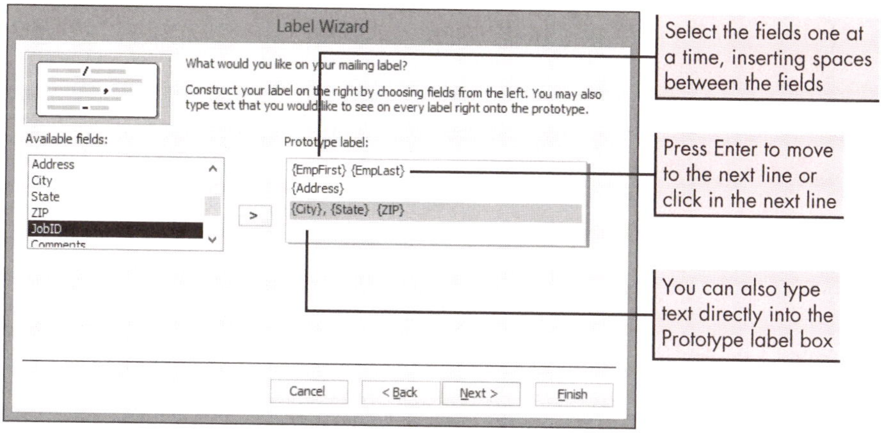
Label Wizard
What would you like on your mailing label?
Construct your label on the right by choosing fields from the left. You may also type text that you would like to see on every label right onto the prototype.
Available fields:
Address
City
State
ZIP
JobID
Prototype label:
{EmpFirst} {EmpLast}
{Address}
{City}, {State} {ZIP}
Cancel
< Back
Next >
Finish
Select the fields one at a time, inserting spaces between the fields
Press Enter to move to the next line or click in the next line
You can also type text directly into the Prototype label box

Next, Elaine specifies the sort order for the labels. She sorts on last name and then first name to organize the labels logically, and names the report rptEmpLabels. Figure 5.28 shows the final result.

Figure 5.28: rptEmpLabels in Print Preview

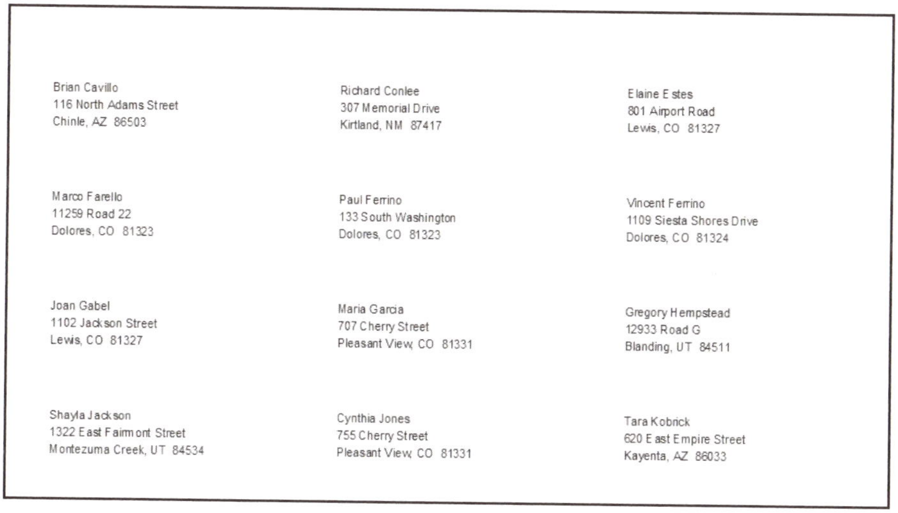
Brian Cavillo
116 North Adams Street
Chinle, AZ 86503
Richard Conlee
307 Memorial Drive
Kirtland, NM 87417
Elaine Estes
801 Airport Road
Lewis, CO 81327
Marco Farello
11259 Road 22
Dolores, CO 81323
Paul Ferrino
133 South Washington
Dolores, CO 81323
Vincent Ferrino
1109 Siesta Shores Drive
Dolores, CO 81324
Joan Gabel
1102 Jackson Street
Lewis, CO 81327
Maria Garcia
707 Cherry Street
Pleasant View, CO 81331
Gregory Hempstead
12933 Road G
Blanding, UT 84511
Shayla Jackson
1322 East Fairmont Street
Montezuma Creek, UT 84534
Cynthia Jones
755 Cherry Street
Pleasant View, CO 81331
Tara Kobrick
620 East Empire Street
Kayenta, AZ 86033

How To

Create a Label Using the Label Wizard

1. In the Navigation pane, click the table containing the data for the labels.
2. Click the CREATE tab and then click the Labels button. The first dialog box in the Label Wizard opens, asking what label size you want to use.
3. Scroll the list to select the appropriate label by product number and size. If necessary, click the Filter by manufacturer list arrow to show product numbers and sizes for other manufacturers such as HP, for example.
4. Click the Sheet feed or Continuous option button as appropriate. Click the Next button.
5. Select the font name, size, and weight for the label text. Note that the default Font weight is set to Light. You might want to change this to Medium for readability. Increasing the font size or changing fonts might affect the amount of information you can fit on a label. Click the Next button.
6. The next wizard dialog box asks what you want to include on the label. In the Available fields list box, click the field you want to display on the label, such as FirstName, and then click the select single field button to add the field to the prototype label. Continue to construct the label by adding fields to the prototype label. Press the Enter key to move to a new line. Insert spaces, additional text, commas, and other punctuation on the label manually. Click the Next button.
7. Select one or more fields on which you want to sort the labels. Sort the labels alphabetically (for first class mail) or by ZIP code (if you have enough to meet postal requirements for bulk mail). Click the Next button.
8. Enter a name for the label report, using the "rpt" prefix. Click the Finish button.
9. If you see an error message about the width of the labels, check your data to make sure it all appears.

Best Practice

Testing Mailing Labels Before Printing

Most mailing labels print on stock paper without any problems, but it is possible to have **print registration errors**, which affect the print alignment when you print many labels. The printing may "creep" so that the text in the second row of labels is lower than the text in the first row of labels. By the end of the page, the labels might be totally out of position on the stock. This is particularly common if you custom design a label, modify the font size, or add lines to a label in Design view and have not calculated exactly how wide and how high each label should be. If you have a large quantity of labels to print, be sure to check for possible problems before wasting label stock. Consider the following suggestions:

- Print the labels on regular paper first to make sure they are printing properly.
- Print only a section of the labels at a time. For example, use the Print dialog box to print pages 1–10, then 11–20, and so on. If there are any problems, you will only waste a few sheets of label stock.

Before creating the labels, Elaine creates a query named qryEmpTitle that includes the EmpFirst and EmpLast fields from tblEmployee and Title field from tblJobTitle. Then she uses the Label Wizard to create name tags for all employees that they can wear as a badge. She bases the name tag report on qryEmpTitle, and selects the Clip Badge product number. She centers the name on one line and formats the labels using a 20-point, semi-bold font so that the text is large enough for elderly customers to read. She also formats the job title using a 16-point, semi-bold font. She changes the text alignment to Center for both lines, and then saves the report as rptBadge.

Now that she is finished creating basic reports for 4Corners Pharmacy, Elaine is ready to create more sophisticated management reports.

Steps To Success: Level 1

Marie Cresson is the store manager of Hudson Bay Pharmacy, and needs to produce information stored in the Hudson database for customers and managers. She asks for your help in creating the reports shown in Table 5.9.

Table 5.9: Basic reports for Hudson Bay Pharmacy

Category	Reports Needed
Customer relations	• Directory of drugs, including possible interactions
Daily operations	• List of health plans and the number of days allowed in each refill
Human resource management	• List of classes approved by the pharmacy for reimbursement • Alphabetical phone list of employees • Mailing labels for employees • Name tags for employees
Management decision support and long-range planning	• Physical count report • Outstanding credit balances

© 2014 Cengage Learning

As you save the new reports, be certain to use the name specified in the following steps, including the "rpt" prefix. Also consult your instructor for instructions about submitting your results.

Complete the following:

1. Start Access and open the **Hudson.accdb** database from the STS folder.

2. Marie wants to create a report for Hudson Bay customers that provides an alphabetical list of drugs, including information such as whether each drug is a generic drug or if it interacts with other drugs such as sedatives or alcohol. However, she doesn't want to list the DIN (an internal drug ID), the selling price, the cost (to the pharmacy) of each drug, the fee (dispensing fee), or the name of the supplier. Create a report that lists all drug information except information that is not appropriate for customers. Use the Hudson Bay Pharmacy logo, which is stored in the **HudsonBay.jpg** file in the Chapter 5\Level 1 STS folder. Save the report as **rptDrugList**.

3. Modify rptDrugList to improve its readability and enhance its appearance according to accepted standards for reports. Add colors to the Report Header and Detail section and apply a theme.

4. Next, Marie needs to create a report for the pharmacists and technicians, which they call a daily operations report. This report shows the number of days a health plan allows for each prescription refill. Apply the theme and name this report **rptRefillDays**. Revise the report title, column headings, and fields as necessary to improve the format of the report.

5. Marie mentions that Kim Siemers, the Human Resources manager, needs a human resources report that shows all classes for which Hudson Bay Pharmacy will reimburse employee costs. Create this report for Kim, naming it **rptClassList**.

6. Modify rptClassList by applying the Hudson Bay Pharmacy theme and revising the report title, column headings, and fields necessary to improve the format of the report.

7. Marie also notes that Kim needs a human resources report that provides an alphabetical phone list for all employees. Name the report **rptEmployeePhoneList**. Select fields that clearly identify the employee and provide all their phone numbers.

8. Modify rptEmployeePhoneList to conform to accepted report standards, resizing and moving fields as necessary.

9. Next, Marie needs an accounting report to track customers who have a balance due amount in their accounts. Create a query to provide this information, saving the query as **qryBalance**. Create a management report based on this query that lists the balance due amount in descending order. Name this report **rptBalance**.

10. Marie meets with the pharmacy technicians, who request a drug physical count report. Create a physical count report that lists drugs in alphabetical order by their supplier. Save the report as **rptDrugSupplier**.

11. Marie has two more requests for basic reports. First, she needs mailing labels for employees. Create this mailing label report, using the Avery 5160 label type and name it **rptEmpLabels**.

12. Finally, create name tags for all employees that they can wear as a badge. Name the report **rptBadge**. Be sure the text is large and dark enough for elderly customers to read.

13. Close the **Hudson.accdb** database and then close Access.

LEVEL 2

Developing Management Reports to Support Decision Making

Creating Custom Reports

Elaine distributed the basic reports she created to the other managers at 4Corners Pharmacy, and they have already started to use them for customer relations, daily operations, human resources, and accounting. They also discussed other reports they need to support these functional areas. Table 5.10 lists their requests for additional reports and improvements to existing reports.

Table 5.10: Additional reports suggested for the pharmacy

Category	Reports Needed
Customer relations	• On-demand report showing drug purchases during particular time periods for insurance reporting • Mailing labels for a health and wellness newsletter and coupons to send to each household • Coupons for customers with no recent refill activity • Drug refill list for all customers
Management decision support and long-range planning	• Monthly sales report

© 2014 Cengage Learning

As Elaine reviews this list, she realizes that the requested reports are more complex than the first set of basic reports she created. For example, to create the customer relations report that lists drug purchases during a given period, she must find a way that users can specify which time period they want. To produce the mailing labels for the newsletters and coupons sent to each household, she must select some fields from tblCustomer and some from tblHousehold, and then select name and address information only for customers who are heads of households. To produce these results, Elaine must create **custom reports**, which are reports that require data from more than one table, have calculated fields, use summary statistics, or require parameter input at the time the report is run. Some may require more layout modification in Design view as well.

Creating a Report Using Fields from Multiple Tables

Many of the reports that Elaine wants to create require fields from more than one table. You can use the Report Wizard to select a table and some or all of its fields in the first wizard dialog box, and then select a different table to add other fields. However, if you want to limit the records included in the report or use parameter values for the user to supply when the report is run, you need to base the report on a query.

Elaine decides to start with the mailing labels for the quarterly health and wellness newsletter, which she wants to send to all households. Regular contact with customers is a good way to have them think of the pharmacy when they need prescriptions filled. Fields to create the mailing labels for customers come from tblCustomer and tblHousehold. Because the Label Wizard allows the use of fields from one table only, she must retrieve the data for this report using a query.

Elaine can specify one mailing per household because of the one-to-many relationship between HouseID in the two tables. By limiting the data to only those designated as head of household, each household will receive only one mailing. Elaine first creates the query in Design view by selecting the CustFirst, CustLast, and HeadHH fields from tblCustomer and the HouseID, Address, City, State, and ZIP fields from tblHousehold. HeadHH is a Yes/No field, so the criterion is "Yes" to limit the query results to heads of household. She saves the query as qryHeadHHOnly. See Figure 5.29.

Figure 5.29: qryHeadHHOnly in Design view

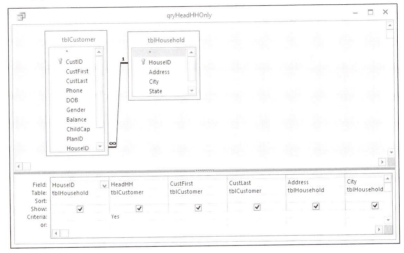

When Elaine starts the Label Wizard, she uses qryHeadHHOnly as the basis for the mailing labels, selecting only the CustFirst, CustLast, Address, City, State, and ZIP fields to appear on the labels, and selects the Avery 5160 product number. Given the large number of customers, Elaine sorts the labels by ZIP code to take advantage of any bulk mail cost savings. She names the labels report rptHeadHHOnly. She can also use this report to create mailing labels for the special promotion coupons she wants to send to all households. Figure 5.30 shows the mailing labels in Design view.

Figure 5.30: Design view of mailing labels

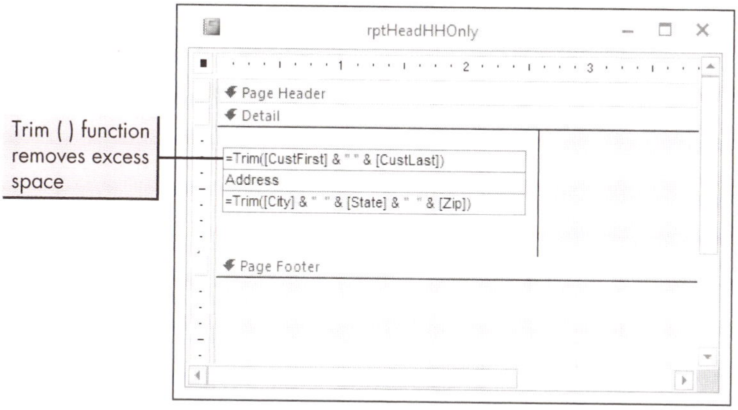

Trim ( ) function removes excess space

Naming Queries Used as the Basis for Reports

If you require a query for a report, it is a good idea to use the same name for both the query and the report, while varying the "qry" or "rpt" prefix as appropriate. You will know the query is the basis for the report and will be less likely to delete the query.

When Elaine runs the report, she sees an error message, indicating that some data may not be displayed, and that there is not enough horizontal space on the page for the labels. This is a common error message when printing mailing labels. Before modifying the columns, Elaine previews the data to discover if any data falls outside the printing area.

It seems that the labels will print correctly, but Elaine decides to modify the labels so that pharmacy employees printing the labels do not receive the same error message each time they print.

Resolving Error Messages in Mailing Labels

Even when using standard mailing label layouts and fonts, you may see an error message when previewing or printing mailing labels. Before modifying column widths, check to see if all the data in the labels is printing. In many cases, no modification is necessary. Especially when using Avery 5160-compatible label stock, the Label Wizard page layout settings require a page width of 8.625 inches—more than the standard 8.5-inch standard paper size. Because this is such a common stock for mailing labels, and because your users may not want to see an error every time they print the labels, you might want to modify the width of the labels to eliminate the message.

How To

Respond to an Avery 5160-compatible Error Message

1. Open the mailing label report in Design view.
2. Hold down Shift while you click to select all the text boxes.
3. Move all text boxes one grid dot to the left.
4. Switch to Print Preview and change the left and right report margins to .25 inches and the column width to 2.583 inches. After you change the column width, you may see the column width reset itself to 2.5826.

Next, Elaine focuses on another customer relations report. Depending on their health plan, customers may need to submit a list of all prescriptions for reimbursement. Elaine wants to create a report that allows a customer to specify a time period, and then generate a list of prescriptions received during that period. Because a technician will print this report for a single customer at a time, the technicians must be able to specify the customer number and the time period before they produce the report. How can Elaine prompt the technicians to enter a customer number before they open and print the report?

Elaine recalls that parameter queries allow user input—when you run a parameter query, it displays a dialog box requesting information to be used as criteria for retrieving records. If Elaine bases the customer relations report on a parameter query, it will stop to wait for user input for each parameter requested, such as the customer number. Elaine creates the query using fields from the tblCustomer, tblRx, tblRefill, tblHealthPlan, and tblDrug tables. She also calculates the total cost of each prescription by multiplying the Quantity, Price, and Days fields. See Figure 5.31.

Figure 5.31: Query to calculate on-demand customer drug purchases

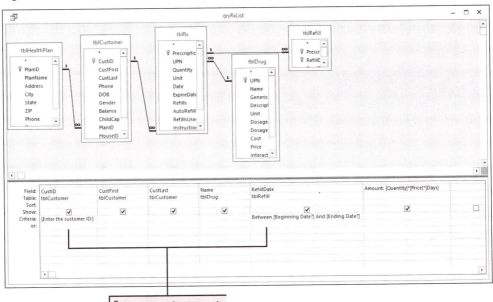

Enter parameter prompts in these two fields

In the Criteria row of the CustID field, she enters the parameter [Enter the customer ID:], and in the RefillDate field, she enters the parameter "Between [Beginning Date?] And [Ending Date?]." By doing so, Access will display three dialog boxes requesting a customer number and date range. She saves the query as qryRxList, and bases a new report on this query, naming it rptRxList. She sorts the report on RefillDate. The finished report lists all prescriptions for a given time period for only one customer, as shown in Figure 5.32.

Figure 5.32: On-demand customer refill report

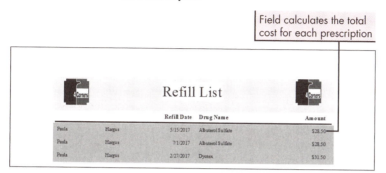

Field calculates the total cost for each prescription

Refill List

		Refill Date	Drug Name	Amount
Paula	Hargus	5/15/2017	Albuterol Sulfate	$28.50
Paula	Hargus	7/1/2017	Albuterol Sulfate	$28.50
Paula	Hargus	2/27/2017	Dyctex	$31.50

Elaine notices that the report contains several fields with repetitious data and decides to group the report so each CustID and name appears only once. She could just start over but decides to add grouping levels in Design view.

Adding or Modifying Grouping Levels to a Report

Custom reports often need to be modified for readability. Repetitious listings of the same field values make it harder to concentrate on the important data in the report. For this reason, you can add a grouping level after creating the original report. The fields that you use to sort data in a report can also serve as grouping fields. If you specify a sort field as a grouping field, you can include a group header and group footer for the group, as you can for any group. A group header typically includes the name of the group, and a group footer typically includes a count or subtotal for records in that group. You use the Group & Sort button on the DESIGN tab to select sort fields and grouping fields for a report. Each report can have up to 10 sort fields, and any of its sort fields can also be grouping fields.

Elaine wants to add a grouping level to her on-demand customer refill report to eliminate the redundant CustID and customer names. She wants to group on CustID because this is the unique field in the query. She clicks the Group & Sort button in the Grouping & Totals group on the DESIGN tab to open the Group, Sort, and Total pane below the report. She clicks the Add a group button in the Group, Sort, and Total pane and selects CustID from the field list. Elaine clicks the second list arrow that appears, then selects from smallest to largest to sort in ascending order. She decides to create a sort by Refill Date, so she clicks the Add a sort button in the Group, Sort, and Total pane. She then selects RefillDate from the field list. By not adding RefillDate as a group, she is only setting the sort order for RefillDate. Figure 5.33 shows the completed group and sort selections.

Figure 5.33: Group, Sort, and Total pane

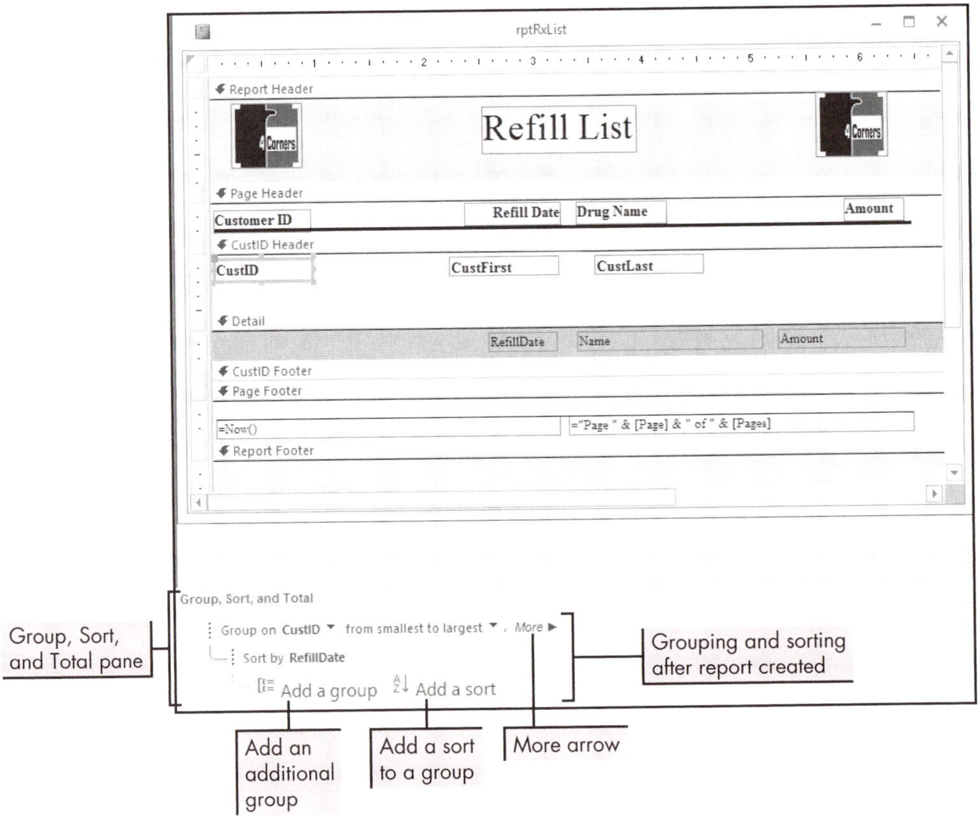

How To

Create a Grouping Level in an Existing Report

1. Open the report in Design view.
2. Click the Group & Sort button on the DESIGN tab to display the Group, Sort, and Total pane.
3. To add a group level, click the Add a group button in the Group, Sort, and Total pane and select a field from the field list. Access displays the fields from the table or query to make your selection easier.
4. To sort the group, click the list arrow, and then select from smallest to largest to sort in ascending order, or from largest to smallest to sort in descending order.
5. To sort on a field under the group, click the Add a sort button in the Group, Sort, and Total pane and select a field from the field list.
6. Click the list arrow next to the sort field displayed in the Group, Sort, and Total pane and select a sort order, such as from oldest to newest.
7. Close the Group, Sort, and Total pane by clicking the close button or clicking the Group & Sort button on the Ribbon.

In Design view for rptRxList, Elaine drags the controls for the CustID, CustFirst, and CustLast fields under the CustID group header so she can display them once before listing all the refills. She modifies the corresponding labels so they have larger fonts. Then she modifies the rest of the controls and adds a line in the Page Header section under the column headings to improve the appearance of the report. She decides to concatenate the customer names so that the first and last names are displayed together. She deletes both CustFirst and CustLast bound controls, creates a new text box control, and then writes the formula for concatenation in the new control: =[CustFirst] & " " & [CustLast]. She changes the property of the new control to match the larger and bold font of CustID. See Figure 5.34.

Figure 5.34: Updated design of the on-demand customer refill report

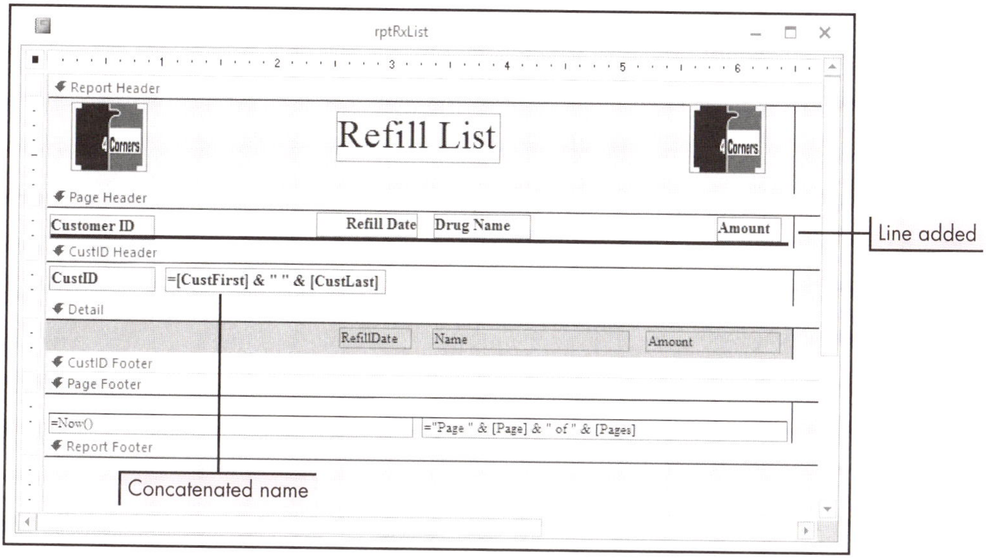

Improving the Information Content of Grouped Reports

Elaine included the **group header** and **group footer** when she created the new grouping level in rptRxList. The group header section is an area on a report used to indicate the start of a new group. Any text or controls located in the group header are shown once for the group. For example, the CustID and customer name located in the group header of rptRxList are only shown once and then the detail about each refill is listed below it in the Detail section. The group footer section is shown only once at the end of any group detail. It can be used to identify the group but it is most often used to contain summary data such as subtotals for the data in the group. Recall that the Report Wizard automatically includes a group header as part of the report if you specify any grouping levels. If you have no information for the group footer, whether you added it as part of a new grouping level or the Report Wizard added it, you can remove it using the Group, Sort, and Total pane. If you want to display a group footer, simply click the More arrow in the Group, Sort, and Total pane and select the footer section arrow until the option with a footer section appears.

Tabular reports that have large amounts of data often contain more information content if the report uses grouping. The groups organize the data into smaller segments that are easier to comprehend. When you use the Report Wizard to create a grouped report, the wizard provides optional summary statistics and percentages to show more information about each group, as well as overall totals for the report.

Elaine wants to add a total for all refills for each customer in rptRxList. Because the report is already created, she wants to add the calculation to the group footer of the report. She recalls that calculated fields are unbound text box controls and that the general format is to use an equal sign followed by the calculation. She opens rptRxList in Design view and adds a text box control in the group footer section of the report. She wants a total, so she types =Sum([Amount]) in the control. Amount was created in an underlying query, so all she needs to do is add up the amounts for each refill. When she checks the report in Print Preview, she notes that the total is not formatted, so she returns to Design view and changes the Format property for the control to Currency. She also changes the label for the control to Refill Total and modifies the report further for best appearance. Figure 5.35 shows the resulting report in Design view and Print Preview.

Figure 5.35: Final rptRxList in Design view and Print Preview

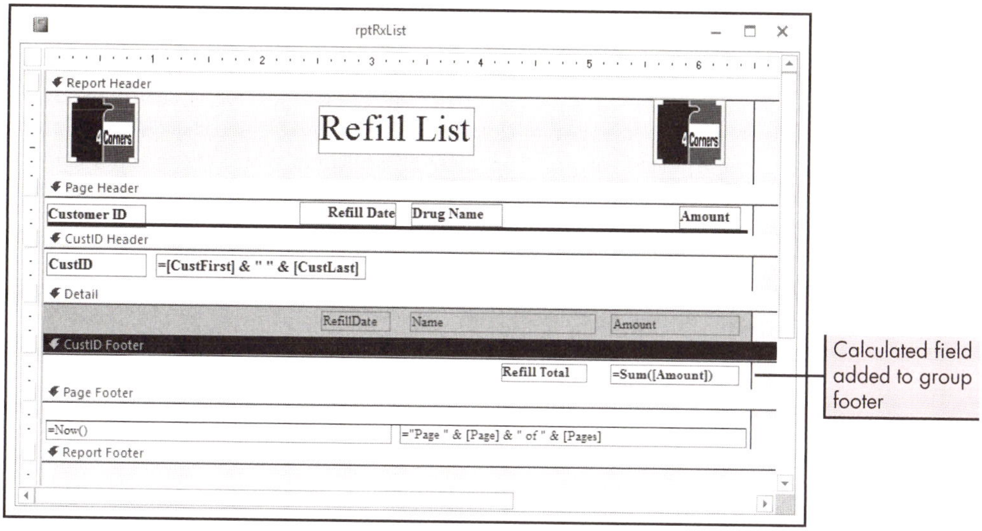

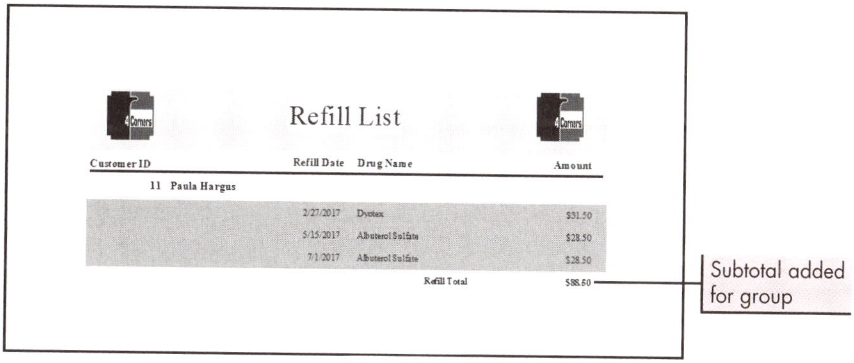

The pharmacy technicians can now use the refill report to show the prescription refills each customer ordered and the total cost of each prescription.

Best Practice

Using Queries to Create Calculated Fields

You can include calculated fields on a report using a text box control. However, most developers recommend creating the calculation in a query and then using the query as the basis for the report. In the query design grid, you can use the Zoom feature to create and modify a calculation and set its format there; Design view for a report does not provide this feature. Using the query design grid is, therefore, preferable for long calculations.

If you do insert a calculated field on a report manually, you can temporarily widen the control or right-click a control, and then click Properties. You can right-click in the field cell and then select Zoom to open a larger window for creating the expression, or click the Build button to open to the Expression Builder dialog box for help in building your expression.

When Elaine shows Paul Ferrino her report for customers showing refills, he becomes interested in seeing the same data—showing all customers in any given time period grouped by year, quarter, and month. He needs to prepare monthly, quarterly, and annual accounting statements for his banker and investors. This report will show the sales values he needs for the income statement. He also wants monthly and quarterly subtotals and a grand total for the period specified. Elaine decides to create a report that will give Paul all of these values by grouping on year, then on quarter, and finally on month. She won't show detail for each refill because Paul doesn't need it.

Best Practice

Understanding That Sometimes Less Is More

It is tempting to print every report showing all the detail. Grouping helps to break the data into subgroups, and summary statistics may help to provide more information content to the user. However, it is often more effective to show only part of the data. Looking at just the top values may help the user to see only what's truly important. For example, a chart showing every drug in inventory, many of which have no sales activity in the time period, is distracting. Looking at only the most-used drugs could be more helpful. Grouped reports also allow the option of printing only summary information using Sum and Avg calculations, for example. A summary report does not show any detail. For long lists of detail, such as all prescription refills for a year, the detail would be overwhelming.

Grouping on Date and Time

Accounting reports are usually prepared for monthly, quarterly, and annual time periods. Accounts receivable and sales values in particular are needed for these time periods, and grouping is a good way to facilitate creating these reports. The Report Wizard has built-in grouping options for Date/Time fields that can use the same date field for multiple time periods.

Because Paul wants to specify the time period in his accounting report, Elaine must first create a query to limit the data. To include the RefillDate and Amount fields, the query uses five tables, because there are no direct relationships between tblRefill, tblRx, and tblHealthPlan, which are the tables that contain the fields necessary for the report and the calculated field. To relate their fields, she must also use intermediate tables—tblCustomer and tblDrug. She adds the calculation for Amount and the parameters to allow Paul to input any dates at the time the report is run. She names the query qrySales. See Figure 5.36.

Figure 5.36: Parameter query to calculate sales and allow input of dates

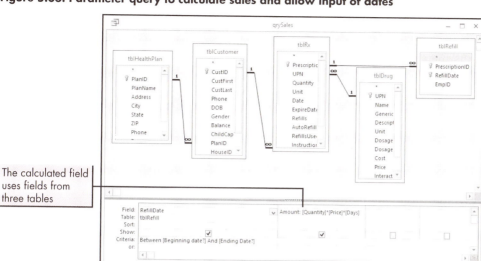

The calculated field uses fields from three tables

Elaine will base the sales report on qrySales. She decides to use the Report Wizard for the basic report because the built-in grouping level options will save her time. She knows she needs three grouping levels dealing with dates, so she selects RefillDate three times as the grouping level. The first level is grouped by Year. The second nested level is grouped by Quarter, and the innermost level is grouped by Month. See Figure 5.37.

Figure 5.37: Three grouping options

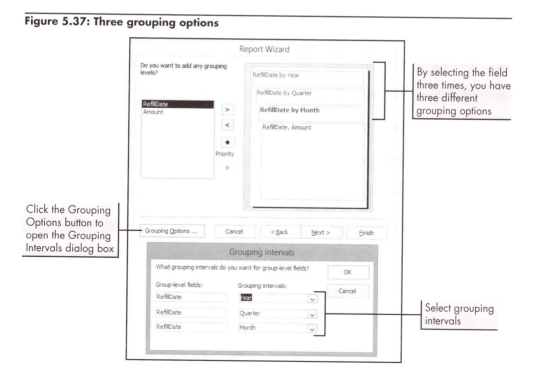

By selecting the field three times, you have three different grouping options

Click the Grouping Options button to open the Grouping Intervals dialog box

Select grouping intervals

Elaine needs sums on the report for each grouping level, so she clicks the Summary Options button. She selects the Sum check box and the Summary Only option button, and checks the Calculate percent of total for sums check box. See Figure 5.38.

Figure 5.38: Specifying summary options

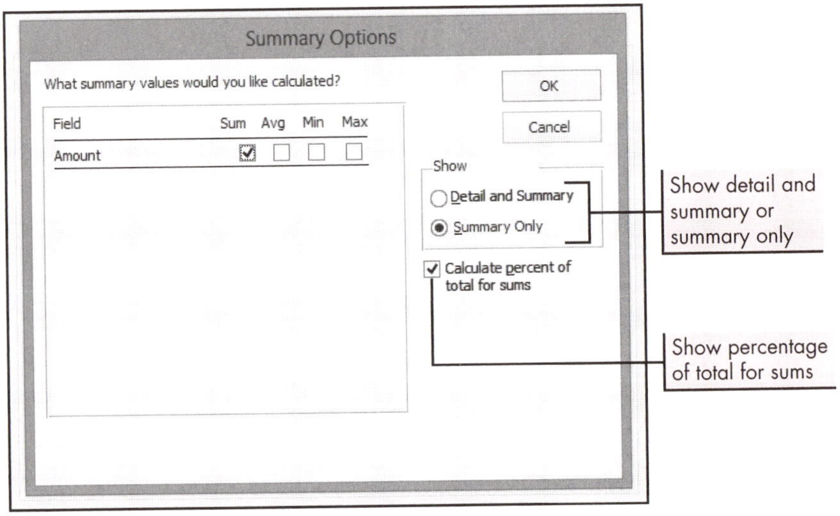

Elaine selects Stepped as the layout to stagger the three grouping levels and saves the report as rptSales.

How To

Group on Multiple Time Periods

1. Start the Report Wizard and select the fields from one or more tables or queries. Then click the Next button.
2. For each time period you want in the report, select the date field as a grouping level. For example, if you want to group on year, quarter, and month, select the date field three times.
3. Click the Grouping Options button to modify the time period for each group level. The first grouping level should be the greatest time period, for example, year.
4. Select the next grouping time period within the greatest time period for the next grouping level. For example, within year, you might select group by quarter and then by month. Note that you can group on year, quarter, month, week, day, hour, and minute. Then click the Next button.
5. Continue the wizard to completion, and then click the Finish button.

Elaine thinks the report looks cluttered and confused, so she follows her checklist and modifies the report until it meets the 4Corners Pharmacy standards. She figures out that she can leave the grouping levels from year to quarter to month the same but, by putting the grouping labels in the group footer for quarter and switching the headings, she can improve the appearance and clarity of the report. She formats the year and report totals for currency and discovers that aligning the results is difficult because the currency format leaves space for parentheses around any negative values. See Figure 5.39.

Figure 5.39: Final sales report in Design view and Print Preview

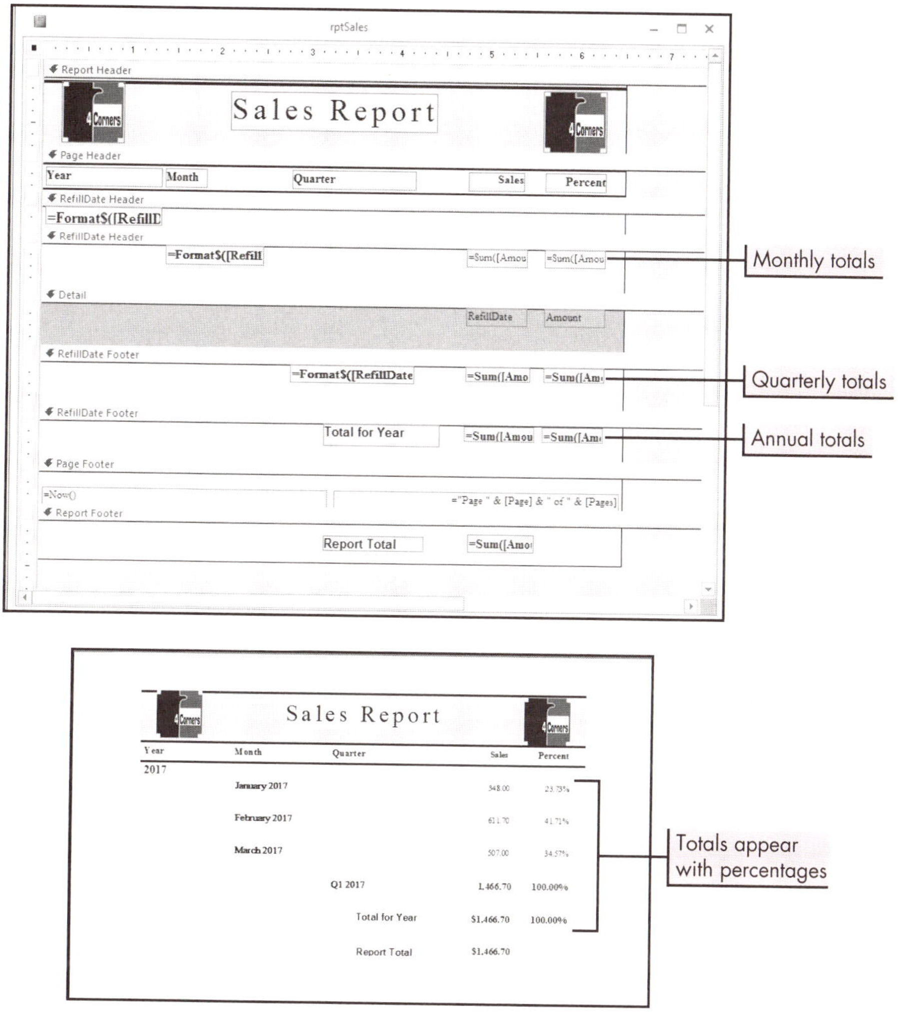

Paul is pleased with the report, and plans to use it for his next meeting with the pharmacy investors. Even as volume for the pharmacy increases, the report will continue to stay concise because it only has summary data.

To increase refill volume at the pharmacy, Elaine wants to create labels to send to customers who have no refill activity within a specified time period. The pharmacy wants to send a coupon to attract these customers back to 4Corners Pharmacy with an offer for a discount on any new or transferred prescriptions. How can she identify these customers?

Elaine recalls that Maria Garcia mentioned using aggregate functions in a query and decides to see if any would identify the last date of a prescription refill. She knows that the labels themselves won't be any different from the household mailing labels. She decides to create the query she needs, make a copy of the mailing label report rptHeadHHOnly, and then modify the record source for the report for the new query.

To identify the households that should receive coupons, Elaine must create a query that shows only the last refill for any customer within a household. She creates a query using the HouseID and RefillDate fields from tblCustomer, tblRx, and tblRefill. She sorts the query on RefillDate in ascending order. This places the last refill for any customer at the bottom of the list. Then she clicks the Totals button on the DESIGN tab, and groups by HouseID. She chooses the Last aggregate function from the list box and names the query qryLastRefill. See Figure 5.40.

Figure 5.40: Identifying the last prescription date for each household

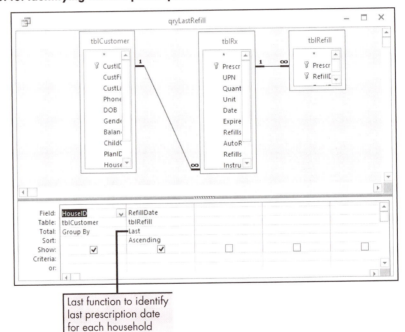

Last function to identify last prescription date for each household

The Last function returns the value for the last row encountered for each group. (See Table 3.10 in Chapter 3 for more information about aggregate functions.) Including the Last function in the Total row for the RefillDate field means that the query will identify the last, or oldest, prescription date for each household.

It doesn't matter who in the household refilled the oldest prescription; Elaine only needs their name and address so she can send only one coupon to each household. To do this, she must create a new query to join the records from qryLastRefill with name and address information from tblCustomer and tblHousehold. She creates the qryAttractOldCustomers query using an outer join to restrict the data and a parameter query to set the cutoff date for no refill activity. Figure 5.41 shows the query design.

Figure 5.41: qryAttractOldCustomers

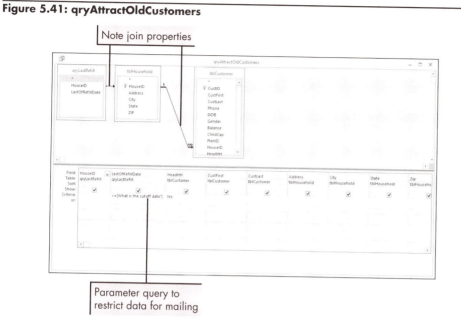

Note join properties

Parameter query to restrict data for mailing

The parameter included in the LastOfRefillDate calculated field means that users will be prompted to enter a date, and the query will select only those customers whose latest refill occurred on or before that date. The right outer join between qryLastRefill and tblHousehold means that the query will include all records in qryLastRefill and only the matching records in tblHousehold that meet the criteria. For example, if Elaine specifies 1/1/2017 as the LastOfRefillDate, the query displays only the names and addresses of household heads whose last prescription refill is on or before 1/1/2017. She tests the results of this query, using 1/1/2017 as the cutoff date, and confirms that the 10 customers the results display are heads of households. She saves the query as qryAttractOldCustomers.

Next, Elaine needs to make a copy of rptHeadHHOnly to use for the coupon mailing and revise the report so that it is based on qryAttractOldCustomers. In this way, she can create mailing labels only for household heads whose last prescription refill is on or before a specified date, and then send these customers a promotional coupon.

Changing the Record Source and Adding Fields

Report designers often need to change the source of data for a report after it is created. For example, if they base a report on a table, but then decide to limit the data using criteria or a parameter query, they can change the record source from a table to the new query. To change the record source for a report, you change the Record Source property in the report's Property Sheet. You can often copy an object such as a query, form, label, or macro, and then modify it for another use. This is particularly useful with reports, which often involve hours of design time. If you copy a report and then change its record source, the field list for the report also changes so that it contains all the fields in the new record source. However, you still need to delete controls on the report for fields that are not included in the current record source or add fields from the field list as necessary.

Elaine copies the mailing label report rptHeadHHOnly and names it rptAttractOldCustomers to match the name of the query that will serve as its record source. Then she opens the property sheet for the report, clicks the Record Source property, and selects qryAttractOldCustomers as the new record source for the mailing labels. See Figure 5.42. Recall that this query selects the names and addresses of household heads whose last prescription refill is on or before a specified date.

Figure 5.42: Changing the record source for a report

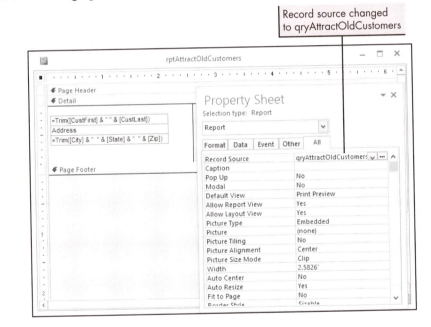

If the fields in the new record source match the fields needed for the report, you only need to change the record source. If not, you might need to remove fields that are not included in the new record source or add fields from the new record source to the report. The fields for Elaine's labels use the same fields as in qryAttractOldCustomers except for the parameter prompt that requests a cutoff date as a criterion. Elaine saves the query, and then switches to Print Preview. The Enter Parameter Value dialog box opens, requesting a cutoff date, and she enters 1/1/2017. The Print Preview window displays 10 mailing labels for the heads of households whose last prescription refill is on or before 1/1/2017.

Next, Elaine meets with a group of pharmacy technicians, who mention that the demand for the refill list report is high and that it is causing a bottleneck in the pharmacy. The refill report shows the prescription refills each customer ordered and the total cost of the prescription. After conferring with Paul Ferrino, Elaine decides to modify the report so it can be sent to every customer. This will provide a list of prescriptions and the associated price for each customer. Elaine and Paul anticipate that they will mail the report annually, but will review this policy after the first mailing.

To create this report, Elaine can revise rptRxList. The original report is based on qryRxList, which is a parameter query that asks for a customer ID and time period, and then lists all the prescriptions for that customer during that time. Elaine plans to change the underlying query to remove the parameter for CustID so that it lists all the customers. She will also add the name and mailing address to the report. For privacy reasons, Paul and Elaine decide to send a separate list to each customer, so she will need to print the prescription information on separate pages, with one or more pages for each customer. If she designs the report carefully, Elaine can use a window envelope to display the mailing address and save the step of printing separate mailing labels.

First, Elaine makes copies of qryRxList and rptRxList and names them qryAllCustRxList and rptAllCustRxList. Next, she modifies the query to remove the CustID parameter and to add the customer address to the query. Because address data is in tblHousehold, she adds the tblHousehold table to the field list area in Design view for qryAllCustRxList. See Figure 5.43.

Figure 5.43: Modified query for rptAllCustRxList

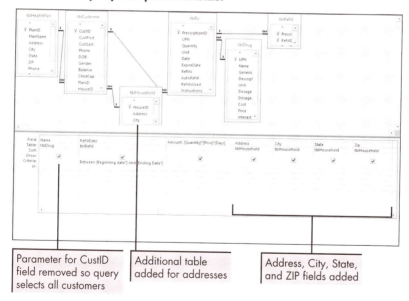

Parameter for CustID field removed so query selects all customers

Additional table added for addresses

Address, City, State, and ZIP fields added

Now she is ready to modify rptAllCustRxList to add address data and revise the formatting. She opens the report in Design view and changes the record source for the report to qryAllCustRxList. The field list for the report now includes the additional fields from tblHousehold.

You can add a field from an underlying table or query to a report by dragging the field name from the field list. Then you can align the field's label and text box for best appearance.

Since Elaine will send this report to each customer, she decides to move the title of the report, Refill List, from the report header to the page header so it prints on each page. She increases the size of the page header, and then moves the Refill List title label into the page header.

She also wants the three column headings—Refill Date, Drug Name, and Amount—and the line in the CustID header to print on each page so that this information appears for each customer. She selects these four controls and moves them into the page header. Now that the page header contains the report title, she no longer needs the report header, which appears on the first page of the report only. She drags the page header bar up to close the report header. Then she removes the CustID label and its text box from the CustID header because this information might be confusing to the customers.

She is ready to create an address block that will show the customer's name and address through the window in a window envelope. To place the address, she drags the Address field from the field list to the report in the CustID header. Access automatically creates a label for the field, but Elaine deletes it because she does not want the address block to include any labels. She decides to create a concatenated field for the city, state, and ZIP information to save space and improve the report's appearance, and does so by typing =[City] & " " & [State] & " " & [ZIP] in an unbound text box control. The report already includes an unbound text box control for the concatenated first and last name, so she aligns this control with the address information.

Elaine measures the distance from the edge of the envelope to its address window and the distance from the edge of the report to the address block, and then uses trial and error to format the address block so that it will appear in the envelope window when the report is printed. As she prints and modifies the report design to accomplish this task, she notices that the report prints more than one customer on the same page. To print only one record per page, she needs to force a page break after each customer.

Forcing a Page Break After Each Group

Many grouped reports are designed to be printed and distributed so that each person receives only the data pertaining to them. To print the data for one person only, you can insert a Page Break control to force a page break so that data for each person prints on a separate page. You can use the Insert Page Break button on the Controls group of the DESIGN tab to insert a page break in the group footer; each new group is then forced to print on a new page. You can also use the Keep Together setting in the Property Sheet to keep a heading and at least part of the detail together.

Elaine inserts the Insert Page Break control in the CustID footer so that the report prints data for a customer, and then starts printing the data for the next customer on a new page. She also notices that the page footer includes page numbers, which are consecutive for the entire report. She consults with Donald Linebarger, database developer, to learn if she can reset the page number to 1 after each customer record prints. He says that she can use a macro or a Visual Basic procedure, which she is not prepared to do, so she decides to simply delete the page numbers in the page footer. The page footer also includes the date, which might be useful to the customers, so she leaves that in the report. Figure 5.44 shows the final report in Design view.

Figure 5.44: rptAllCustRxList in Design View

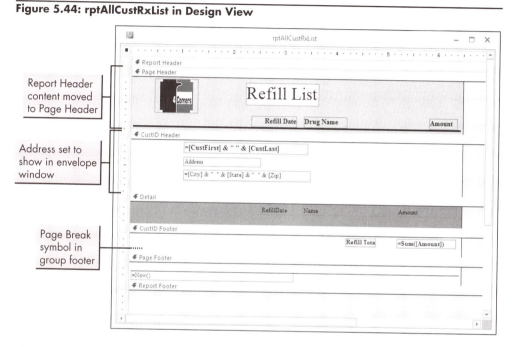

Report Header content moved to Page Header

Address set to show in envelope window

Page Break symbol in group footer

When Elaine prints the report, each page will list the customer's name and address, prescription refills, and total amount spent on the prescriptions.

Steps To Success: Level 2

Marie Cresson of Hudson Bay Pharmacy needs additional reports for the other managers at the pharmacy, and asks for your help in creating the reports shown in Table 5.11.

Table 5.11: Additional reports for Hudson Bay Pharmacy

Category	Reports Needed
Customer relations	• On-demand report showing drug purchases during particular time periods for insurance reporting • Mailing labels for a health and wellness newsletter and coupons to send to each household • Coupons for customers with no recent refill activity • Drug refill list for all customers
Management decision support and long-range planning	• Annual, quarterly, and monthly sales report

© 2014 Cengage Learning

Create queries as necessary to serve as the basis for the reports. As you save the new reports, be certain to use the name specified in the following steps, including the "rpt" prefix. Also consult your instructor for instructions about submitting your results.

Complete the following:

1. Start Access and open the **Hudson.accdb** database from the STS folder.

2. Marie needs to develop a customer relations report. Depending on their health plan, customers might need to submit a list of all prescriptions for reimbursement. Marie wants to create a report that allows a customer to specify a time period, and then generate a list of prescriptions received during that period. Because a technician will print this report for a single customer at a time, the technicians must be able to specify the customer number and the time period before they produce the report. Create an on-demand report showing drug purchases during a particular time period for insurance reporting for a single customer. Base the report on a parameter query named **qryRxList**. This report should also calculate the total cost of refill purchases. Make sure that the report uses the theme specified for Hudson Bay Pharmacy and that it is in good form. Save the report as **rptRxList**.

3. Marie also wants to send a health and wellness newsletter to all households each month. Create the mailing labels for the monthly newsletter that are addressed only to the head of each household. Save the mailing label report as **rptHeadHHOnly**.

4. Marie also wants to send promotional coupons to the head of each household whose last prescription refill is on or before a specified date. Create mailing labels to send to each household for customers with no activity in a specified time period. Name the report **rptAttractOldCustomers**.

5. Besides mailing labels, Marie also needs a few other customer reports. First, she asks you to create a customer telephone directory that includes all customers, their addresses, and their phone numbers listed in alphabetic order and printed in portrait orientation. Because many customers residing in the same household have different phone numbers, the phone number for each customer should be listed with the customer rather than the household. Thus, every customer must have a listing in the directory. Name the report **rptCustomerPhoneList**. Move the address and phone fields under the customer name fields and rearrange the report to make it more readable.

6. The next report Marie needs is a sales report with monthly, quarterly, and yearly sales summary figures. This report should allow input of any time period. Create this report for Marie, naming it **rptSales**. Make sure this report is formatted well and shows the quarterly summary figures after the monthly figures for each quarter.

7. Finally, Marie wants to send a report to all customers listing their drug purchases. Create this report, making sure to include a page break after each customer record so that each page can be mailed to customers individually. Save this report as **rptAllCustRxList**.

8. Close the **Hudson.accdb** database and then close Access.

LEVEL 3

Designing Reports for Data Analysis

Creating Advanced Reports in Design View

Elaine has met with the management team and discussed developing more reports that would help the pharmacy. She has listed them in Table 5.12.

Table 5.12: Advanced reports for the pharmacy

Category	Reports Needed
Daily operations	• Labels for prescription bottles and containers • Customer health plan demographics
Management decision support and long-range planning	• Contribution margin analysis • Graph showing refill activity to analyze coupon promotion effects • Margin data to export to Excel

© 2014 Cengage Learning

These reports are considered to be advanced reports because they include special features such as a chart or a subreport. Elaine might start some reports using the Report or Label Wizard; after that, she will spend most of her time working in Design view. She will also start in Design view for other reports which require maximum layout control.

One of the most important reports Paul Ferrino has requested is a report detailing the contribution margin of the various drugs the pharmacy carries. The sales report Elaine created included information about drugs sold, which is appropriate for creating an income statement, but it doesn't include information to help with decision making about pricing. Paul asks Elaine to create a report that contains details about the volume sold of each drug and its contribution to the overall profitability of the pharmacy.

After some discussion, Paul and Elaine decide to analyze data for a user-specified time period, but will not group the data by quarters or months. Because the database does not contain the tables that are necessary for inventory management, which would help them calculate actual refill days, they assume that every refill is for the maximum number of days allowed under the health plan of the customer. A more sophisticated analysis would also include expenses for variable costs as well as fixed costs, but because Elaine's goal is to compare the profitability of the various drugs, she will not include variable and fixed expenses at this point.

If a drug has a high gross margin, that doesn't necessarily mean it contributes to profits—it might be a drug the pharmacy seldom sells, and then only in limited volume. Lower margin per unit of drugs might make a bigger overall contribution to gross profit due to high-volume sales. This is what Paul wants to examine.

Elaine knows that she must first create a query as the basis of this report because she needs to enter parameters for the time period. She creates a query using data from tblHealthPlan, tblCustomer, tblRx, tblRefill, and tblDrug, and creates calculated fields for sales volume and contribution to profit. She clicks the Totals button in the Show/Hide group on the DESIGN tab and groups by drug name. Because the time period will vary, she uses RefillDate to specify the time-period parameters. She saves this query as qryContributionMarginAnalysis. See Figure 5.45.

Figure 5.45: Query for rptContributionMarginAnalysis

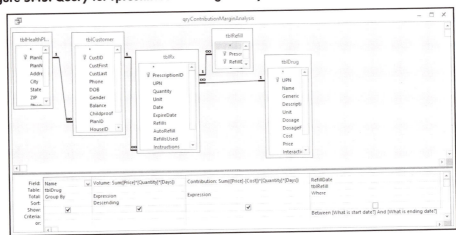

Elaine decides to create the report based on qryContributionMarginAnalysis from scratch in Design view. She will then have complete control over its appearance and properties. Because the contribution margin analysis report is a decision support tool for Paul, she will consult with him frequently as she creates the report.

How To

Create a Report in Design View

1. Click the CREATE tab on the Ribbon.
2. Click the Report Design button in the Reports group. A blank report opens in Design view.
3. Click the Property Sheet button in the Tools group on the DESIGN tab, then click the Data tab in the Property Sheet to choose a record source. If you do not specify the record source at this point, you can specify it later. See Figure 5.46.

Figure 5.46: Selecting a record source in a blank report

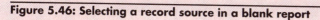

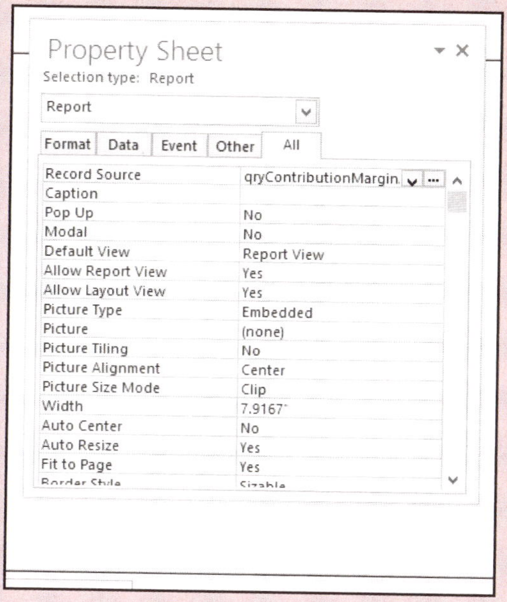

Property Sheet

Selection type: Report

Report

| Format | Data | Event | Other | **All** |

Record Source	qryContributionMargin
Caption	
Pop Up	No
Modal	No
Default View	Report View
Allow Report View	Yes
Allow Layout View	Yes
Picture Type	Embedded
Picture	(none)
Picture Tiling	No
Picture Alignment	Center
Picture Size Mode	Clip
Width	7.9167"
Auto Center	No
Auto Resize	Yes
Fit to Page	Yes
Border Style	Sizable

5

Level 3

4. Add a report header and footer, if desired, by right-clicking the page header and selecting Report Header/Footer on the shortcut menu.

5. Create a report title, if desired, using a label.

6. To display the list of fields for the table or query, click the DESIGN tab and click the Add Existing Fields button in the Tools group.

7. Drag fields to the Detail section from the Field List, as shown in Figure 5.47.

Figure 5.47: Drag fields from Field List into the Detail section of the report

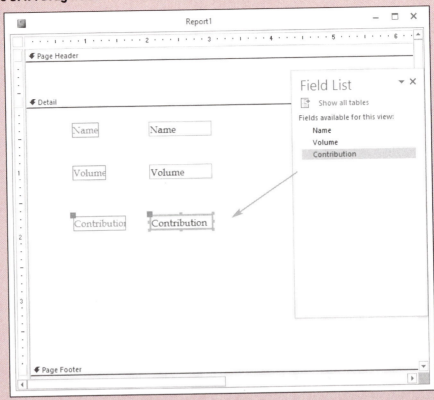

8. Highlight a label in the Detail section, right-click it, and then click Cut on the shortcut menu to separate it from its text box. Paste it where you want it in the page or group header. You can create column headings from label controls as needed if you prefer.

9. Add grouping and/or sorting in the Group, Sort, and Total pane by selecting the Group & Sort button in the Grouping & Totals group on the DESIGN tab. Use the Group, Sort, and Total pane to add other features in the same way you would using the options on the DESIGN, ARRANGE, FORMAT, and PAGE SETUP tabs.

Best Practice

Using the Field List to Create Bound Text Boxes in Design View

When you work from Design view to create a report from scratch, you can create the text boxes used for bound controls by clicking the Text Box button on the DESIGN tab. Then you type the field name into the text box itself or change the Control Source value in the control's Property Sheet.

However, using the field list to create a bound text box offers the following two advantages:

- When you add a text box to a report by dragging a field from the field list, Access provides a corresponding label with the same name as the field. (If the record source defines a caption for that field, Access uses the caption instead.)

- Using the field list also creates a bound text box that inherits many of the same properties the field has in the record source, such as a Currency format for a numeric field. If you don't use the field list to create a text box, you must set these properties in the report manually.

Elaine drags each field in qryContributionMarginAnalysis to the Detail section of the report. She moves the field labels into the Page Header section so that only the fields' text boxes remain in the Detail section. She uses commands on the ARRANGE tab to align the labels with their text boxes and to improve the appearance of the report. She adds formats and clicks the Themes button in the Themes group on the DESIGN tab and applies the Corners theme. Next, she adds the 4Corners Pharmacy logo to the report header. She also changes the label text to 10-point, semibold, modifies the labels to read "Sales Volume" and "Gross Margin Contribution," and then presses Shift+Enter to split the labels into two lines.

Elaine right-aligns the volume and contribution labels, and then moves and aligns the labels and their text boxes. She notices that the Currency format makes the values harder to read, so she changes the format for both volume and contribution to Standard. She uses the Line button on the DESIGN tab to draw a line that separates the labels from the data.

Next, Elaine wants to include the date and page numbers on each page. She creates an unbound text box control in the page footer and deletes its label. In the control, she types =Now() to display the current date, and changes the format to show only the short date. Then she creates an unbound text box control and types ="Page " & [Page] & " of " & [Pages] to place page numbers in the page footer. Now(), [Page], and [Pages] are built-in functions. She also changes the report caption and sets the sort order for the Contribution field to descending by right-clicking the Contribution field and choosing Sort Descending from the shortcut menu. She saves the report as rptContributionMarginAnalysis.

Best Practice

Specifying Sort Order in the Group, Sort, and Total pane

Any sorting you specify in a query is overridden by the sorting you specify in the Group, Sort, and Total pane for a report. To ensure that your data sorts the way you want it to, specify sorting criteria in the Group, Sort, and Total pane, not the underlying query.

When Elaine shows the report to Paul, he asks if she can add totals and a running total to the report. To make room for this additional information, she changes the margin of the report, making sure that the total report width is less than 6.5 inches so she doesn't exceed the paper width of 8.5 inches. (The report width plus two one-inch margins equals the total width of the paper.)

In Design view, Elaine creates a new label called "Running Total" and a new unbound text box with the calculation =[Contribution] to calculate the running total for the Contribution field. Then she modifies the calculated control's properties to set the Running Sum property to Over All and sets the Format property to Standard with two decimal places. (If this report grouped records, she could set the Running Sum property to Over Group.) Figure 5.48 shows the final Contribution Margin Analysis report in Design view and Print Preview.

Figure 5.48: Final Contribution Margin Analysis report in Design view and Print Preview

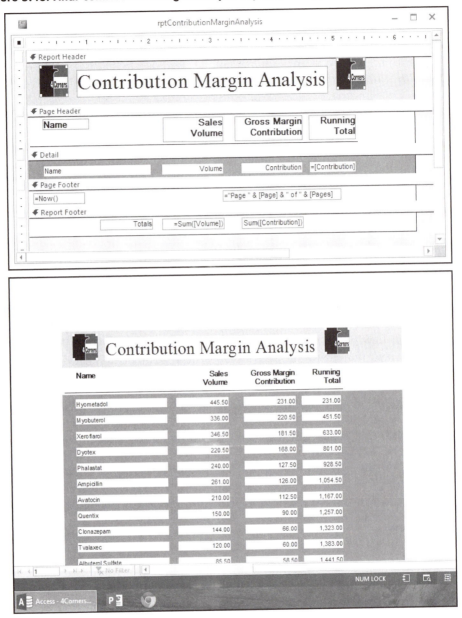

How To

Create a Running Total

1. Create space if necessary in the report for the running total column by widening the report or reducing the left and right margins. Be sure to stay within standard page width.

2. Add a label in the page or group header for the running total field.

3. Add an unbound text box to the detail or group footer section and create the calculation by using =[*Fieldname*].

4. In the Property Sheet for the unbound text box, change the Running Sum property to Over Group (if you have groups and want the running total to reset at each group) or Over All.

Paul and Elaine need to study the new Contribution Margin Analysis report. They may need to raise prices on low-margin, low-volume drugs to justify keeping them in inventory; they may decide to lower prices on high-volume drugs if their margin is sufficient. Comparing margins over time provides valuable input to their decision making.

Exporting Access Data to Microsoft Excel

Paul is much more comfortable analyzing numeric data in Microsoft Excel than he is in Access. He asks Elaine if she could prepare data for him to examine, and perhaps chart, in Excel. Because he wants to analyze margin and pricing over time, Elaine must first create a crosstab query to provide the data he needs.

First, Elaine creates a query that includes the fields necessary for the crosstab query. Paul wants to compare the name of the drug, the margin percentage for each drug, the margin for each prescription in dollars, and the refill date. She calculates the margin percentage for each drug as [Price]-[Cost]/[Price]. Recall that Elaine and Paul are assuming that all refills are filled for the maximum period allowed. Thus, the crosstab query should also include days allowed. She creates the query using parameters for any time period so that Paul can specify this information, and names this query qryDrugMargin. Figure 5.49 shows the design of this query.

Figure 5.49: Design of margin query for the crosstab query

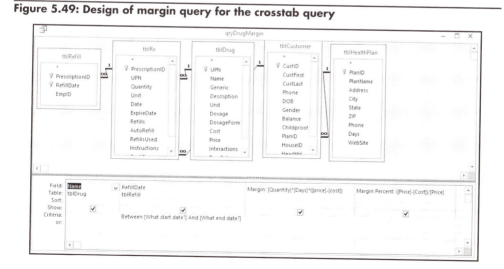

Elaine starts the Crosstab Query Wizard and uses qryDrugMargin as the data source. She includes Name and Margin Percent as the rows—this will list all drugs and their individual percent margin. She selects RefillDate for the columns and monthly for the time period. The sum of the margin is the calculated value. When she tests the query, she notices that the drugs are in alphabetical order. She switches to Design view and sorts the Margin Percent column in descending order to list the drugs with the highest margin first. She considers limiting the drugs to the top 25 or you could select 25%, but Paul wants to look at all of them for now. She saves the crosstab query as qryDrugMargin_Crosstab. Now all she has to do is export the data to Excel for Paul. Figure 5.50 shows the results of the crosstab query.

Figure 5.50: Results of margin crosstab query

qryDrugMargin_Crosstab

Name	Margin Percent	Total Of Margin	Jan	Feb	Mar	Apr	May	Jun	Jul	Aug	Sep	Oct	Nov
Dyotex	76%	$168.00		$24.00		$72.00						$72.00	
Tolbutamide	73%	$39.60					$19.80			$19.80			
Glimepiride	72%	$39.00	$39.00										
Albuterol Sulfate	68%	$58.50					$39.00		$19.50				
Nvalax	67%	$36.00				$18.00			$18.00				
Myobuterol	66%	$220.50				$31.50	$126.00	$31.50		$31.50			
Montelukast sodium	64%	$17.40		$17.40									
Rivastigmine tartrate	62%	$58.50			$58.50								
Quentix	60%	$90.00		$45.00				$22.50		$22.50			
Diazapam	60%	$40.20			$40.20								
Avatocin	54%	$112.50		$22.50	$67.50				$22.50				
Phalastat	53%	$127.50				$25.50	$25.50	$25.50	$25.50			$25.50	
Xeroflarol	52%	$181.50			$66.00				$49.50	$49.50		$16.50	
Hyometadol	52%	$231.00		$21.00	$63.00			$21.00	$63.00		$63.00		
Acebutolol hydrochlor	50%	$33.00							$16.50		$16.50		
Dseurton	50%	$18.00							$18.00				
Levothyroxine	50%	$21.00		$21.00									
Tvalaxec	50%	$60.00	$15.00	$15.00			$15.00	$15.00					
Ampicillin	48%	$126.00			$63.00				$21.00		$42.00		
Haloperidol	46%	$18.00	$18.00										
Clonazepam	46%	$66.00	$16.50	$16.50	$16.50				$16.50				
Epronix	43%	$39.00	$19.50		$19.50								
Didanosine	42%	$28.20									$14.10		
Cefixime	41%	$58.50		$58.50									

Record: 1 of 24   No Filter   Search

How To

Export Data to Microsoft Excel for Further Analysis and Creating Charts

1. Select the query you want to export.
2. Click the EXTERNAL DATA tab on the Ribbon.
3. Click the desired button in the Export group. For example, click the Excel button if you wish to export to Excel.
4. Select the destination and enter a name for the exported query, click OK, and then select whether or not you want to save the export steps and then click Close.
5. Open the query in Excel. You will only see the data, not the underlying query.

Elaine exports the data for Paul and warns him that this data will become obsolete. She can always run the crosstab query again with new dates and then export the data again. Paul should design his worksheet so that he can replace obsolete data with the new data in the future. If he decides to look at only the top margin values, Elaine can modify the underlying query to specify the top-value amount or percent that Paul wants.

Beyond Calculated Fields

Elaine wants to know what proportion of the 4Corners Pharmacy customers are members of each health plan. The pharmacy might be able to negotiate with the various health plans based on the number of members patronizing the pharmacy. She could also use this data to help analyze the effect of any selling price or other limitations that health plans might want to impose. To produce this report, she needs data from tblHealthPlan and tblCustomer. Although the two tables are related on the common field PlanID, they do not use a numeric field to calculate the number of health plans or the percentage of customers who belong to each plan. She wants to use the Report Wizard for this report but needs a numeric field to take advantage of the summary options. She realizes that she must create a totals query first to count the number of customers in each plan and then use the query's numeric field in the report. She creates the query and names it qryHealthplanAnalysis. The results are shown in Figure 5.51. Elaine notes that the numbers are small because the database hasn't yet been put into production. When it is, she will have this report ready.

Figure 5.51: Count of customers in each health plan

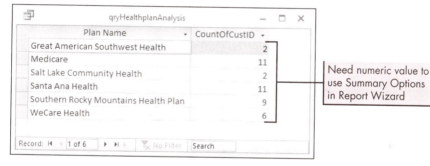

Elaine creates the report using the Report Wizard and uses the qryHealthplanAnalysis query, which counts the number of customers in each plan, as the data source. She groups records on the PlanName field so she can perform calculations for each group, even though the data already appears in a summarized format. Because qryHealthplanAnalysis includes a numeric value, Elaine can select the summary options in the wizard. She selects Sum because the report needs this value to calculate the percentages. She also selects the Calculate percent of total for sums check box, selects the Stepped layout, and applies the Corners theme. Following best practices, she names the report rptHealthplanAnalysis. The report still needs considerable modification to meet the professional standards of the pharmacy, however. She can move the PlanName, Count, and Percentage fields to the grouping header, delete the summary text in the group footer, modify the label for the Percentage field, and generally make the report more attractive. The modified report is shown in Figure 5.52.

Figure 5.52: Health Plan Analysis report

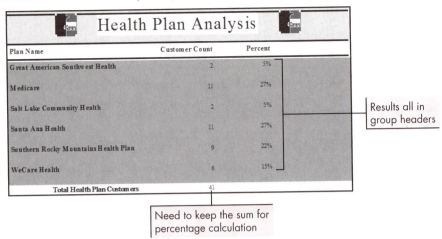

Advanced Label Formatting

Next, Elaine plans to create the labels for all prescription containers and bottles using the Label Wizard. She finds an Avery USA 4168 label (continuous) that measures 2" × 4" in the Label Wizard. This type of label can wrap around the smallest container that 4Corners Pharmacy uses. Larger containers and bottles can also use the same size label. The pharmacy needs to use a printer that can print continuous labels because the technicians will print the labels one at a time throughout the day. She plans to order the labels already printed with the logo, name, address, and phone number of the pharmacy.

Because the Label Wizard allows only one table or query as the basis for the labels, Elaine starts by creating a query with the fields she needs. She will limit the RefillDate in the query to today's date after she finishes modifying the label. She will also add parameter values for the Prescription Number and Use by Date fields. (She can create and test a query more quickly if she uses fixed values in these fields for now.) She sorts the query on RefillDate in descending order so the latest refill is first, and creates calculated fields to calculate the refills remaining and the total quantity in the container. She names the query qryRxContainer.

Next, she lists the data required for the label, the table it comes from, and an approximate order for the contents of the label:

- Prescription number: tblRx
- Date of refill: tblRefill
- Date of prescription: tblRx
- Name of the prescribing doctor: tblDoctor
- Name of drug: tblDrug
- Name and address of the customer: tblCustomer and tblHousehold
- Instructions: tblRx

- Number of refills remaining and expiration date of prescription: tblRx
- Use Before date: Determined by the expiration date on the drug in inventory and input when the refill is processed
- ID of employee who filled the prescription: tblRefill

Elaine is now ready to create the label for the prescription container. She uses the Label Wizard to get started but plans to modify the label significantly.

Modifying Labels in Design View

Elaine can use the properties of the controls to modify the label precisely. Remembering that many of the pharmacy's customers are elderly, she wants the prescription number, the name of the person for whom the prescription is filled, the name of the drug, and the instructions to be large and bold. She also plans to use color to highlight items on the label that a technician might want to know if the customer calls to ask for a refill. Elaine uses the properties in the Property Sheet for the label and its controls. Figure 5.53 displays the label in its final format.

Figure 5.53: Layout of the container label

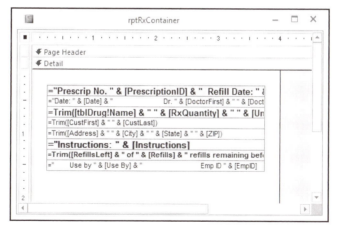

She saves the label report as rptRxContainer. She views that final label format. See Figure 5.54.

Figure 5.54: Finished container label showing test data

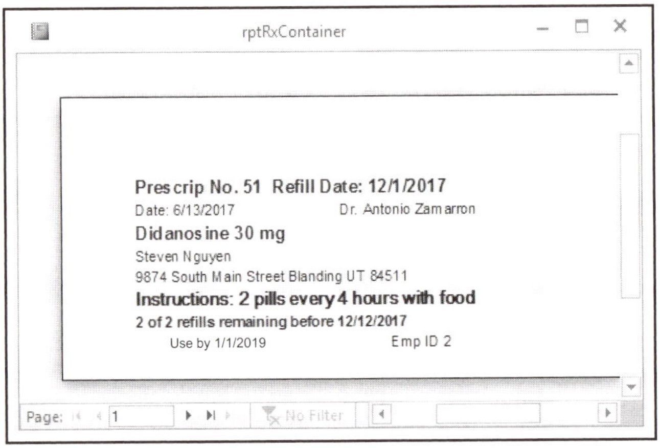

Best Practice

Changing Column Widths and Label Position

You can modify column widths in labels by selecting Columns in the Page Layout group on the PAGE SETUP tab. The Columns tab in the Page Setup dialog box allows you to make changes to the labels the same way you can change the settings in reports. This might be necessary for custom labels and for continuous labels positioned in tractor-fed printers to prevent label "creep" after many labels have printed due to slight misalignment of the labels.

You can change the Number of Columns option to set the number of labels across the page. Left and Top margin settings determine the position for the upper-left corner of the first label. Row Spacing and Height determine the number of labels that will fit vertically on a page and the vertical distance between the labels. Setting Row Spacing to 0 allows the depth of the Detail section to determine the vertical spacing of the labels. Printing on continuous labels might require more adjustments than the sheet-fed labels, so it is a good idea to test print a new label to make sure the alignment is correct.

Elaine is pleased with the labels for the prescription containers. They should save time as each prescription is filled. Next, Paul is preparing for his investor's meeting and has asked Elaine to create a report specifically for 2017 and to add a graph to the sales report to show the 2017 monthly sales.

Including Additional Data for Analysis

To provide additional information on a report from a table or query, you can include a subreport, which provides information similar to that of a subform. You can also apply conditional formatting to a report so that it displays some information in a certain color, for example, if that information meets specified conditions. You might display negative values in red, for example, or values greater than 100,000 in bright blue.

Adding a Subreport to a Report

As you have learned, you can link several tables with one-to-many relationships to display lots of detail in a report. Access supports grouping to help you arrange the data in a hierarchical way by nesting the groups. You can also embed **subreports** or subforms in a report including charts or unrelated data. Subreports are reports you create and then embed in another report. Access allows you to embed subforms as well. (Note that subreports can't be embedded in forms.) Because the Report Wizard does not create main reports and subreports at the same time, you must create the report (or form) you want to use as a subreport first and then add it to the main report in Design view.

After creating the form or report you want to use for the subreport or subform, you add it to the report the same way you added a subform to a form—using the Subform/Subreport button on the DESIGN tab. In many cases, the subreport is linked to a field on the main part of the report, although that is not required. Linked subreports must have a common field in the main part of the report and in the subreport. Unlinked subreports allow you to combine unrelated data on one report. To create a subreport, you can use the Subreport Wizard, one of the Control Wizards Access offers in Design view of a report.

How To

Add a Subform or Subreport to a Report in Design View

1. In Design view, create space for a subreport by increasing the size of the Detail section.
2. Click the Subform/Subreport button in the Controls group on the DESIGN tab.
3. Click where you want to place the subreport. The Subform/Subreport Wizard starts.
4. Select a table, query, form, or report as the source for the subreport. Click the Next button.
5. Select the fields you want for the subreport. Click the Next button.
6. Define the link between the main form and the subform. If there is no link, select None. Click the Next button.
7. Name the subreport. This name will appear on the report. Click the Finish button.
8. Modify the subform and the rest of the report as necessary.

Paul is getting ready for the 2017 annual investors meeting for the pharmacy. Elaine suggests that they create a sales report with only 2017 data. The report will use fixed dates, but she can use it for comparison purposes next year. She will also create a report that shows the profit margin for each prescription drug. Elaine will use this report as a subreport so that Paul can show the investors the sales and the profit margin of the prescription drug at the same time. To create these reports, Elaine must complete the following tasks:

- Copy qrySales, name it qry2017Sales, and modify it to use fixed dates for 1/1/2017 through 12/31/2017 as criteria. She also includes the Name and UPN fields.
- Create a report for qry2017Sales displaying all the fields. Name the report rpt2017Sales. The title of the report should be 2017 Sales Report.

- Create a query from tblDrug that includes the Name and UPN fields and name the query qry2017Margin. Include an expression named Margin that divides the Price field by the Cost Field.
- Create a report for qry2017Margin that includes all the fields.

Elaine opens rpt2017Sales in Design view, increases the size of the Detail section, and uses the Subform/Subreport button to create a subreport with rpt2017Margin. She selects the Choose from a list option button and then selects Show qry2017Margin for each record in qry2017Sales using Name. Figure 5.55 shows her report.

Figure 5.55: rpt2017Sales in Design view

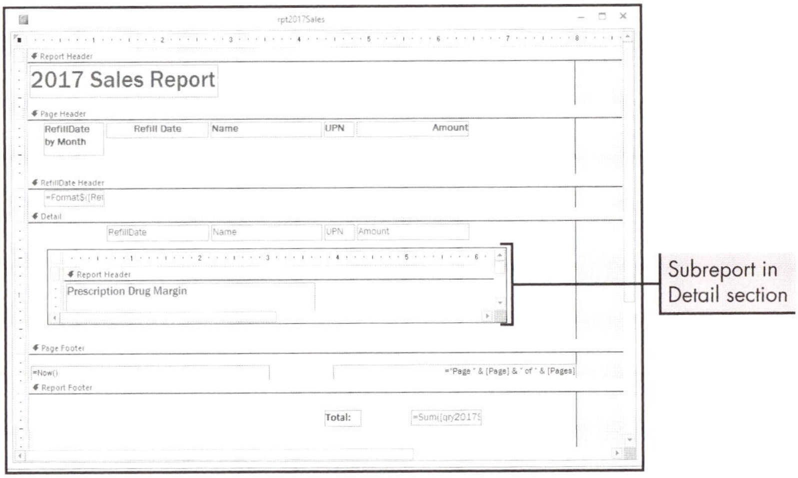

Paul has one more request of Elaine for the investors' annual meeting. He wants the rpt2017Sales report to highlight any sale less than $30 and greater than $100. Elaine suggests changing the color of the value to red to show values less that $30 and blue for values higher than $100. To accomplish this, she can use conditional formatting.

Conditional Formatting for Report Values

Conditional formatting allows the developer to add formatting features such as color, bold, or larger fonts based on the values in the report. Using conditional formatting, you can change the appearance of a control on a report so that it differs from one record to another depending on whether the value in the control meets criteria that you specify. You can use conditional formatting to use a different background color, font style, or text color in a control so that its values are highlighted when they meet a certain condition. If the value of the control changes and no longer meets the condition, Access uses the default formatting for the control. You can specify up to three conditions for a field.

Elaine wants to change the format of the quarterly percentage of sales in rpt2017Sales depending on the values calculated in that field. To do this, she clicks the calculated field for Amount and then clicks the Conditional Formatting button in the Control Formatting group of the REPORT DESIGN TOOLS FORMAT tab. She specifies that the condition is less than $30 and changes the font color to red. For the second condition, she specifies values above $100 and makes these blue. Only those values meeting the conditions will show the changes. Figure 5.56 shows the conditions Elaine sets and the resulting completed report.

Figure 5.56 Setting conditional formatting

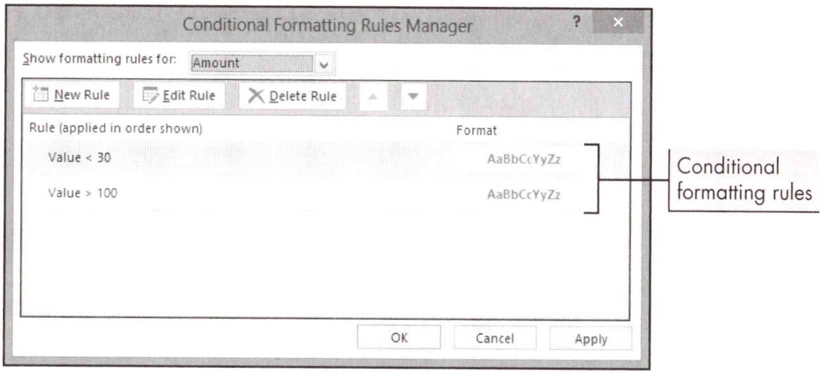

Elaine sets the conditional formatting rules and views the resulting completed report. She scrolls through the report until she finds where both conditional formatting rules are working, as shown in Figure 5.57.

Figure 5.57: Completed 2017 Sales report with conditional formatting applied

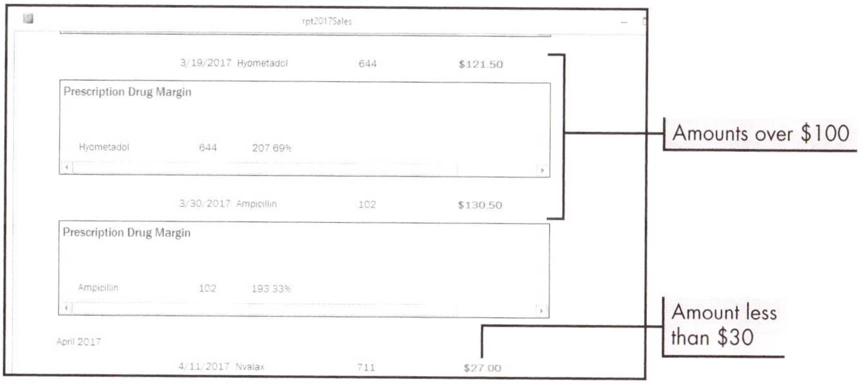

Finally, Paul asks Elaine to create a report with a chart that shows the drugs that are not yet available in a generic form. By keeping track of these drugs, Paul can research these drugs to see when they become available in generic form.

Adding a Chart to a Report

Before she creates a chart in the report for Paul, Elaine reviews the features of a chart. She wants to be sure that the chart has the essential elements and understands them. See Figure 5.58.

Figure 5.58: Chart elements

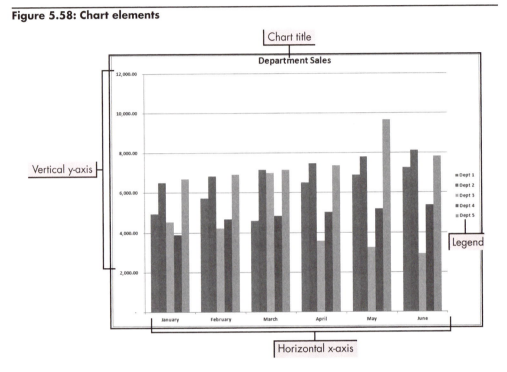

Elaine feels she is ready to create a chart in the report. She first creates a query based on tblDrug that shows the UPN, Name, Generic, and Price fields. She sorts the query in ascending order by Name. In addition, she adds the No criteria in the generic field. She names the query qryDrugWatch. Elaine then creates a report for this query with all the fields except Generic. She uses the Tabular layout and saves the report as rptDrugWatch.

In Design view, Elaine increases the height of the report footer to three inches. She then clicks the Chart button in the Controls group on the DESIGN tab. In the first Chart Wizard dialog box, she selects qryDrugWatch and the UPN, Name, and Price fields for the chart. Elaine chooses the 3-D Column Chart. See Figure 5.59.

Figure 5.59: Selecting a chart type

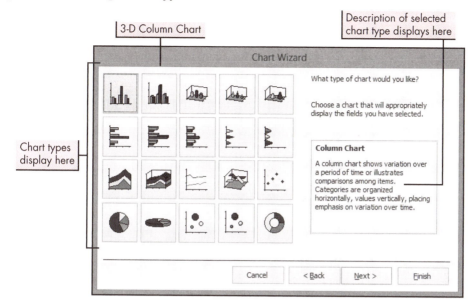

3-D Column Chart

Description of selected chart type displays here

Chart types display here

She clicks the Next button and previews the layout of the chart, as shown in Figure 5.60. The layout is acceptable.

Figure 5.60: Viewing the chart layout

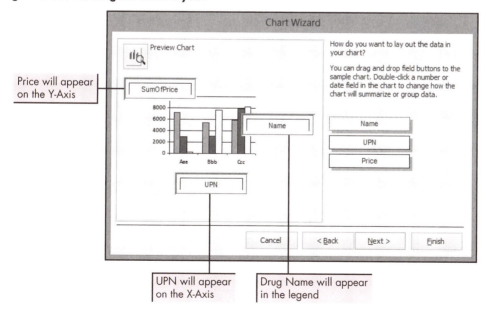

Price will appear on the Y-Axis

UPN will appear on the X-Axis

Drug Name will appear in the legend

After she clicks the Next button, she decides that she does not want the chart to change with each record, so she chooses <No Field> for both the Report Fields and Chart Fields. Elaine enters the name "Generic Drug Watch" for the title of the report. She wants to include a legend and then clicks the Finish button. She realizes that the actual results of the chart will not appear until she views the report when she is not in Design view. She views the chart in Design view and then in Print Preview. Because not all of the data on the X-axis is displayed, she double-clicks the chart so that she can make changes to it. She then clicks on the X-axis and changes the font size to 8 and the size of the chart title to 12. See Figure 5.61.

Figure 5.61: Chart in editing mode

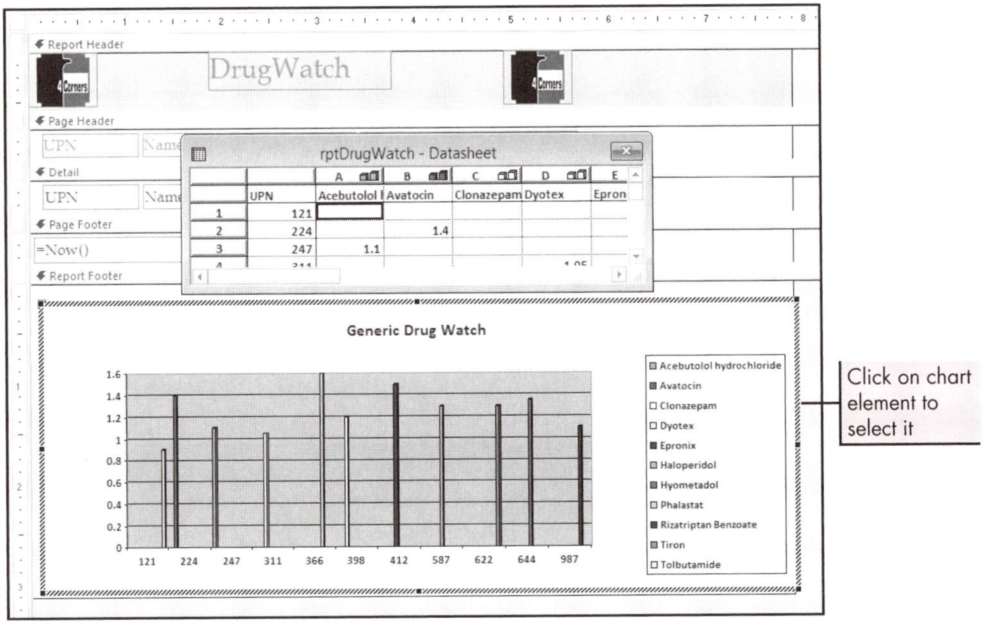

Elaine also changes the Y-axis and legend font size to 8 as well. Figure 5.62 shows the report in Design view and Print Preview.

Figure 5.62: Report with chart in Design view and Print Preview

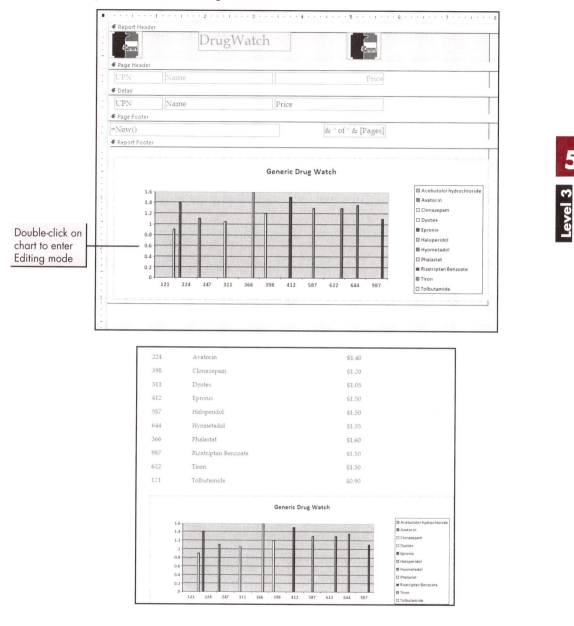

Add a Chart to a Report

1. Create a report or open an existing report, and then switch to Design view.
2. Increase the size of the report section where you want to place the chart.
3. Click the Chart button in the Controls group on the DESIGN tab.

4. In the section for the report, press and hold down the mouse button to draw, from the upper left to lower right, an outline for the size of the chart.

5. In the first Chart Wizard dialog box, select the table or query for the chart and then select the fields to be used in the chart and click the Next button.

6. Choose the chart type in the next wizard dialog box and click the Next button.

7. Drag and drop the fields where you want them to appear in the chart and click the Next button.

8. If you want the chart to change from record to record, select the report field and chart field. Click the Next button.

9. Enter a title for the chart and then click the Finish button.

Now that Elaine has created all the reports Paul needs, he is ready for the annual investor meeting and has reports available to provide important information to improve the efficiency of the pharmacy.

Steps To Success: Level 3

Marie Cresson of Hudson Bay Pharmacy needs additional reports for the other managers at the pharmacy, and asks for your help in creating the reports shown in Table 5.13.

Table 5.13: Advanced reports for Hudson Bay Pharmacy

Category	Reports Needed
Daily operations	• Labels for prescription bottles and containers • Percentage of customers in each health plan
Management decision support and long-range planning	• Contribution margin analysis • Graph showing refill activity to analyze coupon promotion effects • Margin data to export to Excel • 2017 investors' report with graph and conditional formatting

© 2014 Cengage Learning

Create queries as necessary to serve as the basis for the reports. As you save the new reports, be certain to use the name specified in the following steps, including the "rpt" prefix. Also consult your instructor for instructions about submitting your results.

Complete the following:

1. Start Access and open the **Hudson.accdb** database from the STS folder.

2. Create a report from scratch in Design view to analyze contribution margin for all drugs for any given time period. The report should include sales and gross margin subtotals by drug but no detail. Drugs should be sorted by contribution margin in descending order. Be sure the report has a date and page numbers. Add running totals to the report. Modify the report as necessary to conform to the pharmacy standards. Save the report as **rptContributionMarginAnalysis**.

3. Prepare data for export to Excel that shows the drugs, percent margin for each drug, and the margin for each drug over monthly time increments. Name the data **qryDrugMarginforExcel**. Export the data in Excel 2013 format. Save the exported file as **qryDrugMarginforExcel.xlsx**. If necessary, modify the Excel file so that only two places appear for the percentage.

4. Create a summary management report that shows what proportion of Hudson Bay Pharmacy customers are members of each health plan. Show both the total number of customers and the percentage of the total. Save the report as **rptHealthplanAnalysis**, and then modify it as necessary to meet the professional standards of the pharmacy.

5. Create labels for the prescription containers using labels that fit on a typical prescription container. Hudson Bay Pharmacy needs the same information on their prescription labels as does 4Corners Pharmacy. Name the report **rptRxContainer**.

6. Use copies of qrySales and rptSales as the basis for a 2017 sales report with a fixed time period of 1/1/2017 to 12/31/2017. Modify the report as necessary and name it **rpt2017Sales**.

7. In rpt2017Sales, show conditional formatting for each quarter that distinguishes between quarters contributing less than 25% to the pharmacy and those contributing more than 50% to the pharmacy.

8. Close the **Hudson.accdb** database and then close Access.

Chapter Summary

This chapter presented many of the ways you might present data in a database. Because paper reports are still used extensively by management, reports must not only look professional, but must also have the maximum information content to aid in decision making. In Level 1, you learned how to create simple reports using the Report button and the Report Wizard. You also learned how to create grouping levels in a report from a single table and how to create mailing labels using the Label Wizard. You learned how to modify the results of the Report Wizard in Design view and how to add a theme.

In Level 2, you learned about customizing reports using data from two or more tables or queries, about grouping issues such as summary statistics, keeping data together, and page breaks, as well as grouping on date and time or a part of a field's contents.

In Level 3, you learned about many advanced techniques for working with reports. You learned about advanced formatting in labels as well as how to add a subreport or subform to a report.

5

Chapter Exercises

Conceptual Review

1. What are the most popular types of reports produced by Access and why?

2. What methods can you employ to increase the information content of a report?

3. Which items would be on your checklist to make sure your reports all meet the highest standards of professionalism?

4. What other uses are there for labels besides the standard label on an envelope used for mass mailings?

5. Why would you use the Label Wizard instead of just a report for label creation?

6. What naming conventions can you suggest for a large database with many reports, beyond just naming queries and reports with the same name?

7. Why do most database developers create calculated fields in a query rather than just adding them to a report?

8. When would a subreport be a better way to design a report, rather than just grouping?

9. Give an example of how conditional formatting might help with decision making.

10. Explain the difference between a sorted report and a grouped report.

11. Give an example of when you would create a summary report.

12. What can you do to change a report if you want to include fields other than those listed in the report's field list?

13. Where would you insert page numbers if you wanted them to print on every page in the report?

14. In which section would you include running totals for a report?

15. Including conditional formatting in a report is helpful when analyzing what kind of data?

Case Problems

Case 1—Creating Effective Reports for NHD Development Group Inc.

In this project, you continue working on the database for an antiques mall, Memories Antiques in Cleveland, Tennessee. You have been working with Linda Sutherland, the manager of the mall, and with Tim Richards, the chief information officer of the NHD Development group, who owns this mall and several other malls across the country. Tim and Linda are ready to consider what types of written reports they will be able to obtain through the database. In this project, you design several reports that Tim will send to the NHD corporate headquarters about the Memories Antiques Mall. His main goal is to create reports that are clear, appealing, and well organized, using a format that makes information easily accessible.

Human Resources

Complete the following:

1. Start Access and open the **Antiques.accdb** database from the Case 1 folder.

2. Before you start creating reports, Tim suggests that you plan their layout and design. The reports should share a similar format and include the following elements:

   - The NHD logo and name of the mall (Memories Antiques) should appear at the top of every report.
   - An appropriate title should clearly state the purpose of each report.
   - The bottom of every page should include the page number, total number of pages, date, and name of the person who prepared the report in the format "Prepared By: Your Name".
   - Each report should show the appropriate information except for ID numbers, which are meaningful only to the mall, not to the managers at the NHD corporate headquarters.

3. To prepare annual bonuses for employees, the first report Tim needs is an employee compensation report. He'll use this report to determine an appropriate bonus amount for each employee, so it should include detailed information. To compare salaries and wages fairly, the report should group employees by position. Tim also wants the report to show summary statistics for all positions, including the sum, average, maximum, and minimum of the hourly rates. The report should also calculate the total salaries and total wages at the end of the report. Name this report **rptEmployeeSalaryDetail**.

4. Tim also plans to send a summary of employee compensation to his managers at NHD. Instead of including detailed employee information, this report should only summarize wages and salaries by position and provide grand totals. Like the detailed report, the summary report should include the sum, average, maximum, and minimum of the salaries for each position. Name this report **rptEmployeeSalarySummary**.

5. After he analyzes the salary reports, Tim will mail a bonus check to each employee. He needs a set of mailing labels that include all the information necessary to mail the check to each employee's home. He gives you a box of Avery #J8160 labels, and notes that NHD usually uses Times New Roman, 10-point bold text for mailings. Create the mailing label report for Tim, naming it **rptEmployeeLabels**.

6. Tim and Linda are also planning a company meeting to celebrate a successful year of business. Because Tim does not know all the employees by name, he asks you to create name tags for each employee. The name tag should show the NHD logo, and the employee name followed by their position title. He gives you a box of Avery #CB720 labels for the name tags. (*Hint*: If your copy of Access does not include label CB720, choose another label suitable for name tags.) Create the name tags for Tim, naming the report **rptEmployeeNametags**.

7. At the meeting, Tim plans to discuss the classes that are offered at the mall and brainstorm ideas for new classes. He believes that additional classes could boost the mall's profit significantly. He asks you to create a report showing the current class offerings, along with the name of the instructor (in the form Last, First), the number of customers who are currently enrolled and have paid, the cost of the course, and the total amount that has been received for each class. (*Hint*: You can use a query as the basis of this report.) The final page of the report should show the grand total of all collected class fees. Because this grand total is the most important calculation in the report, Tim suggests that you format it so that it stands out from the other information. Name the report **rptClassEnrollment**.

8. Close the **Antiques.accdb** database and then close Access.

Case 2—Creating Financial Reports for MovinOn Inc.

Finance

In this project, you work with Kristina Romano, an accountant in the Washington warehouse of MovinOn Inc. Kristina needs to prepare a series of financial reports to present to David Bowers, owner of MovinOn, the warehouse managers, and the accountants at MovinOn at their annual meeting. They are naturally interested in how much revenue recent jobs have generated, as well as the labor costs that offset this revenue.

Complete the following:

1. Open the **MovinOn.accdb** database from the Case 2 folder.

2. Because Kristina will discuss all the reports at the same time, she wants them to look similar and present a consistent, unified package. She suggests that you use the following guidelines as you design the reports:

   - Include the MovinOn logo at the top of every report.
   - Provide an appropriate title that clearly states the purpose of each report.
   - Show all dollar amounts with a dollar sign and two decimal places.
   - At the bottom of every page, include the page number, total number of pages, date, and name of the person who prepared the report in the format "Prepared By: Your Name".

3. Before the annual meeting, Kristina plans to mail copies of some reports to the warehouse managers. Because she will send materials to each manager at different times, she needs a way to indicate which warehouse she wants before she prints the mailing label. The label she produces should include the manager's warehouse number next to their name, along with other appropriate mailing information. Managers receive a lot of mail, so Kristina asks you to print "Important!" in red text at the top of each label. She plans to use Avery #8663 labels and asks you to create the mailing label report. (Ignore any errors you receive about the size of the labels.) Name this report **rptWarehouseManagerLabels**.

4. The next report that Kristina needs should show the income from recent moving jobs. MovinOn charges $.70 per mile plus $.20 per pound for each job. From this total, Kristina deducts the driver's payment to determine the net income for the moving job. Drivers receive $50 for each job plus their mileage rate (that is, the driver's rate multiplied by the number of miles plus $50). Kristina asks you to create an income report that provides the job ID, the date of the move, the driver's name and rate, the mileage and weight of the job, and the income calculations as described. At the end of the report, Kristina wants to show the total income, the total payments to drivers, and the total net income. (*Hint*: Consider creating a query as the basis for this report.) Name the report **rptJobRevenue**.

5. Kristina also needs a report that shows the income from the storage units. Group the information by warehouse and show the name of the renter so that it's easy to identify the renter by last name. The report should also include the rent per unit, the total rent for each warehouse, and a grand total of rent for all warehouses. Name the report **rptStorageRevenue**.

6. Kristina suspects that MovinOn could increase its income from storage units by encouraging more long-term rentals. Add a calculation to rptStorageRevenue that shows how long each renter has rented a storage unit. Show the figure in years with one decimal place.

7. Close the **MovinOn.accdb** database and then close Access.

Case 3—Creating Meaningful Reports for the Hershey College Intramural Department

Finance

In this project, you help Marianna Fuentes, assistant director of the intramural department at Hershey College, to create reports for the department. First, Marianna needs to print labels that identify the equipment. Then she needs a report of the coaches' purchases. Each coach has been given $700 to spend on each of their assigned sports. This budget is for items that are not supplied directly through the department, such as shirts, water bottles, or trophies. As coaches make their purchases, they are to submit their receipts to Marianna. Marianna has been recording the receipts in a separate database and wants that data now to be incorporated with the department database. She asks if you can import the data into the database and then generate some reports based on this data.

Complete the following:

1. Start Access and open the **Hershey.accdb** database located in the Case 3 folder.

2. Before you can create the coach purchases report, you need to import the data from Marianna's database. The database, **CoachPurchases.accdb**, is located in the Chapter 5\EOC\Case 3 folder. The data you need is in the tblPurchaseByCoach table. Be sure you establish appropriate relationships after you have imported the tblPurchaseByCoach table.

3. Marianna needs a report that shows what each coach has spent from their $700 budget for each sport. The report should show the sport, the coach name, the purchases for that sport, and the total spent. Because this is the first year they are using a budget, the intramural staff is aware that the purchases might exceed the budget.

   She also says that for each sport, you should show the percentage of the budget that has been spent, as well as the remaining amount in the budget. (*Hint*: This could be a negative number.) She also asks you to indicate those sports that have gone over budget by changing the font color of each of the calculated values: the total amount, the percentage of the budget, and the remaining amount in the budget. The date and time of printing should also appear near the title of the report, and the Hershey college logo should appear on all reports. Name the report **rptCoachPurchasesDetail**.

4. Marianna asks that you prepare another report similar to rptCoachPurchasesDetail, but it should provide a summary of the purchases. This report should contain only the total spent, percentage of budget, and remaining budget for each sport. Marianna suggests that you use a line in the report to separate the summary for each sport, and change the font color of the calculated values as you did in rptCoachPurchasesDetail for sports that are over their $700 budget. Finally, this report needs a page header on all but the first page. (*Hint*: Use the report's properties to specify where the page header appears.) Name this report **rptCoachPurchasesSummary**.

5. Provide the labels that are requested for the equipment. In addition to the data pertaining to the equipment, Marianna asks you to include the date the label was printed. The labels should be printed on Avery Label #5386, with large text that nearly fills the labels. After the labels are printed, the department will stick them onto a tag that will then be attached to the equipment. Name the report containing the labels **rptEquipmentLabels**.

6. Close the **Hershey.accdb** database and then close Access.

Automating Database Processing
Operations: Making the Database Easier to Use

LEARNING OBJECTIVES

Level 1

Create a well-designed navigation form to provide a user interface for a database
Automate tasks by creating basic macros
Specify what happens when a database opens

Level 2

Consolidate automated tasks by creating a macro group
Specify conditions and events for macros
Troubleshoot macros

Level 3

Assign a macro to an object event
Run a macro when a form opens or a report prints
Use a macro to validate data

TOOLS COVERED IN THIS CHAPTER

Access Options
Action Catalog
AutoExec macro
AutoKeys
Breakpoints
Events
Macros
Macro groups
Macro security
Navigation forms
Splash screen
Trust Center
Visual Basic for Applications (VBA)

Chapter Introduction

As you add queries, forms, and reports to your database, you will need to manage access to these objects to make the database easy to use without jeopardizing the security of the data. This chapter begins by teaching you how to design and implement a user-friendly menu using a navigation form, so that employees can work with only those parts of the database they need. You will also learn how to restrict the Ribbon tabs and Navigation pane so that users cannot change or modify the design of your database. To automate repetitive tasks you perform frequently and to add more functionality to reports and forms, you will be introduced to basic macros. You will use more advanced macros, including macro groups and special macros, such as AutoExec and AutoKeys, which can save time when working with your database.

Level 1 shows you how to build user-friendly navigation forms and explores introductory concepts about macros. Level 2 discusses advanced macro topics, such as macro groups and event-driven programming. It also explains how to troubleshoot macros so that they are free of error. Level 3 covers macro conditions and using message boxes, techniques that can automate your database to a professional level.

Case Scenario

In previous chapters, Donald Linebarger consulted with the managers of 4Corners Pharmacy and developed a database design. When he releases the 4Corners database for daily use, many employees who work with it will be new to Access. When Rachel Thompson, a pharmacy technician, created the electronic forms for the pharmacy, she began to develop the user interface for the database. (Recall that a user interface is what you see and use to communicate with a computer program such as Access.) Don wants her to customize the organization of the user interface. Instead of using the Navigation pane, which lists all of the objects in the database, Don wants to present a menu of options from which employees can select the forms and reports they use most often. Furthermore, Don needs a way to restrict access to some objects and options. For example, employees can now modify the design of the tables. Accidentally changing the data type of a primary key or inadvertently deleting a field in a table could cause problems in many queries, forms, and reports and even jeopardize the reliability of the data. A specialized user interface that prevents users from working in Design view would also help Don maintain the integrity and security of the database.

Operations Management

Don also wants to reduce the number of steps required to perform common tasks, such as moving from one form to another. In addition, he wants to display a custom message before a record is deleted, change the format of a report or print it depending on its contents, validate the accuracy of data in a form, and make it easier to print frequently used reports.

LEVEL 1

Automating Tasks with Navigation Forms and Macros

Understanding Navigation Forms

A **navigation form** is a special kind of form that provides an intuitive user interface and can appear when you open a database. The use of navigation forms makes navigation in the database similar to that of a Web site. When you view well-designed Web sites, you notice that they typically have top-level navigation commands. And, when you select a command, it will become highlighted or change color so that the user knows which top-level command is selected.

A navigation form has both a main navigation control and subform control automatically built in. To add an object to the navigation form, such as a report, you drag the object directly from the Navigation pane onto the form and a new tab is added. Selecting this tab lets you view the report in the subform control. You can add buttons to the main navigation form to work with the tables, forms, queries, and reports in the database. The navigation form that displays tabs for forms, reports, and queries acts as a main menu. Selecting the tabs on this main menu navigation form lets you instantly view those objects. An example of a main menu navigation form with subforms is shown in Figure 6.1.

Figure 6.1: Example of a main menu navigation form

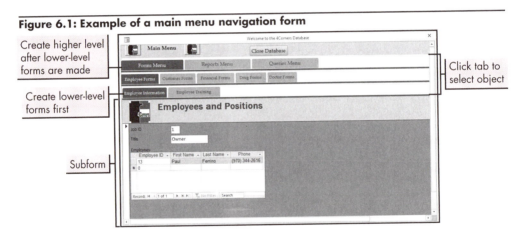

The navigation forms in the database can appear in a hierarchical format to easily select various database objects. A top-level navigation form would be followed by a navigation subform directly below or along the right or left side of the main navigation form. For example, you may have navigation tabs at the top of a navigation form that you select to view groups of reports or forms. If you select the report tab, a group of report tabs displays below the main report tab, and you can choose the next level you want to view, as in the example, Employee Reports, Customer Reports, Financial Reports, or Drug Reports. By dragging objects onto the navigation form to create tabs, the navigation form becomes an interactive part of the database.

Before you begin designing the navigation forms, you should decide on the type of navigation form layout style you want to use. With Access 2013, there are six predefined navigation form layouts. See Figure 6.2.

Figure 6.2: Navigation form layout options

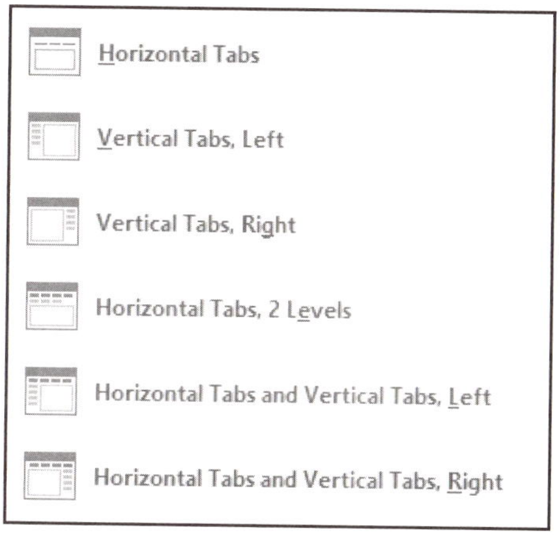

> Horizontal Tabs
>
> Vertical Tabs, Left
>
> Vertical Tabs, Right
>
> Horizontal Tabs, 2 Levels
>
> Horizontal Tabs and Vertical Tabs, Left
>
> Horizontal Tabs and Vertical Tabs, Right

The Horizontal Tabs navigation form places tabs across the top of the form horizontally. If you want tabs to appear vertically on the left or right side of the form, you would select either Vertical Tabs, Left or Vertical Tabs, Right. The Horizontal Tabs, 2 Levels navigation form places two horizontal rows of tabs horizontally across the top form. Using the Horizontal Tabs and Vertical Tabs, Left navigation form places both horizontal tabs across the top of the form and vertical tabs along the left side of the form. The Horizontal Tabs and Vertical Tabs, Right form has tabs across the top and along the right side of the form.

Because a navigation form serves as the user interface for a database, most navigation forms include graphics and labels to provide identification and visual appeal. When you use a navigation form as the main gateway to the database, it's a good idea to set database options that restrict the Ribbon to specified options and to hide the Navigation pane preventing users from accessing commands they could use to change the database design. By implementing these options, a navigation form provides an interface that is more appealing, personalized, and secure than the Navigation pane.

Designing Navigation Forms

Using a navigation form with the Subform/Subreport control lets you present the objects in your database using a logical organization. To provide a user interface in the database with navigation forms, you will need to create the main navigation form. The main navigation form will serve as the main menu when users open the database. You will also construct other navigation forms, such as one for forms and another for reports.

Don starts his work on the 4Corners database by reviewing its objects and planning the categories he will use to organize the objects on the tabs of the navigation form. He does not want to let employees open tables from the navigation form—they can use the forms that Rachel created to enter data and the reports that Elaine Estes developed to view and print information. Furthermore, he wants to prevent most employees from opening tables in Design view so they cannot modify the database design. The queries employees need are now used as the basis for forms and reports, so employees do not need to open queries from the navigation form either.

Don determines that the navigation form should only allow access to the forms and reports. However, the 4Corners database now contains dozens of forms and reports, and employees should be able to open most of them. Instead of listing each form and report on the main navigation form, he can include one tab for forms and another for reports. When users select the tab for forms, a secondary navigation form tab will display. Don considers showing all the forms on this secondary page, but he realizes that there would be so many tabs that users would not be able to easily find the form they need. He decides to organize the forms into five categories: employees, customers, financial, drugs, and doctors. For example, the employee forms include frmEmployee, the main form for entering employee information, and frmEmployeeView, the form that identifies the employees in each job position. He can use the same approach and categories for the reports. For example, the financial reports include rpt2017Sales, the summary sales report for 2017, and rptBalance, the report listing outstanding customer balances. Don sketches a design for his navigation form, as shown in Figure 6.3.

Figure 6.3: Sketch of navigation form design

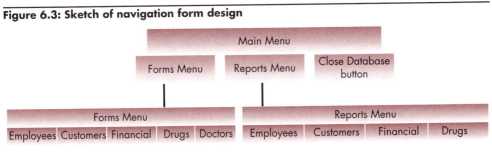

© 2014 Cengage Learning

Don decides to use the Horizontal Tabs layout for the navigation forms so that he will be able to navigate from the top level down. Note that the navigation form for the main menu contains an option to close the database. Including this option means that users can perform all the work they need, and then they close the database without using any other part of the Access interface.

Creating Navigation Forms

Now that Don has sketched the design for the navigation forms, he can create the navigation forms that will be available on the Forms menu and the Reports menu. He will need to create the forms for employees, customers, financials, drugs, and doctors before he creates the main form menu.

Don will need to create these forms first because tabs are created by dragging an object, such as a form, from the Navigation pane onto the navigation form. Tabs in a navigation form are used to display subforms. For example, each subform on the Employee menu will have a tab that you click to view the specific form. Therefore, with navigation forms, forms in the lower level of the hierarchy are produced first. After these forms are created, the navigation form that will be used as the main menu will need to be created.

Recall that Don wants the navigation form for the main menu to contain three options. The first option displays a secondary form showing five form tabs, the second option opens a secondary form showing report tab categories, and the third closes the database. He will use the Horizontal Tabs layout to create all of the subforms, beginning with the Customer Forms menu. Don clicks the Navigation button in the Forms group on the CREATE tab to display the Navigation menu (Figure 6.2). Don selects the Horizontal Tabs layout and the Horizontal Tabs navigation form opens, as shown in Figure 6.4.

Figure 6.4: Horizontal Tabs navigation form

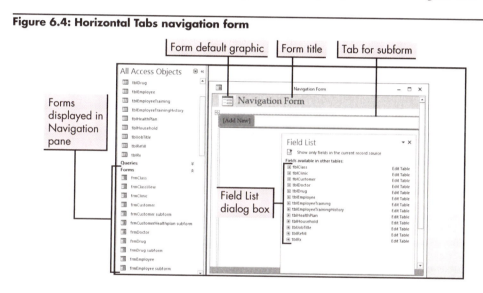

Don notices that the Field List for tables is open, and because he will not use the Field List now, he closes it. The navigation form displays in Layout view because this is the view used to place objects in the navigation form. First, Don deletes the Form title in the Form Header by clicking on the title and pressing Delete. He also deletes the graphic to the left of the title. Then, he minimizes the Form Header so that he can concentrate on the Form tabs.

Don is now ready to drag forms from the Navigation pane into the Customer Forms navigation form. He places his mouse pointer over frmCustomer in the Navigation pane and drags it to the [Add New] tab. Don switches to Design view to see how the form is coming along. The form name frmCustomer displays on the tab and a new [Add New] tab appears, as shown in Figure 6.5.

Figure 6.5: Customer Forms navigation form with frmCustomer added

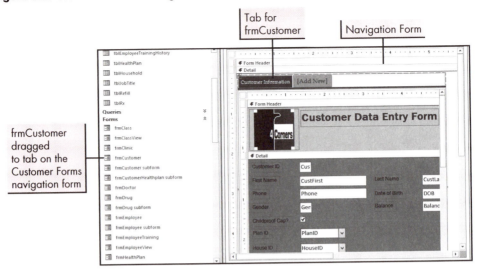

Don is impressed with the ease and simplicity of bringing objects into a navigation form. After switching back to Layout view, he then drags frmHealthPlan and frmHousehold to new tabs in the navigation form. To create more understandable names on the tabs, he double-clicks the frmCustomer tab, and replaces the existing text with Customer Information. He changes the other tab headings to Customer Health Plans and Household Information. To better accommodate the text on the tabs, he uses Shift+click to select each tab heading and changes the font size to 9. The Customer Forms navigation form with the three subforms added is shown in Figure 6.6.

Figure 6.6: Customer Forms navigation form with three subforms added

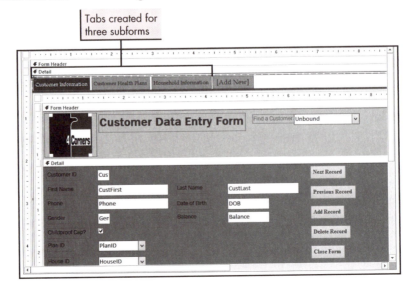

To display as much of the subforms as possible, Don decides to move them closer to the top of the Detail section. To make this adjustment, he switches to Design view. To select all the objects in the Detail section, he clicks the Form Selector button in the upper-left corner of the form and then clicks the Layout Selector , which appears in the upper-left corner of the Detail section. All items in the Detail section are now selected. He places the mouse pointer over the top of the Customer Information tab and drags it to the top of the Detail section. He saves the form as frmNavigationCustomerForms and then views it in Form view, as shown in Figure 6.7.

Figure 6.7: frmNavigationCustomerForms in Form view

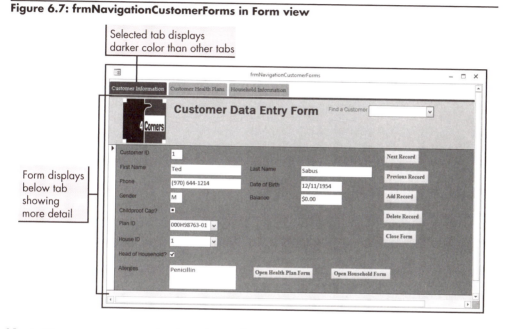

Next Don creates a navigation form for the Employee Forms menu using the frmEmployeeView and frmEmployeeTraining forms. He changes the tab names to Employee Information and Employee Training. After making the same formatting changes he made for the Customer Forms navigation form to the Form Header and tabs in the Detail section, he saves this form as frmNavigationEmployeeForms. See Figure 6.8.

Figure 6.8: frmNavigationEmployeeForms with two subforms

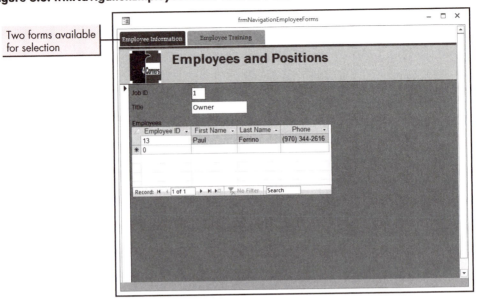

Two forms available for selection

The next navigation form he creates is the Financial Forms navigation form. Don needs to include the frmDrug form because this form shows the margin between the drug price and cost of the drug. Don renames the tab heading for the subform as Drug Margins. Don formats this navigation form like the other two and then saves the form as frmNavigationFinancialForms.

The next form he constructs is the Drug Forms navigation form. He deletes the form title and default graphic. For this form, he includes frmDrug again so the pharmacists and pharmacy technicians can view the drug information. In addition, he adds frmPrimaryActivity2. Don renames the form tabs for the subforms as Drug Information and Prescription Refill Information, formats the form so it is consistent with the two other forms he has created, and then saves it as frmNavigationDrugForms. See Figure 6.9.

Figure 6.9: frmNavigationDrugForms in Form view

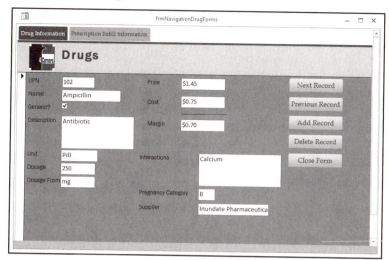

The final navigation form Don creates is for Doctor Forms with frmDoctor as the subform and Doctor Information as the tab name. He saves this navigation form as frmNavigationDoctorForms.

Don is now ready to create the form to be used as the foundation for the navigation forms he created. He creates a navigation form and then saves the form as frmNavigationFormsMenu. In the Layout view, he drags the five navigation forms into this form, as shown in Figure 6.10.

Figure 6.10: frmNavigationFormsMenu in Layout view

As he views the Forms Menu navigation form in Form view, he realizes that he needs to make some changes to this form because both form names and the form tabs are displayed. Switching back to Layout view, he clicks the frmNavigationEmployeeForms tab, selects and deletes the subform title Employee Forms, and then changes the tab name to Employee Forms. He continues this process for each form and tab, saving his changes as he goes along. Finally, he decreases the size of the tabs by clicking on the tab, placing the mouse pointer over the right border and dragging it to the left. Once he completes this task, Don switches to Form view to look at the result. As he places his mouse pointer over each of the tabs, he notices that they change to a darker color. When he clicks a tab, it turns this same darker color, indicating that it is selected. See Figure 6.11.

Figure 6.11: Revised frmNavigationFormsMenu

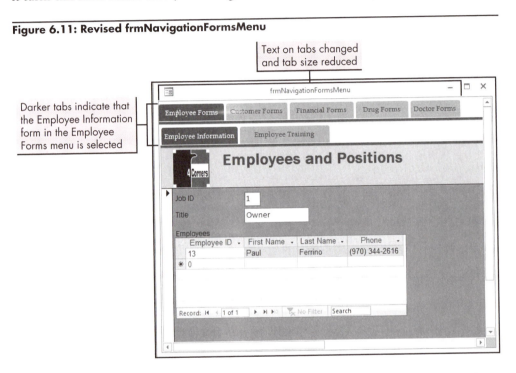

Now Don needs to create navigation forms for reports. He will create navigation forms using the Horizontal Tab layout for the Employee, Customer, Financial, and Drug reports. Based on what he learned about the forms he previously created, he knows that he will need to delete the form title because the tab names for the forms will identify the type of reports that are located in the form. The font, format colors, and theme will also be included in these forms for design consistency. He will add the reports described in Table 6.1 to the navigation forms for reports.

Table 6.1: Navigation forms for reports

Navigation Form Name	Reports Placed on Form	Tab Names for Reports
frmNavigationEmployeeReports	rptEmpLabels	Employee Mailing Labels
	rptBadge	Employee Name Tags
	rptEmployeePhoneList	Employee Phone List
frmNavigationCustomerReports	rptAllCustRxList	Customer Information
	rptHealthPlanAnalysis	Customer Health Plan
	rptHeadHHOnly	Household Information
frmNavigationFinancialReports	rpt2017Sales	Sales Report
	rptContributionMarginAnalysis	Contribution Margin Analysis
	rptBalance	Customers with Account Balance
frmNavigationDrugReports	rptRxContainer	Container Labels
	rptRxList	Rx List
	rptRefillDays	Refill Days

© 2014 Cengage Learning

Don tests these forms and is pleased that they are working correctly: When he selects a report tab that requires beginning and ending dates to be entered in order for the report to display, the dialog boxes open and the report shows with these dates. To change the report tabs for these reports, he switches to Design view.

He then creates the navigation form to be used for the navigation forms he created for the reports. He saves the form as frmNavigationReportsMenu. In Layout view, he then drags each of the four navigation forms for reports to the form. Don then changes these report tabs to Employee Reports, Customer Reports, Financial Reports, and Drug Reports. He decreases the size of the tabs and switches to Form view to view the result, as shown in Figure 6.12.

Figure 6.12: frmNavigationReportsMenu in Form view

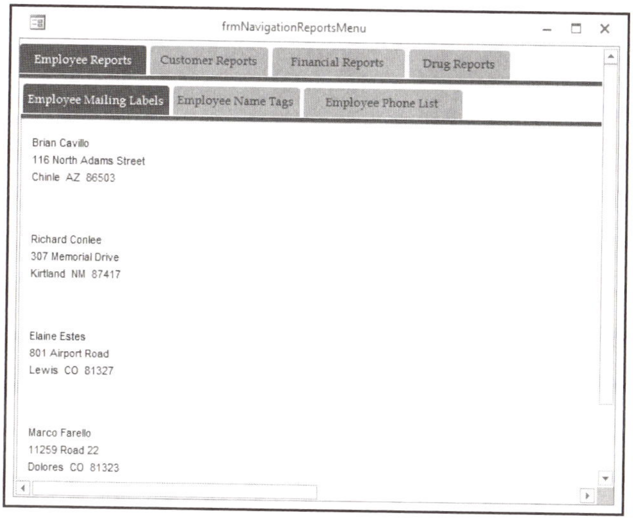

After creating the navigation forms for the Forms Menu and Reports Menu, Don needs to develop the main navigation form that will include these menus. This main navigation form will be the Main Menu for the database. He uses the same layout, Horizontal Tabs, and brings frmNavigationFormsMenu and frmNavigationReportsMenu into the form and changes their tabs to read Forms Menu and Reports Menu and saves the file as frmNavigationMainMenu. Next, he changes the form title to Main Menu and centers it above the Forms Menu and Reports Menu tabs. See Figure 6.13.

Figure 6.13: frmNavigationMainMenu in Layout view

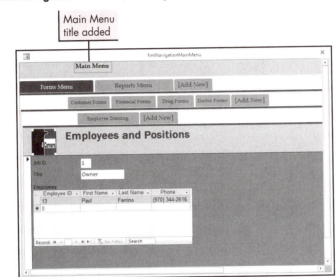

Don switches to Design view and reviews the most recent changes. He first clicks on each tab to be certain they display appropriately. So far, he is satisfied with the form as shown in Figure 6.14.

Figure 6.14: frmNavigationMainMenu in Design view

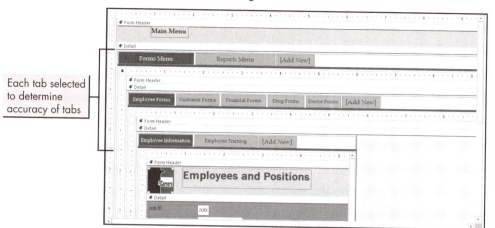

Each tab selected to determine accuracy of tabs

6

Best Practice

Having an Exit Strategy

A computer program should not only provide the information that the user requires, but also be easy to navigate. A well-organized, user-friendly navigation form guides users through a database and helps them find the information they need. Besides organizing navigation form objects into logical groups, database designers recommend that the last item on the main navigation form should be to close the database.

Don decides to modify the appearance of the Main Menu so that it reflects the customized design of other objects in the database. In particular, he wants to add the 4Corners logo and change the title label.

Formatting a Main Menu

First, Don decides to add the 4Corners logo to the Main Menu form header on both sides of the title. He clicks the Logo button in the Header/Footer group on the DESIGN tab and then selects and inserts the 4Corners.jpg image. Access inserts the logo in the upper-left corner of the form. Don adjusts its placement so that it aligns next to the title label. He then repeats this process in the upper-right corner.

When he checks the results in Form view, he decides to enhance the logo by applying a special effect. He returns to Design view, clicks the logo, and clicks the Property Sheet button in the Tools group on the DESIGN tab. On the Format tab of the Property Sheet, he selects the Special Effect button arrow and then clicks the Raised option. He repeats this process for the other logo. Don reviews the Main Menu navigation form and then resizes the window so that it fills most of the screen and displays as much form and report information as possible. He wants Access to use the current size when it opens the Main Menu navigation form, and he wants to prevent users from resizing the form. To make these changes, he opens the Property Sheet for the form. First, he sets the Auto Resize property to No so that Access will not resize the form when it is opened. Then he sets the Border Style property to Dialog to prevent users from resizing the form. Finally, he saves his changes to the form and opens it in Form view. Figure 6.15 shows the completed Main Menu navigation form.

Figure 6.15: Redesigned Main Menu navigation form

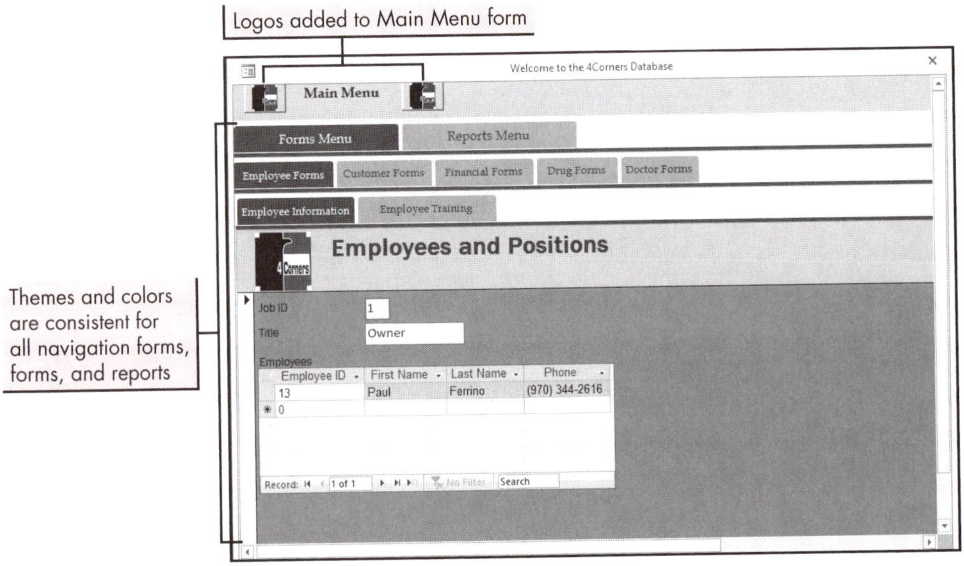

Logos added to Main Menu form

Themes and colors are consistent for all navigation forms, forms, and reports

Change the Format of a Navigation Form

1. Open the navigation form in Design view.
2. Change the format of various elements, such as color, labels, images, and lines, using the tools on the DESIGN tab.
3. To change properties such as the form's size and position, double-click the form selector button, and then change entries on the form's Property Sheet.

Don shows the Main Menu navigation form to Paul Ferrino, who finds it a useful and attractive way for employees to interact with the 4Corners database. Now Paul wants to add a navigation form for queries. Maria Garcia developed a few queries that are helpful on their own and do not serve as the basis for a form or report. Don thinks this over and realizes that he needs to create a macro that opens a query from the navigation form.

Understanding Basic Macros

A **macro** is an action or series of actions that you want Access to perform. Rather than performing a set of instructions repeatedly to perform the same task, you can save time and ensure accuracy by creating a macro that performs those actions for you. Macros automate repetitive tasks, such as opening forms, printing reports, and running queries.

Macros are composed of a series of actions organized in the sequence in which they should be performed. These actions are instructions designed to manipulate database objects, such as opening a form or printing a report. Table 6.2 shows a list of commonly used macro actions.

Table 6.2: Common macro actions

Macro Action	Explanation
Beep	Plays a beep tone when a specified task is completed or is beginning
CloseDatabase	Closes the current database
CloseWindow	Closes a specified database object window
DisplayHourglassPointer	Provides a visual indication, the echo symbol, that the macro is running
FindRecord	Finds the first record that meets the specified criteria; if the action is used again, the macro finds the next record that meets the criteria
MessageBox	Displays a message box containing a warning or informational message
OpenForm	Opens a form in Form view, Design view, Layout view, Datasheet view, or Print Preview
OpenQuery	Opens a select or crosstab query in Design view, Datasheet view, or Print Preview
OpenReport	Opens a report in Report view, Design view, Layout view, or Print Preview or prints a report
QuitAccess	Closes Access

© 2014 Cengage Learning

To create a macro, you work in the Macro window in which you can select actions such as those listed in Table 6.2. You list the actions in the order you want Access to perform them. For example, if you want to create a macro that prints a report, closes the report, and then closes Access, you list three actions in the Macro window: OpenReport, CloseWindow, and QuitAccess.

Best Practice

Protecting the Database from Macro Viruses

Computer viruses pose risks to computer systems and their data. Because millions of computer users are affected by viruses every year, you must protect your data from corruption by these viruses. The best line of defense is to install an antivirus program and update the virus definitions on a regular basis.

Macros are susceptible to a virus attack. To help protect your data from the corruption caused by a virus hidden in a macro, Access lets you set the macro security level on your computer. You set the macro security level by clicking the FILE tab, clicking the Options button, selecting Trust Center, clicking the Trust Center Settings button, and then clicking Macro Settings. The Trust Center dialog box opens, in which you can select one of four macro security levels. See Figure 6.16.

Figure 6.16: Trust Center dialog box

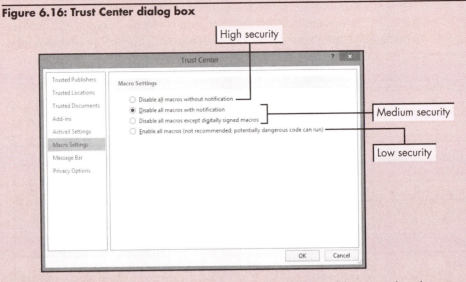

The Disable all macros without notification option disables harmful content, but does not notify you through the Message Bar. If you select the Disable all macros with notification option, harmful content will be disabled, but you will be notified on the Message Bar (which is the area just below the Ribbon that appears when active content, such as ActiveX controls and macros, are blocked). The Disable all macros except digitally signed macros option allows only macros that are digitally signed and come from a trusted source to be executed. The Enable all macros option allows all macros to run, but does not offer any protection. As a best practice, you should set the security level for your database to Disable all macros except digitally signed macros or Disable all macros with notification.

Paul mentions to Don that he is preparing for a meeting with the pharmacy's accountant, and needs to update prescription information and produce the rptContributionMarginAnalysis report for each of the past 12 months. At this point, the 4Corners database contains nearly 20 reports, and Paul thinks it will be tedious to find and generate this report 12 times. Don offers to create a macro for Paul to run the rptContributionMarginAnalysis report. He can also enhance the macro so that Access displays the echo symbol icon, which is the default busy symbol in Microsoft Windows, while the report is being generated and so that it also makes a beep sound when it is complete.

Creating a Macro

Unlike other Microsoft Office products, such as Microsoft Excel and Microsoft Word, which typically record keystrokes to create macros, you create an Access macro in the Macro window. To begin creating the macro for Paul's report, Don selects the CREATE tab and then clicks the Macro button in the Macros & Code group. The new Macro Builder appears with the contextual MACRO TOOLS DESIGN tab displayed. To the right of the Macro Builder is the Action Catalog.

You use the **Action Catalog** to select features you want included in your macro and the actions that you want the macro to perform. You can select an action using one of several methods. First, you can click the Add New Action list arrow in the Macro Builder, and then select the action you want from the list. You can also type the action name in the Search box in the Action Catalog to find the action. Another option is to click the right-facing triangle in front of a folder in the Action Catalog to display actions stored in the folder. See Figure 6.17.

Figure 6.17: Macro Builder for creating a macro

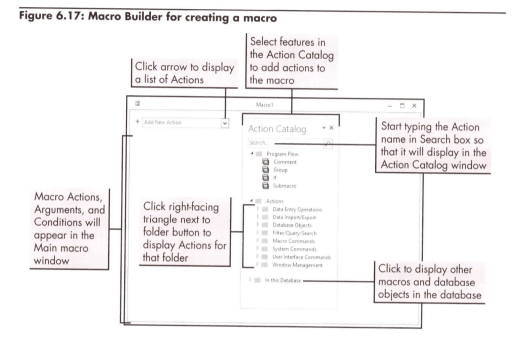

If you use the Action Catalog to select an action, you double-click the action or drag it to the Macro Builder to add it to the macro. Access displays the argument(s) below each action in the Macro Builder. **Arguments** are the additional information that Access needs to perform the task.

Don plans to add three actions and associated arguments to the Macro Builder:

- **DisplayHourglassPointer**—This action changes the pointer to an echo icon while the macro runs. If you turn the hourglass icon off, the echo symbol (or other icon you select) will appear while the macro is running. Access knows to display the busy icon with the DisplayHourglassPointer action. It has one argument that turns the echo symbol icon on or off.
- **OpenReport**—This action opens a report and has five arguments: Report Name (enter or select the report you want to open), View (specify whether to print the report or to open it in Print Preview or Design view), Filter Name (enter the name of a filter

you want to use to sort or restrict the records the report includes), Where Condition (enter a SQL WHERE clause that selects records for the report), and Window Mode (select how to display the report window after Access generates the report).

- **Beep**—This action plays a beep when the macro is finished and has no arguments.

In the Macro Builder, Don clicks the Add New Action arrow and clicks Comment in this list. He then types "Displays an hourglass pointer as the macro runs." Don notices that the comments appear in a bold green format between the symbols /* and */. See Figure 6.18.

Figure 6.18: Macro Builder with comment and Add New Action list arrow

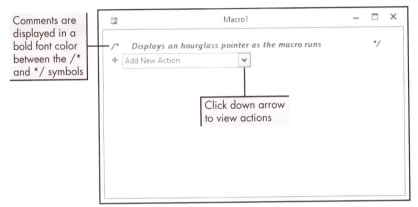

Don clicks the Add New Action arrow and clicks DisplayHourglassPointer. The Hourglass On argument is set to Yes by default, so he doesn't need to change that.

He then adds a new comment in the next row "Opens rptContributionMarginAnalysis in Print Preview." In the next row, he selects the OpenReport action, and then selects rptContributionMarginAnalysis as the Report Name argument and Print Preview for the View argument. The last action he selects is Beep with "Sounds a beep when the macro is finished" as the comment. He saves the macro as mcrContributionMarginAnalysis, using the standard "mcr" prefix for macro objects. Figure 6.19 shows this macro in the Macro Builder.

Figure 6.19: mcrContributionMarginAnalysis in the Macro Builder

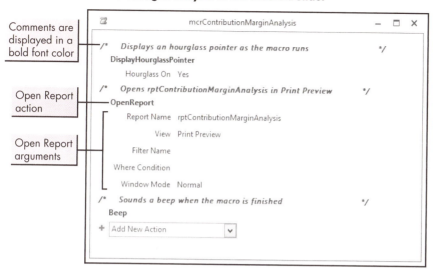

Now that Don has created and saved a macro, he can run it to make sure it performs the task it is designed to perform.

Best Practice

Documenting Macro Actions

Because macros often need to be changed to accommodate a new object or to run more efficiently, you should include a comment for each macro action. Doing so explains the purpose of each action, which is helpful to database designers and others who maintain and update the database.

How To

Create a Macro

1. On the CREATE tab, click the Macro button in the Macros & Code group. The Macro Builder opens with the Action Catalog and MACRO TOOLS DESIGN tab displayed.
2. Add comments to each action to explain its purpose.
3. Add the actions you want the macro to perform to the Macro Builder. You can click the Add New Action arrow and select the action; type the action in the Search box in the Action Catalog, or click to open a folder in the Action Catalog and select an action.
4. Select or enter the appropriate arguments for each action.
5. Save the macro using a name that begins with the "mcr" prefix.

Best Practice

Choosing Tasks to Automate

Macros are designed to perform repetitive actions, so use them to automate tasks you perform often or those that combine basic tasks into a long series, making each step difficult to remember. You should be familiar with the most common actions (refer to Table 6.2) so you can identify tasks as suitable candidates for macros. If you want to automate a task that is not addressed in the built-in macro actions, you can use Visual Basic for Applications (VBA), the programming language for most Microsoft Office programs, to create a program. (You will learn how to use VBA and the Visual Basic Editor in Chapter 7.) VBA does offer advantages over using macros, such as better error-handling features and easier updating capabilities. Macros, however, are useful for small applications and for basic tasks, such as opening and closing objects. Furthermore, you cannot use VBA to assign actions to a specific key or key combination or to open an application in a special way, such as displaying a navigation form. For these types of actions, you need to use macros.

Running a Macro

After you create and save a macro, you can run it in three ways:

- On the MACRO TOOLS DESIGN tab, click the Run button in the Tools group.
- On the DATABASE TOOLS tab, click the Run Macro button in the Macro group, select the macro in the Run Macro dialog box, and then click the OK button.
- In the Navigation Pane, click Macros, right-click the macro name, and then click Run on the shortcut menu.

When you run a macro, Access performs the actions listed in the Macro Builder one after the other.

Now that the mcrContributionMarginAnalysis macro is complete, Don can use the Run button on the MACRO TOOLS DESIGN tab to run the macro. You can also use the commands on the MACRO TOOLS DESIGN tab to edit the macro and extend its functionality.

Don clicks the Run button on the MACRO TOOLS DESIGN tab. The echo symbol appears briefly, and then the Enter Parameter Value dialog box opens. Because the rptContributionMarginAnalysis report is based on a parameter argument query, Don must enter start and end dates to define the period the report covers. When the report opens in Print Preview, a beep plays.

As Don tests the macro by running it several times, he decides that it would be more helpful if the macro printed the report, so he prints and closes the report instead of opening it in Print Preview. The final Beep action can then signal that the report is finished printing. Don realizes that sending the report directly to the default printer is not always a best practice because the report will instantly print when the macro runs without giving additional options. However, he wants to simplify the task of running this report at this time, so he decides to make these changes. Don will edit the mcrContributionMarginAnalysis macro.

Editing a Macro

To edit a macro, you work in the Macro Builder. You can rearrange the order of the actions by clicking the Move up or Move down arrow or dragging the action line to a new position. If you need to add a new action between two existing actions, click the Add New Action arrow, and select the action. Complete the arguments and move or drag the new action to the location between two other actions. To delete an action, click the action and then click the Delete button that appears in the upper-right corner of the selected action.

Don wants to change the View argument of the OpenReport action so that Access prints rptContributionMarginAnalysis instead of opening it in Print Preview. He also wants to insert a CloseWindow action after the OpenReport action to close the report when it is finished printing. He opens the mcrContributionMarginAnalysis macro in Design view, and clicks the OpenReport action. He changes the View argument from Print Preview to Print. He then adds a new comment to explain the CloseWindow action. Next, he clicks the Add New Action list arrow and selects CloseWindow. This action has three arguments: Object Type (select the type of object to close, or leave this argument blank to close the active window), Object Name (enter or select the name of the object to close), and Save (select whether to save the object before closing, prompt to save, or close without saving). Don selects Report as the Object Type, rptContributionMarginAnalysis as the Object Name, and Yes to save the report before closing. He drags the new comment and action before the Beep comment and action. Then he edits the OpenReport comment. Figure 6.20 shows the completed design of mcrContributionMarginAnalysis.

Figure 6.20: Modified mcrContributionMarginAnalysis macro

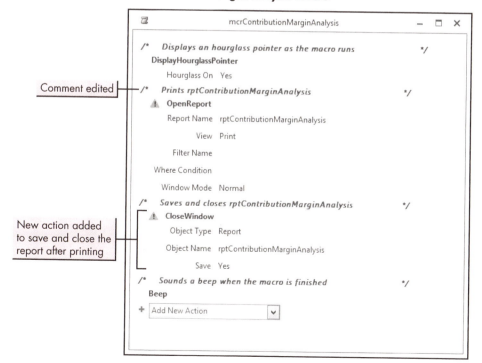

Don runs this macro several times to test it, verifying that the report prints and closes as it is designed to do. He demonstrates the macro for Paul, who plans to use it to print copies of rptContributionMarginAnalysis for his accountant.

Now that Don understands the basics of creating and using macros, he realizes that to solve the problem of including queries on the navigation form, he needs to create one macro per query—he can select the OpenQuery action to run a query, but he must specify which query to run. Even if he includes only five or six queries on the form, creating five or six of the same type of macro seems unnecessarily repetitive. He decides to study more about macros to determine whether he can find a better solution.

In the meantime, Paul asks Don to address the problems of security and personalizing the 4Corners database so that users recognize it as a 4Corners application. Don can accomplish both tasks by specifying what Access does when users open the 4Corners database.

Setting Start-up Options

You can specify certain actions and configurations called **start-up options** that Access performs when a database opens. For example, you can set the name that appears in the Access window title bar, prevent users from using the Navigation pane, or specify a form to open. You can also help to secure the database by hiding selected tabs on the Ribbon and restricting access to the menu commands. These actions allow only authorized users, such as the database manager, to work with tables and other objects in Design view or use commands to make a copy of the database. You set these start-up options using the features in Access Options. After you set the options, they are in effect the next time someone opens the database. If you want to bypass the current database options that you set, you can press and hold down the Shift key when you open the database.

Specifying Current Database Options

Recall that one of Don's goals in creating a navigation form is to hide some of the Ribbons tabs when Access starts and restrict the options so that users cannot tamper with the database design or make unwanted changes. He clicks the FILE tab, clicks the Options command to open the Access Options dialog box, and then selects the Current Database category. See Figure 6.21.

Figure 6.21: Access Options dialog box with options for the current database

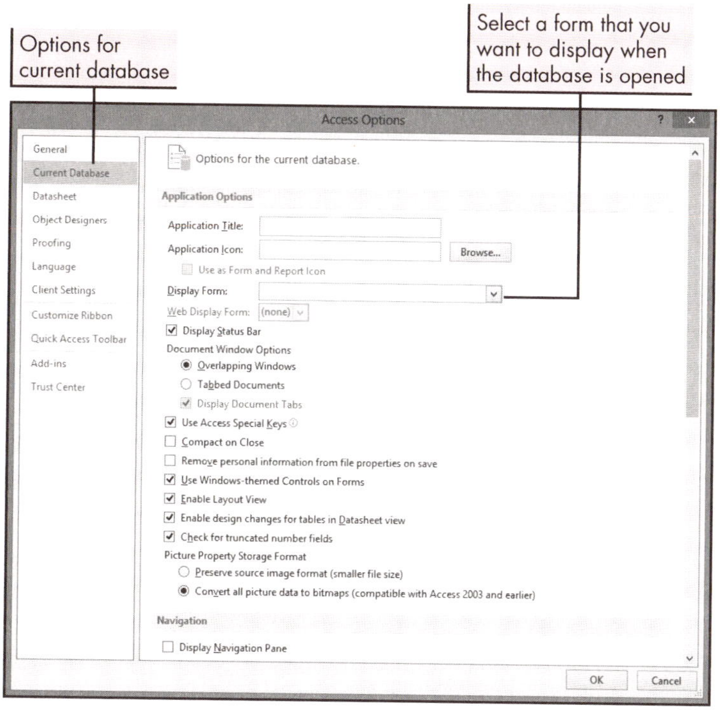

Options for current database

Select a form that you want to display when the database is opened

To control the start-up of the current database, Don performs the following actions:

- **Display Form**—Clicks the arrow and then selects frmNavigationMainMenu as the form that will open upon start-up.
- **Display Navigation pane**—Clicks this check box to remove the check mark so the Navigation pane will not open upon start-up.
- **Allow Full Menus**—Clicks this check box to remove the check mark so users will not have access to the Ribbon tabs and commands that allow users to change the design of the objects in the 4Corners database. Only a subset of the built-in tabs and commands will be available to users.

Don clicks the OK button to close the Access Options dialog box, and then he tests the start-up options by closing and then reopening the 4Corners database. Figure 6.22 shows the main navigation form after Don changed the start-up options.

Figure 6.22: 4Corners database after changing start-up options

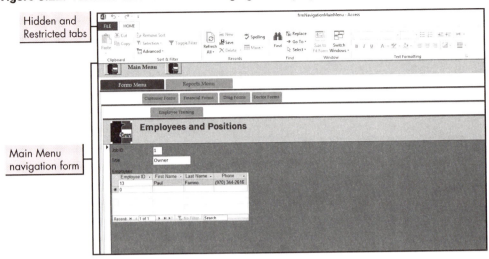

Hidden and Restricted tabs

Main Menu navigation form

Now that Don is satisfied that the options he has set will ensure that unauthorized users can't make changes to the database, he can focus on Paul's next request, to further personalize the 4Corners database.

Creating a Splash Screen

With the Current Database options in effect, Access will display the Main Menu navigation form when someone opens the 4Corners database. However, Don wants to personalize the database by displaying a **splash screen**, which is a form that includes the name of the pharmacy and the database and provides information so that users can contact the appropriate employee for help when necessary. Don already specified that the navigation form appears when users open the 4Corners database. If he changes this option to display a splash screen form instead, the navigation form won't open, meaning users will be on their own when navigating the database. The Current Database category in the Access Options dialog box doesn't allow you to set two objects to open in sequence. How can Don specify that when the 4Corners database opens, first a splash screen appears, and then the Main Menu navigation form opens?

Access provides a special macro called **AutoExec** that runs automatically when a database is opened. When Access starts, it checks for an AutoExec macro. If Access finds a macro by this name, Access runs the macro before performing the tasks specified in the Access Options dialog box. In this case, Don wants to create an AutoExec to display a splash screen form. On the splash screen, he can identify the pharmacy and database name to personalize the database, include his name and phone number so that users can contact him if they have questions, and display instructions for closing the splash screen window. When users follow these instructions, the Main Menu navigation form opens.

To create the splash screen, Don reopens the 4Corners database, but he must press the Shift key as it opens to bypass the Current Database options he set. Then he creates a new form in Design view, using the same colors, fonts, theme, and logo that he used for the navigation forms. He also includes his name and phone number and instructions for closing the splash screen. To specify the size and behavior of the splash screen, he works with the form's Property Sheet and changes the following properties:

- **Caption**—Set to Welcome to the 4Corners database.
- **Scroll Bars**—Set to None.
- **Border Style**—Set to Dialog.
- **Min Max Buttons**—Set to None.
- **Width**—Set to 10 inches.

Don then adds the logo to the Form Header and includes a label with the text 4Corners Database located at the top of the form. He changes the label font color to Black, Text 1, which meets the design specifications of the other forms, and increases the font size to 24. He adds three labels to the Design section of the form to instruct users how to proceed. He saves the form as frmSplash, and then switches to Form view. See Figure 6.23.

Figure 6.23: Initial splash screen for the 4Corners database

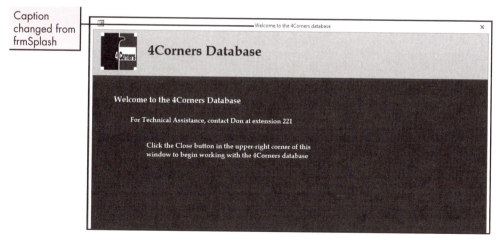

Now that Don has created the splash screen form, he is ready to create the AutoExec macro and specify that it opens the splash screen.

Open a Database and Bypass Current Database Options
1. Press and hold the Shift key at the same time you open the database.

Creating an AutoExec Macro

To create an AutoExec macro, you create a macro that contains the actions you want Access to perform when the database is opened, and then you must save the macro using the name AutoExec. Access looks for this macro when it starts and runs the macro before performing the actions specified in the Access Options dialog box.

Don starts a new macro in Design view, selects OpenForm as the action, and selects the frmSplash form as the argument. He saves the macro as AutoExec. See Figure 6.24.

Figure 6.24: Creating the AutoExec macro

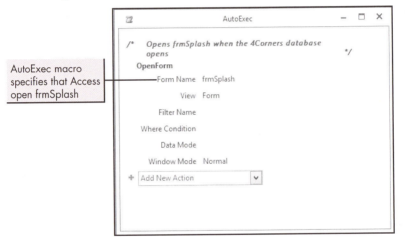

AutoExec macro specifies that Access open frmSplash

Create an AutoExec Macro
1. Click the Macro button in the Macros & Code group on the CREATE tab. The Macro dialog box opens.
2. Add comments to each action to explain its purpose.
3. In the Macro Builder, select the actions you want the macro to perform. You can click the Add New Action arrow and select the action, type the action in the Search box in the Action Catalog until it displays, or click to open a folder in the Action Catalog and select an action.
4. Select or enter the appropriate action arguments for each action.
5. Save the macro using the name AutoExec.
6. Close the Macro Builder.

Don closes Access and then restarts it. When he opens the 4Corners database, Access runs the AutoExec macro, which opens the splash screen form. When he clicks the Close button on the splash screen, the Main Menu navigation form appears with restricted menus and options as specified in the Access Options dialog box.

Now that Don has accomplished his goals of creating a more secure and personalized database, he is ready to solve the problem of including queries on a navigation form.

Steps To Success: Level 1

Glenn Hollander is serving as the database manager for Hudson Bay Pharmacy and asks for your help in extending the user interface for the Hudson database and personalizing its appearance. He also wants to automate a task that Joan Gabel, manager of the pharmacy, performs often.

Complete the following:

1. Start Access and open the **Hudson.accdb** database from the STS folder.

2. Review the objects in the Hudson database and plan the navigation forms that will help users perform their jobs more efficiently and ensure the integrity of the database objects. Glenn does not want to let Hudson Bay Pharmacy employees open tables from the Navigation pane. He wants a main menu from which employees will be able to access the forms they need to enter data and the reports they need to view and print information. He also wants to prevent most employees from opening tables in Design view so they cannot modify the database design. Because queries were used as the basis for the forms and reports, employees do not need to open the queries from the Navigation pane either.

3. Create navigation forms for the Hudson database based on your design. Create two navigation forms, one for the forms and another for reports. Both of these forms should appear in a Main Menu navigation form.

4. Test the Main Menu navigation form to ensure that it is logically organized and provides all the reports and forms that employees need.

5. Glenn wants to add the Hudson Bay Pharmacy logo to the navigation form, change the title label, and change the background color of the navigation forms. Format the navigation form to meet Glenn's goals. Use the logo in the **HudsonBay.jpg** file in the Chapter 6\Level 1 STS folder.

6. Joan is preparing for a meeting with her accountant and needs to print 12 versions of the rptContributionMarginAnalysis report, one for each of the past 12 months. Automate this task for Joan. As the report prints, set Access to display an hourglass (or busy) icon. When the report finishes, a beep should play. Save the macro as **mcrContributionMarginAnalysis**.

7. Glenn wants to set options that will help to secure the Hudson Bay Pharmacy database when users open it. For example, he wants to restrict the Ribbon and menus so that users cannot tamper with the database design. He also needs to specify that Access opens the Main Menu navigation form when it starts. Set these options for Glenn, selecting the ones that will help to secure the database and open the Main Menu navigation form.

8. Personalize the database by creating a splash screen, providing a way for users to close it so they can work with the Hudson Bay Pharmacy database.

9. Glenn wants to display the splash screen first, and then open the Main Menu. Create the appropriate object to meet Glenn's goals.

10. Save and close the Hudson.accdb database.

LEVEL 2
Creating Advanced Macros

Understanding Macro Groups

A **macro group** is two or more macros placed within the same macro file. Instead of creating several separate macros, you can combine them in a macro group. You use macro groups to consolidate related macros and to manage large numbers of macros. When you create a macro group, only its name is displayed as a macro object in the Navigation pane, not all of the macros it contains. For example, suppose Don wants to create a macro to open each report in the database. He would have to create over 20 macro objects. Instead, he can create one macro group named mcrReports, for example, that contains 20 OpenReport actions, one for each report in the database.

Paul has been running the mcrContributionMarginAnalysis macro to print the rptContributionMarginAnalysis report and now wants to print a number of other reports the same way. He asks Don to create similar macros to print the four financial reports that he prints most often: rpt2017Sales, rptBalance, rptRxList, and rptSales. Rather than creating one macro for each report, Don decides that he will create a macro group to solve the problem.

Creating a Macro Group

Although macros within a group are not required to be related, it is logical to organize similar macros within a group. Doing so helps to identify the macros within a group and to reference those macros later as necessary.

Before Don creates a macro group, he plans the macros the group will contain. He needs four macros to print the four reports that Paul specified. Don can use the OpenReport action with the Print argument that he used for the rptContributionMarginAnalysis report. Each macro should also close the report after it prints. To accomplish this, he can use the CloseWindow action, which he also used in the mcrContributionMarginAnalysis macro.

Don needs to bypass the Current Database options that he set, so he presses the Shift key as he opens the 4Corners database. He now has full access to the Ribbon and Navigation pane.

To create a macro group, Don opens a new Macro Builder, and then he reviews the actions in the Action Catalog. To create a group of macros in a single macro, he will need to use the Submacro program flow action. The word Submacro appears before the macro actions are selected. At the end of the submacro, the word End Submacro appears identifying that there are no more actions for that submacro. Don first drags Submacro from the Action Catalog into the Macro Builder, as shown in Figure 6.25.

Figure 6.25: First Submacro action added to the macro group

To distinguish each macro added to a macro group, you must give the macro a unique name. Because a macro can contain many actions, the macro name tells Access where the macro begins. First, in the box to the right of the Submacro action, Don enters "mcr2017Sales" as the name of the first macro in the group. This macro will print and close the rpt2017Sales report. He also adds the comment "Prints and closes rpt2017Sales" by clicking the Add New Action arrow in the Macro window and clicking Comment.

Next, Don adds the OpenReport action and selects the arguments to print the rpt2017Sales report. For the second action in the mcr2017Sales macro, he selects the CloseWindow action and specifies the appropriate arguments for closing the report. He saves the macro group as mcrFinancialReports. Don reviews the first submacro shown in Figure 6.26.

Figure 6.26: mcrFinancialReports macro group with the first submacro added

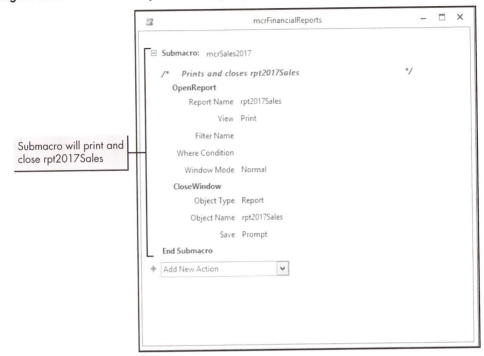

If a macro contains several actions, you continue to select new actions after the first one. Access performs the actions in the Macro Builder and any actions that immediately follow it until End Submacro is reached. Then, if another submacro appears with a macro name, the actions for that macro will perform. To continue building the macro group, you drag Submacro from the Action Catalog, enter a name for the macro and list the actions for it. For the next macro, you skip a row and then drag the Submacro action from the Action Catalog into the Macro Builder again, naming the second macro, listing the actions for it, and so on. You can define the macros in any order and group as many macros as you want.

He repeats this procedure to add three other macros to the macro group: mcrBalance (to print and close rptBalance), mcrRxList (to print and close rptRxList), and mcrSales (to print and close rptSales). He adds comments to each submacro. As a final check before closing the Macro Builder and testing the macro group to make sure it runs without any error messages, Don clicks the Collapse Actions button in the Collapse/Expand group on the DESIGN tab so that he can view each of the submacros in the macro group. See Figure 6.27.

Figure 6.27: Completed macro group

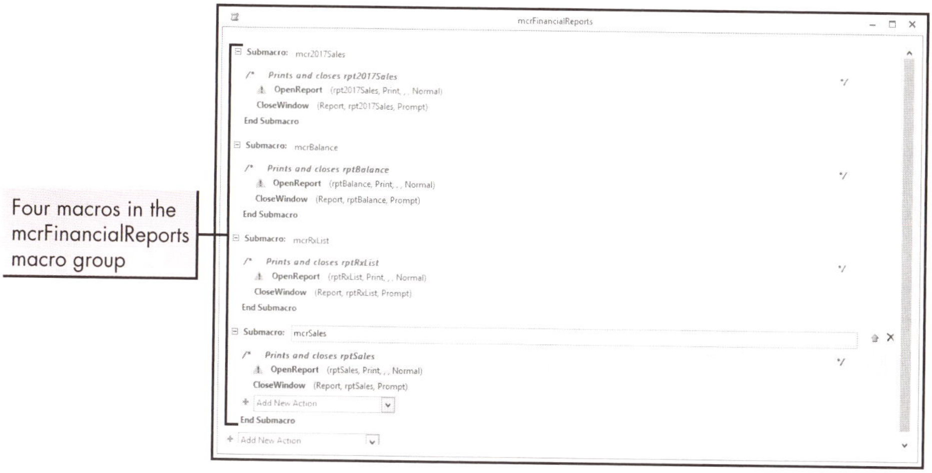

Four macros in the mcrFinancialReports macro group

How To

Create a Macro Group

1. Click the CREATE tab on the Ribbon, and then click the Macro button in the Macros & Code group.
2. If the Action Catalog is not displayed, click the Action Catalog button in the Show/Hide group on the DESIGN tab.
3. Add the Submacro action to the Macro Builder.
4. In the Submacro box, enter the name of a macro. This name must be unique.
5. Click the Add New Action arrow and select an action, and then select or enter the arguments for the action.
6. Repeat Steps 3 through 5 for each macro you want to add to the macro group.
7. Save the macro group, using the "mcr" prefix in the object name.

Running the Macros in a Macro Group

If you click the Run button on the DESIGN tab to run the macros in a macro group, Access runs only the first macro in the group. To run a particular macro within a group, you could click the Run Macro button in the Macro group on the DATABASE TOOLS tab to display the Run Macro dialog box. Then you would click the arrow to display the list of available macros, select the macro you want to run, and then click the OK button.

The options for running the individual macros in the mcrFinancialReports macro group introduce extra steps for Paul: First, he must open the macro group, and then run the appropriate macro. That takes just as much work as opening and printing a report. Don investigates another way to run a macro: He can assign a key combination to each macro in the macro group using an AutoKey.

6

Level 2

Assigning AutoKeys to Macros in a Macro Group

You can assign a key combination to a macro. For example, when you press the key combination, such as Ctrl+T, Access performs the action associated with that key combination. If you assign an action to a key combination that is already being used by Access (for example, Ctrl+C is the key combination for the Copy command), the action you assign can replace the default Access key assignment, though this is not recommended. The new key assignments are in effect as soon as you save the macro group and each time you open the database.

To assign an AutoKey to the macros in the mcrFinancialReports macro group, Don opens the macro group by right-clicking the macro in the Navigation pane and opening the macro in Design view from the shortcut menu. Next, Don clicks the Run Macro button in the Macro group on the DATABASE TOOLS tab. In the Run Macro dialog box, Don clicks the Macro Name arrow. The list of macros in the macro group displays.

In the Macro Name list, highlight the macro to which you want to assign an AutoKey. To specify an AutoKey, you must use a special notation when entering the key or key combinations. Names of single keys, such as the F1 key, must be enclosed within curly brackets ({}). The Ctrl key is represented by a caret (^) and the Shift key by a plus sign (+). (These key combinations are a subset of the syntax used in the SendKeys command, which are built-in commands that send keystrokes to Access databases.) Table 6.3 shows a partial list of key combinations.

Table 6.3: Examples of key combinations for AutoKeys

Key Combination	Macro Name Syntax
F1	{F1}
Ctrl+F1	^{F1}
Shift+F1	+{F1}
Alt+F1	%{F1}
Ctrl+Q	^Q
Ctrl+2	^2
Left arrow	{LEFT}
Backspace	{BKSP} or {BS}
Print Screen	{PRTSC}

© 2014 Cengage Learning

Instead of printing the four financial reports in mcrFinancialReports by selecting and running a macro, Don can modify the mcrFinancialReports macro group to assign key combinations to each macro and then rename the macro group as **AutoKeys**.

Don opens the mcrFinancialReports macro group in Design view. He decides to use a Ctrl key combination associated with the name of each macro. Don opens the Run Macro dialog box. He selects the first macro name, mcr2017Sales, and replaces it with ^L. He replaces the mcrBalance macro name with ^B, mcrRxList with ^R, and mcrSales with ^A. Then he saves the macro group and names it AutoKeys. See Figure 6.28.

Figure 6.28: AutoKeys assigned to macros in the macro group

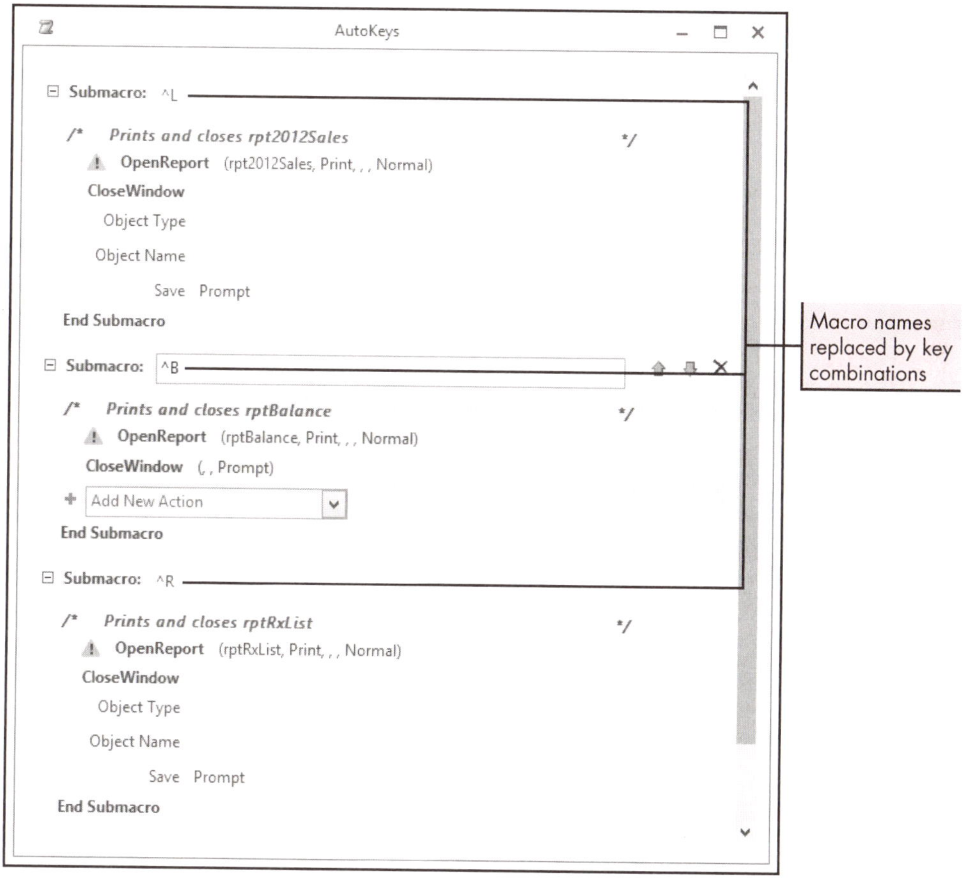

When Don demonstrates the AutoKeys macro, Paul immediately sees how using the key combinations to print and close the four financial reports will save time and effort.

Creating the Navigation Form to Run Macros Using Command Buttons

As you learned in Chapter 4, you can add a command button to a form to execute a series of actions. You can also use a command button to run a macro. First, you create the macro that specifies the actions you want to perform when someone clicks the button. Next, you create a form and add a command button to it, assigning the macro you want to run when the command button is clicked.

Don wants to make running queries easier for the users and make running the queries part of the Main Menu navigation form. He begins by meeting with some of the other managers and determines that they use five queries most often: qryHourlyRateSummary, qryNoTraining, qrySpeakSpanish, qrySubstituteList, and qryYearsOfService. Don creates a new macro group named mcrFrequentQueries with five macros, one for each query. Each macro in the macro group opens the specified query. See Figure 6.29.

Figure 6.29: mcrFrequentQueries with the five query-related submacros added

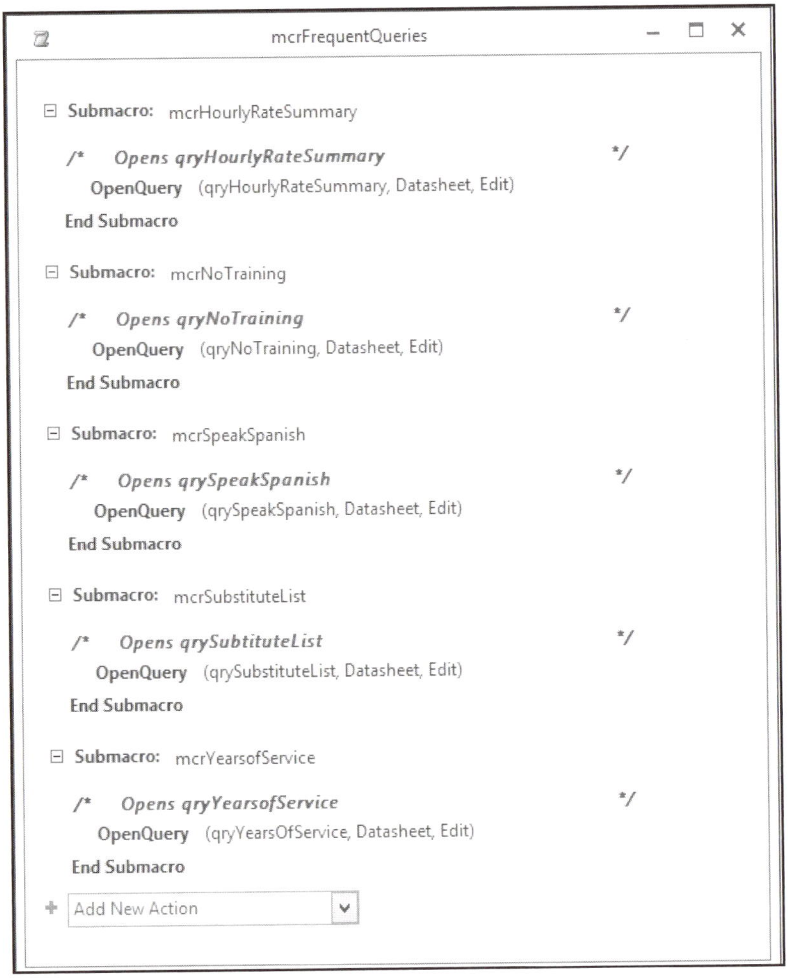

498

Assigning a Macro to a Command Button Control

Next, Don creates a blank form and applies the theme fill color. He clicks the Button control in the Controls group on the DESIGN tab, and then clicks in the form where he wants the first command button placed. The Command Button Wizard starts, and Don selects the Miscellaneous category and the Run Macro action. The macros available in the 4Corners database are displayed in the next dialog box, as shown in Figure 6.30.

Figure 6.30: Command Button Wizard dialog box with available macros

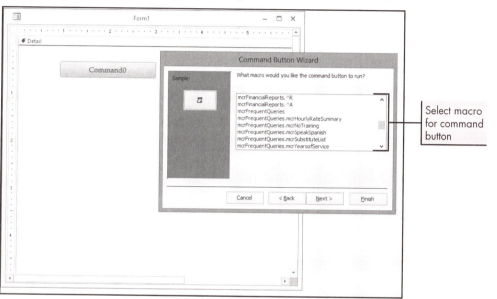

He selects the mcrFrequentQueries.mcrHourlyRateSummary macro and clicks the Next button. In the next wizard dialog box, he types "Run Hourly Rate Summary Query" as the text that will display in the form, and then, in the last dialog box, he enters "mcrHourlyRateSummary" as the name of the button before clicking the Finish button. He continues this process for the other four macros in the macro group. He aligns the text in the command buttons by changing the Alignment property to Left and removing the scroll bars from the form. Don saves the form as frmQueries.

Don now adds this form to a new navigation form he names frmNavigationQueriesMenu. He can then finally add frmNavigationQueriesMenu to the Main Menu Navigation form, as shown in Figure 6.31.

Figure 6.31: Main Menu with frmNavigationQueriesMenu added

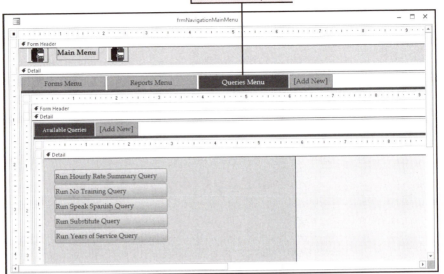

The 4Corners Navigation form allows employees to open any database objects they need. Now that Don has gained experience with macros, learning how to assign macros to key combinations and how to use macros to be used as form controls, Don wants to explore specifying conditions and associating macros with events.

Specifying Conditions and Events for Macros

There are two ways that you can extend the power and usefulness of macros. One way is to specify certain conditions in which the macro actions should perform. For example, suppose you create a macro named mcrTravelExpenses to print a report named rptTravelExpenses, which lists travel expenses incurred by employees. This report is based on a parameter query that requests the start and end date for selecting records. In some months, such as August, employees do not submit any travel expenses. When you run the mcrTravelExpenses macro to print rptTravelExpenses and you enter August 1 as the start date and August 31 as the end date, the report prints with no data. To avoid this, you could set the OpenReport action in mcrTravelExpenses to print a report only if the report contains information, using the logic described in Figure 6.32.

Figure 6.32: Condition testing

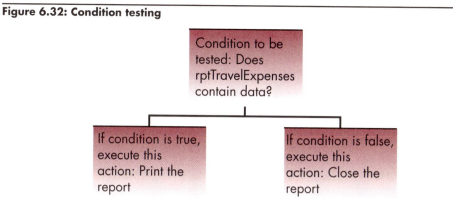

© 2014 Cengage Learning

The other way to make macros more powerful is to associate them with controls, such as a command button or a combo box on a form. When a user clicks the button, Access runs the macro. The technique is called **event-driven programming**, or running a macro when the user interacts with an object, such as clicking a button or moving to a specified field on a form. An **event** is a state, condition, or occurrence that Access recognizes. For example, events occur when you click a field on a form or press a key to choose a menu command. Each event has an associated **event property**, which specifies how an object responds when the event occurs. For example, each form has an On Open event property, which specifies what happens when the form is opened. A text box on a form has an On Click property, which specifies what happens when the text box is clicked. These event properties appear in the Property Sheets for forms, reports, and controls. By default, they do not have an initial value, meaning that the event property has not been set. In other words, when you click a text box, by default, Access takes no special action because the On Click event property for the text box has not been set.

If you set an event property value to a macro name, Access runs the macro when the event occurs. For example, you could create a macro named mcrHighestBalance that opens a form, such as one named frmSales, and then finds the record with the highest value in the Balance Owed field. If you add a command button to a form named frmCustomer, you can open the Property Sheet for that command button, and then set the On Click property to mcrHighestBalance. When users click the command button on frmCustomer, Access runs the mcrHighestBalance macro to open frmSales and to find the record with the highest value in the Balance Owed field.

Paul has a new request for Don that involves specifying conditions and associating macros with events. When Paul works with frmEmployee, which lists all the employees in the pharmacy, he often filters the form by the JobID field so that he can view only employees in a particular position. Doing so involves four steps: He opens frmEmployee, clicks the Next Record button as necessary to find the JobID he wants, clicks the JobID field, and then clicks the Filter by Form button. Instead of performing these four steps for each job category, he would like to somehow automate this process instead. To fulfill Paul's request, Don will place command buttons on frmEmployee that Paul can click to filter the records.

Don first needs to design a macro group that will filter records when executed. He opens a new Macro Builder, and for the first submacro in the macro group, he enters "mcrJobID1" and then selects the ApplyFilter action. This action has two arguments that specify how to apply the filter: Filter Name and Where Condition. You use the Filter Name argument if you are using a query to set the filter conditions. For example, if a query selected only those records from tblEmployee that included the value 1 in the JobID field, Don could enter the name of that query as the Filter Name argument. However, the 4Corners database does not include this query, so Don can use the Where Condition argument to specify the same criteria. For this argument, you can specify a condition to select records as you do in a query. Don enters the following condition in the Where Condition argument:

[JobID] = 1

This condition specifies that the macro will select records in which the JobID field contains the value 1. As in a query, the field name appears in brackets. Don adds four other macros that use the ApplyFilter action and similar conditions to select employee records in the other four job categories. As the final macro in the group, he adds a macro named mcrShowAll and selects the ShowAllRecords action so when the macro is finished the filters will be removed. He also adds comments to document each macro and then saves the macro group as mcrJobID. See Figure 6.33.

Figure 6.33: mcrJobID for filtering employee records by JobID

ApplyFilter actions

ShowAllRecords action

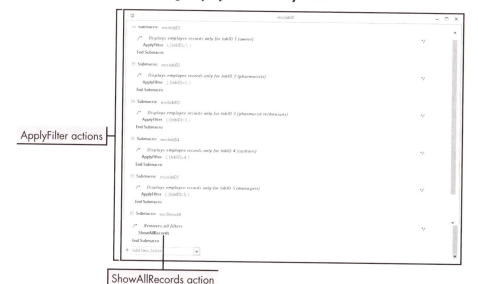

Now that Don has created the necessary macros in the mcrJobID macro group, he can add buttons to frmEmployee and assign the macros to the buttons. He opens frmEmployee in Design view, clicks the Button control in the Controls group on the DESIGN tab, and then clicks in the Form Header to add a button to the form. The Command Button Wizard dialog box opens. Don selects the Miscellaneous category and then selects the Run Macro action. He types "Job ID 1" in the Text box, and then selects the mcrJobID1 macro.

Don needs to repeat this procedure for the four remaining job categories. Rather than using the Command Button Wizard, he can copy the first command button he created, open the Property Sheet for the button, change the caption, and change the macro associated with the On Click event property. Finally, Don adds another command button with the caption Remove Filter, and assigns the mcrShowAll macro to its On Click event property.

Don resizes and moves the buttons and adds a label above them. Don switches to Form view and clicks the Job ID 2 button to verify that the frmEmployee form now shows only pharmacy technicians, who are the employees with Job ID 2. See Figure 6.34.

Figure 6.34: Using a command button to filter records

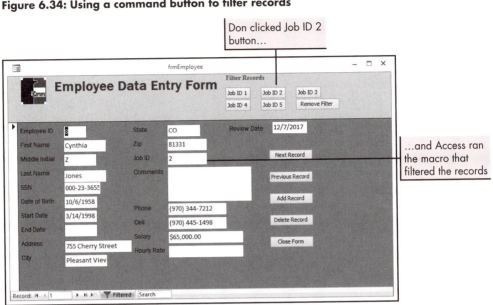

Specifying Where Conditions in a Macro

Don has discovered a new problem that he can solve by using a command button and a macro associated with a button event. When pharmacists and technicians are working with the frmPrimaryActivity form to enter prescriptions and refills, doctors are listed according to their ID. Employees often need to call doctors for information, and they need a quick way to open the appropriate record in the doctor form to find the doctor's name and phone numbers. Don decides to add a button to the prescription form that employees can click to open the doctor form and display the record for the appropriate doctor.

Don creates a macro called mcrViewDoctor. Using the Add New Action arrow, he selects the OpenForm action. For the arguments, he chooses frmDoctor as the form name, Form as the View argument, and Read Only for the Data Mode argument because he does not want the employee to change the doctor's information. For the Where Condition argument, he must construct a condition that filters the records in the frmDoctor form based on the value of the DoctorID field in the frmPrimaryActivity form. Therefore, he must refer to the DoctorID field in the Where Condition argument, using the following syntax for this reference:

[control]![objectName]![controlName]

When referring to controls on a form that are not currently active, Don must use the control's complete name, which includes the type of object that contains the control (*control*), the name of the object (*objectName*), and then the name of the control (*controlName*). Each part of the complete name is separated from the other parts by an exclamation mark (!).

To identify the DoctorID field as a control on a form named frmPrimaryActivity, Don enters the following condition in the Where Condition argument:

[DoctorID] = [Forms]![frmPrimaryActivity]![Doctor]

See Figure 6.35.

Figure 6.35: Macro with a Where Condition argument added

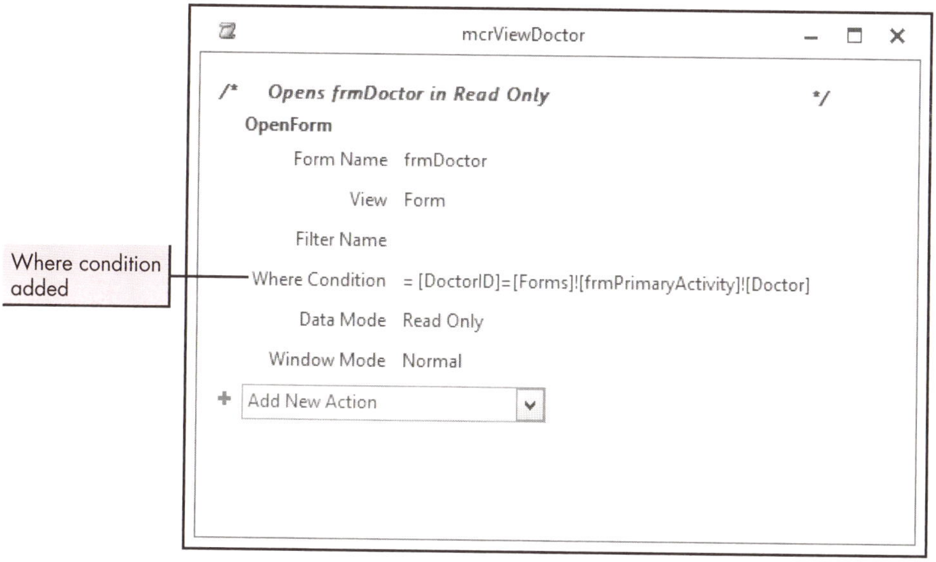

Where condition added

```
                                mcrViewDoctor                    —  □  ✕

     /*    Opens frmDoctor in Read Only                        */
           OpenForm
                     Form Name   frmDoctor
                          View   Form
                   Filter Name
               Where Condition   = [DoctorID]=[Forms]![frmPrimaryActivity]![Doctor]
                     Data Mode   Read Only
                   Window Mode   Normal
        +   Add New Action                ▼
```

6

Level 2

Now the mcrViewDoctor macro will open frmPrimaryActivity and then display the record that meets the criteria specified in the Where Condition argument—the record in frmDoctor that contains a DoctorID value that matches the one for the current record in frmPrimaryActivity. In other words, if employees are working with a record in frmPrimaryActivity that displays 13 in the DoctorID field, they can run the mcrViewDoctor macro to open the appropriate doctor record, the one in frmDoctor that also contains 13 in the DoctorID field.

To run the mcrViewDoctor macro, Don will add a button to frmPrimaryActivity and then associate the mcrViewDoctor macro with the button's On Click event property by using the Command Button Wizard. He opens frmPrimaryActivity in Design view and then adds a command button to the Form Header. He names the button View Doctor.

He saves the changes to frmPrimaryActivity, notes that the DoctorID for the first record is 13, and then tests the macro by clicking the View Doctor button. Don expects the frmDoctor form to open to the record for DoctorID 13, but something is wrong with the macro. Although the frmDoctor form does appear, no information is displayed. Don needs to troubleshoot the macro to solve the problem.

Troubleshooting Macros

Any type of macro is prone to errors, but those containing arguments, such as the Where Condition argument, that you enter rather than select, are especially error-prone. When you first run a macro, it might display a message and stop running, run using the wrong object, or cause other problems that are difficult to trace.

Three types of errors can occur during macro creation and execution. The first type of error is known as a **syntax error**. A syntax error occurs when a macro contains code that violates the macro rules established by Access. Because Access cannot interpret the syntax of the command, it displays a message in a dialog box identifying the error and the statement it cannot interpret. To repair syntax errors, you must find the incorrect statement, identify the missing information or incorrect entry, and then supply the correct information. Often, missing brackets or other symbols cause syntax errors.

The second type of error is known as a **logic error**, which occurs when the macro fails to produce the results you intended. This can be caused by an action placed out of sequence in the macro or incorrect action arguments.

The third type of error is a **run-time error**, or **execution error**, which occurs when the macro tries to perform actions that are not possible to perform. For example, if a macro is designed to open a form that has been deleted, the macro cannot find the form and displays a run-time error.

The possibility of errors increases with the number of actions and conditions you include in a macro. To help you find and repair errors, Access provides several troubleshooting tools, including printing the macro code, single stepping through the execution of the macro, and using the Visual Basic Editor. When you are testing a macro and checking for errors, you are debugging it.

Don decides first to print the macro code in the mcrViewDoctor macro to see if he can identify the problem.

Printing Macros

In Chapter 2, you learned how to print a report of selected objects in the database. One of the simplest ways for Don to troubleshoot a macro is to print it. He can then refer to the printed copy of the macro while the macro runs or while he uses other more sophisticated tools to solve the macro problem. He can choose to print the properties of the macro, its actions and arguments, or the permissions by user and group. He can read through the code on the printed copy and choose the repairs to make.

To print the macro, Don will use the Documenter dialog box, which includes a tab for each type of object in an Access database. He clicks the DATABASE TOOLS tab on the Ribbon, clicks the Database Documenter button, clicks the Macros tab, and then clicks the mcrViewDoctor check box. See Figure 6.36.

Figure 6.36: Documenter dialog box open with the Macros tab selected

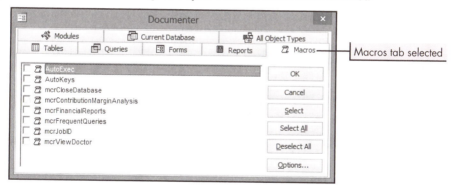

Don clicks the Options button to select which details of the macro he wants to print: properties, actions and arguments, or permissions. He selects the Actions and Arguments check box, deselects Properties and Permissions check boxes, and then clicks the OK button. When he closes the Documenter dialog box, a report appears in Print Preview, listing the actions and arguments set for the mcrViewDoctor macro, as shown in Figure 6.37.

Figure 6.37: Documenter report for mcrViewDoctor

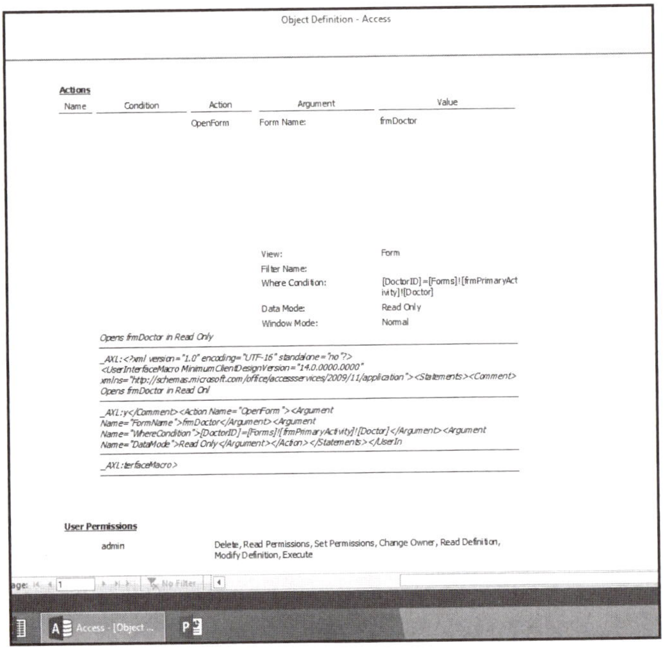

Object Definition - Access

Actions

Name	Condition	Action	Argument	Value
		OpenForm	Form Name:	frmDoctor
			View:	Form
			Filter Name:	
			Where Condition:	[DoctorID]=[Forms]![frmPrimaryActivity]![Doctor]
			Data Mode:	Read Only
			Window Mode:	Normal

Opens frmDoctor in Read Only

_AXL:<?xml version="1.0" encoding="UTF-16" standalone="no"?>
<UserInterfaceMacro MinimumClientDesignVersion="14.0.0000.0000"
xmlns="http://schemas.microsoft.com/office/accessservices/2009/11/application"><Statements><Comment>
Opens frmDoctor in Read Onl

_AXL:y</Comment><Action Name="OpenForm"><Argument
Name="FormName">frmDoctor</Argument><Argument
Name="WhereCondition">[DoctorID]=[Forms]![frmPrimaryActivity]![Doctor]</Argument><Argument
Name="DataMode">Read Only</Argument></Action></Statements></UserIn

_AXL:terfaceMacro>

User Permissions

admin Delete, Read Permissions, Set Permissions, Change Owner, Read Definition, Modify Definition, Execute

How To

Print a Macro

1. Click the DATABASE TOOLS tab on the Ribbon and then click the Database Documenter button. The Documenter dialog box opens.
2. Click the Macros tab, and then select one or more macros to print.
3. Click the Options button to select which details you want to print: properties, actions and arguments, or permissions, and then click the OK button.
4. Click the OK button to open the Documenter report in Print Preview.
5. Print and then close the report.

Don studies the contents of the mcrViewDoctor macro, but he cannot locate the error. He decides to try another troubleshooting technique known as single stepping.

Single Stepping a Macro

Because macros execute very quickly, it is sometimes difficult to identify the action that caused the error. **Single stepping** runs a macro one action at a time, pausing between actions. You use single stepping to make sure that the actions appear in the correct order and with the correct arguments. If you have problems with a macro, you can use single stepping to find the cause of the problems and to determine how to correct them. To single step a macro, open the macro in Design view and click the Single Step button in the Tools group on the DESIGN tab to turn on single stepping. When you turn on single stepping, it stays on for all macros until you turn it off. Now when you click the Run button to run the macro, Access will open the Macro Single Step dialog box that allows you to step through each action.

With the single stepping feature turned on, macros execute one action at a time and pause between actions, displaying a Macro Single Step dialog box that shows the name of the macro, the value of any conditions, the action to be taken, and the arguments for the action. The dialog box also has three buttons you can use to perform the next action in the macro. You can run the next part of the macro by pressing the Step button or stop running the macro (and all other macros in the database) by pressing the Stop All Macros button. Clicking the Continue button stops the single stepping action and resumes the normal operation of the macro.

Don opens mcrViewDoctor in Design view. He clicks the MACRO TOOLS DESIGN tab, clicks Single Step button in the Tools group and then clicks the Run button in the Tools group. The Macro Single Step dialog box opens, as shown in Figure 6.38.

Figure 6.38: Macro Single Step dialog box

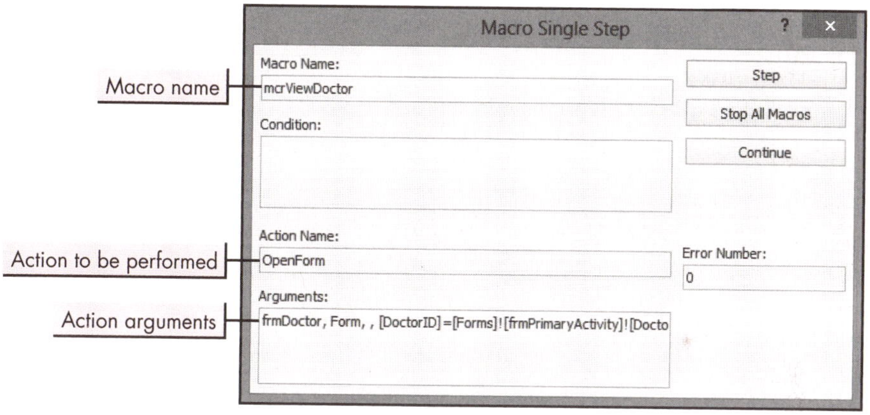

Don examines the dialog box but cannot see anything wrong in this step. He clicks the Continue button to perform the rest of the actions in the macro.

How To

Single Step a Macro

1. In the Macro design window, verify that the MACRO TOOLS DESIGN tab is selected, click the Single Step button and then click the Run button in the Tools group. The Macro Single Step dialog box opens and Access performs the first action in the macro. If necessary, enter desired number or text to perform the action.

2. Click the Step button to execute the next action in the macro. If necessary, click Yes to save the macro.

3. Click the Continue to stop single stepping and resume normal operation of the macro.

4. Click the Stop All Macros button to stop the all macros from running.

Because mcrViewDoctor contains only one action, Don wants to use another troubleshooting tool that will let him examine each part of the action and its arguments.

Setting Breakpoints

When macros become more complicated, you often need to see the details of a macro action and its results. To do so, you can use set a **breakpoint**, which is code you insert in the macro that signals where you want to stop the macro. Stopping a macro at a breakpoint allows you to examine the values of the actions, controls, and arguments the macro is using. To set a breakpoint you need to open the macro in the Visual Basic for Applications window. The macro appears as VBA code, which is the programming language Access uses for macros. If you have already printed a macro and used single stepping to run a macro, you can examine the details of the macro code in the Visual Basic for Applications window, which usually reveals the problems or values that are incorrect and are causing the macro to fail.

Don thinks the problem is with the frmPrimaryActivity form, so he closes the mcrViewDoctor macro and opens frmPrimaryActivity in Form view. He opens the Visual Basic for Applications window by pressing Ctrl+G. See Figure 6.39.

Figure 6.39: Microsoft Visual Basic for Applications window

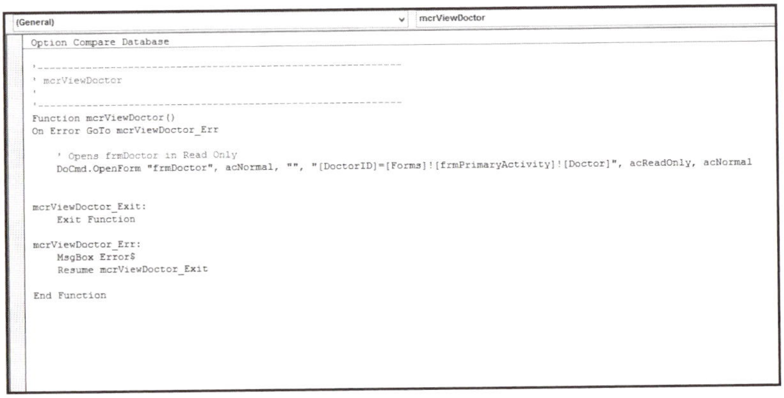

A section of the Visual Basic for Applications window is called the **Immediate pane**, which is used to display the current value of controls and arguments. Don can display a value by using the question mark operator (?) followed by the expression he wants to evaluate. For example, to evaluate a mathematical expression, he can enter "?4 * 5", and the Visual Basic Editor will perform the calculation and show the results. To troubleshoot a macro, Don can view the values used in an action's arguments by typing the value. He wants to determine the results of the expression that he entered as the Where Condition argument for the OpenForm action in mcrViewDoctor:

?Forms!frmPrimaryActivity!Doctor

When he types this expression, the Visual Basic Editor evaluates it and displays the results. In this way, Don can check which DoctorID value the macro is using to select a record in frmPrimaryActivity. When he presses the Enter key, the error message shown in Figure 6.40 appears.

Figure 6.40: Error generated

The results indicate that Access cannot find the Doctor field. Upon closer examination, Don realizes that he mistyped the field and should have entered it as DoctorID. To verify that he has identified the error, he enters the same expression but uses the correct name for the DoctorID field:

<code>?Forms!frmPrimaryActivity!DoctorID</code>

This time, the results are correct. See Figure 6.41.

Figure 6.41: Immediate window shows the results of the expression

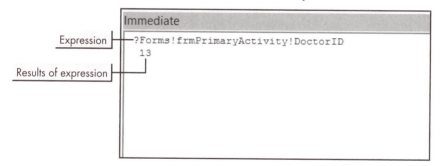

Don changes the macro code and is then satisfied that the macro is working correctly so he closes the Microsoft Visual Basic window. He tests the macro again; this time, frmDoctor opens when he clicks the View Doctor button and displays the correct doctor's information. See Figure 6.42.

Figure 6.42: Testing the View Doctor button and associated macro

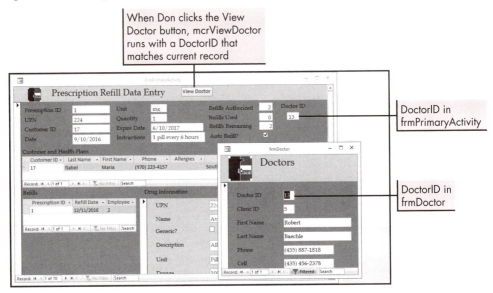

When Don clicks the View Doctor button, mcrViewDoctor runs with a DoctorID that matches current record

DoctorID in frmPrimaryActivity

DoctorID in frmDoctor

Don decides to make one last addition to the frmNavigationMainMenu, adding a Close Database button to the form. He creates the macro using the QuitAccess command with the Exit option so Access closes the database. He adds a command button that will run this macro when the Close Database command button is clicked. He switches to Form view to test the macro, and then he reopens the database to view the form, as shown in Figure 6.43.

Figure 6.43: frmNavigationMainMenu with Close Database button

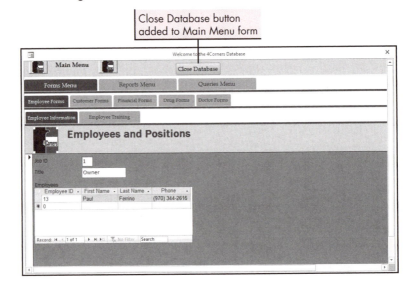

Close Database button added to Main Menu form

Steps To Success: Level 2

Glenn Hollander wants to continue to improve the user interface of the Hudson Bay Pharmacy database. He asks you to create advanced macros that Hudson Bay Pharmacy employees can use to print reports and update the navigation form to include queries. He also wants to include buttons on forms that run macros when users click them.

Complete the following:

1. Start Access and open the **Hudson.accdb** database from the STS folder.

   TROUBLESHOOTING: To complete this exercise, you must press the Shift key while opening **Hudson.accdb** to have unrestricted access to the Ribbon and Navigation pane.

2. Glenn knows that there are four financial reports in the Hudson Bay Pharmacy database that are printed most often: rpt2017Sales, rptBalance, rptRxList, and rptSales. 2017Provide a way to let users automatically print and close each report. Save the macro as **mcrFinancialReports**.

3. Instead of running mcrFinancialReports to print and close the financial reports, Glenn wants employees to be able to press a key combination and run the associated macro. Create a macro named **AutoKeys** that fulfills Glenn's request. Choose key combinations that are easy for employees to remember and associate with each report.

4. Glenn also wants to be able to print and close any report from Print Preview by pressing the Ctrl+P keys. Revise the AutoKeys macro to print and close any report from Print Preview.

5. Modify the Hudson Main Menu navigation form so that it includes a queries navigation form that opens the following queries in the database: qryHourlyRate, qryNoTraining, qrySpeakSpanish, and qryUpToDate.

6. When working with frmEmployee, Joan wants to be able to display only those records that are in a particular job category. Add command buttons to the frmEmployee form so that Joan can filter the records based on JobID by clicking a button. Be sure to include a button that removes the filter.

7. Glenn mentions that when pharmacists and technicians are working with the frmPrimaryActivity form to enter prescriptions and refills, doctors are listed according to their ID. Employees often need to call doctors for information, and need a quick way to open the appropriate record in the doctor form to find the doctor's name and phone numbers. Add a button to frmPrimaryActivity that employees can click to open the doctor form and display the record for the appropriate doctor.

8. Use three troubleshooting tools to test a macro you created for Hudson Bay Pharmacy. Describe the results of each tool.

9. Save and close the Hudson.accdb database.

LEVEL 3

Macro Conditions

Exploring Macro Conditions

Paul frequently uses the rptBalance report that finds customers with outstanding balances greater than zero, but he wants to change the format of this report depending on its contents. He wants to contact customers who have outstanding balances over $25, so he asks Don to modify the report so that any balance greater than $25 is placed in a rectangle and highlighted with an asterisk. Elaine Estes, the pharmacy manager, can then contact these customers and work out a payment plan.

Don considers modifying the report by using conditional formatting but then remembers that he cannot add a rectangle or an asterisk using that feature. Instead, he can create a macro and specify conditions that will produce the same results.

Macro conditions are logical expressions that result in a true or false answer. Depending on the outcome of the condition, the macro can perform one set of actions or another. Using macro conditions, you can add the power and flexibility of decision making, common in computer programming, to your database without directly writing programming code.

Don wants to create a macro that changes the formatting in the rptBalance report depending on the value of the Balance field. He will associate the macro with a report event so that the macro runs when the report opens in Print Preview.

First, Don redesigns the rptBalance report to include a rectangle control to outline the Balance field in the Detail section and a label that contains an asterisk (*). Don right-clicks the rectangle object and sets its Back Style property to Transparent. He names these two objects rectBalance and lblAsterisk and uses their Property Sheets to set their Visible property to No so that these controls do not appear by default. See Figure 6.44.

Figure 6.44: Rectangle and label properties

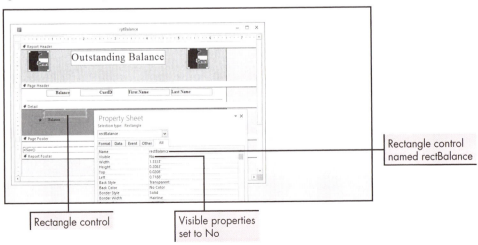

Rectangle control named rectBalance

Rectangle control

Visible properties set to No

Don wants the Visible property to change to Yes when the contents of the report meet the condition that he will specify in the macro he creates next. Don creates a macro named mcrBalanceFormat that contains an If condition to test the value in the Balance field. Don first drags the program flow If action from the Action Catalog into the Macro Builder. Then, in the block next to the If statement, he enters the following condition to test the value:

`[Balance] >= 25`

This expression determines whether the value in the Balance field is greater than or equal to 25. If this condition is true, Don wants to display the rectangle and the asterisk by setting their Visible properties to Yes.

To do so, he can use the **SetValue action**, which changes the property of an object by disabling, updating, hiding, or displaying a control. Don will need to click the Show All Actions button in the Show/Hide group to access the SetValue action. The SetValue action has two arguments: Item and Expression. The Item argument specifies the control whose property you want to change, such as rectBalance or lblAsterisk. The Expression argument specifies the new value for the property, such as Yes. Don enters the following expression as the Item argument to specify the action for this control:

`[rectBalance].[Visible]`

This notation includes the name of the control within square brackets, then a period, then the name of the property to set. In this case, Don wants to change the Visible property of the rectBalance control. For the Expression argument, Don enters "Yes" to indicate that if the value in the Balance field is greater than or equal to 25, Access should set the Visible property of the rectBalance control to Yes, thereby displaying a rectangle around the balance amount. See Figure 6.45.

Figure 6.45: First If Then statement

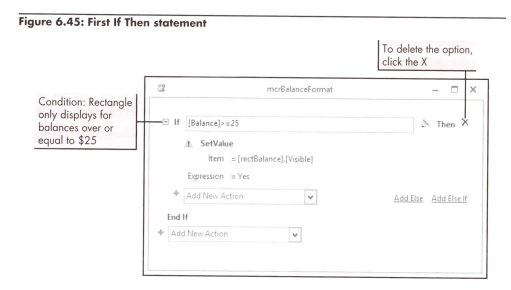

He selects the SetValue action again and then enters "[lblAsterisk].[Visible]" as the Item argument and "Yes" as the Expression argument.

Then he adds an Else If condition to specify what Access should do if the Balance amount is less than 25. He clicks on the last SetValue action to display the Add Else If option located to the right side of the Macro Builder under the selected action. He then specifies [Balance]<25 as the condition, and then enters two SetValue actions to set the Visible property of the rectangle and asterisk to No when the Balance value is less than 25. The completed macro, shown in Figure 6.46, will display a rectangle and an asterisk for balances in rptBalance that are $25 or more, but will not display the rectangle and asterisk for balances that are under $25.

Figure 6.46: Completed mcrBalanceFormat macro

Now that the macro is complete, Don needs to associate it with a report event so that it runs when the rptBalance report opens in Print Preview.

Assigning a Macro to an Object Event

In addition to assigning a macro to a control, such as a command button, by specifying a macro name in a control's event property, you can assign a macro to an object by specifying a macro name in an event property of the object. These events fall into two categories: report events and section events. Report events occur to the report as a whole, such as when the report is opened or closed; section events occur to a section of the report, such as when the section is formatted or printed. Table 6.4 shows a few report events, and Table 6.5 shows some of the section events.

Table 6.4: Report events

Event Name	Action That Triggers the Event
On Open	When report opens, but before it prints
On Close	When report closes
On Activate	When report becomes the active window (receives focus)
On Deactivate	When report loses focus
On No Data	When the record source of the report contains no data
On Page	When the report advances to the next page
On Error	When a run-time error occurs

© 2014 Cengage Learning

Table 6.5: Section events

Event Name	Action That Triggers the Event
On Format	When page layout changes
On Print	After the section is laid out, but before it prints
On Retreat	After the On Format event, but before the On Print event (not available in page header or footer sections)

© 2014 Cengage Learning

Don needs to associate the mcrBalanceFormat macro to the rptBalance report, so when Access formats the report to prepare it for Print Preview, Access will also run mcrBalanceFormat, test the conditions in the macro, and then display the rectangle and asterisk if the first condition is true. Don needs to assign the mcrBalanceFormat macro to the Detail section, which is the section that contains the rectangle, asterisk, and Balance amount, using the report's On Format property, which is a section event.

Don opens rptBalance in Design view, opens the Property Sheet for the Detail section, and then clicks the Event tab. He clicks the arrow for the On Format event property, and then selects the mcrBalanceFormat macro from the list of available macros. He saves his changes and then tests the macro by opening the report and verifying that all balances greater than $25 are appropriately formatted with a rectangle and an asterisk. See Figure 6.47.

Figure 6.47: rptBalance with conditional formatting created by mcrBalanceFormat

Customers with a balance over $25

Don can also attach macros to automate some of the existing forms. To prevent employees from inadvertently deleting records, he wants to open a message box when employees try to delete a record from a form. The message will instruct them to check with a supervisor before completing the deletion. If they click the OK button, the record is deleted. If they click the Cancel button, the record is not deleted. He can accomplish this by using the **MessageBox** command in a macro.

Using Message Boxes with Forms

As with reports, form events can also trigger macros. Use macros with forms to validate data, set values, navigate between forms, and filter, find, and print records. Table 6.6 shows a sample list of form events.

Table 6.6: Form events

Event Name	Action That Triggers the Event
On Load	When the form loads
On Unload	When the form is closed
On Click	When the user clicks the left mouse button on any control on the form
On Dbl Click	When the user double-clicks the left mouse button on any control on the form
Before Update	Before changed data is updated
On Delete	When the user begins to delete a record but before the record is deleted
On Activate	When the form becomes the active window (receives focus)
On Timer	When a specified time interval has elapsed
Timer Interval	Before triggering the event, waits the specified amount of time (milliseconds)

© 2014 Cengage Learning

When users delete a record in a form, Don wants to display a message box asking if they are sure they are authorized to delete the record. (The policy at 4Corners Pharmacy is that employee supervisors must approve all record deletions.) Therefore, the macro he creates must first open such a message box. To achieve this, Don can use the **MessageBox command**, which opens a message box and displays a warning or informational message. When you set a condition that uses the MessageBox command, you write a MessageBox statement using the following syntax:

```
MessageBox("Message",Sum of button and icon values,"Title")
```

The *Message* is the text that appears in the message box. You must enclose the text in quotation marks. The *Sum of button and icon values* is the sum of the values associated with the icons and buttons that you want to display in the message box. Each type of icon, such as an informational icon, or button, such as the OK button, is associated with a value. The button that you want to select by default is also associated with a value. (See Tables 6.7, 6.8, and 6.9.) You select the icons, buttons, and default button that you want, and sum their values. Then you use this sum as the second part of the MessageBox command. The *Title*, which also must be enclosed in quotation marks, is the text that appears in the title bar of the message box.

Table 6.7: Types of buttons and values

Value	Type of Button
0	OK
1	OK, Cancel
2	Abort, Retry, Ignore
3	Yes, No, Cancel
4	Yes, No
5	Retry, Cancel

© 2014 Cengage Learning

Table 6.8: Icon style and values

Value	Icon
0	No icon
16	Critical (white X in a red ball)
32	Warning? (blue question mark in a white balloon)
48	Warning! (black exclamation point in a yellow triangle)
64	Information (blue letter I in a white balloon)

© 2014 Cengage Learning

Level 3

6

Table 6.9: Default buttons and values

Value	Default Button
0	First
256	Second
512	Third

© 2014 Cengage Learning

In the message box that Don is designing, he wants to include the Yes and the No buttons (value 4) and the icon that displays a blue question mark in a white balloon (value 32). He also wants the No button, the second button, as the default (value 256). To specify this argument in the MessageBox command, he must sum the values of the buttons and icons he wants to display: 4 + 32 + 256 = 292. He can use the following MessageBox statement to specify the message box he wants to create, as shown in Figure 6.48:

```
MessageBox("Did you check with supervisor?", 292, "Delete?")
```

Figure 6.48: Sample message box created with the MessageBox action

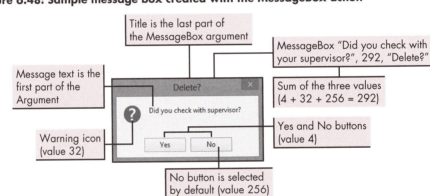

The MessageBox command also returns a value depending on which button is clicked. Table 6.10 shows the values returned depending on which button is selected. Don can use these values to finish setting up the condition for the message box.

Table 6.10: Return value of buttons

Value Returned	Button Selected
1	OK
2	Cancel
3	Abort
4	Retry
5	Ignore
6	Yes
7	No

© 2014 Cengage Learning

He can create a condition that checks to see which button users click. If they click the Yes button, the MessageBox command returns the value 6. If users click the No button, the MessageBox command returns the value 7. The condition can check whether the value returned is equal to 7.

Don creates a new macro named mcrConfirmDeletion, he drags the If action to the Macro Builder, and then enters the following MessageBox statement:

```
MessageBox("Did you check with supervisor?", 292, "Delete?") = 7
```

If a user tries to delete a record in the form, the mcrConfirmDeletion macro will run and test the first condition: MessageBox("Did you check with supervisor?", 292, "Delete?") = 7. If this condition is true—in other words, if the user clicks the No button—the macro cancels the deletion and stops running. To specify these actions, Don clicks in the first row of the Add New Action pane and selects the CancelEvent action. In the next row, he clicks the Add New Action arrow and selects the StopMacro action. Don's entries indicate that, if the condition is true, the macro first performs the CancelEvent action and then the StopMacro action. He adds the comment, "If users click the No button, cancel the deletion and stop." See Figure 6.49.

Figure 6.49: Macro for message box if the No button is clicked

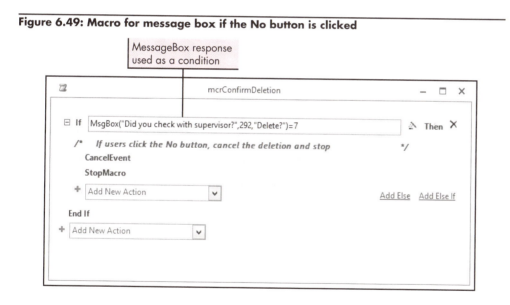

Next, Don must specify what the macro should do if the condition is false (in other words, if the user clicks the Yes button). In that case, the macro should allow the deletion. To specify that action, Don uses the SendKeys action with {ENTER} as the Keystrokes argument for the third entry in the Add New Action pane. If users click the Yes button, the mcrConfirmDeletion macro deletes the record by pressing Enter. See Figure 6.50.

Figure 6.50: Completed mcrConfirmDeletion macro

```
☐                          mcrConfirmDeletion                    —  □  ✕

  ⊟  If  MsgBox("Did you check with supervisor?",292,"Delete?")=7   Then
       /*    If users click the No button, cancel the deletion and stop    */
           CancelEvent
           StopMacro
      End If
       /*    If users click the Yes button, delete the record             */
       ⚠  SendKeys
         Keystrokes  KeyEnter
             Wait  No
    ✦  Add New Action                    ⌄
```

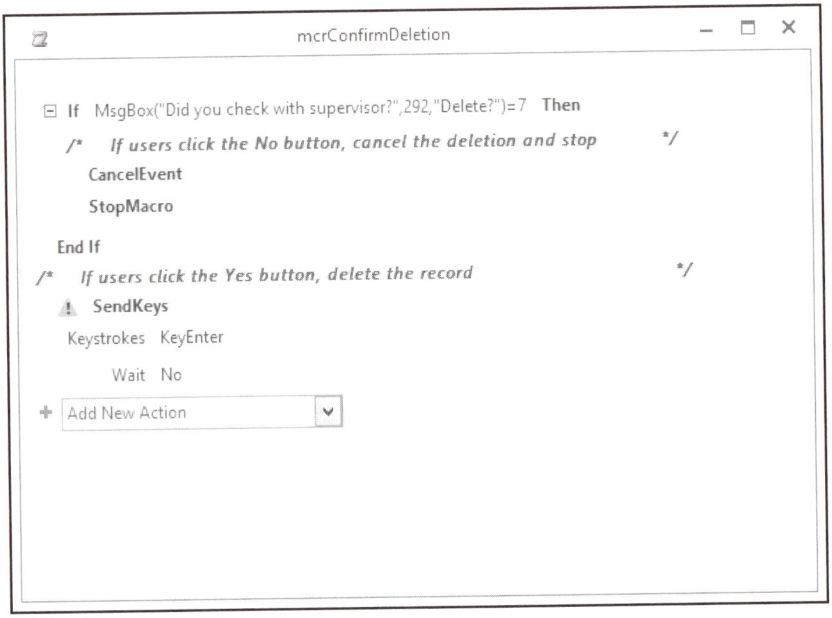

Don wants to test the mcrConfirmDeletion macro on frmCustomer, so he saves and closes the macro, and then opens frmCustomer in Design view. He opens the Property Sheet of the form and assigns the mcrConfirmDeletion macro to the On Delete event. Now, if a user tries to delete a record by using the Delete Record button (or any other technique for deleting a record), the macro displays the message box asking to confirm the deletion. Don tests the mcrConfirmDeletion macro by saving frmCustomer, opening it in Form view, and then clicking the Delete Record command button, trying to delete a record. The message box appears as designed, so he knows that the macro is working correctly, as shown in Figure 6.51.

Figure 6.51: Message box displays based on mcrConfirmDeletion

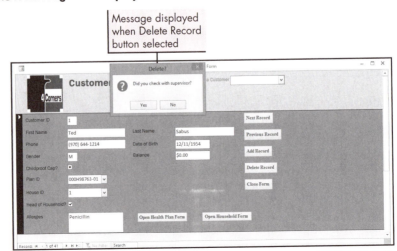

Using Message Boxes with Reports

Next, Paul wants a monthly report to list all the prescriptions issued for the drug Rizatriptan Benzoate. Because this drug is classified as a narcotic, Paul must provide a monthly report to the government if the quantity dispensed is equal to or greater than 100 pills. If the pharmacy dispenses fewer than 100 pills of Rizatriptan Benzoate in a month, he does not need to print the report.

Don begins by creating a query named qryNarcotic that selects all prescriptions for Rizatriptan Benzoate (UPN 987) and displays each customer's last name and quantity of pills dispensed for a particular month and year. Next, he creates a report named rptNarcotic that uses this query as the record source. He adds a text box, named Total, to the UPN footer to sum the quantity dispensed. See Figure 6.52.

Figure 6.52: rptNarcotic in Design view

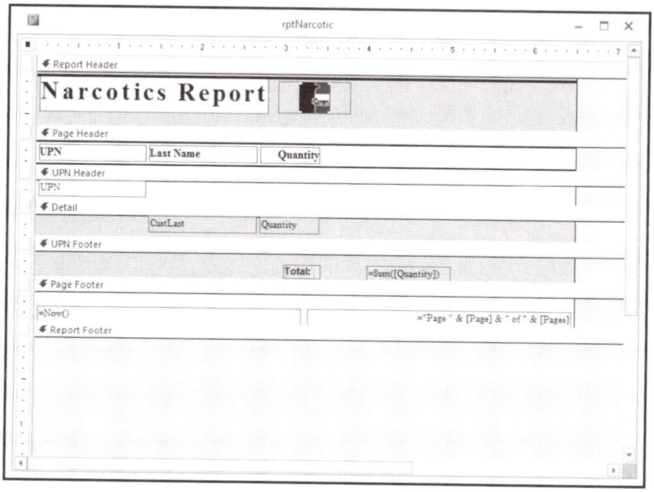

When Paul opens this report, he is going to know if 100 or more pills of Rizatriptan Benzoate have been dispensed. However, Don needs to create a macro that will print the report only if 100 or more pills are dispensed. The macro needs to test the Total field in rptNarcotic to determine if the value in the field is equal to or greater than 100. If it does, the macro will print the report. If the field contains a value less than 100, the macro will display a message and stop.

When conditions in a macro reference the name of a control from a source, such as a form or report, the source must be open when the condition is tested. Therefore, before an action in the macro tests the Total field in the rptNarcotic report, the macro must open rptNarcotic. However, displaying the report might be distracting, so Don can hide the window while the macro tests the condition.

Don creates a macro named mcrNarcotic and adds OpenReport as the first new action. He selects rptNarcotic as the Report Name argument, Print Preview as the View argument, and Hidden as the Window Mode argument. This action means that Access will open rptNarcotic but not display its window when the macro starts. Next, he needs to specify the condition for testing the value in the Total field of rptNarcotic. He adds the If condition and enters the following statement:

$$([Reports]![rptNarcotic]![Total]) < 100$$

This statement checks whether the value in the Total field is less than 100 in a report named rptNarcotic. If the condition is true—if the Total field contains a quantity fewer than 100—Don wants the macro to display a message informing Paul that he does not need to print the report. If this condition is false—if the Total field contains a quantity of 100 or more—the macro should print the report.

Don can use the **MessageBox action**, which opens a message box and displays a warning or informational message. Using the MessageBox action is similar to using the MessageBox command in a condition, *except* with the MessageBox action, you can select the arguments as you do with other actions. A macro containing a MessageBox action does not continue to the next action until the user clicks the OK button, so when you add the MessageBox action to a macro, users will have as much time as they need to read and react to the message box. The MessageBox action requires four arguments:

- **Message**—The text that appears in the message box when it is displayed
- **Beep**—A Yes/No argument that specifies whether a beep sounds when the message box is opened
- **Type**—The argument that determines which icon, if any, appears in the message box to signify the critical level of the message: None (no icon), Critical (white X in a red ball), Warning? (blue question mark in a white balloon), Warning! (black exclamation point in a yellow triangle), and Information (blue letter I in a white balloon)
- **Title**—The title that appears in the message box title bar

Don clicks in the Add New Action pane corresponding to the If conditional statement he entered and selects the MessageBox action. For the Message argument, he enters "Total dispensed is less than 100." For the Beep argument, he selects Yes. For the Type argument, he selects Information. Finally, for the Title argument, he enters "You do not need to print the narcotic report." This means that if the Total field in rptNarcotic contains a quantity less than 100, an informational message box titled "You do not need to print the narcotic report" opens with the Total dispensed is less than 100 message. See Figure 6.53.

Figure 6.53: mcrNarcotic if the value in the Total field is less than 100

Condition: If total less than 100 report does not need to print

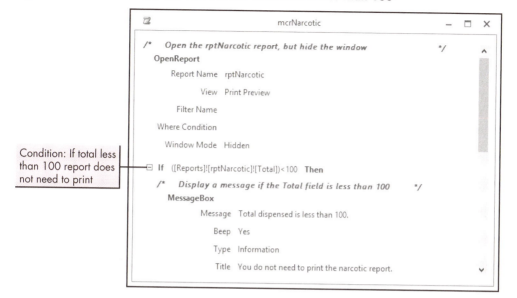

If the condition is true, Don wants to close the hidden report and then stop the macro. In the next row of the Add New Action pane, Don selects the CloseWindow action, specifying Report as the Object Type and rptNarcotic as the Object Name. This means that the macro will close the rptNarcotic report if the condition entered in the first row is true. He now wants to perform one more action if the condition is true—stop the macro. He selects the StopMacro action in the fourth row of the Add New Action pane. Now he can specify the action the macro should perform if the condition in the first row is false— that is, if the total dispensed is equal to or more than 100. He selects the OpenReport action and specifies rptNarcotic as the Report Name argument and Print Preview as the View. The rest of the mcrNarcotic macro is shown in Figure 6.54.

Figure 6.54: Completed mcrNarcotic macro

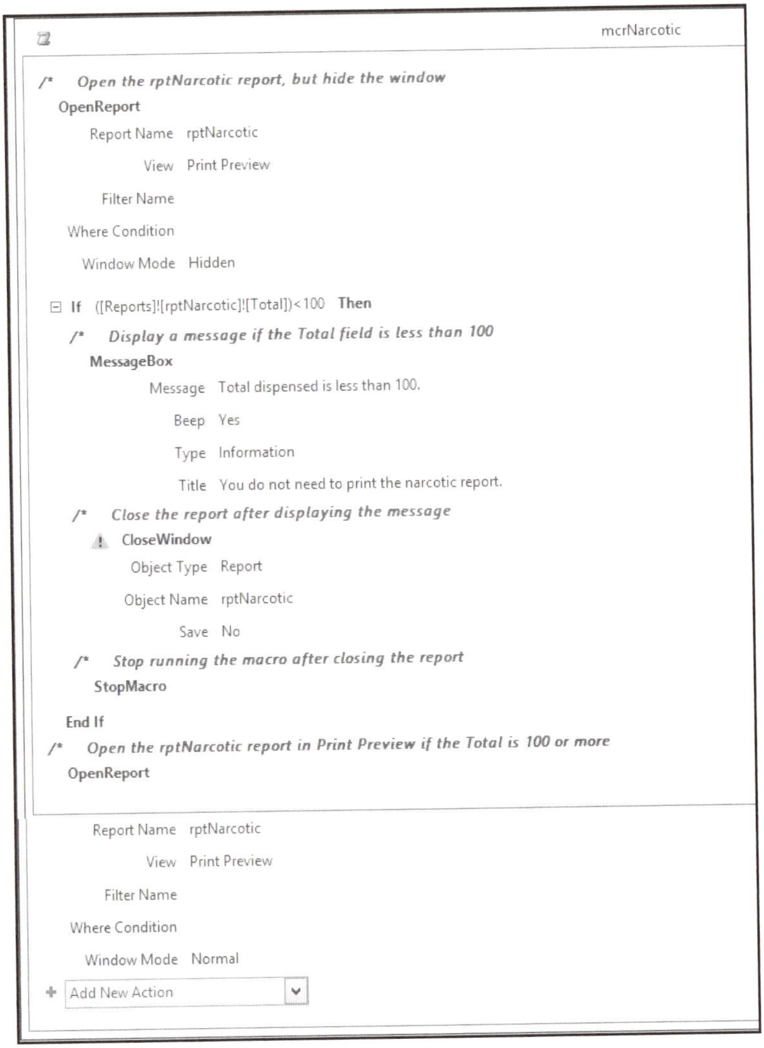

```
                                                              mcrNarcotic

  /*   Open the rptNarcotic report, but hide the window
     OpenReport
           Report Name   rptNarcotic
                  View   Print Preview
           Filter Name
     Where Condition
        Window Mode   Hidden

  ⊟  If   ([Reports]![rptNarcotic]![Total])<100   Then
        /*   Display a message if the Total field is less than 100
           MessageBox
                  Message   Total dispensed is less than 100.
                     Beep   Yes
                     Type   Information
                    Title   You do not need to print the narcotic report.
        /*   Close the report after displaying the message
        ⚠  CloseWindow
              Object Type   Report
              Object Name   rptNarcotic
                     Save   No
        /*   Stop running the macro after closing the report
           StopMacro

     End If
     /*   Open the rptNarcotic report in Print Preview if the Total is 100 or more
        OpenReport


           Report Name   rptNarcotic
                  View   Print Preview
           Filter Name
     Where Condition
        Window Mode   Normal
  ✛  Add New Action                    ▾
```

Don saves the mcrNarcotic macro, opens rptNarcotic in Design view, opens the Property Sheet for the report, and then assigns the macro to the report using the On Page event property. Now, when Paul opens this report, he will trigger the mcrNarcotic macro, which will open and hide the rptNarcotic report. The next action in the macro will test the value in the Total field. If the value is less than 100, three actions will be performed: displaying the message box, closing the rptNarcotic report, and stopping the macro. See Figure 6.55.

Figure 6.55: Information message

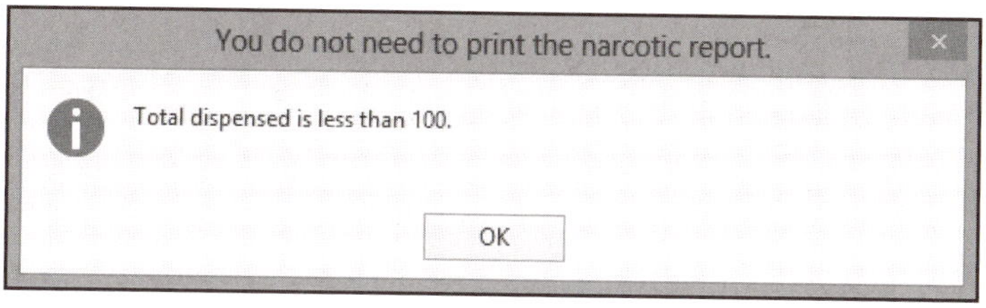

> You do not need to print the narcotic report.   ✕
>
> ℹ Total dispensed is less than 100.
>
> OK

If the value in the Total field is equal to or greater than 100, these three actions are skipped and the report opens in Print Preview so that Paul can print it.

Validating Data with Macros

The most common ways to validate data are to use field properties such as input masks, validation rules, and validation text. However, those field properties have their limits. For example, you can specify only one validation rule for a field and display only one validation message. To validate data using more than one rule and more than one validation message, you can create a macro.

A typical error when entering data in forms is to attempt to enter a record using a primary key value already used in another record. Because a primary key must be unique within a table, Access indicates when you save the form that another record contains the same primary key value, and does not allow you to save the form. The validation rule and input mask control the range and the format of the primary key, but do not prevent you from entering a record with a duplicate primary key value. Only when Access attempts to save the record does it display an error message.

If you have entered many records, it might be difficult to retrace your work and find the one with the duplicate value. It would be more helpful to receive a friendly error message when you enter the duplicate primary key value in the record.

Paul has this problem with the frmDrug form. The primary key field is the UPN, which is a three-character text field. The input mask for the UPN field limits the data entry to three digits and does not use a validation rule. The input mask can ensure that users enter only three digits in the UPN field, but it does not ensure which digits they enter. Paul is finding that when a new drug is entered, employees often mistype a digit, creating an incorrect entry and possibly a duplication of a primary key. Paul feels that it would save time if employees were notified that the field value they entered was a duplicate of another primary key value. Paul speaks to Don about his concerns, and Don decides to create a macro to solve this problem.

Don begins by creating a macro named mcrDuplicateKey. In the first row of the macro, he needs to enter a logical expression to determine if the value entered as the UPN is a duplicate primary key. To perform this task, Don can use a domain aggregate function. Unlike aggregate functions such as Sum and Count, which are used to calculate totals,

domain aggregate functions calculate statistics for a set of records (recordset), or **domain**, from a table or a query. Table 6.11 provides examples of domain aggregate functions.

Table 6.11: Common domain aggregate functions

Function Name	Purpose
DSum	Calculates the sum of a set of values in a specified set of records.
DCount	Determines the number of records that are in a specified set of records.
DAvg	Calculates the average of a set of values in a specified set of records.
DVarP	Calculates the variance across a population in a specified set of records.
DStDevP	Calculates the standard deviation across a population in a specified set of records.

© 2014 Cengage Learning

When users enter a new record in frmDrug and enter a value in the UPN field, Don wants the macro to determine if any records share that value, which is the primary key. To find duplicates, he can use the DCount function to determine the number of records in a set that matches a condition. The DCount function has the following general form:

`DCount(expression, table or query, condition)`

The *expression* represents the field for which you are counting records. The *table or query* identifies the object that contains the entire records. The *condition* limits the data to a subset of the entire recordset; a conditional expression or logical expression.

For the mcrDuplicateKey macro Don is creating for frmDrug, he could use the following DCount function:

`DCount("[UPN]", "tblDrug", "[UPN]=[txtUPN]")`

However, Don notes that UPN is the name of the control on the frmDrug form that contains the UPN number. Don will need to change the name of this text box to txtUPN in the frmDrug to distinguish it from the UPN field in tblDrug, which he will do shortly. If the DCount function finds a record that matches the condition—that is, if a value in the UPN field in tblDrug is the same as the value in the txtUPN text box in frmDrug— the function returns the value of 1. Don uses the following complete condition in the mcrDuplicateKey macro:

`DCount("[UPN]", "tblDrug", "[UPN]=[txtUPN]") = 1`

If this condition is true, Access has found a record that has the same primary key as the one being entered into the form. Don next specifies the action he wants the macro to perform if this condition is true: Display an error message. In the Add New Action pane, he selects the MessageBox action and enters "You have entered a UPN for a drug already entered in this form. Click the OK button and reenter the UPN." as the Message argument. He also selects Critical as the Type argument and enters "Duplicate Primary Key" as the Title argument.

After displaying the message box, Don wants the macro to cancel the event that triggered the macro. He adds a second action, the CancelEvent action, which has no arguments. If the condition is true—if a user enters a duplicate primary key value—a message box appears and the insertion point remains in the UPN text box of the form. If the condition is false, no action needs to be taken. The completed macro is shown in Figure 6.56.

Figure 6.56: mcrDuplicateKey macro

Don opens frmDrug in Design view, opens the Property Sheet for the UPN text box, and changes its name to txtUPN. Then he assigns the mcrDuplicateKey macro to the Before Update event property of the txtUPN. This means that if a user enters a duplicate primary key value, the macro will run before Access updates the record. Don tests the macro by opening frmDrug in Form view, noting the UPN in the first record, 102, and then attempting to enter a new record with the same UPN. When he finishes entering the UPN, an error message appears. See Figure 6.57.

Figure 6.57: Duplicate key error message generated by mcrDuplicateKey

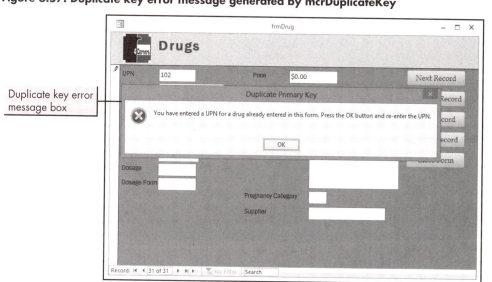

Don feels confident that he has made the database easier to use. Now that the database is getting close to completion, he will meet with key individuals in the pharmacy to see if he can create additional enhancements to the database.

Steps To Success: Level 3

Glenn Hollander is impressed with your work with macros, and wants to continue to use them to improve the Hudson database. He asks for your help in setting macro conditions for forms and reports, displaying custom error messages, and validating data.

Complete the following:

1. Start Access and open the **Hudson.accdb** database from the STS folder.

2. Joan Gabel frequently uses the rptBalance report and wants to display an asterisk next to balances of $20 or more. She also wants to display a rectangle around those balances. Modify rptBalance to display a rectangle and an asterisk for balances of $20 or more. Name the macro for this task **mcrBalanceFormat**.

3. Create a macro that provides a custom message to the users of frmCustomer, reminding them that they should check with a supervisor before deleting a customer record from the form. Name the macro for this task **mcrConfirmDeletion**.

4. Create a query that will determine what quantity of the drug Rizatriptan Benzoate has been dispensed during a particular month. Name the query **qryNarcotic**. Create a report based on qryNarcotic named **rptNarcotic**. Assign a macro to rptNarcotic so that the report prints only if the total quantity dispensed is over 100. Name the macro **mcrNarcotic**.

5. Using a macro, add data validation to the frmDrug form so that a user cannot add a duplicate DIN. This will need to be added to the Form's BeforeUpdate event. Name the macro **mcrDuplicateKey**.

6. If necessary, troubleshoot any macro that is not working correctly.

7. Save and close the Hudson.accdb database.

Chapter Summary

In this chapter, you learned how to design and implement a navigation form for a database. You also learned how to use the Trust Center to set macro security options such as restricting the use of the Access menus, Ribbon tabs, and the Navigation pane so that users cannot affect the design of your database. You created macros to automate repetitive tasks you perform frequently and add functionality to reports and forms.

In Level 1, you designed navigation forms and then created and ran basic macros. You also set Current Database options and created a splash screen. In Level 2, you worked with macro groups to organize macros and then you assigned macros to events to make your forms and reports more flexible and powerful. You also learned how to troubleshoot macros so that they are free of error. In Level 3, you explored macro conditions and using message boxes, techniques that can automate your database to a professional level.

Conceptual Review

1. What is a navigation form?

2. Describe the steps for creating navigation forms that lead up to a navigation form that serves as a main menu when the database is opened.

3. List at least three uses of a macro.

4. What is a macro group?

5. What is the function of the AutoExec macro?

6. What are some of the options you can set using the Access Options dialog box that affect what happens when you open a database?

7. Explain how macros can be used for database security.

8. What is an event? Explain how you can use macros with events.

9. Explain the purpose of macro conditions.

10. Name the techniques you can use to troubleshoot a macro.

11. Explain how a macro can be used to enhance data integrity.

12. Explain the purpose of the following macro commands:

   a.   SetValue

   b.   Beep

   c.   Hourglass

   d.   Close

   e.   Exit

   f.   OpenForm

Case Problems

Case 1 – Providing a User Interface for the NHD Development Group Inc.

In this project, you continue working on the database for an antiques mall, Memories Antique Mall in Cleveland, Tennessee. Tim Richards, the chief information officer of the NHD Development Group, which owns this mall, recently reviewed the work you completed in the Antiques database. The queries, forms, and reports you created are proving to be useful to the mall staff, and are helping to streamline the mall operations. However, Tim is concerned that users who are new to Access will find it difficult to navigate and select the objects they need.

Tim asks you to create a user interface that provides an easy way to view and select queries, forms, and reports in the Antiques database. To personalize the database, he wants it to open with a window showing the company name and logo along with command buttons users can click to display a series of menus. Users should be able to select the objects they need from these menus.

Complete the following:

1. Start Access and open the **Antiques.accdb** database from the Case 1 folder.

2. Tim wants to provide easy access to the forms and reports in the Antiques database without using the Navigation pane. First, plan the navigation forms. Then, create a main navigation form that allows users to access all the forms and reports in the Antiques database. Tim suggests that you group the reports and forms on separate navigation forms. He also reminds you to verify that the appropriate object is displayed when you click each entry.

3. Tim wants to be sure to associate the database with the mall's parent company, NHD Development Group. Include the company logo and identify Memories Antique Mall on the main navigation form. Tim also suggests that you design the navigation form and select colors to coordinate with the company logo. (The logo, **NHD-logo.jpg**, is located in Chapter 6\EOC\Case 1 folder.)

4. After reviewing the navigation form used for the main menu, Tim realizes that it should provide an option to view the queries (lists) you created earlier. Include the queries on a separate navigation form designed to match the ones you created for forms and reports. (*Hint*: First, create macros to open each query, and then run the macros from the navigation form.)

5. In addition to using a navigation form with the main menu, Tim wants to personalize the database by displaying a splash screen when users open the Antiques database. Create a splash screen that includes the name of the mall and identifies NHD as its parent company. It should also contain the NHD logo (NHD-logo.jpg) and *your name* and *phone number* so that users can contact you if they have questions or problems with the database. Finally, the splash screen should provide a command button that users can click to open the main menu navigation form.

6. For security, set the splash screen to appear when the database opens. Specify properties appropriate for a splash screen.

7. Review your work to make sure that the navigation forms and splash screen work properly and are attractive and easy to use. Figure 6.58 will give you an idea of what your splash screen could look like.

Figure 6.58: Splash screen example for Memories Antique Mall database

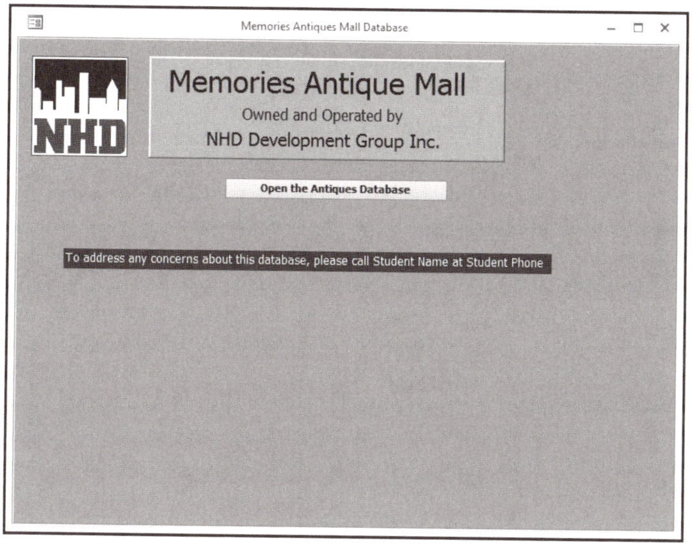

8. Save and close the Antiques.accdb database and Access.

Case 2 – Improving Access to Data and Reports for MovinOn Inc.

Previously, you created tables, queries, forms, and reports to help MovinOn streamline the recording, managing, and viewing of data in the MovinOn database. After you finish your work with the database, Dora Nettles, administrative assistant in the Washington warehouse, will serve as the database manager. Dora is currently training employees on using the MovinOn database, and reports that some employees are not familiar with Access and don't know how to use the Navigation pane to open the queries, forms, and reports that they need. Dora asks you to create an interface that lets users work with the data without using the Navigation pane.

Information Systems

Complete the following:

1. Start Access and open the **MovinOn.accdb** database from the Case 2 folder.

2. Dora says that most employees only need to open queries, forms, and reports. Create navigation forms including a main menu navigation form that provides access to all the forms, queries, and reports in the database. To create a consistent user interface, the company logo should appear on the main menu navigation form. (The logo, **MovinOn-logo.jpg**, is located in the Case 2 folder.) The design and colors of the navigation form should coordinate with the company logo. Dora also makes the following request to consider as you design your navigation form: Group queries into a logical order on a separate navigation form.

3. Dora also wants to clearly identify the database when it is opened. Create a splash screen that includes the company logo (MovinOn-logo.jpg). The splash screen should have a button that users can click to open the main navigation form for the MovinOn database. In addition, the splash screen should show the company name and contact information. Use your name and phone number as the contact information. Figure 6.59 shows what your screen could look like.

Figure 6.59: Splash screen example for MovinOn, Inc. database

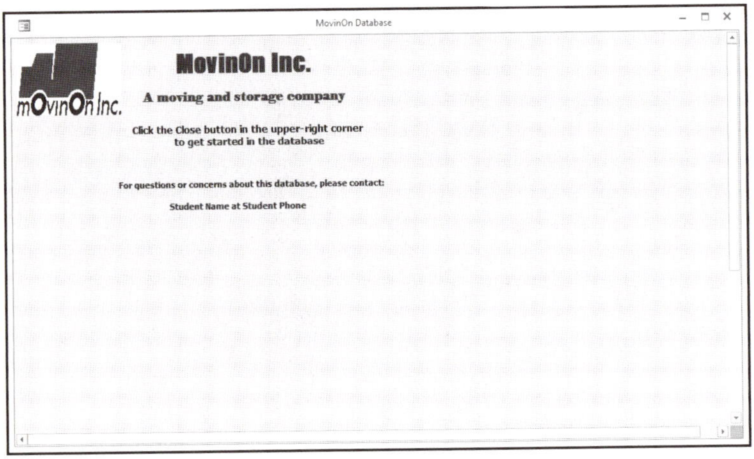

4. For security, set the splash screen to appear when the database opens. Specify properties appropriate for a splash screen. Restrict access to the Navigation pane and the Ribbon tabs.

5. MovinOn is a growing company and expects to add several employees this year. Dora explains that when entering and editing employee data, users often need to find records for employees in a certain job category. On the frmEmployeeData form, provide a way to filter records to show only those employees in a specified job category. For example, users should be able to open frmEmployeeData and then select an option or click a button to view employee records only for warehouse managers.

6. Dora wants you to provide the same kind of functionality in the Driver Data Entry form that you used in the Employee Data Entry form. Modify frmDriverData so that users can filter records in three ways: view records only for drivers with an "A" driving record, view records for drivers with an "A" or a "B" driving record, or view all the records. To maintain consistency, use the same technique and design that you used in frmEmployeeData.

7. Finally, when users are working with the Customer Data Entry form, Dora wants to make it easy to locate a particular customer. Because users usually know the customer by the last name of the contact person, add a control to frmCustomerData that lets you search for a record by selecting a contact's last name. Dora wants you to keep this control separate from the data so that it stands out but is still readily available. (*Hint*: Consider placing the control in the form's header section.)

8. Save and close the MovinOn.accdb database.

Case 3 – Providing a User Interface for the Hershey College Intramural Department

In this project, you continue to work with Marianna Fuentes, assistant director of the Intramural Department at Hershey College. She has some concerns about the purchases that coaches have made and asks that you flag large purchases in the Hershey database. She wants to highlight the large purchases on-screen and on the written purchases detail report.

In addition, to maintain security and make the Hershey database easier to use, Marianna does not want the staff to work directly with the objects in the Navigation pane. Most department employees are not familiar with Access, and she wants to provide a menu system that includes options users can choose to open the queries, forms, and reports in the database.

Finance

Complete the following:

1. Start Access and open the **Hershey.accdb** database located in the Case 3 folder.

2. When you last worked with this database, you imported data pertaining to the purchases made by coaches for their assigned sport. You also created a report containing this data. Now that you have imported this data, Marianna explains that additional purchases will be entered directly in the database. Therefore, she needs an easy way to enter the purchase data. Create a form named **frmPurchaseData** that meets Marianna's needs. Also be sure to coordinate the design of the new form with the rest of the database.

3. Marianna is concerned that coaches are making large purchases without the proper approval. In the frmPurchaseData form, highlight purchases for $150 or more by placing the words **Large Purchase** next to the amount and drawing a box around both the amount and these words. Change the color of these elements to red.

4. To help track and prevent unauthorized large purchases, Marianna asks you to provide a way to display the coach's information in frmPurchaseData for any purchase of $150 or more. Add a button to the form that only appears for a large purchase. When users click this button, it should display the name and other relevant information for the coach who made this purchase. Users should only be able to view, not change, the coach's data. The button should not be visible when the amount is less than $150.

5. In addition to highlighting large purchases in the Purchase Data form, Marianna wants to do the same in the Coach Purchases Detail report. Add the same words, Large Purchase, next to purchase amounts greater than or equal to $150. Format the words in bold red text, and draw a red box around the words.

6. Recently, a coach turned in a purchase receipt, which the intramural staff recorded in the database using frmPurchaseData. Later, a staff member inadvertently deleted the record of that purchase, and no one could find the original receipt or a copy. Marianna wants to avoid this kind of problem in the future. In frmPurchaseData, provide a means to caution users when they are deleting a purchase record. The caution should ask users if they have a receipt for the purchase and then confirm that the record should be deleted.

7. Marianna wants to display a splash screen when the database is opened. Create a splash screen that includes the name of the department and the department logo. (The logo, **HC-logo.jpg**, is located in the Chapter 6\EOC\Case 3 folder.) For security, set the splash screen to appear when the database opens. Include your name and phone number on the splash screen. Figure 6.60 shows what your screen could look like. Specify properties appropriate for a splash screen. If users close the splash screen, the navigation form should appear. Do not allow users to access the Navigation pane.

Figure 6.60: Splash screen example for Hershey College Intramural Department database

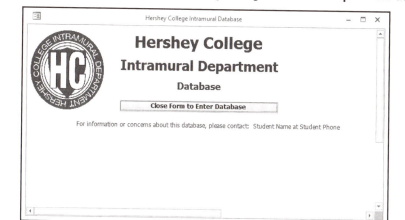

8. Create a main menu navigation form that allows users to access the queries, forms, and reports in the Hershey database. Design the menus so they are attractive and coordinate well with the department logo.

9. Save and close the Hershey.accdb database.

SAM: Skills Assessment Manager

For current SAM information, including versions and content details, visit SAM Central (http://samcentral.course.com). If you have a SAM user profile, you may have access to hands-on instruction, practice, and assessment of the skills covered in this chapter. Since various versions of SAM are supported throughout the life of this text, check with your instructor for the correct instructions and URL/Web site for accessing assignments.

Enhancing User Interaction Through Programming

Human Resources: Extending the Capabilities of the Database Using VBA

"I like thinking big. If you're going to be thinking anything, you might as well think big."
—Donald Trump

LEARNING OBJECTIVES

Level 1

Understand Visual Basic for Applications programming
Design, create, and test a subroutine in a standard module
Design, create, and test an event procedure
Design, create, and test a function in a standard module

Level 2

Design, create, and test a custom function in an event procedure
Verify data using event procedures
Use the case control structure

Level 3

Troubleshoot VBA procedures
Compile modules
Develop sources for learning VBA

TOOLS COVERED IN THIS CHAPTER

Assignment statement	**DoCmd statement**
Breakpoints	**If statement**
Code window	**Immediate window**
DateDiff function	**Variables**
DateSerial function	**Visual Basic Editor**
Debug	**Watch Window**

Chapter Introduction

Users of professionally developed databases work with forms to maintain data and work with forms and reports to display information. In Chapters 4 and 5, you learned about the features and properties of forms and reports and learned how to customize these objects for users. In Chapter 6, you learned how to create navigation forms and automate repetitive form and report tasks with macros. However, you can customize and automate a database only so far by using the features and properties of forms and reports and by using macros. To fully customize and automate a database to perform more complex validity checking and to use functions and actions not available with macros, you must use Visual Basic for Applications (VBA).

This chapter introduces you to VBA and describes how to use VBA to enhance database processing for users. Level 1 compares macros with VBA and explains how to create subroutines and functions in modules. Level 2 discusses how to use VBA to verify data in more complex ways and to extend the functionality of a form. Level 3 explains how to troubleshoot VBA and how to learn more about programming a database application with VBA.

7

Case Scenario

Maria Garcia, the human resources manager for 4Corners Pharmacy, has observed her staff using the new user interface and has talked with other employees about the automated tasks developed by Donald Linebarger. Now that the database is close to completion, Maria meets with Don to review their interaction with the database and prepare a list of improvements they want to make to it.

**Human
Resources**

Although the database contains all the data Maria needs, she must manually calculate some information based on the data stored in the database. For instance, the pharmacy provides special bonuses to employees with at least five but fewer than ten, and ten or more years of service based on the employee's actual annual salary or estimated annual salary for those paid an hourly rate. Therefore, when Maria works with frmEmployee, the form should display estimated salaries for hourly paid employees and a message indicating the employee's tenure if it is more than five but fewer than ten or more than ten years. In both cases, the form should only display information for active employees. In addition, for each active employee, Maria wants to see the current age of the employee displayed on the form. Finally, she wants the database to help verify the accuracy of ZIP codes and phone area codes.

The improvements Maria needs go beyond the capabilities of standard Access objects and macros. To provide the database features needed by human resources, Don needs to enhance the forms in the database by using VBA.

LEVEL 1
Writing Visual Basic for Applications Code

Understanding Visual Basic for Applications

Visual Basic for Applications (VBA) is the programming language for Microsoft Office programs, including Access. VBA has a common syntax and a set of common features for all Microsoft Office programs, but it also has features that are unique for each Microsoft Office program due to each program's different structure and components. For example, because Access has fields, tables, queries, forms, other objects, tab controls, subforms, and other controls that are unique to Access, VBA for Access has language features that support these components. In contrast, because Microsoft Excel does not have these same Access components, VBA for Excel does not support them, but VBA for Excel does support cells, ranges, and worksheets—three of the basic structures of Excel. The basic VBA skills you learn for any one of the Microsoft Office programs transfer to any other Microsoft Office program, but to become proficient with VBA for another program, you first need to master its unique aspects. When you use a programming language, such as VBA, you write a set of instructions to direct the computer to perform specific operations in a specific order, similar to writing a set of instructions for a recipe or an instruction manual. The process of writing instructions in a programming language is called **coding**. You write the VBA instructions, each one of which is called a **statement**, to respond to an event that occurs with an object or control in a database. A language such as VBA is, therefore, called both an **event-driven language**—an event in the database triggers a set of instructions—and an **object-oriented language**—each set of instructions operates on objects in the database. Your experience with macros, which are also event-driven and object-oriented, should facilitate your learning of VBA. Although you must use macros if you need to assign actions to a specific keyboard key or key combination, or if you need to open a database in a special way, such as displaying navigation forms.

VBA provides advantages over using macros, such as better error-handling features and easier updating capabilities. You can also use VBA in situations that macros do not handle, such as creating your own set of statements to perform special calculations, verifying a field value based on the value of another field or set of fields, or dynamically changing the color of a form control when a user enters or views a specific field value. You enter VBA code in the VBA window shown in Figure 7.1.

Figure 7.1: Visual Basic for Applications window

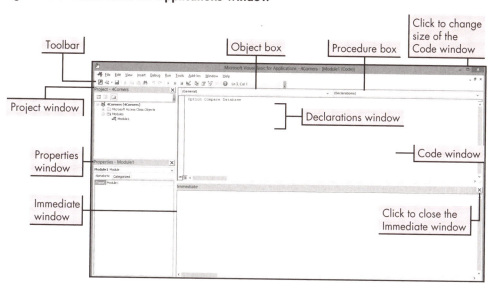

When you write code, you write it in either a class module or a standard module. The VBA window appears slightly different with each module. You will learn more about these modules later. Most objects in the VBA window can be moved, closed, or resized. The Object box shows the name of the object associated with the current code, if you are using a class module. In a standard module the word General appears because it is not associated with a specific object such as a form or report. The Procedures box lists the events supported by the object in a class module. In a standard module, the names of the procedures are displayed. And, as you saw in Chapter 6, the Immediate window can be used to test the code. The Declarations window is where you will spend most of your time writing the code. Notice that there are scroll bars that let you move around and view the code. You can also resize the Declarations window by dragging any of its borders.

Event-Driven Programming

As you learned in Chapter 6, an event is a state, condition, or occurrence that Access recognizes. For example, events occur when you click a field or command button in a form, open an object, change a field value in a form, or press a key to choose a menu option. Each event has an associated event property that specifies how an object responds when the event occurs. For example, each report has an On Open event property that specifies what happens when a user opens the report and triggers the Open event, and each form control has an On Click event property that specifies what happens when a user clicks the control and triggers the Click event. Event properties appear in the property sheet for forms, reports, and controls. By default, event properties are not set to an initial value, which means that no special action takes place when the event occurs.

Level 1

7

If you set an event property value to a macro name, as you did in Chapter 6, Access runs the macro when the event occurs. You can also create a group of statements using VBA code and set an event property value to the name of that group of statements. Access then executes the group of statements, or **procedure**, when the event occurs. Such a procedure is called an **event procedure**. Access has over 60 events and associated event properties. Table 7.1 lists some frequently used Access events.

Table 7.1: Frequently used Access events

Event Name	Action That Triggers the Event
After Update	After changed data in a control or a record is updated
Before Update	Before changed data in a control or a record is updated
Activate	When a form or report receives the focus and becomes the active window
Change	When the value in a text box or combo box changes
Click	When a user clicks the left mouse button on a control in a form
Dbl Click	When a user double-clicks the left mouse button on a control in a form
Delete	When a user takes some action, such as pressing the Delete key, to delete a record, but before the record is actually deleted
Got Focus	When a form or form control receives the focus
Key Down	When a user presses a key in an active form
Key Up	When a user releases a key in an active form
Load	When a form is opened and its records are displayed
Mouse Down	When a user presses a mouse button
Mouse Move	When a user moves the mouse pointer
Mouse Up	When a user releases a mouse button
Not In List	When a user enters a value in a combo box that is not in the combo box list
Open	When a form is opened, but before the first record is displayed; before a report is previewed or printed
Timer	When a specified time interval has elapsed
Undo	When a user undoes a change to a form or form control
Unload	When a form is closed

© 2014 Cengage Learning

Some events apply to both forms and reports, other events apply to only forms or only reports, and still other events apply to certain types of form controls. For example, command buttons, text boxes, option buttons, and combo boxes have different uses and exhibit different behaviors, and, therefore, have different events associated with them. Table 7.2 shows some common events and whether the event applies to forms, reports, and selected form controls. For example, the Not In List event is unique to combo box controls, and the Delete, Load, and Timer events are unique to form objects, whereas other events are common to two or more objects/controls.

Table 7.2: Common events for selected controls

Event	Report	Form	Command Button	Text Box	Option Button	Combo Box
			Object or Control			
Activate	x	x				
After Update		x		x	x	x
Before Update		x		x	x	x
Change		x		x		x
Click		x	x	x	x	x
Delete		x				
Key Down		x	x	x	x	x
Load		x				
Mouse Down		x	x	x	x	x
Not In List						x
Open	x	x				
Timer		x				

© 2014 Cengage Learning

Coding VBA

When you work with VBA, you code a group of statements to perform a set of operations or calculate a value, and then you attach the group of statements to the event property of an object or control. Access then **calls**—executes or runs—these statements every time the event occurs for that object or control. Each group of statements is called a procedure. The two types of procedures are function procedures and subprocedures.

A **function procedure**, or simply, **function**, performs operations, returns a value, accepts input values, and can be used in expressions (recall that an expression is a calculation resulting in a single value). For example, some of the 4Corners database queries use built-in Access functions, such as Avg, Min, and Max, to calculate an average and to determine minimum and maximum values. Don can create new functions to support the unique needs of users for their database processing. For example, he might create a function to determine the number of years between two dates and then use that function to calculate employees' ages and years of service. In the case of determining an employee's age, Don uses the function with the employee's date of birth and today's date, and the function returns the employee's age, which he can display in a form or report.

A **subprocedure**, or **subroutine**, performs operations and accepts input values, but does not return a value and cannot be used in expressions. Most Access procedures are subroutines because you need the procedures to perform a series of actions or operations in response to an event. For example, Don will create a procedure to calculate and display the estimated salary for active hourly paid employees later in this chapter.

You store a group of related procedures together in a database object called a **module**. Each module starts with a **Declarations section**, which contains statements that apply to all procedures in the module. One or more procedures, which follow the Declarations section and which can be a mixture of functions and subroutines, constitute the rest of the module. The two basic types of modules are standard modules and class modules.

A **standard module** is a database object that is stored in memory with other database objects (queries, forms, and so on) when you open the database. You can use the procedures in a database's standard modules from anywhere in the database—even from procedures in other modules. A procedure that more than one object can use is called a **public procedure**. For example, you could create a function to determine the number of years between two dates, store the function in a standard module, and then use that function to determine ages or other year difference calculations in any query, form, report, or macro in the database. All standard modules are listed on the Modules tab in the Database window.

A **class module** is usually associated with a particular form or report. When you create the first event procedure for a form or report, Access automatically creates an associated form or report class module. When you add additional event procedures to the form or report, Access adds them to the class module for that form or report. Each event procedure in a class module is a **local procedure**, or a **private procedure**. Only the form or report for which the class module was created can use the event procedure because private procedures use internal memory more efficiently and release storage space more quickly than public procedures. A private procedure is protected from being inadvertently called by other procedures outside the module. Thus, you eliminate the possibility that an error can occur.

Best Practice

Choosing Between a Function and a Subroutine

By default and by design, all event procedures are subroutines. In all other cases, you should create the module as a function only if you need to calculate a single value without any other processing operations; otherwise, you should create the module as a subroutine.

Best Practice

Setting an Event Procedure

You can set an event property to one of three values: a macro name, an event procedure, or an expression. If you set the event property to a macro name, the macro runs when the event occurs. If you set the event property to an event procedure, the associated subroutine in the object's class module runs when the event occurs. Finally, if you set the event property to an expression, the expression is evaluated and results in a single value when the event occurs.

Creating a Subroutine in a Standard Module

In Chapter 6, Don created a macro named mcrContributionMarginAnalysis to print rptContributionMarginAnalysis. In the macro he included the display of the echo symbol—the default busy symbol in Microsoft Windows 7—while the report is being generated, an action to save and close the report, and a beep sound when the macro is finished. Table 7.3 lists the four actions in the macro and the action arguments and comments that Don used for each action.

Table 7.3: Actions in mcrContributionMarginAnalysis

Macro Action	Action Arguments	Comment
Hourglass	Hourglass On: Yes	Displays the echo symbol as the macro runs
OpenReport	Report Name: rptContributionMarginAnalysis View: Print Window Mode: Normal	Prints rptContributionMarginAnalysis
CloseWindow	Object Type: Report Object Name: rptContributionMarginAnalysis Save: Yes	Closes rptContributionMarginAnalysis
Beep		Sounds a beep when the macro is finished

© 2014 Cengage Learning

Don wants to replace mcrContributionMarginAnalysis with a VBA procedure to accomplish the same task—printing rptContributionMarginAnalysis. This task is part of Don's overall plan to replace most macros with VBA procedures. Don realizes that the VBA code will not be exactly the same as the macro code. He will not replace the simple macros, such as those that open an object when clicking a command button on the navigation form. He will also keep the essential macros that he cannot perform with VBA, such as the AutoKeys macro (which assigns a macro action or set of actions to a key or key combination) and the AutoExec macro (which opens the splash screen when the database opens). Don feels, as do most database developers, that the advantages of using VBA over using macros—better error-handling features and greater capabilities—outweigh the relative ease of creating macros.

Best Practice

Dividing an Application into Parts

Programming is as much an art as it is a science. Before actual coding begins, a team of system analysts usually analyzes how a system needs to work and function and then designs the system accordingly. Part of the analysts' job is to look at large applications and break them down into manageable parts and then distribute the parts to individual modules with each module assigned to specific programmers. Even when writing small VBA applications, you should write only one part of an application at a time. In this way, you focus on smaller portions of the problem at one time rather than trying to make the entire application work at once.

Creating a New Standard Module

Before Don turns his attention to the enhancements Maria wants, he is going to begin his project of replacing the macros with VBA procedures. Don opens the 4Corners database without the splash screen so he has access to all the database objects and Access tools. Don's first task is to create a public procedure in a standard module that will print rptContributionMarginAnalysis, but not interact with the report or cause changes to the report in any way. This procedure will exist externally to the report and will not be part of its class module. Also, because the procedure does not return a value, Don will create the procedure as a subroutine instead of as a function.

Using the actions in mcrContributionMarginAnalysis as a guide (see Table 7.3), Don creates a new standard module by clicking the CREATE tab on the Ribbon, and then clicking the Module button in the Macros & Code group. The Microsoft Visual Basic for Applications window opens.

To begin a new procedure in the module, Don clicks the Insert menu, clicks Procedure, types "PrintReport" in the Name text box, makes sure the Sub and Public option buttons are selected, and then clicks the OK button. Note that you can also click the Insert Module button to start this procedure. Figure 7.2 shows the Visual Basic window with the new subroutine in the Code window.

Figure 7.2: Starting a new subroutine in the Visual Basic window

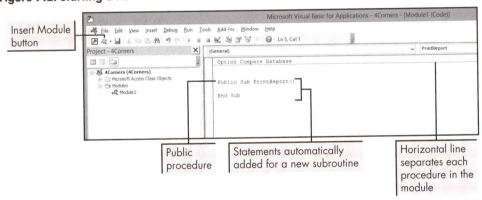

The program you use to create and modify VBA code is called the **Visual Basic Editor** (**VBE**, or **editor** for short), and the **Visual Basic window** is the program window that opens when you use VBE. The **Code window** is the window in which you create, modify, and display specific VBA procedures. You can have as many Code windows open as you have modules in the database. In the Code window, the Object box indicates the current control ("General" means there is no current control), and the Procedure box indicates the procedure name (PrintReport) for the procedure you are viewing or editing. (If the Immediate window is opened on your screen, you can close it while you work.)

Don's subroutine begins with a **Sub statement** and ends with an **End Sub statement**. The Sub statement includes the **scope** of the procedure (private or public), and the name of the procedure (PrintReport), followed by opening and closing parentheses.

A horizontal line in the Code window is used to visually separate each procedure in the module. Notice the Option Compare statement in the Declarations section above the horizontal line. The **Option Compare statement** designates the technique Access uses to compare and sort text data. The default method "Database" means that Access compares and sorts letters in normal alphabetical order, using the language settings specified for Access running on your computer.

How To

Create a Subroutine in a New Standard Module

1. Open the database, click the CREATE tab on the Ribbon, and then click the Module button in the Macros & Code group.

2. Click the Insert menu in the Microsoft Visual Basic window, and then click Procedure.

3. Type the name for the procedure in the Name text box. Note that spaces are not permitted in procedure names. VBA naming conventions and options are discussed later in the chapter.

4. Type the statements between the Sub and End Sub statements.

5. Click the Save button on the toolbar in the Microsoft Visual Basic window, type the module name in the Module Name text box, and then click the OK button.

Creating a Subroutine

Don types the statements in his procedure between the Sub and End Sub statements. He replaces each of the four actions in the mcrContributionMarginAnalysis macro with an equivalent action in the procedure using the **DoCmd statement**, which executes an action in a procedure. For example, to run the Hourglass method, Don types the following VBA statement:

```
DoCmd.Hourglass True
```

DoCmd, an Access object, is separated from Hourglass, a method, by a period, or dot; True is an argument, with the effect of the statement, which changes the mouse pointer to the echo symbol. You use False instead of True to change the echo symbol back to the standard mouse pointer. Note that a **method** is a function or procedure that operates directly on specific objects or controls.

Next, Don enters the DoCmd.OpenReport statement to print rptContributionMarginAnalysis. This OpenReport statement needs arguments to name the report, to identify which view to use for the report (the acViewNormal argument prints the report immediately), and to identify which window type to use for the report (the acWindowNormal argument constant uses the default Report window). Finally, Don uses the DoCmd.Beep statement to sound a beep at the end of the procedure. The Beep statement does not have any arguments.

The underscore character (_), that follows "DoCmd.OpenReport," at the end of the line indicates a statement that continues to the next line. Commas are used to indicate missing arguments or to separate variables. Entering the statement on one line would extend the statement far to the right and possibly require scrolling left and right to view parts of the statement. In these cases, you can split a statement across two or more lines by typing the underscore character to signal that the statement continues on the next line. If you try to go to the next line without completing a statement and without typing the underscore character, you receive an error message.

Figure 7.3 shows the set of statements that Don enters for the PrintReport subroutine.

Figure 7.3: PrintReport subroutine

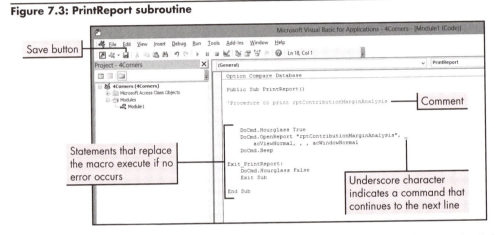

As you can see Don has also added a comment above the first statement after the Sub statement to explain the procedure's purpose. You can include comments anywhere in a VBA procedure to describe what the procedure or a statement does to make it easier to identify the purpose of statements in the code. You begin a comment with the word Rem (for "Remark") or with a single quotation mark ('). VBA ignores anything following the word Rem or the single quotation mark on a single line. Comments appear in green in the Code window.

Best Practice

Documenting VBA Code

Different people can use different approaches to solving a problem, so you should use comments in a VBA procedure to explain the purpose of the procedure and to clarify any complicated programming logic used to the programmers who will be working with the code. Most companies have documentation standards that specify the types of comments that should be included in each procedure. These standards typically require comments that identify the name of the original creator of the procedure, the purpose of the procedure, and a history of changes made to the procedure by whom and for what purpose.

Don knows that he needs to add a statement if an error occurs. He will add the On Error statement and then the DoCmd statement. By adding the statements in this order, first an error needs to occur and if it does happen, then the DoCmd will execute. The statement On Error GoTo Err_PrintReport after the comment line is processed only if an error occurs with one or more of the three DoCmd statements. Remember the rptContributionMarginAnalysis report is based on a parameter query in which the user must enter start and end dates to define the period the report covers. If a user types an illegal date, an error occurs, and the On Error statement is executed. The On Error statement contains GoTo Err_PrintReport, so the next statement processed is the Err_PrintReport: line. This statement is called a **line label**. It serves as the starting point for a block of statements in a procedure; a line label begins a line and ends with a semi-colon (;). If an error occurs, Access changes the busy icon back to the standard mouse pointer (the DoCmd.Hourglass False statement), and then Access displays a message box containing a description of the error that occurred (the MsgBox Err.Description statement).

Don used another line label, the Exit_PrintReport line: to serve as the start of a section of statements consisting of the two statements that follow. These statements are executed if the procedure prints the report successfully. That is, the DoCmd statements complete without an error, Access changes the busy symbol back to the standard mouse pointer (DoCmd.Hourglass False), and then the procedure ends (Exit Sub statement). The completed PrintReport subroutine is shown in Figure 7.4.

Figure 7.4: Completed PrintReport subroutine

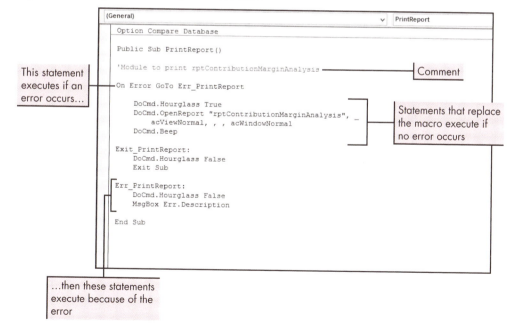

Indenting Statements in Procedures

VBA does not require statements to be indented in procedures. However, most experienced programmers indent statements to make procedures easier to read and maintain. Except for beginning comments and line labels, it is best to indent all lines equally within a procedure. Pressing the Tab key once indents the line four spaces to the right, which is a sufficient amount of indentation, and pressing the Shift+Tab key combination moves the insertion point four spaces to the left. Later in this chapter, you will see statements that are indented more, but always in multiples of four spaces, and you will learn why the additional spacing is necessary.

To run the procedure, Don clicks the Run Sub/UserForm button on the toolbar. The busy icon appears, the Enter Parameter Value dialog box opens, Don enters a start date of 1/1/2016, clicks the OK button, enters an end date of 12/31/2016, clicks the OK button, a beep sounds, the report prints, and then the pointer changes back to its standard shape. As a test, Don runs the procedure again, but this time enters an illegal start date, such as 12/31/201*. Because he entered illegal characters, a Microsoft Access message box appears indicating that it could not process the value. The report, therefore, does not print.

Don has finished his work with the procedure, so he saves the module by clicking the Save button on the toolbar. Don will use *bas* as the prefix for the module name according to the naming convention he has been using throughout the database. He then types "bas4CornersGeneralProcedures" in the Name text box, and then clicks the OK button. Don then closes the Visual Basic window, and the bas4CornersGeneralProcedures module appears in the Modules section of the Navigation pane.

Don now turns his attention to the enhancements requested by Maria. He begins by writing a procedure to display the estimated annual salaries for employees who are paid an hourly rate.

Creating an Event Procedure

When Maria uses frmEmployee, she wants to view each employee's annual salary. For salaried employees, the Salary field value represents the annual salary. However, for active, hourly paid employees, the form displays the hourly rate but not an annual salary. For these employees, Don needs to multiply the hourly rate by 2,080, which is the product of 40 hours per week and 52 weeks per year.

Based on the requirements, Don needs to add a text box with an associated label to frmEmployee. The caption for the label control will be "Est Salary," and the text box control will display the results of the calculated estimated salary. Maria wants to view the two controls only for active, hourly paid employees, so the controls should be invisible for inactive employees and for active salaried employees. Likewise, the calculation should be performed only when the two controls are displayed. Further, Maria wants the estimated salary for hourly rates $12 or more per hour to be formatted in green and in all other cases to be formatted in blue. Don and Maria agree that the controls should be displayed under the Hourly Rate text box.

Designing an Event Procedure in a Form's Class Module

Maria's enhancement applies only to frmEmployee, so Don needs to add a procedure to the form's class module. Each time Maria navigates to a record, Don wants the procedure to run for the current record. Therefore, Don needs to associate the procedure with the form's BeforeUpdate event property, which is triggered when moving to another record.

First, Don adds a text box control to frmEmployee in Design view. Don decides to give both the label and text box meaningful Name property values to help identify what they are in the procedure. The procedure will use these names when setting the controls to visible or invisible. Don sets the label's Name property to EstSalary_Label and the Caption property to Est Salary. He makes font-related changes so this control is consistent with the others. Then he sets the text box's Name property to EstSalary. He also resizes and repositions the controls, as shown in Figure 7.5.

Figure 7.5: Text box and associated label added to form

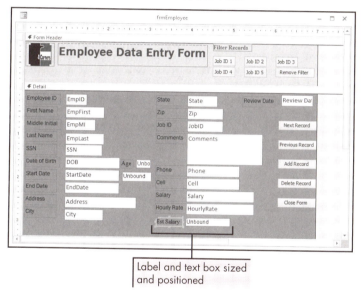

Label and text box sized and positioned

To add the event procedure, Don opens the Property Sheet for the form, switches to the Event tab, clicks the BeforeUpdate box list arrow, and clicks [Event Procedure]. Don then clicks the Build button in the BeforeUpdate box. The Code window opens in the Visual Basic window with the Private Sub and End Sub statements for the new event procedure automatically added. The event procedure name, Form_BeforeUpdate, means the BeforeUpdate event for the form object. See Figure 7.6.

Figure 7.6: Code window contains Private Sub and Exit Sub statements

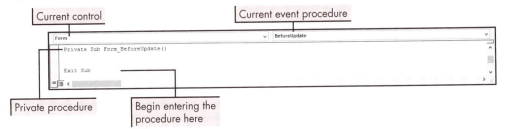

Don writes out the procedure statements he needs before he begins to type them in the event procedure, so that he can review them and make sure they will accomplish what Maria wants accurately and without error. Don's design for the event procedure is as follows:

```
Private Sub Form_BeforeUpdate()
    'For active employees paid an hourly rate
    '    display their estimated salaries
    If IsNull(EndDate) And IsNull(Salary) _
        And Not IsNull(HourlyRate) Then
        EstSalary = HourlyRate * 2080
        EstSalary.Visible = True
        EstSalary_Label.Visible = True
        If HourlyRate >= 12 Then
            EstSalary.ForeColor = vbGreen
        Else
            EstSalary.ForeColor = vbBlue
        End If
    Else
        EstSalary.Visible = False
        EstSalary_Label.Visible = False
    End If

End Sub
```

Note that he changes Exit (the default) to End, which is basically the same, but Access 2013 consistently uses Exit versus End, but he changes it to keep consistency throughout the database. The key statements in this event procedure involve deciding when Access needs to perform the calculation and make the controls visible and when Access needs to display the estimated salary in a blue or green text color. For these statements, Don has used one of VBA's decision-making statements, the If statement.

Using the If Statement in Decision Making

A decision-making statement executes a group of statements based on the outcome of a condition. In the simplest decision-making statement, Access executes a group of statements if the condition is true and executes nothing if the condition is false. You can also write a decision-making statement that executes a second group of statements if the condition is false; in this case, only one set of statements is executed—the true-statement group executes only if the condition is true, and the false-statement group executes only if the condition is false. When the procedure needs to make a decision, you need to identify the condition to test.

One portion of Don's procedure must determine whether to display the estimated salary in blue or green. To test one condition that results in one of two answers, Don uses an **If statement**, which tests a condition and follows one of two paths depending on the outcome of the condition. The general form of a VBA If statement is:

```
If condition Then
    true-statement group
[Else
    false-statement group]
End If
```

Access executes only the *true-statement* group when the condition is true and only the *false-statement* group when the condition is false. In the general form of the If statement, the bracketed portion is optional. Therefore, you must omit the *Else* and its related false-statement group when you want Access to execute a group of statements only when the condition is true

Don's If statement is:

```
If HourlyRate >= 12 Then
    EstSalary.ForeColor = vbGreen
Else
    EstSalary.ForeColor = vbBlue
End If
```

The statement contains one condition (HourlyRate >= 12), true-statement group is (EstSalary.ForeColor = vbGreen) and the false-statement is (EstSalary.ForeColor = vbBlue). If an HourlyRate field value is greater than or equal to 12 (the condition is true), the estimated salary text color is set to green; otherwise, the text color is set to blue. Notice that statements in the true-statement group and the false-statement group are indented to make the procedure more readable.

Statements such as EstSalary.ForeColor = vbGreen are assignment statements. An **assignment statement** assigns the value of an expression—the color constant value vbGreen, in this case—to a control or property—the text color, or ForeColor property, for the EstSalary control, in this case.

Because a property is associated with a control, you use the general form of *ControlName. PropertyName* to specify a property for a control. An assignment statement such as EstSalary. ForeColor = vbGreen, for example, assigns a value to the EstSalary control's ForeColor property. A control's **ForeColor property** determines the control's foreground, or text, color. The expression in this assignment statement uses a built-in color constant named vbGreen. **Color constants** are predefined VBA names that have values that represent the system color value for the color in the constant name. Other color constants you can use are vbBlack, vbRed, vbYellow, vbBlue, vbMagenta, vbCyan, and vbWhite.

Don's If statement also uses the comparison operation >= to test the condition: "Is the hourly rate greater than or equal to $12?" Table 7.4 lists test conditions frequently used in procedures.

Table 7.4: Comparison operators used in procedures

Operator	Meaning	Example
<	Less than	txtTotal < 7
<=	Less than or equal to	txtBill <= 10.50
>	Greater than	EmpAge > 21
>=	Greater than or equal to	StartDate >= #01/01/2008#
=	Equal to	txtName = "Jones"
<>	Not equal to	TestAnswer <> "yes"

© 2014 Cengage Learning

As shown in the examples, text fields and controls can contain values such as names and addresses that need to be enclosed in quotation marks and values such as dates need to be enclosed in pound signs (#).

Best Practice

Using the End If
For If statements that do not require the false-statement group, you can omit the Else part of the If statement. For If statements that have no false-statement group and only one statement in the true-statement group, you can omit the End If part of the If statement and place the statement immediately after the Else part of the If statement as follows:

```
If HourlyRate >= 12 Then EstSalary.ForeColor = vbGreen
```

However, changing business requirements frequently necessitate changes to procedures, and programmers who change the procedures in the future are usually not the same programmers who originated the procedures. Experienced programmers write procedures so that they can be easily maintained by other programmers in the future. One such technique is to use the End If part of the If statement even when there is no false-statement group and only one statement in the true-statement group. Not only does this make the statements stand out more clearly to anyone reading the procedure, it also makes it easier to add additional statements to the true-statement group should new requirements arise that require a programmer to add more commands.

Don's procedure has another, yet more, complicated If statement that will determine whether Access should calculate the estimated salary and make the label and text box visible. Just as you can use the And, Or, and Not operators in queries, you can use these same operators in VBA If statements to test multiple conditions. Don can use the **IsNull function**, which returns a True value when a field or control is null and False when it is not. Don writes out the If statement as follows:

```
If IsNull(EndDate) And IsNull(Salary) _
    And Not IsNull(HourlyRate) Then
```

For the If statement to be true, all three conditions must be true because the And operators connect each separate condition. If the EndDate is null (the employee is an active employee and has no ending employment date), the Salary is null (the employee is not a salaried employee), and the HourlyRate is not null, then Access calculates the estimated salary, makes the two controls visible, *and* determines the text color for the estimated salary. On the other hand, if the HourlyRate is null, that is, the hourly rate has not yet been stored for the employee, there is no hourly rate upon which to base the calculation. Therefore, after entering the If statement, Don addresses this condition by entering a true-statement group—the eight lines following the two-line If statement, as shown in Figure 7.7. When one or more of the conditions is false, the two statements following the second Else constitute the false-statement group and are executed—the two controls are hidden.

Figure 7.7: BeforeUpdate event procedure in the Code window

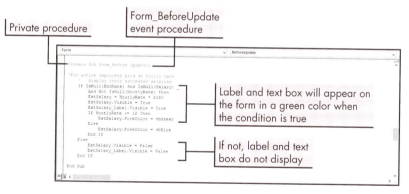

Also note that the EstSalary = HourlyRate * 2080 assignment statement multiplies the HourlyRate field value by 2,080 and assigns the calculated value to the EstSalary control. The Visible property is set in the four remaining procedure statements—setting the Visible property to True displays the control, and setting it to False hides the control.

Note that Don could have entered the If statement on one line without the underscore (_) character, but to make the code easier to read while working with it now and in the future, he uses the underscore to continue the code on the next line.

Best Practice

Properly Matching Clauses in Embedded If Statements

The End If clause terminates an If statement. You can embed, or nest, If statements within other If statements, and each embedded If statement is terminated by its own End If clause. When you have an If statement with a false-statement group, the Else clause terminates the true-statement group and marks the beginning of the false-statement group. You must make sure in procedures that you match Else and End If clauses with the correct If clause. Else and End If clauses match up with the closest previous If clause that has not already been paired with its Else and End If clause. That is, the matching first occurs with the embedded If statement. Although you can nest If statements for several levels, experienced programmers avoid deep nesting because it is too easy to make errors when designing and writing such complicated procedures. Also, other programmers have difficulty understanding and changing them. It is best to redesign and rewrite complicated procedures to make them simpler and easier to understand and maintain.

Testing an Event Procedure

Don carefully reviews his design before entering it in the Code window. He saves the class module, closes the Visual Basic window, and then saves his changes to frmEmployee. To test the event procedure, Don switches to Form view. The first record is for Joan Gabel, an inactive employee with an EndDate field value, so the two new controls are hidden correctly, as shown in Figure 7.8.

Figure 7.8: Testing for an inactive employee

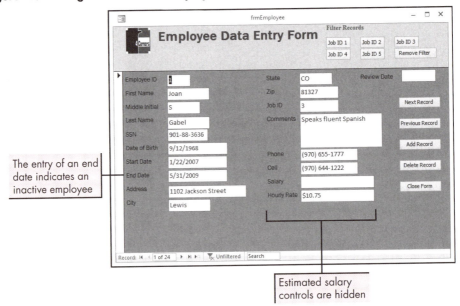

The entry of an end date indicates an inactive employee

Estimated salary controls are hidden

Navigating to the second record for Marco Farello, the two controls are visible because he is an active, hourly paid employee. The estimated salary is displayed correctly in blue because Marco's hourly rate is $11.33, which is less than $12.00, as shown in Figure 7.9.

Figure 7.9: Testing for an active employee

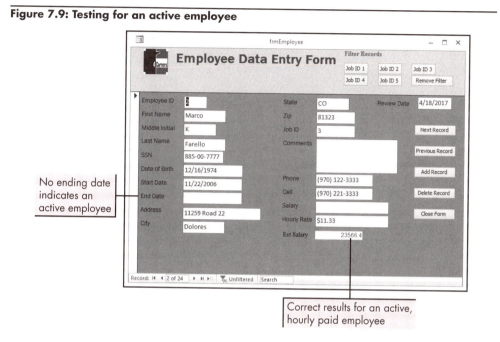

No ending date indicates an active employee

Correct results for an active, hourly paid employee

Don navigates through the other records to make sure the results are correct in the different situations. Don demonstrates the results to Maria, who approves his enhancement but wants the estimated salary values displayed in currency format similar to the salary field values. Also, because the estimated salary is a calculated control, users should not be able to change its value or tab to it, and its appearance should be different from a normal text box to distinguish it as a calculated control. To make these changes, Don switches to Design view, sets the EstSalary text box control's format to Currency, its Border Style to Transparent, its Locked property to Yes, and its Tab Stop property to No. He then decreases the size of the text box so it displays closer to the label. He saves the changes, switches back to Form view, and navigates to the second record. Figure 7.10 shows the estimated salary value for Marco Farello formatted as currency.

Figure 7.10: Testing the event procedure with new formats

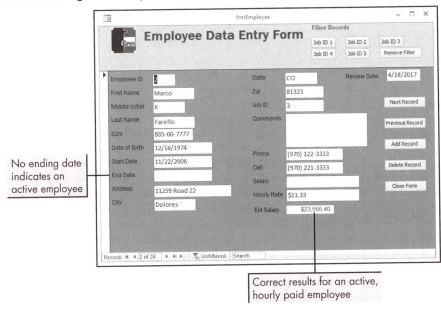

No ending date indicates an active employee

Correct results for an active, hourly paid employee

Using a Function in a Standard Module

Don reviews the remaining enhancement requests and notices that two requests have a similar need. The years of service and employee age requests both require the calculation of the number of years between two dates. For the years of service request, Don needs to calculate the number of years between an employee's start date and today's date to determine the number of years of service. For the employee age request, Don needs to calculate the number of years between an employee's date of birth and today's date to determine the employee's age. When you have similar calculation requests, it is better to create a function to perform the calculation than to place the calculation in multiple places in procedures. Doing so allows you to change the calculation in one place instead of in multiple places if you need to correct an inaccuracy in the calculation or enhance the calculation to meet changing business needs.

Using Functions in VBA

You use a function that you create similarly to the way you use the built-in functions in Access. For example, to calculate the total of the Balance field amounts, you use the expression Sum ([Balance]). The function name (Sum) is followed by the argument(s) it needs, which are enclosed in parentheses. If a function needs more than one argument, commas separate the arguments. When Access encounters a function name in an expression, Access executes the function and passes the argument values to the function. The function uses the values to perform its operations and, when the function finishes, the single value calculated by the function replaces the function in the expression.

There is one remaining new component to the YearDiff function—the SecondDate value is compared to the result of the DateSerial function using the less than operator (<). If the SecondDate is less than the DateSerial result, the comparison is True; otherwise, the comparison is False. When comparing two dates, the first date is less than a second date when the first date chronologically precedes the second date. It is interesting that Access stores a True comparison result as a zero value, and a False comparison result as a value of minus one (-1). Recall that Don's original YearDiff function gave results that were either accurate or one year more than the correct result. In the cases in which the original YearDiff function was accurate, the new version of the function adds zero, which means the result continues to be accurate. And in the cases where the original YearDiff function was one year higher than it should be, the new version subtracts one (by adding minus one), which means that these results are also correct. Figure 7.13 shows Don's revised YearDiff function. Note that you will need as many closing parentheses at the end of the function as you have opening parentheses.

Figure 7.13: Revised YearDiff function in the Code window

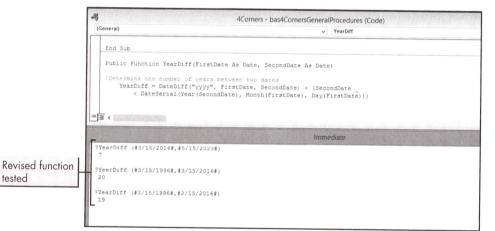

Revised function tested

Don saves the standard module that contains the revised YearDiff function and tests its results. The revised function returns the correct results.

Testing the Logic of a Procedure

Experienced programmers design procedures thoroughly before entering them into the computer. However, these same programmers find logic errors in procedures they thought were flawless. Because the complexity of computer procedure logic is sufficiently high, logic errors are bound to occur. Therefore, it is important for programmers to test, correct, and retest every procedure until it works in all situations. Never release a new or enhanced procedure to users until you are positive it will work for them in all situations. For example, if Don had not tested the YearDiff function with several pairs of dates, he might not have identified the problem that his revised YearDiff function corrects, and users would have received incorrect results some of the time.

Best Practice

Creating Generalized Procedures

Making the YearDiff function a public function in a standard module allows it to be used in any expression in the database. Doing this also isolates any problem with the function to a single location in the database and isolates the follow-up problem correction there too. In addition, the YearDiff function requires two dates as arguments, even though the present requirements specify that today's date (for the years of service request and for the employee age request) is always the second date passed as an argument to the procedure. Don purposely built a two-argument requirement into the function so that he could anticipate meeting future user requirements for the same function. For example, Maria might plan a future awards banquet, in which case she needs to know which employees will have served for 20 or more years with the pharmacy as of a certain future date. In this case, Don can use the YearDiff function as written because he had the experience and foresight to anticipate how useful the function could be as a generalized procedure.

Steps To Success: Level 1

Glenn Hollander is the database manager for Hudson Bay Pharmacy and asks for your help in enhancing the Hudson database. He also wants to automate a task that Joan Gabel, manager of the pharmacy, performs often, such as the need to know how long employees have worked for the company. Before Glenn turns his attention to the enhancements Joan wants, he is going to begin his project of replacing the macros with VBA procedures.

Complete the following:

1. Start Access and open the **Hudson.accdb** database from the STS folder.

2. Review mcrContributionMarginAnalysis. Replace this macro with a VBA procedure. Save the module as **basHudsonGeneralProcedures**.

   TROUBLESHOOTING: Until you get through the pilot testing with the database, it is good practice to keep a backup copy of database that had the macros and forms that used the macros. Then, in the event those testing the database get error messages based on the code you entered to replace the macros, you can refer back to them.

3. Create a public function to calculate the age of the employees using the **YearDiff** function in a standard module that accurately calculates the number of years between two dates. The YearDiff has two arguments, DOB and Date, where DOB is the employee's date of birth, and Date is today's date. Then, test the function.

4. Create a function that will determine the months the employee has worked with the company. The employee's start date and today's date will determine the months of service.

5. Save and close the Hudson.accdb database.

LEVEL 2

Using Custom Functions and Verifying Data

Enhancing an Event Procedure to Use a Custom Function

Don continues his work on enhancing the database. He still needs to work on two of Maria's outstanding requests, both of which can use the YearDiff function he already created. The first request is to add functionality to frmEmployee so it displays a message for active employees who have worked at the pharmacy for at least five years but fewer than ten years or for ten or more years. This added functionality will make it easier for Maria to keep track of salary increases for all employees. The second request is to add functionality to the same form so it displays the current age of all active employees. This added functionality will allow Maria to watch for employees nearing retirement age.

Don could design VBA solutions for both requests at the same time because the requests involve the same form, use the same function, apply only to active employees, and are relatively simple in concept and design. However, he decides to tackle them individually, starting with the years of service request. Designing the requests individually allows Don to concentrate on one problem at a time, reducing the chance of introducing flaws into the design and subsequently implementing a VBA solution that does not work properly. After implementing the VBA solutions individually for the two requests, Don can review them and combine them later, if appropriate.

The years of service request must use the YearDiff function to determine the difference in years between the employee's start date and today's date and display a message for employees with ten or more years of service and employees with at least five but fewer than ten years of service. After conferring with Maria to understand and confirm her requirements, Don maps out the modifications he needs to make to the frmEmployee form and VBA procedure logic he must add to. This procedure will be added to the frmEmployee's Current event procedure.

- Add a text box named YearsOfService to frmEmployee to the right of the StartDate text box, and set its Border Style property to Transparent, Tab Stop property to No, and Locked property to Yes. In the text box, display a message in frmEmployee that indicates the years of service for each employee with at least five but fewer than ten years of service and for employees with ten or more years of service. For employees with ten or more years of service, display "10+ years"; for employees with fewer than ten but more than five years of service, display "5+ years". Use the YearDiff function to determine an employee's number of years of service based on the start date and today's date. Delete the label from the text box control because the positioning of the text box and its displayed message make the text box self-explanatory. Deleting the label will also reduce clutter on the form.

- Add the VBA statements to frmEmployee's BeforeUpdate event procedure so the focus changes to a new record, making it the current record every time a record is added. The frmEmployee's BeforeUpdate event procedure already contains statements to calculate and display the estimated annual salary for hourly employees.
- Design decision-making logic in the VBA procedure for frmEmployee to show the length of time employees have or had been with the company. Show the length of time of inactive employees too, if they meet the greater than 5 year criteria in order to assess employee contentment with the company and their reason for leaving.
- Design additional decision-making logic in the VBA procedure based on the years of service calculation to make the text box control visible and to display one of two messages; otherwise, the text box control should not be visible.

Based on the design requirements, Don writes the following VBA procedure statements that he will add to the form's Current event procedure:

```
'For active employees, display a message for those
'    with at least five but less than ten or ten or
'    more years of service
If IsNull(EndDate) And Not IsNull(StartDate) Then
    If YearDiff(StartDate, Date) >= 10 Then
        YearsOfService = "10+ years"
        YearsOfService.Visible = True
    ElseIf YearDiff(StartDate, Date) >= 5 Then
        YearsOfService = "5+ years"
        YearsOfService.Visible = True
    Else
        YearsOfService.Visible = False
    End If
End If
```

Using an ElseIf Statement in an If Statement

The first three lines of the service-related procedure are comments that describe the purpose of the set of VBA statements. Don's If statement (If IsNull(EndDate)) will select only active employees. In addition, the StartDate field should have a field value (Not IsNull(StartDate)). For each employee record that passes this test (meaning that both conditions are true), it is necessary to determine whether the employee has either five but fewer than ten years of service (display the message "5+ years") or ten or more years of service (display the message "10+ years"), using the expression YearDiff(StartDate, Date) to determine the accurate number of years of service. Note that Date is an argument in the YearDiff function that actually uses the **Date function**. The Date function returns the current computer system date, so that the employee's start date and today's date are the arguments to the YearDiff function.

The ElseIf statement is equivalent to an Else clause followed immediately by an If statement. Figure 7.14 shows the syntax for an ElseIf clause on the left and an Else clause followed by an If statement on the right.

Figure 7.14: Comparing an ElseIf clause with an Else...If clause

ElseIf clause	Else...If clause
| ```
If condition Then
    true-statement group 1
ElseIf condition Then

    true-statement group 2
Else
    false-statement group

End If
``` | ```
If condition Then
    true-statement group 1
Else
    If condition Then
        true-statement group 2
    Else
        false-statement group
    End If
End If
``` |

© 2014 Cengage Learning

The choice of which If statement version you use is a matter of personal preference, although the ElseIf version requires one less End If statement at the end and is not as deeply indented, which makes the code more readable.

Best Practice

Arranging the Order of Condition Testing

The order of condition testing is critical. You must place the conditions in order from least inclusive to most inclusive. Placing the conditions in the wrong order will cause the statements following the ElseIf clause never to execute; only the statements following the initial If condition and following the Else condition execute. And, they should all be placed before the End Sub.

For example, Don's design first tests for ten or more years of service (least inclusive) and, for those employees for whom the condition is true, executes the two following assignment statements and then proceeds with the next statement after the End If. For all other employees, the condition with the ElseIf clause executes and, for those employees with at least five years but fewer than ten years of service (most inclusive), the design executes the two following assignment statements and then proceeds with the next statement after the End If. Finally, for all employees with fewer than five years of service, the design executes the statement following the Else clause, setting the Visible property for the text box to False.

On the other hand, if the design first tests for employees with five or more years of service, then the condition is true for both employees with five or more years of service and for employees with ten or more years of service. Thus, both sets of employees would have the text box message set to "5+ years" and the Visible property for the text box set to True, and then the statement following the End If would be executed. In other words, the design would never result in the display of the "10+ years" message.

Don spots something in his design that he doesn't like. The YearDiff function is used twice—once in the second If statement and again in the ElseIf clause. For those employees with ten or more years of service, only the first function call executes, but both function calls execute for all other employees. Executing the function twice takes more computer time than if he uses an assignment statement, such as Service = YearDiff(StartDate, Date). He can replace the repeated functions if he creates a Service variable and uses an assignment statement.

```
If Service >= 10 Then
ElseIf Service >= 5 Then
```

Don corrects the design by adding the assignment statement for the Service variable and modifying the two conditions. He also adds a declaration statement (Dim Service As Integer) immediately following the comment lines. You use the **Dim statement** to declare variables and their associated data types in a procedure. Figure 7.15 shows the completed procedure.

Figure 7.15: Completed procedure to determine an employee's years of service

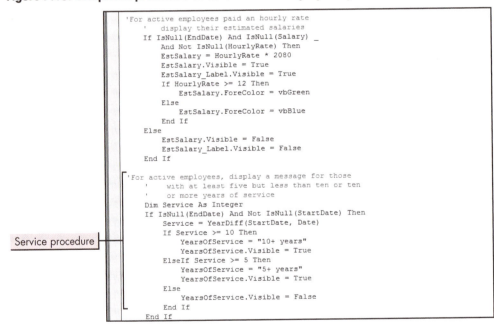

```
'For active employees paid an hourly rate
'    display their estimated salaries
If IsNull(EndDate) And IsNull(Salary) _
    And Not IsNull(HourlyRate) Then
    EstSalary = HourlyRate * 2080
    EstSalary.Visible = True
    EstSalary_Label.Visible = True
    If HourlyRate >= 12 Then
        EstSalary.ForeColor = vbGreen
    Else
        EstSalary.ForeColor = vbBlue
    End If
Else
    EstSalary.Visible = False
    EstSalary_Label.Visible = False
End If

'For active employees, display a message for those
'    with at least five but less than ten or ten
'    or more years of service
Dim Service As Integer
If IsNull(EndDate) And Not IsNull(StartDate) Then
    Service = YearDiff(StartDate, Date)
    If Service >= 10 Then
        YearsOfService = "10+ years"
        YearsOfService.Visible = True
    ElseIf Service >= 5 Then
        YearsOfService = "5+ years"
        YearsOfService.Visible = True
    Else
        YearsOfService.Visible = False
    End If
End If
```

Service procedure

Don tests the enhancement and verifies that it works correctly for all conditions tested in the VBA statements. Figure 7.16 shows the YearsOfService text box for the record for Virginia Sanchez, an active employee with more than ten years of service. The message "10+ years" appears correctly.

Figure 7.16: Testing the procedure to determine an employee's years of service

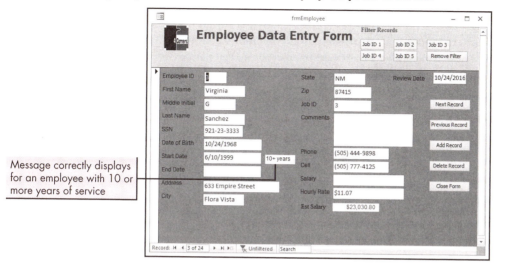

Message correctly displays for an employee with 10 or more years of service

Add and Change Statements in a Procedure

1. Open the object, such as a form, that contains the event procedure in Design view.
2. To add a new procedure, module, or class module, click Insert on the menu bar in the Code window, and then click Procedure, Module, or Class Module.
3. To edit existing statements, scroll the Code window to the desired statement, and then make the necessary changes.
4. Click the Save button on the Visual Basic toolbar, and then close the Visual Basic window.

Next, Don turns his attention to designing the VBA statements to calculate and display the age of active employees. Don's form modifications and VBA statements must address the following:

- Add a text box named Age and an associated label named Age_Label to frmEmployee to the right of the DOB field text box. Set the text box's properties similar to the YearsOfService calculated control. The associated label should display "Age" as its caption.
- Add VBA statements to the form's BeforeUpdate event procedure.
- Design decision-making logic in the VBA procedure to include only those employees who are active (designated by an end date without a value) and who have a date of birth, which is required for the age calculation.
- Use the YearDiff function to determine an employee's age based on the date of birth and today's date.
- Neither the text box nor the label should be visible for inactive employees or employees without a date of birth value.

Figure 7.17 shows the VBA procedure statements Don adds to the form's BeforeUpdate event procedure to calculate and display the age of active employees.

Figure 7.17: Procedure to calculate an active employee's age

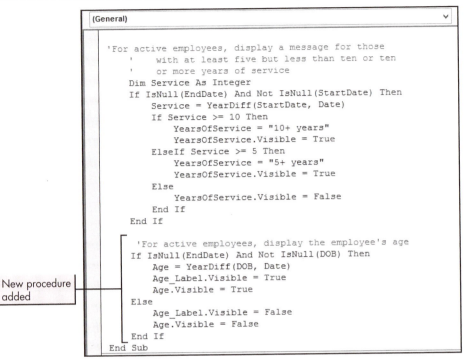

```
(General)                                                                    ˅

    'For active employees, display a message for those
         '    with at least five but less than ten or ten
         '    or more years of service
         Dim Service As Integer
         If IsNull(EndDate) And Not IsNull(StartDate) Then
             Service = YearDiff(StartDate, Date)
             If Service >= 10 Then
                 YearsOfService = "10+ years"
                 YearsOfService.Visible = True
             ElseIf Service >= 5 Then
                 YearsOfService = "5+ years"
                 YearsOfService.Visible = True
             Else
                 YearsOfService.Visible = False
             End If
         End If

          'For active employees, display the employee's age
          If IsNull(EndDate) And Not IsNull(DOB) Then
              Age = YearDiff(DOB, Date)
              Age_Label.Visible = True
              Age.Visible = True
          Else
              Age_Label.Visible = False
              Age.Visible = False
          End If
     End Sub
```

New procedure added

Note that Visible properties have to be set to either True or False each time the statements execute. The resetting of this property is necessary because when the routine executes, it does not remember the settings of the Visible property made the last time the routine was executed. Therefore, you have to set them each time to ensure they are correct for this employee.

Don tests the enhancement and verifies the test results. Figure 7.18 shows the form with the record for Marco Farello displayed. Marco has worked at the pharmacy for more than five but fewer than ten years and is 41 years old as of March 15, 2016.

Figure 7.18: Testing the procedure to display an active employee's age

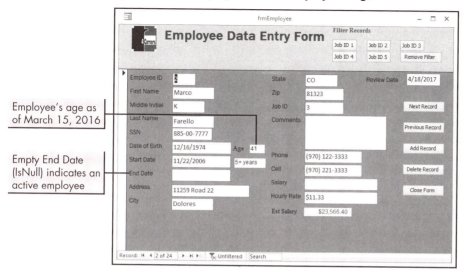

Employee's age as of March 15, 2016

Empty End Date (IsNull) indicates an active employee

7

Level 2

Best Practice

Combining the VBA Statements for Separate Enhancements

Each of Don's enhancements involve the form's BeforeUpdate event. Further, the VBA statements display the controls only for active employees. Don could combine the VBA statements as much as possible or, at the very least, enter the VBA statements for both enhancements at the same time and test them together. However, experienced programmers find that it is easier to test enhancements separately because errors are isolated to the single added enhancement, making it easier to find any problem and correct it. After an enhancement is entered and completely tested, the programmer enters the next enhancement and tests it, this time knowing that any problems detected apply to this enhancement.

After entering and testing all enhancements, should you consolidate code? For example, Don's completed BeforeUpdate event contains the years of service enhancement, and the current age enhancement. All three enhancements apply only to active employees, so he could review the three separate sets of statements, find three If statements that include testing the EndDate field value for a null value, and combine the three sets so that only one If statement tests the EndDate field value. If he chooses not to combine the sets of statements, each enhancement remains implemented as a separate set of statements, which makes it easier to understand the event procedure and modify it in the future. Also, each set of separate statements is simpler than if combined because combining the statements will intermingle them into one more-complicated set. The main argument for combining the enhancements is to make the event procedure execute faster. If Don combines the enhancements, he might reduce the number of conditions tested, which results in less time needed to process the event procedure. As a general rule, you should keep the enhancements separate until execution speed becomes a critical factor.

Don decides not to combine the three separate enhancements in the form's BeforeUpdate event procedure. Next, Don will implement the enhancements Maria requested to verify ZIP codes and phone area codes. He begins by designing the ZIP code enhancement.

Verifying Data with VBA

Maria often makes typing errors when entering Arizona ZIP codes, whose first three digits range between 850 and 865, and New Mexico ZIP codes, whose first three digits range between 870 and 884. She tends to transpose the first two digits. She wants Don to create a procedure to verify that Arizona and New Mexico ZIP codes are in the correct range when she updates the Zip field in frmEmployee. For this procedure, Don can use an event procedure attached to the Before Update event for frmEmployee. The **Before Update event** occurs before changed data in a control or a record is updated in the database. Using the form's Before Update event for this new procedure will find data-entry errors for Arizona and New Mexico ZIP codes and alert users to the errors before the database is updated.

Designing the Field Validation Procedure to Verify ZIP Codes

The subroutine that Don designed for frmEmployee to verify Arizona and New Mexico ZIP codes uses several of the statements from Don's previous designs as well as some others:

```
'Verify the first three digits of zip codes
   '    in Arizona and New Mexico
  Dim ZipFirstThree As Integer
  If Not IsNull(State) And Not IsNull(Zip) Then
      ZipFirstThree = Val(Left(Zip, 3))
      Select Case State
          Case "AZ"
              If ZipFirstThree < 850 Or ZipFirstThree > 865 Then
                  MsgBox "AZ zip codes must start 850 to 865"
                  GoTo CommonProcessing
              End If
          Case "NM"
              If ZipFirstThree < 870 Or ZipFirstThree > 884 Then
                  MsgBox "NM zip codes must start 870 to 884"
                  GoTo CommonProcessing
              End If
      End Select
  End If

  Exit Sub
      CommonProcessing: DoCmd.CancelEvent Me.Undo
          Zip.SetFocus
  End Sub
```

After two lines of comments, the next statement, Dim ZipFirstThree As Integer, declares the integer variable named ZipFirstThree. The subroutine assigns the first three digits of the ZIP code (the Zip field) to the ZipFirstThree variable, and then uses the variable when verifying that Arizona and New Mexico ZIP codes begin in the correct range.

The procedure should not attempt to verify records that contain null field values for the State field and the ZIP field. To screen out these conditions, the procedure uses the statement If Not IsNull(State) And Not IsNull(ZIP) Then, which pairs with the last End If statement. This If statement determines whether both the State and ZIP fields are not null. If both conditions are true, Access executes the next statement in the procedure. If either condition is false, Access skips to the paired End If statement and the final If statement is evaluated.

The procedure statement, ZipFirstThree = Val(Left(Zip, 3)), uses the built-in Val and Left functions to assign the first three digits of the ZIP field value to the ZipFirstThree variable. The **Left function** returns a string containing a specified number of characters from the left side of a specified string. In this case, the Left function returns the leftmost three characters of the ZIP field. The **Val function** returns the numbers contained in a specified string as a numeric value. In this case, the Val function returns the leftmost three characters of ZIP as an integer value.

Using the Case Control Structure

The statements from the Select Case State statement to the End Select statement are an example of a control structure. A **control structure** is a set of VBA statements that work together as a unit. One control structure Don has already used is the If statement, a decision-making or conditional control structure. The **Case control structure** is another conditional structure; it evaluates an expression—the value of the State field, in this case—and then performs one of several alternative sets of statements based on the resulting value (or condition) of the evaluated expression. Each Case statement, such as Case "AZ" and Case "NM", designates the start of a set of alternative statements. Note that you can use a Case Else statement as the last Case statement, if you need to include a false-statement group.

For the Before Update event procedure, the Select Case State statement evaluates the State field value. For State field values equal to AZ (Arizona ZIP codes), the Case "AZ" statement marks the beginning of the statement group that executes for Arizona, and the statement group's end occurs with the next Case statement. For State field values equal to NM (New Mexico ZIP codes), the Case "NM" statement marks the beginning of the statement group that executes for New Mexico, and the statement group's end occurs with the End Select statement. For ZIP codes other than those for Arizona and New Mexico, neither Case statement is true, so execution proceeds to the End Select statement, then the following End If statement, and continues on to evaluate the final If statement.

Because valid Arizona ZIP codes start with the values 850 through 865, invalid numeric values are less than 850 or greater than 865. The next VBA statement, If ZipFirstThree < 850 Or ZipFirstThree > 865 Then, is true only for invalid Arizona ZIP codes. When the If statement is true, the next two statements execute. When the If statement is false, nothing further in the procedure executes, Access performs the default behavior, and control returns to the form for normal processing. A similar If statement detects and acts on invalid New Mexico ZIP codes.

The MsgBox statement displays an appropriate error message in a message box that remains on the screen until the user clicks the OK button. The message box appears on top of frmEmployee so the user can view the changed field values in the current record. After the user clicks the OK button in the message box, the Cancel = True statement tells Access to cancel the BeforeUpdate event. In this case, Access does not update the database with the changes to the current record. In addition, Access cancels subsequent events that would have occurred if the Before Update event had not been canceled. (You will learn more about these subsequent events in Level 3.) For example, because the form's Before Update event is triggered when you move to a different record, the following events are triggered when you move to a different record, in the order listed: Before Update event for the form, After Update event for the form, Exit event for the control with the focus, Lost Focus event for the control with the focus, and the Record Exit event for the form. When the BeforeUpdate event is cancelled, all these events are canceled and the focus remains with the record being edited.

The final if statement checks to see whether the event is to be cancelled. If so, the Zip.SetFocus statement executes. **SetFocus** is a method that moves the focus to the specified object or control. In this case, Access moves the focus to the Zip field in the current record in frmEmployee, making it the current control in the form. Don could have put a Zip.SetFocus statement after each of the two GoTo CommonProcessing statements, but he knows that it is more efficient and less error-prone to avoid duplicating this code, especially since he knows that he will be adding ZIP code validations for other states later. You will learn more about these subsequent events in Level 3.

Testing the Field Validation Procedure to Verify ZIP Codes

Don opens the property sheet for frmEmployee and sets the form's BeforeUpdate property to [Event Procedure]. He clicks the Build button to open the Code window in the Visual Basic window, and enters the VBA procedure statements he wrote. See Figure 7.19.

Figure 7.19: Procedure to verify employee ZIP codes

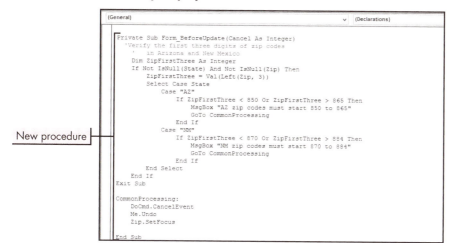

```
(General)                                                        ▼  (Declarations)

Private Sub Form_BeforeUpdate(Cancel As Integer)
    'Verify the first three digits of zip codes
    '    in Arizona and New Mexico
    Dim ZipFirstThree As Integer
    If Not IsNull(State) And Not IsNull(Zip) Then
        ZipFirstThree = Val(Left(Zip, 3))
        Select Case State
            Case "AZ"
                If ZipFirstThree < 850 Or ZipFirstThree > 865 Then
                    MsgBox "AZ zip codes must start 850 to 865"
                    GoTo CommonProcessing
                End If
            Case "NM"
                If ZipFirstThree < 870 Or ZipFirstThree > 884 Then
                    MsgBox "NM zip codes must start 870 to 884"
                    GoTo CommonProcessing
                End If
        End Select
    End If
Exit Sub

CommonProcessing:
    DoCmd.CancelEvent
    Me.Undo
    Zip.SetFocus

End Sub
```

New procedure

Don saves the procedure, closes the Visual Basic window, saves the form, and then switches to Form view to test the ZIP code validation procedure, changing AZ and NM ZIP codes to valid and invalid values, and changing other state ZIP codes in a similar way, making sure each record ends up with its original ZIP code. Note that changing a ZIP code and then moving to another field on the form does not trigger the procedure; only by navigating to another record does the form's BeforeUpdate event occur and cause the procedure to execute. Figure 7.20 shows the message box that opens when Don changes the ZIP code for record 3 from a valid value of 85415 to an invalid value of 97415 and clicks the Next Record button.

Figure 7.20: Testing the procedure to verify employee ZIP codes

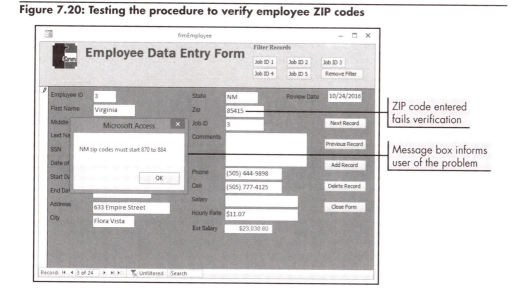

ZIP code entered fails verification

Message box informs user of the problem

After Don clicks the OK button, the BeforeUpdate event is canceled, the changes to the record are canceled, and the focus moves to the text box for the ZIP field. Don will add the ZIP code verifications for other states at a later time.

Best Practice

Using an Event Procedure for a Control or for a Form

Don designed the ZIP code verification procedure to trigger when the form's BeforeUpdate event occurs. Not only is there a BeforeUpdate event for each form, but there is also a BeforeUpdate event for each control on a form. Why didn't Don design the procedure to use the BeforeUpdate event for the ZIP field or for the State field? That is, why not trigger the procedure when a user enters or changes an employee's ZIP code? The reason for not using the BeforeUpdate event for the ZIP field is that users can enter and change data in any order on a form. It's possible that an employee moves from Arizona to Colorado, for example, which would require the user to change both the State field value and the ZIP field value. If the user changes the ZIP field value before the State field value and Don used the BeforeUpdate event for the ZIP field, the procedure would determine that the ZIP code is invalid and would undo all changes made to the record, even though the user *intended* to change the State field value next. When you need two or more fields as part of the validation process, you should use the form's BeforeUpdate event. However, the downside to using the form's BeforeUpdate event in this situation is that *all* changes made to the record are undone, not just the fields involved in the event procedure's validation process. The phone area code validation procedure that Don plans to design next shows an alternative validation approach that doesn't have this drawback.

Designing the Field Validation Procedure to Verify Phone Area Codes

Maria has a similar need to validate the area codes for employees. Don designs a procedure to validate the phone area codes for Arizona and New Mexico and will add the statements to validate the other phone and cell phone area codes at a later time.

To validate phone area codes, the design first tests the first three digits of the phone number, just as the procedure for ZIP codes tests the first three digits of the ZIP code. Note that phone numbers are displayed as (###) ###-####, but the Phone field has an input mask and only the ten-digit phone number is actually stored in the database, which means that the design needs to test the first three digits. The new procedure must display a message for invalid phone area codes, similar to the procedure that displays a message for invalid ZIP codes.

Because new regulations allow people to keep their phone numbers when they move, an employee living in one state might legitimately have a phone number with an area code that is assigned to a different state. So it is possible that the phone number is valid even though it has a different area code than those assigned to the state. The ZIP code rules stipulate that a state *must* have specific ZIP codes, but the phone number rules stipulate that a state is assigned specific area codes but could also have other area codes. The ZIP code procedure prevented users from entering invalid ZIP codes, but the phone number procedure must allow users to use any area code. For this procedure, the message can suggest a potential error, but must accept any phone area code entry, regardless of the person's state of residence.

Don's procedure to verify Arizona and New Mexico phone area codes is as follows (note that lines 8 and 9 may be included on one line as well as lines 10 and 11):

```
Private Sub Phone_BeforeUpdate(Cancel As Integer)
'Verify the phone area code for Arizona and New Mexico
    Dim PhoneFirstThree As Integer
    If Not IsNull(State) And Not IsNull(Phone) Then
        PhoneFirstThree = Val(Left(Phone, 3))
        Select Case State
            Case "AZ"
                If Not (PhoneFirstThree = 623 Or
                PhoneFirstThree = 928) Then
                    MsgBox "AZ phone area codes should be 623
                    or 928"
                End If
            Case "NM"
                If Not (PhoneFirstThree = 505) Then
                    MsgBox "NM phone area codes should be 505"
                End If
        End Select
    End If
End Sub
```

The design considers only records with State and Phone field values that are not null. If the procedure detects a potential error with the first three digits of the phone number, the procedure displays an informative message in a message box and lets the user decide whether the value is valid. Also, the BeforeUpdate event for the Phone field triggers the procedure, meaning that any change to the Phone field value causes the procedure to execute. If, for any reason, there is a possibility that a user could modify Phone field values and then modify State field values and in that update sequence cause a potential error, you should consider making the procedure a public procedure in a standard module and triggering the standard module for the Phone field's BeforeUpdate event and for the State field's BeforeUpdate event.

Don opens the Property Sheet for the Phone field in frmEmployee, sets the field's BeforeUpdate property to [Event Procedure], and then clicks the Build button to open the Code window in the Visual Basic window. Figure 7.21 shows the VBA procedure statements that Don enters.

7

Level 2

Figure 7.21: Procedure to verify employee phone area codes

```
Private Sub Phone_BeforeUpdate(Cancel As Integer)
'Verify the phone area code for Arizona and New Mexico
    Dim PhoneFirstThree As Integer
    If Not IsNull(State) And Not IsNull(Phone) Then
        PhoneFirstThree = Val(Left(Phone, 3))
        Select Case State
            Case "AZ"
                If Not (PhoneFirstThree = 623 Or PhoneFirstThree = 928) Then
                    MsgBox "AZ phone area codes should be 623 or 928"
                End If
            Case "NM"
                If Not (PhoneFirstThree = 505) Then
                    MsgBox "NM phone area codes should be 505"
                End If
        End Select
    End If
End Sub
```

Don saves the procedure, closes the Visual Basic window, saves the form, and then switches to Form view to test the phone area code validation procedure, changing AZ and NM area codes to valid and invalid values, and changing other state area codes in a similar way, making sure each record ends up with its original phone value. Note that changing a phone area code value and then switching to another field on the form triggers the procedure. Figure 7.22 shows the message box that opens when Don changes the area code for the cell phone in record 3 from a valid value of 505 to a potentially invalid value of 555.

Figure 7.22: Testing the procedure to verify employee phone area codes

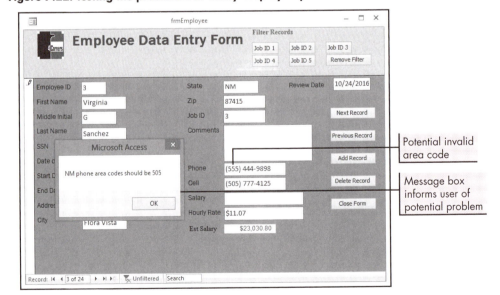

After Don clicks the OK button, the focus returns to the field in the record to which Don navigated after making the area code change. He changes the area code back to 505 and finishes his testing.

Steps To Success: Level 2

Glenn Hollander wants you to continue to automate the Hudson Bay Pharmacy database by adding functionality to four existing forms. He wants to enhance frmEmployee to make it easier to identify an employee's current age and the length of time an employee has been with the pharmacy. He also wants to enhance frmPrimaryActivity and frmPrimaryActivity2 to make it easier to identify the number of months since a customer's last refill and to alert the pharmacist when a customer has no refills remaining. Finally, Glenn wants to enhance frmClinic to ensure that users enter valid phone area codes when entering the record for a new clinic.

Complete the following:

1. Start Access and open the **Hudson.accdb** database from the STS folder.

2. Add a text box named YearsOfService to frmEmployee and place it to the right of the StartDate text box.

3. Add the VBA statement to the frmEmployee's BeforeUpdate event for YearsOfService using decision-making logic in the VBA procedure to include only active employees. Design additional logic on the Years of Service calculation based on the years of service calculation to make the text box control visible and display one of two messages; otherwise the control should not be visible.

4. Add a text box named Age to frmEmployee to the right of the DOB field. The associated label should be Age.

5. Design decision-making logic to determine an active employee's age based on the date of birth and today's date.

6. For frmPrimaryActivity and frmPrimaryActivity2, add a calculated field that displays the number of months between the prescription date and the expiration date, using blue text for the calculated field. Display the calculated field only when both source dates are not null.

7. For frmPrimaryActivity, add a calculated field without its associated label that displays the message **Call the customer** if the number of refills used is zero, and that displays the message **Call the doctor** if the number of refills used equals the number of refills authorized, displaying both messages with red font.

8. Design a Field Validation Procedure to verify Alberta phone area codes of 780 in frmClinic.

9. Save and close the Hudson.accdb database.

LEVEL 3

Testing and Exploring VBA

Troubleshooting VBA Procedures

As an experienced systems analyst and information systems specialist, Don knows that learning to troubleshoot and handle the errors that can occur when coding a program in VBA or any other programming language is a critical part of learning the language. As you have already seen, several types of errors can occur when working with VBA code. These errors are grouped into the general categories of syntax, compilation, logic, and run-time errors.

A **syntax error** occurs when a VBA statement violates the language rules for the statement, such as a misspelling, an incorrect sequence of keywords, or a missing parenthesis. Syntax errors are detected immediately when you complete the statement and move to another statement. An error message opens and explains the error, and the statement is highlighted until you correct the error. For example, if you try to go to the next line in the Code window and there is an error in the current statement, you receive the error shown in Figure 7.23.

Figure 7.23: Compile error message

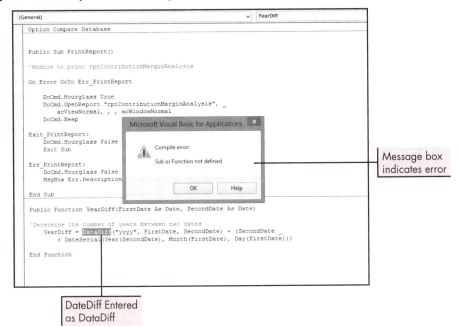

At this point, you can return to the previous line and review the statement. Often, as is the case in Figure 7.23, it is up to the programmer to determine the cause of the error because the error shown in the message box does not specifically tell you that you misspelled the function name; it only tells you that something is not correct. The types of syntax errors that you receive as you are typing statements are usually only typing errors, and with practice and experience, you will be able to easily solve these types of errors.

A **compilation error** occurs when you translate procedures into a form that the computer cannot understand. The process of translating modules from VBA to a form the computer understands is called **compilation**; you say that you **compile** the module when you translate it. When you run a procedure for the first time, Access compiles it for you automatically and opens a dialog box only when it finds syntax errors in the procedure. If it finds an error, Access does not translate the procedure statements. If no errors are detected, Access translates the procedure and does not display a confirmation. Sometimes compilation and syntax errors are not identified until you actually run the procedure. For example, Figure 7.24 shows the bas4CornersGeneralProcedures module in the Code window. When Don typed the YearDiff function, he accidentally typed "DateDiff" as "DataDiff." The compiler did not highlight this misspelling as a syntax error. However, when he attempted to navigate to the second record in frmEmployee, the Code window opened and a message box displayed the message "Compile error: Syntax error." After Don clicked the OK button, the compiler highlighted the YearDiff function as the potential source of the problem.

Figure 7.24: Error corrected

```
Public Function YearDiff(FirstDate As Date, SecondDate As Date)

'Determine the number of years between two dates
    YearDiff = DateDiff("yyyy", FirstDate, SecondDate) + (SecondDate
        < DateSerial(Year(SecondDate), Month(FirstDate), Day(FirstDate)))

End Function
```

DataDiff changed to DateDiff

Don quickly found the problem in the Code window since it is highlighted. He then selected and retyped the function name as DateDiff. In other cases, he might need to spend more time analyzing the problem to find its solution. In this example, frmEmployee would remain locked until Don stops the debugger by clicking the Reset button on the toolbar. A good way to avoid encountering compilation errors in the database object at run time is to compile the module before you save it. In response, Access compiles the procedure and all other procedures in all modules in the database. It is best to compile and save your modules after you make changes to them, to ensure that they do not contain compilation errors.

Compile a Module

1. Click Debug on the menu bar in the Visual Basic window.
2. Click the Compile command.
3. Correct any errors identified by the compiler.
4. Click the Reset button to stop the debugger.
5. Save the module.

If you do not compile each module in the database, each procedure is compiled the first time it is executed by you (or a user), and debugging of the procedure proceeds at this point. To prevent compilation errors at run time, you should use the Compile command on the Debug menu to compile them as your last step before saving the module. If the compiler reports an error, you can correct it; if the compiler does not report any problems, you can save the module knowing that it compiles correctly.

Although you might have entered all procedure statements with the correct syntax and compiled the module with no errors, the procedure might still contain logic errors. You learned in Level 1 that a *logic error* occurs when the procedure completes and produces incorrect results. For example, Figure 7.25 shows frmEmployee with the record for Marco Farello displayed. On May 1, 2016, Marco should be 41 years old. However, the form displays his age as -39.

Figure 7.25: Logic error in procedure

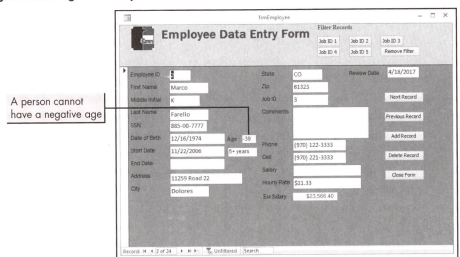

Figure 7.26 shows the Code window for the form. The module does not have any syntax errors and is compiled correctly. However, the programmer transposed the arguments in the YearDiff function, resulting in a logic error and an incorrect result in the form.

Figure 7.26: Identifying a logic error in the Code window

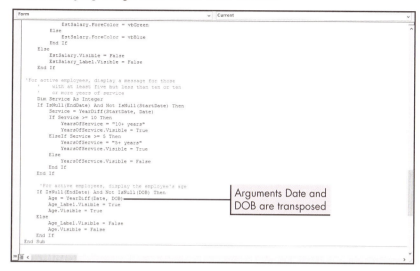

```
        EstSalary.ForeColor = vbGreen
    Else
        EstSalary.ForeColor = vbBlue
    End If
Else
    EstSalary.Visible = False
    EstSalary_Label.Visible = False
End If

'For active employees, display a message for those
'    with at least five but less than ten or ten
'    or more years of service
Dim Service As Integer
If IsNull(EndDate) And Not IsNull(StartDate) Then
    Service = YearDiff(StartDate, Date)
    If Service >= 10 Then
        YearsOfService = "10+ years"
        YearsOfService.Visible = True
    ElseIf Service >= 5 Then
        YearsOfService = "5+ years"
        YearsOfService.Visible = True
    Else
        YearsOfService.Visible = False
    End If
End If

    'For active employees, display the employee's age
If IsNull(EndDate) And Not IsNull(DOB) Then
    Age = YearDiff(Date, DOB)
    Age_Label.Visible = True
    Age.Visible = True
Else
    Age_Label.Visible = False
    Age.Visible = False
End If
End Sub
```

Arguments Date and DOB are transposed

Changing the YearDiff function to YearDiff(DOB, Date) corrects the logic error, and Marco's age is correctly displayed as 41 in the form. As you learned in Level 1, it is critical to test as many situations as possible to discover and correct logic errors in your procedures. The result might display correctly in 19 out of 20, but the last record might alert you to a logic error that you need to correct.

An **execution error**, or **run-time error**, occurs when a procedure executes and stops because it tries to perform an operation that is impossible to perform. For example, the procedure might try to open an object that does not exist or that has been deleted, or divide a value by zero in a calculation.

Using the Debugger to Correct Errors

The source of any error in a procedure can be difficult to debug. To help you to debug a procedure, you can use the commands on the Debug menu in Visual Basic. Setting a **breakpoint** in a procedure lets you run the subroutine or function up until the line on which you set the breakpoint. When a breakpoint is set, the procedure halts execution at that point and displays the module screen. Using one or more breakpoints in a procedure is a good way to isolate the place at which the procedure stops producing the anticipated result.

How To

Set a Breakpoint

1. Right-click in the gray margin area to the left of the statement on which you want to set the breakpoint, point to Toggle and then click Breakpoint.

The statement is highlighted in maroon and a maroon circle appears in the margin to the left of the statement, as shown in Figure 7.27.

Figure 7.27: Setting a breakpoint

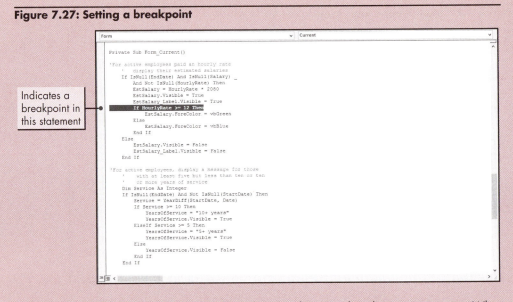

Indicates a breakpoint in this statement

2. Save the module and then open the object that uses the procedure that you are testing. When Access encounters a breakpoint, the Code window opens and a yellow arrow appears in the margin to the left of the statement that contains the breakpoint.

When a procedure is executing and the statement that contains the breakpoint is executed, the procedure halts and the VBA code is displayed. You can use the mouse pointer to get more information about the procedure. For example, pointing to a variable name displays a ScreenTip with the value contained in the variable at the point that the procedure halted. Often, you can use the ScreenTip to isolate a problem in a function or its arguments to identify the cause of an error. You can also execute the procedure one statement at a time to try and identify the cause of an error by clicking Debug on the menu bar, and then clicking Step Into. When you use the Step Into command, the procedure executes the next statement and stops. Clicking Debug on the menu bar and then clicking Step Out executes the current subroutine or function and then halts. By setting breakpoints and stepping in and out of procedures, you can often identify the exact cause of an error. When you identify the error, clicking the Reset button stops the debugger so you can fix the problem, recompile the module, and then save the module. When you no longer need the breakpoints, click Debug on the menu bar, and then click Clear All Breakpoints.

Identifying Errors Using the Watch Window

Another useful tool that you can use to debug a procedure is the Watch Window. The **Watch Window** shows the current value of a specified variable. After clicking a specified variable, you click Debug on the menu bar, and then click Add Watch. The Add Watch dialog box opens, in which you enter the variable name that you want to watch. Figure 7.28 shows the Add Watch dialog box, which is set to watch the Service variable in the procedure.

Figure 7.28: Add Watch dialog box

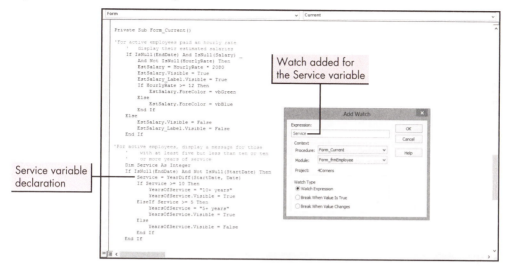

After setting the variable to watch and clicking the OK button in the Add Watch dialog box, the Watch Window opens at the bottom of the Visual Basic window. Figure 7.29 shows the Watch Window with the Service variable as the watch expression and after setting a breakpoint in the Current procedure for the statement after the assignment statement for the Service variable. "<Out of context>" in the Value column in the Watch Window appears for the watch expression when Access is not executing the procedure that contains the watch expression. The Service variable is a variable that is local to the Current procedure and has a value only when the On Current event procedure executes.

Figure 7.29: Watch Window

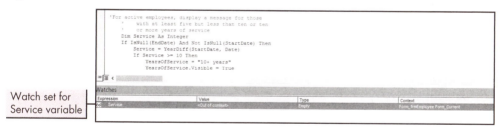

The current value of the specified variable appears in the Watch Window as you step through a procedure. Figure 7.30 shows the fifth record of frmEmployee in Form view with the Service variable assigned the value of 6. This is correct for a start date of 6/14/2010 and using 7/1/2016 as today's date. Repeatedly using the Step Into command, or pressing the equivalent F8 key, executes the statements in the procedure and continues to display the Service variable in the Watch Window. When the procedure ends, the Value column for the Service variable again displays the "<Out of context>" message in the Value column.

Figure 7.30: Watch Window after a breakpoint

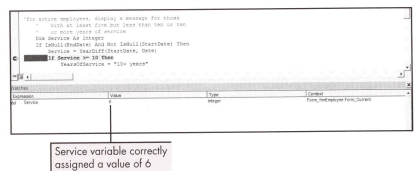

Service variable correctly assigned a value of 6

Instead of setting a breakpoint in the procedure, when you add a watch expression you can specify in the Add Watch dialog box that you want to see the value of the watch expression by setting a breakpoint when the value of the watch expression changes or when the value is true.

Troubleshooting VBA Errors

When VBA procedure errors of any type occur, you must find where the error occurred, what caused the error, and then fix the error. Finding the location of the error is easy for syntax, compilation, and run-time errors because Access highlights the statement that caused the error. Fixing syntax and compilation errors is also easy because the highlighted statement is the location and cause of the error, and you must correct the statement itself. Fixing run-time errors is more difficult because the highlighted statement is not always the cause of the error; the execution of previous statements in the procedure might have set up an error situation that became evident only when the highlighted statement executed. In many ways, troubleshooting logic errors is the most difficult because you have to find the location of the error, find what caused the error, and determine how to fix the error. Having a set of tools to use for troubleshooting, such as breakpoints and watch expressions, is critical for troubleshooting success, as is having a solid understanding of VBA and an inquisitive, open mind.

Building Procedures Slowly to Isolate Problems

Another way to prevent problems in your procedures is to build them slowly using small groups of statements so you can prove them to be correct as you go. It is easier to correct problems in small groups of statements than it is to try to debug a long procedure. If you use this approach, you can write a small group of statements and test them, and then continue adding statements to the procedure and testing them until you have written the entire procedure. Using the Immediate window, which you learned about in Level 1, is also a good way to check your statements as you write them. If you encounter an incorrect result in the Immediate window, you can stop and debug the problem before continuing.

Best Practice

Avoiding Problems with Reusing Code from Other Sources

Creating your first few VBA procedures from scratch is a daunting task. To get started, you should take advantage of the available resources that discuss various ways of designing and programming commonly encountered situations. These resources include, but are not limited to, the Access Help feature, VBA books, blogs, podcasts, and Web sites that provide sample code. These resources contain sample procedures and code segments, often with commentary about what the procedures and statements accomplish and why. However, when you create a procedure, you are responsible for knowing what it does, how it does it, when to use it, how to enhance it in the future, and how to fix it when problems occur. If you simply copy statements from another source without thoroughly understanding them, you won't be able to enhance or fix the procedure in the future. In addition, you might overlook better ways to accomplish the same thing—better because the procedure would run faster or would be easier to enhance. In some cases, the samples you find might be flawed, so that they won't work properly for you. The time you spend researching and completely understanding sample code will pay dividends in your learning experience to create VBA procedures.

Using Help to Learn More About Programming and VBA

Access Help contains useful information about programming in Access and VBA. For example, you can learn more about events in Access Help by pressing F1 to display the Access Help dialog box or clicking the Help button (question mark symbol) on the Ribbon. Help content is installed on your computer when you install Access.

To view the To get help, click in the Search box and type the topic you would like to search and then press Enter. For example, you can type "events" in the Search box and press Enter. Figure 7.31 shows Help topics relating to events.

Figure 7.31: Help topics relating to events

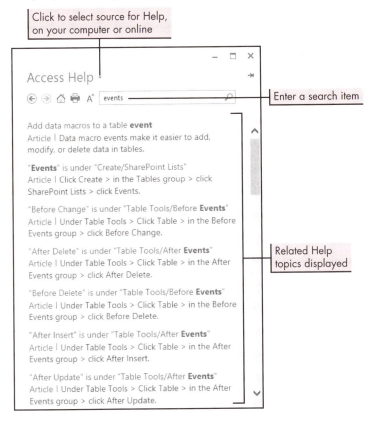

Reading the individual topics can provide excellent background information about new features, tables, and sharing a database on the Web. Other links in the Search results list include event procedures before and after other functions or events.

You can find Help topics about programming language. Type "Visual Basic" in the Search box and then press Enter. See Figure 7.32.

Figure 7.32: Access Help on Visual Basic

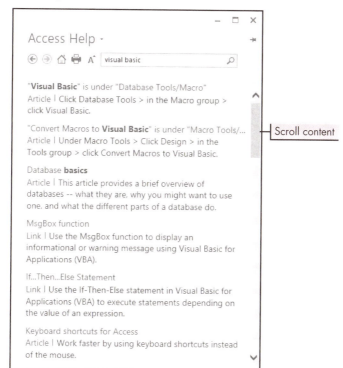

Scroll content

You can then click on links to developing macros or If Then Else statements. Since you were learning about conditions using the If, Else, and ElseIf statements, you might decide to view the ElseIf clause, as shown in Figure 7.33.

Figure 7.33: Access Help for ElseIf clause

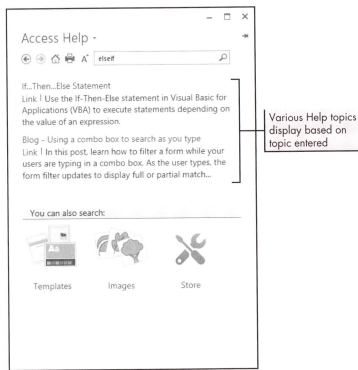

Various Help topics display based on topic entered

If you need more information or help, take advantage of the multitude of books, periodicals, and Web sites that focus on the use of VBA in Microsoft Access.

Steps To Success: Level 3

Complete the following:

1. Start Access and open the **Hudson.accdb** database from the STS folder.

2. Sometimes the information you need about a VBA topic is found in Access Help and other times it's found in Visual Basic Help. Which of the two Help systems contains a topic named "Immediate Window?" Some of the links in this topic cover material, such as breakpoints and watch expressions, discussed in this chapter. Search Access Help to find any additional information you feel you want additional information about.

3. Canadian postal codes consist of six characters with a required format of letter, digit, letter, digit, letter, and digit. Use a make-table query to create a copy of tblEmployee as tblEmployeeCopy and then use a Form wizard to create a form, named frmEmployeeCopy, for the new table. (*Note*: Do not create a copy of the table; you must use a make-table query. Do not save the make-table query in the database.) Format the form using the colors and theme as you did in the other forms.

4. Create and test a VBA event procedure that verifies Canadian postal codes in frmEmployeeCopy. Canadian postal codes have six characters. The letters can be between A and Z and the numbers need to be between 0 and 9. The six postal code characters are in the order letter, number, letter, number, letter, and number.

5. Test the VBA event by entering an incorrect postal code and try moving to the next record. An error message should appear.

6. Close the **Hudson.accdb** database and Access.

Chapter Summary

In this chapter, you learned how to enhance a form using VBA procedures in ways that are not possible using only the tools provided with Access. In Level 1, you learned how to create a subroutine in a standard module, how to create an event procedure, how to code control structures in VBA that add decision making to a procedure, how to assign values to variables, and how to create and test a function. You also learned how to correct problems in procedures.

In Level 2, you learned how to create a custom function to solve a problem in a specific database object. You also learned how to code procedures that can verify data entry by validating the user's entry against a predefined list of acceptable values.

In Level 3, you explored different methods for troubleshooting logic, compilation, run-time, and syntax errors in procedures. You learned how to use breakpoints to isolate logic and syntax problems and explored different ways to isolate problems. You also explored the Access Help and Visual Basic Help to learn more about general programming basics, coding in VBA, and handling errors.

Conceptual Review

1. Why is VBA an event-driven and object-oriented language?

2. What is an event property?

3. What is an event procedure?

4. Why would you choose to use a function instead of a subroutine?

5. When would you choose to use a standard module?

6. What is the difference between a private procedure and a public procedure?

7. When would you choose to use a class module?

8. Which statements begin and end a subroutine?

9. Describe the general syntax of the If statement.

10. What is a variable? How do you declare a variable in a procedure?

7

Chapter Exercises

11. What is the Dim statement? When do you use it?

12. When does the Before Update event occur?

13. What is a control structure and when do you use it?

14. Describe the following types of errors and give an example of each type: syntax, compilation, logic, and run-time.

15. What does it mean to compile a module?

Case Problems

Case 1 – Enhancing Employee Data for NHD Development Group Inc.

Human Resources

Linda Sutherland, manager of the Memories Antique Mall in Cleveland, Tennessee, has been using the database to manage data about dealers, employees, classes, instructors, customers, and booths. She has transferred most of her manual systems to the database and has been very pleased with the database. Linda asks if you can make it easier to print the two reports that she frequently prints, rptEmployeeSalaryDetail and rptEmployeeSalarySummary, because she sends these reports to the NHD corporate offices on a quarterly basis.

Another change that Linda asks you to make is to hide the Hourly Rate controls for salaried employees and to hide the Salary controls for hourly employees in frmEmployeeData. In the same form, Linda mentions that she needs a way to monitor personnel reviews for employees with regard to having advance notice to schedule them and a reminder when they are past due. You tell Linda that she might benefit from having a reminder on frmEmployeeData to indicate how many months remain until the employee's next review date, and a reminder for employees who have not had their reviews when the scheduled date has passed. Linda wants the overdue reminder to appear in red, bold font and the number of months until the next review to appear in blue, bold font. She also wants you to hide the review date when the review is overdue so it does not display a negative number, and to hide the review date for inactive employees.

Complete the following:

1. Start Access and open the **Antiques.accdb** database from the STS folder.

2. Create a new standard module named **basAntiquesGeneralProcedures** and add two procedures to it. The first procedure should print rptEmployeeSalaryDetail, and the second procedure should print rptEmployeeSalarySummary.

3. Open frmEmployeeData. Hide the Salary controls for hourly employees and the Hourly Rate controls for salaried employees. (*Hint*: Salary will need to be greater than zero.)

4. Create a text box control below the Review controls. Name the text box **ReviewMonths** and the label **ReviewMonths_Label**. Change the label caption to **Months Until Next Review**. In the ReviewMonths text box, add a calculated field that accurately displays the number of months between the current date and the employee's next review date. Format the ReviewMonths value in a blue, bold format.

5. If the value in ReviewMonths in frmEmployeeData is less than zero, hide the ReviewMonths and ReviewMonths_Label controls and display the message **Review is overdue!** in a bold, red format. (*Hint*: Set your computer's system clock to the year 2016 or later to test the procedure.)

6. Hide the Review and ReviewMonths_Label controls in frmEmployeeData when the value in the Review field is null.

7. Save and test your procedures and make sure that your changes to frmEmployeeData work correctly.

8. Save and close the Antiques.accdb database.

Case 2 – Enhancing Data Entry and Verifying Data for MovinOn Inc.

David Bowers, general manager of MovinOn, met with his warehouse managers to discuss the progress you have made in developing the MovinOn database. Because MovinOn Inc. recently adopted a pension plan for all employees, the managers want to inform employees when they are fully vested in the plan, which happens after five years of service. David asks if you can add a message to the form that indicates when an employee is fully vested based on the length of service. He also wants you to add a control that calculates an employee's years of service. For active employees, he wants you to hide the End Date field; for inactive employees, he wants you to hide the Review field. Finally, to help with data entry, the warehouse managers want to verify phone and cell phone area codes entered into frmEmployeeData.

Complete the following:

1. Start Access and open the **MovinOn.accdb** database located in the STS folder.

2. Add a new control to frmEmployeeData that uses a calculation to accurately determine the years of service for each active and inactive employee. Set the control's properties so users cannot change it or tab to it, and so its border is transparent.

3. Add a label control to frmEmployeeData in the appropriate position on the form, using the name **Vested_Label** and the caption **Fully Vested**. The message should appear on the form when an active or inactive employee has five or more years of service. Display the message in red font. (*Hint*: Set your computer's system clock to the year 2016 or later to test the procedure.)

4. For active employees, hide the End Date controls in frmEmployeeData. For inactive employees, display the End Date controls in a bold, red font.

5. For hourly employees, hide the Salary controls; for salaried employees, hide the Hourly Rate controls.

Human
Resources

6. Verify telephone area codes for employee phone numbers in frmEmployeeData. For employees living in Oregon, the valid area codes are 541, 503, and 971; for employees living in Washington, the valid area codes are 425, 360, 206, 509, and 253; for employees living in Wyoming, the valid area code is 307. Warehouse managers should be able to enter phone area codes for other states not included in the lists.

7. Verify cell phone area codes for employee cell phone numbers in frmEmployeeData. The valid cell phone area codes are the same as the ones for regular phone numbers. Warehouse managers should be able to enter phone area codes not included in the lists.

8. Save and test your procedures and make sure that your changes to frmEmployeeData work correctly.

9. Save and close the MovinOn.accdb database.

Case 3 – Enhancing the Database for Hershey College

Operations Management

Marianna Fuentes, assistant director of the Intramural Department at Hershey College, is concerned about the purchases that coaches have made. She asks that you "flag" large unapproved purchases in frmPurchaseData with a message box indicating that the purchase requires her approval, and to put a message on the form when the amount exceeds $100. Marianna is also finding transposed phone area codes in the database. Because the college is located in an area with only one phone area code, she asks if there is a way to ask the user to confirm the entry of telephone and cell phone numbers when they do not begin with the 717 area code.

Complete the following:

1. Start Access and open the **Hershey.accdb** database located in the STS folder.

2. Open frmPurchaseData and replace the form's On Current macro with a procedure that displays the message **Please see Marianna Fuentes for approval** in a message box when a purchase amount exceeds $100. In addition, display the message **Needs Approval** to the right of the Amount text box in red font when the amount exceeds $100.

3. Use the Help feature in the Content from this computer area to learn how to use the On Click event.

4. After you have read the information related to the On Click event, consider how you might use it in the database. Write a proposal of how you might use the On Click event in this form and why you would choose to use it.

5. Marianna has learned that there are sometimes discrepancies in the way people enter data. For example, in frmFieldData, users might enter the season as "Fall" or "FALL." Marianna wants to change all entries entered into the SeasonAvailable field to uppercase letters. Use Help to learn how to use the UCase function, and then change the values in the SeasonAvailable field to uppercase.

6. Use Help to learn about the CurrentUser method, and then use this method to display the name of the current user when frmStudentData is opened, which will be the On Load event. Have a message box display with the text "Database currently being viewed by:" (*Hint:* You will add & CurrentUser( ) to the end of the previous statement. Note: If you are working in a secured database, this would be the name of the user who has logged in. If you are using an unsecured database, this function would return Admin, which is the default account name of the user.

7. Save and close the Hershey.accdb database.

SAM: Skills Assessment Manager

For current SAM information, including versions and content details, visit SAM Central (http://samcentral.course.com). If you have a SAM user profile, you may have access to hands-on instruction, practice, and assessment of the skills covered in this chapter. Since various versions of SAM are supported throughout the life of this text, check with your instructor for the correct instructions and URL/Web site for accessing assignments.

Glossary

Action Catalog A pane in the Macro Builder window that provides the types of actions that you want the macro to perform.

action query A special type of query that performs actions on a table, such as changing the contents of a field, adding records from one table to another table, deleting records from a table, or making a new table based on criteria.

actions Instructions designed to manipulate database objects, such as opening a form or printing a report.

aggregate functions The arithmetic and statistical operations such as Avg, Sum, Min, Max, StDev, and Var. You can apply aggregate functions to groups of data to calculate results for each group.

analysis The process of collecting, organizing, and transforming data into information that can be used to support decision making.

AND criteria The conditions that must all be true for Access to select a record.

append query A type of query that selects records from one or more tables and then adds those records to the end of another table.

argument The additional information that Access needs to perform the task. Access provides over 50 different actions, most of which perform multistep tasks, such as selecting a specified report and then opening it in Print Preview.

artificial key A primary key that is created when no natural key exists.

Attachment An Access data type that can store one or more files for each record in the database.

AutoExec A special macro that runs automatically when a database is opened.

AutoKeys A macro group that assigns an action or set of actions to a key or key combination.

AutoNumber The Access data type that generates a unique number in a field to produce unique values for each record in a table.

back up The process of creating a copy of a database that can be restored in the event of a loss.

Backstage view The view in which the File tab commands and tabs are displayed. Typically, two columns of options appear to the right of the screen with the command or tab settings.

base table (underlying table) The table on which a query, form, or report is based.

Beep A macro action that plays a beep sound.

Before Update event The event that occurs before changed data in a control or record is updated in the database.

bound form A form that is bound to an underlying table or query. Most forms are bound forms.

breakpoint A code inserted into a macro or VBA procedure signaling where to stop the macro.

Calculated (data type) An Access data type that uses data from fields in the same table to perform calculations, a few of which include addition, subtraction, and multiplication.

calculated field A field in a query, form, or report containing an expression that is calculated from the data.

call The term used in a programming language to describe the process of executing a statement when an event occurs.

candidate key A field or collection of fields that could function as a table's primary key, but that was not chosen to do so.

Caption property A field property that determines how the field name is displayed in database objects. Also, a feature that determines the text that appears on the title bar of a report.

Cascade Delete Related Records An option that allows Access to delete related records in related tables when the primary record in the primary table is deleted.

Cascade Update Related Fields An option that allows Access to update the appropriate foreign key values in related tables when a primary key value in the primary table is updated.

Case control structure A conditional structure that evaluates an expression and then performs one of several alternative sets of statements based on the resulting value (or condition) of the evaluated expression.

class module A module associated with a particular form or report in a database.

Code window The Visual Basic Editor window in which you create, modify, and display specific VBA procedures.

coding The process of writing instructions in a programming language.

command button An unbound control that users click to perform common tasks, such as moving to a different record or closing a form.

comment The text added to code for the purpose of describing what the procedure or a statement does to make it easier for others to identify the purpose of statements in the code.

common field A field that appears in two or more tables and contains identical data that is used to relate the tables. The common field is called a primary key in the primary table and a foreign key in the related table.

compact To reorganize the data and objects in a database by reassigning and deleting unused space. Compacting a database usually reduces its file size.

comparison operators The operators that allow you to make comparisons, such as > (greater than), < (less than), = (equal to), >= (great than or equal to), <= (less than or equal to) <> (not equal to), and Between.

compilation The process of translating modules from VBA to a form the computer understands. You say that you compile the module when you translate it.

compilation error An error that occurs when you translate VBA procedures into a form the computer cannot understand.

composite primary key (composite key) A primary key composed of two or more fields.

concatenation The process of combining the contents of two or more fields, such as a first and last name, into one string.

conditional formatting The process of applying formatting features such as color, bold, and font size based on whether the values in a report or form meet criteria that you specify.

control An object such as a text box, button, or label that lets users interact with a database object.

control structure A set of VBA statements that works together as a unit. The If statement is an example of a control structure.

criterion The condition you are searching for in the data.

crosstab query A type of totals query that performs aggregate function calculations on the values of one database field and allows you to determine how your summary data appears in the results.

Currency The Access data type that formats numeric values with a dollar sign and two decimal places. Note that the number of decimal places can be changed.

custom report A report that requires data from more than one table, includes calculated fields, uses summary statistics, or requires parameter input when the report is opened or printed.

D

data Raw information, including words, images, numbers, or sounds.

data analyst A person in an organization who transforms data into information by sorting, filtering, or calculating it to perform an analysis.

data duplication The process of creating repeated records in a database, which leads to wasted space and inconsistent and inaccurate data.

data redundancy An undesirable effect of storing repeated data in fields in a table that wastes space and results in inconsistent and inaccurate data. Data redundancy is often avoided by creating additional tables.

data type A field property that determines how to store the data in the field.

database A collection of one or more tables that contain records of information.

database administration (DBA) The group that is responsible for designing, maintaining, and securing a database.

database administrator The person who designs, maintains, and secures a database.

Database Documenter (Documenter) An Access tool that produces a report of every object or selected objects in a database.

database management system (DBMS) A system that creates and defines a database; a software program that creates and accesses the data in a database.

Database window The Access window in which a database opens.

Datasheet view An Access view that displays the records for a table or query in rows and fields in columns. A view of data that displays fields in columns and records in rows.

Date function A VBA function that returns the current computer system date.

Date/Time The Access data type that stores dates or date and time combinations.

DateDiff function A VBA function that calculates the number of time intervals between two dates.

Declarations section The first part of a VBA module that contains statements that apply to all procedures in the module.

Default Value property A field property that enters a default value into a field; can be used for all field types except AutoNumber.

delete query A query that removes records from a table based on criteria you specify.

deletion anomaly The problem that occurs when a user deletes data from a database and unintentionally deletes the only occurrence of that data in the database.

Description property A property of a field used to document its contents.

Design view The window that lets you define the fields and properties for a table, query, form, or report.

detail The main section in a form or report that displays data from the underlying data source.

detailed report A report that lists each row of data from a table or query.

determinant A field or collection of fields whose value determines the value in another field.

Dim statement In a VBA procedure, the statement used to declare a variable and its associated data type.

domain A set of records; a recordset.

domain aggregate function A function that calculates statistics for a domain from a table or a query.

E

End Sub statement The last line of a subroutine.

entity A person, place, thing, or idea.

entity integrity A guarantee that there are no duplicate records in a table, that each record is unique, and that no primary key field contains null values.

event A state, condition, or occurrence that Access recognizes, such as clicking a command button or opening an object.

event property The property associated with an event that specifies how an object responds when the event occurs.

execution error (run-time error) An error that occurs when a macro or VBA code is executed.

expression An arithmetic formula that performs a calculation in a query, form, or report.

Expression Builder A tool to assist in developing complicated expressions for calculated fields that shows the fields, functions, and other objects available in Access.

F

field (column) A single characteristic of an entity in a database. For example, fields that describe a customer might include first name, last name, address, city, and state.

Field Properties pane The lower pane of Table Design view that displays the field properties for the selected field.

Field Size property A property of a field that limits the number of characters to store in a Text field or the type of numeric data to store in a Number field.

filter One or more conditions that restrict viewing of data in a single table to create a temporary subset of records.

Filter by Form An Access feature that lets you specify two or more criteria when filtering records.

Filter by Selection An Access feature that lets you select a field in a datasheet and then display only data that matches the contents of that field.

Find duplicates query A query that is used to locate duplicate records in a table or query.

Find unmatched query A query that is used to locate records with no related records in a second table or query.

first normal form (1NF) A database table that does not contain any repeating groups.

foreign key The common field in the related table between two tables that share a relationship.

form A database object based on a table or query and used to view, add, delete, update, and print records in the database.

form footer The lower part of a form. It displays information that always appears on a form but at the bottom of the screen in Form view and the bottom of the last page when the form is printed.

form header The upper part of a form. It usually contains static text, graphic images, and other controls on the first page of a form.

function (function procedure) In a programming language, a function performs operations, returns a value, accepts input values, and can be used in expressions.

functional dependency A column in a table is considered functionally dependent on another column if each value in the second column is associated with exactly one value in the first column.

G

grid The gray background on a form or report in Design view that displays dots and gridlines to help with aligning controls.

group footer A section of a report that is printed at the end of each group of records. Often used to print summary information such as subtotals for a group.

group header A section of a report that is printed at the beginning of each group of records. Often used to print the group name.

grouped report A report that organizes one or more records into categories, usually to subtotal the data for each category. The groups are based on the values in one or more fields.

H

header section In a form or report, the section located at the top part of the form or report that typically displays the title.

history table A table of data containing archived records.

Hourglass A macro action that changes the pointer to an echo symbol while the macro runs.

Hyperlink (data type) The Access data type that displays text that contains a hyperlink (link) to an Internet or file location.

I

If statement In a programming language, the statement that tests one condition that results in one of two answers and that follows a set of instructions depending on the outcome of the condition.

Immediate window The part of the Code window in Visual Basic Editor that is used to test VBA procedures without changing any data in the database.

index A list maintained by the database (but hidden from users) that associates the field values in the indexed field with the records that contain the field values.

information Data that is organized in some meaningful way.

inner join In a query, a join that displays records from both tables that have similar corresponding records in the related table.

input mask A property of a field that applies a predefined format to field values.

Input Mask Wizard An Access wizard that guides you through the steps of creating an input mask and lets you enter sample values to ensure the correct results.

insertion anomaly The problem that occurs when a user cannot add data to a database unless other data has already been entered.

IntelliSense A built-in Access feature that you can use to build expressions to perform calculations or tasks with the data. As you start typing an expression or field name, a list of expressions or field names appears from which you can make a selection.

Is Null function A VBA function that returns the value True when the field or control is null and the value False when it is not.

J

join A relationship between tables and the properties of that relationship. The relationship is shown by a join line in the Relationships window in Access. Tables that are joined have a common field with the same or compatible data type and the same field values.

junction table An intermediary table created to produce a many-to-many relationship between two tables that do not share a one-to-one or one-to-many relationship.

K

KeyTips A pop-up display of an access key for a particular command or tab.

L

label In Design view, the left side of the field that describes the information found in the field.

Left function The VBA function that returns a string containing a specified number of characters from the left side of a specified string.

literal character A character that enhances the readability of data but is not necessarily stored as part of the data, such as a dash in a phone number.

logic error In a programming language, the error that results when a procedure produces an incorrect result.

logical operators The operators that allow you to make logical comparisons, such as AND, OR, and NOT.

Long Text The Access data type that stores long passages of alphanumeric data.

Lookup An Access data type that creates fields that let you look up data in another table or in a list of values created for the field.

lookup field A field that provides a list of valid values for another field, either using the contents of another field or values in a list.

Lookup Wizard The Access wizard that allows you to set field properties to look up data in another table or in a list of values created for the field.

M

macro An action or series of actions that you want Access to perform.

Macro Builder A window that you use to build a macro.

macro condition A logical expression that results in an answer, such as true or false.

macro group Two or more macros stored in the same macro file.

mailing labels report A type of multicolumn report used to print names and addresses in a format suited for sending mail through the postal service. Labels can also be used for other purposes such as name badges.

make-table query A query that lets you make a new table from data in other tables.

many-to-many relationship (∞:∞) A relationship between tables in which each record in the first table matches many records in the second table, and each record in the second table matches many records in the first table.

method An action that operates on specific objects or controls.

MessageBox action A macro action that opens a message box and displays a warning or other information.

module (VBA) A group of related procedures saved in a database object. A module begins with a Declarations section and includes one or more procedures.

MsgBox command A command you can use in a macro condition to specify what action the macro should take depending on the state of the message box.

multiple-column report A report that displays information in several columns, such as a telephone listing or mailing labels.

N

natural key A primary key that details an obvious and unique trait of a record, such as an ISBN code for a book.

navigation form A type of form that displays when you open a database and provides a controlled method for users to open the objects in a database.

Navigation pane A pane that provides a list of all Access objects in the database. You can collapse the Navigation pane so that you have more room on your screen and then restore it to its original size when you need to access objects.

nonkey field A field in a table that is not part of a table's primary key.

normalization A process that reduces the chance of deletion, update, and insertion anomalies in a database.

null value A field value that is unknown, unavailable, or missing.

Number The Access data type that stores numbers that are used in calculations.

O

Object Definition report A report generated by the Database Documenter.

object-oriented language A programming language, such as VBA, that includes a set of instructions that operate on objects in the database.

OLE Object The Access data type that identifies files that were created in another program and then linked to or embedded in the database.

one-to-many relationship (1:∞) A relationship between tables in which one record in the first table matches zero, one, or many records in the related table.

one-to-one relationship (1:1) A relationship between tables in which each record in one table matches exactly one record in the related table.

Open Exclusive mode A method of opening an Access database that locks out all users except for the current user from opening and using the database at the same time.

Open Exclusive Read-Only mode A method of opening an Access database that locks out all users except for the current user, but the current user can only view the data in the database.

Open mode A method of opening an Access database that lets multiple users open and use the database at the same time; it is the default option for opening a database.

Open Read-Only mode A method of opening an Access database that lets multiple users open the database, but users cannot write any information to the database and are limited to viewing existing data only.

OpenReport A macro action that opens a report.

Option Compare statement A statement in the Declarations section above the horizontal line that designates the technique Access uses to compare and sort text data. The default method "Database" means that Access compares and sorts letters in normal alphabetical order, using the language settings for Access specified on your computer.

OR criteria The criteria that select records that match any of the specified values.

orphaned The term used to describe a record whose matching record in a primary or related table has been deleted.

outer join A left outer join displays all records from the table on the left and only those records from the table on the right that have matching records from the table on the left. A right outer join displays all records from the table on the right and only those records from the table on the left that have matching records from the table on the right.

P

page footer A section of a report or form that appears at the end of every printed page.

page header A section of a report or form that appears at the top of every printed page.

parameter value A prompt used in a query to allow user input when the query is run. The value the user enters is then used as the criterion for that field.

partial dependency The situation in which a field is dependent on only part of a composite primary key.

password A collection of characters that a user types to gain access to a file.

primary key A field or combination of fields that creates a unique value in each record in a table.

primary sort field The field used to sort the records first, which must appear to the left of any other field. Additional fields used to further sort the records must appear to the right of the primary sort field.

primary table In a one-to-many relationship, the table that is on the "one" side of the relationship.

private procedure (local procedure) A procedure in a class module that can be used only by the form or report for which it was created.

procedure (event procedure) A group of statements in a programming language that are executed when an event occurs.

public procedure A procedure that more than one database object can use.

Q

query A database object that stores criteria for selecting records from one or more tables based on conditions you specify.

query by example (QBE) The process of creating a query by entering the values you want to use as criteria for selecting records.

R

record (row) Collectively, the values in each field in a table for a single entity.

record source The underlying table or query object that provides the fields and data in a form.

recordset (query) A datasheet that contains the results of a query.

referential integrity A rule that if the foreign key in one table matches the primary key in a second table, the values in the foreign key must match the values in the primary key. When the database does not enforce referential integrity, certain problems occur that lead to inaccurate and inconsistent data.

related table In a one-to-many relationship, the table that is on the "many" side of the relationship.

relational database A database that contains tables related through fields that contain identical data, also known as common fields.

repeating group In an incorrectly designed database table, a field that contains more than one repeating value.

report A database object that presents the information from one or more database tables or queries in a printed format.

report footer A section of a report that is printed once at the end of the report. The report footer appears last in the report design but is printed before the final page footer.

report header A section of a report that is printed once at the beginning of the report. The report header is printed before the page header.

Report tool An Access tool that allows you to create an instant report that displays all the fields and records in a single table or query.

Report Wizard A wizard that guides you through the steps of creating a report based on one or more tables or queries by asking you questions about the record sources, fields, layout, and format you want to use.

Required property The property of a nonprimary key field that requires users to enter a value in the field.

run-time error (execution error) An error that occurs when a procedure executes and stops because it tries to perform an operation that is impossible to perform.

S

second normal form (2NF) A database table that is in first normal form and that does not contain any partial dependencies on the composite primary key.

select query A query that selects data from one or more tables according to specified criteria and displays the data in a datasheet.

SendKeys action A macro action that sends keystrokes to Access or to another active program.

Short Text The Access data type that stores up to 255 alphanumeric characters that are not used in calculations.

single stepping The process of running a macro one action at a time, pausing between actions.

sort The process of arranging records in a table or query in a particular order or sequence, such as alphabetical.

splash screen A form that opens when an application begins, often listing information such as the name of the application and programmers and contact information.

standard module A database object that is stored in memory with other database objects when the database is opened. Standard modules can be used from anywhere in the database.

startup options A set of actions and configurations that Access performs when a database opens. Using the Access Options dialog box, you can set options such as Display Form, Display Navigation Pane, Allow Full Menus, and so on.

statement A VBA instruction that responds to an event that occurs with an object or control in the database.

Structured Query Language (SQL) The common query language of most DBMSs, including Access. A query created in SQL can run in most database programs.

Sub statement The first part of a subroutine that includes the scope of the procedure (private or public), the name of the procedure, and an opening and closing parenthesis.

subdatasheet A datasheet that displays records from related tables in Table Datasheet view.

subform A form that appears within another form and is usually used to display related data.

subreport A report that appears within another report and is usually used to display related data.

subroutine (sub procedure) In a programming language, a subroutine performs operations and accepts input values, but does not return a value and cannot be used in expressions.

summary report A type of grouped report that calculates totals for each group and a grand total for the entire report, and doesn't necessarily include details.

surrogate key A computer-generated primary key that is usually invisible to users.

syntax error An error that occurs when a VBA statement violates the language rules for a statement, such as a misspelling, an incorrect sequence of keywords, and a missing parenthesis.

T

Tab control A control you can add to a form that contains a subform on each page of the control. Users can move between the control pages by clicking the tabs.

tab order The order in which you move from one control to another in a form when you press the Tab key. The tab order determines the order for data entry.

table (entity) A collection of fields that describe one entity, such as a person, place, thing, or idea.

Theme A predefined format with borders, background colors, shading, and graphic effects that you can apply to forms and reports.

third normal form (3NF) A database table that is in second normal form and the only determinants it contains are candidate keys.

time-series data The data that shows performance over time for periods such as years, quarters, or months.

transitive dependency The situation that occurs between two nonkey fields that are both dependent on a third field; tables in third normal form should not have transitive dependencies.

Trust Center A feature, located in Access Options, which provides various selections for setting macro security levels on your computer.

U

unbound control A text box that displays the results of a calculated field, a label such as the title of a form, or a logo or other graphic used to make the form more attractive. It is unbound because it is not based on an underlying table or query.

unbound form An Access form with no record source, such as one containing instructions to help users navigate through a database.

unnormalized data Data that contains deletion, update, or insertion anomalies.

update anomaly The problem that occurs when, due to redundant data in a database, a user fails to update some records or updates records erroneously.

update query A query that changes the values of data in one or more existing tables based on criteria.

V

Val function The VBA function that returns the numbers contained in a specified string as a numeric value.

validation rule A rule that compares the data entered into a field by a user against one or more valid values that the database developer specified.

Validation Rule property A property of a field that specifies the valid values that a user can enter into the field.

Validation Text property A property of a field that displays a predefined message if a user enters an invalid value into the field.

variable A named location in computer memory that can contain a value.

Visual Basic Editor (VBE, editor) The program used to create and modify VBA code.

Visual Basic for Applications (VBA) The programming language for Microsoft Office programs, including Access.

Visual Basic window The program window that opens when you use Visual Basic Editor (VBE).

W

Watch Window The VBA window that is used to debug a procedure by showing the current value of a specified variable while the procedure is executing.

wildcard character A placeholder that stands for one or more characters. Common wildcards are the asterisk (matches any number of characters), question mark (matches any single alphabetic character), and pound sign (matches any single digit in a numeric field).

Y

Yes/No The Access data type that stores one of two values, such as yes or no, true or false, or on or off.

Index